CONTRACT ON AMERICA

CONTRACT ON AMERICA

THE
MAFIA MURDERS
OF
JOHN AND ROBERT KENNEDY

BY
DAVID E. SCHEIM

Argyle Press   •   Silver Spring, Maryland   •   1983

ISBN number 0–9610272–0–7

Library of Congress catalog card number 82–74146

Printed in the United States of America

בפרח רשעים כמו עשב
ויציצו כל פעלי און
להשמדם עדי עד

When the wicked thrive like grass
and all evildoers flourish
it is that
they may be destroyed forever

Psalm 92

Preface
to the First Publication

"Your evidence indicates that the press in the United States is not quite as free as it is supposed to be," noted Senator Sam Ervin in 1959, following Senate exposure of Mob leverage over several major newspapers.[1] His observation has applied especially well with respect to organized crime and the John and Robert Kennedy assassinations. As documented within the following pages, coverage of these subjects has been repeatedly censored, while journalists investigating them have been threatened, assaulted and murdered.[2] A few personal experiences in the course of researching this book added to my doubts about bringing an explicit exposé on these topics to fruition.

For this reason, *Contract on America* is being released into the public domain through this limited edition, published under tight control, prior to arrangements for dissemination on a larger scale. In addition to allowing for unrestricted distribution, assignment into the public domain is appropriate on two counts. First, I find it difficult to consider this book a private undertaking, considering the contributions of more than thirty people during the past ten years—including assassination researchers and organized crime experts who furnished leads, several students who performed editing and reference checking, friends who offered criticism and encouragement, and many others who helped with proofreading, translations, and production. Second, I believe it fitting that the critical findings contained herein be offered without personal gain to the American people.

---

[1] Robert Kennedy, *The Enemy Within* (New York: Harper, 1960), p. 237.

[2] See the introduction, sections 3.1 and 24.3, and section 26 of Appendix 4.

Contents

Introduction   *1*
1. Precedents   *5*

Part I
Assassins

2. Crossfire in Dealey Plaza   *19*
3. ...   *28*

...rail of Murder   *28*

at
Large

4. The Why and the Wherewithal   *37*
5. Four Suspects   *49*

Part II
Mob
Fixer
in
Dallas

6. Jack Ruby in Chicago: Molding of a Mobster   *65*
7. The Mob and Jack Ruby Move to Dallas   *73*
8. Jack Ruby's Criminal Activities   *79*
9. Jack Ruby's Underworld Contacts   *84*
10. Jack Ruby and the Dallas Police   *98*
11. Jack Ruby, Mobster   *106*

Part III
Murder
on Cue

12. Perjury and Suspicious Activities   *113*
13. Premeditation and Conspiracy   *125*
14. The Startling Testimony of Jack Ruby   *138*

Part IV
Pilgrims
and
Pirates

15. The Cuban Coalition   *156*
16. Post-Assassination Policy   *167*
17. The Warren Commission Cover-Up   *181*
18. Jack Ruby and the Cuban Coalition   *200*

Part V
A
Mafia
Contract

19. Contacts with the Marcello Family   *211*
20. Meeting Mobsters and Teamsters   *218*
21. The Collapse of the Mob's Assassination Alibi   *228*
22. Jack Ruby, Lee Oswald and Officer J. D. Tippit   *239*
23. The Mafia Killed President Kennedy   *251*

24. Epilogue   *264*
Conclusion   *285*

Appendices

1. Documents from the National Archives   *297*
2. Profiles of the Apalachin 58   *302*
3. Background on Jack Ruby's Telephone Records   *306*
4. Mafia Review: References by Subject   *307*
5. A Conversation Between Alex Bottus, Theodore Charach, and the Author   *401*
6. Additional Underworld Contacts of Jack Ruby   *404*
7. Reports on Ruby by "State and Federal officials"   *406*

Notes   *409*
Selected Bibliography   *459*
Index   *469*

In our sleep, pain which cannot forget
falls drop by drop upon the heart until,
in our own despair, against our will,
comes wisdom through the awful grace of God.

Aeschylus, quoted by Robert Kennedy on the death of
Martin Luther King[1]

Introduction

A clearly presented, flawlessly documented exposé of who performed the murder is all that can justify yet another book on the much-confounded Kennedy assassination riddle. But the reader probably requires even more: that the bitter facts offer some glimmer of wisdom to sweeten the unforgotten pain, some historical insight to help America finally overcome this tragedy. Only for this do we dare reflect back to John F. Kennedy's presidency, when it seemed that America could right any wrong, realize any vision. Only for this can we bear to hear again the shattering sound that still rings in our nightmares—echoing in subsequent assassinations, ghetto riots, the Vietnam War, Watergate crimes: the fatal gunshot of November 22, 1963 in Dallas. The horror was not so much that President Kennedy was killed, but that he was cut down by the meaningless act of a deranged individual, or so it appeared. The lesson was clear: moral purpose was for heaven, hell and Sunday school; history was gray and godless.

To some observers across the Atlantic, however, it was the official explanations, not the moral repercussions of Kennedy's slaying that were hollow. Reporting for *Paris-Match* in December 1963, Raymond Cartier observed that Europe "almost in its totality" refused to dismiss the assassination, together with the subsequent slaying of accused killer Lee Oswald by Jack Ruby, as "the chance encounter of an anarchist and an exhibitionist."[2] More likely, certain European journalists deduced, was that "Kennedy was murdered by the Mafia."[3] Particularly forthright was Serge Groussard, the distinguished French journalist and author, who wrote in *l'Aurore*:

> The Chicago gangsters of 1963. . . . are the men whom President
> Kennedy was relentlessly tracking down. . . . Feeling themselves
> to be driven back, little by little, from the labor unions they

controlled and other screens for their activities, and drunk with rage, they must have decided for many months to strike at the very top—to kill the head of the Kennedy family.[4]

Groussard also reported that Oswald's killer, Jack Ruby, was a "front man" for the Mob, sent to Dallas in 1946 to run a night club "for the underworld, or for the Mafia, as you prefer."[5]

The above-quoted observations from Europe were featured in the worldwide best seller *Who Killed Kennedy?* by Thomas Buchanan. The British edition, that is. The American edition, published by Putnam later in 1964, was conspicuously different in one respect: virtually all of the many original references to organized crime were deleted or watered down. Among the items excised, as I found when I first tried to verify my notes from this source, were Groussard's striking accusations of Mafia culpability.[6] Also cut out from the Putnam edition was Buchanan's own conclusion that "gangsters were involved in this case."[7] Further comments along these lines were retained with key words sanitized: "the Mafia" became "gangsters";[8] "a gangster murdered Oswald" became "a man named Ruby murdered Oswald."[9] From "Ruby was one of the most notorious of Dallas gangsters," this nebulous banality emerged: "Ruby was one of the best-known figures in that border world which lives under continual police surveillance."[10]

The censorship of *Who Killed Kennedy?* was, unfortunately, not an isolated occurrence. A larger pattern of cover-up in the Kennedy murder case was discernible to Raymond Cartier as early as December 1963. Buchanan again quotes Cartier's article:

> The professional gangster killing the President's assassin out of patriotic indignation, Europe does not believe it for a moment. ... It justifies suspicion of a deliberate and desperate concealment, carried out by all the organs of authority in the American nation, from the White House to Murder, Incorporated.[11]

Adding ironic emphasis to Cartier's assertion, the concluding seven words—"from the White House to Murder, Incorporated"—were deleted in the American edition of Buchanan's book.[12]

In the spring of 1973, when I joined other researchers at the National Archives to pour through the government's massive files on the Kennedy assassination case, I learned that Groussard's and Cartier's suspicions had been well-founded. One point became particularly clear: despite official denials, Jack Ruby had indeed been a "professional gangster," and had engaged in extensive contacts with underworld figures from across the country in the months before the assassination. Also, the evidence that established his criminal ties had been repeatedly suppressed or distorted by the Warren Commission, the government body initially charged to investigate Kennedy's murder. For example, the Commission reported that "virtually all of Ruby's Chicago friends stated he had no close connection with organized crime."[13] But my trace of the Commission's cited references revealed that one of these "friends" was a notorious Mob executioner, and that several others had racketeering involvements.[14] Another disturbing example of cover-up was the fate of an FBI report that described Ruby's frequent contacts with Joseph Civello, the Mafia boss of Dallas in the 1950s and early 1960s. The Commission published the first page of this report, *with the paragraphs describing the contacts between Ruby and Civello blanked out from an otherwise perfect photoreproduction.*[15]

But Jack Ruby's Mob ties, so incredibly covered up, were only the most obvious of disquieting circumstances surrounding the Kennedy murder. As I probed the National Archives file on the assassination, trading leads with other researchers, I found a gold mine of suspicious activities, shady characters and dubious alibis. The tasks ahead were clear: to piece these activities together, to identify the names of these characters in organized crime sources, and to show that their alibis were in fact fraudulent. It appeared that if these steps could be accomplished, it could be proved, at least, that the November 24th killing of Oswald was a cold-blooded, carefully coordinated conspiracy—an unsurprising conclusion, given Ruby's background. I wondered if the same web of Mob conspiracy would extend back two days to the murder of President Kennedy as well.

Determined to deal with probative evidence only, and to discard suspicions that could not be confirmed, I found progress toward these ends disconcertingly slow. Often weeks of combing government hearings, newspaper articles and books on organized crime passed by before I found another assassination figure among the ranks of the Mob. Yet as the weeks turned into years, the pieces of the Dealey Plaza puzzle began to fall into place. And as my collection of organized crime sources filled out, a larger issue emerged.

During the past century, the Mafia has been slaughtering and terrorizing America's citizens, plundering its unions and businesses, subverting its police, courts and government.[16] The structure and crimes of this vicious army have been documented in countless government hearings and court proceedings dating back to 1890, based on testimony of its defectors, electronic surveillance, observation of its national conclaves, and other police intelligence.[17] Recognizing the intolerable national threat posed by the Mob, John and Robert Kennedy launched a massive campaign to eradicate it, which went into high gear during the Valachi hearings in the fall of 1963.[18] It became increasingly clear to me that America's mandate, regardless of demonstrable culpability in President Kennedy's assassination, was to resume and successfully conclude this anti-Mob crusade.

A turning point in my investigation of the Kennedy assassination came in 1979, with the publication of the report, hearings and exhibits of the House Assassinations Committee. After reexamining the case for two years—twice as long as the Warren Commission's term—the Committee concluded that two gunmen fired at President Kennedy, confirmed that evidence linking the Mob to his assassination had been suppressed, and found that the Mob had the "motive, means and opportunity" to kill him.[19] Although the Committee reached no clear conclusion as to culpability, it released important evidence, including wiretap transcripts and testimony which showed Mobsters discussing and plotting President Kennedy's death.[20]

The Congressional disclosures complemented my research well; they established Mob-assassination links that I had been unable to prove, while a major portion of my findings, bearing on critical facets of the case,[21] had not been covered by either the Committee or other investigators. Between the Committee's findings and my work, there was enough new evidence to finally prove Mob culpability; my task became to discard unimportant details and to structure the evidence into a coherent, readable form. This process was aided greatly by a team of Harvard students who, over the course of three summers, edited the emerging manuscript and verified each of its roughly 5,000 cited references.

The final product of these ten years of work is not a pretty chronicle. Yet tempering the anguish is a revelation: the events recounted, far from random or meaningless, are woven together with a stunning moral unity. And beckoning us to encounter that unity, from the depths of the horrors exposed, are striking moral choices.

Organized crime, gentlemen, has its own scale of justice.
If . . . they have more to gain by someone's death than they
have to lose, then he's a dead man, whether he's a cop, the
President of the United States, or whoever.[1]

> Ralph Salerno, New York City Police organized crime
> expert

From the days of prohibition the "syndicate" has had an
active interest in politics and exerted considerable influence in both city and county elections. Many citizens of this
community will still recall the "bloody" election of March
27, 1934, when "syndicate" hoodlums roamed the city in un-
licensed black sedans slugging and killing. According to the
Kansas City Star of the next day the result was four dead, 11
critically injured and countless numbers severely beaten.[2]

> A Kansas City, Missouri grand jury report of 1961

□ 1 □

Precedents

By 1963, the Kennedy Administration was becoming increasingly
successful in its crusade to eradicate organized crime. Incensed and
obstructed, some Mob figures spouted venomous oaths against brothers
John and Robert Kennedy. Others discussed specific plots to kill them.[3]

Before tracing the background and outcome of these Mafia assassination
plots, however, it is important to put them in perspective. Other prominent
Americans have led sweeping campaigns against the Mob—Chicago Mayor
Anton Cermak was one, labor leader Walter Reuther another. Their fates
provide interesting precedents to the Kennedy murders.

/1/ The Assassination of Mayor Anton Cermak of Chicago

After being elected mayor of Chicago in 1931, Anton J. Cermak "made it his mission to drive the mob from Chicago," reported Judge John Lyle, a political contemporary.[4] Cermak organized special police squads to go after Al Capone's gang,[5] and according to racketeer Roger Touhy, offered the services of "the entire police department."[6] Although Cermak's motives can be questioned (he was apparently aligned with a rival group of racketeers, which included Touhy and Ted Newberry[7]), his determination "to wipe out the Mafia" was clear.[8] The mayor's resolve became increasingly evident as the 1933 Chicago World's Fair approached;[9] by its opening, he pledged, there would be "no hoodlums left."[10] Success seemed within Cermak's grasp when, on December 19, 1932, a special mayoral police squad illegally raided Mob headquarters and sprayed chieftain Frank Nitti with bullets.[11]

But Nitti recovered, and Cermak supporter Ted Newberry was murdered in apparent retaliation three weeks later.[12] Now terrified of assassination, Cermak bought a bullet-proof vest and moved into a penthouse apartment with a private elevator.[13] Believing that Nitti had imported Louis "Little New York" Campagna into Chicago to kill him, Cermak also increased his bodyguard force from two to five and placed guards at the homes of his two daughters.[14] Nitti was in fact gambling that "the crime crusade would blow up if they got rid of Mayor Cermak," two police officers later maintained.[15]

On February 15, 1933, one month after the Newberry slaying, Mayor Cermak was on hand while President-elect Franklin Roosevelt greeted dignitaries at a political rally in Miami's Bayfront Park.[16] Suddenly, Giuseppe Zangara stepped forward and fired a series of shots with a revolver, wounding five people in the crowd.[17] One of those hit was Cermak, who died three weeks later.[18]

On the surface, the case was clear-cut. Zangara claimed that he had been trying to kill President Roosevelt.[19] His grudge: chronic stomach pains, which he blamed on capitalists.[20] He was tried, convicted, and executed within two weeks of Cermak's death, no questions asked.[21] He was a model lone assassin, the Warren Commission concluded many years later: "a failure," and "a victim of delusions."[22] Indeed, he was a natural prototype for the Commission's characterization of Lee Harvey Oswald.[23]

But Zangara's tale of senseless vengeance was as dubious as it was ludicrous. For one thing, an autopsy revealed that Zangara was a "healthy, well-nourished individual" who had nothing wrong with his stomach.[24] Also, it is difficult to explain how, firing from close range and ostensibly aiming for Roosevelt, he managed to hit a cluster of people near Cermak, eight to ten feet from Roosevelt.[25] For Zangara was an experienced marksman,[26] and he told his lawyer that no one grabbed his arm or deflected his aim before he had finished firing.[27]

Other factors discredit the "lone nut" explanation and indicate Mob culpability. Zangara was a drifter who had lived in Philadelphia, Los Angeles, and New Jersey,[28] and whose chief activity during his last two years in Florida was betting on horses and dogs.[29] According to *Lightnin'*, a Chicago magazine which first exposed several instances of Capone-era corruption,[30] Zangara had also worked in a Mob narcotics processing plant in Florida.[31] The magazine's editor, the Reverend Elmer Williams, conjectured that Zangara had run into trouble with the Syndicate, and been given a choice: shoot Cermak, or be killed or tortured himself.[32]

Chicago Crime Commission President Frank Loesch also believed that "Mayor Cermak was deliberately murdered in a Capone gang plot."[33] Loesch stated he had information that Philadelphia Mafia members had assisted the Chicago branch by recruiting Zangara.[34] Judge John Lyle, a well-known Chicago political figure and friend of Cermak,[35] concluded succinctly that Cermak "was killed by the blackhanders," i.e., "the Mafia."[36]

Several historians agreed.[37] So did Cermak himself. On his hospital bed, the mayor told a reporter friend that he had been threatened before his trip to Miami for trying to break up Syndicate control.[38] And when his secretary first visited him at the hospital, Cermak told her, "So you arrived all right. I thought maybe they'd shot up the office in Chicago too."[39] Before he died, Cermak said he thought the Mob was behind his shooting.[40]

Years later, sociologist Saul D. Alinsky confirmed Cermak's suspicions. Alinsky was a member of the prison board supervising Roger Touhy,[41] a Chicago racketeer of the Prohibition era, who was imprisoned from 1934 to 1959 on a kidnapping conviction.[42] After Touhy's death in 1959, Alinsky made public a story of Touhy's which had been "commonly known for many years in many circles in Chicago."[43] As reported by Kenneth Allsop in *The Bootleggers*,

> In the crowd near Zangara was another armed man—a Capone killer. In the flurry of shots six people were hit—but the bullet that struck Cermak was a .45, and not from the .32-calibre pistol used by Zangara, and was fired by the unknown Capone man who took advantage of the confusion to accomplish his mission.[44]

/2/ Mafia Murders and Labor Unions

The Cermak slaying thus established a precedent for Mob murder in the political arena, and for the Mob's use of a "lone nut" to divert suspicion from itself. Examined below is the shooting of another prominent individual—this time in the labor movement—in which the Mob again went to some length to mask its culpability. This second shooting highlights the Mob's long history of labor union terrorism, which is discussed briefly by way of introduction. It was this brutal phase of Syndicate activity, incidentally, that prompted the Kennedys to tackle the Mob.[45]

Wholesale slaughter and intimidation. Captive labor unions are big business for the Mafia. The sources of income are legion: extortion payments from employees, paychecks for ghost workers, on-site racketeering earnings—and welfare deductions from union members who may "end up dead instead of sick if they ever try to collect."[46] And when such labor practices net the Mafia $385 million from Teamster coffers,[47] 15 percent of the price of all meat sold in New York City,[48] or $14 million from a 200-percent cost overrun on a defense contract in St. Louis,[49] everyone foots the bill. Indeed, with virtual control of some of the nation's largest unions,* the Mob extends its tentacles over the entire American economy.

Before a pension fund can be drained or an extortion payment extracted, however, honest union leaders and vocal members must be terrorized into submission—or eliminated. The vicious methods employed by the Mob to conquer and exploit labor unions are illustrated in the following three examples from the early 1970s.

In June 1971, 16 goons descended upon a nonunion construction site near Philadelphia and attacked workers with baseball bats.[52] Six men were left "a mass of bloody flesh, broken arms and fractured skulls"; one was nearly blinded.[53] An assailant who expressed remorse over the vicious attacks was found in a ditch, shot in the head, the next morning.[54] Bloody baseball bats left behind after the beatings bore the emblem of Roofers Local 30;[55] this was one of four unions cited by the *Philadelphia Inquirer* as "suspected by police of being involved with the Mafia."[56] Illuminating this

---

*The extent of such control was noted in a Justice Department report:

> A majority of the locals in most cities of the United States in the International Brotherhood of Teamsters (IBT), Hotel and Restaurant Employees (HRE), Laborers' International Union of North America (Laborers), and International Longshoremen's Association (ILA) unions are completely dominated by organized crime. The officials of these unions are firmly entrenched; there is little hope of removing them by a free election process. Convictions for misconduct have been sparse and when one corrupt official is removed another soon takes his place.... There are many other unions which are hoodlum infiltrated, such as the Laundry Workers and the Operating Engineers.[50]

The report noted that in New York City alone, more than 100 unions have "members of organized crime or their associates in positions of power."[51]

and many similar incidents of assault, arson, and murder[57] was one union member's comment:

> It is a standing phrase in construction work that the Mafia has taken over, thus the violence—and the kickback and bullying systems so obvious to the workers.[58]

Mob violence in connection with labor extortion in the food industry was described to Congress in 1972 by Clarence Adamy, president of the National Association of Food Chains.[59] Adamy testified: "We are suspicious, at least, that some store manager deaths, some food company employee deaths, some warehouse fires, some store fires were the result of reprisals by organized crime."[60] Adamy estimated that deaths from such causes "may run to a hundred."[61] And he added: "Mr. Chairman, a man from my staff disappeared on May 10, 1971, under the most peculiar circumstances ... this is a very personal question to me now."[62]

The third example of Mafia labor violence surfaced in the long battle between the Teamsters, whose leadership functions essentially as a Mob subsidiary,[63] and the United Farm Workers union. During a ten-day reign of terror in June 1973, hundreds of farm workers were injured by 350 Teamsters goons.[64] At least 20 required hospitalization,[65] and one UFW organizer, Nicholas Bravo, was found beaten to death.[66] Spurred by bonuses paid for injuries inflicted, the Teamster thugs attacked the striking farmworkers, women and children included, with lead pipes, chains, brass knuckles, baseball bats, ice picks, and bombs.[67] Thirty Teamsters were arrested on felony charges.[68] The systematic campaign of violence was documented in depositions from hundreds of workers, collected by volunteer law students.[69]

The late George Meany, former president of the AFL-CIO, called the campaign against the UFW "the most vicious strike-breaking, union-busting effort that I have ever seen in my lifetime on the part of the Teamsters."[70] Meany, who supported the UFW with $1.6 million from the AFL-CIO, observed that the Teamsters were signing sweetheart contracts with the growers, making farm workers "actual slaves to the labor contractor."[71]

Such incidents of violence, claiming the lives of dozens of union leaders, have characterized the Mafia's depredation of the labor movement in America since the 1920s.[72] But perhaps labor's most dramatic struggle against the Mob was staged in the auto factories of Detroit.

The shooting of United Auto Workers union President Walter Reuther. Walter Reuther was a self-made man, who worked his way through college as an expert die maker in an auto plant.[73] He was a man of principle, who fought for civil rights well before that cause became popular.[74] He was a man of courage, who in the 1930s delivered messages from the German underground to European contacts at the peril of the Gestapo.[75] And like his friend Robert Kennedy,[76] he was a visionary, who strove to infuse the highest ideals into the labor movement:

> What good is a dollar an hour more in wages if your neighborhood is burning down? What good is another week's vacation if the lake you used to go to, where you've got a cottage, is polluted and you can't swim in it and the kids can't play in it? What good is another $100 pension if the world goes up in atomic smoke?[77]

Given Reuther's courage and vision, it is not surprising that he became a prominent labor leader who was ranked in one widely published poll, along with Churchill and Stalin, as one of the world's ten most influential men.[78] And it was predictable that Reuther, like the Kennedys, would take an uncompromising stand on one important issue:

> American labor had better roll up its sleeves, it had better get the stiffest broom and brush it can find, and the strongest disinfectant, and it had better take on the job of cleaning its own house from top to bottom and drive out every crook and gangster and racketeer we find.[79]

The job would not be easy.

Reuther's first run-in with gangsters occurred on May 26, 1937, when he was viciously beaten during a union leafletting drive at the Ford Motor Company's River Rouge plant in Detroit.[80] His assailants: the Ford "Service Department," an antiunion goon squad of 3,000 "ex-convicts, thugs and musclemen."[81] The head of this Service Department was Harry Bennett, a top assistant to Henry Ford who courted Mob muscle with cozy Ford contracts.[82] A U.S. Senate committee chaired by Senator Estes Kefauver reported one case in which Detroit Mafioso Anthony D'Anna became a 50-percent owner of a Ford dealership a few weeks after meeting with Bennett.[83] The committee was also concerned that Ford had awarded a regional distributorship to a New Jersey firm whose controlling stockholder was Brooklyn Mafioso[84] Joe "Adonis" Doto.[85]

Reuther and his co-workers succeeded in organizing the United Auto Workers despite such efforts by Bennett's men and a thwarted attack against him by two armed thugs in April 1938.[86] But in 1947, when Reuther won the UAW presidency and control of its executive board,[87] he again found himself at odds with the Mob. The issue this time was illegal gambling. A 1948 *Business Week* survey found that large factories nationwide

were rife with gambling; 10 percent of production workers in large factories were gambling consistently on the job.[88] "National syndicates" were
"involved as never before," controlling $20 million in estimated annual
bets from Detroit auto plants alone, *Business Week* reported.[89] The Kefauver Committee concurred that in-plant gambling was "very widespread"
and "very highly organized,"[90] reporting that

> on some occasions organized gamblers would throw very large
> funds into union elections in major locals in the Detroit area in
> the hopes of securing the election of officials who would toler-
> ate in-plant gambling.[91]

The Mob thus had much at stake when Reuther, after winning the 1947 UAW
election, promptly launched a crusade against racketeer-controlled gambling in the auto factories.[92]

On the evening of April 20, 1948, Walter Reuther was seriously wounded
by a 12-gauge shotgun blast fired through his kitchen window.[93] The gunman's careful planning and deadly aim, foiled only by Reuther's last-
second turn to speak to his wife,[94] convinced police that a professional
killer had been responsible.[95] A year later, on May 22, 1949, it was Reuther's
brother's turn.[96] Also a high UAW official, Victor Reuther was hit in the face,
throat and shoulder and blinded in one eye by another shotgun blast.[97]

A prime suspect in these incidents was cited in the *Business Week* article
on in-plant gambling:

> In their search for a murder motive, Detroit police questioned
> gambling syndicate personnel whose in-plant operations were
> being impeded at Reuther's direction. It was an entirely logical
> field for the police investigation.[98]

Two other logical suspects in the shootings were Communists, whom
Reuther had purged from the union after the 1947 election,[99] and antiunion
employers.[100] Interestingly enough, investigations of each of these groups
led right back to the Mob.

Concerning the Communists, wrote Reuther biographers Cormier and
Eaton:

> The UAW's left wing, the Reuther opposition, had mutually prof-
> itable links with underworld figures who dominated illegal gam-
> bling in the auto factories, an operation grossing perhaps $20
> million a year. Because of the freedom of movement accorded
> local union stewards and shop committeemen, they made ideal
> collectors and runners for the crime syndicate. The Reuthers
> realized this and were trying to stop betting in the plants.[101]

Particularly unscrupulous was Melvin Bishop, one of the leaders of the Communist faction which Reuther had purged in December 1947.[102] Curiously, Bishop was discovered to be friendly with Santo Perrone, who was identified in a 1965 U.S. Senate report as one of the top ten Mafiosi in Detroit.[103] Bishop kept Perrone's private number in his telephone pad,[104] and the two were once arrested together for illegal deer hunting.[105]

When UAW investigators of the Reuther shootings focused on employers who had given the union the most trouble, Santo Perrone's name came up again. In 1934, a local of the Congress of Industrial Organizations (CIO) struck the Detroit, Michigan Stove Works, one of the largest nonautomotive manufacturing plants in the Detroit area.[106] Soon afterward, John A. Fry, the stove works president and deputy commissioner of the Detroit Police, enlisted the Perrones to recruit strike breakers.[107] The strike was broken and the union driven out.[108] Santo Perrone was then given a contract to haul scrap from the plant, and Perrone's brother Gaspar a high-paying, do-nothing position.[109]

The Perrones were subsequently sentenced to six years in jail on liquor violations, and the union succeeded in organizing the company's employees.[110] But when the Perrones were released 29 months later, their parole applications supported by John A. Fry, the union organization again disintegrated.[111] After describing these events, the Kefauver Committee noted

> the sinister relationship between the lucrative contracts granted to the gangster Perrones and the ability of the Detroit, Mich., Stove Works to keep labor unions out of its plant.[112]

The same strategy was later used by the Briggs Manufacturing Company of Detroit, then the largest independent auto-body manufacturer in the world, whose president was a close friend of Fry.[113] On April 7, 1945, Briggs awarded a scrap handling contract to Santo Perrone's 28-year-old son-in-law, Carl Renda.[114] Renda, who had "no equipment, know-how or capital whatsoever,"[115] promptly assigned the job to companies that for many years had been removing the scrap.[116] A week later, the first of six vicious beatings was inflicted by unknown assailants on leading labor officials at the Briggs plant.[117] The Kefauver committee concluded, "The inference is inescapable that what Renda, the entirely unequipped college student, was being paid for, was the service of his father-in-law, the 'muscle' man, Sam Perrone."[118]

Such sleazy incidents of collusion grounded Walter Reuther's own suspicions that his shooting was traceable to a coalition of the Mob, Communists, and a "small group of diehard employers ... who also were willing to work for the underworld."[119] The underworld, Reuther later explained, figured that I was the kind of person who would do everything that I could to try to keep them from taking control of this union and using it for the rackets and everything else that they use unions for.[120]

A Detroit police investigation of the Reuther shootings initially shed little light on who was actually responsible. The questionable conduct of the police probe's director, Detective Albert DeLamielleure, appeared to be part of the problem.[121] When a Detroit grand jury looked into the Briggs beatings of UAW organizers, it found that

> much of the investigatory work was done by police detective Albert DeLamielleure. One witness testified his wife had been beaten by hoodlum types after being interviewed, supposedly in confidence, by DeLamielleure.[122]

Also suspicious were instructions DeLamielleure gave to two investigators, Colonel Heber Blankenhorn and Ralph Winstead, whom the UAW hired out of frustration with the police's poor performance.[123] According to UAW official Emil Mazey,

> the first thing DeLamielleure told them was for Blankenhorn to go to Europe to look for some Communists who may have attempted to shoot Walter Reuther and he told Winstead to go to Mexico. We had reason to think that he had done this because he did not want a solution to the shooting.[124]

(Similar diversions were presented in the Kennedy assassination case by New Orleans District Attorney Jim Garrison, as discussed later.)[125]

In 1949, no thanks to Detective DeLamielleure, the UAW received two important leads. Obtained through a *Detroit News* secret witness plan, the first suggested an investigation of one Clarence Jacobs, an ex-con once bailed out by Mafioso Santo Perrone.[126] The second called attention to a Detroit service station owned by Perrone.[127] The second lead proved significant in 1951, when Detroit Police Commissioner George F. Boos disclosed reports that the Reuther shootings had been hatched in a bar two doors away from Perrone's Esso station.[128] Curiously, the bar's secret owner was found to be none other than Detective DeLamielleure.[129] DeLamielleure was demoted[130] and subsequently went to work for the Teamsters,[131] which Reuther was instrumental in expelling from the AFL-CIO in 1957.[132]*

---

*Another who became a Teamster official was Melvin Bishop,[133] the Communist faction leader whom Reuther had purged from the UAW. According to Robert Kennedy, Teamsters President Jimmy Hoffa made Bishop a union official after Bishop had become "closely associated with some of the gangster element in Detroit."[134]

As the long inquiry into the shootings of Walter and Victor Reuther continued, wrote biographers Gould and Hickok, "it became more obvious than ever that thugs and underworld characters were gunning for them, or had been hired to do the job."[135] The biggest break came in 1953, however, when UAW investigators located Donald Joseph Ritchie, a nephew of Clarence Jacobs, in a Canadian jail.[136] Ritchie agreed to cooperate, but fearing murder, asked for a $25,000 payment to his wife; the UAW paid.[137] Brought down to Detroit on December 31, 1953, he was interviewed by Wayne County Prosecutor Gerald O'Brien.[138] Six days later O'Brien issued warrants for the arrests of Mafia members[139] Santo Perrone and Peter Lombardo, Perrone's son-in-law Carl Renda, and Ritchie's uncle Clarence Jacobs.[140] Prosecutor O'Brien also released Ritchie's statement to the public:

> I was in the car the night Walter Reuther was shot. For about four or five years I had been working for Santo [Sam] Perrone. I made about $400 or $500 a week.
>
> In the occupation, I was—well, it just wasn't what people would call work.
>
> Clarence Jacobs approached me for this particular job. He told me I would get five grand.
>
> I was approached about five days before it happened and asked if I wanted to go. This conversation took place in Perrone's gas station. Perrone asked me several days before the shooting if I was going on the job. I said I was.
>
> I didn't ask a lot of questions. These people don't talk things over very much.
>
> All I knew was that Perrone had once said: "We'll have to get that guy out of the way." Did he mean Reuther? Yeah. . . .
>
> Jacobs did the shooting. He was the only one who got out of the car. I don't know how long he was gone. It's hard to remember time.
>
> I heard the report of the gun. Then Jacobs got back in the car and said: "Well, I knocked the bastard down." We took off in a hurry.
>
> After the job they dropped me back at the Helen Bar, about 200 feet from the gas station. I don't know what they did with the car. I heard later it was demolished and junked. I haven't any idea what happened to the gun.[141]

Predictably, Ritchie never took this testimony to trial. Held as a material witness at a Detroit hotel, Ritchie supposedly slipped out by fooling his two police guards into thinking he was taking a shower.[142]* Ritchie then fled to Canada and reportedly disclaimed his story as a hoax to collect the $25,000 from the union.[146] Yet given the Mob's demonstrated ability to strike out at heavily guarded witnesses,[147] the purported retraction is hardly credible; there are better ways to con a buck than to finger the Mafia. Indeed, the circumstances of the case justify the UAW's belief[148] that Ritchie's confession is accurate—that the Mob tried to kill labor paragon Walter Reuther.

The murder of UAW-AFL President John Kilpatrick. Like Reuther's CIO-affiliated United Auto Workers, its counterpart in the American Federation of Labor, the UAW-AFL, came under gangland attack. But the Mafia's infestation of the UAW-AFL was more severe, and its results more lethal. A member described the situation in a letter to George Meany, which was examined during a Senate investigation:

> While living in New York, I was employed in a plant where the union is the AFL Auto Workers. . . . The union is run by an ex-convict John Dio and his henchmen. I tried to protest a contract sellout at a meeting and was called at home by these thugs and told if I loved my children to shut up. . . . I'm no hero, so I did. We moved to Chicago and I got a job . . . where the UAW-AFL is the union. This was worse than before. A local hoodlum, Angelo Inciso, runs this union. . . . I was told to keep my mouth shut or I would be thrown down the steps.[149]

Angelo Inciso, boss of UAW-AFL Local 286 in Chicago, was indeed a hoodlum—a close associate of Chicago Mafia boss Tony Accardo[150] with many arrests and convictions.[151] But when Inciso began to plunder the local,[152] John Kilpatrick, international president of the UAW-AFL,[153] stepped in and had him ousted.[154] Kilpatrick also assisted the federal effort to prosecute Inciso,[155] leading to a ten-year prison sentence for him in June 1960.[156]

Although convicted, Inciso still had almost $500,000 in defrauded union

---

*During the McClellan Committee hearings in the fall of 1963, Detroit Police Commissioner George Edwards cited examples of what he described as "the continual brazen effort of the Mafia" to corrupt police officials.[143] Edwards testified that under a reform administration in 1939 "we saw the former mayor of the city of Detroit, the former prosecuting attorney, the former sheriff, the former superintendent of police, and roughly 250 police officers all go to jail for the acceptance of graft in order to let gambling operate in the city of Detroit."[144] But this massive cleanup failed to expunge the root of the problem, the Mafia; in 1965 and 1971 flagrant cases of Mob-police corruption were again exposed.[145]

funds,[157] so Kilpatrick filed civil suit against him to recover this sum.[158] Detroit Police Commissioner George Edwards described what happened when the case came to trial:

> About 10 a.m. on April 28, 1961, John A. Kilpatrick was standing outside of [the] superior court room on the eighth floor of the County Building in Chicago and Inciso approached him and snarled, "I am going to kill you." When Kilpatrick was taken aback at the threat, Inciso said, "I am not going to do it personally but I'll have it done."[159]

Five months later, on October 20, Kilpatrick was found dead in his car, a single bullet hole behind his left ear.[160] Two men were arrested and convicted for the murder;[161] one fingered Inciso's right-hand man, Ralph Pope, as the one who ordered it.[162] But no other witness would implicate Pope, and neither Pope nor Inciso was prosecuted. "Again the insulation at some point worked,"[163] Commissioner Edwards commented.

Although the Mafia's top brass was thus untouched, the successful prosecution of the Kilpatrick case was an unusual triumph. For not since 1934 had a conviction been obtained for any of Chicago's thousand gangland slayings.[164] But this success was not accidental. When news of Kilpatrick's murder reached the new U.S. Attorney General, Robert Kennedy, he ordered the Justice Department to "find out who's behind this killing, and get him."[165] Fifty FBI agents were then detailed to Chicago,[166] marking the first time the Bureau ever investigated a gangland murder in that city.[167]

Indeed, under the stewardship of the attorney general, the Kennedy Administration was combating the Mob on a national scale[168] as Mayor Cermak had done in Chicago, as the Reuthers had done in the UAW-CIO, and as Kilpatrick had done in the UAW-AFL. Harry Anslinger, the Federal Commissioner of Narcotics, observed in 1963 that this

> determination to wipe out organized crime has had a significant impact all over the United States. The gangsters are running for their lives.[169]

PART I
ASSASSINS AT LARGE

On Friday, November 22, 1963, shortly after 11:50 a.m., President John F. Kennedy left Love Field, the Dallas airport, for a motorcade procession through the city.[1] He rode in the second car of the motorcade with his wife, Jacqueline, Texas Governor John Connally and his wife, Nelly, and two Secret Service agents.[2] At 12:30 p.m., as the presidential limousine turned left onto Elm Street from Houston Street, a series of shots rang out.[3] President Kennedy was hit in the shoulder and Governor Connally was struck in the back; several seconds later, a bullet tore into President Kennedy's head.[4] The mortally wounded president was then rushed to Parkland Hospital, where he was pronounced dead at 1 p.m.[5]

Fifteen minutes later, Dallas Police Officer J. D. Tippit was shot to death as he stopped his patrol car beside a pedestrian in the Oak Cliff section of Dallas.[6] Shortly before 2 p.m., police arrested Lee Harvey Oswald, who worked in the Texas School Book Depository Building, as a suspect in both slayings.[7] The next day, a Dallas Police official announced that the case was "cinched": Oswald, unassisted, had shot President Kennedy from the sixth floor, southeast corner window of that building, beside which a rifle and three cartridges had been found.[8]

On Sunday, November 24, Oswald was escorted to the basement exit ramp of the heavily guarded Dallas Police building for transfer to the county jail.[9] And at 11:21 a.m., as millions of television viewers watched

Oswald approach the ramp, Dallas night club owner Jack Ruby lurched forward and fatally shot him in the stomach with a .38 caliber revolver.[10] Ruby told police that he had killed Oswald in a temporary fit of depression and rage over the president's death.[11]

With Oswald's protestations of innocence[12] silenced by Ruby's revolver, the Johnson Administration hastened to wrap up the case. "Almost immediately after the assassination," reported the Senate Intelligence Committee in 1976, the Administration pressured the FBI to "issue a factual report supporting the conclusion that Oswald was the lone assassin."[13] Indeed, on the day of Oswald's death, both FBI Director J. Edgar Hoover and Deputy Attorney General Nicholas Katzenbach expressed the need to "convince the public that Oswald is the real assassin."[14] Katzenbach also mandated, "Speculation about Oswald's motivation ought to be cut off."[15]

On November 29, as noted in an FBI memo, President Johnson told Hoover that the only way to stop the "rash of investigations" was to appoint a high-level committee.[16] The same day, Johnson issued an executive order creating a commission to probe the assassination case,[17] which would be chaired by Chief Justice Earl Warren.[18] As the presidential commission was being assembled, Hoover orchestrated press leaks proclaiming that Oswald had killed President Kennedy "in his own lunatic loneliness."[19] Ten months later, the Warren Commission issued its final report, with an obliging verdict: Oswald was the lone demented assassin, and Ruby his unassisted avenger.[20]

But the Commission's tranquilizing findings wore thin as its massive files of primary evidence were publicly released and examined. In books, leading journals, legal and medical forums, critics exposed the Commission's serious distortions of its own cited evidence, which characterized virtually every facet of its case.[21] By 1966, joining the call for a new investigation were William F. Buckley, Richard Cardinal Cushing, Walter Lippmann, Arthur Schlesinger, *Life* magazine, the *London Times* and the American Academy of Forensic Sciences.[22] And by 1976, according to a Gallup poll, four out of five Americans believed that the assassination of President Kennedy was a conspiracy.[23]

In September 1976, more than a decade after the first Congressional call for a new probe,[24] Congress chartered the House Select Committee on Assassinations to reexamine the murders of President Kennedy and the Reverend Martin Luther King.[25] Two years later, the Committee terminated its hearings with the dramatic presentation of new scientific evidence.[26] These new findings confirmed longstanding public doubts about the official version of what happened on November 22, 1963. And they underscored ominous questions as to what forces have shaped America's course from that day onward.

> In contrast to the testimony of the witnesses who heard and observed shots fired from the [Texas School Book] Depository, the Commission's investigation has disclosed no credible evidence that any shots were fired from anywhere else.[1]
>
> The Warren Commission, in its report

> Scientific acoustical evidence establishes a high probability that two gunmen fired at President John F. Kennedy. ... The committee believes, on the basis of the evidence available to it, that President John F. Kennedy was probably assassinated as a result of a conspiracy.[2]
>
> The House Select Committee on Assassinations, in its report

■ 2 ■

Crossfire in Dealey Plaza

"You can't say Dallas doesn't love you," Nelly Connally told President Kennedy, as the presidential limousine rode north on Houston Street that sunny Friday, November 22, 1963.[3] At 12:30 p.m., the limousine turned left onto Elm Street, passing the Texas School Book Depository Building at the corner of Houston and Elm.[4] Sloping upward on Elm Street, ahead and to the right of the limousine, was a stretch of grass which came to be called the "grassy knoll." Further ahead, as shown in figure 1,[5] Elm Street ducked beneath a railroad overpass and turned into Stemmons Freeway. Mrs. Connally looked past the overpass toward the freeway, remarking to Jacqueline Kennedy, "We're almost through, it's just beyond that."[6]

Standing on the overpass, enjoying his commanding view of the motorcade, railroad signal supervisor S. M. Holland heard a series of shots.[7] Holland glanced left toward a five-foot picket fence atop the grassy knoll, which bordered a railroad parking lot to the north.[8] His eyes immediately fixed on a cluster of trees 60 yards away, near the corner of the fence.[9] And at that moment, as Holland reported in a sheriff's affidavit later that day, he

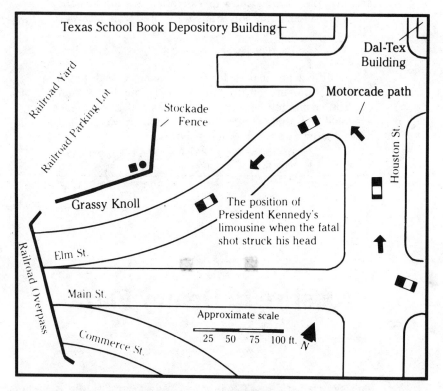

Figure 1. The scene of President Kennedy's assassination. The square behind the stockade fence denotes the area where witnesses saw smoke, cigarette butts and footprints, as reported to the Warren Commission in 1963 and 1964. The dot behind the fence denotes the position of an assassin, as determined by a Congressionally-selected team of acoustical experts from a sound tape of the shooting.

saw "a puff of smoke come from the trees."[10] He subsequently told the Warren Commission, "There was a shot. ... And a puff of smoke came out about 6 or 8 feet above the ground right out from under those trees."[11]

Holland was not alone in this observation. Six other railroad workers situated atop the railroad overpass—Richard C. Dodd,[12] Clemon E. Johnson,[13] Austin L. Miller,[14] Thomas J. Murphy,[15] James L. Simmons,[16] and Walter L. Winborn[17]—reported seeing smoke in the same area just after they heard the shots. The smoke could not be explained as exhaust fumes or steam or otherwise dismissed.* Moreover, two witnesses sniffed gunpowder in that vicinity. Senator Ralph Yarborough, who rode past the picket fence, downwind from it, seconds after the shooting,[23] reported, "you could smell powder on our car" nearly all the way to Parkland Hospital.[24] Dallas Patrolman Joe M. Smith also caught the smell of gunpowder behind the picket fence, in the railroad parking lot.[25] Smith had headed for the fence when a bystander exclaimed to him, "They are shooting the President from the bushes."[26]

Just after the shooting, railroad workers Holland, Simmons and Dodd jumped over a steam pipe, scrambled over a "sea of cars" in the railroad parking lot, and dashed to the picket fence, where they had spotted the smoke.[27] There, between the fence and a station wagon parked just west of the fence corner,[28] they found "about a hundred foottracks in that little spot," going in every direction.[29] Holland later told the Warren Commission he had the impression that "someone had been standing there for a long period."[30] Holland also noted two spots of mud on the bumper, "as if someone had cleaned their foot, or stood up on the bumper to see over the fence."[31] Simmons reported the same thing,[32] and Dodd added, "There were tracks and cigarette butts laying where someone had been standing on the bumper looking over the fence."[33]

Many other witnesses also indicated that a shot had come from that same area.[34] One was William Newman, Jr., who was watching the motorcade with his wife and two children from the curb of Elm Street at the bottom of the grassy knoll.[35] In a Dallas County Sheriff's affidavit of November 22, Newman reported

> the President's car turned left off Houston onto Elm Street . . . all of a sudden there was a noise, apparently gunshot. . . . then we fell down on the grass as it seemed that we were in the direct path of fire. . . . I thought the shot had come from the garden directly behind me.[36]

---

*Johnson suggested that the smoke they observed may have come from a motorcycle abandoned by a policeman.[18] Holland reported, however, that he saw the smoke before the policeman abandoned the motorcycle.[19] Some have alternatively proposed that the smoke was actually steam. But the only nearby steam line ran along the railroad overpass—practically underfoot of the witnesses there—and nowhere near the corner of the picket fence.[20]

A favorite argument of nonconspiracy buffs to dismiss the reported sightings of smoke is that "smokeless powder" used in modern weapons leaves no smoke.[21] But in actuality, the term "smokeless powder" has the same exaggerated connotation as "seedless grapefruit." As reported by a panel of firearms experts commissioned by the House Assassinations Committee, the propellant in modern cartridges "is not completely consumed or burned. Due to this, residue and smoke are emitted."[22]

Newman and his wife fell to the ground, each covering a child.[37]

Mary Elizabeth Woodward was standing on the Elm Street curb near the Newmans watching the motorcade.[38] When the President's car approached, Woodward told a reporter on November 22, "there was a horrible, ear-shattering noise coming from behind us and a little to the right."[39] Behind and to her right was the picket fence.[40] Woodward then fell to the ground, along with the Newmans and three other men in the vicinity.[41]

Dallas law enforcement officers immediately focused attention on the railroad parking lot north of the fence, and on the surrounding railroad property. Just after the shooting, Dallas Police Chief Jesse E. Curry broadcast on his police microphone, "get a man on top of that triple underpass [the railroad overpass] and see what happened up there."[42] Riding in the lead car of the motorcade with Curry, Dallas County Sheriff Bill Decker radioed the order to "move all available men out of my office into the railroad yard to try to determine what happened in there."[43] His deputies proceeded into the railroad parking lot behind the picket fence.[44]

But these official directives were unnecessary. Right after the shots were fired, as reported by witnesses and shown in photographs, dozens of police officers and bystanders charged up the grassy knoll.[45] Among them were two motorcycle policemen in the motorcade: one who rode over the curb and up the grass, and another who dropped his motorcycle on Elm Street and ran up with his pistol drawn.[46] A large crowd also swarmed toward the knoll from the corner of Houston and Elm Streets, near the Texas School Book Depository Building.[47] That building, in contrast, attracted no immediate attention from bystanders.[48] Within minutes after the shooting, at least 50 policemen were searching the railroad parking lot and surrounding railroad yard.[49]

Four of this police contingent—Dallas County Deputy Sheriffs L. C. Smith, A. D. McCurley, J. L. Oxford and Seymour Weitzman—reported that bystanders mentioned smoke or shots coming from the vicinity of the picket fence.[50] Weitzman, for one, was running up the grassy knoll when someone said that a "firecracker or shot had come from the other side of the fence."[51] Weitzman vaulted over the fence into the parking lot,[52] where a railroad yardman told him that the source of gunfire was "the wall section where there was a bunch of shrubbery."[53] The yardman also related that "he thought he saw somebody throw something through a bush."[54] Weitzman eventually joined Holland, Simmons, and Dodd near the corner of the picket fence, where he saw "numerous kinds of footprints that did not make sense because they were going different directions."[55]

Reports from three additional witnesses reinforced suspicions that a gunman had fired from behind the picket fence. Lee Bowers, stationed atop a 14-foot railroad tower, observed three cars cruising around the railroad lot less than half an hour before the assassination,[56] although police had sealed off the area.[57] Two of the cars had out-of-state license plates, one of which, a 1961 or 1962 Chevrolet Impala, was muddy up to the windows.[58] Lone male drivers rode in the Chevrolet and the third car;[59] one held something to his mouth which appeared to be a microphone or a telephone.[60] As the motorcade came within his commanding view, Bowers noticed two men standing behind the picket fence.[61] They were the only people in the vicinity unfamiliar to the 15-year Dallas railroad veteran.[62] When the shots were fired, "a flash of light or smoke" or "some unusual occurrence" near the two strangers attracted Bowers' eye.[63]

J. C. Price watched the motorcade from the roof of the Terminal Annex Building, near the Depository Building.[64] After the volley of shots, Price saw a man running full-speed from the picket fence to the railroad yard.[65] Price noted that the man held something in his right hand, which "could have been a gun."[66]

After the shooting, Dallas Police officer Joe M. Smith encountered another suspicious man in the lot behind the picket fence.[67] Smith told the Warren Commission that when he drew his pistol and approached the man, the man "showed [Smith] that he was a Secret Service agent."[68] But according to Secret Service Chief James Rowley and agents at the scene, all Secret Service personnel stayed with the motorcade, as required by regulations, and none was stationed in the railroad parking lot.[69] It thus appeared that someone was carrying fraudulent Secret Service credentials—of no perceptible use to anyone but an escaping assassin.

In 1966, Haverford College professor Josiah Thompson began a meticulous study of reports, photographs, medical documents, and other evidence bearing on the Dealey Plaza shooting.[70] Thompson focused on indications that a shot had come from behind the picket fence: the accounts and immediate reactions of bystanders, the odor of gunpowder, the rapid convergence of police; the reports describing three cruising cars, two strangers, a fleeing man, and a phantom Secret Service agent.[71] He was particularly interested in the smoke, footprints and cigarette butts observed behind the picket fence by railroad workers at the scene.[72] To pinpoint the details of these observations, Thompson interviewed signal supervisor S. M. Holland on November 30, 1966, at Holland's home in Irving, Texas.[73]

Holland told Thompson that he heard four shots, the last two closely spaced.[74] He saw a puff of white smoke come out from the trees after the third or fourth shot.[75] The smoke was positioned over the picket fence, "about ten or fifteen feet" west of the corner.[76]

Holland then described to Thompson what he found behind the fence minutes later:

> And I got over to the spot where I saw the smoke come from and heard the shot. . . . Well, you know it'd been raining that morn-

ing and behind the station wagon from one end of the bumper
to the other, I expect you could've counted four or five-hundred
footprints down there.[77]

He continued, "And on the bumper, oh about twelve or eighteen inches
apart, it looked like someone had raked their shoes off; there were muddy
spots up there, like someone had been standing up there."[78] Holland summarized his impression of the footprints with the comment, "It looked like
a lion pacing a cage."[79]

Holland's remarks to Thompson were featured in the latter's highly regarded treatise, *Six Seconds in Dallas*, published in 1967. In that book,
Thompson noted that many questions remained unanswered about the
shots fired in Dealey Plaza.[80] But "with regard to the shot from behind the
stockade fence," he concluded, "the evidence indicates unambiguously
that a shot came from that location."[81] The details "may yet fill in," Thompson added, through a "future investigation, a sudden revelation or the pa-
tient labors of other researchers and historians."[82]

Eleven years later, in March 1978, the House Assassinations Committee
located a trunkful of 1963-vintage Dallas Police records in the custody of a
former intelligence director of the department.[83] Among them was a dictabelt recording of "channel one" transmissions by police on the day of the
assassination.[84] And on the dictabelt was a ten-second series of loud clicks
and pops, transmitted from a police motorcycle whose microphone control button had stuck in the "on" position.[85] Police transcripts and testimony covering the assassination-day transmissions, dating back to 1963
and 1964, established that the dictabelt was authentic.[86] Moreover, recorded time annotations fixed the time of the sounds at seconds after 12:30
p.m.—just when the shooting occurred.[87]

Seeking possible clues concerning the shots fired at President Kennedy,
the House Assassinations Committee commissioned two prominent acoustical experts to study the dictabelt sounds. One was Dr. James Barger, chief
scientist of the Cambridge, Massachusetts firm of Bolt, Beranek and Newman, Inc., who supervised the initial phase of this study.[88] His acoustical
expertise had been relied upon in applications ranging from tracking sub-
marines for the Navy to determining the source of gunfire from sound
tapes for a federal grand jury investigating the 1970 Kent State shootings.[89]
The second expert was Professor Mark Weiss of Queens College, the City
University of New York, who reviewed Dr. Barger's work and then
spearheaded a refinement of it.[90] Recommended to the Committee by the
Acoustical Society of America, Professor Weiss had served with Dr. Barger
on the panel of technical experts appointed in 1973 by Judge John Sirica to
examine the Watergate tapes.[91]

On September 11, 1978, after comparing the dictabelt sounds with recorded test firings in Dealey Plaza, Dr. Barger presented his initial findings to the Committee.[92] He concluded that four of the sounds (the last three occurring 1.65, 7.56 and 8.31 seconds, respectively, after the first) were probably sounds of gunshots from Dealey Plaza.[93] The indicated firing positions: shots one, two and four from the Texas School Book Depository, the third shot from the grassy knoll.[94] Each of these four recorded impulses passed several screening tests designed to rule out sounds which were not gunshots fired in Dealey Plaza at the time of the assassination.[95] Nevertheless, given the available data, Dr. Barger could ascertain the origin of the third firing position with only an indeterminate 50–50 probability.[96]

A frustrated House Assassinations Committee then asked Professor Mark Weiss and his research associate, Ernest Aschkenasy, whether an extension of Dr. Barger's work could move that probability off center—one way or another.[97] The refinement Weiss and Aschkenasy proposed was an ingenious application of basic physical principles to pinpoint Dr. Barger's estimates of the firing and microphone positions of the third shot.[98] This refinement would reduce the margin of error six-fold, and make the results far more conclusive.[99] After more than two months of calculations using this refinement, Weiss and Aschkenasy determined the pair of firing and microphone position whose computed echo pattern precisely matched that of the third dictabelt impulse.[100] They had identified the "acoustical fingerprint"[101] of a gunshot fired from the grassy knoll toward the presidential limousine in Dealey Plaza—as distinctive as the sound of a piano playing in a concert hall.

On December 29, 1978, in dramatic public testimony, Weiss and Aschkenasy presented their findings to the House Assassinations Committee.[102] Their conclusion, Professor Weiss testified, was that "with a probability of 95 percent or better," the third shot was fired from the grassy knoll.[103] Aschkenasy added,

> The numbers could not be refuted. . . . The numbers just came back again and again the same way, pointing only in one direction, as to what these findings were.[104]

After reviewing the new acoustical work, Dr. Barger was recalled to testify. He concurred that "the probability of this being a shot from the grassy knoll was 95 percent or better."[105]

The acoustical analysis yielded additional predictions which confirmed its validity. The four determined positions of the recording police microphone traced out a path on Houston Street which fit the actual course and speed of the motorcade.[106] The testimony of a Dallas Police officer established that his motorcycle had been in that vicinity when the shots were

fired, and that his microphone had been mounted in the configuration indicated by the acoustical study.[107] Moreover, an "N-wave," characteristic of
supersonic gunfire, appeared in each dictabelt impulse for which the police
microphone was in an appropriate position to detect it, including the
recorded sound of the third shot.[108]

The most striking finding, however, was the exact location of the grassy
knoll gunman. According to the acoustical calculations, this firing position
was behind the picket fence, eight feet west of the corner.[109] That was just
two to seven feet from where S. M. Holland, a dozen years earlier, had
placed the signs observed by himself and fellow railroad workers: the puff
of smoke, muddy station wagon bumper, cigarette butts, and cluster of
footprints.[110] But it was more than 300 feet from Oswald's alleged firing
position.[111] And it was in front and to the right of the presidential limousine
during the shooting,[112] although at least one bullet struck from behind.[113]
The acoustical evidence thus established "a high probability," as the House
Assassinations Committee concluded, "that two gunmen fired at President
John F. Kennedy."[114] The "logical and probable inference," the Committee
observed, was that President Kennedy was killed "as a result of a
conspiracy."[115]*

The acoustical evidence raised the strong possibility, moreover, that a
third gunman had fired. For the first and second dictabelt impulses, apparently sounds of gunshots from the Texas School Book Depository,[120] were
spaced just 1.65 seconds apart.[121] Yet tests conducted by both the FBI and
the Army firmly fixed the minimum firing interval of Oswald's Mannlicher-
Carcano rifle at 2.3 seconds.[122] And suspicious movements observed in the
Depository Building by three witnesses did in fact suggest that two assassins had been stationed there.[123] The House Assassinations Committee attempted, not very successfully, to finesse this additional embarrassment to
the Warren Commission's findings.[124]

Another backup gunman may have been caught by the camera of Phillip
Willis, a retired U.S. Air Force major, in a photograph he took from Elm
Street immediately after the first shot was fired.[125] This photograph shows
the picket fence in the grassy knoll, a nearby concrete wall, and what appears to be the upper part of a person behind the wall.[126] After performing

---

*There are conflicting indications as to which firing position was the source of
the fatal shot to President Kennedy's head.[116] But common sense dictates the grassy
knoll, given the distinct snap of his head to the left and rear shown in the well-
known motion picture film made by Abraham Zapruder.[117] Furthermore, a profuse
amount of blood and brain matter flew out in the same direction.[118] Dallas Police Officer Bobby W. Hargis, for example, who was riding a motorcycle left and rear of the
presidential limousine, was splattered so forcefully with blood and brain tissue that
he "thought at first [he] might have been hit."[119]

computer analysis of this figure, a panel of photographic experts concluded that it was, indeed, "most probably an adult person standing behind the wall."[127] The panel noted that the figure was no longer visible in a subsequent photograph of the same area, and that its shape, height and distribution of flesh tones were consistent with those of an adult person.[128]

The person in the Willis photo could have been an innocent bystander trying to see President Kennedy. Yet why would such a person have chosen a concealed position behind the concrete wall, when the grassy knoll just yards away provided an open view of the motorcade?[129] A more ominous alternative is suggested by something else near the figure in the photo.[130] "Visible near the region of the hands," the House photographic panel noted, "is a very distinct straight-line feature."[131]

To faithful adherents of Warren Commission doctrine, however, the demonstrated existence of two or more assassins simply required casting more demented gunmen into its meaningless melodrama. As one such believer put it in 1967, the evidence of multiple assassins "is not sensational: it simply means that Oswald must have had an accomplice."[132] In 1971, one of Sirhan Sirhan's lawyers would use a similar argument to dismiss indications that a second gunman fired at Robert Kennedy. Such an attacker would have been someone with no connection to his client, the attorney would claim, "who seized on the impulse of the moment" to fire a bullet into the senator's brain.[133]

Yet to most Americans, the Congressional determination of conspiracy raises more penetrating questions. Was Lee Harvey Oswald merely an expendable participant in a much larger conspiracy, pegged as the lone culprit by officials under pressure to wrap up the case? Was an assassination contract in fact executed by some group with a demonstrated murder capability, a known hatred of President Kennedy, and a rational motive for killing him? An initial clue suggesting this possibility is a sinister series of incidents that followed the assassination.

You can not exist in a society where the ultimate solution to everything is to kill somebody, which is the answer of organized crime to any problem.[1]

Mob defector Michael Raymond, testifying in 1971 before a U.S. Senate committee under a grant of immunity from U.S. District Court Judge John Sirica[2]

What the committee witnessed here yesterday is . . . that fear that is all too often characteristic of people called to testify in matters touching on organized crime. A fear that, frankly must be recognized as justified. Indeed, I would note that . . . between 1961 and 1965 . . . more than 25 informants were lost in organized crime cases, killed by those who would prevent their testimony from being made public.[3]

G. Robert Blakey, chief counsel of the House Assassinations Committee, speaking of one frightened committee witness

□ 3 □

A Telltale Trail of Murder

On December 17, 1969, a federal grand jury indicted Newark Mayor Hugh Addonizio, Mafia boss Anthony Boiardo and 13 others on charges of splitting $1.5 million in payoffs extorted from city contractors.[4] Following the indictment, Michael Dorman reported in *Payoff*, it was feared that Mob violence might subvert the case.[5] A critical prosecution witness was placed under guard after receiving threats from Boiardo.[6] A defendant was "killed in a mysterious automobile crash" after meeting with the prosecutor and offering to cooperate.[7] "Another auto crash took the life of a cooperative government witness."[8] One of those indicted "died of what was officially described as a heart attack."[9]

The same pattern of violence, so characteristic of organized crime cases,[10] was brutally enacted in the aftermath of the Kennedy assassination.

/1/ Three Journalists

Like their European counterparts,[11] some American newsmen quickly came to suspect Mafia ties to the Kennedy murder. Witness the official synopsis of a December 12, 1963 FBI interview of *Chicago Daily News* reporter Morton William Newman.[12] Newman had covered the assassination, and had discussed with colleagues a story suggesting that Jack Ruby had underworld ties:[13]

> Newman informed that as a result of this story, which apparently has been rumored around some, some of the people of the news media think that possibly the "Syndicate" hired Oswald to assassinate President Kennedy.
>
> He further stated that it is his understanding that when [Ruby's sister] Eva Grant was at the police station after Jack Ruby's arrest, as she was leaving the police station, she made a remark to the effect that Jack didn't see why "Kennedy was killed when a man like [Mafia defector Joseph] Valachi was permitted to live."[14]

But Ruby's suspected ties to the Mob, eventually confirmed,[15] received virtually no coverage in the American press for more than a decade. The following series of events may partially explain why.

On Sunday night, November 24, 1963, award-winning journalist Bill Hunter of the *Long Beach* (Calif.) *Press Telegram* and reporter Jim Koethe of the *Dallas Times Herald* went over to Jack Ruby's apartment.[16] There they met with Ruby's roommate, George Senator, and attorneys Jim Martin and Tom Howard,[17] all of whom had visited Ruby in jail that day.[18]

On April 24, 1964, Hunter was in the press room at the Public Safety Building in Long Beach, California when a policeman entered the room with a fellow officer and shot Hunter in the heart.[19] The policeman initially claimed that his gun fired when he dropped it and tried to pick it up.[20] But he later changed his story after the determined trajectory of the bullet proved this impossible.[21]

On September 21, 1964, newsman Koethe was killed by a karate chop to the throat in his Dallas apartment, inflicted by an unknown assailant.[22] His apartment was found ransacked.[23] Koethe had been working on a book about the Kennedy assassination, in conjunction with two other reporters.[24]

Attorney Tom Howard, age 48, died in March 1965 of what was called a heart attack;[25] no autopsy was performed.[26] Friends observed him acting strangely two days before his death.[27]

Ruby's roommate, George Senator, told the Warren Commission that

after November 24, he feared he would be hurt or killed.[28] Senator testified
he was so terrified for ten days afterward that he "was afraid to sleep in the
same place twice," and in fact slept at a different friend's house each
night.[29]

Dorothy Kilgallen, a well-known crime reporter, went to Dallas after the
assassination to investigate the case.[30] In March 1964, she was granted an
exclusive private interview with Jack Ruby in a judge's chambers in the
Dallas Police Building.[31] Author Joachim Joesten noted her continuing
interest:

> [To find *New York Journal American*] columnists Bob Considine
> and Dorothy Kilgallen muckraking the Oswald case and casting
> doubts on the official theory has been both refreshing and
> hopeful. . . . On April 14, 1964, the *Journal American* ran a col-
> umn by Miss Kilgallen which opens up many embarrassing
> questions for the Dallas Police. . . .[32]

Kilgallen's interest may well have disturbed more sinister circles; in another column, she reported that Ruby was a gangster.[33]

On November 8, 1965, Dorothy Kilgallen, age 52, died in her New York
home, the cause of death reported eight days later as ingestion of barbitu-
rates and alcohol.[34] Two days later, her close friend Mrs. Earl Smith died;
the autopsy conclusion: cause of death unknown.[35] Texas newspaper editor
Penn Jones reported that "shortly before her death, Miss Kilgallen told a
friend in New York that she was going to New Orleans in 5 days and break
the case wide open."[36]

/2/ Hank Killam

The Warren Commission speculated that "one conceivable association"
between Ruby and Oswald

> was through John Carter, a boarder at 1026 North Beckley Ave-
> nue while Oswald lived there. Carter was friendly with Wanda
> Joyce Killam, who had known Jack Ruby since shortly after he
> moved to Dallas in 1947 and worked for him from July 1963 to
> early November 1963.[37]

Actually, the middleman of this possible Ruby-Oswald link was Hank Killam, Wanda's husband, who had worked as a house painter with John
Carter.[38]

On March 17, 1964, Hank Killam was found dead, his throat cut, amid the
shattered glass of a department store window in Pensacola, Florida.[39] His

death became the subject of a nationally publicized investigation in 1967 by County Solicitor Carl Harper,[40] during which members of Killam's family were questioned. According to his brother Earl, Hank said he had left Dallas because he was "constantly questioned by 'agents' or 'plotters.' "[41] He had "moved to Pensacola, then Tampa, then back to Pensacola to escape these 'agents.' "[42] Earl Killam told reporters that two days before Hank's death, Hank had told him, "I'm a dead man. I've run as far as I'm going to run."[43] And Hank's mother related that at 4 a.m. on the day of his death, Hank received a call at her home.[44] He dressed and left the house, after which she "heard a car drive off . . . although [he] did not own a car."[45]

The police ruled the death a suicide,[46] the local coroner an accident.[47] But Hank's wife felt that suicide was unlikely,[48] and his brother Earl remarked, "Did you ever hear of a man committing suicide by jumping through a plate glass window?"[49]

/3/ Rose Cheramie

On November 20, 1963, a bruised and battered woman was found lying on a road near Eunice, Louisiana.[50] She was Rose Cheramie, a heroin addict and prostitute with a long history of arrests.[51] Taken to Louisiana State Hospital near Jackson, Louisiana, Cheramie spoke of the assassination of President Kennedy, to occur two days later.[52]

Over the years, Cheramie's remarks were reported by various sources,[53] including a policeman who became associated with the assassination probe of New Orleans District Attorney Jim Garrison.[54] Perhaps most credible is the account of Dr. Victor Weiss, a resident physician at Louisiana State Hospital in 1963.[55] In 1978, Dr. Weiss told an interviewer from the House Assassinations Committee, as the Committee summarized, that

> on Monday, November 25, 1963, he was asked by another physician, Dr. Bowers, to see a patient who had been committed November 20 or 21. Dr. Bowers allegedly told Weiss that the patient, Rose Cheramie, had stated before the assassination that President Kennedy was going to be killed. Weiss questioned Cheramie about her statements. She told him she had worked for Jack Ruby. She did not have any specific details of a particular assassination plot against Kennedy, but had stated the "word in the underworld" was that Kennedy would be assassinated.[56]

On September 4, 1965, Cheramie was struck by an auto and killed on a highway near Big Sandy, Texas.[57] The driver said that he saw Cheramie lying on the road and tried to avoid hitting her, but ran over the top of her skull.[58]

/4/ **Lee Bowers**

Stationed atop a 14-foot tower near Dealey Plaza,[59] as previously related, railroad worker Lee Bowers noticed several unusual incidents on the morning of November 22. Bowers described them to the FBI, the Warren Commission,[60] and later, in a filmed and tape-recorded interview on March 31, 1966, to a private assassination researcher.[61]

As reported in the *Midlothian* (Texas) *Mirror,* Bowers had received death threats and had purchased a large life insurance policy before he was killed in an unusual automobile accident in Midlothian, Texas.[62] In the morning of August 9, 1966, according to two eyewitnesses, his car swerved off the road into a concrete bridge abutment.[63] "The doctor from Midlothian who attended Bowers stated that he did not have a heart attack and that he thought Bowers was in some sort of 'strange shock.' "[64]

/5/ **Nancy Perrin Rich**

Nancy Perrin Rich furnished detailed testimony, to be discussed later,[65] on Jack Ruby's involvement with the Mafia, the Dallas Police, and Cuban gun-running. In her June 2, 1964 appearance before Warren Commission counsel, she also related that about a week beforehand, she had begun to receive telephoned threats on her life.[66] In addition, she had been tailed for several days by different persons in different cars.[67] She testified that she reported the tail, and the Mansfield, Massachusetts Police picked up a Mr. Alberto from Hyde Park in a black Pontiac; he could not explain what he was doing 60 or 70 miles from his home.[68] A recent assassination source reported that Mrs. Rich later joined the roster of assassination witnesses who died violently.[69]

/6/ **Witnesses to the Tippit Slaying**

Approximately 45 minutes after President Kennedy was assassinated, Officer J. D. Tippit stopped his patrol car to speak to a man near the intersection of 10th Street and Patton Avenue in Dallas.[70] As Tippit stepped out of his car, the man shot him three times, and Tippit slumped to the ground.[71] According to eyewitness Jack Tatum, as paraphrased in the House Assassinations Report, the assailant then

> walked around the patrol car to where Tippit lay in the street and stood over him while he shot him at point blank range in the head. The action, which is often encountered in gangland murders and is commonly described as a coup de grace, is more indicative of an execution than an act of defense intended to allow escape or prevent apprehension.[72]

The House Assassinations Committee noted that the upward, front to back trajectory of one bullet which struck Tippit, previously unexplained, was consistent with Tatum's account.[73]

The Warren Commission had determined, on the other hand, that it was Oswald who shot Tippit when Tippit tried to question him.[74] But there were serious problems with this conclusion.[75] Questionable at best, for example, was the Commission's reliance on an identification of Oswald in a police lineup by eyewitness Helen Markham.[76] When asked by Warren Commission counsel, "Did you recognize anyone in the lineup?" Markham replied, "No, sir."[77] She repeated she had "seen none of them, none of these men" in response to five further questions about the lineup.[78] Finally, when counsel asked, "Was there a number two man there [in the lineup]?" she answered, "Number two was the one I picked ... the man I saw shoot the policeman."[79] How did she recognize him? "When I saw this man I wasn't sure, but I had cold chills just run all over me."[80] In the Commission's report, however, this exchange was condensed to one convenient conclusion: Markham "confirmed her positive identification of Lee Harvey Oswald as the man she saw kill Officer Tippit."[81]

Warren Reynolds and Nancy Jane Mooney. Situated at a car lot a block west of the scene of Tippit's shooting, Warren Reynolds observed Tippit's assailant run by.[82] The Warren Commission asserted in its report that

> Reynolds did not make a positive identification when interviewed by the FBI, but he subsequently testified before a Commission staff member and, when shown two photographs of Oswald, stated that they were photographs of the man he saw.[83]

Amazingly, however, the Commission failed to mention[84] a sinister series of events leading up to Reynolds' new-found certainty.

On January 23, 1964, two days after his initial interview with the FBI,[85] at approximately 9:15 p.m., Reynolds walked down to the basement of the auto dealership at which he was employed.[86] He flipped on the light switch, but the basement remained dark; the bulb had been removed.[87] As the FBI reported, "Thinking the light bulb was burned out, he proceeded downstairs to the basement fuse box and, as he reached for the fuse box, was shot in the head with a .22-caliber weapon";[88] fortunately, he survived.[89] Police investigators determined that "Reynolds was not robbed of anything."[90] Yet the assailant had been waiting in the basement for more than three hours before he shot Reynolds.[91]

On February 3, 1964, Darrell Garner was arrested as a suspect in the shooting.[92] Garner was released, however, after Nancy Jane Mooney gave an affidavit two days later stating that she was with Garner at the time of the shooting.[93] But then, as reported by the FBI, "on February 13, 1964, at 2:45 A.M., Nancy Jane Mooney was arrested and charged with disturbing the peace. . . . After being placed in a cell at the Dallas City Jail, Nancy Jane Mooney hung herself with her toreador trousers."[94]

When interviewed by the FBI[95] and questioned by Warren Commission counsel in July,[96] Reynolds stated that he believed he was shot because he had witnessed the flight of Tippit's assailant.[97] Reynolds said that he "had been scared as a result of having been shot through the head after the assassination of President Kennedy."[98] He also related that about three weeks after he got out of the hospital, someone tried to abduct his ten-year-old daughter.[99] About the same time, someone unscrewed the light bulb from his front porch.[100] Reynolds admitted that these incidents made him apprehensive, and felt that they were related to the events of November 22.[101]

By July 1964, as the Commission so neatly recorded, Reynolds was willing to identify Tippit's assailant as Lee Harvey Oswald.[102]

Acquilla Clemons. An eyewitness to the Tippit slaying never mentioned in the Warren Report,[103] Acquilla Clemons was questioned by independent investigators in a filmed and tape-recorded interview.[104] She reported that the gunman was "kind of a short guy" and "kind of heavy,"[105] a description incompatible with Oswald's appearance.[106] Clemons also related that just two days after the Kennedy and Tippit killings, a man who appeared to be a policeman came to her house.[107] His message:

> He just told me it'd be best if I didn't say anything because I might get hurt.[108]

/7/ William Whaley

The testimony of William Whaley, a taxi driver who gave Oswald a ride shortly after the assassination,[109] raised a number of questions. For one thing, Whaley reported that in a police lineup he was shown on November 23, Oswald was the only adult, the only one with a bruise on his head, and that his clothing stood out.[110] Whaley related that he "could have picked him out without identifying him by just listening to him because he was bawling out the policemen, telling them it wasn't right to put him in line with these teenagers."[111] This testimony raised doubts about the identification of Oswald in that same lineup[112] by another eyewitness to the Tippit shooting, William Scoggins; Scoggins later chose the wrong picture when asked by federal agents to select Oswald from several photos.[113] And Whaley related that Oswald started to get out of his cab and offer it to an old lady who wanted a ride.[114] Strange behavior for an escaping assassin.

William Whaley, age 60, was killed in a head-on collision on the Trinity River Bridge in the pre-dawn hours of December 18, 1965. It was the first death of a Dallas taxi driver on duty since 1937.[115]*

/8/ Albert G. Bogard

Albert G. Bogard was a salesman at the Downtown Lincoln-Mercury dealership in Dallas.[121] Bogard testified that on the afternoon of November 9, 1963, a man came into his showroom and asked for a demonstration ride in a Mercury Comet, which he drove somewhat recklessly.[122] The man said his name was Lee Oswald,[123] which Bogard wrote down on a business card.[124] But when Bogard heard on November 22 that Oswald "had shot a policeman,"[125] he tore up the card in the presence of other salesmen.[126] Bogard told his colleagues, "He won't be a prospect any more because he is going to jail."[127]

Bogard passed an FBI-administered lie detector test on his account,[128] and his testimony was corroborated in its essentials by three other employees of the auto agency.[129] One of these employees told the FBI that he also remembered the name "Oswald," and had written it down before the assassination.[130] Bogard and the other employees related that this customer had told them that he had a new job and no cash or credit but expected some money in the next two or three weeks, and had sarcastically remarked that he might have to go back to Russia to get a car.[131]

The perplexing features of this account were that Oswald did not know how to drive,[132] and that the testimony of two other witnesses precluded a visit by Oswald to the auto showroom on November 9.[133] In fact, several incidents were reported in which a man positively identified as Oswald appeared where he could not have been,[134] indicating that he may have been impersonated and framed.

In an interview with a private researcher on April 4, 1966 in Dallas, fellow salesman Oran Brown described what happened to Bogard:

> You know, I am afraid to talk. ... Bogard was beaten by some men so badly that he was in the hospital for some time, and this was after he testified. Then he left town suddenly and I haven't

---

*Another victim of a rare fatal taxicab accident was Dallas attorney Alfred E. McLane.[116] According to the testimony of Jack Ruby, McLane had once met at a Dallas restaurant with Ruby, another attorney, and an owner of the Tropicana Hotel in Cuba.[117] During the years 1959 and 1960, McLane served as general counsel to Rimrock Tidelands, an oil exploration company.[118] The managing director of a key subsidiary, Rimrock International Oil Company, was one Santo Sorge.[119] The McClellan Committee described Santo Sorge as "one of the most important Mafia leaders" and a liaison between "highest ranking Mafiosi in the United States and Italy."[120]

heard from him or about him since. . . . I think we may have seen something important, and I think there are some who don't want us to talk. Look at that taxi driver who was just killed, and the reporters.[135]

Brown might have been even more reluctant to speak had he known Bogard's ultimate fate. On February 14, 1966, Bogard was found dead in his car in Hallsville, Louisiana, with a hose running from the exhaust pipe into the passenger compartment.[136] Suicide, it was ruled.[137]

/9/ Roger Craig

Roger D. Craig, a Dallas deputy sheriff who was in Dealey Plaza during the assassination,[138] gave testimony on Oswald's movements that suggested conspiracy and contradicted the official reconstruction.[139] Shortly afterward, Deputy Craig, who had been voted "Man of the Year" in 1960 by the Dallas County Sheriff's department,[140] was fired.[141] And according to California CBS-TV producer Peter Noyes,

> For a time Craig went into hiding, after receiving information from one of his few remaining friends in law enforcement that the Mafia had put a price on his head.[142]

The House Assassinations Committee disclosed that Craig "reportedly committed suicide on May 15, 1975."[143]

/10/ George DeMohrenschilt

George DeMohrenschilt was a friend of Oswald[144] mentioned frequently in both government and private sources on the assassination.[145] On March 29, 1977, he was found shot to death, just after the House Assassinations Committee had tried to reach him for questioning.[146] Another apparent suicide.[147]

The deaths of more than a dozen additional witnesses, many of them violent or unnatural, have also been reported.[148]

The incidents described above are singularly characteristic of one organization, which routinely kills and intimidates witnesses to cover its crimes. It is therefore not surprising, as will be shown, that the captured slayer of one critical assassination witness—Oswald's killer, Jack Ruby—was an affiliate of that organization. Nor is it surprising, as shown in the next chapter, that this same organization had the motive, means, opportunity, and declared intention to murder President Kennedy.

> Cuba was gone. As long as Kennedy was in the White House there was no chance of getting it back. ... [Hoffa] was under indictment. Nevada was threatened. From coast to coast their activities were under investigation and harassment as never before. And now even the Indochina [narcotics] connection was coming undone. ... The question was whether organized crime could survive another five years of the brothers Kennedy.[1]
>
> Robert Sam Anson, television producer and political correspondent

□ 4 □
The Why and the Wherewithal

Fundamental to the solution of any crime are two considerations. Cui bono—who benefited from it? And who had the capability to commit it? In the case of the assassination of President Kennedy, as this chapter will show, the Mob fit the bill on both counts. For the Mob was obstructed and incensed by the Kennedy Administration's intensive anticrime crusade. Its thirst for revenge was expressed in invectives against John and Robert Kennedy, recorded by FBI electronic surveillance during 1962 and 1963. It was also evidenced, more ominously, in specific assassination plans and predictions by Mob bosses Carlos Marcello and Santos Trafficante and by their Teamster ally, Jimmy Hoffa. Furthermore, the Mafia had both the traditional proclivity and expertise to resolve its desperate dilemma by murder.

/1/ An Attorney General Fights Crime

Early in his political career, as counsel to a Senate committee investigating military procurement, Robert Kennedy learned of the oppressive machinations of America's directorate of crime.[2] As Kennedy noted in 1956, the committee discovered that military uniforms were being supplied by "some of the leading East Coast gangsters. ... We found corruption, violence, extortions permeated all their activities."[3] Later that year, journalist

Clark Mollenhoff gave Kennedy a tip on underworld infiltration of the Teamsters—a union of which Kennedy at the outset "had only a vague impression" as "big and tough."[4] This led to the formation of a special Senate committee to investigate such infiltration of labor, chaired by Senator John McClellan, with Robert Kennedy as general counsel.[5] The ensuing series of hearings exposed the Mob's brutal tyrannization and plunder of labor unions,[6] sickening an American public that had not yet come to accept such subjugation as normal. Kennedy himself was profoundly affected by his ringside view of these atrocities.[7]

While Robert Kennedy conducted a sustained drive against labor racketeering in the late 1950s,[8] the Mob drew little fire from a fragmented, ineffectual Justice Department[9] and an FBI chief who opposed measures against it.[10] But in 1961, when Kennedy assumed the post of Attorney General in his brother's administration, bureaucratic lethargy was shattered. As Victor Navasky noted in *Kennedy Justice*, Robert Kennedy channeled his boundless energy and expertise into a "total commitment to the destruction of the crime syndicates":[11]

> Operating with a direct line to the top, the Organized Crime "whiz kids" [the Justice Department's anti-racketeering section] fanned out across the country and began raiding gambling establishments, closing down bookies' wire services, indicting corrupt mayors and judges, and generally picking off, one by one, the names on the "hit list."[12]

Attorney General Kennedy was personally involved on all fronts. According to former Justice Department official William Geoghegan, Kennedy "got five anti-crime bills moved through the Judiciary Committee so quickly that nobody had a chance to read them."[13] Harry Anslinger, federal commissioner of narcotics in the Kennedy Administration, described the Attorney General's performance in the field:

> He traveled over the country, calling special meetings with our agents, exhorting them to nail the big traffickers. ... He knew the identity of all the big racketeers in any given district, and in private conference with enforcement officials throughout the country he would go down the line, name by name, and ask what progress had been made. ... He demanded action and got it.[14]

Under Robert Kennedy's leadership, by the year 1963 the size of the Justice Department's antiracketeering section had quadrupled,[15] the list of Mob targets for prosecution had grown from 40 to more than 2,300,[16] and the rate of convictions against racketeering figures had more than quadrupled.[17]

But Attorney General Kennedy was not satisfied. As he wrote in the *New York Times Magazine* in October 1963:

> It would be a serious mistake, however, to overestimate the progress Federal and local law enforcement has made. . . . The job ahead is very large and very difficult. We have yet to exploit properly our most powerful asset in the battle against the rackets: an aroused, informed, and insistent public.[18]

Yet even as Kennedy's words appeared in print, the massive public outrage required for a final crushing onslaught was being effectively mobilized. For during the RFK-coordinated Senate rackets hearings that October, a defector from New York's Genovese Mafia Family, Joseph Valachi, dramatically exposed the Mafia to Americans on nationwide television:

> Then they called us [new recruits] in one at a time. . . . there was a gun and a knife on the table. . . . I repeated some words they told me. . . . He [Salvatore Maranzano] went on to explain that they lived by the gun and by the knife and you die by the gun and by the knife. . . . That is what the rules were, of Cosa Nostra. . . . Then he gave me a piece of paper, and I was to burn it. . . . This is the way I burn if I expose this organization.[19]

There were, in fact, more than a dozen other Mafia members and associates before and after Valachi who described the organization's inner workings, in most cases under oath.[20] But Valachi's bold defiance of the Mafia code of silence severely demoralized the Mob.[21] Laced with hundreds of names and corroborated descriptions of dozens of slayings, his week-long, televised testimony stunned the American public.[22] And to pyramid its impact, Attorney General Kennedy pledged during the fall hearings to expand his war on organized crime.[23] According to journalist Robert Anson, Kennedy also "had begun laying plans for a massive, frontal assault" on the Mob's Las Vegas base, involving "all the investigative resources of the federal government, from FBI to IRS."[24]

While the Mafia chafed under the aggressive anticrime program of Robert Kennedy, the root of its problem was his brother, the president. As a senator on the McClellan Committee in the late 1950s,[25] President Kennedy had acquired the same orientation as Robert toward what he called a "nationwide, highly organized, and highly effective internal enemy."[26] And the president gave the drive against organized crime his personal backing,[27] placing it at the top of his domestic priorities.[28] If Attorney General Kennedy were killed, President Kennedy would spare no effort to track down the culprits and continue his brother's work. But if presidential support were severed, Robert Kennedy would effectively become "just another lawyer"—as Jimmy Hoffa gleefully described him on November 22, 1963.[29]

/2/ Up Against the Wall

The Mob's exasperation over the Kennedys was bared in FBI wiretaps of 1962 and 1963, which were made public by the House Assassinations Committee in 1978. Buffalo Mafia boss Stefano Magaddino complained, "They know everything under the sun. They know who's back of it, they know Amici [members], they know Capodecina [captains], they know there is a Commission [the Mafia's national governing body]."[30] In a subsequent conversation, he exclaimed, "they should kill the whole [Kennedy] family."[31] Chicago Mafiosi and political front men complained that local operations were virtually shut down, and made inflammatory remarks about the Kennedys.[32] Philadelphia Mafia associate Willie Weisberg raged, "With Kennedy, a guy should take a knife. ... Somebody should kill the [obscenity]. ... Somebody's got to get rid of this [obscenity]."[33] And New York Mafioso Michelino Clemente observed, "Bob Kennedy won't stop until he puts us all in jail all over the country."[34] Clemente declared that the situation would not change "until the Commission meets and puts its foot down."[35]

/3/ An Assassination Plan by Carlos Marcello

One particular member of the Mafia National Commission[36] had the power, the jurisdiction, and the rabid hatred of the Kennedys to coordinate an assassination contract against the president in Dallas.

A 1977 *Time* cover story on the Mob began quite appropriately, "New Orleans Mafia boss Carlos Marcello. ..."[37] For as head of the Mafia's "first 'family,'" established in New Orleans in the 1880s,[38] Marcello is today among the most powerful, if not the most powerful, of the Mafia bosses in the United States.[39] One manifestation of Marcello's stature is the exceptional financial and political success of his 30-year reign[40] in Louisiana. The *Saturday Evening Post* reported in 1964 that the Mafia's annual income in New Orleans "runs to $1,114,000,000, making it by far the State's largest industry."[41] And as reviewed for Congress in 1970 by Aaron Kohn, director of the New Orleans Metropolitan Crime Commission, Marcello's criminal enterprise

> required, and had, corrupt collusion of public officials at every critical level including police, sheriffs, justices of peace, prosecutors, mayors, governors, judges, councilmen, licensing authorities, state legislators and at least one member of Congress.[42]

In short, Marcello "controlled the state of Louisiana," and "continues to dominate the state" with actions "more flagrant than ever," as summarized by *Life* magazine in 1970.[43]

Yet Marcello's influence extends far beyond his home state, earning him the *Wall Street Journal's* appellation as the "undisputed patriarch of the Cosa Nostra in Louisiana and the nearby Gulf Coast area."[44] Indeed, he has sponsored operations over the years in such diverse locations as California,[45] Las Vegas,[46] Indiana,[47] and Cuba.[48] Of particular interest to the assassination case are his close and longstanding ties with underworld figures in Dallas and other areas of Texas.[49] For example, Marcello has been in telephone contact with two top-ranking Mafiosi from Dallas: Joseph Civello and Joseph Campisi[50] (both associates of Jack Ruby, as later shown[51]). If an important Mob contract were to be performed in Dallas, the strings would be pulled by regional boss Carlos Marcello.

Before Kennedy became president, Marcello enjoyed the dearth of official interference characteristic of his profession. His only major judicial setback occurred in 1930 at age 20, when he was convicted of assault and robbery and sentenced to 9 to 14 years in prison.[52] But in 1935, after serving less than five years of his sentence, he was freed on a pardon by Louisiana Governor O. K. Allen.[53] Over the next several years, Marcello's underworld career was marked by several further offenses for which he was charged but never prosecuted, including sale of narcotics and assault of a policeman with intent to murder.[54] Finally convicted for drug sales in 1938, he settled a $76,830 fine with a $400 payment and served just ten months of a lengthy prison sentence.[55] Although federal deportation proceedings were initiated against him in 1953,[56] and his deportation was later urged by senators Kefauver, Mundt, Curtis and Ervin,[57] Marcello thwarted authorities with endless delaying maneuvers.[58] In the process, he spent a record amount on legal fees for such a case.[59]

But Marcello's free ride came to a halt in 1960, with the election of President Kennedy. Even before the president's inauguration, Attorney General-designate Robert Kennedy targeted the Mafia overlord of Louisiana for special attention by the Justice Department.[60] And just three months after President Kennedy assumed office, under Robert's instructions, Marcello was arrested, handcuffed, and summarily flown to Guatemala, pursuant to a longstanding order to deport him.[61] When the enraged Mafia boss[62] illegally reentered the United States and had his lawyers challenge the order, the Kennedy Justice Department greeted him with federal indictments on charges of fraud, perjury, and illegal reentry.[63] In addition, following Robert Kennedy's guidelines, the FBI intensified its scrutiny of Marcello.[64]

In November 1963, Marcello was cleared of the fraud charge,[65] after a trial marred by alleged jury tampering and a plot to murder a key prosecution witness[66]—two typical Mob courtroom tactics.[67] His acquittal was announced just three hours after the event that spelled his ultimate freedom from the law: the assassination of President Kennedy.[68] And the following report provides an initial clue that this, too, was within the sphere of Marcello's murderous machinations. The information was first disclosed in the *Grim Reapers*, published in 1969, by Ed Reid, a Pulitzer Prize-winning author and former newspaper editor.[69] The source, Edward Becker, confirmed Reid's report and provided additional information in a 1978 interview with the House Assassinations Committee.[70]

In September of 1962, Becker and an associate, Carl Roppolo, met with Marcello to seek financing for a business venture.[71] The meeting was arranged without difficulty because of Roppolo's close relationship with Marcello.[72] The site of the gathering was an elegantly furnished office in a farmhouse on Churchill Farms, Marcello's 3,000-acre plantation outside New Orleans.[73] As author Reid recounted, the conversation began with underworld pleasantries, the talk becoming relaxed and familiar as the Scotch flowed. But Carlos' mood changed when the government's drive against organized crime was brought up and Robert Kennedy's name mentioned:

> "*Livarsi na petra di la scarpa*" Carlos shrilled the Mafia cry of revenge: "Take the stone out of my shoe!"
>
> "Don't worry about that little Bobby son of a bitch," he shouted. "He's going to be taken care of!"[74]

Becker told the House Assassinations Committee that Marcello had been very angry, and had "clearly stated that he was going to arrange to have President Kennedy murdered in some way."[75] Marcello explained his intentions with an analogy comparing President Kennedy to a dog and Attorney General Kennedy to its tail.[76] "The dog will keep biting you if you only cut off its tail," Marcello observed, but the dog would die if its head were cut off.[77] Marcello also offered a less allegorical rationale for the choice of victim, as reported in an FBI synopsis of a 1967 interview with Reid:

> They could not kill Bobby because the President would use the Army and the Marines to get them. The result of killing the President would cause Bobby to lose his power as Attorney General because of the new President.[78]

Becker told the House Assassinations Committee that Marcello's plan to murder President Kennedy appeared serious and deliberate.[79] Marcello had even alluded to the manner in which he intended to carry out the contract.[80] According to Becker, Marcello indicated that an outsider would be used or manipulated to do the job, so that his own lieutenants would not be linked to the crime.[81]

Although Becker was disturbed by Marcello's words, he did not believe Marcello would be able to follow through on his plan, and had grown accustomed to underworld figures making such vituperative remarks about their adversaries.[82] But after the assassination, as the House Assassinations Committee paraphrased, Becker

> quickly came to believe that Carlos Marcello had in fact probably been behind it. He reached this opinion because of factors such as Lee Oswald having been from New Orleans, as well as Jack Ruby's alleged underworld associations. Becker stated that "it was generally thought in mob circles that Ruby was a tool of some mob group." Becker further stated that he had learned after the assassination that "Oswald's uncle, who used to run some bar, had been a part of the gambling network overseen by Marcello. He worked for the mob in New Orleans."[83]

When questioned by the House Assassinations Committee on January 11, 1978, Marcello denied that the meeting or discussion reported by Becker had ever occurred.[84] But two points Marcello advanced in support of his denial were particularly unconvincing. First, in conflict with his own expressed feelings[85] and information from other sources,[86] Marcello claimed he had not been terribly concerned about Robert Kennedy's anti-crime stance until his April 1961 deportation, and that he did not hold a grudge against Robert Kennedy.[87] Second, Marcello testified that he used his Churchill Farms estate only for hunting and not for meetings.[88] This second assertion was directly contradicted by Marcello associate[89] David Ferrie, who told the FBI that he had met there with Marcello on November 9 and 16, 1963, to map "strategy in connection with Marcello's trial."[90]

Notwithstanding the Mobster's denial, Becker's account of Marcello's intention to murder President Kennedy rang true. Becker reiterated to the House Assassinations Committee: "It was [truthful] then and it is now. I was there."[91] Author Ed Reid told the Committee that he believed that Becker was credible and trustworthy, and had previously furnished "unusually reliable" information about organized crime.[92] Independent sources confirmed that Becker went to New Orleans in September 1962,[93] and that Becker's associate Carl Roppolo was close to Carlos Marcello.[94] Also significant were the statements of Julian Blodgett, a former FBI agent and chief investigator for the district attorney of Los Angeles County, for whom Becker did investigative work in the early 1960s.[95] Blodgett told the House Assassinations Committee that Becker was honest and was one of "the most knowledgeable detail men" in the private investigative business.[96] Blodgett said he would believe Becker's account of the Marcello meeting.[97]

/4/ An Assassination Prediction by Santos Trafficante

If Carlos Marcello had exhorted the Mafia National Commission to arrange the murder of President Kennedy, an eager second might well have
been Tampa Mafia boss Santos Trafficante, Jr.

Like his very close associate[98] Marcello, Trafficante is a longstanding Mafia power[99] with influence extending into the Bahamas and the Caribbean.[100] Trafficante's Mob stature was highlighted by his presence at two
Mafia meetings in New York State: the 1957 convention at Apalachin,[101] and
the 1966 mini-conclave at La Stella Restaurant in Queens.[102] Indicative of
their close relationship, Trafficante sat at Marcello's left at the latter gathering of 13 top Mafia figures.[103]

Trafficante had been the leading figure in the Mob's Cuban gambling empire during the 1950s.[104] Following Castro's shutdown of Mob rackets, as
will be discussed, Trafficante became a principal in Mafia-CIA assassination attempts on the Cuban premier.[105] Trafficante was also a key figure in
worldwide narcotics operations[106]—a preoccupation that may explain his
visit in 1968 to Singapore, Hong Kong, and South Vietnam.[107] The Florida
Mafia boss could thus have hardly favored two foreign policy initiatives of
President Kennedy in the fall of 1963: moves toward accommodation with
Castro, and the ordered withdrawal of 1,000 American troops from South
Vietnam, an underworld narcotics stronghold.[108] But Trafficante was hurt
closer to home by the Kennedy Administration's anticrime crusade, as he
expressed in an obscene diatribe recorded by an FBI bug in 1963.[109]

In its 1979 report, the House Assassinations Committee noted Mafia boss
Trafficante's predisposition to participate in a murder contract against
President Kennedy:

> Santos Trafficante's stature in the national syndicate of
> organized crime, notably the violent narcotics trade, and his
> role as the mob's chief liaison to criminal figures within the
> Cuban exile community, provided him with the capability of
> formulating an assassination conspiracy against President
> Kennedy.... In testimony before the committee, Trafficante
> admitted participating in the unsuccessful CIA conspiracy to
> assassinate Castro, an admission indicating his willingness to
> participate in political murder.[110]

One incident carried these suspicions beyond the realm of conjecture.

In September 1962, while an inebriated Carlos Marcello outlined a
presidential assassination contract at Churchill Farms, Trafficante spouted
injudicious remarks of his own at the Scott Byron Motel in Miami Beach.[111]
Trafficante expressed them during a meeting with José Aleman, Jr., a
wealthy Cuban exile, about a $1.5 million Teamster loan.[112] According to

Aleman, as reported by the *Washington Post* in 1976, the subject turned to John and his brother Robert Kennedy, at which point Trafficante became quite bitter:

> Have you seen how his brother is hitting Hoffa, a man who is a worker, who is not a millionaire, a friend of the blue collars [*sic*]? He doesn't know that this kind of encounter is very delicate. Mark my words, this man Kennedy is in trouble, and he will get what is coming to him.[113]

When Aleman suggested that Kennedy would probably get reelected, Trafficante replied, "No, José, he is going to be hit."[114]

Aleman said that he reported this and subsequent conversations with Trafficante to FBI agents,[115] and was questioned closely by the FBI about this threat shortly after the assassination.[116] According to the *Washington Post*, two of the agents named by Aleman, George Davis and Paul Scranton, "acknowledge their frequent contacts with Aleman but both declined to comment on Aleman's conversation with Trafficante."[117] Scranton explained he required clearance to furnish such comment and "wouldn't want to do anything to embarrass the Bureau."[118]

Trafficante was summoned before the House Assassinations Committee on March 16, 1977, and asked if he had known or discussed information that President Kennedy would be assassinated.[119] The Mafia boss declined to answer, citing his Constitutional right to avoid self-incrimination.[120] He likewise remained silent when asked if he had visited Jack Ruby in Cuba.[121] "There was considerable evidence," the Committee reported, that such an encounter "did take place" in 1959.[122] When Trafficante was subsequently granted immunity and recalled to testify, he admitted meeting with Aleman to discuss a Teamster loan, but denied ever predicting President Kennedy's murder.[123]

Aleman was questioned under oath by the Committee on September 27, 1978, and he described his conversation with Trafficante exactly as the *Washington Post* had reported.[124] In particular, Aleman repeated Trafficante's menacing words about President Kennedy, including the phrase "he is going to be hit."[125] Expressing pronounced fear of reprisal from Trafficante,[126] however, Aleman professed he had interpreted this remark to mean Kennedy would be hit "with a lot of votes from the Republican Party or something like that."[127] Yet in two previous interviews with Committee staff members, Aleman said that he had clearly understood this phrase and additional statements by Trafficante to indicate that the president would be murdered before the 1964 election.[128] As one staff interviewer paraphrased, Aleman reported that Trafficante "was not guessing about the killing; rather he was giving the impression that he knew Kennedy was going to be killed."[129] Aleman also told a staff interviewer that he gathered "that Hoffa was to be principally involved in the elimination of Kennedy."[130]

/5/ Assassination Plots by Jimmy Hoffa

To be sure, if any Mafia associate was inclined to assist an assassination contract against President Kennedy, it was Teamster boss James Riddle Hoffa.

Hoffa had been a close ally of the Mob since he courted it to gain control of the Teamsters[131]—turning the union into a "mob subsidiary"[132] and its Central States Pension Fund into a Mob grab bag.[133] In particular, Hoffa was exceptionally close to both Carlos Marcello and Santos Trafficante,[134] each instrumental in a massive Mob campaign which attempted to keep the Teamster boss out of jail.[135] Along with Marcello, Trafficante and Chicago Mafia boss Sam Giancana, Hoffa was a principal target of Robert Kennedy's campaign against organized crime.[136] And Hoffa made no effort to conceal his loathing of both John and Robert Kennedy.[137] For example, on November 22, 1963, Hoffa flew into a rage and became abusive when notified that Teamster headquarters had been closed in President Kennedy's memory.[138]

Hoffa had expressed similar vitriolic sentiments about the Kennedys to a trusted lieutenant, Edward Partin.[139] A tough Teamster official from Louisiana, Partin had been a Hoffa confidant since 1957.[140] The Teamster boss had believed Partin to be a man of proper loyalties, as Partin later explained: "Hoffa always just assumed that since I was from Louisiana I was in Marcello's hip pocket."[141] But in the summer of 1962, when Hoffa's remarks about Robert Kennedy escalated from diatribes to proposed murder plots, Partin was shocked into becoming a government informant.[142] And he became quite an informant—furnishing details of conversations with Hoffa and aides which were repeatedly corroborated.[143] Partin also demonstrated his credibility by passing an FBI polygraph test on his account of the Kennedy murder plot "with flying colors."[144]

Partin told federal officials that Hoffa first spoke to him of killing Robert Kennedy in July or August 1962, when Partin was in Hoffa's Washington office.[145] Hoffa asked Partin if he knew anything about plastic explosives, and mentioned throwing a bomb in Kennedy's car or home.[146] Hoffa explained to Partin, "I've got to do something about that son of a bitch Bobby Kennedy. He's got to go."[147] Hoffa also mentioned that he knew where to get a silencer for a gun.[148] In a subsequent telephone conversation between Hoffa and Partin, which was taped by federal officials, Hoffa asked Partin to bring plastic explosives to Nashville;[149] Hoffa was on trial there for allegedly receiving hundreds of thousands of dollars in payoffs from a trucking firm.[150]

A second murder plan which Hoffa discussed with Partin was strikingly similar to the one carried out against President Kennedy. As the House

Assassinations Committee summarized, Hoffa proposed "the possible use of a lone gunman equipped with a rifle with a telescopic sight. . . . an assassin without any identifiable connection to the Teamster organization or Hoffa himself."[151] He spoke of "the advisability of having the assassination committed somewhere in the South," where extreme segregationists could be blamed.[152] And Hoffa noted "the potential desirability of having Robert Kennedy shot while riding in a convertible."[153]

Partin told the House Assassinations Committee, as it paraphrased, that "Hoffa had believed that having the Attorney General murdered would be the most effective way of ending the Federal Government's intensive investigation of the Teamsters and organized crime."[154] Yet as Hoffa's close friend[155] Carlos Marcello noted soon afterward in September 1962,[156] the assassination of the president was a more logical step. And Partin found it possible that one Kennedy assassination plan by Hoffa could have developed into another.[157] Partin noted that Hoffa "hated Jack as much as Bobby. . . . After all, he was the man who'd always been in charge of Bobby."[158] Hoffa would "fly off" when the name of President Kennedy "was even mentioned."[159]

Both the FBI and the House Assassinations Committee concluded that Partin had been truthful in reporting Hoffa's assassination plots against Robert Kennedy.[160] Indeed, as the Committee reported, "the Justice Department developed further evidence supporting Partin's disclosures, indicating that Hoffa had spoken about the possibility of assassinating the President's brother on more than one occasion."[161] Author Stephan Brill reported, for example, that Hoffa's top aide, Harold Gibbons, had also "overheard parts of a conversation in which Hoffa discussed the possibility of having Robert Kennedy murdered."[162]

/6/ **Masters of Murder**

Thus the Mafia was pushed to desperation and fury by the Kennedys' anticrime crusade. And even more drastic federal action against this national enemy was portended by the televised Valachi hearings of October 1963. On November 22, 1963, however, the Mob's problem was suddenly solved—solved by an assassination that had been outlined or predicted within three months in 1962 by Marcello, Trafficante and Hoffa, all intimate associates. Could the Mob have in fact performed the murder it so chillingly previewed? A decidedly affirmative answer is found in its century-long record of slaughter, which continues to this day.

While it is generally believed that every Mafia member is required at some time to kill,[163] the height of the art is cultivated by salaried hit squads maintained by each of the families.[164] Whether the victim is to be strangled and left in the city dump as an example,[165] punctured through the ear with an ice pick to mimic a natural cerebral hemorrhage,[166] smashed in the face with a baseball bat for effect,[167] shot and robbed at home to appear as "street crime,"[168] or gunned down at a public rally,[169] the Mafia has hundreds of professionals with the expertise to carry it off smoothly.[170] Whether the victim is a cooperative witness,[171] a Mobster out of line,[172] a radio announcer,[173] a reporter,[174] a policeman,[175] a labor leader,[176] or an exiled South American democrat,[177] the Mafia can devise a plan to eliminate the victim with the finest killers and weapons available.[178] And whether the statistics of its workings are one thousand recorded killings in Chicago,[179] or two-thirds of all murders and maimings in Massachusetts,[180] the Mafia holds the uncontested title of number one in murder.

Although local talent is usually abundant, Mafia bosses often handle important contracts with the best of the national field.[181] As New England Mafia defector Vincent Teresa reported,

> The idea of importing gunmen from other mobs isn't new. Anastasia used to send out assassins all over the country [from the infamous "Murder, Inc."] to handle hits for other mobs. Today, every mob has its own assassination squads who are available for lend-lease assignments. Whether you go to Chicago, New York, Montreal, Newark or Boston, they have assassination squads made up of men who get a regular weekly salary just to be ready for the day a hit is needed.[182]

Teresa named both killers and victims in three slayings in which hit men from other families were used, exemplifying this nationwide murder network.[183] He also mentioned one instance in which assassins from his Mafia family were sent to New Orleans to handle a contract for Carlos Marcello; Teresa did not know who the targeted victim was.[184]

As *Look*'s Washington bureau chief, Warren Rogers, wrote in 1969,

> If it was a conspiracy that killed President Kennedy ... the Cosa Nostra should have been a prime suspect. The Mafia *is* a conspiracy, and it had the organization, the assassination know-how, the skilled manpower and a motive.[185] [Emphasis in original.]

And as the House Assassinations Committee concluded in its 1979 report, Marcello, Trafficante, Hoffa, and the Mob as a whole "had the motive, opportunity and means" to kill President Kennedy.[186] This capability was further indicated by the activities of four suspicious assassination figures, as covered in one last chapter of compelling preliminaries.

□ 5 □

Four Suspects

Three men were apprehended as possible suspects soon after the assassination of President Kennedy. A fourth man later drew suspicion by conducting a bizarre assassination probe which thoroughly obfuscated the case. Yet when the evidence was unraveled, there were common features characterizing all four. Every one was linked to the Mob. Every one was active in New Orleans. And every one left a trail that led, directly or indirectly, to New Orleans Mafia boss Carlos Marcello.

/1/ David Ferrie

David Ferrie was a man of dual affiliations. On the one hand, he was a virulent anti-Communist[2] who provided flight instruction, armaments and money to the Cuban Revolutionary Council (CRC), an anti-Castro organization.[3] He associated with men like Guy Banister, a private detective and a reputed bigwig in the ultraright Minutemen.[4] Like Ferrie, Banister was closely involved in the CRC,[5] and shortly before the Bay of Pigs invasion, Banister reportedly stored a large quantity of arms at his 544 Camp Street office in New Orleans.[6] Ferrie was very close with Banister, visiting his office frequently in 1963.[7]

The other affiliation that characterized Ferrie, as *Look* magazine summarized, was his "well-known" and "strong ties to Carlos Marcello."[8] Ferrie knew Marcello well,[9] telephoned him several times,[10] and was reported by

several sources to have flown Marcello back to the United States after Marcello's deportation to Guatemala.[11] Even in his anti-Castro activities, Ferrie
may have served as a financial conduit for Marcello, as suggested by an FBI
report of April 1961.[12] Ferrie's ties with the Mafia boss were particularly intensive in the fall of 1963, when both Ferrie and Banister were employed by
attorney G. Wray Gill on Marcello's deportation case.[13]

[In light of Ferrie's ties to both anti-Castro elements and Marcello, especially intriguing was his association with another noteworthy person: Lee
Harvey Oswald. This association probably began in the mid-1950s, when
Oswald was a cadet in a Louisiana Civil Air Patrol squadron commanded
by Captain David Ferrie.[14] Several witnesses confirmed to the House
Assassinations Committee that Oswald and Ferrie were in the squadron at
the same time; one reported that "it is a certainty."[15] Six other witnesses,
whom the committee found "credible and significant,"[16] testified that Ferrie
and Oswald were definitely together in Clinton, Louisiana, less than three
months before the assassination.[17]

After Kennedy was shot, Ferrie's links to Oswald became especially trou-
bling to Jack Martin of New Orleans. A friend of Ferrie's until mid-1963[18]
and a sometime investigator for Guy Banister,[19] Martin told several people
that he suspected Ferrie might have assisted Oswald in the killing.[20] That
evening, Martin got into an argument over the matter with Guy Banister in
Banister's office.[21] Martin claimed the provoking factor was his remark to
Banister, "What are you going to do—kill me like you all did Kennedy?"[22]
What happened next was described in a police report filed that day:
Banister severely beat Martin on the head with his revolver.[23] According to
Martin, Banister would have killed him but for the intervention of
Banister's secretary.[24]

Within 48 hours of this incident, as the House Assassinations Committee
summarized, "Martin had the entire New Orleans police department hunting for David Ferrie."[25] As with virtually all witnesses whose information
contravened the lone-nut hypothesis, however, Martin's allegations about
Ferrie were dismissed as being "without foundation."[26] And soon after
questioning by the New Orleans Police, the Secret Service and the FBI, Ferrie was cleared of suspicion and released.[27] Yet after FBI documents from
Warren Commission files were declassified in 1970 and other material was
released by Congress, initial suspicions about Ferrie were strongly
reinforced.

A prime point of concern was Ferrie's virulent posture toward President
Kennedy. Questioned by the FBI after Kennedy's death, Ferrie admitted that
following the Bay of Pigs invasion, he had "severely criticized" Kennedy
both in public and private.[28] Ferrie claimed he had no real murderous intent, but "might have used an offhand or colloquial expression, 'He ought
to be shot.' "[29] Ferrie also admitted that he had said anyone could hide in
the bushes and shoot the president.[30]

Ferrie's questionable alibi for November 22 and the few days following hardly precludes the possibility that he followed through on his "offhand" remark.[31] Carlos Marcello, attorney G. Wray Gill, Gill's secretary, and FBI agent Regis Kennedy all asserted that Ferrie was in New Orleans attending to Marcello's deportation case at the time of the assassination.[32] But the only one of the four not actually involved in Marcello's case was FBI agent Kennedy—who had been strangely derelict in his assigned surveillance of Marcello,[33] and who had passed on Marcello's preposterous claim that he earned his living as a tomato salesman and real estate investor.[34] Kennedy and Marcello both said that Ferrie was in the courtroom at Marcello's trial at 12:15 p.m. on November 22.[35] But Gill and his secretary said that Ferrie was at Gill's office at that time.[36]

Ferrie told FBI investigators that later in the day, in "celebration" of Marcello's acquittal, Ferrie and two friends decided on the spur of the moment to go "hunting, drinking or driving."[37] "Merely to relax," his story continued, Ferrie, Alvin Beauboeuf and Melvin Coffey then drove several hundred miles all night in a heavy rainstorm to Houston and Galveston, Texas, hoping to go ice-skating and goose-hunting.[38] But Ferrie's alibi was seriously flawed. According to one witness in Texas, the three men did no ice-skating whatsoever.[39] And they would have had a hard time goose-hunting, since according to Ferrie, they brought no guns.[40] Moreover, Ferrie claimed that he left his home at roughly 6:30 p.m. on November 22 to pick up his friends, eat dinner in Kenner, Louisiana, and continue to Texas.[41] But Gill said that Ferrie was at the Royal Orleans Hotel that evening,[42] while Assistant District Attorney Herbert Kohlman learned that Ferrie left for Dallas that afternoon.[43] And finally, a conflict in the records of two hotels placed Ferrie and his friends in both Houston and Galveston during a 12-hour period between November 23 and 24.[44]

Two aspects of Ferrie's assassination weekend whereabouts, however, were incontrovertible and significant. First, Ferrie was in Texas within hours after, if not during the assassination of President Kennedy. Second, in the same period, Ferrie made several contacts with Marcello and Marcello's attorney, G. Wray Gill. Among these contacts were telephone calls Ferrie placed to Gill from various points in Texas.[45] Ferrie also called the Town and Country Motel, Marcello's headquarters in New Orleans,[46] from one of his stops: the Alamotel in Houston, another Marcello property.[47] Perhaps most interesting, however, were meetings on November 9 and 16 between Ferrie and Marcello at the Mobster's Churchill Farms estate;[48] Ferrie claimed they were there "mapping strategy in connection with Marcello's trial."[49]

The connecting thread to the presentation of Ferrie's alibi was again Carlos Marcello. Alvin Beauboeuf, for one, freely discussed Ferrie with the FBI on November 25, 1963, until asked about their post-assassination travels in Texas.[50] Beauboeuf suddenly refused to say anything more without

Gill's counsel.[51] The same day, Beauboeuf was arrested in New Orleans along with Layton Martens,[52] who had been in contact with Ferrie during the Texas trip.[53] When questioned about Ferrie, they refused to talk without the help of another Marcello attorney, Jack Wasserman[54]—who years later, before the House Crime Committee, repeatedly and improperly prompted Marcello when the Mafioso avowed that he was a "tomato salesman."[55] Also on November 25, when Ferrie presented himself to New Orleans authorities for questioning about the assassination, he showed up with none other than Gill as his counsel.[56]

Initial police suspicions of Ferrie thus proved to be solidly founded. He had made overtly threatening statements against the president. His alibi for November 22 through November 25 was incongruous, contradictory, and curiously reliant on counsel by attorneys of Carlos Marcello. And Ferrie was closely involved with the Mafia boss during and before this period, meeting him personally on the two Saturdays before the assassination. These contacts were especially ominous given Ferrie's contacts with Oswald and the specific assassination plan which Marcello outlined in September 1962.[57]

Yet Ferrie was not the only Marcello associate in contact with Lee Oswald before the assassination.

/2/ Lee Harvey Oswald

Lee Harvey Oswald, a 24-year-old father of two young daughters, had moved from New Orleans, his birthplace, to Dallas in October 1963.[58] His marksmanship was marginal,[59] and barring psychological speculation,[60] his motive for killing President Kennedy was indiscernible. Yet after the Dallas shooting, with remarkable dispatch, Oswald was arrested, proclaimed the lone assassin, and then permanently silenced by Jack Ruby's revolver.

These circumstances, plus serious flaws in the official case against Oswald,[61] suggest questions as to his role in the assassination. Was Oswald set up as a fall guy, as he maintained,[62] possibly recruited to perform some compromising action to link him to the assassination? Was he perhaps assigned to fire some shots at the motorcade, in the vain hope that with a bizarre stroke of luck, the assassin in the grassy knoll would be spared the trouble of shooting? If so, did Oswald follow through, or did he back out at the last minute, perceiving the trap that had been laid? Whatever Oswald actually did, however, recent disclosures of the House Assassinations Committee shed light on a more important issue: the identity of those behind his actions.

A glimpse into Oswald's actual affinities is afforded by an incident in which he was arrested for disturbing the peace. On August 9, Oswald was handing out pro-Castro leaflets in New Orleans for the Fair Play for Cuba

Committee.[63] He got into a scuffle with three Cuban exiles and police intervened, arresting all four men.[64] On the surface, the incident appeared to illustrate Oswald's commitment to Communist causes and his propensity to commit erratic actions to further his beliefs.[65]

Yet two features of Oswald's arrest indicate far different involvements, paralleling the dual affiliations of his August 1963 contact, David Ferrie. First, the building at 544 Camp Street, the address on Oswald's pro-Castro leaflets, housed only Cuban activists of the anti-Castro bent—including the Cuban Revolutionary Council, Guy Banister and David Ferrie.[66] Moreover, as the House Assassinations Committee reported, Oswald was associated with quite a few anti-Castro activists in 1963,[67] despite his professed pro-Castro leanings.[68] The second interesting feature of Oswald's arrest was the identity of the man who arranged his bail: Emile Bruno;[69] Bruno was an associate of two Syndicate deputies of Carlos Marcello.[70]

Charles "Dutz" Murret, Oswald's uncle and a friend of Bruno,[71] was also well-connected with the New Orleans Mafia crowd. Various other relatives of Oswald told the House Assassinations Committee that Murret was heavily involved in New Orleans gambling, and had worked for notorious Marcello Mobster Sam Saia.[72] The FBI and other sources reported additional Mob associations of Murret.[73] And according to Marguerite Oswald, Lee's mother, Murret had probably met Marcello himself.[74]

Although Murret's background provides no more than a hint of suspicion, it is intriguing in view of his exceptionally close relationship with his nephew. Murret was a "surrogate father of sorts" to Oswald in New Orleans, the House Assassinations Committee noted.[75] These ties continued after Oswald went to the Soviet Union, married, and returned to the United States. In the spring of 1963, for example, Oswald spent several days at the Murret residence,[76] which had been almost a second home for Oswald in his youth.[77] In July 1963, Oswald traveled with the Murret family to Mobile, Alabama, where Oswald gave a talk about his experiences in Russia;[78] Dutz Murret paid for the trip.[79] And on the evening of August 11, two days after Oswald's arrest, Murret stopped by at Oswald's apartment.[80] During this period of close contact between Oswald and Murret, Oswald was familiar with his uncle's extensive underworld activities, discussing them in 1963 with his wife, Marina.[81]

Murret and his friend Emile Bruno were not Oswald's only points of contact with organized crime. Oswald had grown up on Exchange Alley in New Orleans, a center of notorious underworld joints and Mafia-affiliated gambling operations.[82] His high school was regarded by some "as the alma mater, so to speak, of kids who frequently graduated to various criminal and underworld careers."[83] Furthermore, Mrs. Marguerite Oswald, Lee's mother, was for many years a close friend of Mobster Sam Termine,[84] who in turn was close to Carlos Marcello.[85] Termine had in fact "spoken of serving as a

Marcello chauffeur and bodyguard," the House Assassinations Committee reported, "while he was actually on the State payroll, in the Louisiana State Police"[86] (such dual affiliation has been demonstrated often in both New Orleans[87] and Chicago[88]). Mrs. Oswald twice refused to provide any specific information about Termine when questioned by the House Assassinations Committee.[89]

/3/ Eugene Hale Brading

Both ballistic evidence[90] and witnesses' reports[91] suggest that one bullet fired on November 22 came from a group of three structures facing Dealey Plaza: the Records, Criminal Courts and Dal-Tex buildings. The Dal-Tex building, in particular, was the scene of a Dallas Police search immediately after the fateful shooting on November 22.[92] And the possibility that an assassination team had been operating in that building was suggested by the prompt arrests of two suspects.

One man, wearing a black leather jacket and black gloves, was led out of the building by two policemen.[93] He was then driven off in a police car to the catcalls of the crowd.[94] The police report states only that this man had been in the building "without a good excuse" and had been taken to the Dallas County Sheriff's office.[95] Incredibly enough, police records contain no further reference to this suspect.[96]

The other man arrested in the Dal-Tex Building shortly after the assassination, in contrast, presented an affluent appearance and a polished alibi.[97] He identified himself as Jim Braden, a 48-year-old Californian in Dallas on oil business.[98] Braden explained his presence in the Dal-Tex Building by relating in some detail how he had gone in to find a public telephone right after President Kennedy was assassinated.[99] Yet according to the Dallas County Sheriff's Office, he was in the building when the president was shot.[100] Braden's identity and address were confirmed by a California driver's license and credit card,[101] and he too was released without fingerprinting or further police investigation.[102]

Braden's assassination-day arrest drew more attention in 1969, however, when the license number he had furnished to police[103] was checked through the California Department of Motor Vehicles.[104] It turned out that "Jim Braden" was a changed name which appeared on a new driver's license requested on September 10, 1963 by a Eugene Hale Brading.[105] In the past, Eugene Brading had in fact used four other aliases.[106] And the need for Brading's many aliases was revealed through an investigation spearheaded by Peter Noyes, the producer of CBS-TV affiliate KNXT in Los Angeles.[107] Among Noyes' sources were federal and local law enforcement agencies,[108] including the Los Angeles Police Department,[109] which had questioned Brading about his presence in Los Angeles—100 miles from his home—on the night of the Robert Kennedy assassination.[110] Concerned about his possible involvement in both Kennedy assassinations, the Los Angeles Police compiled an extensive report on Brading.[111]

It turned out that Brading's associations ranged from "Mafia and oil contacts" to friendships "with 'far-right' industrialists and political leaders" in the Dallas area, noted Robert Houghton, chief of detectives of the Los Angeles Police.[112] Most conspicuous were Brading's Syndicate ties, such as his close contacts with Mafia bosses[113] Eugene and Clyde Smaldone of Denver.[114] Brading was also an associate of California Mafia executioner[115] James Fratianno, Mobster[116] Harold "Happy" Meltzer, California Mafioso[117] Joe Sica, and other underworld figures.[118] And Brading's rap sheet showed 35 arrests,[119] with convictions for burglary, bookmaking and embezzlement.[120] As California television producer Noyes summarized, Brading was "a man linked over the years to the Mafia."[121]

Under critical reexamination, the alibi provided by "Jim Braden" for his November 22 arrest proved flimsy. When questioned by the Los Angeles Police Homicide Division in connection with the Robert Kennedy assassination,[122] Brading said he had viewed President Kennedy's motorcade from outside the Federal Parole Building.[123] Adding a touch of specificity, Brading claimed to have noticed a parole officer there, a "Mr. Flowers."[124] Yet Roger Carroll, chief probation officer in Dallas, reported that all employees of the Parole Building had walked over to Harwood Street to watch the motorcade, since the view from the Parole Building was almost completely obstructed.[125] And Carroll stated that he had no "Mr. Flowers" employed at his office in November 1963 or at any time since then.[126] Also contradicted was a claim of Brading that he left Dallas for Houston on the night of November 22: federal parole records do not place him in Houston until four days later.[127]

Interesting, too, were Brading's whereabouts the day before the assassination. When Brading checked in on November 21 with Officer Carroll, as reported in federal parole records,[128] he stated that he "planned to see Lamar Hunt and other oil speculators" while in Dallas.[129] Brading claimed that he never actually saw Lamar Hunt,[130] but confirmed that three business associates did visit Hunt on November 21, 1963.[131] The three were Roger Bauman, Morgan Brown and Duane Nowlin[132]—all with strong underworld ties.[133] Further information was furnished by Paul Rothermal, a former FBI agent who was chief of security for Hunt Oil in Dallas.[134] Rothermal reported that the company log for November 21 showed a visit to Lamar and Nelson Hunt by Bauman, Brown, Nowlin "and friend."[135] Rothermal said he believed this "friend" was Eugene Brading.[136] What is most significant about Brading's reported visit to Hunt, as will be discussed later, is that Jack Ruby was in or near Lamar Hunt's office on that very day.

Brading's movements reveal another suspicious coincidence. During his several trips to New Orleans in the fall of 1963,[137] he used the office of an oil geologist in room 1701 of the Marquette Building, receiving mail at that address.[138] On one occasion, Brading informed parole authorities that he could be contacted at room 1706 of that building.[139] The office of G. Wray Gill, Marcello's attorney, which David Ferrie frequented in the fall of 1963, was room 1707.[140] Yet the activities of Brading, Ferrie and Ferrie's contact Oswald would become obscured by the subsequent machinations of another New Orleans resident.

/4/ Jim Garrison

By the year 1967, the double-lone-nut theory of the Warren Commission had been trampled to a new low of credibility by an onslaught of independent critical research. After much discussion in leading journals, books, and legal and medical forums,[141] Oswald's capability to fire all of the assassination shots had been seriously disputed.[142] A Congressional resolution calling for a review of the Warren Commission findings had been introduced[143] with the support of several prominent Americans.[144] And the American public, which had accepted the lone-assassin hypothesis almost universally in 1963,[145] rejected it by a three-to-two margin in a 1966 Louis Harris poll.[146]

But critical review of the Kennedy case came to a virtual standstill in February 1967,[147] following a startling development in New Orleans. Jim Garrison, the city's district attorney, announced that he had uncovered an assassination conspiracy and would prosecute the culprits.[148] To an attentive world press, Garrison pegged David Ferrie as a prime suspect;[149] the drama intensified four days later, when Ferrie was found dead in his apartment with a cerebral hemorrhage.[150] In the wake of these developments, Congressional calls for a new investigation were soon forgotten.[151] And thinking the D.A. had a genuine lead, many leading assassination critics rushed down to New Orleans to jump on his bandwagon.[152]

Through the efforts of these critics, a good deal of legitimate information was exchanged and disseminated from Garrison's office. Yet as Garrison's case unfolded, his specific accusations became increasingly outlandish, and the main thrust of his efforts increasingly questionable. Especially bizarre was Garrison's prosecution of Clay Shaw, who became his prime culprit.[153] A retired director of the New Orleans International Trade Mart, Shaw was a soft-spoken liberal who devoted most of his time to restoring homes in the Old French Quarter and writing plays.[154] Although Garrison succeeded in establishing that Shaw was a homosexual[155] whose first name matched that of a reported suspect,[156] it took the jury less than an hour to find Shaw innocent of Garrison's extravagant accusations.[157]

A monumental fraud. Through Garrison's prosecution of Clay Shaw, however, a criminal conspiracy was indeed exposed. As summarized by Walter Sheridan, an NBC investigator and a former aide to Robert Kennedy, Garrison's effort was "an enormous fraud," involving "bribery and intimidation of witnesses."[158] The particulars were reported by *Newsweek*,[159] the *New York Times*,[160] *Look* magazine,[161] the *Saturday Evening Post*,[162] an NBC News special,[163] and the book *Counterplot* by Edward J. Epstein.[164] The methods, as documented in these sources, included promised or transacted bribes of cash, gifts, an airline job, financing for a private club, heroin, and a paid vacation in Florida.[165] Garrison and his aides also resorted to threats of imprisonment and death,[166] a plot to plant evidence in Clay Shaw's home,[167] and indoctrination of witnesses to parrot invented charges under the influence of hypnosis and drugs.[168]

Everyone but the Mafia. Although Garrison made extravagant charges against an assortment of Cuban exiles, CIA agents, Minutemen, White Russians, and Nazis,[169] he conspicuously avoided any reference[170] to one prime assassination suspect: the Mafia. For example, in discussing testimony concerning Ruby's anti-Castro activities, which he quoted at length, Garrison described Ruby as a "CIA bagman" and an "employee of the CIA."[171] But Garrison said nothing about Ruby's organized crime involvement.[172] The cited testimony, in contrast, contains not one allusion to the CIA.[173] Yet it is replete with references to the "Mafia" and the "syndicate" in connection with both Ruby's Cuban activities and his night club operations.[174] Amazingly, Garrison also refrained from mentioning[175] the close and portentous ties of his key suspect, David Ferrie, to Mafia boss Carlos Marcello.

But such ties were of little concern to Garrison, who declared on national television that Marcello was a "respectable businessman,"[176] and who stated that there was no organized crime in New Orleans.[177] According to Garrison, "people worry about the crime 'syndicate', but the real danger is the political establishment, power massing against the individual."[178] Skeptical of Garrison's professed ignorance about organized crime, a team of *Life* magazine reporters once asked him about Frank Timphony, a notorious Syndicate figure in Garrison's own district.[179] Garrison claimed never to have heard of him, and carrying the act further, placed a call to an aide in the reporters' presence.[180] The Garrison aide "promptly assured" his boss that Timphony was "one of the biggest bookies in New Orleans."[181]

Relationships and deference to the Mafia. It became apparent, however, that the district attorney's knowledge of organized crime was quite direct and intimate. Garrison's hand-picked chief investigator during his first years as district attorney was Pershing Gervais,[182] an admitted associate of Carlos Marcello.[183] Gervais was formerly a New Orleans policeman, but was fired after twice stealing the payoff money awaiting distribution to his fellow officers.[184] In 1967, *Life* magazine reported that Garrison had been given free lodging and a $5,000 line of credit on three trips to the Mob-controlled Sands Hotel in Las Vegas.[185] One of Garrison's tabs was personally signed by Marcello lieutenant Mario Marino,[186] who took the Fifth Amendment when questioned about the matter.[187] And in June 1969, as *Life* subsequently reported, Marcello bagman Vic Carona died after suffering a heart attack in Garrison's home during a political meeting.[188]

Throughout his career, Garrison demonstrated his fidelity to his reported friend,[189] Carlos Marcello. This fidelity was exhibited in the early 1960s, when Garrison conducted a cleanup of the Bourbon Street night club district after being elected district attorney as a reform candidate;[190] his raids selectively avoided the clubs controlled by Marcello.[191] From 1965 through 1969, Garrison won just seven cases against Marcello gangsters.[192] Yet he dismissed 84 such cases,[193] including one charge of attempted murder, three of kidnapping and one of manslaughter.[194]

In 1971, Garrison was on the receiving end of an indictment—on the federal charge of accepting $50,000 a year in payoffs to protect illegal gambling.[195] The tax evasion case against Garrison became "airtight," as evaluated by U.S. Attorney G. Gallinghouse,[196] when six of Garrison's codefendants turned state's evidence against him.[197] The jury was presented first-hand testimony describing four $1,000 bribes to Garrison, corroborated by IRS agents, plus actual tape recordings of the bribe transactions.[198] But Garrison was acquitted,[199] possibly with the help of reported bribes of $50,000 and $10,000 offered to rig his trial and swipe evidence.[200] The outcome was reminiscent of Marcello's acquittal on a fraud charge on November 22, 1963, after a juror had been offered a $1,000 bribe and the key witness against him set up to be murdered.[201]

Further exemplifying justice in Marcello's fiefdom was the conduct of Ed Haggerty, the presiding judge in the Clay Shaw trial. Judge Haggerty chose to lodge and feed the trial jury at the Rowntowner Inn,[202] bypassing several motels closer to court.[203] The Rowntowner was run by one of Marcello's partners,[204] Frank Occhipinti,[205] whose construction firm built a cut-rate house for Occhipinti's next-door neighbor: Jim Garrison.[206] According to Warren Rogers, then Washington bureau chief of *Look* magazine, Garrison occasionally dropped in at the Rowntowner,[207] but Judge Haggerty treated it as almost a "nightly wateringhole."[208] When Rogers went there to speak to Haggerty, his childhood acquaintance, the judge jovially introduced Rogers around—first, to Occhipinti.[209]

The Marcello set was also treated congenially in a 1967 New Orleans probe of organized crime.[210] Conducted in response to intense public pressure,[211] the probe was described to Congress by Aaron Kohn, director of the New Orleans Metropolitan Crime Commission:

District Attorney Jim Garrison and his First Assistant, Charles R. Ward, conducted a parody of a grand jury investigation into organized crime. Before doing so, however, both of these prosecutors denied the existence of organized crime in New Orleans. Those who alleged it to exist were publicly denounced as "professional liars, witchdoctors," etc. Witnesses who sought to give information about organized crime were intimidated in and out of the grand jury room over extensive periods of time.[212]

Kohn, a leading organized crime expert[213] who criticized Mob-political corruption in Louisiana,[214] was himself arrested and jailed by Garrison for "intimidating a public official by the use of threats";[215] the case was thrown out of court.[216]

The purpose of the Garrison assassination probe. Thus, Jim Garrison conducted a fraudulent probe of the Kennedy assassination, which deflected attention from Carlos Marcello[217] and disrupted serious investigation of the case.[218] And in view of Garrison's coziness with the Marcello organization, it is logical to ask whether his probe was carried out with precisely this purpose. Such a possibility is indicated by Garrison's false charges against an Edgar Eugene Bradley of California,[219] described in Los Angeles Police files as "the man Garrison mistook for Eugene Hale Brading."[220] There were enough similarities between Bradley and Brading for Garrison's accusations to confound reports about Brading.[221] But to a professional investigator, the distinction between Bradley, an uninvolved Californian, and Dal-Tex felon Brading was apparent.[222]

One blatant maneuver, however, clearly exposed the Mob's hand in Garrison's assassination charade. On March 3, 1967, during the height of the Mob-Teamster campaign to spring Jimmy Hoffa,[223] James "Buddy" Gill tried to bribe government witness Edward Partin to invalidate his testimony against Hoffa.[224] During their discussion, apparently to put additional pressure on Partin, Gill informed Partin that Garrison was going to subpoena Partin in his assassination probe.[225] And on June 23, 1967, Baton Rouge Radio Station WJBO broadcast that Partin had been "under investigation by the New Orleans District Attorney's Office in connection with the Kennedy Assassination investigation."[226] The station quoted a Garrison assistant as saying that a man drove Oswald and Ruby during alleged encounters in New Orleans, and that Garrison's office was "checking the possibility it was Partin."[227]

It was not at all anomalous that the intermediary in this crude Mob ploy, James "Buddy" Gill, had been an administrative assistant and close associate of Senator Russell Long.[228] For as shown later, Long's relationship to Carlos Marcello is similar to Garrison's,[229] and Long assisted the Marcello-coordinated effort to spring Hoffa.[230] To complete the picture, Russell Long was an old political ally of Jim Garrison[231] who encouraged Garrison's assassination probe,[232] and whose "steadfast backing" was acknowledged by Garrison.[233]

Jim Garrison's success in clouding the trail of his patron, Carlos Marcello, was reflected by author Ed Reid in *The Grim Reapers*—the book that first disclosed Marcello's 1962 plot to murder President Kennedy. After recounting Marcello's chilling remarks at Churchill Farms, Reid commented:

> Certainly, many mobsters had every reason to want the Kennedys out of the way. Of course, as District Attorney Jim Garrison is certain he can prove, other interested parties also had reasons for wanting to eliminate John F. Kennedy. Perhaps the truth will emerge one day.[234]

Although Reid was unaware of the synchrony between Marcello's and Garrison's machinations, he was correct in his concluding prediction.

PART II
MOB FIXER IN DALLAS

The telltale murders of witnesses, compelling factors of motivation and means, the vitriolic remarks of Marcello, Trafficante and Hoffa, plus the suspicious involvements of Ferrie, Oswald, Brading and Garrison—all these suggest that the Mafia was behind the assassination of President Kennedy. In the remaining chapters, this hypothesis is borne out through an extraordinary source: a detailed record of the background, activities and contacts of a Mobster involved in the crime. The Mobster is Jack Ruby; the record is the National Archives file generated from an extensive FBI investigation into the background of Oswald's murder. This file contains hundreds of thousands of documents, which on surface examination present a bewildering jumble of details. Yet when significant information is extracted, accounts of witnesses cross-checked, names cross-referenced with organized crime sources, and certain events clarified by recent Congressional disclosures, this voluminous file documents Mob culpability in the assassination.

The Ruby material will be unraveled in three steps. This part, focusing on his activities before 1963, establishes that he was a long-time Mafia functionary. The next part examines the period between November 22 and 24; it shows that the Dallas Mobster shot Oswald not on impulse, but as part of a carefully coordinated conspiracy. The final part goes back to April 23, 1963, when President Kennedy's visit to Dallas was first announced. It

considers a dramatically intensifying series of telephone calls, then meetings in Dallas, between Ruby and numerous Mobsters from across the
country—including many associates of Marcello, Trafficante and Hoffa. It
unmasks a concertedly fabricated alibi with which these Mobsters covered
these contacts, conspiracy in its own right. And it clearly links this timely
series of Mob contacts and Dallas meetings to the assassination of President Kennedy.

It is important to understand, however, that Ruby was by no means a
dominant figure in the assassination conspiracy. Rather, his role emerges
like that of a plant foreman or a stage manager. His qualification for the
final act of this role, the spectacular execution of Oswald, was his special
position in the Syndicate. For Ruby was not so notoriously linked to the
Mafia to have made its assassination involvement obvious. Yet he was
close enough to have been expected to have kept its code of silence—
without the help of yet another execution. But in the last analysis, this bal-
ance of proximity collapsed on both counts. For under post-assassination
scrutiny, Ruby's Mob ties were clearly exposed. And by the time of his final
official hearings, Ruby had neither the criminal loyalty nor the callousness
to maintain his silence about the horrible act in which he had conspired.

To put Ruby's ties to the Mafia in perspective, a brief characterization of
this criminal organization is provided here from testimony before the
House Assassinations Committee. It was presented by Ralph Salerno, retired organized crime expert of the New York City Police Department,
whom the *New York Times* credited with "the reputation of knowing more
about the Mafia than any other nonmember."[1]

> There is a national conspiratorial criminal organization
> within the United States whose members refer to as La Cosa
> Nostra. The organization is made up of groups known to the
> members as families. The families are headed by a leader who is
> referred to as a boss or the Italian word capo is used. The fami-
> lies have a second in command, executive officer to the leader,
> who is referred to as the underboss, and they use the Italian
> word sottocapo.
>
> The families have a position known as counselor, or they use
> the Italian word consigliere, who is considered to be an adviser
> and who is available to all of the members of the family.
>
> The family has within it subunits, known originally as Decina.
> ... The subunits are headed by a person with a title of capore-
> gime, or the head of the regime. This position is often referred
> to in the anglicized word captain. The individual members of
> the family are referred to as members, soldiers, or as a made
> man or as a button man.
>
> The families are governed in matters of import of policy and

in matters arising between families by the national commission whose numbers can vary, which is made up of the leaders of the major families. Those families whose leaders do not serve on the commission may have their interests represented by a commission member.

Other terms for the organization or its individual families, often used by outsiders, are the Mafia, the organization, the clique, the boys, the office, the arm.

There are rules which are known to members, though not written anywhere. They use relatives and friends as couriers. ... They have elaborate systems of prearranged times and telephone numbers in order to communicate with each other and to thus avoid electronic surveillance.

They engage in political activity to an inordinate degree. They make direct political contributions. They engage in fundraising in obtaining contributions from others for political purposes. ...

They will hold elective and appointive positions at all levels of government. They will help relatives achieve elected and/or appointed positions at all levels of government. They will try to influence the outcome of government decisions. They will lobby in favor of legislation they consider in their best interests. ...

They will campaign against candidates considered to be inimical to their best interests. They will assassinate other family leaders in order to replace them. They will employ public relations efforts, such as protesting Italian defamation, when the term Mafia or La Cosa Nostra are ever used.

They will make illegal deals with high and lower level labor leaders. They will get finders fees for arranging union loans. They will get percentages for helping someone obtain Government loans.

They will operate an intelligence-gathering capability. ... They will intimidate or kill informants and witnesses. They will fake illnesses, and once even a kidnapping, in order to avoid legal process. They will utilize bribery as a tactic. They will utilize other forms of corruption. They will engage in blackmail. They will try to influence media stories.[2]

The Mafia's incursion into America was reported by a New Orleans grand jury in 1890: "the existence of a secret organization known as the Mafia has been established beyond doubt."[3] Since then, its "existence, structure, activities, personnel," to quote a government report of 1972, "have been confirmed and reconfirmed beyond rational dispute."[4] As detailed in numerous government hearings and court proceedings, its structure and workings have been penetrated through these sources: i) the testimony of more than a dozen defected Mafia members and associates, spanning the past 60 years; ii) tape-recorded conversations of Mafiosi in operation, obtained through electronic surveillance; iii) a pattern of thousands of convictions, indictments, and arrests involving associated individuals and related crimes; and iv) police busts of national Mafia conclaves, in which previously identified Mafia members were apprehended together.[5] When provided the opportunity to refute the findings derived from these sources, Mafia members have repeatedly declined by invoking their Fifth Amendment right to avoid self-incrimination.[6]

To clarify the terminology used in this volume, the word "Mafia" denotes the specific criminal organization characterized above by Salerno. The words "Mob" and "Syndicate" refer to a larger conglomeration composed of the Mafia plus thousands of underlings and other criminals from assorted ethnic groups who function as semi-autonomous satellites. Since the Mafia works closely with these underlings and satellites, however, the distinction between "Mafia" and "Mob" applies mainly to the underworld status of individuals, not to criminal operations. For variety, or to describe criminal activity without clear Mafia affiliation, looser terms such as "organized crime," "underworld," "gangster," and "racketeer" are used with their usual connotations.

A final comment is in order concerning the Italian origins of the Mafia—as noted above by Ralph Salerno, himself of Italian descent. The Mafia is to Italians as bone cancer to bone tissue: an aberration that victimized those of its own extraction before metastasizing to other domains. The preposterous notion that frank discussion of the Mafia slights Italians has been promoted almost exclusively by Mafia members themselves.[7]

Jack Ruby . . . would be important in history even without
the events in Dallas because of his relation to the history of
organized crime in Chicago.[1]

Peter Dale Scott, professor of English at the University
of California, Berkeley, and author of several books and
articles on the Kennedy assassination

□ 6 □

Jack Ruby in Chicago: Molding of a Mobster

Jack Ruby's involvement with the Mob dates back to his earliest years in Chicago. The story of how it was forged provides both background for the assassination case and insight into the workings of organized crime in America. Moreover, it is an engrossing personal drama, which builds to a poignant climax in Ruby's final testimony before the Warren Commission.

/1/ 1911–36: Juvenile Delinquency and Underworld Introductions

Jack Rubenstein was born to Joseph and Fanny Rubenstein in 1911 in a poor Jewish neighborhood in Chicago.[2] During his youth, he lived with his family in several apartments in similar areas, generally near Italian neighborhoods.[3] Then, in 1923, because of his "bad behavior" and family problems, he was placed in a foster home by a Chicago juvenile court, and spent the next four or five years in foster homes.[4] Without the influence of a stable family, young Ruby was predictably attracted to the glamorous Prohibition riches of the gangsters, rather than to the canons of a hypocritical law enforcement in the corrupt Capone era.

Ruby's induction into Mob circles began under a prominent mentor. Boxer Barney Ross, a friend of Ruby,[5] told the FBI that in 1926 he "associated with a group of about twelve youths, among whom was Jack Ruby."[6]

Ross said that members of this group became acquainted with Al Capone, who would give them a dollar "to run innocuous errands."[7] Ross told the FBI that Ruby "might have run innocuous errands for Capone."[8]

Ruby's association with this young band of Capone minions continued for several years,[9] leading to further criminal associations. Three sources reported that around 1940, Ruby belonged to the South Side "Dave Miller Gang," headed by Chicago boxing referee Dave Miller.[10] The Warren Commission touched on this early affiliation of Ruby, reporting his disruption of pro-Nazi Bund meetings with other Miller gang members.[11] But it failed to point out that Miller was a notorious gambling boss[12] with a long police record.[13]

Dave Miller's gym, where Ruby hung out and boxer Barney Ross trained,[14] was a place to observe and associate with still more important racketeers. Indeed, fans of Ross included Ralph Capone, Matty Capone, Murray Humphreys, Frank Nitti, Sam Hunt and Tony Capezio[15]—all notorious Capone gang members. Another Ross follower was Al Capone himself,[16] who would buy up all the tickets to some early Ross fights, allowing other fans free admission.[17]

Ruby also hung out at the Sherman Hotel Lobby and the Gym Club.[18] A friend of his told the FBI that Ruby would "accept or make bets amongst the group of individuals who used to frequent both locations."[19] The old Gym Club crowd, according to the same friend, "currently hangs around the H&H Restaurant located on North La Salle Street";[20] the H&H was described in a contemporaneous FBI report as "a known hangout for Chicago bookmakers, gamblers, juice men, and petty hoodlums."[21] The manager of the H&H Restaurant, Maish Baer,[22] who knew Ruby,[23] was identified by a U.S. Senate Committee as a nonmember associate of the Chicago branch of the Mafia.[24] (Baer was murdered in 1977 after he "allegedly failed to heed a suggestion that he stop competing with the mob in the loanshark business.")[25]

Ruby rapidly acquired the precepts of his peers, as indicated by his arrest at age 19 for selling pirated music sheets.[26] He was sentenced to 30 days in jail because, according to Ruby, he "wouldn't tell the judge who was behind the business."[27] And his budding criminal character was unblemished by any steady employment.[28] An old friend related that "Ruby seemed to be always well off financially, and former friends often wondered where he obtained his income."[29]

In 1933, a lean year for the Chicago Mob with the repeal of Prohibition, Ruby and some neighborhood buddies headed out to the Santa Anita Race Track in Los Angeles.[30] This racetrack was described in testimony before the Kefauver Committee as a meeting place for Mobsters.[31] After a few months at Santa Anita, Ruby moved on to San Francisco.[32] There he worked for "gambler"[33] Frank Goldstein[34] and spent time with a racketeer associate from Chicago,[35] Solly Schulman.[36]

/2/ 1937–40: Union Official

Ruby returned to Chicago in 1937, and until 1940 was active in Local 20467 of the Scrap Iron and Junk Handlers Union.[37] Initially, Ruby organized and collected dues;[38] eventually he became a top union official.[39] A fellow boss of Local 20467, Paul Dorfman, told the FBI he believed "Ruby was never a salaried employee of the union but probably drew some expense money from collected dues."[40] Dorfman also reported that there was approximately six cents left in the treasury when he took charge in 1940.[41]

Ruby maintained that he worked for the union because he "always wanted to be a humanitarian."[42] Yet he was as qualified to have been a labor leader as his brother Hyman—once declared an "incorrigible" delinquent by a Chicago juvenile court[43]—was to have worked for Governor Horner and obtained a political patronage job.[44] A more credible explanation for Ruby's labor involvement was furnished by Paul Roland Jones, a Mobster[45] and long-time acquaintance of his.[46] Jones told the FBI he "knew that the syndicate had an interest in this union and presumed this was Ruby's connection."[47] Indeed, during Ruby's tenure in the local, the State of Illinois seized its books on the grounds that it was a "front for organized crime."[48] The AFL-CIO arrived at the same assessment, deeming it "largely a shakedown operation,"[49] and the *Chicago Tribune* cited its criminal ties.[50] Jones also told the FBI that Ruby "was accepted and to a certain extent his business operations [were] controlled by the syndicate."[51]

On December 8, 1939, the founder of Local 20467,[52] Leon Cooke, was fatally shot, under circumstances described in conflicting accounts.[53] According to a friend of Ruby, Cooke was the son of a scrap iron dealer who wanted to help the workers, and was "a very high type of individual."[54] Ruby's sister Eva Grant testified that Cooke "was a highly reputable lawyer. That's why they killed him."[55] Immediately after the shooting, the local was taken over by Paul Dorfman, the Chicago Mob's notorious trade-union liaison,[56] who brought the local into the Teamsters.[57] A subsequent Senate investigation termed the Local 20467 leadership a "link between Mr. Hoffa and the underworld," and attributed to it incidents of graft, beatings, and killings.[58] Dorfman invoked the Fifth Amendment when questioned by Senator McClellan about his position and function in the local.[59]

Ruby's role in the Mob takeover of Local 20467 was illuminated in union minutes two months after Dorfman became its head: his name appeared right after Dorfman's on an apparently hierarchical list of Local officials.[60] And Ruby retained his leadership position until the AFL temporarily took control.[61] Furthermore, the possibility that Ruby was involved in the killing itself is raised by a Chicago Police homicide report. The report states that Ruby was arrested on the day of the Cooke shooting, and "was held at the Police Station in the investigation."[62] The assumption that Ruby was held as a suspect is supported by a remark of Ruby's acquaintance Lenny Patrick, that "Rubenstein had been involved in the investigation into the murder of Leon Cooke but had been cleared."[63] Yet the Chicago homicide report strangely failed to record either the disposition of Ruby's arrest or the outcome of the murder investigation,[64]* casting doubt on the assertion that Ruby was cleared.

Nor was Ruby convincingly absolved by a story, related by both himself[68] and Paul Dorfman,[69] that union official John Martin shot Cooke in an argument. Although the Warren Commission reported this story as fact,[70] it cited in support only the account of a *Chicago Tribune* employee describing an article that allegedly pegged Martin as the killer.[71] This article, however, was apparently neither produced nor excerpted by the Commission.[72] And the report of the *Tribune* employee reveals that the source of the article was Ruby![73]

Thus with no credible exculpation of Ruby, the one person whose arrest was reported in connection with the Cooke homicide,[74] the following account must be given serious consideration. It was related by David Byron, general manager of the Automotive Division of Federated Industries in Antioch, Illinois, and a neighborhood acquaintance of Ruby in Chicago.[75] Byron told the FBI he remembered reading in a Chicago newspaper that Ruby had been

> president of some "Junk Dealers' Union" in Chicago. . . . A shooting occurred and Rubenstein was charged with killing a man. He was arrested, convicted and sentenced in Chicago on this charge and served in prison . . . for "a little over a year."[76]

The Cooke murder typifies the tactics used in the Mob's wholesale assault upon the unions, which began in the 1930s.[77] A similar case was related to the McClellan Committee by a St. Louis law enforcement officer:

> [St. Louis Mafioso] John Vitale is the boss of local 110, Laborers' union. . . . Joe Gribler was the business agent, and George Meyers worked there. . . . Both of them were killed. . . . Shot in the head . . . Raymond Sarkus was appointed business agent. . . . he was close to Vitale.[78]

---

*The disappearance of criminal records and reports on Mobsters from Chicago Police files has been a common occurrence. Chicago journalist Ovid Demaris cited several such instances,[65] and related that at one time Chicago policemen did not even bother to make a written report on a racketeer "because if they did it would be stolen from the files and sold to the hood within an hour."[66] Similar flagrant gaps and misinformation on Mobsters in the police files of several other cities have been reported.[67]

Vitale, who was seen with Gribler ten minutes before he was murdered,[79] took the Fifth Amendment when questioned about the killings.[80]

(Although names and images have changed since Ruby's years in Chicago—Allen Dorfman has succeeded his stepfather, Paul, as a top Teamster power[81]—the Mob's labor pillage continues as brazenly as ever.[82] At the 1976 Teamsters' convention in Las Vegas, for example, President Frank Fitzsimmons proclaimed, "To those who say it's time to reform this organization, that it's time the officers quit selling out the membership, I say to them, go to hell!"[83] On cue, an obscenely affluent, Mob-studded slate of officials was then returned to power, with a 25-percent pay hike.[84])*

/3/ 1941–1946: Racketeering in the Chicago Night Club District

After leaving Local 20467, Ruby became involved in several sales ventures, interspersed with long stretches of unemployment.[90] Between 1941 and 1943, Ruby and relatives reported, he sold everything from punchboards to novelties to miscellaneous items such as salt-and-pepper shakers.[91] The true nature of these ventures, however, was illuminated by Ruby's acquaintance Paul Roland Jones. Jones told the FBI that he had once given the name of a large bootlegging customer in Oklahoma to Hyman Rubenstein, Jack's brother.[92] Jones said that Hyman then shipped whiskey to the customer from Chicago, "in cases labeled to indicate they were *salt and pepper shakers.*"[93] † And representative of Ruby's associates in such operations was Ben Epstein, a bookmaker until his retirement in 1951,[94] who was involved in a "business venture" with Ruby in the 1930s.[95]

But these ventures were merely supplemental to Ruby's operations in Chicago strip joints, which have been Mob-controlled for decades.‡ One

---

*Disgusted with the rape of the Teamster membership, one elected delegate from Detroit, Pete Camarata, submitted proposals calling for a reduction in officers' salaries and the expulsion of any officer who took an employer's bribe.[85] Although properly filed, the proposals were not included in the convention agenda;[86] when Camarata introduced them on the floor, he was booed down.[87] Later, at a Fitzsimmons "victory cocktail party," Camarata was escorted out and severely beaten by two Teamster thugs.[88] It was subsequently revealed that three Teamster gunmen from Louisiana had been brought to Las Vegas to kill Camarata, but had refrained from firing when they found him accompanied by several colleagues on the night of the planned contract.[89]

† An italicized phrase denotes author's emphasis, unless a specific note to the contrary follows the phrase in question.

‡ A federal report issued in the late 1960s stated, "The criminal element is in complete control of many establishments serving liquor to patrons and all the cabarets featuring strip tease entertainment in the [six] main Chicago night life

report of Ruby's operations there came from John Cairns, who operated a jukebox route in Chicago from 1942 to 1947.[98] His route included McGovern's bar, described by the FBI as a "bar and bookmaking establishment that was frequented by gamblers and hoodlums,"[99] and characterized by the Illinois Crime Commission as a notorious criminal establishment.[100] Cairns told the FBI that he often saw a Jack Rubenstein at that bar, whom he later recognized as Oswald's killer from news photos.[101] Cairns stated that Rubenstein "was well known to others frequenting McGovern's and it was rumored that he was also a connection for narcotics traffic in the area."[102] Cairns said he had learned in addition that Ruby "had an interest" or was "employed in some managerial capacity" in a strip joint on North Clark Street.[103]

Edward Morris Jr., another Chicago resident, told the FBI that Ruby ran the Torch Club on Walton and Clark Streets in Chicago in the early 1950s.[104] Morris identified Ruby by photograph and recollected that his name was Rubenstein "or similar."[105] Jack Kelly, who had sporadic contacts with Ruby through the 1940s and 1950s, reported that Ruby sold combination gambling tickets for horse racing in 1945 or 1946 at the Gaity Club.[106] Robert Lee Shorman, who knew Ruby in Dallas, said that Ruby told him he had worked floating crap games in the Chicago area,[107] confirming Ruby's illegal gambling involvement. Also interesting was the report of Maish Baer, a Chicago Mafia nonmember associate,[108] that he and Ruby had been "hustlers" in the Maxwell Street Market area during the late 1940s.[109]

Because Ruby was identified in these reports through acquaintances or from photographs, as well as by name, quite perplexing were claims that he was being confused with another man: "Harry Rubenstein."[110] This "Harry Rubenstein," not Jack, was active in the Chicago night club district in the 1940s, according to Club 19 manager Leo Denet.[111] The same was reported by Nate Zuckerman,[112] an employee of James Allegretti,[113] whom the FBI described as a "top local organized crime figure."[114] This story was also presented, with great conviction, by Frank Loverde, described by federal sources as a Chicago Mafia member "active in the management of strip shows in Chicago's north side."[115] Loverde insisted that Ruby was not connected with organized crime in Chicago.[116] He further "indicated that he believed the [FBI] agents were questioning him in the mistaken belief that the Oswald killing had some organized crime overtones."[117] He advised that many people in Chicago confused Ruby with Harry Rubenstein, whom Loverde claimed had killed a man in 1946, was run out of Chicago and was believed to have gone to Texas.[118] Loverde declined to furnish any particulars about Harry Rubenstein to the FBI.[119]

---

areas."[96] In fact, the *Chicago Daily News*, which ran a series of Mob exposes in 1964, called special attention to one Chicago night club that it discovered was *not* outfit-sponsored.[97]

But it appeared that Loverde was confused, for the only Harry Rubenstein who turned up for the FBI said that he resided continuously in Chicago from 1925 to 1963, and had never been to Texas.[120] This Harry Rubenstein listed several night clubs he had run or owned, but mentioned neither the Torch Club, the Gaity Club, nor McGovern's[121]—three bars where Ruby was reported to have operated.[122] And any possibility of mistaken identity was precluded by further reports of Ruby's activity in the Chicago night club district by three additional persons who knew him.[123] Thus the man described by several witnesses as a gambler, night club operator and rumored narcotics connection in this Mob-controlled domain was unmistakably Jack Ruby.

Although Ruby's military service between 1943 and 1946[124] provided a respite from Chicago night club operations, it did not entirely disrupt his life style. The corporal of Ruby's training unit was Hershey Colvin, who "considered himself Ruby's closest associate during the training period," and who often traveled with Ruby to New Orleans on weekends.[125] Colvin was described by Ruby's brother Hyman as a "professional gambler" who dealt cards or ran a crap table and "maybe booked horses."[126] Consistent with this assessment, Colvin was employed at the hoodlum-owned[127] Vertigo Key Club in Chicago when interviewed by the FBI on November 26, 1963.[128] A further indication of Ruby's interests was provided by his fellow soldier Urban Roschek. Roschek told the FBI Ruby informed him that "after the war, he could get Roschek a job picking up numbers in Chicago, and Roschek could make about $200 a week."[129]

/4/ The Fine Reports of "Ruby's Chicago Friends"

The details of Ruby's early underworld involvements take on special significance in light of an utterly fantastic conclusion advanced by the Warren Commission. In its review of Ruby's Chicago background, the Commission reported, "There is no evidence that he ever participated in organized criminal activity."[130] And not to put the lie to its own assertion, the Commission omitted mention of almost all of the evidence in its own files presented in this chapter.[131]

But Ruby's Chicago underworld ties could not be concealed by mere omission, since they had been too well reported (e.g., an article of November 26, 1963 in the *New York Times*, entitled "Ruby Linked to Chicago Gangs; Boasted of Knowing Hoodlums"). So the Commission fashioned a specific denial of such ties, based solely on the following observations:

> Virtually all of Ruby's Chicago friends stated he had no close connection with organized crime. In addition, unreliable as their reports may be, several known Chicago criminals have denied any such liaison.[132]

Of course, it is ludicrous to expect that such men as Chicago Mafiosi John Capone,[133] James Allegretti,[134] and Frank Loverde[135] would reveal any of Ruby's Mob connections if they knew of them, and predictably they did not.[136] But the Commission's first sentence, concerning "Ruby's Chicago friends," seems persuasive—until the 11 documents cited in the supporting footnote are examined and cross-checked against other sources.

For one of these "Chicago friends" turns out to be Lenny Patrick, who absolved Ruby of sinister involvements by telling the FBI, "No matter how much you investigate, you'll never learn nothing, as he [Ruby] had nothing to do with nothing."[137] It so happens that Lenny Patrick is a notorious Syndicate killer,[138] identified in a U.S. Senate report as a Chicago Mafia nonmember associate.[139] He was described in a source on organized crime as a reputed "expert on gangland executions," credited by police with "masterminding some of the Syndicate's more important liquidations."[140] A second cited friend "admits knowing Lenny Patrick."[141] A third was a bookmaker;[142] a fourth, a gambler and employee of a hoodlum-owned bar;[143] a fifth, a Chicago bar owner from the gang which ran errands for Al Capone;[144] a sixth, a partner with Ruby in the sale of gambling devices.[145] Needless to say, the unmentioned backgrounds of Mob killer Patrick and others of "Ruby's Chicago friends" puts the Commission's denial of Ruby's underworld connections in drastically different light.

The Commission exhibited an equally grotesque disregard for the evidence in a similar claim it advanced about Ruby's underworld ties in Dallas: "Numerous persons have reported that Ruby was not connected with [organized criminal] activity."[146] One of this group of "numerous persons" turns out to be Joseph Campisi,[147] a leading Dallas Mafia figure.[148] Another is Roy Pike,[149] alias Mickey Ryan,[150] a close contact of Ruby during the fall of 1963,[151] whose alibi for November 22 was suspicious.[152] A third such person is union official Irwin Mazzei.[153] That Mazzei is used as a reference is incredible, for the only portion of his cited FBI interview relevant to Ruby's underworld connections was his comment that he

> knew nothing of his [Ruby's] background, hoodlum or gambling connections or Police Department connections, other than those mentioned by Ruby. Ruby had mentioned that he had connections with the "Syndicate" and labor in Chicago and used to work for the "Syndicate" in Chicago.[154]

It is indeed bizarre that the Warren Commission represented Mazzei as absolving Ruby of underworld ties, when Mazzei merely confirmed the extensive evidence of Ruby's such ties as a young man in Chicago. Yet Chicago racketeering was but a training arena for Ruby's Syndicate career, which was launched in earnest with the Mob's plunge to plunder the rich frontiers of the American West.

The rats had become bloated and all-powerful rodents, rulers of an invisible empire whose boundless billions surpassed those of Detroit's motor industry. This enormous wealth . . . gave the rodents in charcoal suits the resources to buy New York skyscrapers; to gain control of brokerage houses and banks; to muscle into competition in major industries, hotels and motels, steel and oil, vending machines and racetracks, dress factories and meat-packing plants.

Wherever they went, the rulers of this nether world carried with them the taint of their money and the contamination of their tactics. A proprietor didn't want their vending machines? Wreck his joint and teach him a lesson. A union was causing trouble? Buy off its business agent or murder him. A bank wasn't returning a Shylock's profit? Substitute phony paper for its good securities—loot the till and bankrupt it. Meat prices were high? Well horses come cheap; so do dead and diseased cows. . . .

These things have happened, do happen, are happening.[1]

Fred Cook, journalist

□ 7 □

The Mob and Jack Ruby
Move to Dallas

/1/ Mob Incursion into Dallas

While Texas has long been a haven for racketeering,[2] Dallas boasts particular notoriety.[3] From the 1930s to the mid-1940s, according to expert testimony before the Kefauver Committee, "all forms of gambling, including policy, flourished in Dallas."[4] And in 1946, when Steve Guthrie was elected sheriff of Dallas County, the city "was 'wide open' with prostitution and gambling and other vices running full steam."[5] These activities were punctuated by "an average of 2 or 3 murders a month which looked like murders by gangs."[6]

The Chicago branch of the Mafia decided that it was time to bring these lucrative rackets within its more disciplined clutches, as the Mob had already done in its westward expansion to such cities as St. Louis,[7] Detroit,[8] and Kansas City.[9] An unusually detailed account of this invasion of Dallas was given to the Kefauver[10] and McClellan[11] committees by Dallas Police Lieutenant George Butler.

According to Lt. Butler, in 1946 the "boys from Chicago came in, looked the situation over, and decided that they wanted to take over not only Dallas but the whole State of Texas and the Southwest."[12] About 20 Chicago Mobsters came down, including hoodlums Danny Lardino, Paul Labriola, James Weinberg, Martin Ochs, Marcus Lipsky, and Paul Roland Jones,* bankrolled by top-ranking Chicago Mafioso Pat Manno.[20] While Lipsky wanted to "kill the four top gamblers in the Dallas area ... and let everybody know how tough he was,"[21] Jones deemed it wiser to make a deal with the officials.[22] Jones' approach prevailed, and he entered into negotiations with newly elected Sheriff Guthrie and Lieutenant Butler, who were secretly reporting to the Dallas police chief and taping the conversations.[23]

Jones offered Sheriff Guthrie a substantial cut of the profits in exchange for completely protected gambling operations, including bookmaking, slot machines, and card and dice games.[24] As Jones later told the FBI, "the substance of the arrangements made was simply that the syndicate group would run the County and the Sheriff was to take their orders and that the syndicate group would provide sufficient people to handle the operations."[25] The Mob was also eager to gain a foothold in its drive to take over the unions.[26] In particular, Butler testified, it aimed to "*unionize every truckdriver in the Nation*," so it could "*bring industry to its knees, and even the Government*."[27]

During the bribery negotiations, Jones told Guthrie that his cut could add up to $150,000 a year or more.[28] And when the next election came around, Jones promised, the Mob would "buy off all competition and pay all of his campaign expenses."[29] In addition, they would furnish letters

---

*The labor racketeering activities of Lardino, Labriola, and Weinberg were described in testimony before the McClellan Committee in the late 1950s.[13] The committee reported that Lardino, in particular, was a top Chicago Syndicate figure,[14] and that Labriola at one point held the longest arrest record in Chicago history.[15]

Marcus Lipsky was a partner with Chicago Mafioso[16] Ross Prio in the Blue Ribbon Dairy Company and the L&P (Lipsky and Prio) Milk Company.[17] Lipsky also owned the Reddi-Wip Corporation, manufacturers of a well-known whipped topping, until it was sold to Hunt & Wesson in 1970.[18] While Lipsky was in control, Angelo Polizzo, a captain in the California Mafia family of Nicola Licata, was on the Reddi-Wip payroll.[19]

praising Guthrie from important people throughout the nation.[30]* Jones indicated that the Syndicate, which operated "from coast to coast and in Canada and Spain,"[32] already had this arrangement in St. Louis, Kansas City, New Orleans, Little Rock, and several other cities.[33] When Guthrie and Butler asked Jones if they could "meet some of these people that he had been bragging about,"[34] Jones brought down Pat Manno—reputed fifth-ranking Chicago Mafioso at the time[35]—whose conversation with Jones, Butler, and Guthrie was recorded.[36]

/2/ A "Small Time Peanut" with the Chicago Mob

Jack Ruby, too, went from Chicago to Dallas in 1947, after an earlier visit.[37] And his arrival at about the same time as the Chicago Mob was not a coincidence. Sheriff Steve Guthrie told the FBI that at the time of the bribery negotiations,

> there were approximately 25 "thugs" and hoodlums from Chicago in Dallas from time to time. ... Jack Ruby at that time was a "small time peanut" with this group who were going to bribe Guthrie. Ruby's name came up on numerous occasions ... as being the person who would take over a very fabulous restaurant at Industrial and Commerce Streets in Dallas. ... the upper floor would be used for gambling. ... Ruby's name constantly came up as being the person who would run the restaurant.[38]

Guthrie stated, "if the records can still be heard, Ruby's name will be heard on numerous occasions."[39]

The Warren Commission dismissed Guthrie's report of Ruby's involvement, claiming that "22 recordings of the conversations between Guthrie, Butler, and Jones fail to mention Ruby."[40] But the Commission's claim was based merely on "incomplete transcriptions of the recordings," and the recordings were "almost completely inaudible," the House Assassinations Committee later clarified.[41] The Commission also neglected to note that the FBI agent who reviewed these incomplete transcriptions found one of the recordings inexplicably missing.[42]

*By the 1950s, Michael Dorman wrote in *Payoff*,

> the racketeers dominated the election machinery in many parts of Texas. Even more than the oilmen and the giant construction companies looking for public works contracts, the racketeers served as financiers of political campaigns. They decided long in advance of elections whom they would run for office. Their money, influence, and other assets determined who would win various positions from the top to the bottom of the ticket.[31]

In a further attempt to discount Sheriff Guthrie's report, the Commission marshaled the account of Lieutenant Butler,[43] as paraphrased in December 1963 by the FBI:

> Ruby was not involved in the bribery attempt. In fact he [Butler] had never heard of Ruby until after the investigation and trial had been completed [in 1947[44]]. He stated the way Ruby came into the picture was . . . [when] Paul Roland Jones began hanging out at Ruby's club after the sentence.[45]

But Lieutenant Butler's credibility on this matter evaporated in 1978, when he told the House Assassinations Committee that he had discussed Jack Ruby during the bribery negotiations in 1946.[46] In Butler's new version of events, Ruby was known to the Chicago Mob delegation, but was considered "too emotional" and insignificant.[47] Indeed, having "known Jack Ruby for years,"[48] and having related a story that Oswald was Ruby's illegitimate son,[49] Butler was not the most reliable source concerning Jack Ruby. And in contradiction to Butler's conflicting denials of Ruby's Mob involvement, *Chicago Daily News* reporter Morton William Newman told the FBI that Ruby was definitely involved in the Mob bribe attempt—based on information from Lieutenant Butler.[50]

Another *Chicago Daily News* reporter, Jack Wilner, also corroborated Sheriff Guthrie's description of Ruby's association with the Chicago Mob group. Wilner stated his " 'syndicate sources' reflect that Ruby was reportedly involved in 1947 with Nick St. John [Nick DeJohn], Paul Labriola, Marcus Lipsky and Paul Roland Jones in [an] effort to take over gambling in the Dallas, Texas area."[51] All of these cited associates of Ruby were linked to the Dallas Mob incursion in Butler's pre-assassination Senate testimony.[52] Confirmation from an additional Chicago source was reported by Milton Viorst in *The Washingtonian*:

> Louis Kutner, a Chicago attorney who had worked for the Kefauver Crime Committee, said Ruby had appeared before Kefauver's staff in 1950, and in the course of subsequent investigation it was learned that Ruby was a syndicate lieutenant who had been sent to Dallas to serve as a liaison for Chicago mobsters.[53]

Giles Miller, a Dallas businessman who knew Ruby well, provided further insight into Ruby's move to Dallas:

> Jack Ruby would sit at the table where I was seated and discuss how he was sent down here by "them"—he always referred to

"them"—meaning the syndicate in Chicago. He always complained that if he had to be exiled, why couldn't he have been exiled to California or Florida?[54]

And Mobster Paul Roland Jones, while denying that Ruby's name came up in the bribery negotiations,[55] confirmed Ruby's association with the other Chicago Mob delegates in Dallas. Jones told the FBI that after his bribery conviction, he ran into Ruby in Chicago in the company of Labriola, Weinberg, and possibly Lardino,[56] who "addressed Ruby by name and introduced him" to Jones.[57] The gangsters assured Jones that "Ruby was 'O.K.'" which Jones understood "to mean that he was known . . . to have some acceptance at least by 'the syndicate.'"[58] Jones also told the FBI that Ruby had operated a restaurant on Industrial and Commerce Streets in the early 1950s;[59] this supported Sheriff Guthrie's assertion that the Mob had designated Ruby to operate a restaurant at that intersection.[60]

Although the Mob's attempt to bribe Sheriff Guthrie backfired, its conquest of Dallas proceeded as planned. According to Lt. Butler's testimony before the McClellan Committee, the Chicago gang "took over coin machine and amusement companies in Texas, Louisiana and Arkansas,"[61] including slot machine, pinball machine and jukebox routes.[62] By 1957, as a U.S. Senate committee reported, Dallas was graced with its own Mafia boss, Joseph F. Civello,[63] who represented the city at the famous Mafia convention in Apalachin, New York.[64] And by 1967, Dallas rated inclusion in a federal report as one of 25 centers of Mafia activity in the United States.[65]

/3/ Settling in Dallas

Ruby himself established permanent residence in Dallas in the latter part of 1947,[66] and officially changed his name from Jack Rubenstein to Jack L. Ruby on December 30 of that year.[67] His first business venture there was the Silver Spur Club at 1717 South Ervay, of which he was manager and part owner for several years.[68] This club was described by Lt. Butler as a hangout during the late 1940s of Paul R. Jones and other Chicago Mobsters involved in the Dallas bribe attempt.[69] In a medical interview, Ruby himself said of the Silver Spur,

> You had to know this place to know what went on. You could get exonerated for murder easier than you could for burglary.[70]

In 1952, Ruby and two associates purchased the Bob Wills Ranch House on Corinth and Industrial Streets.[71] After a short stay in Chicago later that year, Ruby returned to Dallas and secured an interest in the Vegas Club at 3508 Oaklawn.[72] He also managed the Ervay Theater and Hernando's Hideaway, and became a distributor for pizza crusts and medicine within the next few years.[73]

One element of Ruby's "magic touch" in his business acquisitions was manifested in his takeover of the Vegas Club. Irving Alkana, the club's previous owner, told the FBI that Ruby purchased a one-third interest in it from him in the early 1950s.[74] Then, in April or May 1954, Alkana related, Ruby attacked and beat him during an argument over finances.[75] Describing this or a similar altercation with Alkana, Ruby remarked: "They had me for assault to murder."[76] Alkana related that two months after this beating, he sold his remaining two-third's interest to Ruby and later left Dallas.[77] Assisting Ruby in the takeover and operation of the Vegas Club was Joseph Locurto, alias Joe Bonds,[78] a thug with six arrests in three states.[79]

Although Ruby's other ventures were temporary, he retained ownership of the Vegas Club through November 1963.[80] But in 1959, its management was assumed by his sister Eva Grant[81] when Ruby and business partner Joe Slatin established the Sovereign Club, a plush private club at 1312½ Commerce Street.[82] In 1960, the Sovereign was converted into the Carousel Club, a public club serving beer, champagne, setups for drinks and pizza, and featuring striptease shows.[83] Jack Ruby and his associate Ralph Paul assumed ownership of the Carousel Club,[84] and Ruby operated it from its opening until the assassination.[85]

While these and similar ventures[86] provided Ruby a front and base of operations, as in Chicago, the focus of his life lay in a different realm.

> For at least the past half-century, organized crime was permitted to establish octopus-like tentacles throughout this nation and its communities. It is now identified as our biggest industry in dollar volume. Through violence, corruption and deception the underworld established itself as a conglomerate industry and grew to proportions which now influence every aspect of American life: our mores, our economy, our political system, government processes and competitive free enterprise.[1]
>
> Aaron Kohn, president of the New Orleans Metropolitan Crime Commission

□ 8 □

Jack Ruby's Criminal Activities

While the Mafia plays a major or dominant role in every criminal activity—from the traditional standbys of narcotics,[2] loan sharking,[3] fencing,[4] counterfeiting,[5] extortion,[6] and prostitution,[7] to more recent exploits such as securities theft,[8] child pornography,[9] cigarette smuggling,[10] bankruptcy fraud,[11] cargo theft,[12] and drug counterfeiting[13]—its leading money maker since the repeal of Prohibition has been illegal gambling.[14] Spurred by annual revenues estimated between $20 and $50 *billion*,[15] the Mafia has secured a virtual monopoly in this activity, collecting from every bookmaking operation, numbers bank and casino in the cities it infests.[16] In this context, Jack Ruby's major role in Dallas gambling operations, established below by several corroborating sources, is particularly significant. Indeed, when considered with his other underworld activities and contacts, to be discussed, the unmistakable picture of a Mobster emerges.

/1/ Gambling

In April 1959, the Dallas Police received a list of names found on Dallas gambler Sidney Seidband when he was arrested in Oklahoma City.[17] Of the 15 persons named, the Dallas Police described 12 as known gamblers and two as known associates of gamblers.[18] The other name on the list—the only one not identified in any way—was Jack Ruby's.[19] His mention there was not at all anomalous, given the following three accounts of Ruby's illegal gambling operations.

William Abadie: Ruby's slot-machine warehouse and bookmaking establishments. William Abadie was sought out by FBI agents and questioned in Los Angeles on December 6, 1963.[20] The agents told him that they "wanted to interview him concerning his knowledge and associations with Jack Leon Ruby, of Dallas, Texas."[21] Relieved to learn he was not being nabbed for jumping bail on a drunken driving charge, Abadie advised them that "he hardly knew Ruby and was entirely willing to discuss anything concerning Ruby."[22]

Abadie told the FBI that beginning in March 1963, he "was hired by Ruby's shop foreman as a slot machine and juke box mechanic" for a period of about seven weeks.[23] He stated that while performing his duties as a mechanic, he "did see Ruby in the warehouse shop,"[24] adding that "on one occasion for a few days he 'wrote tickets' as a bookie in one of Ruby's establishments."[25] When asked about Ruby's political affiliations, Abadie volunteered that Ruby and his gambling employees were all "anti-integrationists" who "would not allow Negroes to place bets,"[26] hardly unusual for that region and period.

Abadie said that while working in Ruby's warehouse, he gathered "it was obvious that to operate gambling in the manner that he did, that he must have racketeering connections with other individuals in the City of Dallas, as well as Fort Worth, Texas."[27] This opinion "applied also to police connections with the two cities."[28] And Abadie reported that "while he was making book for Ruby's establishment, he did observe police officers in and out of the gambling establishment on occasion."[29]

The FBI report of Abadie's interview spans five consecutive pages of Commission Document 86 in the National Archives.[30] Yet the version published in the Warren Commission Hearings and Exhibits, Commission Exhibit 1750, contains only four pages. The first page of this report, which describes Abadie's employment in Ruby's slot machine warehouse and bookmaking establishment, is missing.[31] This omission is most curious, particularly since the unpublished first page lists Abadie's full name, his address and other important matters of record[32] routinely included in published exhibits.

Jack Hardee: control of numbers operations. Jack Hardee, an inmate at the Mobile County Jail in Alabama, was interviewed by the FBI on December 26, 1963.[33] Hardee told agents that "approximately one year ago, while in Dallas, Texas, he attempted to set up a numbers game, and he was advised ... that in order to operate in Dallas it was necessary to have the clearance of Jack Ruby."[34] He was also told that "Ruby had the 'fix' with the county authorities."[35] Hardee is a credible witness, since other particulars he furnished concerning Ruby were corroborated.*

Harry Hall: a cut for official connections. Harry Hall, a reliable witness,† told Secret Service and FBI agents that in the early 1950s he was involved in a scheme to bilk rich Texans through high-stake bets.[41] The report of his interview states that

> Ruby on occasion provided Hall with a bankroll and introduced him to likely victims, with Ruby taking 40% of any deal. ... because he was supposed to have influence with the police, so that [Hall] would have no worry about any gambling arrest.[42]

Hall related that one of these victims, from whom they won a large sum of money on football bets, was Texas billionaire H. L. Hunt.[43] Hunt had in fact patronized an illegal gambling casino and had been swindled in gambling deals, other sources reported,[44] lending credibility to this assertion. Hall also reported that while on a trip with Ruby, they passed through Tulsa, Oklahoma, and Shreveport, Louisiana, and he observed that "Ruby seemed to have good connections in gambling circles" in these cities.[45]

/2/ Narcotics

Another important facet of Ruby's underworld career was his involve-

---

*Hardee reported that Ruby was well acquainted with a "Sol," who operated and owned Sol's Bar and Restaurant on either Main or Elm Street in Dallas.[36] Several sources established that Ruby knew Dallas gambler E. R. Solomon, known as "Sol," who operated Sol's Turf Bar on Commerce Street, directly between Main and Elm Streets.[37] And Hardee's account of Ruby's "hustling the strippers" of his club while keeping half of the prostitution earnings[38] was confirmed by other witnesses.[39]

†The Secret Service report of Hall's interview states:

> Harry Hall was an informant for the Los Angeles Office several years ago, giving information which resulted in the seizure of a counterfeiting plant. He has since given information to the Intelligence Division of the Treasury and the Federal Bureau of Investigation. ... his information in many cases has been reliable.[40]

ment with narcotics. According to an atypically informative Warren Commission memo, in 1947, Jack Ruby "became the subject of a narcotics investigation along with his brother, Hyman, and Paul Roland Jones."[46] Ruby was in fact interrogated by federal narcotics agents that year in connection with this case, as summarized in an official report which lists "Mafia" as a related file.[47] Ruby was not prosecuted,[48] however, although Jones was convicted of flying 60 pounds of opium over the Mexican border.[49] But when Ruby again came to the attention of federal authorities a decade later, there was little doubt that he was participating in a major narcotics operation.

On March 20, 1956, the FBI filed a report of an interview with Eileen Curry, an informant for the FBI and the Los Angeles Police.[50] Curry told the FBI that about the first of the year she moved to Dallas with her boyfriend James Breen after they had jumped bond on narcotics charges.[51] While in Dallas, she related, Breen told Curry that he had "made connection with a large narcotics setup operating between Mexico, Texas, and the East."[52] Curry reported in that FBI interview, filed seven years before the assassination, that "in some fashion James got the okay to operate through *Jack Ruby of Dallas*."[53]

In an FBI interview after Ruby killed Oswald, Eileen Curry confirmed her 1956 account and elaborated on Ruby's operation.[54] She told the FBI that early in 1956 she saw Ruby drive up to her apartment on Gaston Boulevard in Dallas, pick up her boyfriend James Breen, and depart.[55] Later that day, when Breen returned, he told her that "he had accompanied Ruby to an unnamed location, where he had been shown moving pictures of various border guards" plus narcotics agents and contacts on the Mexican side.[56] She said that "Breen was enthused over what he considered an extremely efficient operation in connection with narcotics traffic."[57] Curry had seen Ruby several times at her apartment and at Ruby's club, and recognized him as Oswald's killer from news photos;[58] there was no question of identification.

Eileen Curry's two detailed and consistent accounts to the FBI describing Ruby's narcotics involvement are difficult to discount. Moreover, they are consistent with earlier indications of such involvement by Ruby,[59] and with close contacts between Ruby and narcotics trafficker Joseph Civello, soon to be discussed.[60] Yet, as in Ruby's gambling operations, the chief significance of his narcotics dealings is his level of function—a controlling role in a "large narcotics setup operating between Mexico, Texas, and the East."[61] Just as Ruby was described by Abadie, Hardee, and Hall as supervising or granting clearance for bookmaking, numbers, and other gambling ventures, so he was cited by Curry as the person who approved James Breen's narcotics dealings in Dallas.

/3/ **Prostitution and Other Criminal Activities**

Also fitting the underworld mold were some less significant criminal activities of Ruby. Former Dallas County Sheriff Steve Guthrie told the FBI that he believed "Ruby [had] operated some prostitution activities and other vices in his club since Ruby had been in Dallas."[62] Jack Hardee, who knew Ruby in 1962, reported that "Ruby hustled the strippers and other girls who worked in his club," setting up dates for them and taking half the earnings.[63] This arrangement explained a transaction involving Chicago businessman Larry Meyers and Carousel stripper Joy Dale; Meyers got to know Dale and then made out a check for $200 to Jack Ruby, half of which Ruby paid to Dale.[64]

Restaurant operator Carl Maynard informed the FBI that one of his waitresses, who had once worked at the Carousel, told him "all girls employed did fill $100 a night dates after work."[65] Maynard believed that Ruby "got a percentage of prostitution dates."[66] Joe Bonds, a close associate and business partner of Ruby in the early 1950s, told the FBI that Ruby would "make women available" to Dallas police officers.[67] And Kenneth Dowe, a Dallas disc jockey, testified that Ruby "was known around the station for procuring women for different people who came to town."[68]*

Ruby used his time at the Carousel Club, his base of operations, to pursue other criminal sidelines. Jack Marcus, a Chicago attorney, spoke with Ruby at the Tropicana Night Club in Havana in 1959.[78] Marcus told the FBI that Ruby "indicated he had 'everything' at the night club [the Carousel] including gambling."[79] Other witnesses reported that Ruby operated a number of criminal activities out of the Carousel Club, including the distribution of stolen razor blades[80] and pornography,[81] both of which are lucrative Mob rackets.[82]

Of course, Ruby's most infamous criminal exploit was murder. And as will be shown later, the killing of Oswald, like Ruby's other activities, was Mafia-directed.

---

*One curious feature of the relatively few specific reports of Ruby's criminal activities is the location of their sources. William Abadie was interviewed in Los Angeles,[69] Jack Hardee in Mobile, Alabama,[70] Harry Hall in Los Angeles,[71] Eileen Curry in Los Angeles[72] and Chicago,[73] and Carl Maynard in Burbank, California.[74] Virtually all other witnesses who provided such specifics also lived far from Dallas when they were interviewed.[75] This strange lack of information from Dallas is comparable to the consistent denial of Ruby's underworld involvement by Chicago Mobsters.[76] It suggests that an edict of silence may have been issued throughout the Dallas underworld and underworld fringe circles—the most likely source of information on Ruby's criminal activity. The frightened behavior and perjury of Ruby's Dallas associates, as examined later,[77] supports this possibility.

So much is being written and filmed and spoken today that glamorizes the Mob. This is a gross misrepresentation of what these people are really like. They are the scum of the earth.[1]

Mob defector Patsy Lepera, testifying in 1973 before a U.S. Senate committee under a grant of immunity by U.S. District Court Judge John Sirica.[2]

□ 9 □
Jack Ruby's Underworld Contacts

Complementing Jack Ruby's gambling and narcotics activities was an extraordinary collection of associations with notorious underworld figures from across the nation. Some, such as Paul Roland Jones, Dallas Mafia boss Joseph Civello and versatile Mob "gambler and murderer" Lewis McWillie, maintained longstanding ties with Ruby. But others, including several associates of Marcello, Trafficante and Hoffa, were in touch with Ruby only during a brief period: the seven months between the first report of President Kennedy's visit to Dallas and his assassination.

Discussed below are the backgrounds and links with Ruby of 17 of his most significant underworld and Teamster contacts (seven more are covered in Appendix 6). These associations of Ruby are considered here to demonstrate his overall involvement with organized crime; contacts in the pre-assassination period, to be covered in depth later, are only summarized at this point. In the course of establishing Ruby's Mob affiliation, however, this chapter also profiles the Mob's infiltration into various spheres of American enterprise—from unions to gambling casinos, from medicare clinics to the U.S. Senate. Many of the Mobsters listed are still active.

A close associate of Jimmy Hoffa,[3] **Barney Baker** worked as a Teamster "organizer" under Hoffa's direct orders[4] until jailed on a federal racketeering conviction in 1961.[5]

Baker started out in the late 1930s and early 1940s as a strong-arm man for a racketeering outfit on the New York City waterfront.[6] During this period he was wounded in one gangland-style execution,[7] questioned about another,[8] and was at one point on the lam himself for a dock murder.[9] After a stretch in the mid-1940s as doorman for Mobsters Jake Lansky and Mert Wertheimer at the Colonial Inn in Florida,[10] and a stint with Bugsy Siegel in Las Vegas,[11] Baker had the necessary background for a leadership role in the Teamsters. In 1952 he was "elected" president of Teamsters Local 730,[12] and soon became organizer for the Central States Conference.[13]

Baker functioned in the Teamsters as "a versatile labor goon,"[14] or as Robert Kennedy phrased it, one of Hoffa's "roving emissaries of violence."[15] The FBI identified him as "a reported muscle and bagman for Teamster President James Riddle Hoffa."[16] And the House Assassinations Committee described him as a "hoodlum with organized crime and Teamsters connections."[17] Baker maintained close and frequent contacts with notorious Mobsters throughout the country.[18]

Contacts with Ruby. On November 7, 1963, Baker called Ruby from Chicago;[19] Ruby called Baker the next day.[20] The name "Barney," with three of Baker's phone numbers, was found in one of Ruby's notebooks.[21]

Joseph Campisi is identified in Drug Enforcement Administration files as a member of organized crime,[22] and is linked to organized crime in several other sources.[23] He is by all indications a top-ranking Dallas Mafia member. Illustrating his standing in the Mafia hierarchy is his close friendship with Joseph Civello,[24] the former Mafia boss of Dallas, who represented the city at the 1957 Mafia convention at Apalachin, New York.[25] According to one FBI informant, Campisi was slated to take over Civello's position.[26] Complementing Campisi's associations with Civello and other Dallas crime figures[27] are his reported close contacts with state judges and Dallas law enforcement officials.[28]

Although Campisi has been connected with illegal gambling for years, he was arrested only once, in 1944, for murder;[29] Campisi pleaded self-defense and no indictment was pressed.[30] His business operations have included promotion of Las Vegas gambling junkets and partnership in an insurance firm.[31] He has also run the Egyptian Lounge, a Dallas restaurant and bar, since the late 1950s; his brother Sam was a partner until Sam's death in 1970.[32] That establishment was so notorious as a Dallas underworld hangout, according to one Dallas intelligence officer, that you could not go in "without getting your picture taken by the FBI."[33]

Yet Campisi has attracted most attention from law enforcement officials through his very close friendship with the Marcellos of Louisiana. Campisi often visited Carlos Marcello and four brothers of Carlos who are reportedly also Mafia-involved.[34] In addition, telephone records show calls between Marcello-tied enterprises in New Orleans and Campisi's Egyptian Lounge in Dallas,[35] and between Campisi and Carlos Marcello himself.[36] The Campisi-Marcello relationship was reported by intelligence agencies in Texas and Louisiana,[37] and was recently confirmed by Campisi.[38]

Contacts with Ruby. Joseph Campisi was described by Ruby's sister Eva Grant as a close friend of Ruby.[39] Ruby's roommate, George Senator, named "a Mr. Campisi, who operates the Egyptian Lounge" as one of Ruby's three closest friends.[40] But Campisi had difficulty presenting a consistent account of his relationship with Ruby. On December 6, 1963, Campisi told the FBI he had known Ruby casually since 1948, but "never associated with him. ... never socialized with him," and knew "nothing of Ruby's background or associates."[41] But in 1978, Campisi provided the House Assassinations Committee with a rather detailed description of Ruby's background and associates,[42] and reported that he had once invited Ruby home for a barbecue.[43] Campisi also gave conflicting accounts concerning a large sum of cash found on Ruby when Ruby shot Oswald.[44]

In December 1963, Campisi told the FBI that he had visited Ruby on November 30, 1963 in the Dallas County Jail,[45] as confirmed by police records.[46] During the same FBI interview, Campisi reported that his "last contact with Ruby" prior to then occurred on the night before the assassination, "when Ruby came to the Egyptian Restaurant for a steak."[47] In 1978, however, Campisi once again reversed himself and denied this assassination-eve contact.[48]

Frank Caracci was identified in a 1970 Judiciary Committee hearing as a "Cosa Nostra involved" gambler and strip joint operator.[49] He was described by *Life* magazine as a "Marcello Mobster,"[50] and the *Wall Street Journal* reported that he was "closely affiliated" with Carlos Marcello.[51]

In 1969 Caracci was involved in an incident which once again demonstrated how Marcello, as *Life* magazine put it, "controlled the State of Louisiana."[52] In September of that year, Caracci was arrested when police raided a Syndicate gambling operation at the Royal Coach Inn in Houston, Texas.[53] Nabbed with Caracci were three men who all showed up later, along with the Marcello clan, for the Dallas wedding of a son of Joseph Campisi.[54] The arrest proved particularly embarrassing for one of them, Frank "Tickie" Saia—a prominent political, business and sports figure in Louisiana,[55] who was caught with a bunch of gambling slips on his person.[56]

When police examined the phone records of the raided gambling operation, they found calls to Mobsters across the country.[57] Juxtaposed with these were calls to top Louisiana politicians, including Saia's close friend,[58]

Senator Russell Long.[59] Long had in fact sponsored Saia for a job as regional adviser to the U.S. Small Business Administration.[60] By 1974, as the *New York Times* reported, "millions of dollars" in Louisiana SBA money had gone to "persons with known Mafia backgrounds" as a result of Mob subversion of the regional office.[61]

Given Saia's gambling arrest and his ties to Caracci,[62] Campisi,[63] and Marcello himself,[64] his sponsorship for a federal post by Senator Long was disturbing. A similar situation was noted in a staff report of the House Assassinations Committee:

> On June 16, 1961, the FBI received a report that a U.S. Senator from Louisiana might have sought to intervene on Marcello's behalf [in his fight to avoid deportation]. This Senator had reportedly received "financial aid from Marcello" in the past and was sponsoring a Louisiana official for a key INS [Immigration and Naturalization Service] position from which assistance might be rendered.[65]

"Financial aid from Marcello" was apparently a reference to substantial campaign contributions which Senator Russell Long received from Carlos Marcello, as documented, according to *Life*, in a 1951 internal staff report of the Kefauver Crime Committee.[66] Marcello's beneficence to Long was further reciprocated when both Long and Caracci's associate Saia assisted the Marcello-sponsored campaign to spring Jimmy Hoffa.[67]*

Additional information on Caracci was presented by Aaron Kohn, director of the New Orleans Metropolitan Crime Commission, during a Congressional hearing in 1972:

> There were close connections between the Cosa Nostra organizations of Zerelli in Detroit and of Carlos Marcello in Louisiana.
> ... A major figure in the Marcello organization, Frank Caracci, recently convicted and imprisoned on three counts of conspiracy to bribe a Federal tax agent, was in the Detroit area in 1969

---

*"Two generations of the Long family," *Life* magazine summarized, "have coexisted with the Mafia."[68] The alliance began in 1934, when Huey Long, Russell's father, "invited New York Mob boss Frank Costello to come into Louisiana and organize gambling for a percentage of the take."[69] For his personal bodyguard, Huey hired James Brocato,[70] also known as "Diamond Jim" Moran, a convicted racketeer close to Carlos Marcello.[71] The continuity of political traditions was later demonstrated when Robert Brocato, a nephew of James and friend of the Marcellos,[72] became chairman of the New Orleans Board of Health.[73] Not to be inhibited by his official position, Brocato tried to run down a police officer during a traffic altercation in 1971;[74] no charges were pressed by the district attorney's office.[75]

in company of Zerelli Mob members. With him was his brother-in-law, Nicholas J. Graffagnini of Jefferson Parish, Louisiana.[76]

Contacts with Ruby. Caracci was one of those Mob figures whose contacts with Ruby were apparently confined to the pre-assassination period. Between June and October of 1963, as detailed later, Ruby visited one of Caracci's New Orleans night clubs, telephoned another several times, and met with Caracci on at least one occasion.[77]

Frank Chavez was a thug with arrests for obstruction of justice and for attempted murder by hurling a firebomb.[78] This background made him an ideal choice to head the Teamsters in Puerto Rico,[79] and to lead Hoffa's drive to take over the AFL-CIO-affiliated Union Gastronomica.[80] The drive succeeded after the union's headquarters was blown up by five Molotov cocktails in February 1962.[81]

After President Kennedy was killed, Chavez sent Robert Kennedy a letter stating that he was soliciting money to supply Lee Harvey Oswald's grave with flowers.[82] In 1964 and again in 1967, Chavez set out from Puerto Rico with the reported intention of killing Robert Kennedy.[83] But Chavez's designs were squelched a year after the latter trip, when he was killed by one of his own bodyguards.[84]

Contacts with Ruby. Between 1960 and 1962, Leopoldo Ramos Ducos was Chavez's organizer for Teamster Local 901.[85] Ramos Ducos told the FBI on November 27, 1963 that he had heard Chavez "mention the name of one Jack Ruby as someone connected with the Teamsters union."[86] Ramos Ducos also stated that in the fall of 1961, Chavez had told him he "had an appointment to meet Richard Kavner, International Vice President of [the] Teamsters Union, and Jack Ruby as well as a third Teamster official."[87] Kavner, described by author Dan Moldea as "another key member of the Hoffa circle" who "carried a gun," was linked to several dynamite bombings and had been to Puerto Rico on Teamster business.[88]

A link between Ruby and Chavez was further documented by a Justice Department memorandum of November 26, 1963, indicating "a connection between Rubenstein [Jack Ruby] and Frank Chavez and Tony Provenzano."[89] The third man, Provenzano, was a Teamster international vice president and a captain in Genovese Mafia Family.[90] He was convicted of extortion in 1963[91] and of murder in 1978.[92] The connections are credible in view of Ruby's one-time involvement with Paul Dorfman in a Chicago Teamster local[93] and other Teamster links of Ruby to be discussed.

Joseph Francis Civello was the Mafia boss of Dallas during the 1950s and 1960s[94] and was one of the 59 delegates apprehended at the 1957 Mafia convention in Apalachin, New York.[95] (Civello was temporarily put out of commission by his arrest, and intelligence officers believe that New York Genovese Family representative Peter Pelligrino was sent to Dallas to watch Mob interests during that period.)[96] Civello's criminal record dates back to 1928, and includes an arrest for murder and a conviction for a federal narcotics violation.[97] Born in Louisiana, Civello was friendly with Carlos Marcello,[98] to whom he was connected by toll call records.[99]

Contacts with Ruby. In an FBI interview on January 14, 1964, Civello stated that he had known Ruby casually "for about ten years."[100] Like fellow Mafioso Joseph Campisi,[101] however, Civello was being modest about the extent of his association with Ruby.

The Ruby-Civello relationship was illuminated by Bobby Gene Moore, who grew up in Dallas and worked for Ruby at various times between 1952 and 1956 as a pianist in the Vegas Club.[102] After the assassination, Moore was prompted to contact the FBI by a statement on television that his former employer had no gangster connections.[103] He was interviewed by agents on November 26, 1963 in Oakland, California.[104]

Moore told the FBI of deals involving Ruby, two Dallas policemen, and local underworld figures; several of his allegations were verified years later by arrests for the activities he described.[105] But most interesting was Moore's report about an Italian importing company on 3400 Ross Avenue in Dallas, at which Moore was employed during the early 1950s.[106] Moore was characteristically accurate when he told the FBI he suspected that his employers, Joseph "Cirello" and Frank LaMonte, might have been importing narcotics.[107] For the Dallas directory listed the store at 3400 Ross Avenue to a brother of Mafia boss Joseph Civello.[108] The Joseph "Cirello" transcribed by the FBI was thus Joseph Civello, whose business fronts included import-export, olive oil, and cheese,[109] and whose criminal activities did in fact include narcotics dealings.[110]

Given Civello's top Mob status, an additional statement of Moore is quite significant. Moore told the FBI in his November 1963 interview that Ruby was "a *frequent visitor and associate of Cirello* and LaMonte."[111] Interviewed in 1964 by the FBI, LaMonte admitted having known Ruby since the early 1950s,[112] further corroborating Moore.

Bobby Gene Moore's FBI interview, spanning two pages in National Archives files,[113] was published by the Warren Commission as Exhibit 1536 (both are reproduced in Appendix 1). But the Commission's published version gave no inkling of Ruby's frequent visits with Dallas Mafia boss Joseph Civello. Also excluded was Moore's expressed belief that Ruby "was connected with the underworld in Dallas."[114]

In fact, the entire second page of the original National Archives report was omitted in Commission Exhibit 1536. And three paragraphs of the original's first page, mentioning Joseph "Cirello," were *blanked out from an otherwise perfect photocopy of that page.* In this fashion, with seven of the original nine paragraphs omitted or excised, Moore's account became almost compatible with the Warren Commission's denial of a "significant link between Ruby and organized crime."[115]

Mickey Cohen was a notorious West Coast Mobster.[116] Active in gambling, politics and murder,[117] he spent ten years in prison for income tax evasion, serving part of his sentence at the Alcatraz federal penitentiary.[118]
Contacts with Ruby. New York Times reporter Gladwin Hill told the FBI he had "heard from unrecalled sources that Ruby was acquainted with Mickey Cohen."[119] And former Vegas Club owner Irving Alkana advised the FBI that Ruby had told him he knew Mickey Cohen.[120] These accounts are credible in light of Ruby's close friendship[121] with Mickey Cohen's one-time girl friend[122] "Candy Barr," a former pornographic movie star who was jailed on a narcotics charge.[123]

Ruby's sister Eva Grant testified that **Joseph Glaser** was one of New York City's wealthiest booking agents, who "probably could have been in rackets."[124] This last phrase was characteristic of Mrs. Grant's mild or euphemistic descriptions of such individuals as Lewis McWillie,[125] Lenny Patrick,[126] and Dave Yaras[127]—all of whom were described by independent sources as Mobsters and killers.[128]

Glaser's Syndicate connection was recently confirmed in a *New York Times* series on Los Angeles attorney and Mobster Sidney Korshak.[129] Describing Korshak as "the most important link between organized crime and big business,"[130] the *Times* related that senior Justice Department officials ranked him among "the most powerful members of the underworld."[131] His underworld clout was suggested by one incident in 1961, in which Jimmy Hoffa was displaced from the best suite in the Las Vegas Riviera Hotel to accommodate him.[132]

The *Times* reported that one of the companies over which Korshak "has virtually absolute control," an investment "he has sought to keep secret," is the Associated Booking Corporation.[133] "In 1962, according to court documents," as the *Times* further noted,

> Joseph Glaser, the head of Associated Booking Company, the nation's third-largest theatrical agency, assigned all of the "voting rights, dominion and control" of his majority stock in the concern to Mr. Korshak and himself. The agreement meant that Mr. Korshak, who through the 1960's had seemed merely to be the agency's legal counsel, was able to assume complete control over the company upon Mr. Glaser's death in 1969.[134]

Contacts with Ruby. On August 5, 1963, Jack Ruby visited Joseph Glaser in New York City.[135] Ruby placed two calls to Glaser ten days later.[136]

Alexander Gruber described himself to the FBI as an all-American guy who was a member of no organization "other than the Democratic Party or the Boy Scouts of America."[137] While the Warren Commission published the four-page FBI interview of Gruber containing this self-appraisal,[138] it omitted an accompanying two-page FBI report[139] which was suppressed even from National Archives files until 1970. This FBI report summarizes Gruber's police record of six arrests under two aliases in Illinois, Indiana and California, with a conviction for grand larceny.[140] According to Seth Kantor, a White House press corps reporter, Gruber was "running with Frank Matula, whom Hoffa had installed as a Teamsters official shortly after Matula got out of jail on perjury charges. Gruber also maintained known connections with hoodlums who worked with racketeer Mickey Cohen."[141]

Contacts with Ruby. Al Gruber was a friend of Ruby from Chicago, where they had roomed together for a year.[142] In mid-November 1963, after a ten-year separation, Gruber paid an extended visit to Ruby in Dallas.[143] Ruby then called Gruber in Los Angeles three hours after President Kennedy was shot.[144] The two described these contacts in grossly conflicting accounts.[145]

Paul Roland Jones is best known for leading the Chicago Mob delegation in the Dallas bribe attempt,[146] but his criminal record is quite well-rounded. His first major infraction was the murder of a state witness in Kansas,[147] for which he was sentenced to life imprisonment in 1931.[148] But in 1940, with typical Mob political aplomb, Jones secured a pardon from Governor Husman.[149] In 1946, after extricating himself from a felony warrant issued in Cleveland,[150] Jones arrived in Dallas to represent the Chicago Mob in its abortive bribe attempt.[151] While appealing his 1947 conviction in that affair,[152] Jones was convicted of flying 60 pounds of opium over the Mexican border.[153] In 1960, Jones was indicted for perjury in connection with the Texas Adams Oil Company swindle.[154]

Contacts with Ruby. Jones told the FBI that he got to know Ruby quite well in the late 1940s in Dallas, visiting him occasionally thereafter.[155] Jones claimed the relationship was just a friendly one,[156] but Ruby's interrogation by the Federal Bureau of Narcotics in connection with Jones' opium smuggling arrest[157] may indicate otherwise. Jones dropped in from out of state to see Ruby at the Carousel Club a week before the assassination of President Kennedy.[158]

Russell D. Matthews was described in one FBI report as a burglar, armed robber, narcotics pusher, and murderer.[159] He worked for Mob-controlled Cuban casinos in the late 1950s,[160] and turned to Dallas underworld pursuits in the 1960s.[161] The *Dallas Morning News* reported that "Matthews was arrested more than 50 times by Dallas area law authorities but served time in prison only once—two years on a federal narcotics viola-tion."[162] In January 1974, Matthews was subpoenaed by a federal grand jury in Houston concerning a reported contract to kill informants of corruption in the Houston Police Narcotics Division.[163] He is now employed at the Horseshoe Club in Las Vegas.[164]

Matthews is an associate of Mafia figures Santos Trafficante[165] and Joseph Campisi.[166] Matthews and Campisi were seen together in both Dallas and Las Vegas in 1978.[167]

Contacts with Ruby. Four witnesses described Matthews as an associ-ate or friend of Ruby.[168] On October 3, 1963, a call was placed from the Carousel Club to a number in Shreveport, Louisiana listed to Elizabeth Matthews, Russell's former wife.[169]

Lewis J. McWillie, described by Dallas Police as a "gambler and mur-derer,"[170] served the Syndicate in several domains. After moving to Dallas as a young man, he became a "prominent figure in illegal gambling" in the 1940s, according to an FBI report.[171] Social Security records establish Mc-Willie's employment in 1942 and 1943 for local rackets bosses[172] Lester "Benny" Binion and Benny Bickers at the Southland Hotel in Dallas,[173] owned by New Orleans Mafioso[174] Sam Maceo.[175] Throughout the 1940s and 1950s, McWillie was involved in the operation of several gambling spots in the Dallas area,[176] including the Top of the Hill Club,[177] Cipango's,[178] and a gambling house at 2222 Jacksboro Highway in Fort Worth.[179]

From September 1958 until May 1960, McWillie was manager of the Mob-owned Tropicana Hotel in Havana;[180] the hotel's other top men included Mobsters Giuseppe Cotrini, John Guglielmo, Norman Rothman, Willie Bis-choff, and Meyer and Jake Lansky.[181] After being expelled from the Tropi-cana by the Castro regime, McWillie managed to stay on as the pit boss of the Capri Hotel Casino,[182] in which Santos Trafficante held a major inter-est.[183] While in Havana, according to an FBI report in the National Archives, McWillie associated with Meyer and Jake Lansky, Santos Trafficante, Willie Bischoff, Dino Cellini, and other top Mobsters.[184] He was finally forced out of Cuba in January 1961, along with the rest of the Mob,[185] with most of his as-sets confiscated.

After his departure from Cuba, McWillie spent several months working on the Caribbean islands of Aruba and Curacao.[186] He then became pit boss at the Cal Neva Lodge in Lake Tahoe, Nevada,[187] the same hotel in which Frank Sinatra was forced to relinquish his 50-percent ownership because of contacts with Chicago Mafia boss Sam Giancana.[188] Shortly afterward, Mc-Willie became pit boss at the casino of the Riverside Hotel in Reno,[189] which was owned by Mobsters from Detroit.[190] In 1962, following the receipt of a $2.75 million Teamsters Pension Fund loan, the Riverside declared bank-ruptcy,[191] and McWillie landed a job at the Thunderbird Hotel in Las

Vegas.[192] In all instances, McWillie testified, he was in a supervisory role, "overseeing the gambling."[193] McWillie was still at the Thunderbird, in which Meyer and Jake Lansky held interests,[194] at the time of the assassination.[195] When McWillie testified before the House Assassinations Committee in 1978, he was employed at the Holiday Inn casino in Las Vegas.[196]

Contacts with Ruby. Ruby, McWillie and others reported that the two were close friends.[197] Their close association was exhibited during a week-long trip to Havana by Ruby in 1959, during which he saw McWillie frequently.[198] Moreover, Ruby reported, he once had four guns shipped to McWillie in Cuba.[199] And on May 10, 1963, according to sales records confirmed by McWillie, Ruby had a .38 Smith and Wesson revolver shipped from Ray's Hardware Store in Dallas to McWillie in Las Vegas.[200] Over the following four months, Ruby called McWillie eight times at the Thunderbird in Las Vegas.[201]

Murray W. "Dusty" Miller was the head of the Southern Conference of Teamsters in 1963[202] and later became Secretary-Treasurer of the Teamsters International.[203] The House Assassinations Committee reported that Miller "was associated with numerous underworld figures."[204]

Contacts with Ruby. On November 8, 1963, Ruby called Miller person-to-person at the Eden Roc Hotel in Miami.[205]

Lenny Patrick was identified in a 1965 U.S. Senate report as a high-ranking nonmember associate of the Chicago branch of the Mafia.[206] His activities included "extortion, mayhem and murders," plus gambling, loan sharking, and narcotics dealing, which he reportedly controlled on Chicago's West Side.[207] He is profiled in *Captive City* as the "Syndicate overlord of the 24th and 50th wards" in Chicago,[208] with business interests including hotels, restaurants, supermarkets, liquor stores, aluminum products, a disposal service, vending machines, insurance, and industrial uniforms.[209] His police record includes 28 arrests on charges including murder,[210] a 1933 conviction for bank robbery,[211] and a 1975 conviction for contempt of court.[212]

According to one FBI informant, Patrick was a close contact of Sam Giancana,[213] the former Mafia boss of Chicago.[214] Like several of Ruby's other Mob contacts, Patrick reportedly once held an interest in a Cuban gambling casino.[215] But Patrick was best known as one of the Mob's leading killers.[216]

Contacts with Ruby. Patrick told the FBI that he and Ruby were casual friends in Chicago,[217] but had not been in touch since the early 1950s.[218] According to Ruby's sister, however, Ruby called Patrick in 1963.[219]

Aaron Kohn, director of the New Orleans Metropolitan Crime Commission, described **Nofio J. Pecora** of New Orleans as an "exconvict with extensive past history in the heroin traffic" and a partner of Carlos Marcello.[220] G. Robert Blakey, chief counsel of the House Assassinations Committee, testified that "the FBI, Justice Department, and Metropolitan Crime Commission of New Orleans have identified Pecora as one of Marcello's three most trusted aides."[221] The *New York Times* also identified Pecora as an associate of Marcello and the recipient of a $210,000 loan from the New Orleans office of the Small Business Administration.[222]

Contacts with Ruby. On August 4 and October 30, 1963, telephone calls were exchanged between a Dallas phone listed to Ruby and a New Orleans phone of Pecora.[223] Each had virtually exclusive use of his respective telephone.[224]

Johnny Roselli was a prominent Mafia figure active in Las Vegas and Los Angeles.[225] A former associate of Al Capone,[226] Roselli was convicted in 1944 with other top Mobsters for conspiring to extort $1 million from Hollywood's major motion picture studios.[227] The group perpetrated the extortion scheme by gaining control over the International Alliance of Theatre Stage Employees, then demanding massive payoffs with the threat of a nationwide strike.[228] During the early 1960s, Roselli was a principal in joint plots by the Mob and CIA to assassinate Fidel Castro.[229] In August 1976, Roselli's body was found floating in an oil drum in Florida's Biscayne Bay, shortly after he had testified to the Senate Intelligence Committee about those plots.[230]

Contacts with Ruby. Roselli told columnist Jack Anderson that he knew Ruby,[231] and described Ruby as "one of our boys."[232] The two may have first met in 1933, when both became involved with the newly opened Santa Anita Race Track in Los Angeles.[233] Federal sources report that during the fall of 1963, when Roselli was under FBI surveillance, he met twice with Ruby in Miami.[234]

A Chicago bail bondsman with no felony record, **Irwin S. Weiner** maintains his office a few doors away from Chicago Police headquarters.[235] He is also one of the Mob's leading front men in Chicago,[236] "thought to be the underworld's major financial figure in the Midwest."[237] "A comprehensive list of his associates," the House Assassinations Committee noted, "would include a significant number of the major organized crime figures in the United States."[238] Among them have been Jimmy Hoffa, Santos Trafficante, Sam Giancana, Paul and Allen Dorfman, Sam Battaglia, Marshall Califano, and "lord high executioner"[239] Felix ("Milwaukee Phil") Alderisio.[240]

Weiner's activities illustrate how the Mob operates in America. One of them, as reported by the House Assassinations Committee, "defrauding the national welfare and medicare systems located in Chicago,"[241] was typical. He did this "through the manipulation of funds" and "the deliberate burn ing of medicare clinics for insurance claims."[242] He has also "been linked to the arson of restaurants and nightclubs, resulting in insurance fraud."[243] Weiner's business interests have included partnerships with Felix Alderisio in three meat-shortening firms and a real estate company.[244] One shortening firm was closed by a Chicago judge in 1961 after allegations of strong-arm sales techniques;[245] Weiner was charged as an accessory when Alderisio was later indicted for extortion.[246] A 1973 FBI report "states that Weiner was handling all the skimmed money from Las Vegas for Chicago's organized crime community."[247] And a 1974 FBI transcript of electronic surveillance, again summarized by the House Assassinations Committee, "reports an alleged bribe by Weiner to an assistant U.S. Attorney in Chicago to have organized crime figure Sam Battaglia released from prison."[248]

Like many of Ruby's other Mob contacts, and like Ruby himself,[249] Weiner had been involved in the Mob's Cuban operations. For example, a 1962 FBI memo reported that "Weiner has boasted, and those who were in the know in Cuba have confirmed, that for his services to Phil Alderisio[,] Santos Trafficante, etc., he was given a substantial interest in the Deauville Gambling Casino and the Capri Gambling Casino in Havana. When Weiner last talked about this he was crying about the loss of a vast fortune occasioned by Castro."[250]

Weiner was also active in the Teamsters, as demonstrated by his frequent mention in FBI files with Jimmy Hoffa and union bigwig Allen Dorfman.[251] In one 1959 transaction, a company headed by Weiner was promoted by the Teamster International leadership to handle the multimillion-dollar bonding requirements of the locals.[252] But the letter of endorsement came the day before Weiner's company was even incorporated.[253]

In 1974, Weiner, Allen Dorfman, two trustees of the Teamster's central states pension fund, and other Mobsters were indicted by a Chicago federal grand jury on charges of defrauding the fund of more than $1.4 million.[254] The case involved a Teamster pension fund loan to a New Mexico firm which was then drained bankrupt by the Mob;[255] federal officials have estimated that similar transactions have defrauded the Teamsters of at least $385 million.[256] As the House Assassinations Committee summarized, "the prosecution's seemingly strong case" against Weiner and his codefendants "crumbled when its key witness, David Siefert, was brutally murdered on September 27, 1974, just before the trial was scheduled to begin."[257]

Contacts with Ruby. Ruby and Weiner knew each other, at least casually, as youths in Chicago.[258] On October 26, 1963, Ruby placed a 12-minute call from the Carousel Club, person-to-person, to Weiner in Chicago.[259] When questioned by the FBI three days after Ruby shot Oswald, Weiner refused to provide any information about this call.[260] He subsequently furnished a series of contradictory explanations.[261]

Like his close associate[262] Lenny Patrick, **David Yaras** was included in a U.S. Senate list of Chicago Mafia nonmember associates, characterized by an activity code indicating "extortion, mayhem and murder."[263] Arrested 14 times,[264] Yaras is described in *Captive City* as "a prime suspect in several gangland slayings"—one of "more than a score of top-rated exterminators who work strictly on contracts for the board of directors."[265] Yaras was one of a group of Mobsters monitored by an FBI bug in 1962 while planning a murder contract in Miami and discussing previous killings.[266] The bug provided grisly transcripts detailing Mob executions, later published by *Life* magazine,[267] and saved the life of the intended victim.[268]

Yaras served as a go-between for Carlos Marcello and Santos Trafficante,[269] the Mafia bosses who had spoken of President Kennedy's murder in the summer months of 1962. Yaras was also a crony of Jimmy Hoffa,[270] who had outlined plans to kill Robert Kennedy within the same brief period. Along with Trafficante, Yaras was instrumental in founding Teamster Local 320 in Miami.[271] As author Dan Moldea reported, that local "served as a front for many of the Mob's gambling and narcotics activities."[272]

Like Marcello, Trafficante, Hoffa, Ruby, Matthews, McWillie, Patrick, Roselli, and Weiner,[273] Yaras had engaged in Mob operations in Cuba.[274] According to Charles Siragusa, a federal narcotics officer, Yaras "ran a number of gambling operations on the island and was also the Chicago mob's liaison to the Cuban exile community after the fall of Batista."[275] And the House Assassinations Committee reported that "Yaras has served, it is alleged, as a key lieutenant of Chicago Mafia leader Sam Giancana."[276]

Yaras also played a part in a conquest which brought the Mob nationwide control over bookmaking operations—the takeover of Continental Press, the leading racing wire service of the 1940s.[277] In 1946, while Mafiosi Carlos Marcello and Jack Dragna muscled into regional distributorships of Continental's,[278] national manager James Ragen tried to hold out against the Mob.[279] At the same time, Paul Roland Jones bragged to Sheriff Guthrie and Lt. Butler in Dallas about how his backers were going to take over the wire service, and how Ragen was going to be killed.[280] Thus it came as no surprise when, soon afterward, Ragen was ambushed and shot.[281] Six weeks later, he was fatally poisoned by mercury slipped into his soft drinks despite a 24-hour guard at his hospital bed.[282]

Lt. Butler testified he learned that the Chicago Mob group, specifically Dave Yaras, was behind the Ragen slaying.[283] Indeed, in 1947, Dave Yaras, Lenny Patrick, and William Block were indicted for Ragen's murder.[284] Charges were dropped, however, after one witness was murdered, one fled, and two changed their testimony.[285]*

---

*In contrast to the fate of the three Mobsters was that of Chicago Police Captain Thomas E. Connell and Lieutenant William Drury, who secured the indictment against them.[286] When the two policemen brought in Chicago Mobster Jake Guzik for questioning about the case, Guzik was ordered freed within two hours.[287] Con-

Contacts with Ruby. Yaras told the FBI that he knew Ruby for about 15 years in Chicago,[291] and related enough details about Ruby's habits and personality to indicate more than a remote acquaintance.[292] Yaras also confirmed that Ruby knew Lenny Patrick.[293]

Although Yaras had no recorded contacts with Ruby in 1963, a curious indirect link brings us full circle alphabetically among Ruby's associates. Recall that on November 7 and 8, 1963, Jack Ruby exchanged calls with Teamster thug Barney Baker.[294] Two weeks later on November 21, 1963, at 6:17 p.m., the night before the assassination, a 3-minute call was placed from the home phone of Baker in Chicago to a "Dave" in Miami, Florida.[295] The "Dave" called person-to-person by Baker,[296] as identified by telephone records,[297] was none other than Ruby's old friend, Syndicate killer Dave Yaras.

Further indications of Ruby's Mob affiliation were furnished by two witnesses. Louisville tavern operator Carlos Malone told the FBI that in the summers of 1957 and 1958, he visited the Ellis Park Race Track in Kentucky with Jack Ruby;[298] Malone identified Ruby by name and photograph.[299] Accompanying the two was Ellis Joseph, a former Louisville policeman who had resigned from the force in 1952 after being charged with theft.[300] Malone reported that Joseph, who appeared well-acquainted with Ruby, had described Ruby as a "syndicate man out of Chicago."[301] Joseph also mentioned to Malone that Ruby had some tips on horses from the Syndicate,[302] and Malone observed that Ruby had several winners that day.[303]

Mrs. Nancy Perrin Rich, a former bartender and waitress at the Carousel Club,[304] told the FBI that "she saw syndicate men from Chicago and St. Louis in Ruby's night club."[305] Mrs. Rich "entertained them as hostess and observed money payments made to Ruby."[306] In subsequent sworn testimony, she related:

> Ruby had had various characters visit him, both from New York, Chicago, and even from up in Minneapolis. . . . I was introduced to some of them. I was asked to go out with some of them. . . . I saw them come and go.[307]

It is explicitly clear from context[308] that she was referring to the Syndicate. And Mrs. Rich was among dozens of witnesses[309] who described Ruby's remarkable association with the flip side of the Dallas criminal establishment: the Dallas Police department.

---

nell and Drury, on the other hand, were indicted for depriving Guzik of his civil rights and thrown off the force.[288] Drury fought for reinstatement in the courts until September 25, 1950, the night before he was scheduled to give information to a Kefauver Committee investigator—he was then shotgunned to death in his garage.[289] Attorney Marvin Bas, another scheduled witness, was also murdered, a few days before the Kefauver Committee opened hearings in Chicago.[290]

The iron-fisted rulers who control the Mafia have locked a strangle hold on American politics. Using such tactics as bribes, campaign contributions, threats, blackmail, ballot box manipulation and delivery of large voting blocks, they have spread their tentacles of power through every level of government. From city halls to state capitols and from the halls of Congress even to the White House, no public official is regarded by the Mob as exempt from possible corruption.[1]

Michael Dorman, journalist and author

You and I know what the problem is. They buy off the judge, they buy off the prosecutor, they buy off the sheriff, and they buy off the law enforcement officers locally, directly or indirectly.[2]

Senator Henry Jackson, referring to Syndicate gambling operatives

□ 10 □

Jack Ruby
and the Dallas Police

All levels of American government are subverted by the Mafia, as reflected by its estimated annual corruption expenditure of more than $15 billion.[3] But the most pervasively infested segment is local law enforcement.[4] As the Massachusetts Crime Commission concluded in 1957, the Mafia mainstay of illegal gambling "could not exist within a community without the knowledge and protection of the local police."[5] And as organized crime expert Rufus King wrote, whoever controlled a community's illicit gambling operations more often than not "also controlled—the word is responsibly chosen, controlled—the community's local law enforcement agencies."[6] Indeed, the police corruption required for Mob operation has been exposed by countless local and Congressional investigations in cities across the nation.[7] The resulting erosion of both police and judicial effectiveness is all too evident in the rampant street crime which terrorizes and devastates urban America.

A textbook model of Mob-police corruption is provided by the city of Dallas. Even before the Mafia takeover of Dallas rackets in the late 1940s, according to two sources quoted in *Green Felt Jungle*, "The police force was rotten from top to bottom"; gangsters controlled "the sheriff, the police, the judges ... everything in the state."[8] The standard pattern of gambling nonenforcement was represented by the criminal record of Isadore Max Miller—a major Dallas bookmaker active for decades.[9] He was finally convicted on federal gambling charges in 1965,[10] but had not been arrested by Dallas authorities since 1949.[11] Mob associate Russell D. Matthews, on the other hand, was arrested 59 times by Dallas police but convicted only once on a federal narcotics violation.[12] It appeared that Matthews was accurate when he told an associate that he had Dallas all wrapped up ("It is my town").[13]

By all indications, the corruption in Dallas approached the venal level of Ruby's native Chicago, where the Mafia still helps to determine police promotions,[14] and where policemen are regularly convicted of various Syndicate-tied crimes, including murder.[15]* During the 1950s, several Dallas-area gambling houses continued to operate[18]—well after most such establishments had been closed in the heat of the Kefauver hearings. In 1967, in fact, one Dallas Police lieutenant was arrested by federal authorities for running his own bookmaking business.[19] And 30 days of telephone conversations of a local gambling boss, taped by the FBI prior to gambling raids in 1972, reportedly included the voices of at least a dozen Dallas Police officers.[20]

Bill Decker, the Dallas County sheriff, was reportedly a key figure in underworld corruption. During the November 7, 1946 session of the Dallas bribery negotiations, tape-recorded by police, Mobster Paul Roland Jones described Decker, then under-sheriff, as an "oldtime bootlegger here."[21] Sheriff Steve Guthrie added, "We all know Bill Decker is a payoff man with [rackets boss[22]] Bennie Binion."[23] Dallas Police Lieutenant George Butler concurred with Guthrie.[24] Consistent with this assessment was Decker's admitted long-time acquaintance with hoodlum R. D. Matthews[25] and his friendship with Mobster Joseph Campisi.[26]

It is hardly comforting to note that the same Sheriff Decker rode in the

---

*In a December 6, 1968 article entitled "Corruption Behind the Swinging Clubs," *Life* magazine concluded that a major cause of the wholesale misconduct by Chicago Police at the 1968 Democratic convention was rampant Mob corruption in the department.[16] The article detailed several shocking cases of payoffs, favors, and Mob-police ties, and summarized: "There is a climate around Chicago police in which organized crime thrives like jungle shrubbery."[17]

"rolling command car" in front of President Kennedy's limousine on November 22, 1963.[27] And Decker was also involved in the abortive arrangements to transfer Oswald from the Dallas Police jail.[28] Yet it was Oswald's killer and Decker's prisoner,[29] Jack Ruby, who perhaps focused the most penetrating glimpse into Mob-police corruption in Dallas. Although some of Ruby's police contacts appear typical for a night club operator, their exceptional scope and nature demonstrate a connection of far greater consequence.

/1/ Ruby's Extensive Police Contacts

Ruby was "well acquainted with virtually every officer of the Dallas Police force," noted his friend Lewis McWillie.[30] Amazing as it seems, given the roughly 1,200 officers on the force,[31] this claim was confirmed by many other acquaintances of Ruby.

"Ruby knew every police officer in Dallas," reported Robert Craven.[32] "He knew most of the policemen on the police force," said Breck Wall;[33] "all the policemen in town," related Joseph Cavagnaro.[34] Reagan Turnman told the FBI that Ruby "was acquainted with at least 75 percent and probably 80 percent" of the police force.[35] Another acquaintance of Ruby commented that he "seemed to know every policeman in Dallas and every important official and newspaper man."[36]

"Ruby was well known among members of the Dallas Police Department," noted a police lieutenant who said he knew Ruby well.[37] "Many Dallas Police officers" were on a "first name basis" with Ruby, according to a former Dallas policeman.[38] Ruby was "on speaking terms with about 700 out of the 1200 men on the police force";[39] he was "very friendly with members of the Dallas Police Department";[40] he "knew everyone on the Police force," three other witnesses reported.[41]

But Dallas Police Chief Jesse Curry, under fire for permitting Oswald's killing in his own headquarters, held a different opinion. According to Chief Curry, "no more than 25 to 50 of Dallas' almost 1200 policemen were acquainted with Ruby."[42] Not surprisingly, this paraphrase of Curry's testimony is the only estimate of the extent of Ruby's police ties printed in the Warren Report.[43]

Complementing Ruby's extensive Dallas Police ties were other official contacts, as indicated by documents he kept. Among the items found in his possession were the business cards of the chief of the Narcotics Division in Austin, Texas[44] and of the captain of the Traffic Division in El Paso;[45] a card of the Chicago Police Department;[46] permanent passes to the Carousel Club, signed by the recipients, issued to Dallas Assistant District Attorney W. F. Alexander, Garland Deputy J. T. Ivey, and city hall officials Ray Hawkins and John D. Bailey;[47] five bail bond cards;[48] and various lists with the notations "Rosemary Allen ... Deputy Sheriff Decker's secretary,"[49] "Buddy Walthers ... Deputy Sheriff,"[50] "Travis Hall ... County Clerk Deputy,"[51] and "Clint Lewis ... Deputy Sheriff."[52] Also found was a card bearing Ruby's name and the Dallas County official seal, signed by Justice of the Peace Glen W. Byrd.[53] Similar to a card once furnished to Capone Mobster Jack Zuta,[54] it read:

> To all public officials: kindly extend to the individual whose signature appears above any and all assistance which may be properly given in keeping with your official duties and obligations.[55]

/2/ Police Favors and Paychecks from Jack Ruby

One place of contact between Ruby and the Dallas Police was his Carousel Club. The Carousel "was frequented by most of the officers of the Dallas Police Department," most of whom Ruby knew "on a first-name basis," according to a hostess at the club.[56] "Law enforcement officers, both plain-clothes and uniformed police and deputy sheriffs frequently came to the Sovereign Club to converse with Ruby," according to the food service manager at Ruby's Sovereign Club, precursor of the Carousel.[57] Others reported that "many officers of the Dallas Police Department came in and out of the Carousel";[58] "Ruby's club was frequented by Dallas Police officials";[59] "numerous officers came into the club."[60] These statements were corroborated by the accounts of three former Dallas Police officers.[61]

A former Carousel bartender, James Rhodes, told the FBI that Ruby "gave orders to the bartender and waitresses that the officers should never be charged for anything they received at the club."[62] Nancy Perrin Rich, a former bartender and waitress at the Carousel, testified that Ruby had given a standing order to serve hard liquor free to any Dallas policemen who wanted it,[63] even though it was illegal for Ruby to serve hard liquor in the club.[64] Robert Shorman, a musician at the Carousel Club, said that he saw "between 150 to 200 police officers at the Carousel at one time or another," including Captain Fritz, but he "never saw a police officer pay for a drink."[65] Five others, including two Dallas Police officers, also reported that Ruby routinely gave free drinks and food to Dallas policemen.[66]

Other witnesses reported more substantial favors. Herbert Kelly, food service manager of Ruby's Sovereign Club, told the FBI that each Sunday night Ruby would "entertain as many as eight law enforcement officers, furnishing them gratis expensive dinners and drinks."[67] James Rhodes reported that he once bartended for Ruby at a Carousel Club party for "thirty or forty police officers."[68] Ruby told Rhodes that the group included the chief,[69] and Rhodes gathered that Ruby paid for the party.[70] Rhodes also described an after-hours party held at the Carousel by Ruby for 14 members of the Dallas Police vice squad.[71]

Mrs. Janice Jones, once a waitress at the Carousel, told the FBI that Ruby gave a fifth of whiskey to each Dallas policeman who came by around Christmas[72]—a rather expensive proposition considering the number of Ruby's police acquaintances. Dallas Policeman Hugh Smith confirmed that Ruby gave bottles of liquor to numerous policemen.[73] He also related that a bachelor on the Dallas Police Force had "used Ruby's apartment on several occasions."[74] Ruby's acquaintance Joe Bonds advised the FBI that Ruby "made women available to officers."[75] And Dallas hardware store owner Ray Singleton told the FBI that Ruby once came into his store to purchase a revolver—accompanied by a police officer.[76]

Also significant were many reports that Ruby employed off-duty policemen as bouncers in his night clubs.[77] This arrangement violated Dallas Police regulations,[78] which is perhaps why E. E. Carlson, a detective on the force, refused to discuss it when questioned by the FBI.[79] And it was incongruous given Ruby's proficiency as a fighter,[80] which he often demonstrated by abusive ejections of unruly patrons at his clubs.[81] In fact, six witnesses specifically reported that Ruby served as his own bouncer.[82] It thus appears likely that this reported "employment" arrangement was a fiction to cover payoffs by Ruby to policemen who frequented his clubs.

/3/ No Police Problems for Jack Ruby

Ruby's police favors certainly bought him personal immunity from law enforcement, beginning with his night club operations. James Barrigan, a Dallas night club owner, told the FBI that Ruby illegally served drinks after midnight in the Carousel Club, even when Dallas policemen were present.[83] Ruby's friend Paul Roland Jones stated that Ruby "could not have operated his businesses [or] been permitted to put on the 'raw shows' that he did" without payoffs to the police.[84] Carousel employee Joan Leavell said that the Dallas Police permitted Ruby to run shows rougher than those of other Dallas clubs.[85] And Carousel stripper Janet Conforto ("Jada") told the FBI that Ruby boasted that the police let him "get away with things at his club" because of his friendship with them.[86]

Ruby was "known to have brutally beaten at least 25 different persons," as reported in a February 24, 1964 memo by two Warren Commission staff members.[87] But the police seemed as reluctant to arrest Ruby for assault as for liquor violations. Dallas attorney John Wilson, Jr. told the FBI that he saw Ruby assault a man in a local bar without apparent provocation, probably using brass knuckles, causing a large amount of bleeding.[88] Wilson related that when policemen arrived, they intended to arrest the man Ruby had beaten, but not Ruby.[89] They took no action against Ruby, even after Wilson told them what happened.[90] Wilson observed that the officers "were extremely reluctant to do anything about Ruby."[91]

Mrs. Paul Calgrove, who had worked for Ruby, reported that she had complained to the Dallas Police of physical abuse by him.[92] The police told her that she was crazy to press charges against him, and laughed at her desire to do so.[93] Similarly, when Carousel employee Nancy Rich complained that Ruby had pushed and injured her, the police warned her that by filing suit against him, she would only get herself "in more trouble than [she] bargained for."[94] Mrs. Rich testified that when she tried to prosecute Ruby, she was arrested twice on phony charges,[95] and told by the police that she might find the climate outside Dallas more to her liking.[96] One witness told the FBI that in reference to this or a similar incident, Ruby once boasted that "he had just squashed [sic] a complaint against him for beating one of his dancers."[97] In contrast, Ruby's sister Eileen Kaminsky was reportedly given the VIP treatment by the Dallas Police when she visited the city a year before Kennedy's assassination.[98]

/4/ Ruby's Police Record

Ruby's police record directly demonstrates his immunity from the law. Ruby was arrested nine times between 1949 and 1963 on charges including assault, carrying a concealed weapon, and liquor infractions.[99] But he was convicted only once, in 1949, paying a $10 fine.[100] The dispositions of the other arrests were recorded as "complaint dismissed," "no charges filed," "no further disposition shown," and acquittal in one case.[101] Likewise, Ruby's traffic record shows no payments on nine violations committed after 1956, including negligent collision, speeding and running a red light.[102] As concluded in an atypical Warren Commission staff memo of February 24, 1964, Ruby avoided prosecution "through the maintenance of friendship with police officers, public officials, and other influential persons in the Dallas community."[103]

The handling of one of Ruby's infractions is probably representative. On December 5, 1954, at 1:30 a.m., Ruby was arrested by Dallas policemen E. E. Carlson and D. L. Blankenship for permitting the consumption of alcoholic beverages in his night club during forbidden hours.[104] The arresting officers' report states that the officers saw beer on the table, and observed that a customer attempted "to hold the bottle and said that it was her beer."[105] In an interview with a physician, Ruby described his arrest that night by Officers Carlson and Blankenship, adding "but then they found out I had good friends and they came out the next night sort of apologetic."[106] Not surprisingly, the charge against Ruby was dropped two months later.[107] Signed by Dallas District Attorney Henry Wade, the motion dismissing the charge asserted:

The police report states that they [Blankenship and Carlson] observed customers consuming beer after hours. Both officers stated that this is incorrect and they did not observe the customers consuming beer. It is recommended that this case be dismissed because of insufficient evidence.[108]

Yet both Carlson and Blankenship later told the FBI that their police report was accurate.[109] Blankenship stated that he did not know why the charge was dismissed.[110]

/5/ Frequent Visits to Police Headquarters

Perhaps the most important indication of unusual ties between Ruby and the Dallas Police was his frequent presence at police headquarters. "It was common knowledge that Ruby spent time almost every day at the Dallas Police Department," Benny Bickers told the FBI on November 24, 1963.[111] "On numerous occasions after receiving a telephone call Ruby would go to the police station," according to Herbert Kelly, food service manager of Ruby's Sovereign Club.[112] Indeed, Ruby was in the Dallas Police building several times between Thursday, November 21 and Sunday, November 24,[113] although perhaps not for his usual business. The many accounts of Ruby's contact with the police were well summarized by Carousel employee Nancy Rich, who testified,

> I don't think there is a cop in Dallas that doesn't know Jack Ruby. He practically lived at that station. They lived in his place.[114]

/6/ Mob-Police Liaison

Ruby's extensive and often irregular ties with the Dallas Police thus indicate a connection beyond the realm of corrupt night club politics. Given these extraordinary police ties, in fact, quite credible was an allegation that Ruby was "the pay off man for the Dallas Police" (it was reportedly stated,[115] and then denied,[116] by Mickey Ryan, alias Roy Pike, an associate of Ruby*). Regardless of Ruby's precise role in the underworld's corruption

---

*Ryan, a close contact of Ruby during the fall of 1963,[117] had a suspicious alibi for the time of the assassination. The only thing Ryan could recall about his activities November 22–24 was that he was watching television with his wife when "he heard a news flash that President Kennedy had been shot."[118] Yet Carousel stripper Nancy Powell testified that she was with Ryan and a friend Pete—no mention of Ryan's wife[119]—when Ryan was informed of the assassination in a telephone conversation.[120] Powell related, "Then [Ryan] came out of the bedroom and he said, the President has just been shot, he walked right to the TV and turned it on."[121] Ryan left Dallas for California at the end of November 1963,[122] having arrived in the city only two months earlier.[123]

network, however, it is clear that he was an important intermediary in arranging the gambling fix. To review three previously cited observations, Harry Hall told the FBI that Ruby received 40 percent of Hall's gambling profits because Ruby "was supposed to have influence with the police, so that he [Hall] would have no worry about any gambling arrest."[124] William Abadie saw Dallas officers frequenting Ruby's gambling establishment and concluded, "It was obvious that to operate gambling in the manner that he did," Ruby must have had both "racketeering connections" and "police connection[s]" in Dallas and Fort Worth.[125] And Jack Hardee reported being told that "Ruby had the 'fix' with the County authorities, and that any other fix being placed would have to be done through Ruby."[126]

Although "Mob-police liaison" has a sinister ring, the reality of Ruby's police connection can be comprehended in human terms. Ruby enjoyed playing the glad-hander, speeding around town with impunity, delivering bribes to police and officials, and doling out the favors of his Carousel Club strippers. Jack Ruby, the slum hustler, had become the generous benefactor—buying popularity among a high-placed constituency as an intermediary for the gangster elite he had idolized since childhood. And for the Mob, Ruby filled a critical role, spreading the fix with the happy-go-lucky aura that its corruption specialists would ordinarily take great pains to cultivate.[127]

Yet the murderous roots behind Mafia corruption inevitably penetrate its innocuous facade. And there would come an undertaking in Dallas that would require police collusion—that would demand full payment of Satan's lien on the glad-handing of Jack Ruby.

> The [FBI] files make clear that the Warren Commission failed abysmally to pursue FBI leads linking Oswald's own assassin, Jack Ruby, to the Mob. Ruby had ties to mobsters in Chicago, New York, Los Angeles and Dallas, and even, as a boy, to the infamous Al Capone.[1]
>
> *Time* magazine, December 19, 1977

> Wasn't it pretty well known to the FBI that Jack Ruby, No. 1, was a member of organized crime, No. 2, he ran a strip joint and has been somewhat commonly referred to as a supplier of both women and booze to political and police figures in the city of Dallas.[2]
>
> Congressman Stewart McKinney, addressing FBI representative James Malley in the House Assassinations hearings

□ 11 □

Jack Ruby, Mobster

Notwithstanding the fine recommendations of his "Chicago friends,"[3] Ruby's Mob connection is apparent from the activities, contacts and background considered in the previous chapters. Yet Ruby's underworld position is difficult to reconcile with certain of his character traits, such as his gregarious nature and generosity,[4] which are quite human and in some instances even likable. In order to better understand Ruby's criminal nature, it is thus helpful to examine other of his personality traits more compatible with his occupation.

/1/ Ruby's Life Style

Ruby played the part of a gangster in classic Chicago style. He dressed extravagantly; his outfit the day of the Oswald shooting included a silk necktie with gold-plated tie clasp, an imported leather belt, a ring with three diamonds, a 14-carat gold Le Coultre diamond-studded wristwatch, and his "Chicago hoodlum hat."[5] Sometimes he also wore brass or aluminum knuckles[6] to complement his natural proficiency with his fists;[7] two sets of them were found in his car.[8] One acquaintance described Ruby as an "intense racketeer and hustler," who was "interested solely and entirely in his businesses and gambling."[9] A close friend testified, "He always reminded me of a gangster. . . . he just reminds me of a real hood."[10] And another friend of Ruby testified that "because of his character automatically people would take him as a thug."[11]

Ruby's "one outstanding characteristic . . . was his own personal intense interest in gambling of any kind," former employee William Abadie told the FBI.[12] A one-time acquaintance reported that Ruby "bet heavily, made frequent telephone bets on horse races and basketball games."[13] And according to Harry Hall, Ruby once won $5,000 on a telephone bet with a Montreal bookie and sent Hall there to collect the winnings.[14] Ruby's affinity for betting was also demonstrated in the summer of 1957, when he went to the races in Hot Springs, Arkansas with Mobster Lewis McWillie.[15]

Ruby's relationships with women were characteristic of his profession. Carousel employee Larry Crafard testified that Ruby told him he had had a sexual relationship with every one of the women who worked for him;[16] Carousel stripper Karen Carlin named some of her fellow entertainers with whom Ruby went to bed.[17] Another Carousel employee said that Ruby "was always on the make," and would frequently date female employees and other women.[18] One woman told the FBI that Ruby had tried to rape her when she was a waitress at his Silver Spur Club at age 14.[19]

Ruby's reading material included articles pertaining to his business. A "partially complete" copy of the November 18, 1963 *Wall Street Journal*, including the first page, was found in Ruby's car.[20] That issue featured a front-page article entitled "Mafia and Business," which mentioned Ruby's associate Joseph Civello.[21] A "partial copy" of the September 8, 1963 *New York Daily Mirror* was also found in Ruby's car.[22] Page 11 of that day's *Mirror* contained an article about Mafia defector Joseph Valachi.[23] That article also described how one Mafia figure went about "setting up a patsy and luring him into a narcotics conspiracy."[24]

Ruby observed the Mob custom of carrying and stashing away large sums of cash. The *Dallas Morning News* reported that police detectives found two large wads of bills of undisclosed amounts when they searched Ruby's apartment on November 24[25] ($256.80 was found according to police accounting.[26]) Police inventories reported that Ruby was carrying more than $2,000 in cash when he shot Oswald.[27] Bank bags containing an additional $1,015.78 in small bills and change, probably night club receipts, were found among his possessions.[28] And a printer who did some work for Ruby noticed about five to twenty $100 bills in Ruby's wallet when he took it out on one occasion.[29]

Ruby's spending habits also typified success in his affiliation. When out of town, he stayed at such luxury hotels as the Sheraton Lincoln in Houston (on May 9, 1963[30]) and the New York Hilton (from August 4 to 6, 1963[31]). Johnny Branch, manager of the Empire Room in Dallas, said that Ruby would come in there from time to time and hand out $5 bills to random customers.[32] Even during his last year in Chicago, while still a relatively small-time operator, Ruby lived at the Congress Hotel[33]—also the home of Mayor Anton Cermak in the 1930s.[34] Yet Ruby reported no earnings to the Social Security Office between 1940 and 1956.[35]

Indeed, Ruby was consistently modest about his finances in his official accounts, declaring a median income of $6,000 on his tax returns for the years 1956 through 1962.[36] But the Internal Revenue Service did not find his appraisals too reliable, holding a claim against him for $44,400 in delinquent excise and income taxes in 1963.[37] And this IRS scrutiny, which had put so many of Ruby's predecessors in prison,[38]* explains his thrift in documentable transactions. Thus it makes sense that Ruby resided in a small apartment in Dallas,[46] but lodged at the Sheraton in Houston[47] and the Hilton in New York;[48] that he owned a 1960 Oldsmobile,[49] yet was seen by two witnesses driving a Cadillac.[50]

Ruby's frequent travels across the country provided a further indication of his apparent affluence. The assassination material contains reports of Ruby's visits to the following cities after he moved to Dallas in 1947: New York,[51] Chicago,[52] Los Angeles,[53] San Francisco,[54] Wichita,[55] Tulsa,[56] Hot Springs (Arkansas),[57] Henderson (Kentucky),[58] Las Vegas,[59] New Orleans,[60] Miami,[61] and Havana, Cuba.[62]

/2/ Ruby's Status in the Mob

With this personal glimpse into Ruby's criminal side, his underworld activities and associations begin to fall into place. Although all of the material in this part helps illuminate Ruby's status within the Mob, the following points deserve special attention.

Ruby served an elite criminal apprenticeship in Chicago, starting out in a group that ran errands for Al Capone, appropriating a union with notorious Mobster Paul Dorfman, and learning the basic rackets in the Chicago

---

*Ever since such notables as Al Capone, Frank Costello, Johnny Torrio, Waxey Gordon, and Moe Annenberg were convicted on tax evasion charges,[39] Syndicate figures have been careful to maintain a low financial profile. Top boss Vito Genovese, for example, owned a modest home and auto.[40] So did Meyer Lansky,[41] who was investigated for income-tax evasion from 1950 to 1953.[42] "Don Peppino," a former top New England Mafioso,[43] would drive around in an old Chrysler for fear of the IRS.[44] And Louisiana Mafia boss Carlos Marcello once carried the act a bit further by successfully pleading poverty to settle a $76,830 fine for a rare conviction with a $400 payment.[45]

night club district. In the late 1940s, Ruby earned hi⸜
Chicago delegation that muscled in on the Dallas are
years, several members of this group died,[63] were murⴑ
las.[65] Thus, although Ruby came to Dallas as a "small tin⸜
the Chicago gang, by 1963 he had become one of a select ⸜
cate pioneers there.

During his years in Dallas, Ruby made contact with dozeⴑ   ⸜der-
world figures in the area and across the country. These includeⴑ ⴍarcello
associates Joseph Campisi, Frank Caracci, and Nofio Pecora; Teamster
goons Barney Baker and Frank Chavez; notorious Mobsters Mickey Cohen,
Paul Roland Jones, Lewis McWillie, Lenny Patrick and Irwin Weiner; and
Dallas Mafia boss Joseph Civello. A common interest probably led to Ruby's
visits with Civello, since Civello was convicted on federal narcotics
charges,[67] and since Ruby's name came up twice before 1963 in federal narcotics investigations.[68] Indeed, it is unlikely that Ruby could have given
"the okay to operate" in a major narcotics network "between Mexico,
Texas and the East"[69] without an okay, in turn, from Civello.

But of all the criminal arenas in which Ruby operated, the most important was undoubtedly the Mob's top-dollar monopoly,[70] illegal gambling. As
reported by three credible witnesses and corroborated by other sources,
Ruby operated his own slot machine warehouse and bookmaking establishments, and was instrumental in coordinating the "fix" with police and
local authorities. It is this key niche in illicit gambling operations, in conjunction with his Mob ties, that establishes Ruby's position in the upper
echelons of the Dallas Mob organization.

But there is probably a dichotomy between his functional importance
and his clout. As a Jew, Ruby found opportunities in the Dallas underworld
that were closed to him in the more established East and Midwest, where
the Mafia had beaten the competition into subservience or oblivion.[71] It
was indeed such areas as California, Nevada, Florida, the Caribbean and
the Bahamas that nurtured the rise of Meyer Lansky, Moe Dalitz, Mickey
Cohen, Bugsy Siegel and other ethnic counterparts of Ruby prominent in
the Syndicate.[72] Yet in any region, a sharp distinction is always drawn between associates of the Mafia, however valuable, and the core group of
members.[73] For example, leading Syndicate financier[74] Meyer Lansky can
take no action without the approval of Mafia superiors, who, during one
period, kept him under the constant escort of Vincent Alo ("Jimmy Blue
Eyes"),[75] a Genovese Family caporegime.[76]* It is thus likely that despite Ru-

---

*Vincent Teresa, the highest ranking and most valuable defector to date from the
Mafia,[77] who had dealings with Lansky,[78] wrote in his memoirs in 1973 that Lansky

can't give orders to any Mob guy unless he has an okay from that guy's
boss, and to do that he has to go through Jimmy Blue Eyes. . . . [Lansky

nportance in Dallas Mob operations, he had virtually no governing
)ower.

Whatever Ruby's exact position in the underworld pecking order, however, it is clear from his background, activities, life style and associations
that he was intimate with the Mob. Ruby himself hinted to the Warren Commission that some thought he was "put here as a front of the underworld
and sooner or later they will get something out of me that they want done
to their advantage."[80] That particular service of Ruby—and more of his remarkable testimony—will be covered in the following part.

---

is] a very valuable friend of the mob—always has been and always will
be. .... He can sit with the bosses because he makes them so much
money. But if he got out of line, if he defied them, they'd wipe him out in
a second.[79]

PART III
MURDER ON CUE

It was Sunday morning, November 24, 1963, two days after the assassination of President Kennedy. Police were making final preparations for the transfer of suspect Lee Harvey Oswald from Dallas Police headquarters to the county jail.[1] At the same time, Jack Ruby was in the downtown Dallas Western Union office[2] wiring $25 to his Carousel entertainer, Karen Carlin.[3] According to her husband Bruce,[4] Ruby,[5] and herself,[6] Karen had requested the money for rent and groceries in a 10:19 call to Ruby that morning.[7] Ruby received a receipt for the $25, time stamped 11:17 a.m.,[8] and headed for the Dallas Police building one block away.[9]

Three minutes later, at 11:20 a.m.—an hour and 20 minutes after the scheduled transfer time—Oswald was moved from his cell in the Dallas Police building.[10] Police escorts guided him down through the basement, which was swarming with reporters, to the ramp of the garage.[11] The transfer had been elaborately planned,[12] and word had been given that everything was ready.[13] Yet when Oswald reached the ramp, as described by police escort L. D. Montgomery, he

> had to stop, because [the transfer] car wasn't in position. . . . It was supposed to have been in position when we got there, but it wasn't there, so, we had to pause, or slow down for the car to come on back.[14]

And at 11:21 a.m., as Oswald paused at the garage ramp, standing in place of the out-of-position transfer car was Jack Ruby.[15] Ruby pulled out a .38-caliber revolver, and fired one fatal shot into Oswald's abdomen.[16]

The murder of Lee Oswald simplified the Kennedy assassination case in several respects. The long and cumbersome trial necessitated by Oswald's protests of innocence was circumvented by Ruby's professedly impetuous act.[17] And the perplexing questions about November 22 were overshadowed by a straightforward series of events on November 24. The 10:19 a.m. call from the Carlin residence in Fort Worth to Ruby's apartment in Dallas.[18] The 11:17 a.m. telegram from Ruby to Karen Carlin.[19] And then the 11:21 a.m. televised shooting in the police basement.[20] They all seemed just the series of fateful coincidences that Ruby described.

Yet the Oswald murder provided another, more disquieting simplification. For Lee Oswald, a man of assorted involvements, was upstaged by Jack Ruby—a man whose singular identification could not, despite the best of efforts, be concealed. Jack Ruby was a professional gangster, who would hardly commit a crime aimlessly or explain it truthfully. And Jack Ruby was intimately tied to the Mob—an organization with the motive, means, and declared intention to kill President Kennedy.

As a critical preliminary step toward unraveling the Kennedy assassination, this part will dissect the evidence concerning the Oswald murder. It will show that Ruby's alibi for his assassination-weekend activities was totally fraudulent. The Carlin call and telegram were staged. And the shooting of Oswald was a meticulously coordinated murder contract. These are underscored in the amazing final hearings of Jack Ruby himself—in which, on record, Ruby indicated his alibi was prepared with others, mocked his recitation of it, and stated he could not tell the truth because his life was in danger. A preview:

> Who else could have timed it [the Oswald shooting] so perfectly
> by seconds. If it were timed that way, then someone in the po-
> lice department is guilty of giving the information as to when
> Lee Harvey Oswald was coming down.[21]

Clearly, neither the timing of the shooting nor the existence of a conspiracy could have been hypothetical issues to Jack Ruby. But the cited conspiracy will assume grippingly real dimensions in the coordinated perjury of some very frightened witnesses.

> In the underworld that Ruby had frequented since his
> childhood, when a witness who is soon to testify in court is
> murdered, it is for a single purpose: to prevent him from
> confessing, and from implicating his associates in some
> crime that has been committed.[1]
>
> Thomas Buchanan, a journalist who covered the trial of
> Jack Ruby for the French weekly *l'Express*

☐ 12 ☐

Perjury and Suspicious Activities

In official interviews following the fatal shooting of Oswald, Ruby and several associates presented detailed accounts covering Ruby's activities prior to that event.[2] The contradictions are virtually endless. A good starting point to examine these stories and the events leading up to the Oswald murder is the afternoon of President Kennedy's assassination.

/1/ A Visit to Parkland Hospital

Jack Ruby told the FBI and the Warren Commission that on Friday afternoon, November 22, 1963, he placed a night club ad at the Dallas Morning News building and then went to the Carousel Club.[3] At no time that day, claimed Ruby, did he visit Parkland Hospital,[4] where President Kennedy and Governor Connally were treated. But journalist Seth Kantor reported in the Scripps-Howard newspapers,[5] told the FBI,[6] and testified before Warren Commission counsel[7] that he saw Ruby there on Friday afternoon. A member of the White House press corps, Kantor related that at 1:30 p.m., he met, shook hands and spoke with Ruby in a corridor at Parkland Hospital.[8] Kantor was quite sure it was Ruby, since they had become well-acquainted when Kantor was a reporter in Dallas.[9] Kantor stated that he would testify to the Parkland encounter in a court of law,[10] reiterating that he was "indelibly sure"[11] it took place. And Kantor's account was corroborated by another witness, Mrs. Wilma Tice. Tice testified that she saw a man at Parkland Hospital Friday afternoon whom she heard addressed as "Jack"; she identified him as Ruby from news photos.[12]

But the Warren Commission, faithful to its lone-nut dogma, accepted Ruby's denial of his Parkland Hospital sojourn.[13] Noting an inconclusive matter of timing,[14] the Commission proposed that Kantor had been confused; he had really spoken with Ruby at a news conference Friday night which they both attended.[15] But this conjecture was absurd given Kantor's account of what transpired during his encounter with Ruby. As Kantor reported, "Ruby shook hands numbly, having minutes earlier witnessed the tragic events of the President's assassination," and was anxious "for news about the President's condition."[16] Indeed, as recently asserted by both the House Assassinations Committee[17] and a Warren Commission staffer who investigated the matter,[18] Kantor's corroborated account of Ruby's visit to Parkland Hospital was in all likelihood accurate.

/2/ **Visits to the Dallas Police Building**

Ruby did, in fact, also attend a news conference around midnight, November 22, in the Dallas Police building.[19] As can be heard on videotape, Ruby interjected the correction "Fair Play Cuba" when District Attorney Henry Wade told reporters that Oswald belonged to the "Free Cuba Committee."[20] But the midnight press conference was not the only occasion that Ruby visited the Dallas Police building during the assassination weekend. Detective August Eberhardt, who had known Ruby five years,[21] testified that he spoke with Ruby in the third-floor hallway of the police building between 6 and 7 p.m. Friday.[22] Detective Roy Standifer, also well-acquainted with Ruby,[23] testified that they exchanged greetings in the same place at about 7:30 p.m.[24] The encounter occurred shortly after Standifer's supper break, which he routinely began at 6:30 p.m.[25]

Dallas television reporter Vic Robertson, Jr., another acquaintance of Ruby,[26] was positive that early Friday evening he saw Ruby try to open the door of Captain Fritz's office, where Oswald was being questioned.[27] Robertson then heard a voice say, "You can't go in there, Jack."[28] John Rutledge, a *Dallas Morning News* reporter, also saw Ruby directly across from Captain Fritz's office before 6 p.m. that night.[29] And other witnesses reported Ruby's presence in the Dallas Police building Friday between 4 and 7 p.m.[30]

About noon on Saturday, November 23, Ruby visited the police building again. His presence was noted in a rather amusing account to the FBI by *France-Soir* reporter Phillippe Labro:

Ruby encountered Mr. Labro and asked him who he was and what he did for a living. Mr. Labro advised Ruby that he was a French newspaper reporter. Ruby's response was "ooh la la Folies Bergere," which, according to Labro, were probably the only French words known to Ruby. Ruby then presented Mr. Labro with a card advertising his night club "The Carousel" containing the picture of a nude woman and invited him to stop and have a drink with him. ... There is no question in his mind as to the identity of the person whom he talked with on November 23, 1963, as Ruby.[31]

Possibly in reference to this encounter, Ruby told a medical interviewer, "I even passed out some of my cards to those newspaper men from all over the world."[32]

Thayer Waldo, a Fort Worth reporter, ran into Ruby in the police building at 4 p.m. Saturday.[33] Waldo testified that Ruby introduced himself, gave Waldo a Carousel card, and invited him and other newsmen over to the club for free drinks.[34] NBC News Producer-Director Fred Rheinstein testified that Saturday afternoon before 5 p.m., he saw a man in the police building who he was "reasonably certain was Ruby."[35] This man entered a police building office in which District Attorney Henry Wade was reportedly working and from which newsmen had been excluded.[36] UPI photographer Frank Johnston,[37] French journalist Francois Pelou,[38] and others[39] also saw Ruby at police headquarters Saturday afternoon and evening.

In Ruby's version of his assassination-weekend activities, however, his only visit to the Dallas Police building before Sunday morning occurred on Friday, shortly before midnight.[40]

/3/ Mood During the Assassination Weekend

Ruby's exuberant behavior Saturday afternoon at the police station—handing out Carousel cards and inviting reporters for drinks—typified his mood during much of the assassination weekend. Friday night at police headquarters, "Ruby appeared to be anything but under stress or strain," noted T.V. newsman Vic Robertson, Jr. "He seemed happy, jovial, was joking and laughing."[41] At radio station KLIF early Saturday, Ruby "was not grieving," and, "if anything," was "happy that the evidence was piling up against Oswald," announcer Glen Duncan said.[42] Ruby even commented that Oswald was a good-looking guy who resembled Paul Newman, and expressed "no bitterness against the man," according to Russ Knight, a disc jockey.[43] Johnny Branch, manager of the Empire Room, testified that Ruby came into his club Saturday night at about 10 p.m., mentioned nothing about the assassination, and handed out some $5 bills to customers as he did on other occasions.[44]

But Ruby told the FBI he was "in mourning" Friday and Saturday.[45] He said he cried when he heard the president was shot,[46] "cried a great deal" Saturday afternoon,[47] and was depressed Saturday night.[48]

/4/ Feelings for the Kennedys

Ruby explained that his tremendous grief, so little in evidence, was caused by his great love for the martyred president and his sympathy for the Kennedy family.[49] This anguish over the assassination, Ruby stated, finally "reached the point of insanity,"[50] suddenly compelling him to shoot when Oswald walked to the police ramp that Sunday morning.[51]

But a handwritten note from Ruby to one of his lawyers exposed this story, in the words of the House Assassinations Committee, as "a fabricated legal ploy."[52] Disclosed by *Newsweek* in 1967, the note from Ruby to attorney Joe Tonahill read:

> Joe, you should know this. Tom Howard told me to say that I shot Oswald so that Caroline and Mrs. Kennedy wouldn't have to come to Dallas to testify. OK?[53]

Indeed, the patriotic sentiments Ruby professed were quite out of character. Harry Hall, his partner in a gambling operation, told the FBI that "Ruby was the type who was interested in any way to make money."[54] Hall "could not conceive of Ruby doing anything out of patriotism."[55] Jack Kelly, who had known Ruby casually since 1943, "scoffed at the idea of a patriotic motive being involved by Ruby in the slaying of Oswald."[56] And Ruby's friend Paul Roland Jones was paraphrased by his FBI interviewers as affirming that

> from his acquaintance with Ruby he doubted that [Ruby] would have become emotionally upset and killed Oswald on the spur of the moment. He felt Ruby would have done it for money....[57]

Perhaps Ruby himself shed the most light on his "tremendous emotional feeling"[58] in testimony before the Warren Commission on June 7, 1964, following his conviction for first-degree murder:

> [Rabbi Seligman] eulogized that here is a man that fought in every battle, went to every country, and had to come back to his own country to be shot in the back [starts crying].
> I must be a great actor, I tell you that.[59]

In a polygraph hearing a month later, Ruby offered even bolder indications of his true feelings. At one point he remarked, "They didn't ask me another question: 'If I loved the President so much, why wasn't I at the parade?'" (referring to the president's motorcade).[60] Ruby added, "It's strange that perhaps I didn't vote for President Kennedy, or didn't vote at all, that I should build up such a great affection for him."[61] Although Ruby volunteered this remark under the pretext of defending himself against unspecified detractors,[62] his reference to the private matter of his vote could only have been a candid confession. And Ruby dropped the hypothetical guise when he later interjected, speaking of himself, "Here's a fellow that didn't vote for the President, closes his clubs for 3 days, made a trip to Cuba...."[63]

An indication of Ruby's actual feelings for the Kennedys was perhaps expressed in a November 24 ABC-TV interview with "Jada," a Carousel Club stripper.

> **Jada**: I have heard Jack talk about the Kennedys and I've been trying to think and it's so confusing today, but I believe he disliked Bobby Kennedy.
> **Q**: Get no recollection of what he had ever said about the President?
> **Jada**: Yes. He followed that statement up about Bobby with something about Jack Kennedy....[64]

/5/ Early Saturday Morning at KLIF

After Ruby left the Friday midnight press conference in the police building, he told the FBI, he went directly to the newsroom of Dallas radio station KLIF.[65] Ruby said he arrived there at about 2 a.m. and stayed for an hour.[66]

There are two problems with this account of Ruby's visit to KLIF. For one thing, Ruby, disc jockey Russ Knight and another KLIF employee conflict sharply on how Ruby got into the newsroom that night.[67] A second point of controversy was whether or not Ruby met with Ike Pappas, then a New York radio announcer, who was using the KLIF newsroom early Saturday.[68] Danny McCurdy of KLIF testified that Ruby "spent the majority of the time in the newsroom with our newsman, Glen Duncan, ... and also a gentleman named Pappas."[69] And Russ Knight testified that Ruby listened in on a conversation between himself and Pappas.[70] But Pappas, who had met Ruby briefly at the midnight news conference,[71] emphatically denied that Ruby was in the KLIF newsroom while he was there.[72]

The discrepancies over Ruby's alleged Saturday morning visit to KLIF are particularly suspicious in light of Ruby's close relationship with station personnel. Ruby was well-acquainted with Gordon McLendon,[73] the owner of KLIF and many other radio stations throughout the United States.[74] McLendon gave Ruby "a lot of free plugs," Ruby reported,[75] and Ruby called McLendon's home the night of the assassination.[76] According to government witness Ed Partin, radio magnate McLendon was later named by Marcello associate D'Alton Smith as someone lined up to assist the Mob's spring-Hoffa campaign.[77]

Ruby's ties to KLIF personnel were also demonstrated by more than a dozen entries of their names and phone numbers in documents found among his possessions.[78] Of particular interest was the phone number of Ruby's friend[79] Russ "Knight" Moore,[80] the KLIF disc jockey, written on the back of an envelope found in Ruby's pocket when he shot Oswald.[81] The other notation on the back of that envelope was the name, address, and phone number of Thomas Hill of Belmont, Massachusetts.[82] Hill was a John Birch Society official cited in a Warren Commission staff memo of February 24, 1964 as among possible "sources of contact between Ruby and politically motivated groups interested in securing the assassination of President Kennedy."[83]

/6/ Early Saturday Morning with Dallas Policeman Harry Olsen

When questioned by the FBI in December 1963, Ruby reported that he "left Radio Station KLIF at about 3:00 A.M. on November 23, 1963, and drove to the Dallas Times Herald newspaper building."[84] But in his subsequent Warren Commission hearing, Ruby revised this story to acknowledge an encounter with Dallas Police Officer Harry Olsen and Olsen's girlfriend, Kathy Kay, a Carousel Club stripper:

> **Mr. Ruby**: . . . I left the KLIF at 2 a.m., and I spent an hour with the officer and his girlfriend, so it must have been about 3:15 approximately. No, it wasn't. When you are not concerned with time, it could have been 4 o'clock.
> **Chief Justice Warren**: It doesn't make any difference.
> **Mr. Ruby**: Forty-five minutes difference.[85]

Ruby was astute to challenge Warren's indifference to the adjustment in timing, for accounts of Ruby's meeting with Olsen are once again fraught with conflicts. But this time the perjury is transparent, the perjurers several in number, and the realm of conspiracy thus broached.

Circumstances and timing of the meeting. Olsen and Kay both testified that they were at a Dallas bar on November 22 until about midnight, the bar's closing time.[86] They then went directly to Simon's Garage nearby, they reported, to chat with garage attendant Johnny Simpson.[87] Kay testified that she, Olsen, and Simpson were sitting in a parked car talking when Ruby drove by.[88] They waved and Ruby pulled in, she related.[89] According to Olsen and Kay, Ruby arrived about half an hour to an hour after they left the bar,[90] thus no later than 1 a.m.

Garage attendant Johnny Simpson presented a totally different story. He told the FBI that around 1 a.m., November 23, Olsen "came to Simon's garage exit to wait for his girl friend."[91] Next, "the girl friend came and got into Olsen's car, they started to drive off, but the girl apparently saw Jack Ruby walking down the street and she yelled a greeting to him."[92] Ruby, on the other hand, testified that he drove past Simon's Garage after leaving KLIF, heard a loud honk, and saw Olsen and Kay in a car "very much carried away."[93] Ruby also said that he did not leave KLIF until after 2 a.m.,[94] consistent with the account of a KLIF employee who reported that Ruby was there for a 2 a.m. newscast.[95]

Ruby testified that he stayed with Olsen and Kay for an hour.[96] But Olsen told the FBI in December 1963 that the early Saturday morning conversation between himself, Ruby, Simpson, and Kay lasted "about ten minutes."[97] In subsequent testimony before Warren Commission counsel, Olsen stated this conversation lasted "two or three hours."[98]

Simpson's participation in the conversation. Olsen testified that Simpson took part in the conversation with Ruby, Kay, and himself,[99] and related Simpson's response to a statement by Ruby.[100] But Simpson told the FBI he "did not take part in any of the conversation."[101] Except for one overheard remark, Simpson said, he did "not know what the three talked about."[102] And Ruby never mentioned Simpson at all when he described the meeting with Olsen and Kay.[103]

Content of the conversation. Harry Olsen, Kathy Kay, and Jack Ruby testified that most of their conversation concerned the assassination, and that they were all upset.[104] In particular, Kay said that Ruby was "real upset"[105] and "would sit back and stare off into space, and . . . just keep saying over and over how terrible it was."[106] Olsen agreed that Ruby was "pretty emotionally upset."[107] Yet Olsen had previously told the FBI on December 12, 1963 that they had all "*mentioned*" the assassination of President Kennedy," but that Ruby "did not appear to be any more upset over the tragedy than the average individual."[108] Also, Ruby quoted a purported remark by Kay about what would have happened to Oswald in England,[109] which Olsen did not recall[110] and which Kay denied stating.[111]

Evaluation. The basic discrepancies in the circumstances, time, participants, and content of the Ruby-Olsen conversation show that perjury was committed by some or all of the witnesses. Considering the firm testimony of newsman Ike Pappas,[112] it appears likely that Ruby never visited KLIF on the morning of November 23; rather he met Dallas Policeman Harry Olsen at Simon's Garage around 12:30 or 1 a.m. for "two or three hours," as Olsen testified in his second version of events.[113] Uncertainty also surrounds the roles of Kay and Simpson, whose presence adds an innocent flavor to the encounter. This suggests that Kay was not there and that Simpson just observed from a distance, as he told the FBI.[114]

Harry Olsen and Kathy Kay. More suspicions concerning Dallas policeman Harry Olsen and Carousel stripper Kathy Kay, both quite friendly with Ruby,[115] were raised by conflicts in their testimony about their own assassination weekend activities. Olsen testified that he spent all day Friday, November 22 guarding an estate whose name and address he could not recall.[116] The job was arranged through a fellow police officer whose name he could not recall,[117] and Olsen stated twice that he finished his shift around 8 p.m.[118] Yet Kathy Kay testified first that Olsen left his guard duty at 4 p.m.,[119] then changed the time to 6 p.m.[120]

As for their activities between Friday and Saturday night, Olsen and Kay were vague and inconsistent.[121] Both mentioned persons they reportedly encountered but whose names they could not furnish.[122] Both did recall, however, running into Jack Ruby again on Saturday night, in front of the Carousel Club,[123] which was closed for the weekend.[124]

Olsen and Kay were more specific about their activities on Sunday, November 24. Olsen testified he spent all day Sunday with Kay at her home.[125] Then, at 9 or 10 p.m. that evening, they visited Dealey Plaza.[126] But Kay testified that on Sunday, November 24, she and Olsen visited Olsen's parents in Henrietta, Texas, 160 miles from Dallas.[127] Kay said that they left Dallas at about 4 p.m., spent three hours in Henrietta, headed back at about 10 p.m., and went directly to bed after returning to Dallas.[128] Also conflicting were Olsen's and Kay's reports about how they learned of an event that morning memorable to both: the uncannily timed shooting of Oswald by their friend Jack Ruby.[129] And given these striking disparities, one can only wonder whether the whereabouts of police officer Olsen were related to the slaying.

After the assassination, Olsen and Kay seemed anxious to leave Dallas. Kay did not go back to work at the Carousel Club after Ruby was arrested,[130] and about a week later began an engagement in Oklahoma City.[131] Tom Palmer, a Dallas union official, testified that Kay did not return to work because she "said she was afraid to and wanted to get out of town."[132] Palmer said that when he saw Kay on Tuesday, November 26, and told her that her contract was still valid, she replied, "I don't care, I just want to get out of town. I don't like it."[133]

On December 7, 1963, Olsen was driving his car when it veered off the road and crashed into a telephone pole, injuring him seriously enough to require two weeks of hospitalization.[134] After he was released from the hospital, Olsen left the Dallas Police,[135] and he and Kay moved to California on February 1, 1964.[136]

/7/ A Saturday Morning Photography Excursion

Filling out Ruby's Saturday morning activities, after the meeting with Olsen and a trip to the Times Herald building,[137] was a strange alleged sojourn.

Jack Ruby, Carousel employee Larry Crafard, and Ruby's roommate, George Senator, testified that at about 4 a.m. Saturday, they all went to photograph an "Impeach Earl Warren" billboard near the expressway.[138] Ruby claimed it had aroused his curiosity because of its similarity to an anti-Kennedy ad in the newspaper on Friday.[139] Afterward, the three testified, they proceeded to a post office to check the box number which had appeared in that ad, and then to the Southland Hotel Coffee Shop.[140] This strange excursion was described with some degree of consistency, despite discrepancies concerning the presence of Crafard during different parts of the trip[141] and the order of events.[142]

But there was one major problem. George Senator was interviewed by the FBI on Sunday, November 24,[143] the day Ruby shot Oswald—just one day after the events in question. And in that interview, Senator described his Saturday morning activities rather differently. As paraphrased by the FBI,

> After Senator and Ruby talked for awhile in the apartment, they got into a car and came downtown to a coffee shop of the Southland Hotel for a cup of coffee, this being about 4:30 or 5 o'clock in the morning of November 23, 1963. They talked considerably during this time of the shooting.[144]

When Senator described his Saturday morning activities in a subsequent interview that Sunday, he again omitted any reference to the purported photography excursion.[145]

During his hearing before Warren Commission counsel, Senator was questioned intensively about the discrepancy between his testimony concerning the photography excursion and his original accounts.[146] He was cross-examined skeptically when he claimed it initially had just slipped his mind.[147] Indeed, more likely, the story of this excursion—explaining three photos of the "Impeach Earl Warren" sign found on Ruby's person after he shot Oswald[148]—was communicated to Senator only after November 24. And it is interesting that the part of the story originally reported by Senator,[149] which was corroborated by independent witnesses,[150] was Ruby's visit to the Southland Hotel. That hotel was a long-time Mafia hangout,[151] owned by Mafioso Sam Maceo.[152]

George Senator. Senator's testimony concerning the entire assassination weekend was suspect, as even the Warren Commission was compelled to observe:

> The Commission also experienced difficulty in ascertaining the activities of Senator on November 22 and 23. He was unable to account specifically for large segments of time when he was not with Ruby. And, as to places and people Senator says he visited on those days prior to the time Oswald was shot, the Commission has been unsuccessful in obtaining verification.[153]

The House Assassinations Committee also noted that Senator's testimony was "extremely vague" and "not consistent."[154]

Senator's behavior after Ruby shot Oswald was unusual. For ten days, Senator so feared being hurt or killed that he "was afraid to sleep in the same place twice"—and didn't.[155] Senator claimed he had no particular reason for this fear and that it was just "a natural instinct in a situation such as this";[156] his interrogator replied, "I am saying it is not natural."[157]

Attorney Jim Martin told the FBI that Senator was practically "overwhelmed with fear,"[158] and this fear was "one of the primary reasons he left the Dallas area."[159] Martin was one of those present, along with Senator, attorney Tom Howard, and newsmen Bill Hunter and Jim Koethe, at a meeting in Ruby's apartment on the night of November 24.[160] Perhaps Senator had cause, however, to be so afraid of some person or group as to refuse to specify even whom he feared.[161] For within 16 months after the meeting in Ruby's apartment, as related in chapter 3, Howard died of a reported heart attack, and Hunter and Koethe were brutally murdered.

Larry Crafard. Carousel employee Larry Crafard left Dallas around noon on Saturday, November 23, without telling anyone, and hitchhiked to Michigan with $7 in his pocket.[162] He was located by the FBI several days later in a remote part of that state.[163]

/8/ Saturday Afternoon Calls From Nichols Garage

The following three incidents and circumstances concern the matter of premeditation, so pivotal to this case. For if Ruby shot Oswald on the spur of the moment, just after wiring $25 to Karen Carlin and more than an hour after the scheduled transfer time, it could only have been a solitary action expedited by freak coincidence. But if the shooting had been planned in advance, Ruby's movements were then timed "perfectly, by seconds"—as he testified[164]—to place him where the transfer car should have been when Oswald appeared.[165] In this case, the Carlin telegram, the shooting and the fabrication of Ruby's alibi could only have been the workings of a well-coordinated conspiracy.

At about 1:30 p.m. on Saturday, November 23, Ruby placed a phone call from Nichols Garage.[166] Tom Brown, a garage attendant, told the FBI that during this call, he "overheard Ruby inform the other party to the conversation as to the whereabouts of Chief of Police Curry."[167] Around 3 p.m., Ruby made another call from the garage to someone he called "Ken."[168] Garrett Hallmark, general manager of the garage, overheard Ruby discuss the transfer of Oswald.[169] Ruby seemed to be seeking confirmation of its scheduled time, and said in that context: "You know I'll be there."[170]

KLIF announcer Ken Dowe testified that he was the party Ruby called on Saturday afternoon to inquire about Oswald's transfer,[171] and that Ruby merely offered to cover the event for the radio station.[172] But his story is suspect, considering Ruby's questionable involvement with KLIF personnel[173] and conflicts in Dowe's account.[174] In particular, Dowe told the FBI that when Ruby identified himself on the telephone Saturday afternoon, the name Jack Ruby "meant nothing to him."[175] But Dowe subsequently testified that he had been introduced to Ruby at KLIF before the assassination, and had learned that Ruby ran a night club and procured women for record promoters.[176] Indeed, Ruby indicated familiarity with the person to whom he spoke by his statement, "You know I'll be there"—referring to the Oswald transfer[177] with apparent specific intent.

/9/ Saturday Evening: "Are you crazy? A gun?"

Ruby further exposed his plans for the Oswald transfer during a later telephone conversation which was overheard by Wanda Helmick, a carhop at the Bull-Pen Drive-In Restaurant in Arlington, Texas.[178] The Bull-Pen was operated by Ralph Paul, a financial partner in the Carousel Club.[179]

Helmick testified that on Saturday evening, November 23, she was sitting in the Bull-Pen three to six feet from a pay telephone when it rang at about 8 or 9 p.m.[180] She said that it was answered by another waitress, who handed it to Ralph Paul after calling out, "It is for you. It is Jack."[181] Helmick testified that during the course of the conversation, Ralph Paul "either said 'are you crazy? a gun?' or something like that, or he said something about a gun."[182] Helmick was sure Paul "did say something about a gun, and he asked him if he was crazy."[183] She reported that after the Oswald shooting, "these people that I worked for, they was trying to keep everything so much of a secret ... they was trying to keep Ralph Paul hid, sort of."[184]

It is difficult to interpret Paul's remarks to Ruby as anything but a response to Ruby's decision to murder Oswald with a gun—the plan he carried out the next day. But this demonstrates premeditation, thus destroying the foundation of Ruby's alibi for killing Oswald.

/10/ **Ruby's Gun**

When Ruby ostensibly felt a sudden urge to kill Oswald, just as Oswald reached the police basement ramp,[185] he conveniently had a loaded gun in his trouser pocket.[186] When first questioned by the FBI on Monday, November 25, Ruby "declined to say why he brought his revolver with him when he came downtown."[187] A month later, however, Ruby explained to the FBI that "he had his revolver in his right front trouser pocket" the entire assassination weekend, "because he had a lot of money on his person and always carried his gun when he carried money."[188] During his June hearing before the Warren Commission, Ruby was again asked if he carried a gun prior to the Oswald killing, specifically during the Friday midnight press conference. This time Ruby testified, "I lied about it. It isn't so. I didn't have a gun."[189] Ruby now explained that during the assassination weekend, he kept his gun in its customary place, in a money bag.[190] Five of his associates testified, in fact, that Ruby rarely kept the gun anywhere but in such a bag.[191]

Therefore, when Ruby carried his gun without a bank bag into the police basement that fateful Sunday morning, it was but a final step in a well-conceived plan—a murder plan he had discussed with Ralph Paul the preceding night. Some of the details were illuminated in the final hours before he carried it out.

> If there was a conspiracy, then this little girl that called
> me on the phone in Fort Worth then is a part of the
> conspiracy.[1]
>
> Jack Ruby, referring to Carousel stripper Karen Carlin,
> from the transcript of his July 18, 1964 polygraph
> examination at the Dallas County Jail

> Mrs. Carlin was highly agitated and was reluctant to make
> any statement to me. She stated to me that she was under
> the impression that Lee Harvey Oswald, Jack Ruby and
> other individuals unknown to her, were involved in a plot to
> assassinate President Kennedy and that she would be killed
> if she gave any information to the authorities.[2]
>
> Secret Service agent Roger C. Warner, in a report of a
> November 24, 1963 interview with Karen Carlin

□ 13 □

Premeditation and Conspiracy

The telegram of $25 from Ruby to Karen Carlin at 11:17 Sunday morning
is the key to the shooting in the police headquarters four minutes later. If
the telegram were legitimate, as noted earlier, the killing could only have
been impetuous; if the telegram were staged, only a carefully coordinated
conspiracy.

The critical clues to this telegram, in turn, are two transactions between
Ruby and Carlin that preceded it. The first was a loan of $5 Ruby reportedly
made to Carlin the night before.[3] The second was a call one hour prior to
the telegram, in which Carlin reportedly requested the additional $25 from
Ruby.[4] Presentations of both incidents relied heavily on Karen and Bruce
Carlin.

/1/ **The Carlins**

Karen Bennett Carlin. Karen Carlin ("Little Lynn") was a Carousel Club stripper during October and November of 1963.[5] Like her co-workers,[6] Carlin reportedly doubled as a prostitute for Ruby.[7] And it appears that the 20-year-old[8] Carlin was at most a pawn—a very reluctant pawn—in a more important underworld activity.

In her first official interview on November 24, 1963, Carlin "was reluctant to make any statement."[9] She explained that she suspected an assassination conspiracy and that she "would be killed if she gave any information to the authorities."[10] As Secret Service agent Roger C. Warner described, she "twisted in her chair, stammered in her speech, and seemed on the point of hysteria."[11] She would give information only "through the aid of her husband,"[12] and then asked "that all information she had related be kept confidential to prevent retaliation against her in case there was a plot afoot."[13]

Carlin's fears persisted, as indicated by her arrest for carrying a gun at Ruby's bond hearing.[14] And when questioned by Warren Commission counsel, she related a further incident of interest:

> **Q**: Do you recall that during the course of the Ruby trial when you were waiting to testify that there was a jail break there and some people got out of the jail, and I think they passed right near by you, I believe?
> **Mrs. Carlin**: Yes.
> **Q**: Do you remember what you screamed or said?
> **Mrs. Carlin**: "Oh, my God, they're after me."
> **Q**: Yes—what made you believe that "they" were after you?
> **Mrs. Carlin**: Because I was scared I was going to get killed before I ever got to court.[15]

According to a recent source on the assassination, shortly after the trial, Karen Carlin "was found shot to death in her Houston hotel."[16]

Bruce Carlin. Karen's common-law husband,[17] Bruce, age 23,[18] was described by Ruby as a "pimp" whom Karen "was supposed to be married to."[19] This characterization was supported by a reliable[20] Dallas Police informant, who observed several suspected prostitutes and pimps going in and out of the Carlins' Fort Worth residence.[21] And Nancy Powell, a stripper at the Carousel Club, testified that Bruce didn't work, "and Lynn was pregnant, and he beat her up all the time."[22]

The testimony of Tom Palmer, Dallas branch manager of the American Guild of Variety Artists, further illuminated Bruce Carlin's character:

Q: What was Little Lynn's boyfriend or husband or whatever he is attempting to do for her?

[testimony apparently deleted]

Mr. Palmer: I had that feeling. I had no proof of that.

Q: Anything else that you think he was attempting to do?

Mr. Palmer: Not that I am aware of, no. I thought that was what it was, plus having her in a club where he could call as her manager and probably circulate and pander for her.[23]

The only clue to Palmer's missing response to the first question was the preceding topic of discussion: diet pills and narcotics.[24] Also suggestive of criminal involvement was Carlin's habit of calling assorted public pay phones, including one at "Cy's Wee Wash It" in Hialeah, Florida.[25]

Most suspicious, however, was Carlin's assassination alibi. He testified that on November 20 or 21 he and his partner Jerry Bunker embarked on a sales trip for the "Motel Drug Service" to supply various motels with drugs and sundries.[26] The firm had no office or telephone number.[27] Carlin testified that they left Dallas together in a station wagon,[28] spent November 21 in Houston,[29] and were in a motel in New Orleans when they heard about the assassination.[30] Yet under extensive questioning, Carlin could provide no further details concerning this trip,[31] nor could he recall his activities on November 23.[32] Carlin could not even remember that President Kennedy had visited Houston on November 21,[33] although he claimed that he was there that same day and had picked up some Houston newspapers.[34]

Carlin was sure, however, that he made the 250-mile trip from Dallas to Houston by car with Jerry Bunker on the 20th or 21st of November.[35] But telephone records prove this quite impossible. For on November 20 at 9:42 p.m., Bunker, in Houston, placed a person-to-person call to Bruce Carlin at the Carousel Club in Dallas.[36] And four hours later, another call was placed from Houston to the Carousel Club—this time *from* Carlin.[37] Thus, if the telephone records are correct, Carlin could not have driven to Houston with Bunker.

Another conflict concerning Bruce's whereabouts around the time of the assassination was introduced by the testimony of his wife:

Q: Do you remember whether he had been on a trip that weekend?

Mrs. Carlin: No, I don't even remember that.

Q: Was he in town when the President was killed, do you remember that?

Mrs. Carlin: Yes—well, I don't know. I don't know whether he was or not, I believe he was, though.[38]

Karen's inability to account for Bruce's assassination whereabouts is particularly suspicious in light of a point noted in 1978 by former Texas Governor John Connally:

> Ask any adult person, over the age of 30, in this country, or over the age of 35 we will say, where they were when they first heard the news of the assassination. They can tell you where they were, what they were doing, and who they were with. I have not asked one human being in the world, not anywhere in the world, that hasn't been able to tell me. . . .[39]

Thus Bruce Carlin, a pimp, and Karen Carlin, a terrified Carousel Club stripper, do not appear to be especially credible witnesses. Their accounts of the evening before Ruby shot Oswald confirm this impression.

/2/ A Saturday Night Loan of $5 to Karen Carlin

The story of a loan of $5 from Ruby to Karen Carlin on Saturday night, November 23, established a reasonable precedent for the $25 telegram on Sunday. Perhaps for this reason, it was recited by so many people: Carousel stripper Nancy Powell, Nichols Garage attendant Huey Reeves, Ruby's sister Eva Grant, plus the Carlins and Ruby.[40] Yet the presentations of this group suffered from conspicuously flawed direction. For not one facet of the purported incident was described consistently—not the date, the participants, the reason for the loan, or the payment. Indeed, only through a few common elements is it possible to determine that any two witnesses were attempting to narrate the same events.

The basic story. On Saturday evening, November 23, 1963, Karen Carlin testified, she, Bruce and Carousel Club stripper Nancy Powell took Powell's car from Fort Worth to Dallas.[41] They arrived at Nichols Garage, next door to the Carousel Club, at about 8:30 p.m., and Karen walked up to the club to perform in the evening's show.[42] Finding it closed, however, they decided to go home.[43] But first they called Ruby to request a small loan, since all three were broke,[44] and Ruby asked to speak to garage attendant Huey Reeves.[45] The outcome was that Ruby told Reeves to give $5 to Karen and keep a receipt: Reeves did so.[46]

Below are some of the most flagrant of a virtually continuous succession of contradictions in the accounts of the various witnesses.

The reason for the trip. Telephone records show a call from the Carousel Club to the Carlin residence at 1:45 p.m. Friday, November 22.[47] According to Carousel handyman Andrew Armstrong and Karen Carlin, the call was from Armstrong to Karen to notify her that the club would be closing.[48]

Armstrong told her that the club would not open Friday night, Karen testified, but "would open the next night."[49] And so, believing the club would open Saturday night, the three made the futile trip.[50]

In January 1964, however, Armstrong told the FBI that on Friday afternoon he had notified Karen and other Carousel employees that "the club would be closed Friday night, Saturday night and Sunday night."[51] Armstrong knew the club would be closed Saturday when he called Karen, he reported.[52] Carousel employee Larry Crafard, who was at the club Friday afternoon,[53] also testified that Armstrong had learned of the Saturday closing before he called any employees.[54]

In testimony before Commission counsel in April 1964, Armstrong tried to be more accommodating to Karen's alibi.[55] This time he testified that he never called Karen on Friday afternoon,[56] as he reiterated in the following exchange:

> **Q**: But you are positive that you did not reach Karen—Little Lynn—Bennett to call her?
> **Mr. Armstrong**: Sure I didn't.[57]

A page later in the transcript of his testimony, however, Armstrong asked to "straighten a little something out here," and presented yet a third version of events.[58] But his multiple revisions only underscore the absence of any credible reason for the Saturday night trip to the Carousel Club.

Means of transportation to Dallas. Karen Carlin had some difficulty relating how she got from Fort Worth to Dallas that Saturday night:

> **Q**: How did you come?
> **Mrs. Carlin**: Bus.
> **Q**: Did you come alone?
> **Mrs. Carlin**: No, I didn't. I didn't come by bus. I came with Tammi True [Nancy Powell], another stripper.[59]

Karen then specified that she, Bruce and Nancy drove to Dallas and back to Fort Worth in Nancy's car,[60] as the other two also reported.[61] But when interviewed by the FBI on November 26, Karen had mentioned no companions on her Saturday night trip to Dallas,[62] and had asserted that she "called Ruby as she did not have enough money for transportation back to her home in Fort Worth."[63] This precluded a ride back with Nancy, since Nancy mentioned no problem with gas or other expenses for the short trip back to Fort Worth.[64] Thus, Karen's account of November 26 implied that she traveled by public transportation, as she initially specified in the testimony quoted above.

The payment. Karen, Bruce, and garage attendant Huey Reeves testified that Karen received $5 from Reeves that night.[65] And in June 1964, Reeves was shown a receipt for $5 from Ruby to Karen, time-stamped "1963 Nov 23 PM 10 33."[66] Reeves then stated that he believed he stamped the receipt, but was unsure when he did so.[67] But in December 1963, Reeves had told the FBI that he had given Karen $5 and issued a receipt at about 7:30 p.m.[68] And in March 1964, when asked whether he time-stamped the receipt to Karen, Reeves replied, "I don't believe I did—I don't think so."[69] Also curious was Reeves' initial response when asked whether Karen was accompanied by anyone when she came to the garage that night:

> I don't remember whether her husband was with her or not. Let's see, I didn't think about having to go through this. . . .[70]

But the witness who fumbled the story most seriously was Nancy Powell. Nancy testified that she was with Karen at Nichols Garage when Karen called Ruby.[71] And both Nancy and Bruce testified that they were with Karen essentially the whole time during the Saturday night trip to Dallas.[72] Yet when asked by the Warren Commission about the purported payment to Karen, Nancy adamantly denied that Karen received any money:

> **Q:** Did she get any money there in the parking lot?
> **Mrs. Powell:** No.
> **Q:** Were you at the parking lot?
> **Mrs. Powell:** Yes. . . .
> **Q:** You don't remember getting any money on Saturday night?
> **Mrs. Powell:** Her getting any money?
> **Q:** Yes.
> **Mrs. Powell:** I don't know where she would get it from, because she was with me, and we didn't go any place to get any money.[73]

Nancy testified instead that she believed Karen had asked for $25 in her conversation with Ruby,[74] and that Ruby could not comply that night, but promised to send the money the next day.[75] Thus it appears that Nancy Powell confused the script for the Saturday night $5 loan with that of the Sunday morning $25 telegram.

The date of the incident. Ruby told the FBI that "on Friday night, November 22, 1963, he had to give her [Karen] $5.00 so she could get home."[76] Yet Karen testified that she stayed in Fort Worth all evening on Friday, November 22,[77] so Ruby evidently cited the wrong date for the same Saturday night incident. Although a lapse in memory could account for one such error, it is harder to overlook that same mistake by three others;

Andrew Armstrong,[78] Eva Grant,[79] and Nancy Powell[80] were all similarly confused about whether Friday or Saturday night was the date of the $5 loan to Karen Carlin.

Particularly dubious was Nancy Powell's insistence that the incident occurred the same night that Ruby went to synagogue,[81] which according to Ruby was Friday night.[82] She explained, "Maybe somebody told me, but I know he went to the synagogue that day [of Karen's trip]. ... I am saying this is a fact, you understand?"[83] Perhaps Nancy's eagerness to support Ruby's alibi was inspired by her boy friend,[84] Ralph Paul, Ruby's night club partner[85]—the one overheard that night telling Ruby, "Are you crazy? a gun?"[86]

The person who received the loan. Ruby's sister Eva Grant was one of the witnesses who confused the date of the loan at Nichols Garage.[87] Yet it is clear that she could have referred only to the Saturday night loan of $5 to Karen Carlin. For that $5, Huey Reeves testified, was the only money he had ever lent on Ruby's behalf to any of Ruby's employees.[88] Reeves worked the 7 p.m. to 7 a.m. shift at Nichols' garage from November 22 through November 24, as he had for more than a year before the assassination.[89]

Mrs. Grant also muddled a more critical point in her version of the story, which she eagerly volunteered during her testimony:

> **Q**: Well, Mrs. Grant, just let—
> **Mrs. Grant**: And [Vegas Club pianist] Leonard Wood wanted some money, and I think it was Friday night.
> **Q**: I don't want the details.
> **Mrs. Grant**: Wait a minute, this is very important.
> **Q**: All right.
> **Mrs. Grant**: He wanted some money, so I think, it seems to me, I said—Jack was in the house—"You will tell the guys at the garage next door to the Carousel Club, you give him your name, and he will put $10 in an envelope." Now, Jack made this call from the house. ...[90]

Mrs. Grant later stated that the conversation may have occurred on Saturday, November 23,[91] rather than on Friday. Yet she insisted that it was Leonard Wood, pianist at the Vegas Club which she managed,[92] who telephoned her and requested a loan.[93] And she testified that Ruby then telephoned the garage and gave instructions to leave money for Leonard Wood.[94]

With the testimony of Eva Grant, the variety in renditions of the $5 loan from Ruby to Carlin reaches ludicrous proportions. The lack of even a core of consistency in the accounts demonstrates that the entire incident was manufactured, apparently to support Ruby's Sunday morning alibi—which proves equally spurious.

/3/ A Sunday Morning Call from Karen Carlin

Telephone company records show a call at 10:19 a.m., Sunday, November 24, 1963, from the Fort Worth residence of the Carlins to the Dallas residence of Jack Ruby.[95] Ruby and the Carlins testified that in this call, Karen asked Ruby for money for rent and groceries.[96] This would have accounted for Ruby's $25 wire to Karen Carlin at 11:17 a.m., four minutes before the Oswald shooting—if the witnesses had not all been lying, once again, about the call.

The accounts of Jack Ruby and George Senator. Ruby told the FBI and the Warren Commission that on Sunday morning, soon after the call from Karen Carlin, he left his apartment and drove to the downtown Western Union office.[97] He mentioned no activities that morning before the trip downtown.[98] In April 1964, Ruby's roommate, George Senator, also testified that Ruby was home Sunday morning until he left for downtown, about half an hour after receiving a call from Karen Carlin.[99]

Yet Senator had presented a different story when questioned on November 24, 1963, just hours after the events in question, as paraphrased by the FBI:

> Ruby and Senator arose on November 24 and Senator noticed Ruby had brought one of four dogs which he ordinarily keeps at the Carousel Club home with him. At about 10:30 A.M. Ruby left the apartment with the statement he was going to "take the dog to the club." Senator denies any knowledge of subsequent activities of Ruby until he heard of his having shot Oswald. *The only thing*, therefore, Senator knew Ruby was going to do when he left the apartment was take the dog back down to the club.[100]

In testimony before Commission counsel, Senator claimed that the Carlin call, like the Saturday morning photography excursion,[101] had just slipped his mind.[102] Both explanations were received by counsel with justified skepticism.[103]

In fact, neither of Senator's conflicting accounts was truthful. For Ruby spent Sunday morning not in his apartment, but in the vicinity of the Dallas Police building; he could not possibly have received the call from Karen Carlin. This was established through the testimony of three television crewmen who were stationed in front of police headquarters that morning, preparing to cover the Oswald transfer.

The testimony of three WBAP-TV crewmen. WBAP crewman Ira Walker testified that shortly after 10:30 a.m., a man came up to Walker's TV truck and asked, "Has he [Oswald] been brought down?"[104] Soon after Oswald was killed, a mug shot of Ruby was telecast on a monitor in the truck.[105] At that time, Walker testified, he recognized the man as Ruby:

> Well, about four of us pointed at him at the same time in the truck, I mean, we all recognized him at the same time.[106]

Walker testified that because of the close conjunction in time between talking with the man and seeing Ruby's mug shot, he was positive that the man was Ruby.[107] And Walker reaffirmed this positive identification in testimony at Ruby's trial.[108]

Warren Richey reported that while on top of the TV truck with his camera, he took note of a man in front of the police building at approximately 8 a.m. and again about 10 a.m.[109] Richey testified that he was "positive, pretty sure in [his] own mind" that this man was Jack Ruby.[110] He explained that he recognized Ruby from videotapes and news photos without knowing of the on-the-spot identification made by the men inside the truck.[111]

John Smith, stationed inside the TV truck, testified that he saw a man twice between about 8 and 10 a.m. Sunday.[112] The second time, the man came up to the window of the truck, within three feet of him, and inquired about the transfer of Oswald.[113] When the mug shot of Ruby was telecast, Smith immediately associated the face with the man he had seen; "I was convinced to myself that that was the same man."[114] Smith testified that he would positively identify the man as Ruby except for "this thing of the hat. . . . I couldn't see his hairline and I couldn't see the complete face."[115] When asked if "with that reservation," he "would have no doubt it is the same person," Smith responded affirmatively.[116] In prior FBI interviews of December 4, 1963, both Richey and Smith had identified the man as Ruby with no reported qualification.[117]

The testimony of Walker, Richey and Smith was corroborated by Donald C. Roberts, then West Coast editor of NBC's Huntley-Brinkley report, who was monitoring NBC transmissions from Dallas affiliate WBAP-TV that morning.[118] Roberts told the FBI that three WBAP-TV technicians

> instantly recognized Ruby on TV transmission immediately after Oswald was shot and so advised Roberts by telephone before Ruby's name was announced over the air. Technicians told Roberts that Ruby had been present at the WBAP mobile remote unit at Dallas City Hall [in the same building as police headquarters], about two hours before Oswald was shot. . . .[119]

Treatment in the Warren Report. In its typically lame fashion, the Warren Commission attempted to dismiss the three crewmen's observations. First, it noted that none saw Ruby "for an extended period" or "on a previous occasion,"[120] rather stringent criteria which it never applied to purported identifications of Oswald.[121] Second, it claimed that "Richey described Ruby as wearing a grayish overcoat," but "Ruby did not own an overcoat."[122] In fact, witnesses described Ruby carrying[123] and wearing[124] an overcoat during the assassination weekend. And an overcoat was indeed appropriate for the 32-degree temperature at 8 a.m. Sunday.[125]

Third, the Commission related that Smith had described Ruby as "unkempt," but Ruby was characteristically well-groomed,[126] and "Senator testified that Ruby shaved and dressed before leaving their apartment that morning."[127] It failed to recall, however, that Ruby had scurried around Dallas the preceding two days with virtually no sleep,[128] and that it had itself found Senator an unreliable witness.[129] Finally, the Commission mentioned a man near the TV van "who might have been mistaken for Ruby."[130] But the photo on which this assertion is based shows a man of little resemblance to Ruby.[131]

The collapse of Ruby's alibi. The observations of Ruby by WBAP-TV crewmen Walker, Richey, and Smith demonstrate that Ruby was at the police building awaiting Oswald's transfer—not at his apartment talking to Karen Carlin—in the hours before the shooting. This was corroborated by the reports of two additional witnesses.

Ray Rushing was a preacher from Plano, Texas, who attempted to visit Oswald at police headquarters on the morning of November 24.[132] In an interview with Dallas Police Lt. Jack Revill, Rushing reported that he saw Ruby and had a short conversation with him during a ride in a police elevator at about 9:30 a.m.[133] Lt. Revill evaluated Rushing as "truthful" and treated his information as fact.[134] Revill noted, however, that the district attorney "didn't need [Rushing's] testimony, because he had placed Ruby there the morning of the shooting."[135] This placement was apparently credible to the jury that found Ruby guilty of premeditated murder.[136]

The second corroborating witness was Mrs. Elnora Pitts, who testified that she had done housecleaning for Ruby every Sunday for several weeks before the assassination.[137] Pitts explained that she would call each Sunday morning to make sure Ruby wanted her to come that day.[138] On November 24, however, when she called Ruby's home sometime after 8 a.m., a male voice answered the phone and their conversation proceeded as follows (arranged into responsive form, for clarity, from the transcript of her testimony):

> **Voice**: What do you want?
> **Mrs. Pitts**: What do I want? This is Elnora.

Voice: Yes, well, what—you need some money?
Mrs. Pitts: No, I was coming to clean today.
Voice: Coming to clean?
Mrs. Pitts: This is Elnora.
Voice: Well, what do you want? . . .
Mrs. Pitts: Do you want me to come today?
Voice: Well, yes, you can come, but you call me.
Mrs. Pitts: That's what I'm doing now. . . .[139]

Mrs. Pitts testified, "He sounded so strange to me," and she asked "Who am I talking to? Is this Mr. Jack Ruby?" The party responded "Yes. Why?"[140] She said that she was scared by "the way he talked. He didn't talk like—he never did sound like hisself."[141] Indeed, the man did not sound like Ruby, did not recognize Mrs. Pitts, and had no knowledge of their weekly cleaning arrangement, because Ruby was outside the Dallas Police building when she called.

/4/ A Meticulously Coordinated Conspiracy

Thus the 11:17 a.m. Sunday telegram to Karen Carlin was just an act, staged to support Ruby's performance as the demented avenger—the crowning element of a totally fraudulent assassination-weekend alibi. The production was elaborate, requiring coordination and coercion to elicit the somewhat synchronized recitations of the cast. Yet most critical was the cue for Ruby to stroll to the Western Union office, and to arrive in the police basement just as Oswald reached the ramp. Possible clues to how it was transmitted so quickly from police headquarters to Ruby are provided by three incidents which occurred just before the shooting.

Shortly before 11:21 a.m., Ruby's attorney Tom Howard entered the Dallas Police building, Detective H. L. McGee reported later that day.[142] McGee related that Howard

came in through the Harwood Street entrance and walked up to the jail office window. At this time, Oswald was brought off the jail elevator and Tom Howard turned away from the window and went back toward the Harwood Street door. He waved at me as he went by and said, "That's all I wanted to see." Shortly after that I heard a shot.[143]

When questioned by the FBI on December 11, Howard confirmed almost every detail of the movements described by McGee.[144] But Howard claimed his remark to the detective had been the innocent question, "Are they fixing to take him out of here?"[145] And Howard reported that he "said nothing to anyone except the detective" about Oswald's movements before the shooting.[146]

Just as Oswald became visible to the spectators in the police basement, a car horn let out a blast, as heard on both television and radio sound-tracks.[147] A further event which occurred just then was noted by Tom Pettit, an NBC News correspondent who was broadcasting live from the police basement.[148] Pettit told the FBI that "almost simultaneously with the shoot-ing, a blue car, which had been parked on the ramp immediately behind the armored car, backed rapidly down the ramp and came to a stop with a screeching of brakes at the bottom of the ramp."[149] This was one of the cir-cumstances that caused Pettit to conjecture that "a conspiracy existed to kill Oswald."[150]

Pettit was also disturbed by the seemingly purposeless loitering of Cap-tain Will Fritz, chief of the Police Homicide Detail, who was at the scene of the Oswald shooting, but not in uniform.[151] Similar misgivings about Fritz were reported by Travis Kirk, an established Dallas attorney who was well-acquainted with local law enforcement officials.[152] Kirk told the FBI he sus-pected that "Fritz had deliberately arranged to have Oswald shot in order to close the case."[153] Kirk "based this on the fact that Fritz and Jack Ruby were very close friends, and that Jack Ruby, in spite of his reputation of being a 'hood,' was allowed a complete run of the Police station and partic-ularly the Homicide and Inspectors Bureau."[154] In fact, as noted previously, two reporters saw Ruby near Fritz's office on the evening of the assassina-tion, and one saw Ruby try to go in.[155]

Kirk also furnished background on Tom Howard, the lawyer who popped in to observe Oswald's transfer with such uncanny timing. Kirk told the FBI, as the interviewing agent paraphrased, that

> at one time Howard had several prostitutes working for him and, as far as he, Kirk, was concerned, Howard is still a hoodlum himself. He stated Howard had been prosecuted in Federal Court for the Mann Act several years ago, but that the matter had been hushed up and attempted action against him by the Texas Bar association had been dismissed.[156]

Another potential police-underworld liaison for Oswald's murder was Dallas County Sheriff Bill Decker. Decker played an important role in the assassination case, riding ahead of the presidential limousine,[157] helping to plan Oswald's transfer,[158] then supervising the custody of Jack Ruby.[159] At the same time, Decker was well-connected in the underworld, having been characterized in the Dallas bribe tapes as an "old-time bootlegger" and an underworld "payoff man,"[160] and maintaining friendships with two notori-ous local hoodlums.[161] Equally suspicious was another of Ruby's friends on the force, Harry Olsen, who met with Ruby in Nichols Garage during the early morning of November 23.[162] Olsen's alibi for the entire assassination weekend was questionable.[163]

In any event, it was clear that "someone in the police department," as Ruby intimated in his testimony, was "guilty of giving the information as to when Lee Harvey Oswald was coming down."[164] Also assisting the plot was Karen Carlin, so instrumental in establishing Ruby's alibi, whom Ruby again described with his thin hypothetical facade as "part of the conspiracy."[165] Another who lent a hand was the man in Ruby's apartment who impersonated him in the telephone conversation with Elnora Pitts. And the conspirators included whoever secured the perjured testimony of the terrified Karen Carlin, murdered soon after; of the equally terrified George Senator; of the frightened Kathy Kay, who left Dallas with Harry Olsen after his auto accident; and of the fleeing Larry Crafard, who hitchhiked to Michigan on November 23 with $7 in his pocket.

Finally, of course, the star of Oswald's murder contract was the long-time Dallas Mobster and police fixer, Jack Ruby. His performance was masterful; the shot was fired with deadly accuracy and right on cue. But when the Warren Commission came to Dallas the following June, Ruby proved much too outspoken for his part.

I would like to request that I go to Washington. . . .[1]

I want to tell the truth, and I can't tell it here.[2]

Gentlemen, my life is in danger here.[3]

Jack Ruby, from the official transcript of his June 7, 1964 hearing before the Warren Commission

Representative Ford: Is there anything more you can tell us if you went back to Washington?

Mr. Ruby: Yes; are you sincere in wanting to take me back?[4]

From the same transcript

□ 14 □

The Startling Testimony of Jack Ruby

On November 25, 1963, the day after he shot Oswald, Jack Ruby's prospects did not seem particularly bleak. For Ruby had every reason to expect that through his Mob connections, some way could be found to evade a serious sentence—just as he had escaped all but a $10 fine on his previous nine arrests,[5] as his friend Paul Roland Jones had been pardoned for killing a state witness in Kansas,[6] as his friends Patrick and Yaras had gone free for the murder of James Ragen.[7] Moreover, Ruby's portrayal of an enraged patriotic avenger had been accepted readily, even sympathetically.[8] A reduced sentence was thus a distinct possibility, even without the usual Mob tactics: bribery, jury tampering, intimidation and murder of witnesses.[9]

It was thus understandable that in his first FBI interview of November 25, 1963, Ruby recited the chronicle of an aggrieved loner who desired only to spare the Kennedy family the anguish of a trial.[10] He briefly described his activities during the assassination weekend, but refused to tell the FBI why he was carrying a gun when he shot Oswald.[11] He also refused to say how he got into Dallas Police headquarters that morning,[12] or to detail his activities and contacts.[13] Ruby filled in these specifics on December 21, when the FBI interviewed him again.[14]

But Oswald's murder was an exceptional case; a fix yielding Ruby a light sentence would have aroused too much public suspicion. And on March 14, 1964, Ruby was convicted of first-degree murder and sentenced to death.[15] Within a month, through letters from his sister Eileen Kaminsky and his lawyers, he petitioned the Warren Commission for a hearing.[16] His request was finally granted, and on June 7, 1964, he testified in Dallas before Commission chairman Earl Warren, member Gerald Ford, Texas special counsel Leon Jaworski, and other officials.[17]

The transcript of Ruby's testimony is startling both as history and as drama. During part of the hearing, Ruby recounted the same pat alibi that he had recited to the FBI.[18] Yet Ruby repeatedly interrupted his narrative with statements of a completely different character. The significance of both these statements and the official response to them is particularly clear in light of the background presented in the preceding chapters. For as shown, Ruby's pat alibi was a complete sham, and the accumulated evidence blared this to the Commission by the time Ruby's testimony was taken. Let us now go back to this June 1964 hearing in the Dallas County Jail, as recorded by the government stenographer, for a first-hand sampling of this amazing testimony.

/1/ Indications of a Canned Alibi

After some preliminary dialogue, Chairman Warren instructs Ruby, "tell us your story";[19] Ruby complies.[20] But it soon becomes quite clear that this "story" is not Ruby's alone. At one point, after denying his Friday afternoon visit to Parkland Hospital, Ruby interjects, "Does this conflict with my story and yours in great length?"[21] Secret Service agent Elmer Moore replies, "Substantially the same, Jack, as well as I remember."[22] At another point, while describing his activities after the assassination, Ruby remarks, "I may have left out a few things. Mr. Moore remembers probably more...."[23]

One remark by Ruby's attorney, Joe Tonahill, indicates just how carefully Ruby's alibi has been rehearsed. When Ruby digresses from this alibi at one point during the hearing, Tonahill instructs him, "You go on and keep telling it to *Caroline* and *the truth*."[24] Sure enough, later in his narrative, Ruby describes "a most heartbreaking letter" to "*Caroline*" Kennedy.[25] Fifteen transcripted lines later he interjects, "I am going to tell *the truth* word for word."[26]

/2/ "I would like to request that I go to Washington"

Ruby first departs from his prepared narrative after an interruption caused by the entrance of a Commission staff member:[27]

> **Mr. Ruby**: Is there any way to get me to Washington?
> **Chief Justice Warren**: I beg your pardon?
> **Mr. Ruby**: Is there any way of you getting me to Washington?
> **Chief Justice Warren**: I don't know of any. I will be glad to talk to your counsel about what the situation is, Mr. Ruby, when we get an opportunity to talk.
> **Mr. Ruby**: I don't think I will get a fair representation with my counsel, Joe Tonahill, I don't think so. I would like to request that I go to Washington and you take all the tests that I have to take. It is very important.[28]

After more dialogue concerning Ruby's plea, Chief Justice Warren directs Ruby to resume his story.[29] But a page later in the transcript, Ruby interrupts and repeats his request:

> Gentlemen, unless you get me to Washington, you can't get a fair shake out of me.
> If you understand my way of talking, you have to bring me to Washington to get the tests.[30]

Ruby is again directed to continue his narrative, this time by his lawyer, Joe Tonahill.[31]

/3/ "I want to tell the truth, and I can't tell it here"

Later in his hearing, after receiving no response to his requests to be taken to Washington, Ruby once more departs from his prepared alibi. He begins by asking Sheriff Decker and other policemen to leave the room.[32] The conversation continues:

> **Mr. Decker**: You want all of us outside?
> **Mr. Ruby**: Yes.
> **Mr. Decker**: I will leave Tonahill and Moore. I am not going to have Joe leave.
> **Mr. Ruby**: If you are not going to have Joe leave—
> **Mr. Decker**: Moore, his body is responsible to you. His body is responsible to you.
> **Mr. Ruby**: Bill, I am not accomplishing anything if they are

here, and Joe Tonahill is here. You asked me anybody I wanted
out.
    Mr. Decker: Jack, this is your attorney. That is your lawyer.
    Mr. Ruby: He is not my lawyer.
    (Sheriff Decker and law enforcement officers left room.)[33]

Ruby then requests once again to be taken to Washington, this time explicitly stating the reason, thereby indicating that everything he has already
recited is a sham:

    I want to tell the truth, and I can't tell it here. I can't tell it here.
    Does that make sense to you?[34]

    At this point, Ruby questions two of the people in the room. He first asks
Commission staff member Joe Ball, an attorney from Los Angeles, whether
he has any connection with another California lawyer, Melvin Belli.[35] Ruby
has reason to be wary of a connection with Belli, a member of his defense
team.[36] For Belli went out socially many times with notorious California
Mobster[37] Mickey Cohen,[38] and provided favors, including a $3,000 loan, to
the hoodlum.[39] Also, together with attorney Tonahill, Belli handled the narcotics case of pornographic film star Juanita Slusher ("Candy Barr"),[40] a
close friend of both Cohen[41] and Ruby.[42] Moreover, Belli was brought into
Ruby's case by Michael Shore[43]—a Los Angeles record executive[44] who
was a business partner and very close associate of Chicago Mobster Irwin
Weiner.[45]
    Ruby next asks Secret Service agent Elmer Moore, "Where do you stand,
Moore?"[46] Then Ruby remarks, "Boys, I'm in a tough spot, I tell you that."[47]
He soon afterward returns to his original request:

    Mr. Ruby: When are you going back to Washington?
    Chief Justice Warren: I am going back very shortly after we
finish this hearing—I am going to have some lunch.
    Mr. Ruby: Can I make a statement?
    Chief Justice Warren: Yes.
    Mr. Ruby: If you request me to go back to Washington with
you right now, that couldn't be done, could it?
    Chief Justice Warren: No; it could not be done. It could not
be done. There are a good many things involved in that, Mr.
Ruby.
    Mr. Ruby: What are they?[48]

/4/ "My life is in danger here"

Ruby continues with an extended but futile argument to persuade Warren to take him to Washington;[49] Warren's incredible responses will be considered shortly. Although Ruby fails to sway Warren, he does put on the record exactly why he cannot tell the truth in Dallas:

> **Mr. Ruby**: Gentlemen, my life is in danger here. Not with my guilty plea of execution.
> Do I sound sober enough to you as I say this?
> **Chief Justice Warren**: You do. You sound entirely sober.
> **Mr. Ruby**: I tell you, gentlemen, my whole family is in jeopardy. My sisters, as to their lives.[50]

/5/ "Would you rather I just delete what I said and just pretend that nothing is going on?"

When Ruby finally sees there is no hope of going to Washington, he briefly drops all pretense. He plunges in by naming an organization to whom he had no direct allegiance, and from whom he had least to fear.

> **Mr. Ruby**: All right, there is a certain organization here—
> **Chief Justice Warren**: That I can assure you.
> **Mr. Ruby**: There is a certain organization here, Chief Justice Warren, if it takes my life at this moment to say it, and Bill Decker said be a man and say it, there is a John Birch Society right now in activity, and Edwin Walker is one of the top men of this organization—take it for what it is worth, Chief Justice Warren.
> Unfortunately for me, for me giving the people the opportunity to get in power, because of the act I committed, has put a lot of people in jeopardy with their lives.
> Don't register with you, does it?
> **Chief Justice Warren**: No; I don't understand that.
> **Mr. Ruby**: *Would you rather I just delete what I said and just pretend that nothing is going on?*
> **Chief Justice Warren**: I would not indeed. I am only interested in what you want to tell this Commission. That is all I am interested in.
> **Mr. Ruby**: Well, I said my life, I won't be living long now. I know that my family's lives will be gone. When I left my apartment that morning—
> **Chief Justice Warren**: What morning?

> **Mr. Ruby**: Sunday morning.
> **Chief Justice Warren**: Sunday morning.[51]

By his blank response to Ruby's indication of conspiracy and his sudden curiosity about Ruby's resumed alibi, Warren cuts off further meaningful discussion about the assassination. During the remainder of the hearing, however, Ruby slips in some significant disclosures in other digressions. Then, toward the end of the session, Ruby engages in extraneous and at times disjointed discourse, and otherwise attempts to prolong the hearing.[52] For example:

> **Chief Justice Warren** [addressing Commissioner Ford]: Congressman, do you have anything further?
> **Mr. Ruby**: You can get more out of me. Let's not break up too soon.[53]

This behavior is clearly understandable, given Ruby's several explicit statements expressing fear of being killed shortly after the interview.[54] One example is this remark:

> Mr. Bill Decker said be a man and speak up. I am making a statement now that I may not live the next hour when I walk out of this room.[55]

In fact, Ruby does not let the hearing end before securing repeated assurances from Warren that he will be given a lie detector examination, which would allow him further contact with federal officials.[56]

Ruby's explicit fears of death may appear fanciful, but only to someone unfamiliar with the assassination evidence. Recall the case of Rose Cheramie, a criminally involved drug addict, who told doctors in a Louisiana hospital that the "word in the underworld" was that Kennedy would be assassinated.[57] Less than two years later, in September 1965, she was run over by an automobile in Texas.[58] Two days after Ruby shot Oswald, Teamster official Leopoldo Ramos Ducos informed FBI agents of contacts between Ruby and two top Teamster officials.[59] His decision to talk was evidently known, for earlier that day he had received the message, "We killed Kennedy and the next will be Ramos Ducos."[60] Dallas Sheriff Roger Craig, who reported incidents indicating conspiracy, went into hiding after he learned "the Mafia had put a price on his head."[61] Craig "committed suicide" several years later.[62] Nancy Perrin Rich, who reported Ruby's Mafia ties, was tailed in Massachusetts by a man in a black Pontiac who could not explain to police what he was doing 60 miles from his home.[63] She later died violently.[64]

Ruby's intimations of death threats are indeed credible given the aftermath of a November 24, 1963 meeting at his apartment between his roommate, George Senator, two journalists, and two attorneys. Within 16 months, both journalists were brutally murdered,[65] and one attorney died of what was called a heart attack.[66] Senator was terrified for days after the meeting.[67] Others who backed Ruby's alibi exhibited similar fears or unusual behavior—including Kathy Kay, Larry Crafard, and Karen Carlin.[68] Carlin, in the words of an interviewing Secret Service agent, "seemed on the point of hysteria," believing there was "a plot to assassinate President Kennedy" and that she "would be killed if she gave any information to the authorities."[69] She was shot to death several months later.[70] Other cases of murders, assaults, and intimidation of witnesses have been described in Chapter 3.

And Ruby's Dallas jail cell was hardly a sanctuary from Mob retribution. As he knew well from personal dealings, the Mafia can kill a witness in a maximum security cell as easily as a loan shark defaulter in a dilapidated tenement.* Indeed, Ruby could hardly have felt secure in the custody of Sheriff Bill Decker[76]—a reputed underworld payoff man.[77] Nor could Ruby have been reassured by the Mob murder of another witness in Dallas Police custody, of which he knew well: the murder of Lee Harvey Oswald. The message was perhaps reiterated to Ruby by Mafioso Joseph Campisi, an associate of the Marcellos,[78] who visited Ruby in jail on November 30, 1963.[79]

/6/ The Commission's Conduct of Ruby's Hearing

Mafia intimidation and police payoffs were not the only factors, however, that inhibited Ruby from speaking freely at his Dallas hearing. As discussed in a subsequent chapter, Mafia corruption also compromised the federal government's handling of the assassination probe.[80] And it is inescapably clear that one member of the Warren Commission took extraordinary steps to encourage Ruby's silence at the hearing—steps that defy any legitimate explanation.

---

*In 1941, for example, Mob informant Abe Reles plunged to his death from a hotel window while under guard by six New York City policemen.[71] In 1945, Peter LaTempa was poisoned in a maximum security cell in a Brooklyn jail while waiting to testify against Mafia boss Vito Genovese.[72] In 1954, Gaspare Pisciotta, a witness against the Sicilian Mafia, was poisoned in his isolated cell in Palermo with enough strychnine to kill 40 dogs.[73] And during the 1970s, four Mob defectors were murdered and six others died unnatural deaths under a federal alias program which was allegedly compromised by corrupt officials.[74] Almost 20 of the FBI's Mob informants were killed in 1976 and 1977.[75] Fortunately for Ruby, however, killing him would have aroused too much suspicion following his own murder of Oswald.

Reluctance to interview Ruby. Jack Ruby, the most important assassination witness then alive, was not called to testify until June 1964, and then only because of his repeated requests.[81] Three times during the hearing, in fact, Ruby expressed regret that the Commission had not interviewed him earlier.[82] Chairman Warren explained, "I wish we had gotten here a little sooner after your trial was over, but I know you had other things on your mind, and we had other work, and it got to this late date."[83] Later on, Warren added, "Unless you had indicated not only through your lawyers but also through your sister ... that you wanted to testify before the Commission, unless she had told us that, I wouldn't have bothered you."[84]

Lack of questioning on relevant matters. By waiting until June to question Ruby, however, the Commission gained one advantage. For the evidence amassed by then had demonstrated that Ruby's alibi and his actual activities prior to Oswald's murder were extremely suspicious. And sufficient time had elapsed to prepare questions on dozens of critical points. Several important areas of interrogation were listed in just one memorandum of February 24, 1964, by Commission staff members Leon Hubert and Burt Griffin.[85] This memo stated that Ruby "became the subject of a narcotics investigation," and was "peripherally, if not directly connected with members of the underworld" in Dallas.[86] It noted that Ruby "very carefully cultivated friendships with police officers and other public officials," and "became interested ... in the possibility of opening a gambling casino in Havana."[87] The memo also listed groups, persons, and locations to investigate in connection with the assassination.[88] These included the Teamsters Union, the "Las Vegas gambling community," the Dallas Police Department, radio station KLIF, H. L. Hunt, and the City of New Orleans.[89] It was also apparent that Ruby's pre-assassination telephone conversations and visits with Mobsters from across the country,[90] including top lieutenants of Carlos Marcello,[91] merited close scrutiny.

Yet Ruby was grilled by the Commission on none of these matters, and was rarely even questioned about his transparently perjured alibi.[92] The Commission's complete lack of interest was illustrated by one flagrant gap in his ten-page narrative of his assassination-weekend activities, in which he skipped over a 28-hour period with only brief references to watching television and visiting a night club.[93] It was clear that much was omitted; several witnesses described more than a dozen activities of Ruby during this period.[94] But the Commission was forced to report conjectures of what "Ruby apparently did" in that interval,[95] because it had allowed Ruby to skip over this gap without even one question.[96]

Indeed, most of the interventions by Warren, who took almost complete charge of the hearing, were efforts to steer Ruby back to his canned story whenever he digressed.[97] Warren did this when Ruby asked to be taken to

Washington,[98] reported that his life was in danger,[99] stated he could not tell the truth in Dallas,[100] and finally made one attempt to do so.[101] Warren's exclusive interest in Ruby's canned story was illustrated when he responded "I don't understand that" to Ruby's disclosure about the Birch Society.[102] Later on, however, Ruby resumed the recital of his alibi, and stated, "I realize it is a terrible thing I have done, and it was a stupid thing, but I just was carried away emotionally. Do you follow that?"[103] This time Warren replied, "Yes; I do indeed, every word."[104]

"I want you to feel absolutely free to say that the interview is over." When the most important witness in the nation's most important inquiry asked to be taken to Washington to provide information he felt endangered to disclose in Dallas, there was only one conceivable official response. Even if these requests had not been so persistent, Ruby's pat alibi so obviously fraudulent, or his background and pre-assassination contacts so markedly suspicious, Warren had only one legitimate option—to assure Ruby that the government would protect him and enable him to tell the full truth. The following excerpt from Ruby's hearing can therefore be read only with amazement.

> **Mr. Ruby**: ... Chairman Warren, if you felt your life was in danger at the moment, how would you feel? Wouldn't you be reluctant to go on speaking, even though you request me to do so?
>
> **Chief Justice Warren**: I think *I might have some reluctance* if I was in your position, yes; I think I would. I think *I would figure it out very carefully* as to *whether it would endanger me or not.*
>
> If you think anything that I am doing or anything that I am asking you is endangering you in any way, shape, or form, I want you to feel absolutely free to say that the interview is over.[105]

The subsequent dialogue reveals that the silence Warren advised for Ruby was to be permanent, although the opportunity to talk freely which Ruby requested could have been easily arranged.

> **Mr. Ruby**: What happens then? I didn't accomplish anything.
>
> **Chief Justice Warren**: No; nothing has been accomplished.
>
> **Mr. Ruby**: Well, then you won't follow up with anything further?
>
> **Chief Justice Warren**: There wouldn't be anything to follow up if you hadn't completed your statement.
>
> **Mr. Ruby**: You said you have the power to do what you want to do, is that correct?

Chief Justice Warren: Exactly.

Mr. Ruby: Without any limitations?

Chief Justice Warren: Within the purview of the Executive order which established the Commission. We have the right to take testimony of anyone we want in this whole situation, and we have the right, if we so choose to do it, to verify that statement in any way that we wish to do it.

Mr. Ruby: But you don't have the right to take a prisoner back with you when you want to?

Chief Justice Warren: *No; we have the power to subpoena witnesses to Washington* if we want to do it, but we have taken the testimony of 200 or 300 people, I would imagine, here in Dallas without going to Washington.

Mr. Ruby: Yes; but those people aren't Jack Ruby.

Chief Justice Warren: No; they weren't.

Mr. Ruby: They weren't.[106]

Warren later repeated his advice to Ruby: "I want you to feel that you are free to refrain from testifying any time you wish."[107]

Warren's inexplicable* behavior had tragic personal as well as historical consequences. For Jack Ruby had nothing to gain by implicating himself in premeditated murder and conspiracy while his appeals were pending; evidently he had much to fear in doing so. Nevertheless Ruby, a lifelong criminal, briefly rose to a level of nobility by attempting to put the truth on the record. And it must have been a stunning blow to him to discover, as he phrased it toward the end of his hearing, "Maybe certain people don't want to know the truth that may come out of me."[118]

---

*Any hope that Warren's conduct had a reasonable explanation was quashed by J. Lee Rankin, chief counsel of the Warren Commission, in 1978 testimony during the House Assassination hearings. When asked about the Commission's strange denial of Ruby's persistent pleas, Rankin said, "We were all convinced that Ruby was interested in a trip to Washington rather than how much he could enlighten the Commission."[108] If, indeed, the Commission knew as little about Ruby's situation as Rankin claimed, then its investigatory incompetence was almost as appalling as the more sinister possibilities otherwise suggested.

Warren himself discussed the assassination in a May 1972 television interview.[109] His remarks were analyzed by a private researcher using the Psychological Stress Evaluator (PSE), a lie-detecting device that measures stress by voice pattern analysis.[110] Demonstrated reliable in several tests,[111] it is used by hundreds of U.S. law enforcement agencies and accepted as evidence in more than a dozen states.[112]

Warren's remarks in the interview were found to have been generally unstressed,[113] but when the conversation turned to the assassination, a completely different pattern emerged.[114] Warren answered a series of questions by contending the Commission had explored all angles and found no evidence of conspiracy.[115] "The PSE showed hard stress" in each response,[116] revealing at one point "a perfectly trimmed hedge"—the strongest possible indication of deception.[117]

/7/ The Polygraph Examination

Several times in his testimony, Ruby expressed a desire to take a polygraph test.[119] As his hearing drew to a close, and the moment approached when he would be left alone with his Dallas Police custodians, Ruby became even more insistent about this request:

> **Mr. Ruby**: All I want is a lie detector test, and you refuse to give it to me. . . . And they will not give it to me, because I want to tell the truth.
> And then I want to leave this world. . . .
> **Chief Justice Warren**: Mr. Ruby, I promise you that you will be able to take such a test.
> **Mr. Ruby**: When?[120]

Ruby put little stock in Warren's assurance:

> **Mr. Ruby**: . . . these things are going to be promised, but you see they aren't going to let me do these things.
> Because when you leave here, I am finished. My family is finished.
> **Representative Ford**: Isn't it true, Mr. Chief Justice, that the same maximum protection and security Mr. Ruby has been given in the past will be continued?
> **Mr. Ruby**: But now that I have divulged certain information . . .[121]

Ruby's skepticism persisted, and he repeated his request for a polygraph test in his last statement of the hearing[122]—even after both Warren and Ford had promised that he would be given such a test.[123]

Ruby's skepticism was not groundless. On June 11, 1964, FBI Director J. Edgar Hoover sent a letter to the Warren Commission denying its request to have the FBI administer a polygraph test to Ruby.[124] Hoover claimed the test was unreliable[125] (although the FBI had administered such a test to at least one other assassination witness[126]) and that Ruby's appeals were in progress[127] (they were still going on in late 1966[128]). The Warren Commission then sent Hoover a letter repeating its request,[129] and on July 13 Hoover refused again.[130]

Nevertheless, perhaps because of the unequivocal pledge that Ruby secured from it, the Commission scheduled the test for July 16, 1964.[131] A few days beforehand, however, the Commission received word from Ruby's sister and attorneys that they opposed the test.[132] They objected on the grounds that "his mental state was such that the test would be meaningless," and that the test "would affect Ruby's health and would be of questionable value."[133] But finally, on July 18, 1964, the test was administered to Ruby.[134]

There are two reasons why Ruby would have desired such a test. First, it could have provided an avenue out of the clutches of the Dallas Police—although, as it turned out, it was administered in the Dallas County Jail,[135] as was his June 7 hearing.[136] Second, it could have allowed Ruby to appease anyone threatening him by relating his alibi, yet still expose the truth through the polygraph readings. He had to insure only that the right questions were posed to him. Ruby probably did not realize, however, that the polygraph apparatus only measures stress, and that death threats could generate as much stress as considerations of integrity. In any event, as the House Assassinations Committee concluded, the results were impossible to interpret because of "numerous procedural errors made during the test."[137]

/8/ Ruby's Disclosures

Despite Ruby's failure to escape Dallas Police custody and to generate a mechanical record of the truth, he did succeed in putting valuable disclosures on record. In some cases, his statements were made in the guise of attempting to bolster his alibi,[138] as with this remark:

How can we give me the clearance that the ads I put in [announcing the closing of the Carousel and Vegas clubs November 22–24] were authentic, my sincerity, my feeling of emotionalism were sincere; that that Sunday morning I got carried away after reading the article, a letter addressed to Caroline and then this little article that stated Mrs. Kennedy might be requested to come back and face the ordeal of the trial?

Also, *if there was a conspiracy, then this little girl that called me on the phone in Fort Worth then is a part of the conspiracy.*[139]

Yet in other cases, there was no such covering preface,[140] as with this additional statement about Oswald's murder, which also merits repeating:

Who else could have timed it so perfectly by seconds. If it were timed that way, then someone in the police department is guilty of giving the information as to when Lee Harvey Oswald was coming down.[141]

Especially noteworthy are Ruby's repeated requests during his polygraph session to be questioned about the underworld. At one point, Ruby mentioned, "I also had numerous phone calls, long-distance calls, all over the country," and asked to be questioned about organized crime contacts.[142] When Assistant District Attorney William Alexander then proposed the question, "Did any union or underworld connection have anything to do with the shooting of Oswald?" Ruby replied, "Very good."[143] Ruby later repeated, "How about the underworld? . . . There were a lot of phone calls."[144]

After further discussion, Ruby was asked whether he wished to be questioned about any other topic.[145] Ruby replied, "Yes—whether or not I was ever mixed up with the underworld here or involved in any crime?"[146] Asked later whether he wished to be posed further questions, Ruby replied, "Oh, yes, sir. Has the underworld ever contributed money to me for my clubs, or was I put here as a front for the underworld or things to that effect."[147] He then commented that people thought

> maybe I was put here as a front of the underworld and sooner or later they will get something out of me that they want done to their advantage.[148]

Additional disclosures by Ruby are considered later.

/9/ Ruby's Final Statement

Ruby got another brief chance for public contact on March 19, 1965, when he was met by reporters between the Dallas jail and the court.[149] His remarks were telecast that evening on CBS-TV, as reported by Sylvia Meagher,[150] the author of the only comprehensive index to the Warren Commission exhibits.[151] According to Meagher's notes, Ruby pleaded to be removed to federal jurisdiction and made a statement including the words "complete conspiracy . . . and the assassination too . . . if you knew the facts you would be amazed."[152]

Ruby's chance to elaborate appeared imminent when his longstanding request to be extricated from Dallas Police custody was finally granted. On December 7, 1966, a Texas court ruled favorably on his appeal and scheduled a new trial for him in Wichita Falls.[153] But three days later, Ruby was reported ill of lung cancer.[154] He died the following month, on January 3, 1967.[155]

Before his death, Ruby was thus able to indicate conspiracy in the Oswald shooting, and to hint boldly at Mafia involvement. Moreover, as Ruby's background surfaced, it became clear that he had indeed been "mixed up with the underworld,"[156] put in Dallas "as a front of the underworld."[157] But only a series of documents scattered in National Archives files could unravel his "numerous phone calls, long distance calls, all over the country,"[158] and resolve whether he had in fact been "used for a purpose"[159] to accomplish something the Mob wanted "done to their advantage."[160] Only these documents could reveal Jack Ruby's final legacy—the identification of President Kennedy's killers.

PART IV
PILGRIMS AND PIRATES

With leads to the Mob backed up by Jack Ruby himself, a demonstration of its long-suspected[1] assassination role is now within reach. Yet such a demonstration would still leave critical questions unanswered. Were other individuals or groups involved in the plot? Did the Mafia in fact benefit from President Kennedy's murder? Why was the Warren Commission so blind to evidence of multiple assassins and Mafia involvement, so unresponsive to Ruby's attempts to speak freely?

Before following the final stretch of the trail to President Kennedy's killers, this part provides an interlude to consider these questions. The response sweeps through broad ground—from Cuban armaments to Southeast Asian heroin, from the Bobby Baker scandal to Watergate. And it features assorted villains who, despising America's ideals and its democratic system, came to desire President Kennedy's demise. Yet tying together these events and villains, in almost every case, were entanglements with the Mafia. This common connection will underscore the Mafia's central role in Kennedy's murder, whatever the roster of additional assassination conspirators.

The alliances and antipathies to be considered can perhaps be illuminated by brief reflection on their historical roots.* Since Columbus's

*This paragraph and the three following express only a philosophical outlook, and are not directly related to the rest of the text.

voyage in 1492, two classes have settled and shaped the United States: pilgrims and pirates. The pilgrims sought sustenance: they planted, crafted and nurtured. The pirates sought plunder: they extorted, ravaged and murdered. In the nation's westward expansion, this dichotomy was reflected by industrious homesteaders, on the one hand, and by the feverish hordes of the gold rush, whose big winners were not the shrewdest prospectors but the best gunmen. Unfortunately, in some of the richest economic domains, where control of oil wells, watering holes and other natural resources was pivotal, the ruthless prevailed.

The ultimate antecedent of this dichotomy in values was perhaps a clash between nations two millennia ago. One protagonist, whose values strongly influenced the early Pilgrim and Puritan settlers of Massachusetts,[2] was the ancient nation of Israel. It believed in one incorporeal God, in whose image man and woman were created. It aspired to "love thy neighbor as thyself"[3] and to imitate God's holiness: "You shall be holy, for I the Lord your God am holy."[4] And it observed a Sabbath to keep its divine perspective on the community, the land and its fruits.

Israel's antagonist and for six centuries its occupier was the Roman empire, which spurned the noble heritage of the republic it had destroyed. The empire placed its faith in its idols, its edifices, its armies and its deified Caesars.[5] It relegated human beings to fodder for its lusts—in its slave markets, its gladiatorial arenas, its extortionately taxed provinces. And it shared enough of its booty and vice, with its corn dole and free circus extravaganzas, to lull its citizenry into acquiescence.

This clash in values sparked an abortive armed uprising of Judea against Rome, culminating in the year 73 with the Jews' last stand at Masada.[6] During the course of the long rebellion, the empire martyred thousands of Jews, many on the mere suspicion of promoting national independence.[7] Some were burnt alive, others slaughtered in the arena, and masses crucified, until, in the words of Josephus, "there was no room for the crosses, and no crosses for the bodies."[8] Among the Jewish martyrs was a carpenter from Nazareth. Although his manner was gentle, no less treasonous to Caesar was his belief in one God,[9] his nationalism,[10] and his rousing messianic proclamation.[11] Yet in the end, his life and death were made palatable to Caesar's sensibilities. Jesus was worshiped instead of obeyed, his fellow victims portrayed as his killers,[12] the empire absolved and emulated.[13]

America's guiding principles inherited all—the noblest and basest values, often in a bewildering amalgamation. There were those, for example, who coupled the practices of exploitation, manipulation and deception with moral pronouncements, charitable donations, and sponsorship of public television broadcasts in proper British accents. Yet one group retained its ultimate, unadulterated commitment to extortion: the Mafia. Forged by the brutality of assorted conquerors during centuries of foreign subjugation in Sicily,[14] many of its members came to the United States during the turn of the 20th century seeking richer pastures of plunder.[15] They started out as henchmen and merchants of vice; by the end of World War II, they had regrouped into a new American confederation which dominated organized criminal activity.[16] And over the course of three postwar decades, the Mob completed its evolution from servant to master of America's darker side. It no longer cracked skulls for ruthless labor bosses or country club executives—it controlled major unions[17] and elite country clubs.[18] It no longer robbed banks—it bought, sold, and drained them.[19] It no longer bribed just mayors and policemen—it dictated votes to Congressmen and hobnobbed with presidents.[20] The events described in the following chapters illustrate this ominous transformation.

> Others might hate Kennedy. The mob was in a unique
> position to do something about it. Unlike Kennedy's other
> enemies, the Minutemen or the exiles, the Cosa Nostra was
> not a small band of fanatic zealots. It was a cool, well-
> disciplined conspiracy of enormous dimensions.[1]
>
> Robert Sam Anson

□ 15 □
The Cuban Coalition

The Mafia has formed opportune alliances with parties across the political spectrum, ranging from labor bosses to industrial magnates, from
American Communists to Italian Fascists.[2] And in 1959, upon the victory of
Castro's revolutionary forces in Cuba, the Mafia acquired bedfellows of
three persuasions: Cuban exiles, extreme right-wingers, and certain
elements of the CIA. All cooperated in efforts to eliminate the new Cuban
premier; by 1963, frustrated in this and other objectives by the Kennedy
Administration, all joined in antagonism toward President Kennedy as well.
The antipathy which developed between the president and this anti-Castro
alliance was drawn in part across conventional lines of political ideology.
But vituperative rhetoric, murderous methods, and murky entanglements
all exposed it as primarily a Pilgrim-Pirate struggle.

/1/ "Wanted for Treason"

Planned in the Eisenhower Administration under White House Action Officer Richard Nixon,[3] and approved by newly elected President Kennedy,[4]
the Bay of Pigs invasion was touted by the CIA as an operation meriting
American assistance.[5] But from the first hours of the abortive April 1961 incursion into Cuba, it became clear that it could be salvaged only by American military intervention, in particular, by the air support that the CIA had
promised the exiles;[6] President Kennedy refused.[7] The reaction of the CIA
and the exiles was bitter,[8] as reflected by sharp criticism of Kennedy in the
memoirs of E. Howard Hunt, a CIA anti-Castro operative.[9] And the presi-

dent, unhappy with the CIA's handling of the invasion, shook up its top leadership,[10] telling aides he wanted to splinter the CIA "into a thousand pieces and scatter [it] to the winds."[11] The continuing antagonism between President Kennedy and the CIA was exhibited and probably exacerbated just before his death, when he ordered a task force to review American intelligence activities.[12]

In October 1962, the discovery of Soviet missiles in Cuba precipitated a major crisis; President Kennedy averted nuclear war by pledging not to invade Cuba in return for removal of the Russian weapons.[13] The president subsequently ordered the CIA to cut off all support to the Cuban exiles.[14] And in 1963, after several CIA-sponsored raids were carried out despite this order, President Kennedy issued strong warnings against further such anti-Castro activity.[15] The Minutemen, an extreme right-wing group, partially tempered the effect of this ban, however, by providing arms and other assistance to the exiles.[16] In November 1963, President Kennedy further dissociated the United States from violent efforts against Castro by setting up preliminary talks on diplomatic accommodation with Cuba.[17]

Seeking a humane national posture on other fronts, President Kennedy took initiatives viewed radical and treacherous by those who thrived on racial subjugation, international polarization, and the profits derived therefrom. His administration pioneered civil rights measures and sent federal troops to Alabama to enforce court-ordered integration.[18] In August 1963, after the Reverend Martin Luther King gave his famous "I Have a Dream" address to 250,000 Americans in front of the Lincoln Memorial, President Kennedy warmly greeted him at the White House.[19]

On June 10, 1963, President Kennedy shattered hopes for aggressive military action against the Communist bloc in a noteworthy address at American University, concerning "the most important topic on earth—peace."[20] Nikita Khrushchev responded on July 2 with a sharp departure from his own hard-line stance; the two leaders swiftly negotiated a test-ban treaty, signed on August 5.[21] At a reception for the signers, a Soviet band played Gershwin's "Love Walked In."[22] Later that year, a wheat sale agreement was concluded between the two superpowers.[23]

On November 18, 1963, Defense Secretary Robert McNamara told the New York Economic Club, as summarized in *Business Week*, that "a major cut in defense spending [was] in the works,"[24] similar to the cut proposed by Khrushchev in July.[25] McNamara made it plain that "a fundamental strategic shift" was involved, "not just a temporary slash."[26] Such a cut was poorly received by the armaments industry, which was heavily represented in Texas.[27]* And in a January 1963 tax message, President Kennedy af-

---

*The Mafia too had a share in Pentagon dollars. For example, Medico Industries of Pennsylvania received a $3.9 million contract to produce 600,000 warheads for use in Vietnam.[28] The company's general manager, William Medico, was an associ-

fronted the oil industry by calling for a sharp reduction in the oil depletion allowance.[37]

In the spring of 1963, President Kennedy told aide Kenneth O'Donnell of his determination to withdraw American forces from Vietnam after the November election, commenting, "I'll be damned everywhere as a communist appeaser. But I don't care."[38] On October 2, 1963, Defense Secretary McNamara and General Maxwell Taylor reported that it was their objective to terminate the 'major part' of U.S. military involvement in Vietnam by 1965.[39] Specifically, they predicted that 1,000 U.S. troops would be withdrawn from there by the end of 1963.[40] On October 31, in a news conference, President Kennedy reaffirmed his administration's intention to pull out these 1,000 troops.[41] The first 220 of them were withdrawn on December 3, 1963, as directed by President Kennedy's prior order.[42]

Their Pirate sensibilities inflamed, extreme right-wing elements openly expressed their loathing of Kennedy. In April 1963, a flyer was sent to Cubans in Miami, which read:

> Only through one development will you Cuban patriots ever live again in your homeland as freemen ... [only] if an inspired Act of God should place in the White House within weeks a Texan known to be a friend of all Latin Americans ... though he must under present conditions bow to the Zionists who since 1905 came into control of the United States, and for whom Jack Kennedy and Nelson Rockefeller and other members of the Council of Foreign Relations and allied agencies are only stooges and pawns. Though Johnson must now bow to these crafty and cunning Communist-hatching Jews, yet, did an Act of God suddenly elevate him into the top position [he] would revert to what his beloved father and grandfather were, and to their values and principles and loyalties.[43]

The flyer was dated April 18, 1963, and signed "a Texan who resents the Oriental influence that has come to control, to degrade, to pollute and enslave his own people."[44]

---

ate of Russell Bufalino,[29] the northeastern Pennsylvania Mafia boss,[30] who frequently visited the Medico offices.[31] Company President Phillip Medico was described in an FBI wiretap as "a capo" (chief) in Bufalino's Mafia Family.[32] And a third Medico official was apprehended at the 1957 Mafia conclave in Apalachin, New York.[33]

Medico Industries figured prominently in the 1978 scandal surrounding Pennsylvania Congressman Daniel Flood;[34] *Time* magazine dubbed it "the Flood-Medico-Bufalino triangle."[35] According to *Time*, "the FBI discovered more than a decade ago that Flood steered Government business to the Medicos and traveled often on their company jet."[36]

Dallas oil magnate and extreme right-wing propagandist H. L. Hunt reportedly had similar designs for President Kennedy. During a party before the president's visit to Dallas, according to German journalist Joachim Joesten, several witnesses heard Hunt remark that there was "no way left to get those traitors out of our government except by shooting them out," referring to President Kennedy.[45] Edwin Walker, a well-known Dallas official of the John Birch Society, exhibited similar sentiments. Walker flew the flag in front of his house upside-down days before President Kennedy's visit, as a UPI dispatch reported.[46] But he flew it at full staff during President Johnson's proclaimed period of half-staff mourning.[47]

A few days before the assassination, handbills with President Kennedy's photo and a "Wanted for Treason" caption appeared on the streets of Dallas.[48] They were printed by Robert A. Surrey, a close associate of Walker's.[49] And on the day of the president's visit, a local newspaper carried a full-page, black-bordered ad harshly critical of his policies.[50] The sponsors of the ad included Nelson Bunker Hunt, son of H. L. Hunt, and Birch Society members.[51]

/2/ Alignment Against Castro

Thus President Kennedy secured the enmity of Cuban exiles, extreme right-wingers and some CIA operatives through his moderation toward Castro, his peace and civil rights initiatives, and his proposed reduction in the oil depletion allowance. At the same time, he incurred the wrath of the Mob through his administration's crusade against organized crime. But the issue that brought the Mob and these other groups together was Castro's disruption of a massive enterprise in Cuba: Mafia-controlled gambling.

The Mob's dealings in Cuba were chronicled in a recent report furnished to Congress by the Cuban government.[52] "The Mafia began its activities in Cuba during the '20's, taking advantage of the corruption of the successive governments of that period."[53] During the 1940s, it infiltrated Cuban trade unions, while investing "in real estate companies and the building of luxury hotels, casinos and other tourist facilities."[54] The casinos were administered by "Cubans or foreign figures linked to the Mafia," and "directed by Mafia-appointed chiefs"; Florida chieftain Santos Trafficante "represented the Mafia leadership."[55] The Mafia "also controlled the traffic in drugs, jewels, the currency exchange, white slavery and pornographic film shows."[56] Indeed, by the mid-1950s, Havana had become a multibillion-dollar Mob center of gambling, narcotics and vice, paralleled only by Las Vegas.[57]

Like his friend Santos Trafficante and several other Mobsters, Carlos Marcello kept a finger in the Cuban pie through an interest in a gambling casino there.[58] Marcello was also heavily involved in the Cuban narcotics trade,[59] and was rumored to have associated with Cuban exiles and dealt in armaments.[60] The third member of the Mob's anti-Kennedy triumvirate, Jimmy Hoffa, likewise became involved in the Cuban scene by sponsoring an arms smuggling operation from southern Florida to Cuba.[61]

As Castro began making headway during the mid-1950s, the Mob followed the same strategy it used for domestic political challengers.[62] Certain Mob casino operators, including Norman Rothman, supplied Castro with guns and cash, while the bulk of the Mob payoffs still went to Batista.[63] A group of Mobsters even formed a corporation, Akros Dynamics, which sold a fleet of C-74 airplanes to the new Castro government; Hoffa tried unsuccessfully to secure a $300,000 Teamsters pension fund loan for the venture.[64] So when Castro took power in 1959, only prominent Batista allies like Meyer Lansky fled, and the Mob as a whole was not alarmed.[65] In fact, an accommodation was worked out that permitted gambling to continue from March 1959 through September 1961.[66] Supervising was the Castro-appointed "Minister for Games of Chance," a casino operator who had run guns for Castro.[67] This appointee was Frank Fiorini, alias Frank Sturgis of Watergate fame.[68] Along with Norman "Roughhouse" Rothman, Sturgis became an important liaison between the CIA and Mafia in their anti-Castro collaboration.[69]

But Castro had little regard for the American hoodlums, and by September 1961 had expelled all the Mob casino operators from Cuba.[70] Castro declared, according to Sturgis, "I'm going to run all these fascist mobsters, all these American gangsters, out of Cuba ... Cuba for Cubans."[71] As Jack Anderson commented, this expulsion dealt the Mob "a financial blow ... as hard as the 1929 stock market crash rocked Wall Street."[72] Whereas *Fortune* magazine placed the largest loss from expropriation for a U.S. firm at $272 million,[73] the *New York Times* had estimated the Mob's annual gambling take from Cuba at between $350 and $700 million.[74*] It was not surprising, therefore, that Castro's distaste for the Mob was vociferously reciprocated.

/3/ The CIA and the Mafia

The common desire to eliminate the Castro regime eventually led to cooperative activity by the Mob and the CIA.[77] But such sinister collusion between the two groups was not unprecedented. During World War II, William Donovan, chief of U.S. Intelligence (OSS), decided that a "corps of skilled safecrackers, housebreakers and assassins" could further the war

---

*The enormous magnitude of the Mob's Cuban gambling profits was indicated by John Scarne, an American gambling expert, who spent five hours observing one dice table in a Havana casino.[75] He counted a fantastic $3 million change hands that evening at that single dice game in that one casino.[76]

effort.[78] Donovan secured the best—Mafia boss Charles "Lucky" Luciano[79]—who used his influence to protect Mafia-infested American docks from Axis sabotage.[80] In return, Luciano was granted a commutation of a long prison sentence, and was deported to Italy in 1946.[81] There he helped revitalize the Mafia's international narcotics ring,[82] later moving to Havana to control operations in that key American supply point.[83] Between 1946 and 1952, the number of heroin addicts in the United States tripled.[84]

While the details of Luciano's war involvements are hidden in classified files,[85] the better-known activities of fellow boss Vito Genovese reflect the Mafia's contribution to the war effort. In 1937, Genovese fled from New York to Italy after Brooklyn police secured two witnesses to his murder of a Mafia colleague.[86] Genovese ingratiated himself with the Mussolini regime,[87] reportedly contributing $250,000 to the construction of Fascist Party headquarters out of the take he was still drawing from American rackets.[88] Genovese also showed his friendship to the Mussolini regime by ordering the January 1943 murder of Carlos Tresca, editor of the New York anti-Fascist newspaper *The Hammer.*[89]

When the Allies occupied Italy, Genovese got himself appointed translator-liaison for U.S. Army headquarters.[90] Based in a luxury apartment in Naples, traveling freely with government passes in his chauffeur-driven limousine,[91] Genovese traded in stolen American supplies and was a kingpin in Italy's black market.[92] He also served as whoremaster to certain top Allied officers.[93] In one of his more cunning ventures, Genovese used U.S. Army trucks, later found destroyed by fire, to steal flour and sugar from American supplies in Nola.[94]

Genovese's activities were finally uncovered by O. C. Dickey of the U.S. Army Criminal Investigation Division, who sought to return Genovese to the United States for his Brooklyn murder trial.[95] But Genovese used his influence to stay in Italy until one of two witnesses against him, Peter LaTempa, was murdered.[96] While in a maximum security cell in a Brooklyn jail on January 15, 1945, LaTempa suffered from a gallstone condition and asked for medicine to relieve the pain.[97] Later that day he was dead; a city autopsy revealed enough poison in his body "to kill eight horses."[98]

The favoritism shown to Luciano and Genovese was representative of a broader Pentagon courtship of the Sicilian Mafia. Fearing potential Communist advances in postwar Italy, American military officials cut back support for the anti-Fascist underground and turned instead to this underworld organization.[99] The Mafia was glad to cooperate, having been purged almost to extinction by Mussolini.[100] With arrangements apparently made through intermediaries from the American branch, the Sicilian Mafia arranged enthusiastic welcomes, protected the road from snipers, and provided guides for General George Patton's troops on their July 1943 march to Palermo.[101] The Allied military command subsequently appointed many of the Mafiosi, including top don Cologero Vizzini, as mayors of towns in western Sicily.[102] These appointments led to a "recrudescence of Mafia activities," including homicides, noted British Major General Lord Rennell, chief of the Allied Military Government of Occupied Territories.[103] And thanks to this Allied benevolence, the Mafia soon regained its former power[104]—as reflected in the economic weakness, political instability, and terrorism in today's Mafia-infested[105] Italy.

Centralized into the CIA by the National Security Act of 1947,[106] American intelligence forces formed a similar relationship with the Corsican syndicates in France,[107] close allies of the Sicilian Mafia.[108] In the first year of its existence, the CIA hired the Corsicans to disrupt a Communist-inspired dock strike at Marseilles;[109] it was broken after a number of strikers were murdered.[110] The CIA again called upon the Corsicans in 1950, with similar results, when Marseilles dock workers refused to ship war materials to Indochina.[111]

When the CIA and the Mafia cooperated during the early 1960s in Cuba, however, as considered below, a questionable relationship mushroomed into a monstrous alliance. One manifestation was noted by Seymour Hersh in the *New York Times*, based on a 1974 interview with a CIA undercover agent "whose knowledge of the CIA seemed extensive"; Hersh reported that "the Mafia was relied upon" to "assault targets selected by the CIA."[112] The extent of such cooperation was suggested when the Nixon Administration intervened for the defense—ostensibly to protect "intelligence sources and methods"—in at least 20 trials of organized crime figures.[113] A further example of this Mafia-CIA alliance run amuck was a joint counterfeiting operation in Southeast Asia, reported in July 1975 by staff members of the Senate Permanent Investigations Committee.[114]

/4/ Anti-Castro Raids and Assassination Attempts

Returning to the setting of Cuba—where Castro had expropriated a vast gambling empire and inflamed Cold War sentiments—the Mob, the CIA, and extreme right-wing elements initiated a series of operations against the Cuban leader.[115] The Mob contributed in several capacities, supplying arms, ammunition and aircraft to the Cuban exiles, and launching its own paramilitary operations.[116] This involvement surfaced on July 31, 1963, when the FBI raided a dynamite cache in Mandeville, Louisiana, which was used to supply Cuban exiles; it had been stocked by the Mob.[117] Later in 1963, the Kennedy Administration learned of raids being launched into Cuba by six Americans, including CIA undercover agent Frank Sturgis and his friend Alexander Rourke.[118] According to Rourke's attorney, Hans Tanner, the anti-Castro group backing Sturgis was apparently "financed by dispossessed hotel and gambling room owners who operated under Batista."[119] The Mob also reportedly funneled millions of doll gambling receipts to one prominent exile leader, Dr. Pauline Martinez.[120]

The most infamous joint effort between the Mob and CIA in Cuba was a series of assassination plots against Premier Fidel Castro.[121] In December 1959, CIA Director Allen Dulles, who would later serve on the Warren Commission, approved a recommendation that "thorough consideration be given to the elimination of Fidel Castro."[122] In August 1960, CIA officials Richard Bissell and Sheffield Edwards initiated the recruitment of underworld figures to perform the murder.[123] By then, however, as noted in a staff report of the House Assassinations Committee, the Mob had "probably initiated independent assassination plots against Castro," which were to continue for a few years.[124] It was thus likely that the CIA "found itself involved in providing additional resources for an independent operation that the syndicate already had commenced."[125]

The collaboration between the CIA and Mob to kill Castro was most intense at its outset, between August 1960 and April 1961.[126] That stage was followed by more attempts on the Cuban leader between late 1961 and 1962.[127] Although some operations never advanced beyond the planning stage, killers were supplied with weapons on two occasions.[128] As the Senate Intelligence Committee summarized, the proposed assassination devices "ran the gamut from high-powered rifles to poison pills, poison pens, deadly bacterial powders, and other devices which strain the imagination."[129] The go-between who enlisted the Mafia's cooperation for the CIA was Robert Maheu, then an investigator for Washington attorney Edward Bennett Williams.[130] Maheu had conducted questionable investigations on behalf of William's Teamster clients, including Jimmy Hoffa.[131] The principal underworld figures involved were West Coast Mafioso Johnny Roselli, Chicago chieftain Sam Giancana and Florida boss Santos Trafficante.[132]

/5/ Possible Connections to the Kennedy Assassination

One of this Cuban hit squad, Johnny Roselli, was subsequently in contact with Jack Ruby, as discussed later,[133] suggesting a possible connection between murder plots against Castro and plots against President Kennedy. Roselli claimed, in fact, that Castro arranged for President Kennedy's murder, in retaliation for American plots against him.[134] Roselli contended that Castro discovered Mobsters in Havana planning to kill him and persuaded them to switch targets; they then lined up Oswald to kill the president.[135] Yet this retaliation theory, which conveniently draws the main focus of attention away from the Mob, has been rejected on several grounds by both the House Assassinations Committee[136] and several private commentators.[137]

First, given Castro's knowledge about the murder plots against him,[138] it is questionable whether he would have blamed them on President Kennedy. For the evidence indicates that these plots were hatched before John F. Kennedy took office,[139] and were carried on without the authorization of either Kennedy brother.[140] Second, the notion that Oswald became involved with Castro is far-fetched. Although such a connection was suggested in letters discovered by the FBI, the Bureau's investigation revealed that they were fabricated.[141] Indeed, as noted in chapter 5, Oswald's proclaimed pro-Castro sympathies are questionable given his many anti-Castro associations.[142]

Finally, Castro's attitude toward President Kennedy was hardly murderous. Castro appeared chagrined at the news of Kennedy's death,[143] later expressing admiration and respect for his adversary,[144] as did Khrushchev.[145] Castro called him a "bold man" with "initiative," "imagination" and "courage."[146] Moreover, American and Cuban delegations had arranged preliminary talks on bilateral accommodation just before Kennedy's death;[147] ironically, Kennedy's emissary was meeting with Castro when the president was shot.[148] Thus, as summarized in a staff report of the House Assassinations Committee,

> with the prospects of renewed diplomatic relations in the air and the knowledge that Kennedy possessed a more favorable attitude toward Cuba than other military or political leaders, Castro would have had every reason to hope that Kennedy maintained the Presidency.[149]

Castro himself noted that he had nothing to gain by President Kennedy's assassination, and wondered "if someone did not wish to involve Cuba in this."[150]

A more logical connection between Cuban events and the Kennedy assassination has been widely hypothesized. By the fall of 1963, the Mob was chafing under the Kennedy administration's anticrime assault, with even more drastic action portended by the televised Valachi hearings.[151] The aspirations of the Mob's anti-Castro bedfellows were dashed by President Kennedy's steps toward detente, his civil rights initiatives, and the Vietnam troop withdrawals he ordered.[152] Thus, it is conjectured,[153] when their common efforts to eliminate the Cuban premiere were frustrated with increasing firmness by the Kennedy Administration,[154] the target of assassination shifted to this more immediate obstacle—President Kennedy.

/6/ A Parallel Alliance in Southeast Asia

"The Caribbean was bad enough,"[155] noted Robert Sam Anson, a political correspondent captured by Communist troops during his coverage of the

Vietnam War for *Time* magazine.[156] But

> Kennedy was also making peace overtures in Southeast Asia,
> where CIA-supported dictators had allowed the syndicate to
> flourish. The Mafia's interest in Southeast Asia was heroin. . . .[157]

Since the 1950s, the so-called Golden Triangle of Burma, Thailand, and Laos has been a worldwide source of heroin—harvested by local underworld suppliers, processed by the Corsican Mafia, and distributed by the closely allied American Mafia.[158]* When Communist forces began making headway in the region, the CIA, with characteristic shortsighted pragmatism, organized and supported a small army of Laotian and Vietnamese heroin-dealing, anti-Communist mercenaries.[164] To stabilize this arrangement, the CIA courted local heroin overlords, a powerful factor in Vietnamese politics, as French intelligence had done before it.[165] And the State Department covered up the heroin involvements[166] of two top South Vietnamese politicians: President Nguyen Van Thieu and Vice-President Nguyen Cao Ky.[167]

By the early 1960s, as Anson wrote,

> CIA money was indirectly financing a vast opium industry. CIA-
> employed troops grew it, harvested it, and shipped it to Vien-
> tiane and Saigon aboard planes of Air America, the CIA airline.[168]

The same collaboration was noted by Russell Bintliff, former special agent of the Army's Criminal Intelligence Command, as reported by the *Washington Star*.[169] Bintliff said it was widely known in the Far East that the CIA had maintained a close working relationship with opium producers in Southeast Asia's "Golden Triangle."[170] He cited the case of an American soft drink company, Pepsi-Cola,[171] which set up a bottling plant in Vientiane, Laos, with U.S. government financing.[172] But the plant "never produced a single bottle," Bintliff said.[173] "It was for processing opium into heroin. I think this narcotics connection was responsible for most of the GIs who were turned into addicts during the Vietnam War."[174]

*"The American Mafia followed the U.S. army to Vietnam in 1965," noted Alfred McCoy in *The Politics of Heroin in Southeast Asia*.[159] "Attracted to Vietnam by lucrative construction and service contracts, the mafiosi concentrated on ordinary graft and kickbacks at first, but later branched out into narcotics smuggling as they built up their contacts in Hong Kong and Indochina."[160] One Florida Mobster, Frank Carmen Furci, "became a key figure in the systematic graft and corruption that began to plague U.S. military clubs in Vietnam," as exposed in a lengthy Senate investigation.[161] In 1968, Tampa Mafia boss Santos Trafficante visited Furci in Hong Kong and proceeded to Vietnam, where he met with powerful Corsican gangsters.[162] It is suspected that the purpose of Trafficante's visit was "to secure new sources of heroin for Mafia distributors inside the United States."[163]

America was thus led to collaborate with underworld narcotics traffickers in a war which insured the flow of heroin, as well as defense and oil profits, into the United States. Neither the Mafia nor the war suppliers, however, shared in the losses: the corpses, mutilated limbs, acquired drug habits and shattered lives of millions of American soldiers. Nor did one powerful friend of both, who rescinded President Kennedy's troop disengagement order immediately after the assassination, and marched America into its Vietnam debacle.

The oilmen, the politicians, the construction firms and organized crime—call it the Mafia, the Cosa Nostra, the Syndicate, the Mob, whatever you will—have all grown up in Texas together in an orgy of mutual back-scratching.[1]

Ramparts magazine

I think it is evident that organized crime and the mob couldn't possibly operate without the duplicity of judges, of public office holders, public officials and politicians, banks, . . . commissions, commissioners and their staffs, and also law firms.[2]

Senator Charles Percy

□ 16 □

Post-Assassination Policy

It is a common belief among Americans that the assassination of President Kennedy inaugurated a profound and disturbing change in our national course. This chapter examines some of the ugly events underlying this transformation and indicates who benefited from the murder.

/1/ The Johnson Administration

When Lyndon Johnson was sworn in as president on November 22, 1963, he declared, "We shall continue," the slogan of his first two years in office.[3] Johnson did follow through on his predecessor's civil rights initiatives, and sated liberals with massive government spending and the rhetoric of peace. For the most part, however, the record on Johnson's policies reflects anything but continuity.

Guns and oil. Two days after the assassination of President Kennedy, Johnson called a meeting of his top advisers to discuss Vietnam.[4] The results of this meeting were embodied in National Security Action Memorandum 273 of November 26, 1963, parts of which were released in the Pentagon Papers.[5] This memorandum pledged total commitment to "denying" Vietnam to communism,[6] authorized "specific covert operations, graduated in intensity, against the DRV" (North Vietnam),[7] and reversed President Kennedy's movement toward military disengagement.[8] The remaining 780 of the 1,000 troops that Kennedy had ordered out of Vietnam were never withdrawn.[9] And after Johnson won the 1964 presidential election by styling himself as a peace candidate, his administration began to escalate American involvement.

President Kennedy's initiatives toward accommodation with Cuba were also promptly abandoned under Johnson.[10] According to *New York Times* columnist Tad Szulc, the CIA reactivated Cuban invasion and assassination plans in the following two years.[11] And in 1965, Johnson sent U.S. Marines to the Dominican Republic, the Mob's new Caribbean gambling base,[12] to prevent its former leader, Juan Bosch, from returning to power.[13] President Kennedy had supported Bosch, a democratic, non-Communist politician hostile to the Mob, who had been ousted by a coup in September 1963.[14]* Johnson also supported the oil depletion allowance,[18] stifling his predecessor's plan to repeal the mammoth tax loophole. These actions were undoubtedly applauded by Texas oil tycoon Clint Murchison, one of Johnson's earliest political supporters[19] and reportedly a big contributor to Richard Nixon.[20] Another political backer[21] and long-time friend[22] of Johnson was H. L. Hunt, the billionaire oilman and extreme right-wing propagandist.

Antipoverty dollars and race riots. While defense and oil interests profited from the war in Vietnam, Johnson's extravagant "war on poverty" proved a boon to contractors and corrupt city administrators. The paucity of real assistance to the needy was perhaps reflected by some of the nation's worst ghetto riots during his last years in office. Congressman Joseph McDade highlighted another deficiency in Johnson's approach, noting that "organized crime takes from the urban poor far more money than the government puts in."[23] Twenty-two Republican colleagues also expressed concern about this problem, as Congressman McDade summarized:

> The warlords of this cycle of poverty and crime are the organized crime racketeers. If their activities could be curtailed, the

Life Magazine reported in 1967 that Rafael Trujillo, the dictator of the Dominican Republic until his assassination in 1961, had been "fast friends" with New Jersey Mafioso Joe Zicarelli.[15] According to *Life*, Zicarelli sold more than $1 million in arms to Trujillo and arranged the 1952 Manhattan murder of anti-Trujillo exile Andres Requena.[16] Zicarelli was also linked to the 1956 kidnapping and presumed killing of another exile, Jesus DeGalindez, a teacher at Columbia University.[17]

growing crime rate would be dramatically reduced, and the War on Poverty might have a better chance to succeed.[24]

But there was no such action under Johnson, whose abysmal record on organized crime[25] reversed another policy of his predecessor. Within four years of the assassination, in fact, the field time spent by the Justice Department's organized crime section had declined by 48 percent, the time before grand juries by 72 percent, and the number of District Court briefs from that section by 83 percent.[26] Did Johnson's actions in this area also reflect a rapport with the affected parties? At least two sources indicate that the answer is yes.

The Halfen connection. Jack Halfen had a dizzying ascent in the underworld, from passing counterfeit coins at age 15, to exploits with desperadoes "Pretty Boy" Floyd, Bonnie Parker and Clyde Barrow, to criminal associations with such Mafia kingpins as Vito Genovese, Carlos Marcello and Frank Costello.[27] In the 1940s and 1950s, Halfen was a Mob coordinator and fixer for gambling in the Houston area.[28] Bookmaking alone netted more than $15 million a year in Houston;[29] 40 percent went to Carlos Marcello, 35 percent to Halfen and 25 percent to police and politicians for bribes.[30] These arrangements were illuminated during Halfen's 1954 trial for income-tax evasion, which brought him a four-year prison sentence.[31] But prosecutor Charles Herring, a friend and former aide of Lyndon Johnson, never pressed the embarrassing issue of where Halfen's myriad payoff dollars stopped.[32]

Although Halfen never informed on his Mob associates, his loyalty to political collaborators wore thin as the months in jail rolled by.[33] And in conversations with U.S. Marshal J. Neal Matthews in 1956, Halfen provided incriminating information on several of them, including one of his closest political affiliates: Lyndon Johnson.[34] Halfen reported that his Mob-franchised gambling network had given $500,000 in cash and campaign contributions to Johnson over a ten-year period while Johnson was in the Senate.[35] In return, Senator Johnson repeatedly killed antirackets legislation, watered down the bills that could not be defeated, and curbed Congressional investigations of the Mob.[36] For example, a U.S. Senate committee chaired by Estes Kefauver held hearings on organized crime in more than a dozen cities during the early 1950s.[37] But the committee never made it to Texas, reportedly as a result of Johnson's intervention.[38] Halfen had concrete substantiation of his association with Johnson, including a letter from Johnson to the Texas Board of Paroles on his behalf[39] and photographs showing Johnson, Halfen and other Texas politicians on a private hunting expedition.[40]

The campaign to spring Jimmy Hoffa. Mob payoffs to Johnson were also indicated in sworn testimony by Jack Sullivan, a former administrative assistant to Senator Daniel Brewster of Maryland.[41] During a 1964 cocktail party at Teamster headquarters which Sullivan attended, Brewster and Teamster boss Jimmy Hoffa walked off to talk privately on the terrace overlooking Capitol Hill.[42] Afterward, Brewster told Sullivan that Hoffa had asked him to take $100,000 in cash for Johnson to presidential aide Cliff Carter.[43] The payoff was meant to enlist Johnson's support in blocking Hoffa's prosecution for jury tampering and pension fund fraud,[44] for which Hoffa was ultimately convicted.[45]

A few days after the party, Sullivan testified, Teamster lobbyist Sid Zagri came into Senator Brewster's office and gave Brewster a suitcase full of money.[46] Sullivan then accompanied Brewster to Cliff Carter's office, and waited in the car as Brewster went into the office with the suitcase and left without it.[47]*

Corruption credible. Disturbing as they are, these two allegations of Mob payoffs to Johnson are credible for a number of reasons. Johnson secured his first federal office, a U.S. Senate seat in 1948, by winning a Democratic primary election in Texas.[53] He won by 87 votes—when 203 new votes suddenly turned up in alphabetical order late in the ballot tabulation.[54] The federal government launched an investigation for vote fraud,[55] and suspicions were finally confirmed in 1977 when a Texas election judge confessed that the election had been stolen at Johnson's suggestion.[56]†

During his years in Washington, Johnson followed through on this crooked start, as recently disclosed by Pulitzer Prize-winning author Robert Caro:

> For years, men came into Lyndon Johnson's office and handed
> him envelopes stuffed with cash. They didn't stop coming even

---

*In 1969, a federal grand jury in Baltimore indicted Senator Brewster for corruption;[48] he was ultimately convicted.[49] But Attorney General Mitchell refused the recommendation of Baltimore U.S. Attorney Stephen Sachs to indict Russell Long,[50] another senator who had assisted the Mob-Teamster campaign to keep Hoffa out of jail.[51] Long had previously been identified in a 1951 internal staff report of the Kefauver crime committee as the recipient of heavy campaign contributions from Mafia boss Carlos Marcello.[52]

†Of the 203 new votes, all but two were cast for Johnson, earning him the nickname "Landslide Lyndon."[57] Texas election judge Luis Salas told the Associated Press in 1977 that those votes were entered in alphabetical order, as confirmed by FBI agent T. Kellis Dibrell, who participated in the probe of the 1948 election.[58] Salas reported that the 203 votes were fabricated on Johnson's suggestion after a meeting between Johnson and political boss George Parr at which Salas was present.[59]

when the office in which he sat was the office of the Vice President of the United States. Fifty thousand dollars (in hundred-dollar bills in sealed envelopes) was what one lobbyist—for *one* oil company—testified that he brought to Johnson's office during his term as Vice President.[60] [Emphasis in original.]

It was perhaps through such envelopes and the blatant use of political power to further his private business interests[61] that Johnson accumulated a $20 million fortune during his political career.[62]

Johnson sponsored the infamous Senate staff career of Bobby Baker,[63] a man deeply involved with the Mob,[64] whom Johnson called "one of my trusted friends."[65] As discussed in the next chapter, Johnson allegedly helped to conceal Baker's dealings.[66] Finally, Johnson's reported Mob ties would also be hard to ignore in light of his administration's striking inaction against organized crime.

/2/ The Nixon Administration

In 1968, after Edward Muskie's campaign was sabotaged and Robert Kennedy murdered, Richard M. Nixon took over the reigns of government. During Nixon's presidency, the cover-up of the Kennedy assassination was continued. So was the Johnson Administration's shoddy record on organized crime.

Nixon's associations with the Mob dated back to the beginning of his political career—"he began as a Syndicate person in direct connection with Syndicate people," observed Carl Oglesby.[67] Noting Nixon's early ties to Cuban gambling circles,[68] Oglesby concluded that the underlying factor behind Nixon's anti-Castro involvement[69] was "the issue of the Lansky casinos that were being run in Havana."[70] If Nixon's past was murky, however, his record was ultimately clarified—as summarized by journalist Jeff Gerth—through the "unparalleled panoply of organized criminal activity and offenses committed by his White House during his years in office."[71] Below is a sampling, progressing from questionable relationships to flagrant misconduct.

Bebe Rebozo and the Bahamas. Nixon's dealings with organized crime were perhaps modeled after those of his closest associates. One was Bebe Rebozo,[72] who had been heavily involved with Cuban exiles in Mafia-sponsored activities against Castro,[73] and who maintained longstanding legal and financial ties with "Big Al" Polizzi, a Cleveland Mobster and drug trafficker.[74] Both Rebozo and Nixon were friends of James Crosby,[75] chairman of the board of Resorts International,[76] a company which has been repeatedly linked to top Mob figures.[77] Rebozo's Key Biscayne Bank, which did a good deal of business with Resorts,[78] was a suspected conduit for Mob dollars skimmed from the firm's Paradise Island Casino in the Bahamas.[79] And in January 1968, Nixon appeared as Crosby's guest at the opening of the casino.[80] The previous year, *Life* had reported that it was to be controlled by "Lansky & Co."[81]

Nixon's relationship with Resorts proved rewarding to him in at least two ways. During the 1968 Republican national convention in Miami, the Paradise Island Casino's company yacht was put at Nixon's disposal.[82] And, as the *New York Times* reported, Crosby contributed $100,000 to Nixon's presidential primary campaign.[83] These were but a few of Nixon's many underworld-linked involvements in the Bahamas and Florida.[84]

C. Arnholt Smith and the U.S. National Bank. One of Richard Nixon's most generous benefactors and closest friends was San Diego millionaire C. Arnholt Smith.[85] This association proved rather embarrassing in 1973, however, when the U.S. National Bank, controlled by Smith, collapsed.[86] The reason for the failure was that Smith had siphoned off $400 million of its assets into 86 shell companies.[87] The Internal Revenue Service subsequently filed a $22.8 million tax lien against Smith, the largest for a single year in its history.[88] Smith also drew fire from three other federal agencies and a federal grand jury.[89]

The ultimate beneficiary of the U.S. National Bank scam was indicated in a front-page article of September 10, 1973 in the *New York Times*. In particular, the *Times* noted that "Mr. Smith and his enterprises [had] a long history of dealings with organized crime."[90] Senior vice president of the U.S. National Bank, for example, was Lewis Lipton, alias Felix Aguirre, who was "well-connected in the Southern California underworld."[91] Lipton helped a Mafia boss and a Mafia-controlled firm secure loans from the bank.[92] And a one-time director of Smith's Westgate-California conglomerate was John Alessio, a Syndicate figure convicted of income-tax evasion.[93] The *New York Times* cited "Mr. Smith's long business and personal relationship with John S. Alessio" as what federal agents considered "the most obvious example of Mr. Smith's connections to organized crime."[94] Like Smith, Alessio was a benefactor of Nixon, contributing $26,000 to his 1968 presidential campaign.[95]

The collapse of the U.S. National Bank was at the time the largest bank failure in American history,[96] triggering the collapses of the Franklin National Bank and of another creditor bank in West Germany.[97] It typified the Mob's dominant role in the epidemic of U.S. bank failures beginning in 1964.*

---

*Between 1944 and 1964, only a few federally insured banks failed each year.[98] But seven collapsed in the boom year of 1964 and four more collapsed in the first months of 1965.[99] As Fred Cook wrote in *The Secret Rulers*, "Federal officials on

Murray Chotiner and the finale of the spring-Hoffa campaign. Another of Nixon's closest advisers and friends was Murray Chotiner,[105] a lawyer who had represented leading Syndicate figures during his career.[106] Dubbed "the one that made Nixon,"[107] Chotiner helped him achieve his first public position.[108] Chotiner also conceived the melodramatic "Checkers" speech when a secret fund scandal threatened to force Nixon off the Eisenhower ticket in 1952.[109] This close relationship continued throughout Nixon's presidency, as demonstrated by a private office Chotiner occupied in the Nixon White House.[110]

Chotiner's several Mob associates[111] included D'Alton Smith,[112] who was close with Carlos Marcello[113] and produced rock music festivals in California under Marcello's sponsorship.[114] Both Chotiner and Smith were instrumental in the last stage of the seven-year Mob-Teamster campaign to thwart Jimmy Hoffa's criminal prosecution.[115] This campaign was marked by a barrage of bribery, intimidation and perjury,[116] whose "audacity and sweep," as *Life* magazine noted, few Mob fixes "could top."[117] It finally succeeded, with the intervention of Chotiner and Smith,[118] when Nixon pardoned Hoffa in December 1971.[119]

Walter Sheridan, a former Kennedy Justice Department official, had warned journalist Clark Mollenhoff earlier: "It's all set for the Nixon Administration to spring Jimmy Hoffa. . . . I'm told Murray Chotiner is handling it with the Las Vegas Mob."[120] The commutation was granted four months after a U.S. parole board unanimously rejected such a release.[121] It allowed Hoffa to serve just five years of a 13-year sentence for jury tampering and defrauding the Teamsters of almost $2 million.[122]

"Nixon, the Teamsters, the Mafia." The *New York Times* called Nixon's pardon of Hoffa "a pivotal element in the strange love affair between the Administration and the two-million-member truck union, ousted from the rest of the labor movement in 1957 for racketeer domination."[123] This strange kinship was further demonstrated by the Nixon Administration's repeated interventions to quash prosecutions and investigations of Team-

---

every level hold that gangland mobs, entering the banking field, are mainly responsible."[100] This view was expressed by Congressman Wright Patman, former chairman of the House Banking Committee, who charged "hoodlum connections with some of the biggest banks in the country."[101]

In 1971, Claude Pepper, chairman of the House Crime Committee, noted "how extensively organized criminal elements have infiltrated the banking, securities and insurance industries."[102] The result, he observed, was a "pervasive influence of organized crime in the banking and securities industries."[103] According to investigative reporter Jeff Gerth, the nation's three largest bank failures—those of San Diego's U.S. National Bank and New York's Franklin National and Security National Banks—which occurred in the 1970s, were caused by Mob infiltration and draining.[104]

ster criminal activity, as outlined in a *Los Angeles Times* lead editorial entitled "Nixon, the Teamsters, the Mafia."[124]

One such intervention began with a conclave at La Costa Country Club in California, the "Mafia watering hole,"[125] on February 9 through 12, 1973.[126] The participants were Teamster President Frank Fitzsimmons, Allen Dorfman, Chicago Mafia boss Anthony Accardo, and other Mob figures.[127] The meeting soon turned to routine business: a massive scam of Teamster welfare funds.[128] The particular scheme under consideration called for Teamster members to be enrolled in prepaid medical plans, which would kick back 7 percent of their business to People's Industrial Consultants—a Los Angeles front for the Mob.[129] The take would then be divided among Mob and Teamster bosses.[130] The potential bonanza was huge, with $1 billion in projected annual business.[131] The conversations at La Costa outlining the scheme were disclosed by several sources—most notably by FBI electronic surveillance of People's Industrial Consultants.[132]

On February 9, 1973, while the Mob-Teamster discussions were in progress, White House aides H. R. Haldeman, John Ehrlichman, John Dean and Richard Moore also met at La Costa Country Club, for about 12 hours, to discuss Watergate strategy.[133] Some of Nixon's own staff members found the proximity shocking.[134] On February 12, the last day of the Mob-Teamster discussions, Teamster boss Fitzsimmons flew back to Washington with President Nixon on Air Force One.[135] A month later, Attorney General Richard Kleindienst denied an FBI request to continue electronic surveillance of People's Industrial Consultants.[136] Through aides, Kleindienst characterized the surveillance as "unproductive," to the amazement of FBI agents.[137] On the contrary, as the *New York Times* reported, the surveillance "had begun to penetrate connections between the Mafia and the teamsters union."[138] The *Times* called the termination of surveillance an instance of "the perversion of justice that pose[d] as law and order" in the Nixon Administration.[139]*

Nixon's efforts on behalf of the Mob did not go unrewarded. Citing government informants and a secret FBI report, *Time* disclosed in 1977 that the White House had received a $1 million underworld bribe shortly before the dual conclaves at La Costa.[145] The principals in the payoff were Frank

---

*Kleindienst had quashed several prosecutions and investigations of the Mob and Teamsters.[140] As deputy attorney general, he had been offered a $100,000 bribe to stop prosecution of several underworld figures in a stock fraud case, but reported it a week later only when he learned that federal agents were investigating the case.[141] He also lied to a Senate committee about an antitrust case and later drew a criminal conviction for that offense.[142]

After he left public office, Kleindienst collected $125,000 for a few hours' time arranging a health insurance contract between the Teamsters and an insurance firm of dubious reputation.[143] The outcome was classic: $7 million in union members' premiums were siphoned off into several shell companies.[144]

Fitzsimmons and Tony Provenzano;[146] Provenzano is a Mafia captain, former Teamster International Vice President, and recently convicted murderer.[147] Also involved was Allen Dorfman,[148] a Chicago Mob associate, convicted labor racketeer, and Teamster pension fund adviser.[149] Dorfman's role in the Teamsters, noted author Dan Moldea, was to ensure that "every section of organized crime got its fair share of the union's billion-dollar pension and welfare funds."[150] *Time* reported that "the $1 million was intended as a payoff for the Administration's cooperation in preventing Jimmy Hoffa from wresting the union presidency from Frank Fitzsimmons."[151] The *Manchester Union Leader* observed that the bribe was also given in return for short-circuiting various government investigations of the Teamster-Mafia connection.[152]

According to government informants, *Time* reported, Dorfman provided half of the bribe for Nixon on Fitzsimmons' orders.[153] The other $500,000 was handled by Provenzano, again at Fitzsimmons' behest, and delivered to a White House courier in Las Vegas.[154] Provenzano told government informants that the Nixon-Teamster intermediary was White House aide Charles Colson, and the FBI believed that Colson received the money in Las Vegas on January 6, 1973.[155] The FBI called the information on the million-dollar transaction "solid."[156]

One FBI agent commented, "This whole thing of the Teamsters and the mob and the White House is one of the scariest things I've ever seen."[157] Also ominous was the possibility, as *Time* reported, that Nixon may have desired the Dorfman-Provenzano cash to subvert the democratic process further: to provide hush money for the Watergate conspirators.[158] *Time* noted the "crucial timing" of demands for payoffs by Watergate burglar E. Howard Hunt in late 1972, and of a meeting between Hunt's lawyer and Colson on this matter on January 3, 1973.[159]

A Mob-Watergate connection was discussed, in fact, in the White House tape transcripts of March 21, 1973. Presidential aide John Dean told Nixon that $1 million in Watergate hush money was needed, to which Nixon responded,

> We could get that. . . . You could get a million dollars. You could get it in cash. I know where it could be gotten.[160]

Dean remarked that laundering money is "the sort of thing Mafia people can do."[161] Playing the innocent, Nixon replied, "Maybe it takes a gang to do that."[162]

In a second White House tape, Ehrlichman told Nixon that Hunt and Gordon Liddy had gone to Las Vegas for covert purposes,[163] supporting allegations that both had picked up cash from Mob gambling interests there.[164] And in a third tape of May 5, 1971, Nixon and Haldeman considered another role for the Mob—attacking anti-war protesters:

Haldeman: ... do it with the Teamsters. Just ask them to dig up those, their eight thugs.

President: Yeah. ... they've got guys who'll go in and knock their heads off.

Haldeman: Sure. Murderers. ... it's the regular strikebuster-types ... and then they're gonna beat the [obscenity] out of some of these people.[165]

Some such "thug-type guy" was in fact used by Nixon's men to disrupt the Muskie presidential campaign of 1968, as mentioned by Haldeman on that White House tape of May 1971.[166] But the underworld resource upon which Nixon had drawn most heavily over the years was cash. Mobster Mickey Cohen wrote in his memoirs that he had contributed $5,000 to Murray Chotiner for Nixon's first Congressional campaign in 1946.[167] For Nixon's 1950 senatorial race against Helen Gahagan Douglas, Cohen wrote, he had raised $75,000 from Las Vegas gamblers.[168] And in 1960, just before the first of the Kennedy-Nixon debates, Mafia boss Carlos Marcello funneled $500,000 in cash to Nixon through Jimmy Hoffa.[169] That bribe was reported by Edward Partin,[170] a former Hoffa aide turned government informant; Partin's information has been corroborated on several occasions[171] and he has been found credible by both juries and federal officials.[172] Indeed, as noted by Army criminal investigator Russell Bintliff, "There were strong indications of a history of Nixon connections with money from organized crime."[173]

In short, in the words of one Justice Department official, Richard Nixon was "a man who pardoned organized crime figures after millions were spent by the government putting them away, a guy who's had these connections since he was a congressman in the 1940s."[174] And Nixon apparently maintained these connections after resigning his presidency. In October 1975, the *New York Times* reported Nixon's presence with Teamster President Frank Fitzsimmons in a golf tournament at La Costa Country Club.[175] Among Nixon's golfing companions that day was Jackie Presser,[176] a top Teamster official reputedly controlled by the Mob, who has helped dole out millions of dollars in Teamster loans to Mafia enterprises.[177]* Two other golfing companions of Nixon that day were his million-dollar benefactors: Allen Dorfman, the Mob-Teamster financial coordinator, and Tony Provenzano, the former Teamster vice president and convicted Mafia killer.[179]

Nixon's involvement with a man of Provenzano's background drives home an important axiom. The Mafia's millions are extracted by murder. And its bribes are bathed in blood. Which brings us to the most revolting instance of Nixon Administration misconduct on behalf of the Mob.

---

*In December 1980, President-elect Ronald Reagan appointed Presser as a senior economic adviser on his transition team.[178]

The pardon of Angelo "Gyp" DeCarlo. Louis D. Saperstein was in debt to the Mob for $400,000 and could no longer make the interest payments of $5,000 per week.[180] On September 13, 1968, as Mob defector Gerald Zelmanowitz later testified, Zelmanowitz arrived at the headquarters of New Jersey Mafioso Angelo "Gyp" DeCarlo.[181] Zelmanowitz found Saperstein "lying on the floor, purple, bloody, tongue hanging out, spit all over him."[182] Zelmanowitz related,

> I thought he was dead. He was being kicked by Mr. Polverino and Mr. Cecere. He was lifted up off the floor, placed in a chair, hit again, knocked off the chair, picked up and hit again.[183]

DeCarlo then instructed the men to stop the beating and told Saperstein to repay the loan by December 13 or he would "be dead."[184]

On November 26, 1968, Saperstein died of what was initially listed as gastric upset.[185] But the day before, he had written to the FBI describing how DeCarlo and his henchmen had threatened his life.[186] Saperstein wrote that they had "stated many times" that his "wife and son would be maimed or killed."[187] An autopsy prompted by Saperstein's letters disclosed enough arsenic in his body to kill a mule.[188]

The murder of Saperstein was just a day's work for Angelo DeCarlo, a captain in the Genovese Mafia Family[189] described by the FBI as a "methodical gangland executioner."[190] Some of his expertise was revealed in the "DeCavalcante Tapes" of the FBI's electronic surveillance of New Jersey Mafia hangouts during the early 1960s. This 1,200-page transcript was released to the public by court order in 1970,[191] providing a wealth of information about the Mafia.[192] In one conversation, DeCarlo told fellow Mobsters that a good way to handle a murder was to poison the victim and prop him behind the wheel of his auto.[193] DeCarlo then described how he had shot one victim to death: "Itchie was the kid's name. ... I hit him in the heart."[194]

DeCarlo was finally forced to account, in part, for one of his crimes. On March 1970, he was sentenced to 12 years in prison for extortion against Saperstein, based upon the testimony of prosecution witness Gerald Zelmanowitz.[195] But less than two years later, DeCarlo, reportedly terminally ill,[196]* was freed by Richard Nixon on a presidential pardon.[201] Shortly afterward, *Newsweek* reported that DeCarlo, though ailing, was "back at his old rackets, boasting that his connections with Sinatra freed him."[202]

---

*In August 1977, ex-Nazi Herbert Kappler, suffering from terminal cancer, was smuggled out of an Italian military hospital.[197] This escape caused an international scandal and a crisis in Italy.[198] Yet DeCarlo's murderous organization, unlike Kappler's, is still active. And Mobsters have repeatedly feigned illness[199] and even staged a bogus death and funeral[200] to duck the law.

According to FBI informants, as reported by the *New York Times*, the release was obtained through Frank Sinatra's intervention with Vice President Agnew; the details were arranged by John Dean and Agnew aide Peter Malatesta.[203] The release followed an "unrecorded contribution" of $100,000 in cash and another contribution of $50,000 forwarded by Sinatra to a Nixon campaign official.[204] The FBI dismissed these allegations,[205] but Senator Henry Jackson, chairman of the Senate Permanent Investigations Subcommittee, charged that the pardon "bypassed normal procedures and safeguards."[206] Indeed, no one had taken the routine step of consulting officials involved in the prosecution.[207] Citing "serious and disturbing questions as to the reasons and manner" governing the release, Jackson declared, "Something smells and I want to know what."[208]

While DeCarlo was free and back at his rackets, Zelmanowitz, who had been relocated under a new identity,[209] was treated very differently by the Nixon Justice Department. In 1973, Zelmanowitz's cover was destroyed when a background check disclosed that none of the documents which the Justice Department had promised to supply for his relocation had been filed.[210] The Internal Revenue Service then enforced a tax lien against him, contrary to a prior agreement.[211] Amazingly, enforcing the lien were the very same IRS agents whom Zelmanowitz had previously identified to federal investigators as recipients of bribes in connection with his earlier Mob activity.[212]

The incredible conduct of the Justice Department was highlighted in Zelmanowitz's testimony in 1973 before Senator Jackson's Permanent Investigations Subcommittee:

> While DeCarlo lives in luxury and leisure in his home, I and my family are once again dislocated with our property seized and in fear for our lives. Unfortunately, it seems that there is no one left but this committee to heed me.
>
> Even at this moment I still do not have protection from the U.S. Marshal's Service although it has been requested. I have been living for the last week, since last Saturday night, in a motel room. But for the courtesy of your staff, who picked me up this morning and brought me to this committee, armed, I was able to come here.[213]

At the conclusion of his testimony, Zelmanowitz stated,

> I don't know what happens now when I leave this committee room. . . . I am in fear of my life. I do not know where to go or what to do when this is over.[214]

Zelmanowitz had genuine reason for concern. For as *Newsweek* reported in 1977, four Mob defectors under the Justice Department witness protection plan were murdered between 1971 and 1977.[215] And six others died from "such ambiguous causes as drug overdoses, suicides and an auto accident."[216] The Justice Department conducted an 18-month investigation of corruption in the program, leading to the indictment of one U.S. Marshal and the resignation of four others.[217] One marshal learned that "the word was you could buy the location of a witness for $5,000 in Jersey."[218] But these marshals were merely emulating their boss, Richard Nixon, who had well earned the appellation "the Syndicate's President."[219]

/3/ The Ford and Carter Administrations

In August 1974, when President Nixon resigned the presidency in the face of imminent impeachment, his term was completed by his appointed second, Gerald Ford. A go-along politician and Warren Commission alumnus, Ford promptly pardoned his sponsor. This was not the first time, however, that a Mob-involved figure benefited from Ford's lax judgment.

Ralph Salerno, described by the *New York Times* as the nation's leading organized crime expert,[220] estimated in 1969 that the votes of about 25 members of Congress could be delivered by Mob pressure.[221] He also reported that "hundreds of private bills have been slid through at the tail end of congressional sessions to forestall deportation proceedings against Syndicate men."[222] Two examples were furnished in a 1977 story by NBC News on the Mafia takeover of a rural Wisconsin cheese factory, which defrauded supplying dairy farmers of $500,000 and left 55 workers unemployed.[223] NBC reported,

> Through what is believed to be a virtual monopoly of the companies which produce and import Italian cheeses, the mob has been able to get immigration approval for Sicilian gangsters, who come here posing as cheesemakers.* In one case, in 1971,

*To revive traditions and restore discipline, as the *New York Times* noted, American Mob bosses have recently "been importing Mafiosi from Sicily and adding them to their ranks."[224] According to immigration officials, the late New York Mafia boss Carlo Gambino brought in at least 2,000 aliens.[225] Other Mafia bosses who have followed Gambino's lead include Steve Magaddino, Carmine Tramunti and Carmine Galente,[226] the last of whom has "brought in an army of men."[227] As top Mafia defector Vincent Teresa commented, "These Sicilian Mafiosi will run through a wall, put their heads in a bucket of acid for you if they're told to ... because they're disciplined."[228]

One of the better known imports was Tomaso Buscetta, former chief executioner for the Sicilian Mafia.[229] According to the *New York Daily News*, he was "brought here to lend his lethal expertise to Carlo Gambino."[230] But Buscetta is "only one of several professional killers imported from Italy by Cosa Nostra chiefs."[231]

legislation was introduced in Congress on behalf of a cheese company with ties to organized crime, to help keep one of its cheese makers in the country. In the House, the bill was introduced by then-Congressman Gerald Ford; in the Senate, by William Proxmire of Wisconsin. Both Proxmire and Ford said they were responding to a routine request by a constituent. Neither bill passed.[232]

NBC also reported that "under the Nixon and Ford administrations, the federal strike forces against organized crime were hampered by political interference and bureaucratic wrangling," with three strike forces shut down in 1976.[233]

In 1976, Jimmy Carter, a decent man, became the first U.S. president chosen without the specter of assassination since the shooting in Dallas 13 years earlier. Under the Carter Administration, the FBI was refocused against organized crime, the CIA restrained from immoral intrigues, and conspiracy finally acknowledged by Congress in President Kennedy's murder. But by then, more sweeping measures were required to jar America from its post-assassination course.

Thus, facing extinction under President Kennedy's Administration, the Mafia mushroomed to new heights of power after his assassination—murdering its thousands and plundering its billions with ever increasing impunity. And it greased the wheels for its murderous machinations with a massive campaign of corruption, nurtured to obscene proportions by at least one post-assassination president. Yet as *Life* magazine found,

> if the Fix is the Mob's most useful tool, the Cover-up is of equal importance to public officials who allow themselves to be fixed or who ignore Fixes. Case in point: the censoring of the official report on organized crime of President Johnson's own crime commission.[234]

The following chapter will consider the cover-up of another Johnson commission report, whose ultimate subject was the same.

□ 17 □

The Warren Commission Cover-Up

The two fatal shootings generated unprecedented attention and controversy. A committee, named after its distinguished chairman, was charged to investigate. After several weeks of hearings and deliberations, it presented a report to the chief executive.[2]

The report found two maladjusted men responsible for the killings, and appeared to allay nagging suspicions that others were involved.[3] The *Boston Herald* reported that the misgivings of "serious and earnest minded people" were "dissipated by the calm and dispassionate recital of the evidence."[4] The *New York Times* concluded that the committee had done "a great public service" in "assuring the American people and the world that no intentional or notorious injustice [had] been done."[5] Another leading newspaper attributed to the report "the earmarks of fairness, consideration, shrewdness and coolness."[6] It seemed pointless, even presumptuous, to question the findings of a committee chaired by such an eminent figure: Harvard University President Abbott Lawrence Lowell.[7] And so in 1927, with all doubts dissolved by the Lowell Committee's report, shoe worker Nicola Sacco and fish peddler Bartolomeo Vanzetti were sent to the electric chair.[8]

But history returned a radically different verdict on the Sacco and Vanzetti case. Over the years, it became clear that prejudice more than evidence had linked the two Italian "anarchists" to the April 15, 1920 robbery and murders at the Slater and Morill Shoe Company in South Braintree, Massachusetts.[9] In 1977, 50 years after their executions, the "very real possibility that a grievous miscarriage of justice occurred" was finally recognized by the State of Massachusetts.[10] In a proclamation signed by Governor Michael Dukakis, the state designated a Sacco and Vanzetti Memorial Day, stipulating that "any stigma and disgrace should be forever removed" from their names.[11]

The passage of time also revealed the identity of the real South Braintree killers. In 1920, before he became a top Mafia don, Frank "Butsey" Morelli and four brothers had specialized in rifling railroad cars filled with textiles and shoes.[12] The Morellis had been indicted in connection with a shipment of shoes stolen from, of all places, the Slater and Morill Company in South Braintree.[13] Within weeks after the April 15 robbery and murders at that factory, the Morelli brothers were put under police surveillance as prime suspects.[14] And a subsequent confession, physical evidence, eyewitness descriptions, and factors of motivation all implicated the Morellis in the crime.[15]

This evidence was corroborated in 1973, with the publication of the memoirs of Mafia defector Vincent Teresa.[16] Teresa wrote that in the mid-1950s, he visited Butsey Morelli, who had terminal cancer, shortly after an article in the *Boston Globe* accused Morelli of the Slater and Morill robbery-murders.[17] During that visit, Morelli told Teresa "we whacked them out, we killed those guys in the robbery. Those two greaseballs [Sacco and Vanzetti] took it on the chin."[18] Teresa noted that Morelli "didn't brag about anything—ever."[19]

In 1964, the Warren Commission once again implicated two lone nuts—this time a crackpot and a clown—in another case that had all the earmarks of Mafia culpability. This chapter will consider some factors behind this shameful misjudgment, including administration coercion, Commission credulity, Mob subversion, and the misconduct of America's most overrated hero.

/1/ A Predetermined Solution

Before the Kennedy assassination probe even began, certain top government officials had stipulated who the culprit would be. Reviewing the Government's performance in that investigation, the Senate Intelligence Committee reported in 1976:

> Almost immediately after the assassination, [FBI] Director Hoover, the Justice Department and the White House "exerted pressure" on senior Bureau officials to complete their investigation and issue a factual report supporting the conclusion that Oswald was the lone assassin.[20]

Reflecting this bias in a telephone conversation of November 24, 1963, immediately following Oswald's murder, Hoover stated:

> The thing I am most concerned about, and so is Mr. Katzenbach, is having something issued so we can convince the public that Oswald is the real assassin.[21]

The next day, Deputy Attorney General Nicholas Katzenbach wrote a memo asserting:

> The public must be satisfied that Oswald was the assassin; that he did not have confederates who are still at large; and that the evidence was such that he would have been convicted at trial.[22]

Katzenbach continued, "Speculation about Oswald's motivation ought to be cut off."[23]

During early December, as the Warren Commission began its investigation, Hoover orchestrated press leaks proclaiming Oswald to be the "lone and unaided assassin."[24] According to William Sullivan, former number-three man at the FBI, Hoover's motive was "to blunt the drive for an independent investigation of the assassination."[25] On December 13, in harmony with Hoover's cues, *Time* magazine previewed a confidential FBI report to the Warren Commission.[26] The report would find, *Time* proclaimed, that "Oswald, acting in his own lunatic loneliness, was indeed the President's assassin."[27]

/2/ Withheld Evidence

In line with the Hoover-Katzenbach quest for a simple solution and a satisfied public, evidence that contradicted official dogma was withheld or ignored. The Senate Intelligence Committee reported in 1976, as summarized by the *Washington Post*, that "senior officials of both the CIA and the FBI covered up crucial information in the course of investigating President Kennedy's assassination."[28] A similar conclusion was offered by Judge Burt W. Griffin, former assistant counsel for the Warren Commission. In 1978, Judge Griffin told the House Assassinations Committee that "evidence in the possession of government agencies was deliberately withheld from the Warren Commission."[29]

Particularly derelict in his performance was Commission member Allen Dulles—the former CIA chief who resigned following the Bay of Pigs invasion.[30] Curiously, at the Commission's first executive session, Dulles gave each of his colleagues a book purporting to show how American assassinations were always perpetrated by lone, demented men.[31] Then, throughout the Commission meetings, Dulles concealed his knowledge of relevant CIA-Mafia assassination plots against Castro, including the so-called "AMLASH" plot.[32] The Senate Intelligence Committee concluded in 1976 that the AMLASH operation "should have raised major concerns within the CIA about its possible connection with the Kennedy assassination" but that information on it "was not supplied to either the Warren Commission or the FBI."[33]

/3/ Accommodation

Although Chief Justice Earl Warren was heavily involved in his Commission's investigation,[34] the other Commissioners had little touch with its affairs,[35] while the staff members each explored limited areas.[36] And without an adequate grasp of even the limited evidence that the Commission had been provided, these Commissioners and staffers found themselves trapped by the FBI's predetermined conclusion. This dilemma was noted in executive session by J. Lee Rankin, the Commission's general counsel:

> Part of our difficulty ... is that [the FBI officials] have no problem. They have decided that it is Oswald who committed the assassination, they have decided that no one else was involved. ...[37]

The same complaint was expressed by Commission members Russell and Boggs.[38] Working under tight time constraints,[39] with no serious exploration of alternatives,[40] the Commission thus became increasingly committed to this simplistic solution.*

Commission curiosity may have also been contained by fabricated national security concerns. Just such a situation occurred during the Watergate maneuvering, when a CIA directive citing bogus security considerations aborted an FBI probe of the White House "plumbers."[43] And in fact, Hoover justified his opposition to an independent assassination probe by alluding to "aspects which would complicate our foreign relations."[44] No such "aspects" emerged, however, when the case was reviewed in the late 1970s by the Senate and House.[45] Also, the FBI discovered forged letters linking Oswald with Fidel Castro;[46] these may have been used to raise a smoke screen of national security for some unsuspecting Commission investigator.

---

*Considering Chief Justice Warren's central role in the investigation and his amazing handling of Jack Ruby's testimony, it is more difficult to fathom an innocent explanation for his behavior. Whatever his role in the cover-up, however, it was not performed readily. For Warren initially declined President Johnson's offer to preside over the assassination investigation.[41] And when Warren finally acquiesced in a private meeting with LBJ, he emerged with tears in his eyes.[42]

The credulity required to swallow such a ruse was subsequently displayed by one Commission member, Gerald Ford. As reported in *Time* on February 4, 1974,

> After meeting with Nixon for nearly two hours, Vice President Gerald Ford declared that the White House was in possession of evidence that "will exonerate the President" of complicity in the conspiracy to conceal the origins of the Watergate wiretap-burglary.[47]

When asked what the evidence was, Ford replied that

> the President had offered to show it to him, but he had "not had time" to look at it.[48]

The cynic might easily conclude that the subservience Gerald Ford exhibited on the Warren Commission was the same quality sought and achieved by Richard Nixon in his vice presidential appointee.

One glaring manifestation of the Warren Commission's lack of critical judgment was its infamous "single bullet theory." To reconcile the filmed sequence of assassination events[49] with the capabilities of Oswald's rifle,[50] the Commission proposed that a single bullet fired from the Depository Building struck President Kennedy in "the base of the back of his neck," exited from his throat, and then passed downward through Governor Connally's back, chest, wrist and thigh.[51] But this proposition is incredible given the conclusions stated during Kennedy's autopsy by Dr. James Humes, the chief surgeon. As noted in FBI reports of November 23,[52] November 26,[53] December 9,[54] and January 13,[55] and as subsequently reaffirmed by two agents present at the autopsy,[56] a bullet struck the president "just below the shoulder," at "an angle of 45 to 60 degrees downward." It "penetrated to a distance of less than a finger length," leaving "a hole of short depth with no point of exit," and apparently "worked its way out of the victim's back during cardiac massage."[57] Bullet holes in Kennedy's shirt and jacket in fact pinpointed the wound's position in the shoulder,[58] several inches below the neckline location invented by the Warren Commission.[59] It was thus unlikely that a bullet entering there at a downward angle passed upward through Kennedy's throat, flipped in midair, and plunged downward into Connally's back, as the Commission's hypothesis required.[60]

Continuing in its flight of fantasy, the Commission proposed that the body wounds to Kennedy and Connally were inflicted by one bullet which was found on a stretcher at Parkland Hospital and matched to Oswald's rifle.[61] But it was difficult to explain how this bullet, in nearly perfect condition,[62] could have shattered Connally's fifth rib and right wrist and left metal fragments in his chest, wrist and thigh.[63] Indeed, two of the president's autopsy surgeons[64] and forensic experts[65] found it highly unlikely that this bullet could have inflicted all of this damage. And in U.S. Army ballistic tests simulating Connally's wounds, bullets fired in either rib or wrist bones were significantly deformed.[66]

In an attempt to salvage its single-bullet theory from this contrary evidence, the Commission tangled itself in a spectacular self-contradiction. The results of the Army ballistic tests did not apply, it proposed, because

> the bullet which entered the Governor's chest had already *lost velocity* by passing through the President's neck. Moreover, the *large* wound on the Governor's back would be explained by a bullet which was *yawing*. . . .[67]

Later in the report, however, the Commission addressed another dilemma: how could a bullet transitting Kennedy's neck have retained enough momentum to have penetrated five layers of Connally's skin and shattered two of his bones?[68] This time, citing the same Army ballistic tests, the Commission stated, "From these tests, it was concluded that the bullet *lost little of its velocity* in penetrating the president's neck."[69] Now, the bullet exiting his neck "*had retained most of its stability*."[70] This explained the character of Governor Connally's back wound, as noted elsewhere in the Warren Report:

> Because of the *small size* and clean-cut edges of the wound on the Governor's back, Dr. Robert Shaw concluded that it was an entry wound.[71]

The Commission's attempts to bend evidence to fit its desired conclusions thus reached schizophrenic proportions. Yet some of its representatives were bothered by the discrepancies. Staff member Wesley Liebler, for one, described the testimony of the chief witness against Oswald in the Tippit slaying as "contradictory" and "worthless."[72] Liebler also wrote a 26-page memo criticizing the first draft of the Warren Report, calling Oswald's asserted capability to easily fire the assassination shots "a fairy tale."[73] Several staff members were skeptical of the testimony of Marina Oswald,[74] a key witness against her husband.[75] One was Norman Redlich, who wrote a memo stating that she had "lied to the Secret Service, the FBI, and this Commission repeatedly."[76]

/4/ **Beyond Blundering**

For the Commission's accommodation to the lone-assassin line there were thus many explanations. Administration pressure. Incomplete information. Credulity. And a misdirected initial focus on Oswald—a versatile mercenary, apparently, whose worldwide trail of involvements was difficult to untangle.[77] Indeed, it is tempting to write off the assassination cover-up as an unfortunate exercise in blundering—as the meaningless, lunatic crime that the assassination was represented to be.

Benign excuses fail, however, to cover the Commission's gross mishandling of its second target of investigation, Jack Ruby. In early news reports and in voluminous FBI files, one fact plainly emerged: Ruby was affiliated with the Mob—the same organization with the clear motive and means to murder President Kennedy.[78] But amazingly, the Commission concluded that there was "no credible evidence that Jack Ruby was active in the criminal underworld."[79] This bizarre reversal of reality was noted by Congressman Stewart McKinney in a question to an FBI spokesman during the House Assassinations hearings:

> Wasn't it pretty well known to the FBI that Jack Ruby, No. 1, was a member of organized crime, No. 2, he ran a strip joint and had been somewhat commonly referred to as a supplier of both women and booze to political and police figures in the city of Dallas.
>
> Didn't you find it a little difficult to accept the Warren Commission's final output on Ruby with the knowledge that the FBI had put into the Commission?[80]

In a similar vein, *Time* noted how "the Warren Commission failed abysmally to pursue FBI leads linking Oswald's own assassin, Jack Ruby, to the Mob."[81]

Indeed, it was only by the crudest suppression and distortion of evidence that the Warren Commission could hide Ruby's Mob connection. Again and again, materials in National Archives files relating to organized crime were omitted from the 26 volumes of hearings and exhibits published by the Commission.[82] Sometimes, documents were published in the hearings and exhibits excluding the particular pages dealing with underworld involvement.[83] In one instance, the paragraphs reporting Ruby's frequent association with the Mafia boss of Dallas were blanked out of an otherwise perfect photoreproduction.[84]

Even after such censorship, however, many more clues to Ruby's Syndicate involvement remained in the published hearings and exhibits on which the Commission's report was based. For its absolution of Ruby, therefore, the Commission was forced into such audacious sleights-of-hand as this previously quoted gem: "Virtually all of Ruby's Chicago friends stated he had no close connection with organized crime."[85] The Commission neglected to report that one of the cited "Chicago friends" was in fact a top Mob executioner,[86] and that five others had assorted criminal involvements.[87]

/5/ **Mob Subversion**

Without any legitimate explanation, therefore, glaring clues to Mafia assassination culpability were buried, distorted and disingenuously deflected in the Warren Commission's final report. But this cover-up of Mob involvement was hardly surprising. For the assassination investigation was compromised and obstructed by the same network of corruption through which the Mafia routinely subverts the government and press. Following are examples of how this network operates, and how it encompassed the assassination probe.

Watchdog for justice. Our brief excursion through underworld corruption begins with a courtroom fix. It is often a sophisticated affair, featuring an error in testimony, a prosecution oversight or some other technical ploy staged by the Mob, allowing the bribed judge to thwart conviction with all the trappings of decorum.[88] Yet sometimes, the arrangement is contemptuously transparent.

Such was the case in the 1972 murder conspiracy trial of Joe Bonanno, Jr., son of the top Mafia don. The prosecution's case was solid; five of Bonanno's codefendants had already pleaded guilty to various charges.[89] But when U.S. attorney Ann Bowen questioned government witnesses in the Arizona courtroom, Walter E. Craig, the presiding judge, ridiculed her presentation by rolling his eyes, burying his face in his hands, laughing openly, and mimicking one witness in a falsetto voice.[90] Juror Robert Clark noted that Judge Craig "had incredulous looks" on his face, and that "his conduct was anything but impartial."[91] Such conduct was not out of character for Craig, however, who was noted for questionable leniency and personal ties to Mob defendants in his courtroom.[92]

Despite Judge Craig's grotesque efforts to discredit the prosecution's case, the jury found Bonanno guilty of conspiracy to murder as charged.[93] Six weeks after the conviction, however, Craig held a 70-minute hearing and freed Bonanno; he claimed that the jury might have mistakenly based its verdict on Bonanno's involvement in a shakedown attempt.[94] Juror Robert Clark subsequently filed a petition to the U.S. Supreme Court calling for Craig's impeachment.[95] Clark said Craig's speculations about the jury's basis for conviction were "as slanderous as they are false."[96] Prosecutor

Ann Bowen was likewise incensed by Craig's peculiar reversal of the government's hard-fought conviction.[97] And jury foreman Jerry Boyd was "flabbergasted" by his action.[98]

Although unusually flagrant, the conduct of Judge Craig typifies the Mob's pervasive, crippling influence in America's criminal courts[99]—an influence underscored by Craig's earlier tenure as president of the American Bar Association.[100] Yet even more unsettling was the pivotal role that Craig had played in the Kennedy assassination probe. As related in the Warren Commission report, Craig was designated "to participate in the investigation and to advise the Commission whether in his opinion the proceedings conformed to the basic principles of American justice. Mr. Craig accepted this assignment and participated fully and without limitation. He attended Commission hearings in person or through his appointed assistants. All working papers, reports, and other data in Commission files were made available. . . ."[101]

A story about Ruby. Another avenue through which the Kennedy assassination probe was subverted was Mafia manipulation of the press. The technique was hardly novel; in 1964, a New York Mafioso told an FBI informant that

> money was being gathered to fight Valachi's testimony and the Senate [rackets] hearings. They are getting in touch with people in the news media and political figures to hold up any legislation which may result.[102]

Indeed, the Mob has secured major influence over America's press through widespread payoffs to accommodating reporters,[103] intimidation,[104] and control of many outlets of distribution.[105] Over the past two decades, this growing Mob influence has been exhibited by censorship of organized crime coverage[106] and, in some cases, favorable publicity for Mobsters.[107] Yet even back in 1959, following Senate exposure of Mob leverage over several major newspapers, Senator Sam Ervin could conclude, "Your evidence indicates to me that the press in the United States is not quite as free as it is supposed to be."[108]

The Mob's penetration into the Fourth Estate is illustrated by the involvements of three of Ruby's Dallas acquaintances, all prominent media figures. One was Gordon McLendon, owner of the Liberty Broadcasting Network and of radio stations throughout the country, including KLIF in Dallas.[109] A friend of Jack Ruby,[110] as were several KLIF employees,[111] McLendon gave Ruby "a lot of free plugs."[112] In 1971, he reportedly offered assistance to the campaign to spring Jimmy Hoffa.[113] A second influential press figure well-acquainted with Ruby was Matty Brescia.[114] Employed at one point by McLendon's Liberty Network, Brescia headed a public relations firm whose accounts included a major basketball team.[115]

Rounding out the bunch was Tony Zoppi, a locally prominent entertainment columnist for the *Dallas Morning News*[116] who moved to Las Vegas after 1963.[117] Zoppi was close to Ruby, McLendon and Brescia.[118] He also knew Mobsters Joseph Campisi,[119] Russell D. Matthews[120] and Lewis McWillie,[121] sending "regards to McWillie" in a letter to Brescia.[122]

Of the journalistic services Zoppi performed for the Mob, most mundane were his repeated promotions of the Campisi-owned Egyptian Lounge,[123] a Dallas Mafia hangout.[124] Although Zoppi himself frequented that restaurant,[125] he assured the House Assassinations Committee that Dallas "had no syndicated or organized crime that he was aware of."[126] Zoppi also emphasized that Ruby "was not involved in gambling," and lamented that "quick buck artists are saying Jack went down there to plan the assassination. . . . All of a sudden he's a CIA agent, a Mafia don, etc, etc. Sickening."[127]

Zoppi stuck his neck out even further to mask Ruby's Mob connection in a 1973 column entitled "Ruby in Retrospect."[128] Attempting to provide an innocent explanation for Ruby's August 1959 trip to Cuba, to be discussed in the next chapter, Zoppi wrote:

> Jack had a good friend named Lewis McWillie who was a casino executive at the Tropicana in Havana. He asked McWillie if he would like me to fly to Cuba and do a story on the Tropicana's show. Lew agreed. . . . The date was set for December 17, 1960. By coincidence, I received a call from . . . Las Vegas inviting me to the "summit meeting"—an unprecedented show featuring Frank Sinatra, Dean Martin, Sammy Davis, Joey Bishop and Peter Lawford. I called Ruby and told him I would have to postpone the trip. . . . He said he would depart as scheduled. . . .[129]

When questioned by the House Assassinations Committee in 1978, Zoppi repeated this story with major modifications,[130] and McWillie backed him up.[131] But the charade proved embarrassing to both since in 1964, McWillie had detailed a totally different explanation for Ruby's visit to Cuba.[132] Moreover, that visit occurred five months before the "summit meeting" show Zoppi was to review, as pointed out by skeptical Committee interviewers.[133]

Suppressing the Marcello assassination threat. A particular flair for press manipulation has been displayed by Mobster-attorney Sidney Korshak, whom senior Justice Department officials described in 1976 as one of "the most powerful members of the underworld."[134] The *New York Times* noted that Chicago newspapers repeatedly mentioned Korshak's business and social dealings, but sidestepped his underworld affiliation by describing him "with such vague phrases as 'wheeler-dealer' and 'mystery man.' "[135] One senior Chicago reporter cited two instances in which editors deleted unfavorable references to Korshak, noting "you couldn't get a story about him in the paper."[136] And a friend recalled Korshak's boasts that he was able to influence the *Chicago Tribune* to soft-peddle stories about him.[137] Such censorship has long been par for the course in Chicago, where as *Life* reported in 1967, gangsters "swing enough influence in city rooms to get a story killed or softened to the point where it is almost an apology."[138]

A recent incident involving Korshak again demonstrated censorship protecting the Mob. In the summer of 1979, a sequence of "Doonesbury" cartoons satirized Korshak's links with Governor Jerry Brown of California.[139] The sequence mentioned, among other things, a $1,000 campaign contribution Korshak gave Brown on May 4, 1974.[140] But Californians were spared the embarrassing circumstances when major newspapers in Los Angeles, San Francisco and other cities which normally printed "Doonesbury" dropped that particular sequence.[141] Like the Voice of America transmitting across the Iron Curtain, some radio stations in San Francisco filled in by broadcasting the suppressed cartoons.[142]

Korshak's most noteworthy effort to suppress information occurred in connection with the Kennedy assassination. The event in question was Carlos Marcello's careless diatribe of September 1962, as discussed earlier, in which the Mafia boss outlined a plot to murder President Kennedy.[143] The incident was made public when informant Edward Becker described it to Pulitzer Prize-winner Ed Reid, who related it in *The Grim Reapers*, which was published in 1969.[144] The FBI, in turn, learned of Becker's account when Reid showed his manuscript to Los Angeles Bureau officials on May 6, 1967.[145]

On May 7, just one day after Reid first informed it of Marcello's assassination threat, the FBI's Los Angeles office received allegations discrediting Becker.[146] As reported in an FBI memo of May 17, the FBI learned through an intermediary that Korshak had been discussing Becker; Korshak

> advised that Becker was trying to shake down some of Korshak's friends for money by claiming he is the collaborator with Reid and that for money he could keep the names of these people out of the book.[147]

Korshak further stated that "Becker was a no-good shakedown artist."[148] Subsequent FBI documents contain repeated references to the Bureau's use of Korshak's allegations, but no references to his own background, activities, or possible motives in defaming Becker.[149] This was rather surprising, since Korshak had been repeatedly linked to organized crime in the FBI's own files.[150]

Although charged to pursue any new developments in the Kennedy assassination case,[151] the FBI accepted Korshak's allegations and took no action to investigate the Marcello threat.[152] Instead, as noted in a staff report of the House Assassinations Committee, it assisted the effort to suppress Becker's report, exhibiting "a strong desire to 'discredit' the information without having actually to investigate it."[153] On May 26, 1967, for example, the man who forwarded the Korshak allegations to the FBI contacted author Ed Reid; an FBI agent visited Reid five days later.[154] Their mission, as noted in a June 5 FBI memo to FBI Director Hoover, was to "discredit Becker to Reid in order that the Carlos Marcello incident would be deleted from the book by Reid."[155] The only FBI directive issued regarding the entire Becker affair was a handwritten notation by Assistant Director Cartha DeLoach; it requested the Bureau to "discreetly identify the publisher" of the Reid book.[156]

/6/ The Two FBIs

The FBI's handling of the Marcello assassination threat "had highly disturbing implications," noted a staff report of the House Assassinations Committee.[157] So too did the overall conduct of FBI Director Hoover and other top-level FBI officials in the Kennedy assassination probe. Hoover, who immediately mandated that Oswald was the lone assassin,[158] opposed the creation of any public commission to study the case.[159] After the Warren Commission was established, the Senate Intelligence Committee noted, it "was perceived as an adversary by both Hoover and senior FBI officials."[160] William Sullivan, former FBI assistant director, observed that Hoover "did not want the Warren Commission to conduct an exhaustive investigation."[161] And on two occasions, the Senate Intelligence Committee reported, Hoover "asked for all derogatory material on Warren Commission members and staff contained in the FBI files."[162]

The dichotomy between the diligent performance of agents and the questionable conduct of leadership—most notably Hoover—extended to a broader area of FBI functioning. As observed by Ralph Salerno, retired organized crime expert of the New York Police Department,

> There are, in fact, two FBIs. . . . One is the splendid organization itself; the other is its long-time director.[163]

Salerno was referring, in particular, to J. Edgar Hoover's atrocious record on organized crime.[164]

Hoover directed the FBI to fight car thieves, bank robbers, and the Communist menace decried by his friend[165] Joe McCarthy.* But he left organized crime almost totally unscathed,[172] and until the early 1960s, steadfastly denied that a national crime syndicate existed.[173] Hoover refused to acknowledge that fact even after the spectacular police bust of the Mob's 1957 conclave in Apalachin, New York, which was investigated in depth by his own New York agents.[174] Illustrating his position, in 1958 he had an FBI report on the Mafia rescinded, calling it "baloney."[175] FBI personnel who probed the Mob found their work thwarted, their careers jeopardized.[176] Moreover, Hoover consistently opposed special efforts to fight the Mob;[177] it was largely his opposition that caused a federal task force on organized crime to disband in 1958, with its recommendations rejected.[178] Only after Robert Kennedy became attorney general in his brother's administration was Hoover prodded into action against the Syndicate.[179]

While ignoring the Mob in his official capacity, Hoover was less exclusive in his personal relationships. He often stayed for free at the Las Vegas hotels of construction tycoon Del E. Webb,[180] whose holdings were permeated with organized crime entanglements.[181] Hoover and Webb also met frequently on vacations in Del Mar, California.[182] During Hoover's annual trips to that city's luxurious Del Charro Motel, his bill was paid by its owner, Clint Murchison, Jr.,[183] Hoover's "bosom pal."[184] Murchison, a Texas oil tycoon who backed Lyndon Johnson,[185] was questionably involved with both Bobby Baker and the Teamsters.[186] But Hoover continued to accept Murchison's hospitality, even while Murchison's dealings with Baker were being investigated by both the Senate[187] and Hoover's own FBI.[188]

Hoover's free vacations at the Del Charro, during which he often attended the nearby Murchison-owned Del Mar Race Track,[189] did not lead to the best of company. As Jack Anderson reported in 1970,

> The late Clint Murchison picked up Hoover's tab ($100-a-day suites) year after year at the ... Del Charro near their favorite race track ... at the same time some of the nation's most notorious gamblers and racketeers have been registered there.[190]

---

*Tips from Hoover's FBI formed the basis for most of McCarthy's allegations about Communists in government, few of which were ever substantiated.[166] Hoover was also friendly with McCarthy aide Roy Cohn,[167] an attorney who enjoys good relations with the Mob-Teamster set[168] and who assisted its campaign to spring Jimmy Hoffa.[169]

In 1955, the leadership of the Senate Permanent Investigations Subcommittee passed from Joseph McCarthy to John McClellan, one of McCarthy's earliest critics.[170] It was only then that the subcommittee stopped investigating the Communist Party, which has been linked to little except outrageous rhetoric, and focused on the Mafia, which has been linked to countless murders and other crimes.[171]

Given Hoover's position as the nation's top law enforcement officer, these and other contacts[191] with individuals linked to organized crime were certainly questionable. But the real shocker was his contact with Frank Costello, a top Mafia boss of the 1940s.[192] According to *Time*, in a 1975 cover story on Hoover, some FBI agents spoke of his "sometimes traveling to Manhattan to meet one of the Mafia's top figures, Frank Costello. The two would meet in Central Park."[193] Historian Arthur Schlesinger, Jr. reported, "The fact that Hoover met with Costello is confirmed by William Hundley and Edward Bennett Williams";[194] Hundley, a former Justice Department official, is a credible source. The impropriety was glaring—the FBI chief meeting the top Mafia chieftain, impeding efforts to fight the Mob, and resisting a proper investigation of the Mob's suspected assassination of a president.

Hoover's affinity for organized crime was consistent with other aspects of his character. Contrary to the heroic image Americans projected upon him, Hoover was a "bureaucratic genius," as *Time* observed, with an "acute public relations sense"; he "cared less about crime than about perpetuating his crime-busting image."[195] He amassed files of derogatory information on many people,[196] including tapes of an extramarital affair of Dr. Martin Luther King which he sent to King's wife and played for reporters.[197] In addition to loathing blacks,[198] Hoover harbored considerable animosity toward Robert Kennedy.[199] And Hoover demonstrated his contempt for both, as reported by former assistant William Sullivan, by delaying the announcement of James Earl Ray's capture "so he could interrupt TV coverage of Bobby's burial."[200] Equally antagonistic toward Robert Kennedy was Clyde Tolson, Hoover's FBI deputy and companion,[201] who was extensively briefed on the FBI's activities during the Kennedy assassination probe.[202] According to Sullivan, Tolson once said of Robert Kennedy, "I hope someone shoots and kills the son of a bitch."[203]

/7/ Base Alliances in the White House

Sharing Hoover's opposition to an independent assassination probe was President Lyndon Johnson. On November 29, 1963, a week after President Kennedy's death, Hoover told Johnson over the telephone that the FBI's report on the case, portraying Oswald as the lone assassin, was almost finished.[204] In a memo that day recounting the conversation, Hoover wrote:

> The President stated he wanted to get by just with my file and my report. I told him I thought it would be very bad to have a rash of investigations. He then indicated the only way to stop it is to appoint a high-level committee to evaluate my report and tell the House and Senate not to go ahead with the investigation.[205]

The same day, President Johnson signed an executive order creating the Warren Commission,[206] which would so faithfully obey the Hoover-Katzenbach injunction to "convince the public that Oswald is the real assassin."[207]

Given Johnson's alleged underworld ties, it is indeed questionable if he would have wanted an objective probe of the assassination. And incidents in his career, beginning with his years at the Texas State Teachers College in San Marcos, amply demonstrate his ability to coordinate a cover-up. As reported by Pulitzer Prize-winner Robert Caro, Johnson "stole his first election in 1930" for a seat on the college senior council, and won another school election by blackmail.[208] Through many such underhanded political tricks, Johnson became "so deeply and widely mistrusted" by his classmates that they called him "Bull," for "Bullshit"—the nickname recorded in his yearbook.[209] And Johnson's incessant lying earned him the reputation of being "the biggest liar on campus."[210]

Yet prior to 1981, not one biography of Johnson reported this information about his college years.[211] The reason, Caro explained, was that while Johnson was still an undergraduate at San Marcos, he

> arranged to have excised (literally cut out) from hundreds of copies of the college yearbook certain pages that gave clues to his years there (luckily for history, some copies escaped the scissors). Issues of the college newspaper that chronicle certain crucial episodes in his college career are missing from the college library. A ruthless use thereafter of political power in San Marcos made faculty members and classmates reluctant to discuss those aspects of his career.[212]

A second precedent of cover-up involving both Johnson and the Mob was, as previously quoted from *Life*, "the censoring of the official report on organized crime of President Johnson's own crime commission."[213] A third was the Bobby Baker affair.

Bobby Baker was secretary to the Senate majority leader for eight years,[214] during which time he accumulated an estimated $2 million.[215] He resigned on October 7, 1963, a month after his grand-scale influence peddling was exposed by the *Washington Post*.[216] The ensuing scandal proved embarrassing to his mentor and boss, Lyndon Johnson, who had called Baker "one of my trusted friends."[217] As a result of the scandal, in fact, Johnson had been expected to be dumped by President Kennedy from the second spot on the 1964 Democratic ticket.[218]

Baker's far-flung corruption eventually brought him a one-to-three year prison sentence on seven counts of tax evasion, theft, and fraud involving nearly $100,000 in political payoff money.[219] Among the transactions unraveled were dealings with Mobsters and Teamsters in Texas, Las Vegas, the

Caribbean, and his home base of Washington, D.C.,[220] where he functioned as the Mob-Teamster "man in Washington."[221] But little information was obtained from Baker himself, who during his appearances before the Senate Rules Committee repeatedly invoked the Fifth Amendment.[222] And the day after Vice President Lyndon Johnson succeeded Kennedy as president, the Organized Crime Section of the Justice Department stopped receiving information on Baker from Hoover's FBI.[223]

A possible insight into the hush on Baker was provided in a five-page narration of a conversation between Johnson and House Speaker John McCormack, reported in *The Washington Payoff* by ex-Washington lobbyist Robert Winter-Berger.[224] Winter-Berger had met McCormack through Nat Voloshen,[225] a Mob fixer of enormous influence[226] and a close contact of McCormack.[227] On February 4, 1964, Winter-Berger was discussing public relations with McCormack in McCormack's Washington office.[228] President Johnson then barged in and began ranting hysterically, Winter-Berger reported, oblivious to the lobbyist's presence.[229] During his long tirade, Johnson said:

> John, that son of a bitch [Bobby Baker] is going to ruin me. If that cocksucker talks, I'm gonna land in jail. ... I practically raised that motherfucker, and now he's gonna make me the first President of the United States to spend the last days of his life behind bars.[230]

When Johnson finally noticed Winter-Berger's presence, McCormack explained that the visiting lobbyist was a close friend of Nat Voloshen.[231] Johnson then became enthusiastic, exclaiming, "Nat can get to Bobby. They're friends. Have Nat get to Bobby."[232] When Winter-Berger volunteered that he had an appointment with Voloshen the next day, Johnson told Winter-Berger

> Tell Nat that I want him to get in touch with Bobby Baker as soon as possible—tomorrow if he can. Tell Nat to tell Bobby that I will give him a million dollars if he takes this rap. Bobby must not talk. I'll see to it that he gets a million-dollar settlement.[233]

Given a subsequent scandal involving intercessions for Mobsters from McCormack's office at Voloshen's behest,[234] the recounted tirade would hardly have been exceptional in that office. And the Baker case did indeed involve some close friends of LBJ. Through Caribbean contacts acquired in casino gambling ventures,[235] Baker interceded to reverse a Department of Agriculture ruling prohibiting the importation of unsanitarily processed meat from Haiti to Puerto Rico.[236] The meat company for which Baker acted was Hampco,[237] owned by Texas oil magnate Clint Murchison, Jr.[238] Also, when Baker's problems began in September 1963, the attorney he chose was Johnson's close friend[239] Abe Fortas,[240] who later achieved notoriety as the first U.S. Supreme Court justice to resign under pressure.[241]

But in November 1963, Fortas was replaced as Baker's counsel by Edward Bennett Williams,[242] who specialized in clientele of Baker's ilk—including New York Mafia boss Frank Costello,[243] Teamster boss Jimmy Hoffa,[244] Chicago Mafia boss Sam Giancana,[245] and Chicago Mafia "lord high executioner"[246] Felix Alderisio.[247] Fortas had quit the defense of Johnson's protégé Baker to accept a new position, as described in a November 26, 1963 memo by Texas Attorney General Wagoner Carr:

> Mr. Fortas informed me that he has been assigned to coordinate the FBI, Department of Justice and Texas Attorney General's efforts regarding the assassination of President Kennedy.[248]

/8/ Bobby Baker Follow-Up

If these alliances appear murky, at least Baker's status was clarified through his dealings in the late 1960s, as described in 1972 hearings of the House Select Committee on Crime. The focus of the hearings was a multimillion-dollar scam of the Datacomp and Dumont corporations of New Jersey,[249] spearheaded by New York Mafioso[250] Salvatore Badalamente and front man Seymour Pollock.[251] It was a classic case of the Mafia takeover of a business:[252] the companies' assets were drained, their stocks manipulated, and their offices turned into meeting places for Badalamente's criminal associates, who on one occasion discussed robbing the bank next door to Datacomp.[253]

Datacomp President Norman Forsythe testified that Bobby Baker was introduced to him through Pollock, who indicated that Baker could possibly help the company.[254] Baker did indeed help—help siphon off the company's assets, that is—by taking an extensive tour to Europe paid by Datacomp.[255] Baker also helped at one point when death threats from Badalamente and Pollock failed to silence a Datacomp vice president, Dorothy O'Halloran.[256] Mrs. O'Halloran had been describing the hoodlums' transactions to Roger Nichols, an attorney representing a defrauded Los Angeles brokerage firm.[257] After the Mobsters threatened Mrs. O'Halloran, Nichols related to the Committee, Baker "engaged in a softer sell technique to get her to keep quiet."[258] Mrs. O'Halloran was unable to testify about the threats herself, because "she died under very strange circumstances in New York City about March of 1969."[259]

Continuing along the trail exposed by the House Crime Committee, it turned out that the Datacomp-Dumont scam was perpetrated using worthless stock of the Baptist Foundation of America.[260] Amazingly enough, this so-called foundation was just another shell for Badalamente and his Mafia crew.[261] Its only activity was collecting money, which it accomplished with the help of a corrupt minister, a corrupt certified public accountant and a brochure describing a nonexistent hospital, retirement home and pension plan.[262] Through this foundation, the Mob drained the American public of $26 million.[263]

As Chairman Claude Pepper summarized the situation, "The organized crime crowd had a ripe plum ready for picking." The Baptist Foundation of America "went into receivership about 1970, about 1½ or 2 years from the time it was started, with assets of $15,000 and outstanding notes that people had given value for in the amount of $26 million." But "the benefit would come not to the foundation ... the gain derived to this organized crime crowd that manipulated all of this."[264]

/9/ Conclusion

In conclusion, the Kennedy assassination cover-up fit the pattern that Tacitus had characterized earlier: "a shocking crime ... committed on the unscrupulous initiative of few individuals, with the blessing of more, and amid the passive acquiescence of all."[265] This time, the complacent multitudes were credulous Warren Commission members, uncritical journalists, and other Americans who jumped on the lone-assassin bandwagon rather than seek the difficult truth behind the tragic killing. Hoover, Johnson, Zoppi, and Craig were more actively compliant, while Kennedy's enemies from the anti-Castro coalition undoubtedly gave their blessings. And once again the common denominator, actively intervening to subvert the assassination investigation, was the Mob. Indeed, Mob sabotage of the probe was clearly displayed in the Korshak-Becker escapade, and will be further exposed later. It is thus hardly coincidental that in the aftermath of the Kennedy murder, shielded by this cover-up, the Mob has enjoyed a brazen resurgence—as manifested in depleted national treasuries, augmented graveyards, and a tightening "strangle hold on American politics,"[266] which reached even into the White House.

If, in hindsight, the cover-up of conspicuous Mob links to the Kennedy murder is still difficult to fathom, we need only consider the ongoing cover-up of the Mob's wholesale butchery, subversion and plunder. We still say "union" in connection with the Teamsters, a Mafia subsidiary and extortion franchise, even as members suffer under its dictatorial control.[267] We still say "honorable" in connection with Mafia minions in Congress, such as Senator Russell Long and Representative Frank Annunzio.[268] We still pay homage to Mob-sponsored entertainers who front its casinos, launder its cash, and carry messages to its captive politicians.[269] We still regard Vietnam as a senseless tragedy, Watergate as a matter of improper wiretaps.

We sit idly by as the Mafia drains billions from the many pension funds and financial institutions it controls,[270] turns our fields and streams into bargain-rate dumping grounds for toxic chemicals,[271] peddles diseased meat[272] and counterfeit prescription drugs,[273] leads our children into pornography and addiction.[274] In the tradition of J. Edgar Hoover, we rattle our sabers at distant adversaries, yet accommodate our vicious internal enemy like vanquished before a conqueror. We let the Mafia's nationwide army of assassins murder and terrorize our citizens.[275] We dutifully pay billions of dollars in inflated costs for its major influence in trucking, shipping and construction.[276] We pretend all is normal as it paralyzes our police and courts,[277] subverts our government and press.[278] We look the other way as it reaches into all facets of American life,[279] from grocery stores and country clubs[280] to hospitals[281] and Medicare clinics.[282]

The final part of this book will document Mob culpability in the ultimate act of subversion against the United States: the murder of a president. But the time has past for sorting out which triggermen fired the lethal shots in Dallas, which proportions of credulity and corruption supported the assassination cover-up. The mandate is rather to end the ongoing Mafia assault on America with appropriate, legitimate force—just as America responded to the Pearl Harbor attack 30 years ago. Specific measures and statutes to do so will be presented in the Conclusion.

By the late 1950s, according to his own Warren Commission testimony, Ruby had developed a particular affinity for all things Cuban. That was where the money was and that was where the Mafia was. It was through his Cuban intrigues that Ruby's trail crossed those of some of the most powerful organized crime bosses in America.[1]

William Scott Malone, in *New Times*

Now they're going to find out about Cuba, they're going to find out about the guns, find out about New Orleans, find out about everything.[2]

Jack Ruby, in jail after his murder conviction, as reported by a visiting Carousel Club employee

□ **18** □

Jack Ruby
and the Cuban Coalition

Our extended interlude draws to a close, and the suspended chronicle of President Kennedy's assassination awaits its conclusion. Yet Jack Ruby, the key Mob functionary and witness in this chronicle, is not easily put off. For while the Syndicate was engaged in the Cuban dealings described earlier, flying high with its rackets in the 1950s and desperately trying to reestablish them in the early 1960s, Ruby was right in on the action. The circumstances of his Cuban activities provide further insight into both his background and the events previously described.

/1/ Arms Shipments from Florida in the 1950s

Jack Ruby's first Cuban involvement was reported by FBI informant Blaney Mack Johnson, a pilot who had flown cargo to Cuba and had been affiliated with a Miami gambling casino.[3] According to Johnson, "in the early

1950's, Jack Ruby held [an] interest in the Colonial Inn" in Hallandale, Florida.[4] A famous night club and gambling house, the Inn's principals were Meyer and Jake Lansky, New York Mafioso Joseph Doto ("Joe Adonis"), and Mobster Mert Wertheimer.[5] At that time, Johnson told the FBI, Ruby "was active in arranging illegal flights of weapons from Miami to the Castro organization in Cuba."[6] Johnson furnished specifics about these operations, including the name of one of Ruby's collaborators—Edward Browder[7]—whose Cuban entanglements were corroborated by federal sources.[8]

A storage point in Browder's gunrunning operations was the Florida Keys,[9] where Ruby turned up later in connection with similar activity. According to an FBI report, around May 30, 1958, Mrs. Mary Thompson took her daughter, Dolores, and her son-in-law to visit her brother, James Woodard, in Islamorada, in the eastern end of the Florida Keys.[10] The first night there, Dolores and her husband were put up in a nearby cottage owned by a friend of Woodard's named Jack.[11] This "Jack," as Mrs. Thompson later identified from a photograph, was Jack Ruby.[12] Dolores, too, said that photos of Ruby resembled this man.[13]

The two women's identification of Ruby was confirmed by details they learned of his background and life style. Mrs. Thompson told the FBI that "Jack" drove a car with Texas license plates, ran a drinking place in Dallas, was originally from Chicago, and was said to have killed a couple of men.[14] She said that his actual first name was "Leon,"[15] which was Ruby's middle name.[16] And she related being warned by Woodard's wife to "get Dolores out of Jack's house, because Jack might try to rape her."[17] Dolores added that he wore a diamond ring and appeared accustomed to a high standard of living.[18] She also told the FBI that she had been led to believe Jack was part of the Syndicate[19]—a fact not generally known then outside underworld circles.

The witnesses gave the following descriptions of Ruby's smuggling activities. Dolores told the FBI that one night when Woodard got drunk, he mentioned that "he and Jack would run some guns to Cuba" and that Jack had several guns.[20] Mrs. Thompson reported that Woodard's wife told her that Jack had a trunk full of guns.[21] And Dolores saw several boxes and trunks in Jack's garage,[22] which Jack's girlfriend Isabel claimed "contained her furs."[23]

Federal reports concerning Ruby's attested collaborator, James Woodard, give every indication that Ruby's trunks indeed contained arms bound for Cuba. In an FBI interview in September 1963, Woodard admitted having "furnished ammunition and dynamite to both Castro and Cuban exile forces."[24] Included with the FBI report of this interview was a U.S. Customs official's description of Woodard as "armed and dangerous."[25] And on October 8, 1963, when questioned about stolen dynamite found at his residence, he told authorities that it was to be used by Cuban exile forces against Castro.[26] Given Woodard's background and the reported details about "Jack," therefore, the Thompson account of Ruby's Cuban gunrunning activity appears accurate.

Further confirmation of Ruby's arms dealings during the 1950s was contained in U.S. government files. In 1958, Ruby wrote a letter to the State Department's Office of Munitions Controls "requesting permission to negotiate the purchase of firearms and ammunition from an Italian firm."[27] And the name "Jack Rubenstein" was listed in a 1959 Army Intelligence report on U.S. arms dealers.[28] Although located by clerks of these two federal agencies in 1963, both documents are today inexplicably missing.[29]

/2/ Dealings and Travels in 1959

On January 1, 1959, with the help of armaments and cash supplied by the Mob—which it also supplied to Batista—revolutionary leader Fidel Castro gained control of Cuba.[30] But Castro double-crossed his double-dealing benefactor by jailing some of its top emissaries and closing the casinos.[31] Although in late February he permitted operations to resume, extracting millions more from the Syndicate, the accommodation was shaky at best.[32] The Mob's panic following Castro's initial shutdown of the casinos and its dealings in the subsequent period of accommodation are illuminated by some of Jack Ruby's activities in 1959.

In his FBI interview of December 21, 1963, Ruby related that

> at a time when Castro was popular in the United States he read of an individual in the vicinity of Houston, Texas, having been engaged in "gun running to Castro." He said he attempted by telephone to get in touch with this individual as he had in mind "making a buck" by possibly acquiring some Jeeps or other similar equipment which he might sell to persons interested in their importation to Cuba. He said nothing came of this.[33]

Further details provided by Ruby[34] led the FBI to conclude that "the most logical individual to whom Ruby referred" was Robert McKeown[35]—a resident of Bay Cliff, Texas who had smuggled goods to Cuba and whose support Castro had publicly acknowledged.[36]

The FBI thus interviewed McKeown,[37] who related the following information. About a week after Castro's takeover on January 1, 1959, Deputy Sheriff Anthony "Boots" Ayo told McKeown that someone from Dallas was "frantically calling the Harris County Sheriff's Office in an effort to locate McKeown."[38] When questioned by the FBI, Deputy Sheriff Ayo also recalled this "exceedingly intent" caller from Dallas.[39] About an hour later, McKeown reported, a man identifying himself as "Rubenstein" from Dallas telephoned him.[40] The caller asked McKeown if he would use his influence with Castro to free three people held in Cuba.[41] He offered McKeown $5,000 for each person released, indicating that the money would come from Las Vegas.[42]

As McKeown told the FBI, a man who did not disclose his identity visited him three weeks later and offered him $25,000 to write a letter of introduction to Castro.[43] The visitor said that he had an option on a large number of jeeps in Shreveport, Louisiana, which he wished to sell in Cuba.[44] McKeown told the FBI that he made preliminary arrangements to carry out this deal but never heard from the man again.[45] After viewing photos of Ruby, McKeown told the FBI he felt "strongly that this individual was in fact Jack Ruby."[46]

Further information about this or a similar contact is provided in a February 24, 1964 memorandum by Warren Commission staff members Leon Hubert and Burt Griffin.[47] The memo states that "in about 1959, Ruby became interested in the possibility of selling war materials to Cubans and in the possibility of opening a gambling casino in Havana."[48] This squares with the statement by FBI informant Blaney Mack Johnson that Ruby left Miami after his gunrunning dealings "and purchased a substantial share in a Havana gaming house."[49]

But the most definite indication of Ruby's Cuban involvement was his travel to Havana in 1959, during the temporary period of accommodation between Castro and the Mob. One of these trips, a visit of eight or ten days in August with Ruby's friend Lewis McWillie, was reported by both Ruby[50] and McWillie.[51] Ruby noted that McWillie was "a key man over the Tropicana down there," adding, "that was during our good times."[52] Ruby also reported that during his Cuban visit he met with one of the owners of the Tropicana.[53] But he failed to mention that the Tropicana's top men, in addition to manager McWillie,[54] were Mobsters Meyer and Jake Lansky, Norman Rothman, Willie Bischoff, Giuseppe Cotrini and John Guglielmo.[55] He also failed to state that McWillie was a top man in Syndicate gambling operations,[56] who was associated with Santos Trafficante and the Lansky brothers.[57]

Ruby testified that his August visit with McWillie was strictly a vacation, and insisted that it was the only trip he ever made to Cuba.[58] But several sources contradict this testimony. Records of the Cuban government show that a Jack Ruby of Dallas, Texas, arrived in Cuba on August 8 and left on September 11, only to return September 12 and leave again September 13.[59] U.S. Immigration and Naturalization Service documents confirm Ruby's overnight trip to Cuba September 12–13,[60] hardly long enough to have been a casual visit. Three Chicago men saw Ruby at the Tropicana Night Club during the weekend of September 4–6,[61] one reporting that Ruby "appeared to know his way around and was familiar with the employees."[62] A girlfriend of Ruby's received a postcard dated September 8 written by him from Cuba,[63] and a former employee of his told the FBI that Ruby "vacationed in Cuba" the entire summer.[64] Yet bank and FBI records reveal that Ruby was in Dallas August 6, August 21, August 31, and September 4.[65] The House Assassinations Committee thus concluded that if the evidence were correct, "Ruby had to have made at least three trips to Cuba."[66]

Ruby's offhand comments provide the most credible indication of the purpose of his Cuban visits. One acquaintance of his told the FBI that Ruby had said he went to Cuba "trying to get some gambling concessions at a casino there."[67] During his official medical interview, Ruby discussed "his involvement with a deal in Cuba with one Mack Willey [*sic*], a gambler, and explained how this was a chance to make a quick dollar."[68] And according to a Dallas Police informant, Ruby had told his physician that he was bitter about a federal tax claim against him (amounting to $44,000[69]) and "was going to Cuba to 'collect' his income tax and take a 'breather.' "[70]

Also significant was the report of Elaine Mynier, a mutual friend of Ruby and McWillie, who worked at a car rental agency at the Dallas airport.[71] Mynier told the FBI that in May 1959, she visited Cuba and delivered a short coded message from Ruby to McWillie.[72] Mynier's credibility was demonstrated by the accuracy of details she furnished concerning McWillie's gambling operations.[73] It thus appeared that at least during his one day visit to Cuba in September, Ruby "was most likely serving as a courier for gambling interests,"[74] as the House Assassinations Committee concluded.

The House Assassinations Committee also deemed it "likely" that "Ruby at least met various organized crime figures in Cuba, possibly including some who had been detained by the Cuban government."[75] During the summer of 1959, in particular, one of those detained by Castro was Mafia chieftain Santos Trafficante,[76] who later reciprocated by spearheading Mafia-CIA assassination plots against his former host.[77] Another reportedly involved in these plots,[78] Lewis McWillie, visited the Trescornia detention camp where Trafficante was held.[79] So too, apparently, did Jack Ruby.

When asked who went with him to the camp, McWillie testified, without prompting, that "Jack Ruby could have been out there one time with me."[80] In addition, British journalist John Wilson Hudson, who was also detained at Trescornia,[81] reported that he met "an American gangster-gambler named Santos" who "was visited frequently by an American gangster type named Ruby."[82] The House Assassinations Committee found that "the 'Santos' referred to by Hudson was probably Santos Trafficante."[83] And the Committee concluded that "there was considerable evidence" of a meeting between Trafficante and Ruby in Cuba.[84]

If the two Mobsters met in Cuba, their business was probably just routine underworld dealings. Mobster Johnny Roselli reportedly told a close friend that "Ruby was hooked up with Trafficante in the rackets in Havana."[85] And mercenary Gerry Hemming related that Ruby met with an American close to Castro, apparently to help secure Trafficante's release from Cuban detention;[86] this provided a possible follow-up to the McKeown incident.

/3/ Anti-Castro Activity in 1961

Although Trafficante was freed by the Cuban government in August or September 1959,[87] and casino operations were temporarily resumed,[88] the Mob's days in Cuba were numbered. Lewis McWillie, for one, was expelled from Cuba, with all of his assets confiscated, around January 1, 1961[89] (two months after the departure of another of Ruby's Mob associates, Russell D. Matthews[90]). Ruby testified that McWillie "was the last person to leave, if I recall, when they had to leave, when he left the casino."[91] And in 1961, when the Mob embarked with other groups on a campaign to eliminate Castro,[92] Jack Ruby was once again involved. His activities in this phase of the Cuban scenario were described by just one witness, whose credibility could not be successfully impeached.

The testimony of Nancy Perrin Rich[93] belied the Warren Commission's denials of Ruby's ties to Cuba,[94] organized crime,[95] and the Dallas Police.[96] And just as Mobster-attorney Sidney Korshak stepped forward to discredit informant Edward Becker,[97] so an attorney, a Dallas policeman and others offered disparaging remarks about Mrs. Rich.[98] One detractor was Dave Cherry, whom she described as a collaborator in Cuban gunrunning and a contact in a call-girl ring.[99] Cherry told the FBI that Rich was "mentally deranged" and "incoherent in her speech."[100] But Cherry's statements are less than reliable considering that he worked at a night club owned by Benny Bickers,[101] a Dallas underworld figure acquainted with Jack Ruby.[102] Another person who contradicted Rich[103] had a criminal record,[104] while a third[105] was a former dealer and manager at Las Vegas casinos.[106]

Also discrediting to Mrs. Rich was a Secret Service report which concluded that "she told many stories about doing undercover work and working on counterfeiting cases which appeared to be obvious fabrications."[107] But these "stories" were in fact confirmed in a letter written by Oscar A. Kistle, the chief deputy district attorney of Sacramento County, California;[108] it was verified for the Warren Commission by the Sacramento County district attorney's office.[109] This letter, dated October 25, 1963, described undercover work Rich had performed for the Oakland Police Department which led to a criminal conviction.[110] It praised her "utmost cooperation" and "excellent judgment," relating that she "handled herself in the manner of an experienced investigator."[111] It also cited her qualifications "to be a success in the investigative field wherever her services can be used."[112] There is thus no reason to question the account she consistently related in an FBI interview of November 27, 1963,[113] in three subsequent FBI interviews,[114] and in testimony of June 2, 1964.[115]

Mrs. Rich reported that she had become involved in a Cuban smuggling operation through her former husband, Robert Perrin, with whom she had lived in Dallas during 1961.[116] Perrin had been a bodyguard for California Mafioso[117] Jack Dragna and had performed other services for the Mob, Rich admitted after some hesitation.[118] He was ideally qualified for an arms smuggling assignment, since he had been a gunrunner during the Spanish Civil War and was familiar with boats and Cuba, as described by Mrs. Rich.[119] And Mrs. Rich, too, had experience that proved significant: employment in mid-1961 at Ruby's Carousel Club,[120] as confirmed by a Dallas Police officer.[121]

In 1961,[122] Mrs. Rich testified, she accompanied her husband to a Dallas apartment to meet with bartender Dave Cherry and a military officer in uniform.[123] At that meeting, her husband was offered $10,000 to pilot a boat to bring refugees from Cuba to Miami.[124] At a second meeting five or six days later, her husband was told that the deal would also involve bringing armaments into Cuba that the officer had stolen from a military base.[125] During this meeting, Mrs. Rich related, "a knock comes on the door and who walks in but my little friend Jack Ruby."[126] Mrs. Rich inferred that Ruby had brought money to the group, because he came with a "rather extensive bulge" in his jacket that was gone when he left ten minutes later.[127] Also, he received an enthusiastic reception, and plans suddenly became firmer after his arrival.[128]

Mrs. Rich testified that after a third meeting, she became uneasy about the operation and persuaded her husband to drop out.[129] Her fears had magnified when a new man appeared at that meeting who so resembled Vito Genovese that she believed he might have been his son.[130] At that point,

> everything had fallen into place, because Ruby had had various characters visit him, both from New York, Chicago, even from up in Minneapolis. ... I was introduced to some of them. I was asked to go out with some of them. ... I saw them come and go.[131]

Her feelings were summarized in the following exchange:

> **Q**: And you came to the conclusion, then, that Vito Genovese and that group of people were involved in this matter.
> **Mrs. Rich**: Within my own mind; yes. I thought—then I got thinking that perhaps the higher-up that the colonel spoke of was perhaps the element I did not want to deal with that was running guns in, and God knows what else.[132]

Her conclusion was hardly far-fetched, considering Ruby's Mob affiliation, his prior Cuban involvements, and the Mob's central role in the anti-Castro campaign, which reached its peak of activity in 1961.[133]

/4/ Ruby's Ties to Extreme Right-Wing Elements

It was perhaps through the anti-Castro campaign that Ruby formed certain ties with extreme right-wing elements. Suggesting such ties were three photographs of an "Impeach Earl Warren" sign which were found on Ruby's person after he shot Oswald.[134] As discussed, Ruby's explanation of how he obtained these photos is dubious.[135] Also found on Ruby was an envelope marked "box 1757,"[136] the box number which appeared on the "Impeach Earl Warren" sign.[137] On the back of this envelope were the name, address, and phone number of Thomas Hill, a John Birch Society official from Belmont, Massachusetts.[138] Hill was listed in the February 24 memo of Warren Commission counsels Hubert and Griffin as among possible "sources of contact between Ruby and politically motivated groups interested in securing the assassination of President Kennedy."[139]

Two other persons listed in the same category as Hill in the February 24 memo were H. L. Hunt, the Dallas oil billionaire and extreme right-wing propagandist, and his son Lamar Hunt.[140] Indeed, the Hunts were worthy of scrutiny; H. L. had reportedly spoken of shooting "those traitors out of our government,"[141] and another of his sons, Nelson Bunker, had co-sponsored the black-bordered assassination-day ad attacking President Kennedy.[142] Also, a *Houston Post* reporter formerly employed at the Hunt Oil Company disclosed that Hunt personally approached him about plotting to kill either Fidel Castro or the prime minister of Guyana.[143] A participant in the murder plan, later scrapped, was notorious Mobster R. D. Matthews[144]—an associate of Trafficante, McWillie and Ruby.[145]

According to an informant judged reliable by the Secret Service, Ruby had met H. L. Hunt in the early 1950s through some large football bets made between them.[146] Two other sources confirmed Hunt's fondness for high-stakes gambling,[147] and a third indicated that Ruby and Hunt had patronized the same Dallas gambling club in the 1940s.[148] Also, the name "Lamar Hunt" appeared in one of Ruby's notebooks.[149] And several transcripts of "Life Line" radio broadcasts sponsored by H. L. Hunt were found among Ruby's personal articles.[150] But the most intriguing link between Ruby and the Hunts was exhibited on the day before President Kennedy's assassination, as will be discussed later.[151]

In summary, from the 1950s through the early 1960s, Cuba was a hub of Mob activity. And through all phases of this activity, Mobster Jack Ruby was right in the thick of things. Gambling, gunrunning, courting Castro, and then conspiring with extreme right-wing elements to destroy him—Ruby was involved in the Mob's Cuban imbroglio every step of the way. Not as a principal, certainly, but not one to be left out either. And in 1963, when the Mafia redirected its efforts toward a critical new undertaking in Dallas, Jack Ruby was there.

PART V
A MAFIA CONTRACT

On Sunday, September 15, 1963, two months before President Kennedy was assassinated, another tragic crime shocked the nation: four black girls were killed when dynamite ripped apart the Sixteenth Street Baptist Church in Birmingham, Alabama.[1] As the 1960s and most of the 1970s rolled by with the killer still at large, it appeared that the case would never be solved. But in November 1977, Robert Edward Chambliss was brought to trial for the murder of one of the victims.[2] The prosecution established that Chambliss had spoken of performing the bombing, had been seen near the church that morning, had stored explosives in his home, and had been linked to similar violence in the past.[3] The defense countered that the case against Chambliss was "circumstantial."[4] The jury convicted Chambliss of first-degree murder.[5]

Returning now to the Kennedy murder case, in which justice has also been long delayed, recall that two important conclusions have been established. The Mafia had the motive, means and stated intention to kill the president. And a Mobster, Jack Ruby, pulled the trigger in the November 24 sequel: the liquidation of Lee Harvey Oswald. Through the following steps, this part now proves Mob culpability in the assassination itself.

First, after President Kennedy's trip to Dallas was announced, Ruby called and visited more than a dozen Mobsters across the nation, including several associates of Marcello, Trafficante and Hoffa. As November 22 approached, these Mob contacts sharply intensified, and then shifted focus to Dallas. Second, the Mobsters called and visited by Ruby presented a collusively fabricated alibi to explain their contacts—directly exhibiting conspiracy, and precluding an innocent explanation. And third, in the final days before November 22, Ruby's contacts with this Mob pack were punctuated with actions that exposed his participation in a contract to murder the president. Thus, as will be shown, the evidence demonstrates motive, means, specific murder plans, pre-assassination contacts, post-assassination collusion, and the direct involvement of a Mobster in the murder arrangements. Short of a group photo of gun-toting Mobsters in Dealey Plaza, a more convincing demonstration of Mob conspiracy is difficult to contemplate.

The Mafia assassination contract against President Kennedy, as exposed through the National Archives file on Jack Ruby, begins in a key Mob base: New Orleans.

Organized crime involves itself in the life of every single human being. It causes prices to be raised; it affects your pocketbook when you go to a laundry or dry cleaner; the price you pay for food in the market. I have been involved in and know of bad meat being purchased, unfit for human consumption, that has been converted into salami in delicatessens and forced to be sold through grocery stores. . . .

When I testified about Mr. DeCarlo, I, too, had the native feel of what organized crime was.

I saw photographs of graves dug in New Jersey, with over 35 bodies over a period of years, melted with lye. I sat and heard the voices at dinner talking over murdering a 12-year-old child and burying bodies in New Jersey. . . .

Narcotics, manipulation of businesses that cause prices to spiral, we can go on for a long, long time. . . . It goes on and on.[1]

Mob defector Gerald Zelmanowitz, testifying in 1973 before a U.S. Senate Committee

The Chairman [Senator McClellan]: Are you a member of the Mafia?

Mr. Carlos Marcello: I decline to answer on the ground it may tend to incriminate me.[2]

From Senate rackets hearings of 1959

□ 19 □

Contacts with the Marcello Family

A boss among bosses in the Mafia hierarchy,[3] Carlos Marcello had much to lose from the Kennedy crime crusade. Not only was his immensely profitable Louisiana fiefdom threatened, but he found himself high on the attorney general's "hit list" of Mobsters targeted for prosecution.[4] Particularly galling to Marcello were his 1961 deportation to Guatemala[5] and the string of federal indictments that greeted him upon his illegal return.[6] It is thus natural to suspect that Marcello would settle the Kennedy score with the Mob's "ultimate solution to everything":[7] murder. And his chance would come in November 1963, when President Kennedy would enter Marcello's Gulf Coast domain for a motorcade ride through Dallas.

As discussed in Chapter 4, however, Marcello's connection to a Kennedy assassination conspiracy is not merely hypothetical. Informant Edward Becker recounted to reporter Ed Reid[8] and the House Assassinations Committee[9] how he met Marcello in September 1962 at the Mobster's Churchill Farms plantation to discuss a business deal. When the conversation turned to Marcello's problems with the law, Becker reported, the enraged Marcello "clearly stated that he was going to arrange to have President Kennedy murdered in some way."[10] Becker noted that Marcello's assassination plan appeared quite deliberate.[11] To avoid implicating his own lieutenants, for example, Marcello had planned on using a "nut" for the crime.[12] Someone, perhaps, like Lee Harvey Oswald—who was indirectly tied to the Mafia boss through Charles "Dutz" Murret, Oswald's uncle and surrogate father, and through David Ferrie.

This chapter shows that Oswald's killer, Jack Ruby, likewise had ties to the Marcello Mafia Family. But in Ruby's case, the contacts were intensive, often direct, and timely.

/1/ Mafia Bars and Mafia Managers

On April 23, 1963, the *Dallas Times Herald* reported the itinerary of a proposed presidential trip to Dallas.[13] On May 7, as shown by telephone records, Ruby placed a call to the Sho-Bar on Bourbon Street,[14] beginning a long series of contacts with parties in New Orleans. The Sho-Bar was owned in the 1960s by Pete Marcello,[15] a brother and lieutenant of Carlos and a convicted narcotics felon.[16] Ruby called the Sho-Bar again on June 11,[17] and was seen there in early June by three of its employees.[18] One of these employees, Nick Graffagnini, conversed with Ruby at that time, according to Graffagnini and three other witnesses.[19] Graffagnini was identified in Congressional testimony as the brother-in-law of Frank Caracci,[20] whom he accompanied to Detroit in 1969 to meet members of the Zerelli Mafia Family.[21]

But more significant were Ruby's links to Frank Caracci himself—a New Orleans Mobster closely affiliated with Carlos Marcello.[22] In mid-May 1963, Ruby visited the Old French Opera House on Bourbon Street,[23] owned by Caracci.[24] Ruby called that club at least eight times over the next three months.[25] And during Ruby's June visit to New Orleans, he stopped at the 500 Club,[26] of which Caracci was co-owner.[27] Furthermore, an FBI chronology states that Caracci "saw Ruby" in New Orleans during his visit there;[28] Caracci denied this.[29] A subsequent meeting between Ruby and Caracci, reported by a New Orleans Police detective, will be discussed shortly.

/2/ Telephone Contacts with Nofio Pecora

On August 4, 1963, a telephone call was placed from the number 242–5431 in New Orleans to Ruby's telephone in Dallas.[30] Three months later, on October 30, a call was placed from Ruby's phone to the same New Orleans number.[31] That number was listed to a telephone at the Tropical Tourist Court trailer park, in the private office of its manager, Nofio Pecora.[32] When questioned by the House Assassinations Committee, Pecora first declined to respond, then claimed no recollection of a call from Ruby.[33] But he admitted that "he was probably the only person who had access to his Tropical Court telephone in 1963."[34]

Nofio Pecora, Ruby's two-time telephone contact, was a long-time associate and partner of Carlos Marcello.[35] "A multiple ex-convict in the heroin traffic," as described to Congress in 1970, Pecora dealt in narcotics with Marcello before the latter achieved his boss status.[36] Chief Counsel Blakey of the House Assassinations Committee testified that "the FBI, Justice Department, and Metropolitan Crime Commission of New Orleans have identified Pecora as one of Marcello's three most trusted aides."[37] Exemplifying this relationship, Pecora received a telephone call from Marcello on June 24, 1963—at the very same Tropical Court phone from which Pecora called Ruby a month later.[38]

/3/ Alibis

Predictably, innocuous explanations were presented to cover Ruby's extensive contacts with Marcello-affiliated Mobsters. But lame and inconsistent, they serve only to emphasize the absence of any legitimate explanation.

In search of night club talent. When questioned by the FBI about Ruby's June visit to New Orleans, half a dozen witnesses related that Ruby had been seeking entertainers for his night club.[39] In particular, they said that Ruby had inquired about Janet Conforto ("Jada"),[40] a striptease dancer who did, in fact, begin working at the Carousel Club in July 1963.[41]

This quest to hire Jada might be credible, were talent scouting not the stock cover story for so many of Ruby's suspicious activities. When he visited New York in August 1963, for example, he told a Hilton Hotel clerk that he was there to seek night club talent.[42] An associate provided the same story for Ruby's 1959 trip to Cuba.[43] Yet when Ruby testified before the

Warren Commission, he gave totally different explanations for each of these trips, mentioning nothing about night club talent.[44] And given a pattern of orchestrated perjury by Ruby's underworld associates, to be discussed later,[45] there is little reason to believe the witnesses narrating the Jada story: Mobsters Frank Caracci and Nick Graffagnini, union official Leon Cornman, striptease dancer Janet Conforto, Blue Angel Club manager Paul Cascio, and a manager of Marcello's Sho-Bar, Henry Morici.[46]

The ubiquitous Harold Tannenbaum. A second alibi is even more dubious. All of Ruby's New Orleans telephone calls between May and November of 1963, so this story goes, were contacts between Ruby and just one New Orleans acquaintance: Harold Tannenbaum.[47] Reminiscent of "Harry Rubenstein," to whom all of Ruby's criminal dealings in the Chicago night club district were attributed,[48] Tannenbaum purportedly accounted for at least 18 calls between Ruby's phone and five New Orleans numbers.[49] Tannenbaum also told the FBI that he visited Ruby once in New Orleans and twice in Dallas.[50] A curious feature of this allegedly close relationship between Ruby and Tannenbaum, however, is its lack of independent confirmation. Although dozens of Ruby's obscurest associates are mentioned in the Warren Commission's report and hearings, Tannenbaum's name never cropped up in the report,[51] and was raised just once in the hearings—in a question drawing a blank response from the interviewed witness.[52]

Indeed, the specifics of the Tannenbaum alibi confirm its incredibility. In an unpublished FBI interview, Tannenbaum reported that he first met Ruby around May 15, 1963, when they struck up a conversation outside Frank Caracci's Old French Opera House.[53] An FBI chronology fixes the date precisely as May 15[54] by events which, according to Tannenbaum, occurred the following day.[55] But the name "Harold Tannenbaum" appears in an official log identifying Ruby's call to the Sho-Bar on May 7[56]—a week before Ruby was supposed to have met him. Another source indicates that Ruby and Tannenbaum made their introductions yet a third time. According to Jada, the striptease dancer, when she and Tannenbaum met Ruby in June, "Ruby had apparently never met Tannenbaum on any previous occasion."[57]

Whenever their purported introductions were made, however, Tannenbaum would surely have filled a pressing need for Ruby. For as noted earlier, Ruby claimed that his purpose in traveling to New Orleans in early June was to hire Jada. And it so happened that Ruby's new friend Harold Tannenbaum was a booking agent,[58] identified as such or as "Jada's agent" in handwritten notations on telephone logs.[59] In fact, Tannenbaum told the FBI that his phone calls to Ruby on May 16 and on June 5, just before Ruby's New Orleans trip, were "to discuss the hiring of Jada and Jada's contract."[60]

But as the FBI paraphrased it, Mob associate Nick Graffagnini reported that

Jack Ruby came into the Sho-Bar a few days before Janet Conforto (Jada) completed her engagement [on June 12[61]] and
wanted to know how he could go about hiring Jada for a club he
had in Dallas, Texas. Graffagnini said he told him he did not handle the hiring or signing of contracts with the entertainers and
he sent him to the 500 Club on Bourbon Street.[62]

When Ruby came to the 500 Club, according to Marcello associate Frank
Caracci, he inquired about hiring dancers, only for Caracci to communicate through his manager that none was available.[63] Thus, although Harold
Tannenbaum was supposedly Ruby's close contact and "Jada's agent," Ruby
nevertheless went on a wild-goose chase to hire Jada—in two bars which
happened to be owned by criminal associates of Marcello.

Although Jada began working for Ruby in mid-July,[64] Ruby's telephone
contacts with parties in New Orleans continued into the late summer and
fall of 1963.[65] For Tannenbaum to have accounted for these calls, therefore,
a topic of conversation other than negotiations for Jada's contract was required. Tannenbaum obliged: he told the FBI that these later calls concerned "the possibility of his being employed as manager of the Vegas
Club," owned by Ruby.[66] This explanation might have been reasonable except that Ruby's sister Eva Grant had managed the Vegas Club for three-
and-a-half years before the assassination, excluding a two-week absence
for illness in November 1963.[67]

In contrast to these implausibilities and inconsistencies, certain items of
background may explain Tannenbaum's actual role in Ruby's New Orleans
contacts. During the Kennedy Administration, the government conducted
intensive electronic surveillance of Mobsters.[68] This surveillance caused
them to use "elaborate systems of prearranged times and telephone numbers" to elude it in their communications.[69] And as noted in the House
Assassination hearings, Tannenbaum was a "friend and colleague" of Marcello lieutenant Nofio Pecora,[70] the latter a prime target for such surveillance. Tannenbaum in fact lived at lot 32 of Pecora's Tropical Tourist
Court,[71] and four telephone calls were exchanged with Ruby's phones from
a telephone at that lot.[72]

If at all cautious, therefore, Pecora would have used his Tropical Court
office phone in Mob dealings only to touch base and signal for subsequent
contact; this may account for his two contacts with Ruby from that
phone.[73] But for substantive discussions with his Dallas Mob counterpart,
the Marcello aide would have undoubtedly used a less traceable phone—
such as that of his neighbor and colleague, Harold Tannenbaum. Indeed, if
the matter at hand were a sensitive Mafia contract, such a precaution
would have been routine.

Finally, it is significant to note, as disclosed by the House Assassinations

Committee, that Tannenbaum ran "several Bourbon Street clubs controlled allegedly by the Marcello interests";[74] one was Frank Caracci's Old French Opera House.[75] Whether Tannenbaum was a convenient Mob front or an actual Ruby contact, therefore, his alibi hardly sanitizes the Marcello connection underlying Ruby's numerous New Orleans telephone communications. And this connection was further demonstrated through a subsequent personal contact between Ruby and a close Marcello associate.

/4/ A Second Visit With Frank Caracci

On November 27, 1963, FBI agents interviewed Detective Frederick O'Sullivan of the New Orleans Police Intelligence Unit.[76] Detective O'Sullivan told the FBI that six to eight weeks earlier, he had seen a man in New Orleans who he believed was Ruby.[77] O'Sullivan

> felt fairly certain that he had seen Ruby in the French Quarter in the company of Frank Caracci, owner of the 500 Club, Bourbon Street. Also present was Nick Korano [Carno], partner of Frank Caracci.[78]

Two points corroborate O'Sullivan's account. First, Nick Carno was in fact Frank Caracci's partner in the 500 Club,[79] and had been there with Caracci when Ruby visited in June.[80] Second, there were only two gaps of more than a day in Ruby's toll call records for October and November, 1963; they occurred between October 3 and 7 and between October 8 and 12.[81] Both of these gaps fall within the period of October 1 to 15 estimated by Detective O'Sullivan for Ruby's encounter with Caracci. Also consistent with out-of-state travel by Ruby in early October is a notation in one of his notebooks: "American Airline[s], Tuesday October 9 - 985, 11–11:30 A.M."[82]

When questioned by the FBI on November 27, 1963, Caracci denied any contact with Ruby.[83] And four years later, when subpoenaed with Carlos Marcello during a grand jury probe of the Mob, Caracci proclaimed that the probe was "off base" and that he knew nothing about organized crime.[84] Caracci's level of credibility in such declarations, however, is perhaps indicated by his subsequent conviction for attempting to bribe a federal agent.[85]

Thus, the record of Ruby's activities between June and November of 1963 exhibits several points of contact with the Marcello Mafia Family. A visit and two telephone calls to Pete Marcello's Sho-Bar. Two visits with Frank Caracci, a close Mob associate of Carlos Marcello, plus one visit and several calls to a night club owned by Caracci. Two phone calls exchanged with Nofio Pecora, a top Mafia lieutenant of Marcello. Plus an assassination-eve contact in Dallas with Marcello intimate Joseph Campisi, to be discussed later.[86] These calls and visits by Ruby are suspicious, given Carlos Marcello's injudiciously disclosed intention to murder President Kennedy. But they are just a small sampling of Ruby's nationwide Mob contacts in the pre-assassination period.

> The mob is a cancer on this land. ... They reach
> congressmen just as quickly as they reach state houses and
> police precincts. They corrupt businessmen and unions, you
> name it. ... There isn't a state in the union where the mob
> doesn't have influence. They have stolen so many billions in
> securities that you can't dream that high, let alone count.[1]
>
> Mob defector Vincent Teresa

□ 20 □

Meeting Mobsters
and Teamsters

During the summer months of 1962, as discussed earlier, while Carlos
Marcello outlined a plot to murder President Kennedy, Tampa Mafia boss
Santos Trafficante, Jr. and Teamster boss Jimmy Hoffa expressed similar
assassination designs. "Kennedy is in trouble, and he will get what is
coming to him," Trafficante raged, referring to the president. "He is going to
be hit."[2] Hoffa targeted Robert Kennedy for murder, and considered having
him killed by a lone rifleman somewhere in the South, where extreme
segregationists could be blamed.[3] Noting Hoffa's rabid hatred of President
Kennedy, a Hoffa aide found it quite possible that one Kennedy assassination plan by him developed into another.[4]

If Marcello, Trafficante and Hoffa, all close associates, had in fact joined
forces to assassinate President Kennedy, the progression of a conspiracy
would be easy to surmise. Powerful as they were, the two Mafia bosses and
their Teamster ally would have needed approval for such a monumental
undertaking from the full Mafia National Commission—particularly from
key bosses representing New York, Chicago, and the West Coast. A hit
squad would have then been selected from the Mob's nationwide network
of expert executioners. And someone would have been needed at the

assassination site to coordinate communications among the various elements of the conspiracy: associates of the instigating triumvirate, representatives of other top Mafia families, and Mob executioners. Hardly needed by the Mob, however, was someone to generate an incriminating, documentary trail of precisely such contacts.

Following is a chronology of Jack Ruby's underworld contacts in the period between April 23, 1963, the date President Kennedy's trip to Dallas was first reported,[5] and mid-November 1963. It is based largely on toll call records from Ruby's home and Carousel office telephones,[6] plus other sources which identify the parties he called. Barring unidentified, freak exceptions, as discussed in Appendix 3, all such calls were placed by Ruby himself and will be referenced as such.

To present a complete record for the period covered, the New Orleans contacts examined earlier are highlighted here. Additional contacts that Ruby made during the latter part of November will be covered in chapter 23.

/1/ May Through July, 1963: Focus in New Orleans

May 7. Ruby placed a 3-minute call to Pete Marcello's Sho-Bar in New Orleans (523–9468).[7]

May 10. At Ruby's request, a .38 Smith and Wesson revolver was shipped to his friend Lewis McWillie in Las Vegas, according to records of the Dallas gun supplier.[8] Curiously, McWillie never picked up the gun and it was returned to the supplier.[9] In his polygraph exam hearing, Ruby repeatedly brought up another gun sent to McWillie and a message Ruby transmitted about it,[10] remarking, "This is incriminating against me very bad."[11]

McWillie claimed he asked Ruby to ship the gun because he didn't know where to get one in Las Vegas: "I didn't even know you could buy a gun in a store."[12] Coming from a prominent Syndicate figure[13] described by Dallas Police as a "gambler and murderer,"[14] this explanation is less than credible.

May 12. Ruby placed a 6-minute call to the Mob-owned[15] Thunderbird Hotel in Las Vegas.[16] This and many subsequent calls to that number were apparently to McWillie, who was then employed there.[17] For McWillie told the FBI that he received calls from Ruby in August both at the Thunderbird and at home,[18] and Ruby's sister Eva Grant testified that Ruby called McWillie at least ten times between September and November of 1963.[19] The explanations of McWillie and other Mobsters for their contacts with Ruby will be examined in the next chapter.

Also on May 12, Ruby placed an 11-minute call to the Dream Bar in Cicero, Illinois.[20] That bar was identified by the FBI as "an alleged strip joint and gambling operation allegedly operated by several Chicago area hoodlums."[21] The testimony of Ruby's brother Hyman and sister Eva suggests that the call was to Jack Yanover,[22] an official of the American Guild of Variety Artists and one of the two "officers of record" of the bar.[23]

June 5. President Kennedy, Vice President Johnson and Governor Connally met in El Paso, Texas, and decided to proceed with the president's proposed November trip to Texas.[24] Also on that day, Ruby placed a 28-minute call to the Old French Opera House, a New Orleans bar owned by Marcello associate Frank Caracci.[25] During the next few days, Ruby visited New Orleans, where he was seen by several persons in the Bourbon Street night club district.[26] Among them were Caracci and Nick Graffagnini, Caracci's Mafia-involved brother-in-law.[27]

June 8. Many out-of-state Mobsters, including "one of the nation's top vice lords," began to converge in Dallas, according to a Dallas Police report cited by journalist Seth Kantor.[28] On June 9, they held the first of a series of meetings with local colleagues.[29] Among their meeting places were Ruby's Carousel Club and a Howard Johnson's restaurant on the Fort Worth Turnpike in Arlington.[30]

June 10. Ruby placed a 1-minute call to that Howard Johnson's restaurant in Arlington.[31] The next day, Ruby placed a 3-minute call to Pete Marcello's Sho-Bar in New Orleans.[32] On June 13, Ruby again called the Howard Johnson's restaurant in Arlington, speaking for seven minutes.[33]

June 14. Ruby placed a 7-minute call to the Old French Opera House, owned by Caracci.[34] Ruby also placed 8-minute and 4-minute calls on June 19 and an 11-minute call on June 21 to that same number.[35]

June 27. Ruby placed a 7-minute call to the Las Vegas home phone of Lewis McWillie.[36]

July 6, 24. Ruby placed 12-minute and 1-minute calls, respectively, to the Old French Opera House.[37]

/2/ August: The West Coast and New York

August 2. Ruby placed a 7-minute call to Michael Shore at his home in Beverly Hills, California.[38] That day, Ruby also placed a 1-minute call to Shore's office at the Reprise Record Company in Los Angeles.[39] An executive of Reprise,[40] Shore is exceptionally close to Irwin Weiner, one of the most prominent Mafia associates in the Chicago area.[41] When questioned by the House Assassinations Committee in 1978, Weiner admitted that he was "a very close friend" and business partner of Shore, in constant telephone contact with him.[42]

Ruby's contact with Shore, who reportedly knew Frank Sinatra,[43] typified Ruby's diverse connections in the entertainment field.* By no means rou-

*Ruby told a Dallas musician that he "had connections with Reprise," which "Frank Sinatra had something to do with," and "would have no trouble getting a record promoted and distributed nationally."[44] These claims were borne out by

tine, however, was the intensity of Ruby's contacts in the following few days. On August 2, the same day he called Shore, Ruby placed a 3-minute call to the Thunderbird Hotel in Las Vegas[56]—presumably again to McWillie.[57] That day, he also placed a 2-minute call to the Los Angeles home of William Miller,[58] and then a 7-minute call to Miller at a Beverly Hills residence where Miller was visiting.[59] Miller was a booking agent, night club operator and one-time co-owner of the Riverside hotel-casino in Reno, Nevada.[60] He knew Lewis McWillie[61] and was close to Benjamin Dranow,[62] the latter convicted of helping to drain $1.7 million from the Teamster pension fund.[63] Miller himself had applied for a $2.75 million Teamster loan for the Riverside, which was granted with unusual haste—just in time for the hotel to declare bankruptcy in 1962.[64]

August 4. Ruby placed a 5-minute call to the Thunderbird Hotel in Las Vegas,[65] presumably to McWillie.[66] The same day, a call was placed to one of Ruby's phones from the Tropical Court office phone of Marcello lieutenant Nofio Pecora.[67] Pecora later reported that he had exclusive access to that New Orleans phone.[68]

Also on August 4, Ruby placed a 3-minute call to a New York number listed to the Milton Blackstone Advertising Agency.[69] Employed there, in "public relations," was Ruby's old buddy Barney Ross,[70] a former boxer and former drug addict.[71] A slip of paper with the name "Barney Ross," that New York telephone number, and the message "Hurry north" was later found among Ruby's personal effects.[72]

Ruby did in fact "hurry north," taking American Airlines flight 186 to New York that same day;[73] he checked into the New York Hilton at 10:59 p.m.[74] A fellow passenger, Walter Blassingame, told the FBI that Ruby remarked "he was going to be met at the New York airport by a Barney Ross."[75] When they arrived, Blassingame heard Barney Ross paged.[76] Alfred Lurie, also on

---

Ruby's contacts with Shore and others in the entertainment and public relations field—ranging from record promoters for whom he procured women[45] and employees of radio station KLIF[46] to three prominent press figures from Dallas: Gordon McLendon, Matty Brescia and Tony Zoppi.[47]

As highlighted in Appendix 4, the Mafia's overall influence in entertainment is manifested by its infiltration into the actor's union (IATSE),[48] its domination of the movie industry since the 1930s,[49] and its major involvement in rock concert promotion and payola.[50] Representative was the "extensive influence" among Hollywood actors and executives, noted the *New York Times*, of Mobster-attorney Sidney Korshak.[51] "Sidney Korshak is probably the most important man socially out here," reported Joyce Haber, the Hollywood columnist.[52] Equally ominous is Korshak's major involvement in the affairs of Gulf and Western,[53] the large conglomerate that owns Paramount Pictures and other entertainment interests.[54] A similar dual role is played by Frank Sinatra, whose extensive dealings and friendships with Mafia figures have been documented in several sources, including a 19-page Justice Department report.[55]

the flight, reported that Ruby said he was on his way to see Ross.[77] Another witness reported that Ruby's New York trip "was to go see a friend," evidently Ross,[78] and Ruby himself confirmed contact with Ross during that trip.[79]

But Ross told the FBI that he last saw Ruby "accidentally" in Chicago around the end of 1961, and had only talked to him by telephone since then.[80] Equally dubious was Ross' account to the FBI of his former relationship with Al Capone. Ross admitted that "about 1926," when he began his boxing career, he and his friends ran "innocuous errands" for Capone.[81] Ross claimed that he believed Capone gave them these errands only "to keep them from hanging around the streets," and that he did not realize Capone was a big-time racketeer until "about 1927."[82] Capone was in fact notorious by early 1925, however.[83] The report of Ross' FBI interview also notes a direct admission of his duplicity:

> Ross pointed out that in his autobiography although he stated that he had at one time worked for Al Capone, he never did actually work for Capone.[84]

Ruby made other contacts during his New York trip. Within an hour after checking into the Hilton Hotel, Ruby called Caracci's Old French Opera House[85] and Michael Shore's Los Angeles residence.[86] Ruby's activities of the following day were also noteworthy.

August 5. Ruby visited Joseph Glaser in the New York office of Associated Booking Corporation, as reported by both Ruby[87] and Glaser.[88] Glaser was president of Associated Booking,[89] the nation's third largest theatrical booking agency, which has handled such stars as Louis Armstrong, Duke Ellington and Barbra Streisand.[90] But the man who had "virtually absolute control of Associated Booking," the *New York Times* exposed in 1976, was Mobster Sidney Korshak.[91] A year before Ruby's visit, in fact, Glaser transferred a major share of the company's voting rights to Korshak, paving the way for Korshak later to assume complete control.[92] And Glaser himself "probably could have been in rackets," testified Eva Grant,[93] who offered similar gentle characterizations of three Mob killers.[94]

Also on August 5, Ruby placed another call to Michael Shore in Los Angeles.[95]

August 6. Ruby checked out of the Hilton at 4:40 p.m.[96] He told the FBI that "on the return to Dallas he went via Chicago and that members of his family joined him briefly at O'Hare Field, the Chicago airport."[97] But he neglected to mention that while in Chicago he stopped at Henrici's Restaurant, as reported by a woman who met him there.[98] Across the street from Henrici's was the Sherman Hotel,[99] a Mafia hangout conveniently situated near Chicago Police Headquarters and City Hall.[100] Henrici's similar underworld character is suggested by the patronage there of two Mob figures with long criminal records: Teamster official Gus Zapas[101] and narcotics trafficker Vincent "Piggy Mack" Marchesi.[102]

August 15. Ruby placed two 3-minute calls to Joseph Glaser, Korshak's partner, in New York.[103]

August 19. Ruby placed a 1-minute call to the Thunderbird Hotel in Las Vegas, followed by a 2-minute call on August 20 and a 7-minute call on August 22 to that phone.[104] Since Lewis McWillie acknowledged calls from Ruby at the Thunderbird in August,[105] these again were probably to that Mob "gambler and murderer."[106]

August 22. Ruby placed a 7-minute call to the Beverly Hills home of Michael Shore.[107]

/3/ October Through Mid-November: Intensive Nationwide Contacts

Ruby's recorded activities in September were minimal—only three out-of-state calls, all to relatives, and no trips.[108] At the end of the month, however, a critical decision was reported in Washington: President Kennedy would in fact visit Texas, on November 21 and 22.[109] And in the following weeks, Ruby's intensive telephone activity and travel resumed in earnest.

A compilation of Ruby's toll calls by date, as charted below,* provides a striking measure of this spurt in activity. In October, following the confirmation of the president's trip, Ruby's rate of out-of-state calls rose tenfold over September's rate. In the week of November 3, this rate skyrocketed to 25 times the average rate of January through September. Then, in the weeks before the assassination, it plummeted just as dramatically—at the same time that Ruby received several Mob visitors in Dallas, as will be discussed in Chapter 23.

October 3. Ruby placed a 13-minute call to the Shreveport, Louisiana home of Elizabeth Matthews,[113] who had been recently divorced from Russell D. Matthews.[114] Since Russell was an associate of Ruby,[115] and Elizabeth reported she had no acquaintance with Ruby nor recollection of any call from him,[116] it appears that Ruby was trying to contact Russell. Russell D. Matthews was described by federal sources as "a burglar, armed robber, narcotics pusher and murderer."[117] He is an associate of Mafia boss Santos Trafficante,[118] and visited Cuba in the late 1950s on Trafficante's behalf.[119] Matthews is also a close associate of Dallas Mafioso Joseph Campisi.[120]

Within a week of the Matthews contact, Ruby made another visit to the

---

*The chart below shows toll calls from Ruby's Carousel office phone, compiled from telephone records subpoenaed by the FBI[110] and telephone bills found in Ruby's possession.[111] Calls from his home phone, much less frequent,[112] are not included, since no records for such calls before May 1963 are available.

FIGURE 2

Rate of Toll Calls from
Ruby's Carousel Office Phone During 1963

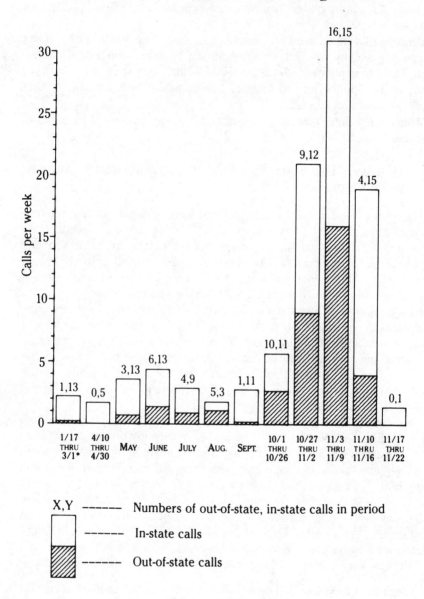

*No information is available for the periods January 1–16 and March 2 through April 9, 1963.

nightclub district of New Orleans.[121] He was seen there with Frank Caracci,[122] a close associate of Carlos Marcello.[123] About this time, Ruby also ventured into Trafficante territory. That visit was detected through federal surveillance of Johnny Roselli,[124] a notorious West Coast Mafioso who was a principal with Trafficante and Chicago Mafia boss Sam Giancana in assassination plots against Castro.[125] According to *New Times*, federal sources disclosed that

> two Miami motel rooms have been identified as the locations of two meetings between Roselli and Jack Ruby. The meetings occurred during the two months preceding the Kennedy assassination.[126]

In the mid-1970s, an aging Roselli began to describe his contacts with Ruby to associates, Senate investigators and columnist Jack Anderson.[127] Roselli admitted knowing Ruby, Anderson reported, and described him as "one of our boys."[128] Anderson reported, "When Oswald was picked up, Roselli suggested, the underworld conspirators feared that he would crack and disclose information that might lead to them. . . . So Jack Ruby was ordered to eliminate Oswald."[129] Amazing candor from a Mobster? The Mafia apparently thought so. A few months after he testified in secret session before the Senate Intelligence Committee in 1976, Roselli's dismembered body was found in an oil drum in Miami's Biscayne Bay.[130] He had last been seen on a boat owned by a Trafficante associate.[131]

On June 19, 1975, three days before Roselli had first been questioned by the Senate Intelligence Committee, staff members of the committee arrived in Chicago to arrange for Mafia boss Sam Giancana's testimony about Cuban assassination plots.[132] That evening, Giancana was shot seven times and killed in his Oak Park home.[133] One of his daughters insisted that he was slain by the same people responsible for killing the Kennedys.[134] A staff report of the House Assassinations Committee noted that "Trafficante has most often been the person assigned responsibility" for the murders of both Giancana and Roselli.[135]

October 25. Ruby placed an 18-minute person-to-person call to Michael Shore in New York, where Shore was visiting.[136]

October 26. Ruby placed a 12-minute person-to-person call to Irwin S. Weiner at Weiner's Chicago home.[137] Weiner is a prominent Chicago Mafia associate, who has been linked to arson, extortion, Medicare fraud, gambling, bribery and murder.[138] He is instrumental in coordinating the flow of cash between the Teamsters, Las Vegas casinos and the Chicago branch of the Mob.[139] His close associates have included Trafficante, Giancana and Hoffa.[140] When questioned by the FBI five days after the assassination, he refused to discuss the call from Ruby;[141] he later provided a series of contradictory explanations.[142] Weiner was also curiously uncertain about what he was doing at the time of the assassination; he could not even remember what city he was in or how he first heard the news.[143] Weiner did confirm, however, that he met with Trafficante in Miami at about that date.[144] Their subject of discussion: "just trivialities."[145]

Ruby's brother Hyman testified that after Ruby "tried to call" Weiner he then "tried to call Lenny Patrick,"[146] whom Ruby had known as a young man in Chicago.[147] Ruby's sister Eva testified that Ruby did in fact call Lenny Patrick in 1963.[148] Patrick was a notorious Mob assassin.[149] "Police credit him with masterminding some of the Syndicate's more important liquidations," one source noted.[150]

On October 26, Ruby also placed a 3-minute person-to-person call to Michael Shore at his Beverly Hills home.[151] Recall that Shore is a record company executive and a good friend, business partner and close contact of Chicago Mobster Irwin Weiner.

October 30. At 9:13 p.m., Ruby placed a 1-minute call to the office phone of Marcello lieutenant Nofio Pecora at the Tropical Court in New Orleans.[152]

October 31. Ruby placed a 4-minute call to the Beverly Hills home of Michael Shore.[153] Over the next three weeks, while Larry Crafard was employed at the Carousel Club,[154] Ruby "talked to Mike Shore two or three times a week on the telephone," Crafard recalled.[155] Ruby apparently spoke to Shore from a Fort Worth telephone, number ED5–1266, which was listed with the notation "give to Mike Shore only" in a notebook Crafard kept for Ruby.[156] Crafard testified, "That would be a number where Jack Ruby could be reached and he didn't want me to give the number to anyone but Mike Shore."[157]

November 7. Ruby received a collect call from "Barney Baker, Chicago, Illinois," and spoke for seven minutes.[158] Baker, who admitted telephoning Ruby in November,[159] was a Hoffa aide described by federal sources as "a reported muscle and bagman" for Hoffa and "a hoodlum with organized crime and Teamster connections."[160] He had been released from prison in June 1963 after serving two years for shaking down a Pittsburgh newspaper.[161]

November 8. Ruby placed a 4-minute call to the Eden Roc Hotel in Miami, person-to-person to Dusty Miller.[162] Murray W. "Dusty" Miller, who confirmed this contact,[163] was the head of the Southern Conference of Teamsters in 1963 and later became Secretary Treasurer of the Teamsters International Union.[164] The House Assassinations Committee disclosed that Miller "was associated with numerous underworld figures."[165]

Also on November 8, Ruby placed a 14-minute call to Barney Baker, the Teamster goon, at Baker's Chicago residence.[166]*

*Baker's telephone records show two calls in November 1963 to the Denver number of boxer Sonny Liston.[167] These contacts lend credibility to the 1973 account of

November 12. Ruby placed a 10-minute call person-to-person to Frank Goldstein in San Francisco.[172] Goldstein, who confirmed the call,[173] described himself as a "professional gambler."[174] Mob killers Russell Matthews,[175] Lewis McWillie[176] and Lenny Patrick[177] were similarly described in the assassination evidence.

November 17. Al Gruber of Los Angeles placed an 8-minute call to Ruby.[178] Gruber, who had six arrests under three different names,[179] also visited Ruby for several days in mid-November, as will be discussed in chapter 23.

These timely and intensive contacts of Ruby suggest that a Mob conspiracy was in progress. The existence of such a conspiracy is confirmed by the concertedly fabricated alibi presented to cover these contacts.

Mafia defector Patsy Lepera that Liston deliberately lost the 1964 championship match against Muhammed Ali on the Mob's orders: "This guy didn't just take a dive—he did a one and a half off the highboard."[168] The Mafia's hold on Liston—typical of its influence in sports[169]—was reflected in an FBI-recorded conversation of December 7, 1961 between Liston's manager, Bernie Glickman, and Mafia boss Sam Giancana.[170] During the conversation, Glickman asked Giancana's permission to take unspecified action regarding Liston.[171]

I believe there should be some integrity in what the hell we do and do not believe in the whole question of the drift toward a police state and McCarthyism with its new name, Mafiaism.[1]

You could get out of the Mafia business, and we could perhaps pay more attention to some of the greater problems, which is the breakdown of law and order on the streets. Organized crime does not embrace murder and rape and muggings and robberies* and this sort of thing.[7]

Cornelius E. Gallagher, U.S. Congressman from New Jersey, 1959–1972, and member of a House subcommittee that investigated organized crime[8]

Neil Gallagher . . . time and again has served as a tool and collaborator of a Cosa Nostra gang lord.[9]

Life magazine, in a 1968 article that excerpted FBI-recorded conversations between Gallagher and Mafia boss Joe Zicarelli

□ 21 □

The Collapse of
the Mob's Assassination Alibi

Lying is second nature for Mobsters; self-serving explanations of their activities are not to be taken seriously. In some cases the fabrications are

*See Appendix 4 concerning, among other things, the brutal murder of a U.S. Senator's daughter by a Mafia-backed band of thieves,[2] the New Year's Eve murders of two black servants by Mobster "Fatty" Russo,[3] the Mafia murder of a Kansas City witness covered by rape and robbery,[4] Mafia-sponsored robberies, hijackings and stock thefts amounting to billions of dollars each year,[5] and the Mob's nationwide fencing network which supports most street crime.[6]

improvised, in others they are coordinated. A classic example of the first situation was presented during a memorable police bust 25 years ago.

In November 1957, New York State Police detained 58 Mafia figures from across the country as they met at Joseph Barbara's home in Apalachin, New York.[10] Police intelligence indicated that the meeting had been called to discuss realignments in the New York Mafia families, the Narcotics Control Act of 1956, and the organizing activities of a garment workers' union in some Mob-owned factories.[11] Fifty of the arraigned Apalachin conferees had criminal records,[12] and half were related by blood or marriage.[13] Their joint detention confirmed the existence of a nationwide Mafia organization, as had been exposed by local grand juries, law enforcement agencies and Congressional committees since 1890.[14]

With assorted improvisations, however, the Apalachin delegates tried to justify their presence at the site of the meeting. Vito Genovese of New York City maintained that host Joseph Barbara was sick and that all of his visitors "just came to wish him speedy recovery."[15] Some of the conferees caught in the woods surrounding Barbara's house said that they had been "looking at real estate."[16] Two others picked up outside claimed that they had been "walking to the railroad station";[17] small matter that the nearest railroad station was 70 miles away.[18] John Montana of Buffalo, New York explained that he was on his way to Medico Industries in Pittston, Pennsylvania when the brakes of his Cadillac started acting up.[19] Believing that Barbara, who owned a fleet of trucks, would have a good mechanic on hand, Montana took a 20-mile detour to Barbara's house and went in for a cup of tea.[20] Then, as Montana related, there was suddenly a big commotion and he decided to take a walk in the woods.[21]

More sinister than the Mob's habitual lying is its routine use of outsiders to bolster its fabrications. To cite an example considered by the House Judiciary Committee, in 1966

> Jerry Angiulo, underboss in the Patriarca family and controller of Boston's criminal syndicate . . . was convicted for assaulting a federal officer. FBI agents, electronically monitoring boss Patriarca's headquarters, recorded how Angiulo discussed his pending prosecution in detail, plotting to defeat it by procuring a blind man to perjure himself and establish an alibi, then getting a second "standup" witness to lie that he, too, saw the phantom encounter.[22]

In a similar case reported by sociologist Donald Cressey, some Mafia "soldiers" were indicted for killing a man.[23] At the trial, the Mafiosi were provided a false alibi by a hotel owner whom they had once assisted.[24] "He had to perjure himself or be killed," Cressey noted.[25] Cressey also described two cases in which witnesses against the Mob received death threats to recant their testimony; one was later murdered.[26]

Carlos Marcello spearheaded a textbook example of Mob perjury, corruption, and intimidation during the 1960s in the epic campaign to extricate Teamster President Jimmy Hoffa from federal prosecution.[27] Among the maneuvers used was jury tampering, as exposed by Hoffa's conviction on that charge.[28] Also employed were affidavits from prostitutes presenting a bizarre tale of judicial improprieties,[29] which supported a motion to grant Hoffa a new trial.[30] The court found this tale a "total fabrication and fraud";[31] one prostitute subsequently recanted her testimony and another was convicted of perjury.[32]

Like the tales of Barbara's house guests and Hoffa's prostitutes, and the stories of Ruby's acquaintances discussed earlier,[33] the alibi presented to explain Ruby's pre-assassination contacts with underworld figures was also a complete fabrication. But this time, the alibi was recited in collusion by Mobsters—a prima facie demonstration of Mob conspiracy.

/1/ Background

> Recently, I had to make so many numerous calls that I am sure you know of. Am I right? Because of trying to survive in my business.
>
> My unfair competition had been running certain shows that we were restricted to run by regulation of the union ... and consequently I was becoming insolvent because of it.
>
> All those calls were made with only, in relation to seeing if they can help out, with the American Guild of Variety Artists. Does that confirm a lot of things you have heard?[34]

To explain his many pre-assassination calls to Mobsters, Ruby testified that he made these calls only to secure assistance in a problem with the American Guild of Variety Artists (AGVA).[35] This AGVA story, echoed by many of the Mobsters he called,[36] was rooted in two points of fact: AGVA had jurisdiction over Ruby's night club entertainers, and the parties he called included some officials of that union.[37] An examination of AGVA's background and of Ruby's relationship with it, however, removes any shred of credibility from the alibi.

Problems with the American Guild of Variety Artists. In 1962, the U.S. Senate Permanent Investigations Subcommittee conducted a series of hearings on AGVA's treatment of the striptease dancers in its ranks.[38] The conditions revealed by union members and officials, law enforcement officials and other witnesses were summarized in a blistering closing statement by Senator John McClellan, the subcommittee's chairman, as briefly excerpted below:

> For the past 2 weeks we have seen unfolded before us a sordid and distressing picture of a labor union which has miserably failed to meet its responsibilities to the profession of artists ... and to the members whom it represents....
>
> The so-called exotic dancers in the vicious and degrading establishments of the underworld ... are required to mix with customers, induce customers to buy drinks, and assist their employers in relieving suckers of every cent that can be taken from them by whatever means may be effective, from short-changing and padded checks to prostitution, jackrolling, knockout drops, and every other means that can be devised or imagined....
>
> The AGVA members employed in these clubs are under complete domination and control of hoodlum owners....
>
> Because of the failure of AGVA to enforce its contracts, the rank and file members are deprived of social security, workmen's compensation, unemployment insurance and other benefits guaranteed them....
>
> Hoodlums and racketeers are able to reap fantastic profits through the exploitation of AGVA members, who are required to work as "B" girls and worse simply because the union will not protect them....[39]

AGVA's character in the early 1960s was perhaps most succinctly summarized by a subcommittee member, Senator Karl Mundt:

> The testimony indicated yesterday ... the AGVA dues-paying members get nothing but their receipt for their dues. It is purely a racket to collect money....[40]

A Chicago Police official who interviewed almost a hundred members likewise concluded, "The union was merely a dues collecting agency."[41]

Its pattern of operation typical of a Mob-controlled union,[42] AGVA was found, not surprisingly, to have many Mob connections. Ernest Fast, former Midwest regional director of AGVA,[43] had meetings with several top Chicago gangsters[44] and admitted close association with Chicago Mafia kingpin James Allegretti.[45] Another Chicago AGVA representative was a reputed Teamster goon,[46] while a number of local AGVA booking agents were reportedly involved in vice operations.[47] In Philadelphia[48] and New Orleans,[49] more AGVA links to the Teamsters were discovered, and a federal official investigating AGVA was found to have been selling information to Hoffa associates.[50] When one active dissident, Penny Singleton, criticized official misconduct at union meetings, a series of false charges were drawn up against her by Irwin Mazzei, the West Coast regional director.[51] Now president of AGVA, Singleton characterizes the union during that period as totally corrupt, its situation "abominable."[52]

AGVA's character in Texas was illustrated by the rap sheet of James Henry Dolan, described by the FBI as "one of the two most notorious hoodlums" in Dallas.[53] Although Dolan specialized in armed robbery, confidence swindles, and shakedown rackets,[54] his seven-state trail of arrests and convictions indicates even more diverse criminal skills.[55] His associates included such Mob heavies as Santos Trafficante, Nofio Pecora, Irwin Weiner, and James Fratianno.[56] In 1962, an informant reported, Dolan was in the "fire business"[57]—reflected by his one-to-three year sentence for arson in December 1963.[58]

From 1958 to 1961, as the House Assassinations Committee noted, "Dolan was employed as the Dallas representative of the American Guild of Variety Artists."[59] Basically, "he was concerned with enforcing minimum standards for entertaining employees in the Dallas area."[60] Although one knowledgeable source labeled Dolan's post "a racketeer position,"[61] Dolan was apparently too busy planning armed robberies in Texas, Arkansas and Mississippi during his tenure[62] to extort payoffs with undivided attention.[63] Dolan might have clarified his AGVA duties to federal interviewers in 1978 had they not been interrupted by Dolan's "pre-dinner 'lock-up' ritual" at Atlanta Federal Penitentiary.[64]

Ruby's contacts with AGVA officials. Predictably, it was several of the same AGVA officials cited for misconduct or underworld affiliation whom Ruby contacted in the months before the assassination. In the early fall of 1963, former AGVA official Dolan saw Ruby in a downtown Dallas restaurant.[65] This encounter punctuated a four-state crime spree by Dolan,[66] which may have included contacts with Marcello associates in May 1963.[67] On August 2 and November 9, Ruby called Irwin Mazzei,[68] the AGVA official who drew up charges against dissident Penny Singleton. In one of these calls, Mazzei later told the FBI, Ruby revealed that he was a friend of Chicago official Ernie Fast,[69] the close associate of a Mafia boss.

Also representative of Ruby's contacts in AGVA was Jack Yanover, one of the "officers of record" of the Dream Bar Lounge in Cicero, Illinois,[70] a reputed underworld strip joint and gambling front.[71] Ruby called the Dream Bar on May 12, 1963,[72] apparently for Yanover.[73] And on November 20, Ruby called another AGVA official from Chicago, Alton Sharpe;[74] Sharpe telephoned a message for Ruby three days later.[75] Sharpe told the FBI that these contacts concerned a letter Ruby wished to send Sharpe about his AGVA problem.[76] But when questioned about Sharpe's explanation, Dallas branch manager Tom Palmer replied, "I don't accept it."[77] Palmer testified, "I couldn't understand his [Ruby's] sending any pertinent data to Chicago, which was not a regional office and had no jurisdiction over this area. . . . I still cannot understand what was of importance, of such importance that would require a weekend transaction of AGVA business."[78]

As demonstrated by telephone records, Ruby's pre-assassination contacts also included two national AGVA officials in New York: Joey Adams,[79] who was reputedly "well connected" with Joseph Glaser,[80] and Bobby Faye.[81] But the most revealing facet of Ruby's New York AGVA contacts is the maze of contradictions surrounding his August visit to that city.

Ruby testified that he was desperately concerned about his AGVA problem:

> I even flew to New York to see Joe Gla[s]er, and he called Bobby Faye. He was the national president. That didn't help. He called Barney Ross and Joey Adams.[82]

But when Ruby registered at the Hilton Hotel, the chief room clerk told the FBI, Ruby said only "that he was in New York City looking for talent for his night club. . . . he was not going to go to any legitimate booking agents, but rather was going to look around the New York night clubs."[83] Barney Ross also said that Ruby discussed talent searching in a call to Ross just before that trip.[84] And Ross claimed that he had last seen Ruby about two years before the assassination;[85] this further contradicted reports that Ruby went to New York specifically to see Ross, and did see him.[86]

The second series of contradictions concerned Ruby's reported contact with AGVA President Bobby Faye. As quoted above, Ruby claimed that Glaser called Faye for him. But Glaser told the FBI that when Ruby requested his assistance in New York, he refused to do anything and "immediately thereafter terminated the interview" with Ruby.[87] If Glaser was telling the truth, perhaps Ruby contacted Faye directly as described by AGVA official Irv Mazzei. Mazzei told the FBI that he received a call from Faye, and

> learned from Faye that Ruby was dissatisfied and had flown from Dallas to New York to see Mr. Faye and was, in fact, sitting in Faye's office when the call was made by Faye.[88]

But Faye told the FBI that he "never had any personal contact with Jack Ruby."[89] Thus the only credibly established contacts of Ruby during his New York trip were with Joseph Glaser, Mobster Sidney Korshak's partner, and with Capone-tied boxer Barney Ross.[90]

/2/ Ruby's AGVA Problem

In summary, AGVA was a Mob-infiltrated "dues collecting" agency, and Ruby's contacts with union officials were particularly questionable. It is consequently difficult to believe that these contacts, much less Ruby's numerous calls to underworld figures, concerned any legitimate union grievance. It is not surprising, therefore, that the story of Ruby's AGVA difficulty proves fraudulent in its basic premises.

The basic alibi. The stories of Ruby, his Mob contacts, and some AGVA officials followed this basic line. Jack Ruby, along with night club operators Abe and Barney Weinstein, had been running "amateur strip shows" at their burlesque establishments for at least two years before the assassination.[91] These shows featured about five or six women paid $10 to $15 per show, and were presented about once a week at each of the clubs.[92] But Ruby ran such shows only to keep up with the competition,[93] believing the Weinsteins were scheduling them to destroy his business.[94] And since 1961 he had attempted to persuade AGVA officials to prohibit them.[95]

When AGVA did ban amateur strip shows early in 1963,[96] Ruby stopped running them.[97] The Weinsteins, on the other hand, continued them under various subterfuges.[98] Ruby, his business suffering,[99] then repeatedly called AGVA officials to complain about the Weinsteins.[100] Ruby also called numerous Mobsters solely to request their intervention with AGVA.[101]

Incongruities and disparities concerning the AGVA situation. There is no facet of this AGVA alibi—the purported threat to Ruby's business, Ruby's concern over it, or his method of solving it—that bears any relation to reality. First, Ruby was at no competitive disadvantage because of AGVA's policy on amateur strip shows. Although Abe and Barney Weinstein ran such shows at one club each,[102] Ruby ran them at both the Carousel and Vegas clubs.[103] And contrary to a key contention of his alibi,[104] Ruby continued to run such shows into the latter part of 1963,[105] well after AGVA issued its directive banning them.[106]

Second, the whole issue was old and inconsequential. According to a one-time Dallas board member of AGVA, the Weinsteins had run amateur strip shows for about 13 years,[107] long before Ruby professed concern over the matter. And AGVA regulations, if they had ever been enforced, merely required Ruby to pay his amateur strippers about $20 more per night to meet union scale.[108] These extra payments, once a week to six women,[109] could hardly have been significant to Ruby—a ranking Dallas gambling and narcotics operative[110] who carried thousands of dollars[111] and paid off hundreds of police officers.[112] Indeed, in November 1963, when his telephone activity peaked,[113] Ruby indicated anything but concern over his night club operations. For during that month, Ruby was constantly away from the Carousel Club, engaged in unknown activities,[114] in contrast to his regular presence there before November.[115]

Ruby's lack of concern over any night club problem was also indicated in the 1978 Congressional testimony of Andrew Armstrong, his handyman and assistant at the Carousel Club during 1963:[116]

> **Q**: Well, was there a time in the fall of 1963 ... that the club was in financial trouble because the competition was doing a lot better because of their use of amateur nights?
> **Armstrong**: No.
> **Q**: They were drawing a lot more customers in and Jack's business was hurting. Do you remember that in the fall of 1963?
> **Armstrong**: No. We was using amateurs, too. ....
> **Q**: Were there any problems that Jack and the club were encountering in the fall of 1963 that was different from before? Were there any special things that were bothering Jack Ruby or bothering the club?
> **Armstrong**: No.[117]

Armstrong noted, in fact, that Ruby's night club business was "picking up" during the fall of 1963.[118]

A third fallacy in the AGVA alibi is the absurd assumption that this Mob-tied racketeering outfit would enforce any regulation covering Ruby's operations. Indeed, Ruby habitually and flagrantly violated AGVA regulations far more serious than the amateur show directive. Ruby pandered his Carousel strippers[119] and expected them to mix with customers to promote the consumption of liquor.[120] Although he regularly funneled cash to AGVA,[121] Ruby was delinquent in paying welfare benefits to his AGVA-affiliated employees.[122] And Ruby physically abused his employees, as many witnesses reported.[123] In short, Carousel house rules included mixing with customers, prostitution, cash transactions, delinquent welfare payments and physical abuse—precisely the practices of hoodlum night club owners described in the Senate AGVA hearings.[124]

Despite his flagrant violations of AGVA regulations, however, Ruby maintained cozy relationships with local AGVA officials. Dallas branch manager Tom Palmer testified that his relationship with Ruby was "amicable in all instances."[125] Palmer explained that he "exercised extreme leniency" in his dealings with Ruby,[126] and that he reacted only by "collecting data that indicated Jack was continuing to violate certain rules of AGVA that could have been awkward for him."[127]

Ruby had also enjoyed friendly relations with Palmer's infamous predecessor, James Henry Dolan. On one occasion, Dolan stood by while Ruby assaulted a band leader in Dolan's AGVA membership; Dolan then joined

Ruby in appropriating the proceeds of the musician's act.[128] On another occasion, when a woman complained that Ruby had struck her at the Carousel Club, Dolan reportedly told her to "forget the incident."[129] Another AGVA official, Jack Cole, had similarly ignored a union member's complaint of abuse by Ruby.[130] Also indicative of Ruby's preferred treatment by AGVA was the report of one Carousel stripper that he had obtained a favorable AGVA rating, allowing him to pay lower salaries, "because he had connections."[131]

A particularly useful contact of Ruby in AGVA was Breck Wall, president of its Dallas council.[132] Responsible for reviewing complaints by performers against night club operators,[133] Wall told the Warren Commission that Ruby called him four times in November 1963 concerning a problem with AGVA.[134] But remarkably, given the purported urgency of Ruby's problem, Ruby's close friendship with Wall,[135] and Wall's AGVA position, Wall could not remember what the problem was:

> **Wall**: ... he was having some sort of problem with his girls and the union was going to make him do something, which I didn't think was right. I told him I would help him out and make sure his case was presented correctly.
> **Q**: What was the union trying to make him do?
> **Wall**: I don't recall.[136]

Later in his testimony, however, Wall did recollect the cause of the trouble with the AGVA: Ruby was not allowing enough break time between striptease acts.[137] Wall never mentioned any problem with amateur strippers.[138]

Even if the issue of amateur strip shows had been a genuine, timely or significant concern of Ruby's, however, it was not a reasonable explanation for his nationwide contacts with Mobsters. The incongruity was pointed out by Congressman Floyd Fithian to one such Chicago contact, Irwin Weiner, and applied equally to others:

> Doesn't that strike you as being a little curious ... [for Ruby to have] bothered to call somebody in Chicago when his little difficulty over an amateur stripper was in Dallas? That does not seem to be a very credible story.[139]

Indeed, if some freak enforcement of AGVA regulations had caused Ruby any genuine concern, there was only one hoodlum whose intervention was needed. That was the man who had routinely subverted AGVA rules through "amicable" relationships with union officials: Dallas Mobster Jack Ruby.

/3/ **Mob Conspiracy**

The totally fraudulent character of the AGVA alibi is further reflected in its various contorted renditions by Ruby's Mob contacts. Teamster goon Barney Baker, for one, told the FBI in 1964 that Ruby called Baker's Chicago home from Dallas in November 1963 and left a message with Baker's wife.[140] Baker related that he then called Ruby, a complete stranger to him, at which point Ruby complained that his "competitors through the help of the AGVA were 'giving [him] a fit.'"[141] Telephone records show, however, that Baker placed a collect call to Ruby *the day before*, not after, Ruby called Baker.[142]

When questioned by the House Assassinations Committee in 1978, Baker gave a rambling account of his contacts with Ruby,[143] punctuated by sudden bursts of recollection, dubious explanations, and reversals.[144] At one point, however, Baker responded with unconscious candor when confronted with some of Ruby's testimony: "Yes, that refreshes me a lot in memorizing exactly what it was about."[145]

On June 1, 1964, Los Angeles felon Al Gruber told the FBI that during their mid-November contacts, Ruby often

> expressed concern about his business being poor. Ruby mentioned that he had been forced by the union to stop having amateur night at his club, and indicated that his competitors had continued having their amateur night programs.[146]

When initially questioned by the FBI on November 25, 1963, however, Gruber provided a detailed account of his conversations with Ruby that omitted any reference to such a problem.[147]

Also interrogated too soon to have received the AGVA line, apparently, was Capone-tied boxer Barney Ross. In June 1964, Ruby testified that in the heat of his AGVA dispute, he "flew to New York to see Joe Gla[s]er," who "called Barney Ross."[148] But when Ross was interviewed in New York on November 25, 1963, as previously related, Ross told the FBI that Ruby had contacted him in 1963 only "to secure talent for Ruby's club in Dallas."[149]

Questioned four days later in Los Angeles, William Miller apparently confused a hastily conveyed AGVA story with the talent-scouting alibi. A one-time Nevada casino owner and beneficiary of Teamster pension fund money, Miller told the FBI that Ruby had telephoned him and complained to him that AGVA "would not let him run the amateur strip nights, but that his competitors were doing so."[150] Yet Miller told the FBI that in the same call, Ruby had asked Miller "if he could obtain some girls to help sponsor an amateur striptease contest in his [Ruby's] Dallas clubs."[151]

The most flagrant fabrications came from Chicago Mobster Irwin Weiner.

When questioned by the FBI on November 27, 1963, as agents noted, Weiner "refused to furnish any information concerning Jack Ruby."[152] In 1974, a private investigator seeking this information was threatened over the telephone by Weiner.[153] Later, Weiner told a reporter, "Ruby was a friend of mine. He called me. I talked to him. What I talked to him about was my own business."[154] And in January 1978, Weiner told an investigator that the call from Ruby had nothing to do with AGVA or any labor problem.[155]

Weiner finally came around to the AGVA line in May 1978, when questioned by the House Assassinations Committee. Weiner testified that his previous accounts had been false, and that he habitually lied to reporters.[156] Instead, he explained, Ruby had called and asked him to write a bond in connection with a lawsuit against a competitor who was running amateur strip shows.[157] But the Committee could not find any indication that Ruby was contemplating such a suit, nor any explanation "for his having to go to Chicago for such a bond."[158] Needless to say, "the Committee was not satisfied with Weiner's explanation of his relationship to Ruby."[159]

Other variations on the AGVA theme were presented by these pre-assassination contacts of Ruby: Lewis McWillie,[160] the Mob "gambler and murderer" and associate of Santos Trafficante;[161] Dusty Miller,[162] the Teamster executive and organized crime associate;[163] Michael Shore,[164] the partner of Irwin Weiner;[165] Frank Goldstein,[166] the "professional gambler";[167] and Joseph Glaser,[168] the Korshak partner who "probably could have been in rackets."[169] Similar stories were also provided by columnist Tony Zoppi,[170] and by three AGVA officials who were curiously fired within three days preceding the assassination of President Kennedy:[171] Alton Sharpe,[172] Irv Mazzei[173] and Bobby Faye.[174] But these synchronized accounts could not bolster the fatally flawed AGVA alibi. They only exhibited a coordinated Mob effort to cover its assassination trail—a Mob conspiracy on its own account.

The House Assassinations Committee noted that "AGVA has been used frequently by members of organized crime as a front for criminal activities."[175] As demonstrated in this chapter, Ruby's AGVA alibi typified this pattern. And the extraordinary criminal activity behind this alibi is further exposed through his activities in the final weeks before the assassination.

> [Organized crime] has already crippled or weakened vital
> organs of our body politic, and it is still spreading and
> spreading rapidly. Unless we act effectively, and with
> dispatch, organized crime may well destroy the social,
> political, economic and moral heart of our Nation.[1]
>
> Senator John McClellan

> If we do not on a national scale attack organized crimi-
> nals with weapons and techniques as effective as their own,
> they will destroy us.[2]
>
> Robert F. Kennedy

☐ 22 ☐
Jack Ruby, Lee Oswald
and Officer J. D. Tippit

There is a fable about a boy who spied a leprechaun burying a hoard of gold in a forest. The boy tied a scarf around a nearby tree, grabbed the leprechaun and made him promise not to untie the scarf. The next day, when the boy returned to snatch some of the treasure, he found scarves tied to every tree in the forest.

A similar predicament confounds the study of possible ties between Jack Ruby and Lee Harvey Oswald. For the Warren Commission volumes contain almost a hundred reports of such ties, many of which are far-fetched and some of which appear deliberately fabricated.[3] Similar to Jim Garrison's allegations, for example, was a report related by Dallas Police Lt. George Butler that Lee Harvey Oswald was the illegitimate son of Jack Ruby.[4] Yet other accounts linking Ruby and Oswald are quite credible, as are many which establish a close association between Ruby and slain police officer J. D. Tippit. And particularly interesting are remarks by Ruby himself highlighting the possibility of each relationship.

/1/   Oswald at the Carousel Club in Mid-November 1963

On November 24, 1963, shortly after Ruby shot Oswald, the Associated Press distributed the following release:

> Entertainer Bill DeMar of Evansville, Ind. told the Associated Press by telephone Sunday that he was positive that Lee Harvey Oswald was a patron about nine days ago in the Dallas night club of Jack Ruby. . . .[5]

A performer at the Carousel Club in November, DeMar stated to the AP,

> I have a memory act . . . in which I have 20 customers call out various objects in rapid order. . . . I am positive that Oswald was one of the men that called out an object about nine days ago.[6]

When shown a photo of Oswald in an FBI interview of November 24, De-Mar stated that he believed "this is the man he saw seated among the patrons of the Carousel Club."[7] And when interviewed by Warren Commission counsel in June 1964, DeMar declined to modify his previous remarks.[8] In that last hearing, however, DeMar asserted only that the man he saw at the Carousel Club might have been Oswald, and that the story of his sighting of Oswald "started snowballing" from an initially tentative identification.[9]

Such belated accommodation to the lone-assassin line was not uncommon among assassination witnesses. Warren Reynolds, for example, came to identify Tippit's slayer as Oswald only after being shot in the head and further intimidated.[10] And George Senator, expressing grave fear of being hurt or killed, drastically modified his initial accounts of assassination-weekend events to fit Ruby's alibi.[11]

Indeed, DeMar's actions on November 24 demonstrate that he was anything but hesitant about his observation of Oswald in Ruby's club. The manager of the Dallas motel where DeMar lodged that day told the FBI that a few minutes after Oswald was shot, DeMar rushed into the motel office, reported the shooting, went immediately to his cabin, and called a number in Evansville, Indiana.[12] This call, placed by DeMar at 11:32 a.m., was to David Hoy, news director for radio station WIKY in Evansville and an old acquaintance of DeMar.[13] Within the next half hour, Hoy then placed two short calls to DeMar at his Dallas motel, a call to the Associated Press in Indianapolis and a 60-minute call again to DeMar.[14] During the afternoon and evening, Hoy called the Dallas Police Homicide Division and DeMar twice,[15] once cutting in on a busy line, telling the operator it was an "emergency call."[16] DeMar placed at least ten more calls that day from his motel, including six other long distance calls and two calls to the Dallas Police Homicide Division.[17]

Dale Burgess of the Associated Press in Indianapolis told the FBI that Hoy called him around noon on November 24 specifically to relate DeMar's sighting of Oswald at the Carousel Club.[18] It is thus curious that in June 1964, David Hoy, then a mind reader in a Boston night club, told the FBI that DeMar had not mentioned his observation of Oswald until about 1:50 p.m. that afternoon.[19] From the frantic telephone activity of both DeMar and Hoy just after the Oswald shooting, it is clear that the AP representative and not Hoy was reporting accurately.

And doubts about DeMar's sincerity that Hoy claimed in June 1964[20] were not evident in Hoy's counsel to him on November 24. For as both reported, Hoy advised DeMar to hide out because of possible danger to his life.[21] Hoy recalled counseling DeMar that DeMar "was in a dangerous position if, in fact, there was a compact between Oswald and Ruby and other members of the underworld."[22] And DeMar testified that Hoy had learned from his news media contacts that the people possibly interested in killing him were "friends of Jack's."[23] DeMar in fact followed Hoy's advice so carefully that federal agents had to call Hoy in Evansville to locate him.[24]

The prompt and drastic actions of both DeMar and Hoy thus lend credibility to DeMar's positive account of Oswald's presence in Ruby's club one week before the assassination. And Carousel stripper Karen Carlin also "vaguely remembered Oswald being at the club" when questioned by the Secret Service on November 24.[25] Although uncertain and hesitant on this point,[26] Carlin subsequently stated that she had seen either Oswald or someone resembling him at or near the club.[27]

/2/ Ruby with Oswald at the Carousel Club on October 4, 1963

On December 3, 1963, Dallas attorney Carroll Jarnagin sent the FBI a seven-page letter[28] detailing a conversation at the Carousel Club on October 4;[29] Jarnagin confirmed this account in a subsequent FBI interview.[30] The participants in this conversation, which Jarnagin said he overheard from a table ten feet away, were Jack Ruby and an "H. L. Lee," whom Jarnagin positively identified as Oswald from news photographs.[31] The Dallas attorney provided a verbatim transcript of much of the conversation,[32] later explaining to a reporter that he had an excellent memory and could probably still recite the chemical formulas on a college exam for which he had received a perfect grade.[33] This claim was reasonable given Jarnagin's attendance at Southern Methodist University, Vanderbilt University and the University of Chicago, as reflected in his credit record.[34]

Two things cast doubt on Jarnagin's story. First, Jarnagin admitted that he and his date, Shirley Maudlin, had consumed more than a bottle of liquor at the Carousel Club the night he reportedly saw Oswald.[35] And second, questioned at a jail in Omaha, Nebraska, Maudlin denied that she and Jarnagin had observed any such encounter.[36] On the other hand, it is farfetched to assume that practicing attorney Jarnagin invented this detailed report, which was consistent with Oswald's movements,[37] Ruby's Syndicate connection,[38] and similar accounts of Ruby-Oswald associations.

Summarizing the dialogue Jarnagin reported, the man using the name H. L. Lee told Ruby that he had just arrived from New Orleans, had not yet notified his family of his presence, and needed money;[39] Oswald had in fact arrived in Dallas from New Orleans on October 3 in just those circumstances.[40] Ruby told Lee "you'll get the money after the job is done," to which Lee countered, "What about half now and half after the job is done?"[41] The job, as the conversation later revealed, was for Lee to kill Governor Connally of Texas when he visited Dallas.[42] Ruby suggested that Lee shoot from the roof of some building or from the Carousel Club, but Lee was skeptical about Ruby's proposed arrangements and assurances of success.[43]

Lee then inquired about the reason for the job:

> **Lee**: Not that it makes me any difference, but what have you got against the Governor?
>
> **Ruby**: He won't work with us on paroles; with a few of the right boys out we could really open up this State, with a little cooperation from the Governor. The boys in Chicago have no place to go, no place to really operate; they've clamped down the lid in Chicago; Cuba is closed; everything is dead, look at this place, half empty. . . .
>
> **Lee**: How do you know that the Governor won't work with you?
>
> **Ruby**: It[']s no use, he's been in Washington too long, they're too straight up there: after they've been there awhile they get to thinking like the Attorney General. The Attorney General, now there's a guy the boys would like to get, but it[']s no use, he stays in Washington too much. . . .
>
> **Lee**: Killing the Governor of Texas will put the heat on too, won't it?
>
> **Ruby**: Not really, they'll think some crack-pot or communist did it, and it will be written off as an unsolved crime.
>
> **Lee**: That is if I get away.
>
> **Ruby**: You'll get away.[44]

Ruby and Lee then discussed other plans for shooting Connally, Jarnagin reported, until Lee noticed that Jarnagin was observing them and they lowered their voices.[45]

If Jarnagin's report was correct, then Oswald was what he claimed, "just a patsy,"[46] set up to be the "crack-pot or communist" Ruby described.

/3/ Ruby with Oswald at the Carousel Club in Early November 1963

In an affidavit of December 2, 1963, Wilbur Waldon Litchfield reported that he visited the Carousel Club on a Tuesday or Thursday night in the first or second week of November 1963.[47] Litchfield sat down at a table, waiting to keep a 10 p.m. appointment with Ruby, and saw three persons enter Ruby's office before his turn came.[48] Ruby's first visitor, Litchfield learned, was a friend of Ruby from California;[49] this may have been Al Gruber of Los Angeles, who visited Ruby at the Carousel Club in mid-November.[50] The second visitor Litchfield observed was a magazine photographer who photographed some of Ruby's strippers that night;[51] another witness confirmed that a magazine photographer took pictures at the Carousel Club two or three weeks before the assassination.[52]

The next to see Ruby, Litchfield reported, was a man in a white V-neck sweater who had been sitting four tables in front of Litchfield.[53] Litchfield had paid particular attention to that man, he explained, "because of his sloppy dress"; the man's "hair was not combed," and he stood out from the other men in suits or sport jackets.[54] In an FBI document not made public for several months after Litchfield was questioned, attorney Carroll Jarnagin had similarly observed that Ruby's Carousel visitor of October 4 "need[ed] a haircut ... his general appearance [was] somewhat unkempt, and he [did] not appear to be dressed for night-club[b]ing."[55]

Fifteen or twenty minutes after entering Ruby's office, the man in the white V-neck sweater came out with Ruby, Litchfield reported.[56] As the man left, he passed within two feet of Litchfield underneath a bright light.[57] Litchfield observed that the man was "in his middle 20's, 5'7" - 5'9"; and very slender."[58] Litchfield then spoke with Ruby about a possible night club venture, and left the Carousel Club at about 1:30 a.m.[59] "After President Kennedy was assassinated," Litchfield related, "and this fellow Oswald's picture was on television and in the paper, I remembered that he was the man I saw in the white V-neck sweater."[60] Litchfield positively identified the man as Oswald.[61]

Following his report, which undermined the lone-nut explanation of events, the Dallas Police immediately took the highly unusual step of giving Litchfield a polygraph exam.[62] The police's curt conclusion was that Litchfield "ha[d] been untruthful."[63] Next, related Litchfield, officials attempted to shake his testimony through a questionable means of pressure, again highly irregular:

. . . when the police were questioning me, they said, "Are you positive, are you positive, are you positive?"

I said, "It looks like him, it looks like him, it looks like him." And they came back, "Are you positive, are you positive?" And then the fact that when the Federal agents talked to me, they said, "You know, if you say you are positive and it wasn't him," it's a Federal charge. . . .[64]

As a result of this official grilling, Litchfield qualified his initial positive identification and affirmed instead that the man in the white V-neck sweater "closely resemble[d]" Oswald.[65] But Litchfield later testified that he had been positive "in [his] mind" that the man was Oswald; "it sure as heck looked like him."[66]

/4/ The Testimony of Jack Ruby and Marguerite Oswald

The testimony of both Jack Ruby and Mrs. Marguerite Oswald, Lee's mother, also provides strong indications of contact between Ruby and Oswald. Ruby's remarks, considered first, are best understood in light of his fear to speak candidly in Dallas, as he expressed to the Warren Commission: "I want to tell the truth and I can't tell it here. . . . my life is in danger here."[67] Because of this fear—hardly unfounded, as discussed earlier—Ruby expressed his candid disclosures in a hypothetical guise, often rather transparent, while maintaining the facade of his fabricated alibi.[68] His reluctance to speak directly became particularly clear during his polygraph hearing, when he explained to attorney Clayton Fowler why he wanted prosecutor Bill Alexander present at the session:

Mr. Ruby: I feel I don't want him to think I'm holding out on anything. I don't want him to have any idea that I'm reluctant to answer things in front of him, believe me.

. . . the thing is that I have a few other thoughts in my mind, as you well know about.

Mr. Fowler: What are they, Jack?

Mr. Ruby: That I spoke to you about for your consideration.

Mr. Fowler: Jack, I'm not worried, I'm not concerned about anybody trying to do away with me. . . .[69]

Later in the hearing, when the forthcoming analysis of his polygraph examination was mentioned, Ruby asked Alexander, "Bill, will I still be around when the answers come back?"[70]

Many statements by Ruby in his polygraph hearing called attention to possible contacts with Oswald.[71] Most interesting was Ruby's disclosure that he and Oswald had private boxes "close together in the post office."[72] The responses of officials at his hearing confirmed this fact,[73] which Ruby found so significant.[74] Further highlighting his reported connection to Oswald, Ruby requested that the polygraph examiner ask him, "Did you ever meet him at the post office or at the club?"[75] Ruby then proposed that he be asked, "How many times did he come up to the club?"[76] It would have been a strange question if Oswald had never been there. Indeed, the many remarks Ruby volunteered about this matter[77] would be puzzling if the contacts described by DeMar, Jarnagin and Litchfield had not occurred.

If Ruby had not been linked to Oswald, also quite puzzling would be the FBI's reported investigation of such a link *the day before* Ruby shot Oswald. Oswald's mother, Marguerite, told the Warren Commission that on the evening of November 23, 1963, FBI agent Bardwell Odum showed her a photograph—a glossy black-and-white photograph of a man "with a big face and shoulders."[78] Agent Odum held this photo up to Mrs. Oswald's face, and she examined it carefully but was unable to recognize the man.[79] Then, on "about the 26th—it was a few days after Lee was shot," Mrs. Oswald testified, she walked into the hotel room where she and Oswald's wife, Marina, were being interrogated.[80] Mrs. Oswald testified,

> On the table were a lot of newspapers ... and I picked this paper up and turned it over, and I exclaimed, "This is the picture of the man that the FBI agent showed me."
> And one of the agents said, "Mrs. Oswald, that is the man that shot your son."[81]

Mrs. Oswald remembered the FBI photograph vividly, and believed she could identify it "out of a hundred pictures."[82] And she testified under oath, "I know it was Mr. Jack Ruby's picture I saw."[83]

The Warren Commission subsequently presented Mrs. Oswald a purported copy of the photo she had been shown on November 23, which did not depict Ruby.[84] But Mrs. Oswald promptly pointed out that it was not the photo she was originally shown; among other things, the top two corners were cut differently.[85] The Commission confirmed her observation, mysteriously asserting that the photos were cropped "to prevent the viewer from determining precisely where the picture had been taken."[86] Yet the Commission asserted that the second photo was a copy of the first, citing "affidavits obtained from the CIA and from the two FBI agents who trimmed the photographs."[87] This lame story loses all credibility in light of subsequent Senate exposure, as discussed earlier, that "senior officials of both the CIA and the FBI covered up crucial information" in the Kennedy assassination investigation.[88]

There is thus no solid basis to question the positive sworn testimony of

Marguerite Oswald, which further indicated a Ruby-Oswald association. And regarding all visual identifications discussed in this chapter, it is pertinent to note that human visual memory is quite acute;[89] subjects shown more than 2,500 slides in one scientific study achieved 85- to 95-percent accuracy in subsequent recognition tests.[90]

/5/ Ruby with Oswald at the Lucas B&B Restaurant in the Early Morning of November 22

Mrs. Mary Lawrence was working as head waitress at the Lucas B&B Restaurant in Dallas during the early morning of November 22.[91] At about 1:30 a.m., she told the FBI, a young man came into the restaurant and sat down at a table.[92] When approached, the man "stated he was waiting for Mr. Ruby."[93] Mrs. Lawrence knew Jack Ruby, a regular patron, but had never seen that man before.[94]

About an hour later, "Jack Ruby came into the B&B Restaurant and, after looking at the young man at the table, sat down at a table behind the cash register. He did not order his usual food, stating he didn't feel good, and ordered a large glass of orange juice. A few minutes later, the young man who was seated at the table went over to Ruby's table. Thereafter, Ruby paid the bill for both himself and the young man who had eaten."[95]

After President Kennedy was shot and Oswald arrested later that day, Mrs. Lawrence was struck by a close resemblance between the man with Ruby and photographs of Oswald.[96] She told the FBI that both she and the night shift cashier "agreed that he appeared very similar to Lee Harvey Oswald."[97] She further reported that the man was "in his 20's, 5'7" - 9", medium build, 140 lbs.," with "dark hair."[98] This exactly matched Oswald's characteristics: 24 years old, 5'9", 140 lbs., with brown hair.[99] Later in her FBI interview, however, Mrs. Lawrence added one detail which seemed to preclude this man being Oswald—he had "a small scar near his mouth, either on the right or left side."[100]

When subsequently questioned by the Dallas Police, Mrs. Lawrence provided a virtually identical account of the assassination morning encounter, and stated that the man with Ruby "was positively Lee Harvey Oswald."[101] Later in that interview, however, she backed down from her positive identification and once more reported a scar on Ruby's visitor, this time "a small deep scar on his left cheek."[102] The scar, once again, got Mrs. Lawrence off the hook as a witness to a very timely meeting between Ruby and Oswald. It is perhaps pertinent to note that on December 3, 1963, two days before her FBI interview, an unknown male called Mrs. Lawrence and told her, "If you don't want to die, you better get out of town."[103]

Superficially, the encounter described by Mrs. Lawrence can be explained by an assertion of Carousel employee Larry Crafard that he accompanied Ruby for breakfast at the Lucas B&B Restaurant early that morning.[104] Yet the rendezvous described by Lawrence hardly appeared to have been a casual breakfast between acquaintances. And since Crafard had "no front teeth," was "creepy," and "looked like a bum," as one witness reported,[105] it was not likely that he could have been mistaken under close observation for Oswald, who was good-looking and had all his front teeth.[106] Another witness likewise noted that Crafard was missing four front teeth and reported that he had "sandy hair,"[107] whereas Lawrence reported that Ruby's visitor had "dark hair"[108] (Oswald had brown hair[109]). Furthermore, if Crafard's account had been the truth, rather than another fabricated cover for Ruby's suspicious activities, there would have been no reason for Ruby to have lied about his whereabouts during that period: Ruby told both the FBI and the Warren Commission that he went directly home and to bed after closing the Carousel Club at about 2 a.m. Friday.[110]

Given the conflicting accounts of Ruby and Crafard and the death threat to Lawrence, Ruby's assassination-morning rendezvous at the Lucas B&B can only be viewed with suspicion. And in light of reports by Albert Bogard and other witnesses describing a man in Dallas who impersonated Oswald,[111] even if Ruby's visitor were not Oswald, but someone of striking resemblance to him, the implications of conspiracy are still strong. Yet when the reported encounter at Lucas B&B is considered with the similar independent observations of DeMar, Jarnagin and Litchfield, plus the testimony of Ruby and Mrs. Oswald, the possibility of contact between Ruby and Oswald is difficult to discount.

/6/ Jack Ruby and Police Officer J. D. Tippit

According to an eyewitness account discussed earlier,[112] an assailant shot Dallas Police officer J. D. Tippit from the sidewalk.[113] The assailant then walked around to where Tippit lay in the street and "shot him at point blank range in the head."[114] The House Assassinations Committee noted that such a "coup de grace," often employed in gangland murders, "is more indicative of an execution than an act of defense."[115] And one report about Tippit did indeed impute that he might have more readily abetted a gangland plot than apprehended a fleeing criminal. Dallas attorney Travis Kirk told the FBI that a female client once approached him about Officer J. D. Tippit, with whom Kirk was personally acquainted.[116] The woman sought Kirk's advice "about a proceeding against Tippit, in that he had apparently raped her during one of his investigations."[117]

Perhaps tying together both Tippit's alleged corruption and his timely execution was his well-established association with one Dallas Mobster—Jack Ruby. Jack Hardee, Jr., an acquaintance of Ruby, told the FBI that Tippit "was a frequent visitor to Ruby's night club" and that "there appeared to be a very close relationship" between Ruby, Tippit and another officer.[118] Two Carousel Club employees, Andrew Armstrong and Larry Crafard, advised the FBI that Ruby had declared he knew Tippit when he learned of Tippit's shooting.[119] Crafard told the FBI that Ruby had "referred to Officer Tippit by his first name or a nickname . . . and said he knew him quite well."[120]

Ruby's sister Eva Grant stated in a telephone interview that Tippit "used to come into both the Vegas Club and the Carousel Club," that "Jack called him buddy," and that "he was in and out of our place many times."[121] And when questioned by the Warren Commission, Mrs. Grant confirmed that "Tippit was in our club" about a month before the assassination.[122] But Tippit's police supervisor told the FBI that Tippit had never been assigned to an area covering Ruby's night clubs or residences.[123] These contacts, therefore, could not have developed through routine police business.

Another contact between Ruby and Tippit was reported by Harold Williams of Dallas. Williams related that early in November 1963, he had been picked up in a police car during a raid of the Mikado Club in Dallas, where he worked as a chef.[124] There were two men sitting in the police car, one of whom Williams recognized then as Carousel owner Jack Ruby, the other of whom he realized was Tippit after seeing news photos following the assassination.[125] When asked if he was sure of his identification, Williams replied, "I am sure. I have no doubt. . . . I am sure because I wanted to pay particular attention to who was in the car and who the officer was."[126] Williams reported that shortly after he told this account to various people, he was picked up by some Dallas policemen and threatened with arrest if he did not change his story.[127]

Mrs. Stella Coffman, head waitress of Ruby's Silver Spur Club from 1948 to 1953, told the FBI that "Ruby knew numerous officers of the Dallas Police force, including officer Tippit who was killed by Lee Harvey Oswald."[128] She reported that Tippit "was a close friend of Jack Ruby."[129] Dallas Police Lt. George C. Arnet also affirmed that Ruby knew Tippit.[130]

But the most significant contact between Ruby and Tippit was reported by Mark Lane, a New York attorney whose initial efforts in the assassination case were creditable. Citing a confidential source who witnessed the encounter, Lane told the Warren Commission that on November 14, 1963, Ruby, Tippit and another man met at the Carousel Club.[131] The third man reportedly at the meeting was Bernard Weissman,[132] one of the signers of the black-bordered assassination-day ad attacking President Kennedy.[133]

Independent accounts of Ruby's association with Weissman provided some support for the report of this encounter. Carousel employee Larry Crafard, who was shown a picture of Bernard Weissman, told the FBI that Weissman had been in the Carousel Club "on a number of occasions."[134] Crafard also advised the FBI that he had "heard Ruby refer to Weissman by the name of 'Weissman,' and on several occasions [had] served Weissman drinks at the Carousel Club."[135] And Bruce Carlin, who frequented the club in November 1963,[136] told the FBI that the subject in Weissman's photo did "look familiar ... I just know he looks familiar."[137]

The most telling confirmation of the reported November 14 meeting between Ruby, Tippit and Weissman, however, was provided by Ruby himself. The segment of his testimony concerning this meeting was introduced by a question from Warren Commission Counsel J. Lee Rankin:

> There was a story that you were seen sitting in your Carousel Club with Mr. Weissman, Officer Tippit and another who has been called a rich oil man, at one time shortly before the assassination. Can you tell us anything about that?[138]

If the "rich oil man" was inserted as a test, Ruby passed it perfectly by his response:

> **Mr. Ruby**: Who was the rich oil man?
> **Mr. Rankin**: Can you remember? We haven't been told. We are just trying to find out anything that you know about him.
> **Mr. Ruby**: I am the one that made such a big issue of Bernard Weissman's ad. *Maybe you do things to cover up, if you are capable of doing it. ...*[139]

When asked once more about a conversation with "Weissman and the rich oil man," Ruby again focused only on the fictional oil man, pointing out that he had not recently been in touch with any rich oil man.[140] Thus failing to elicit any denial from Ruby of the encounter reported by Lane's informant, the Commission Chairman finally interceded:

> **Chief Justice Warren**: This story was given by a lawyer by the name of Mark Lane ... that in your Carousel Club you and Weissman and Tippit, Officer Tippit, the one who was killed, and a rich oil man had an interview or a conversation for an hour or two.
> And we asked him who it was that told him, and he said that it was confidential and he couldn't tell at the moment, but that he would find out for us if whether he could be released or not from his confidential relationship.
> He has never done it, and we have written him several letters asking him to disclose the name of that person, and he has never complied.
> **Mr. Ruby**: Isn't that foolish. If a man is patriotic enough in the first place, who am I to be concerned if he wasn't an informer.

I am incarcerated, nothing to be worried about anyone hurt-
ing me.[141]

Of course, Ruby's description of Lane's informant as "patriotic" makes
sense only if Ruby knew that the informant was telling the truth.
Chief Justice Warren then continued:

Mr. Ruby, I am not questioning your story at all. I wanted you
to know the background of this thing, and to know that it was
with us only hearsay. But I did feel that our record should show
that we would ask you the question and that you would answer
it, and you have answered it.[142]

Contrary to Warren's complacent assurance, however, Ruby had uttered
not one word denying the reported meeting between himself, Weissman
and Tippit.[143] Indeed, given Ruby's demonstrated association with both,
there is every reason to believe it did occur. And Ruby raised further questions about the meeting that would have been pointless if it had not:

Mr. Ruby: How many days prior to the assassination was
that?
Chief Justice Warren: My recollection is that it was a week
or two. Is that correct?
Mr. Ruby: Did anyone have any knowledge that their beloved
President was going to visit here prior to that time, or what is
the definite time that they knew he was coming to Dallas?
Chief Justice Warren: Well, I don't know just what those
dates were.
Mr. Ruby: I see.[144]

As highlighted by Ruby's remarks, the timing of the reported meeting
with Tippit and Weissman raised the suspicion that it was linked to the
Dealey Plaza killing. And events in the final days before November 22 confirmed quite clearly that Ruby was involved in a Mob contract to murder
President Kennedy.

I am now firmly of the opinion that the mob did it. It is a historical truth.[1]

> G. Robert Blakey, chief counsel of the House Assassinations Committee, referring to the assassination of President Kennedy

You can only meet a force with weapons appropriate to the firepower possessed by your enemy. And if the enemy tactics emphasize nuclear attacks, you do not respond with an automatic rifle.

We have got to quit kidding ourselves that we can overcome organized crime by conventional weapons.[2]

> Earl Faircloth, former attorney general of Florida

□ 23 □

The Mafia Killed President Kennedy

Jack Ruby's meetings in New Orleans, New York, Chicago and Miami, four key Mafia bases, were behind him. Following its spectacular, 25-fold peak in the first week of November, as charted earlier, his rate of out-of-state calls plummeted.[3] Now, as November 22 approached, the focus of the Mob activity occupying Ruby shifted to Dallas.

One indication of Ruby's exceptional local activity during this final period was offered by Nancy Powell, a two-year employee of the Carousel Club.[4] Asked about Ruby's behavior "the couple of weeks or months before President Kennedy was shot," Powell testified

> He became more relaxed about the club. At first, he would never leave the club. He was there all the time, but he got to where he would go out and come in later like at 10 o'clock or something.[5]

Larry Crafard, who worked full-time at the Carousel Club for one month in November 1963,[6] was more specific. Crafard told the FBI that during November, Ruby would typically spend one or two hours in the early afternoon at the club.[7] He would then leave for the day, return at about 10 p.m., and remain there until closing at about 1:30 or 2 a.m.[8]

Crafard amplified when subsequently questioned by Warren Commission counsel:

> **Q**: So as I understand it ... he would spend 8 or 10 [of] what would presumably be waking hours away from the club each day.
> **Mr. Crafard**: Yes.
> **Q**: Did he ever talk about what he was doing during that period of time?
> **Mr. Crafard**: No.
> **Q**: Did you ever hear anything or do you have any idea of what he was doing during that period of time?
> **Mr. Crafard**: No.[9]

Crafard also testified that during November 1963, "people would come to the club to see him, he would go downstairs, leave with them, and sometimes would be gone the rest of the afternoon."[10]

By mid-November, however, Ruby no longer had time for routine Carousel-based racketeering; he no longer had any reason for placing calls from his night club office to Mobsters across the country. Now, as documented in National Archives files, Ruby was busy receiving Mob guests from out of town, meeting with other underworld figures from Dallas, and assisting in the final preparations for President Kennedy's murder.

/1/ Visits of Paul Roland Jones and Al Gruber

"About a week before the assassination of President Kennedy," Paul Roland Jones told the FBI, Jones took a two-day trip to Dallas.[11] During that trip, Jones "stopped at Ruby's club and spoke to him just briefly and generally."[12] Living then in Alabama,[13] Jones was an old acquaintance of Ruby and a go-between for the Chicago Mob in the Dallas bribery negotiations of the 1940s.[14] His criminal credentials included convictions for bribery, narcotics smuggling and murder, plus an indictment for perjury.[15]

Al Gruber, another underworld acquaintance of Ruby, dropped in to see him about the same time. Based in Los Angeles, Gruber had six arrests in three states under his name and two aliases, with a conviction for grand larceny.[16] He listed himself as a self-employed scrap dealer working from his residence,[17] but the focus of his activity was probably reflected better by his management of a "card room" in the "Veteran's Cabin" during the 1960s.[18] Seth Kantor, a journalist in the White House press corps, reported further that Gruber was "running with Frank Matula, whom Hoffa had installed as a Teamster official shortly after Matula got out of jail on perjury charges. Gruber also maintained known connections with hoodlums who worked with racketeer Mickey Cohen."[19] Barney Ross, the Capone-tied boxer, was another associate of Gruber.[20]

In a 1964 interview, Gruber told the FBI that he had not been in touch with Ruby since 1947.[21] But about two weeks before the assassination, Gruber related,

> en route to Los Angeles from New York, where he attended a relative's wedding, he stopped at Joplin, Missouri, to get some information on a car wash facility. Since Dallas, Texas was about 100 miles from Joplin, he decided to visit Ruby in Dallas.[22]

When interviewed in 1978 by the House Assassinations Committee, however, Gruber insisted that he had not come from a wedding in New York: "From a wedding? No. . . . I might have said that, but that ain't true."[23] Gruber now explained that he was "driving a Cadillac across for somebody" when it broke down in Joplin, and he decided to visit Dallas,[24] which is actually 300 miles away. "And I figured I would just go see Jack I guess," Gruber related.[25] "I don't know why I went there really."[26]

Ruby, on the other hand, recalled exactly why Gruber visited: "He came to try to interest my brother, Sammy, in this new washateria deal to wash cars."[27] But Gruber testified that he never contacted Sam Ruby[28] and didn't even know him.[29] Similar flagrant contradictions characterized the date of Gruber's visit with Ruby (from a few days[30] to two weeks[31] before the assassination), its duration (one day[32] to several days[33]) and the subject of their conversations.[34] Gruber also provided sharply conflicting accounts[35] for another timely contact: a 3-minute call from Ruby to Gruber in Los Angeles two hours after the assassination.[36]

/2/ The Night of November 20: A Mafia Party

Following the usual pattern, Ruby and two associates related conflicting innocuous activities to explain his whereabouts on the night of November 20.[37] This time, however, the cover was penetrated by detailed independent reports.

Beginning in the late evening of November 20, Frank T. Tortoriello held an all-night party at his residence in the Tanglewood Apartments in Dallas.[38] According to the FBI's first report of this party, Tortoriello's guests were Jada, the Carousel stripper, Jack Ruby, Joe F. Frederici, plus Frederici's wife Sandy and Tortoriello's next-door neighbor, Ann Bryant.[39] Subsequent FBI reports provided more information about the party and about the intriguing relationships of three of those present.

Frank T. Tortoriello, the host, was a partner in a Mob-linked construction company[40] and a buddy of Mafioso Joseph Campisi.[41] Another friend of Tortoriello was Jada, the Carousel stripper, who spent several nights in his apartment during and before November 1963.[42]

Joseph Frank Federici, aliases Frederici, Frederica and Frederico,[43] was described to the FBI as a nephew of Vito Genovese, the notorious former Mafia boss from New Jersey.[44] Federici's background was consistent with that relationship. For one thing, he was a New Jersey resident who lived in Dallas, at the Tanglewood Apartments, only between February 1963 and January 1964.[45] During that period, another Tanglewood resident reported, he was "allegedly employed in the management consultant business at Dallas for his father, who allegedly resides in Trenton, New Jersey."[46] Federici confirmed that his position in Dallas was "Occupation Management Consultant"[47]—a rather nebulous job title for a man with three aliases.

When asked by the FBI about his reported connection to Genovese, Federici admitted that he had told others he was Genovese's nephew.[48] But only "in jest," he explained.[49]

Given Federici's background, it is understandable that recollections about Tortoriello's Wednesday night party were blurred. Tortoriello and Federici denied that Federici attended the party.[50] So did Ann Bryant, who stopped in briefly from next door early Thursday morning.[51] But another Tanglewood resident related that Bryant had told her that Federici had indeed been there.[52] And the resident apartment manager, who investigated complaints of noise from the all-night party, also told the FBI that Federici had attended.[53] As for Ruby's presence, Tortoriello denied it,[54] but Bryant observed a guest "who resembled Ruby's photograph."[55] Moreover, Bryant's description of this man's companion ("about twenty-five years of age, tall brunette," with "a theatrical appearance"[56]) characterized photos of Gloria Fillmon,[57] who was with Ruby late that evening.[58] The indicated presence of Ruby and Fillmon at the party is particularly credible given the conflicts in their alibis for that evening.[59]

The most striking clue to Ruby's presence at Tortoriello's party, however, was his association with the others present. Jada, of course, was Ruby's employee and the alibi for his June visit to New Orleans.[60] Tortoriello was a close associate of Ruby, as Tortoriello told the FBI.[61] Finally, Federici's name was found among Ruby's personal effects,[62] and Federici confirmed his acquaintance with Ruby.[63]

Whatever the nature of Tortoriello's party—strictly a social function, a break from organization business, or a pre-assassination gala—it was another timely Mafia contact of Ruby covered by a suspicious maze of contradictory accounts. Timely, too, was Federici's departure from Dallas to Providence, Rhode Island "during the early morning of November 22, 1963."[64] Federici explained that he left Dallas with his wife "to visit relatives."[65]

/3/ November 21, Late Morning: Hunt and Brading

About 10:30 or 11 a.m., Ruby told the FBI, he drove a young friend, Connie Trammel, to the office of Lamar Hunt.[66] According to Trammel, who supported Ruby's account, she went to see Hunt, a son of oil tycoon H. L. Hunt, for an employment interview.[67] After dropping Trammel off, Ruby related, he met with one of two attorneys—he couldn't remember which one—in the building in which Lamar Hunt's office was located.[68] Ruby then waited around in the lobby for Trammel to come down, he reported, and finally left the building.[69] A more direct contact with Lamar Hunt, however, is indicated in the February 24, 1964 memo of Warren Commission counsels Hubert and Griffin: "Ruby visited his office on November 21. Hunt denies knowing Ruby. Ruby gives innocent explanation."[70]

The reported contact between Ruby and Lamar Hunt is consistent with the appearance of the name "Lamar Hunt" in one of Ruby's notebooks[71] and Ruby's acquaintance with Lamar's father, H. L. Hunt.[72] And it raises suspicion in view of the Hunts' sharp antagonism toward President Kennedy. During a party before the fateful Dallas visit, as previously noted, H. L. reportedly remarked that there was "no way left to get those traitors out of government except by shooting them out," referring to President Kennedy.[73] Also, H. L.'s son Nelson Bunker Hunt co-sponsored the black-bordered ad attacking President Kennedy that appeared in the *Dallas Morning News* on November 22.[74]

At about noon on November 21, Ruby was seen in City Hall by Dallas Police Officer W. F. Dyson.[75] According to Dyson, Ruby entered the sixth floor office of Assistant District Attorney Ben Ellis and handed out Carousel Club cards to Dyson and other policemen in the office.[76] Ruby introduced himself to Ellis, telling him, "you probably don't know me now, but you will."[77] Ruby also visited Assistant District Attorney Bill Alexander;[78] Alexander reported that they discussed some bad checks issued to Ruby.[79]

Also about noon, November 21, Eugene Hale Brading of Los Angeles checked in with Roger Carroll, the chief parole officer in Dallas.[80] Then on parole for embezzlement,[81] Brading was a Mobster with 35 arrests and three convictions under several aliases.[82] According to a report Carroll filed that day, Brading "advised that he planned to see Lamar Hunt and other oil speculators" while in Dallas.[83] Brading claimed that he never actually saw Hunt during that trip,[84] but confirmed that three underworld-involved associates of his did visit the Hunt Oil Company that day to see

Lamar and Nelson Hunt.[85] According to Paul Rothermal, then chief of security for Hunt Oil, however, the company log for November 21 showed a visit by Brading's three associates, Bauman, Brown and Nowlin, "and friend."[86] Rothermal believed that this "friend" was Brading.[87]

/4/ November 21, Afternoon: Houston

On December 4, 1963, Secret Service agent Elmer Moore questioned Ruby "regarding his whereabouts and movements" on Thursday, November 21.[88] Ruby reported visiting the Merchants State Bank downtown;[89] according to Connie Trammel, he stopped in on the way to Lamar Hunt's office.[90] As for Ruby's activities that afternoon, however, the usual contradictions plagued his alibi.

The only other thing that Ruby could recall about his activities Thursday was that he "talked to a bartender named Mickey Ryan" at the Carousel Club, "probably in the early afternoon hours."[91] Andrew Armstrong, the Carousel's handyman, also reported that Ruby was at the club Thursday afternoon "with Mickey Ryan, a bartender who wanted to borrow money from Ruby."[92] But Ryan told the FBI he did not recall meeting Ruby at the Carousel Club that day.[93] In fact, Ryan believed that he "last saw Ruby approximately two weeks prior to November 22."[94] In further support of Ruby's alibi, Andrew Armstrong reported that he believed Ruby called some AGVA officials from the Carousel Club Thursday afternoon "regarding auditions of amateurs."[95] But telephone records show no calls from the Carousel Club that day.[96]

What was Ruby actually doing Thursday afternoon? His telephone records provide a further clue. Mrs. Billy Chester Carr, a Houston booking agent, told the FBI that Ruby called her on November 19, and again on November 21 between 2:30 and 3 p.m.[97] Ruby's toll call records show the reported call to Carr in Houston on November 19,[98] but show no such call on November 21.[99] By Thursday afternoon, however, Ruby did not have to place a toll call to reach Houston. For Ruby was there, monitoring President Kennedy's movements in preparation for the next day's assassination in Dallas.

On December 2, 1963, Secret Service agent Lane Bertram filed a detailed report of a three-day investigation conducted in Houston.[100] It opened with this synopsis:

> Numerous witnesses identify Jack Leon Rubenstein [also known as] Jack Ruby, as being in Houston, Texas on November 21, for several hours, one block from the President's entrance route and from the Rice Hotel where he stayed.[101]

On November 26, as his report describes, Special Agent Bertram interviewed five witnesses who saw Ruby on the 400 block of Milam Street in Houston Thursday afternoon.[102] One was a Houston Deputy Sheriff, Bill Williams, who "saw the man on two or three different occasions and talked to him about 3 p.m."[103] Williams "was sure the picture of Ruby appearing in the paper was identical with the man he observed."[104] After conducting these interviews, Bertram secured police photographs of Ruby and presented them to the five witnesses.[105] "All agree[d] that in their opinion Jack Rubenstein was in Houston on November 21 from about 2:30 to 7:15 p.m., in close proximity to the President's route to the hotel and the Rice Hotel itself."[106]

It is noteworthy that Ruby was first sighted in Houston at about 2:30 to 3 p.m.,[107] the same time that Mrs. Carr received a call from him.[108] This is also the time at which he would have arrived in Houston if he had left Dallas at about noon and driven the 243 miles on the freeway to Houston at an 80- to 100-miles-per-hour Texas clip. Such a speed would have been natural for Ruby given his many traffic violations, including four for speeding.[109]

The only conceivable doubt about the identifications of Ruby was introduced by Marshall Bradley, a witness who got a close view of Ruby from the left.[110] Bradley reported that on the left side of Ruby's face, which had a "one to three day's beard," he saw a very faint cut scar.[111] No other Houston witness observed such a scar,[112] and such a scar was not visible under superficial observation of Ruby.[113]

Yet Ruby's medical history supports the possibility that he had some such faint scar, perhaps noticeable only in the background of a heavy stubble. Dr. Martin Towler testified that in interviews with Ruby and his siblings, "numerous fights and 'brawls' were described during which the subject was frequently struck about the head and face."[114] For example, at age 14 or 15, Ruby recalled, he had "a fight with two grown men in which he sustained lacerations of his lip requiring sutures for repair."[115] At age 16 or so, Ruby was "pistol whipped" by two policemen, causing "bleeding from the scalp."[116] A medical document in the National Archives also describes several incidents in which Ruby was struck on the head or face.[117] In one he suffered a concussion, and in another he was cut by a jug of wine broken over his head.[118] And in 1956, according to a police informant, Ruby was treated by a private physician for abrasions of the head, eye and face received in a fight.[119]

The possible anomaly introduced by one witness, however, is more than offset by the positive identifications of Ruby by the other four.[120] And these identifications are confirmed by further observations fitting Ruby's known characteristics. The five Houston witnesses "advised that the subject was a smooth talker, but talked rather rapidly and appeared nervous."[121] One witness reported that the subject said he had money and a Cadillac parked around the corner;[122] another said he exhibited some money.[123] Two said he asked about a club on Washington Street operated by a man named Jack,[124] a natural instant improvisation for Ruby in that circumstance. Most telling, however, was the composite physical description of the subject (the FBI's description of Ruby is inserted in brackets): "white male, 5–7 - 5–8 [5'9"], 180–210 [175 pounds], brown hair receding, thin on top ["brown hair thinning on top"], brown eyes [brown eyes], dark complexion [medium complexion]."[125] The witnesses also reported that the subject was wearing "heavy material possibly making subject appear larger,"[126] accounting for the discrepancy in weight.

Ruby's interest in President Kennedy's movements was explicitly reported by one witness, Gloria Reece. Reece reported that

> the subject asked her if she was going to the "President's dinner." She advised him that she had not been invited and asked him to buy her a beer and attempted to make a date with him. The subject declined, stating that he was in a hurry and departed going in the direction of the Coliseum where the President was to appear at the Albert Thomas Appreciation Dinner.[127]

It is therefore difficult to dispute Special Agent Bertram's conclusion that Ruby's visit "very probably had some connection with the President's appearance in Houston."[128]

Also in Houston on Thursday was Bruce Carlin, the reputed pimp,[129] who frequented the Carousel Club in November 1963.[130] Carlin claimed that he was there servicing motels with assorted drugs and sundries for the "Motel Drug Service,"[131] a firm with no office or telephone,[132] although Karen Carlin said that he was unemployed at that time.[133] Under intensive questioning, he could furnish virtually no specifics about his whereabouts that day.[134] And one of his few concrete claims was proven impossible, as discussed previously, by an early Thursday morning call he placed from Houston to Ruby's Carousel Club.[135]

/5/ November 21, Night: Three Contacts

At about 10 p.m., as reported by several sources, Ruby stopped in for about 45 minutes at the Egyptian Lounge,[136] a Dallas underworld hangout.[137] One of its owners was Joseph Campisi,[138] a top-ranking Dallas Mafioso close to Carlos Marcello and Marcello's Mafia-involved brothers.[139] When questioned by the House Assassinations Committee in 1978, Campisi said that he was not at the Egyptian Lounge on the night of November 21 and had not known Ruby was there.[140] But on December 7, 1963, Campisi had told the FBI of his "contact with Ruby" that Thursday night, "when Ruby came to the Egyptian Lounge for a steak."[141]

About midnight, Ruby stopped in at a restaurant in the Teamster-financed[142] Dallas Cabana Hotel.[143] With Ruby was Larry Meyers,[144] who had checked into the Cabana that day,[145] as had Mobster Eugene Brading.[146] A sales executive for a Chicago sporting goods firm, Meyers smoothly explained this contact with Ruby as a social encounter, and cited specific business engagements to justify his presence in Dallas.[147] Yet there are hints of suspicion about Meyers and this rendezvous with Ruby.

Although married, Meyers traveled to Dallas from Chicago with "a rather dumb, but accommodating broad" named "Jean West,"[148] "Jean Aase"[149] or "Ann."[150] He was described by one of Ruby's strippers, with whom he had apparently had a similar, $200 encounter,[151] as a "real swinger" with business interests in Chicago, Minneapolis and Las Vegas.[152] Meyers related in detail how Ruby "poured out his troubles" about the AGVA situation,[153] the phony alibi presented mainly by people tied to organized crime.[154] During interrogation by Warren Commission counsel, the mention of Meyers' name prompted a blank pause from Ruby's associate Ralph Paul[155] and a tirade about Ruby's racketeering acquaintances from his sister Eva, who denied knowing Meyers.[156] And in different interviews, Meyers presented detailed but totally contradictory accounts of subsequent contact with Ruby on November 23.[157] Meyers' accounts of activities Friday afternoon and Sunday morning were also inconsistent.[158]

Following his encounters with Joseph Campisi at the Egyptian Lounge and with Larry Meyers at the Cabana, Ruby met a third man at a third Dallas restaurant. At about 1:30 a.m. Friday, a young man walked into the Lucas B&B Restaurant and sat down at a table.[159] About an hour later, Ruby entered and sat down at a table behind the cash register.[160] Instead of his usual order, Ruby asked for orange juice.[161] A few minutes later, the other man came over to Ruby's table.[162] Shortly afterward, Ruby picked up their bill and they left together.[163] B&B waitress Mary Lawrence reported that the man with Ruby "appeared very similar" to photographs of Oswald, and she believed he was Oswald.[164]

Meanwhile, during the early Friday morning hours, ten Secret Service agents enjoyed liquid refreshments at the Cellar Door night club in Fort Worth.[165] As disclosed in a Secret Service report, among those present were five of the eight agents who would ride in the car directly behind President Kennedy's, plus two other members of the White House detail.[166] Most stayed until at least 2:45 a.m. and one stayed until 5 a.m.,[167] although many had to report for duty by 8 that morning.[168]

During their stay at the Cellar Door, at least five of the agents assigned to protect the president were served a grapefruit beverage called a "Salty Dick."[169] These "imitation mixed drinks" were all nonalcoholic, Cellar Door owner Pat Kirkwood later assured,[170] and they were provided on the house.[171] It was on Kirkwood's specific invitation, in fact, conveyed through a press representative, that the Secret Service party went there that night.[172]

Like his underworld acquaintance[173] Jack Ruby, however, Kirkwood's generosity to officials usually had some ulterior purpose. Karen Carlin, who worked at the Cellar Door in the spring of 1963, testified that she

> told the police, the vice squad about him [Kirkwood] and identi-
> fied some policemen that were being paid off by him and every-
> thing, and of course, he had so many friends he got out of it real
> easy.[174]

Among Kirkwood's vice activities, one police informant reported, were "sex parties" he ran at his residence, apparently for profit.[175] And a possible clue to the character of Kirkwood's crowd was Mobster Lewis McWillie's partnership with Kirkwood's father in at least two local gambling operations.[176]

The purpose of Kirkwood's hospitality to President Kennedy's Secret Service guards was suggested in the testimony of another Carousel strip-per, Nancy Powell. After several hours of questioning, Powell mentioned Kirkwood's Cellar Door night club, "where the Secret Service men go."[177] She then threw out this comment: "Pat said he would probably be called to ask him about *getting them drunk on purpose*."[178]

/6/ November 22: A Ringside View

Between 9 and 9:30 a.m. on November 22, Dallas Police Officer T. M. Han-sen, Jr. saw Jack Ruby outside the Dallas Police building.[179] Hansen told the FBI that Ruby was standing with four or five others "directly to the side of the stairway which leads to the basement" at the Harwood Street en-trance.[180] As Hansen passed Ruby, whom he knew casually, Hansen "shook his hand and said good morning."[181]

Filling in Ruby's alibi for later that morning was Tony Zoppi, the enter-tainment columnist who lamented reports of "quick buck artists" linking Ruby to the Mob and the assassination.[182] At about 10:30 a.m. Friday morn-ing, according to Zoppi and Ruby, Ruby stopped in at Zoppi's office in the Dallas Morning News building.[183] Zoppi said that Ruby had come to discuss "an ESP expert he wanted Zoppi to plug";[184] Ruby testified that he picked up a brochure about a memory expert while in Zoppi's office that morning.[185]

Like Zoppi's preposterous alibi for Ruby's trip to Cuba,[186] however, this story was fatally flawed. For in a Congressional interview of 1978, Zoppi de-tailed his assassination morning conversation with Ruby; Zoppi noted that Ruby appeared "too calm that morning to have been involved in a conspir-acy."[187] Ruby's script of events, however, included no actual meeting with

Zoppi. Ruby told the FBI in 1963 that a few hours before the assassination, he "went to the office of Tony Zoppi, but Tony was not there."[188] Ruby subsequently testified that he "went down there Friday morning to Tony Zoppi's office, and they said he went to New Orleans for a couple of days."[189]

Ruby related that he remained in the Dallas Morning News building all morning to place his regular weekend ads for his night clubs.[190] Even after the noon deadline for the ads had passed, Ruby hung around another half hour,[191] although President Kennedy's motorcade was to drive by just a few blocks away.[192] It was especially curious that Ruby missed the chance to see his professed "idol,"[193] since two "partial" Wednesday newspapers showing the motorcade route were found in Ruby's car.[194] During his polygraph hearing of July 1964, Ruby himself noted this problem in his story:

> Oh yes; they didn't ask me another question: "if I loved the President so much, why wasn't I at the parade?"[195]

But in fact, Ruby observed the critical event of that day from a perfect vantage point. An FBI chronology summarized,

> Ruby was on the second floor, front of the Dallas Morning News Building which looks out at the TSBD [Texas School Book Depository] Building. At about the time the President was shot, Ruby allegedly would have a perfect view of the front of the TSBD Building. . . .
> [Ruby was] allegedly sitting in the only chair from which he could observe the site of the President's assassination. . . .
> Georgia Mayor, secretary in the Advertising Division, Dallas Morning News, advised that when she returned from lunch at approximately 12:30 p.m., Jack Ruby was sitting in a chair directly in front of her desk. She believes that Ruby had been looking out at the scene when the President was shot. . . .[196]

There is little to add to Ruby's own testimony on this matter:

> Now, what about my being present in the News Building that morning? Here—the assassination took place across the street from there? . . . if I was in a conspiracy, wouldn't it start off with that point?[197]

/7/ Lethal Finale

At 12:30 p.m., as Ruby anxiously watched, a shot was fired at President Kennedy from the Texas School Book Depository; it inflicted a minor, shallow wound in Kennedy's shoulder.[198] In the limousine of Vice President

Johnson, Secret Service Agent Rufus Youngblood reacted instantly; Johnson reported that Youngblood "turned in a flash, immediately after the first explosion, hitting me on the shoulder, and shouted to all of us in the back seat to get down."[199] During the next eight seconds, however, not even a warning was shouted from the agents in President Kennedy's follow-up car[200]—five of whom had been so solicitously hosted early that morning at Kirkwood's Cellar Door.[201] And then, a bullet was fired from behind the stockade fence in the grassy knoll; President Kennedy's skull splintered backward.[202]

Soon afterward, a man who identified himself as Jim Braden was arrested in the Dal-Tex Building opposite Dealey Plaza.[203] According to police reports, Braden was in the building "without a good excuse" when President Kennedy was assassinated.[204] Six years later, a trace of Braden's driver's license revealed that he was actually Eugene Hale Brading, a prominent California Mobster with 35 arrests and three convictions under six aliases.[205] Questioned then by Los Angeles Police, Brading provided a highly dubious alibi for his whereabouts at the time of the assassination.[206]

Dallas Mafioso Joseph Campisi reported that he was driving his car when he heard about the assassination, but could not remember where.[207] Campisi also had trouble remembering whether he had met with Ruby the night before,[208] but police records confirmed that he did meet with Ruby in jail on November 30.[209]

At 1:30 p.m., an hour after viewing Kennedy's shooting from his prime vantage point, Ruby dropped in at Parkland Hospital to ascertain its outcome.[210] At about the same time, in the Oak Cliff section of Dallas, Police Officer J. D. Tippit, a close associate of Ruby,[211] was shot to death.[212] During the next two days, as detailed earlier, Ruby met with another Dallas Police crony, Harry Olsen,[213] and repeatedly visited the police building,[214] where Lee Harvey Oswald was held. At 11:17 a.m. Sunday morning, as others established an elaborate alibi for him and coordinated the split-second timing, Ruby left the downtown Western Union office to pay another such visit.[215] And at 11:21 a.m., in the crowning action of his Mob career, Ruby fired the shot that ensured Oswald's everlasting silence.

Following a classic pattern, many others with potentially incriminating information were subsequently murdered or intimidated.[216] Representative was the fate of Karen Carlin, who Ruby hinted was "part of the conspiracy."[217] In a Secret Service interview the evening of Oswald's murder, hysterical with terror, Carlin stated that she was "under the impression that Lee Harvey Oswald, Jack Ruby and other individuals unknown to her, were involved in a plot to assassinate President Kennedy."[218] She feared that "she would be killed if she gave any information to authorities," and asked that "all information she had related be kept confidential to prevent retaliation."[219] Carlin also testified that after the president was shot, Cellar Door owner Pat Kirkwood called and told her, "I want you down here in about 20 minutes."[220] When she refused, Kirkwood told her, "If you're not down here, you won't be around too long."[221] Several months later, she was found shot to death in a Houston hotel.[222]

Yet some witnesses survived to present highly incriminating testimony. Three informants detailed assassination designs against the Kennedys that were expressed in 1962 by New Orleans Mafia boss Carlos Marcello, Tampa chieftain Santos Trafficante, and their Teamster ally, Jimmy Hoffa.[223] Crucial too was the testimony of one tormented conspirator, who had come to face the other end of the silencers' gun. On June 7, 1964, stating that he could not tell the truth in Dallas and repeatedly expressing fears for his life, Jack Ruby pleaded with Chief Justice Earl Warren for a hearing in Washington.[224] Although Warren inexplicably refused,[225] Ruby was able to slip in many candid disclosures during his testimony in Dallas.

Ruby mocked his canned alibi ("I must be a great actor"[226]) and indicated conspiracy in the Oswald murder ("If it were timed that way, then, someone in the police department is guilty of giving the information as to when Lee Harvey Oswald was coming down"[227]). He repeatedly called attention to his underworld connections,[228] his opportunity for contacts with Oswald and Tippit,[229] his "numerous phone calls, long-distance calls, all over the country."[230] And it was clearly his own confession, not another's accusation, when he said, "Maybe I was put here as a front of the underworld and sooner or later they will get something out of me that they want done to their advantage."[231]

Other witnesses filled in the details and reported further incriminating incidents: Ruby's visits with Caracci in New Orleans, with Ross and Glaser in New York, with Roselli in Miami, his mid-November contacts in Dallas with several more underworld figures, and his November 21 trip to Houston to preview the president's motorcade. Telephone records showed the striking, 25-fold increase in his out-of-state calls, peaking in early November and then plummeting during his final weeks of activity in Dallas. And covering all was the endless stream of fabrications issued by Ruby's local associates and his distant Mob contacts—some ad-libbed, others coordinated—precluding any last chance that this timely Mob confluence in Dallas was unrelated to the assassination.

And so, when the evidence is sorted and arranged, the pieces of the assassination puzzle fall neatly into place. Gracing the tableau are neither crackpots nor clowns, freak coincidences nor senseless crimes. Rather, coming sharply into focus is the vicious combine of killers suspected by Europeans from the start,[232] a group with the motive and capability to perform the assassination. Indeed, the conclusion is clear: the Mafia killed President Kennedy.

And now, as you can see,
the Sicilian ballad singer has arrived:
he has arrived to sing the story
of Turiddu Carnivali,
the young man who was killed
at Sciara, in the Province of Palermo,
who was killed by the Mafia. . . .
who died, murdered, like Christ.

> From the "Ballad of Turiddu Carnivali," by the popular
> Sicilian poet, Ignazio Buttitta. It was set to music by
> Sicilian balladeer Ciccio Busacca.[1]*

☐ 24 ☐

Epilogue

The Mafia murder of President Kennedy achieved its desired objective.
Under the corrupt new administration of Lyndon Johnson, federal initiatives against the Mob were abandoned as the public was tranquilized with
an assassination cover-up. Instead of battling the Mob, Johnson led America into the Vietnam debacle, which kept Syndicate heroin, Hunt oil and
American blood flowing without accomplishing any strategic objective.
And emboldened by the political control it had so murderously secured,
the Mob plundered America with new heights of brazenness.

Also among the post-assassination horrors were the additional murders
of Black America's favorite sons, Malcolm X and Martin Luther King, and of
presidential front-runner Robert Kennedy. Each tried to help the poor;
each tried to rectify America's twisted course. And by courageously pursuing these ends, each gave the Mob reason to want him dead. Indeed, as

---

*Carnivali, the greatest of Sicilian postwar peasant heroes, became the 38th
trade union victim of the Mafia when assassinated in 1955 at the age of 31.[2] His
indiscretion: protesting the 11-hour day forced upon workers at a stone quarry
operated by the Mafia in partnership with a feudal landlord.[3]

reviewed below, there are hints that the Mob may have been tied to these first two slayings. Yet in the case of the Robert Kennedy murder, as revealed in a chilling climax, the Mafia link goes far beyond the hypothetical.

/1/ The Assassination of Malcolm X

Civil rights activists of the 1960s braved bombings, beatings and killings to dislodge an entrenched system of segregation in the South. But when black American leaders focused on the North's inner cities, they found an empire of exploitation far more vicious and powerful.

"Raping the ghetto." The Mafia's role in the ghetto was illuminated by a cash flow study of New York City's three main slum areas. The New York State Crime Committee determined that in 1968, the state spent $273 million for welfare payments in those areas.[4] And the committee estimated that in the same year, the Mob drained $343 million in gambling and narcotics revenues from those same areas—$70 million more than the state welfare expenditure.[5]

John Hughes, chairman of the Crime Committee, observed that "the flow of money from the ghetto to organized crime is so great that there can be little meaningful economic improvement in New York City's ghettos until it is stopped."[6] Massachusetts Senator Edward Brooke put it more bluntly:

> The black man has been the victim of crime, more than anything else. . . . The Mafia moves in, and the black man does the paying.[7]

And Congressman Joseph McDade of Pennsylvania concluded, "We are losing ground in the war on poverty because organized crime takes from the urban poor far more money than the government puts in."[8]

Yet economic plunder is only one aspect of the Mafia's devastation of the ghetto. As related to Congress by organized crime expert Ralph Salerno,

> Mr. Whitney Young . . . said that he thought it was laughable for anyone to suggest that there is violence in Harlem, for example, because television is showing "Gunsmoke. . . ." He said if they really want to know what causes violence among young people in Harlem, let them study heroin trafficking and the reluctance of public officials to do something about the Mafia.
> . . . in the city of Newark, which had a very bad riot in 1967, . . . while the riot was still going on, and buildings were still on fire, Mr. Floyd McKissick, who was then the executive director of CORE, was asked in a television interview what caused the riot.

His answer was blame it on the Mafia, they controlled all of the narcotics, all of the gambling, all of the loan sharking in Newark.[9]

Shortly before the 1967 Newark riot, in fact, residents picketed City Hall with leaflets proclaiming, "We're tired of our Mafia government."[10] And two state commissions[11] concluded that residents' anger against the Mob and Mob-corrupted government was a major cause of the ghetto riots of the 1960s. As Salerno put it, "Organized crime has been raping the ghetto."[12]*

"All-out war against organized crime." No one understood the ghetto's problems better than its resident and spokesman, Malcolm X. A former regular numbers player, betting up to $20 a day,[17] Malcolm X observed that "practically everyone played every day in the poverty ridden black ghetto of Harlem."[18] In his autobiography, written with Alex Haley, he noted the large profits extracted from numbers operations, commenting, "And we wonder why we stay so poor."[19] Also, when he became a Muslim minister, Malcolm X often preached against the moral degradation wrought by the ghetto rackets.[20]

To combat the devastating effects of ghetto vice, Malcolm X attacked on two fronts, with striking success. First, he attracted hundreds of thousands of converts to the Black Muslim movement,[21] which forbade its members to gamble, use narcotics or patronize prostitutes.[22] Second, he exhorted the black community to deal directly with the root of its problems:

> Since the police can't eliminate the drug traffic, we have to eliminate it. Since the police can't eliminate organized gambling, we have to eliminate it. Since the police can't eliminate organized prostitution and all of these evils that are destroying the moral fiber of our community, it is up to you and me to eliminate these evils ourselves. . . .
>
> *We must declare an all-out war against organized crime in our community.*[23]

Neither such instructions nor the boycott of ghetto rackets he led were likely to have endeared Malcolm X to the Mob.

---

*In contrast, no link between ghetto problems and organized crime was noted by the National Advisory Commission on Civil Disorders, chaired by Governor Otto Kerner of Illinois.[13] But Kerner had apparently acquired a peculiar blindness toward organized crime during his stint as U.S. Attorney of Chicago. At a law-enforcement conference in 1950, Kerner stated that there was "no organized gambling" in Chicago.[14] He also told the conference that he "did not know that the Capone syndicate exist[ed]. I have read about it in the newspapers. I have never received any evidence of it."[15] In 1973, Kerner was sentenced to three years in prison for accepting $150,000 in bribes from horse racing interests.[16]

Muslim revenge or Mafia contract? On February 21, 1965, Malcolm X was beginning a speech at the Audubon Ballroom in New York City when two men in the audience stood up and started an argument.[24] During the commotion, a man with a shotgun and others with pistols advanced toward Malcolm and fatally shot him.[25] One of the assailants, Talmadge Hayer, was shot in the leg and captured;[26] the others escaped.[27]

Suspicion immediately focused on the followers of Elijah Muhammad, the top Muslim leader with whom Malcolm X had split.[28] And when fire destroyed the Muslim mosque in Manhattan the night of the assassination, wreaking further havoc within the movement, it was written off as the retribution of Malcolm's followers.[29] Several days later, proceeding on the theory that Muslims were behind Malcolm's murder, police arrested Norman 3X Butler and Thomas 15X Johnson.[30] Hayer, Butler and Johnson were subsequently convicted of the homicide.[31]

But there were problems with the official reconstruction of the crime. Talmadge Hayer, the apprehended and admitted[32] assailant, had a criminal record[33] but no credibly established Muslim ties.[34] Butler and Johnson, on the other hand, were proud and well-known Muslims.[35] But they were picked up at home well after the fact,[36] maintained their innocence throughout,[37] and were implicated by witnesses of dubious credibility.

Particularly questionable was the prosecution's star witness,[38] Cary Thomas, a one-time narcotics pusher with several arrests and Army courts-martial.[39] A bodyguard for Malcolm X at the fateful Audubon Ballroom engagement,[40] Thomas "stood there transfixed through the shooting ... and then ignominiously ducked."[41] He did not furnish any information about the killing for six weeks,[42] and then presented contradictory accounts incriminating Hayer, Butler and Johnson.[43] Also shaky was the testimony of Charles X. Blackwell, the only other witness who implicated all three men.[44] Blackwell first told police that he didn't know who did the shooting,[45] then rearranged the roles of the alleged assassins.[46] Finally, under cross-examination, he admitted that he had lied under oath.[47]

Another gap in the case against Butler and Johnson was the absence of any physical evidence implicating them.[48] The pistol allegedly fired by Butler was never found,[49] and the shotgun allegedly fired by Johnson could not be traced to him by either fingerprints or purchase history.[50] Further clouding the case was the failure of police to identify or apprehend others whom they believed ordered and abetted the killing.[51] According to *Newsweek* editor Peter Goldman, "Their guesses at the number of men actually involved ranged from four to six or seven—three guns, plus one or two people to create diversions and maybe get in the way of the bodyguards, plus one or two getaway drivers."[52]

Some of these suspects were apparently within Malcolm's organization;[53] as one investigator remarked, "He was definitely set up for it."[54] Malcolm's bodyguards were not armed, nobody was searched, police presence was limited, and no one was on stage with Malcolm at the time of his slaying.[55] All this was purportedly done on Malcolm's instructions, yet was contrary to usual procedure.[56] Particularly suspicious was one bodyguard whom police described as a "professional hood,"[57] who suddenly came into money just before the assassination.[58] When the diversionary quarrel started he left his post,[59] and he skipped town before police could question him.[60]

The theory that co-religionists killed Malcolm X suffered another setback when assailant Talmadge Hayer addressed the judge toward the end of his trial. Hayer stated he had just been telling Butler and Johnson

> that I know they didn't have anything to do with the crime that was committed at the Audubon Ballroom February 21, that I did take part in it and that I know for a fact that they wasn't there, and I wanted this to be known to the jury and the court, the judge.[61]

Hayer refused to name his confederates,[62] but did furnish this information:

> **Q**: ... did somebody ask you and others to shoot and kill Malcolm X?
> **Hayer**: Well, yes, sir. ...
> **Q**: Did this person tell you why he wanted to hire you and these others to assassinate Malcolm X?
> **Hayer**: No, sir.
> **Q**: Were any of them, to your knowledge, Black Muslims?
> **Hayer**: No, they weren't. ...
> **Q**: What was your motive?
> **Hayer**: Money.[63]

There was one organization which Hayer would not have fingered at any cost—the same organization known for using associates of the victim,[64] perjured witnesses[65] and corrupted officials[66] to assist and cover its murders. And given the crusade of Malcolm X against ghetto rackets, plus his exhortation to "declare an all-out war against organized crime,"[67] the same group had a clear motive for his murder. Indeed, the possibility that the Mafia killed Malcolm X was proposed by CORE leader James Farmer, as reported in *Ebony* magazine:

> Farmer had conferred with Malcolm in his Greenwich Village apartment shortly before the young firebrand departed for a trip to Mecca. Without revealing the content of their conversa-

tion, Farmer has since repeatedly hinted that Malcolm was killed because of his crusade against the drug traffic.

In his book, *Freedom When?*, Farmer writes: "Malcolm's killers have not been convicted and I have a hunch that the real story of his death will surprise those who saw it as a case of Muslim revenge. Malcolm was warring on the international narcotic interests in Harlem and they were not pleased about it."[68]

If indeed the Mob was behind the Malcolm X murder, a choice of attorneys in the case was appropriate. For in the late 1960s and early 1970s, Talmadge Hayer's appeal was handled by Edward Bennett Williams,[69] who refused *Newsweek* editor Peter Goldman an interview with his client.[70] Williams had defended the nation's most notorious Mafia members and associates, including New York boss Frank Costello,[71] Chicago boss Sam Giancana,[72] Teamster President Jimmy Hoffa,[73] Senate fixer Bobby Baker,[74] and Chicago Mafia "lord high executioner"[75] Phil Alderisio.[76]*

A postscript. A poignant postscript to the Malcolm X slaying was provided by the fate of his protégé, Charles Kenyatta. As recounted by Frank Hercules in a *National Geographic* essay of 1977 on life in Harlem, Kenyatta "speaks of the overlordship of vice in the community" and of "the seduction of the community's children into using narcotics."[80] He

> excoriates the "overseers of vice." The suffering on his ascetic face deepens. "Why don't they leave our children alone?"
> Some time ago, an automobile in which Kenyatta was riding was ambushed. His body was honeycombed by bullets, and he was left for dead. But, as by a miracle, the crusading idealist recovered.[81]

/2/ The Assassination of Martin Luther King

The Reverend Martin Luther King proclaimed:

> I have a dream ... deeply rooted in the American dream ... that one day this nation will rise up and live out the true meaning of its creeds—"we hold these truths to be self-evident that all men were created equal."[82]

*During the McClellan Committee labor hearings of the late 1950s, Williams outdid his client Hoffa in expressing vehement antagonism toward the Kennedy brothers.[77] On February 19, 1964, Williams invited the U.S. Senate to investigate electronic eavesdropping by federal crime fighters.[78] His statement was the opening salvo of a massive Mob-Teamster campaign which exploited this issue to blunt federal action against organized crime.[79]

Yet he realized that for the inner city resident, this dream was overshadowed by an ever-present nightmare:

> Permissive crime in the ghettos is the nightmare of the slum family. Permissive crime is the name for the organized crime that flourishes in the ghettos—designed, directed and cultivated by the white national crime syndicates operating numbers, narcotics and prostitution rackets freely in the protected sanctuaries of the ghettos. Because no one, including the police, cares particularly about ghetto crime, it pervades every area of life.[83]

The inherent risks of Dr. King's stance were noted by the well-known black journalist Louis Lomax:

> By making a national public issue of the plight of Chicago's Negroes, Martin was on the verge of exposing not only a corrupt political system but the influence of the underworld in ghetto economic life as well. I was surprised, and honestly so, that Martin did not disappear into Lake Michigan, his feet encased in concrete.[84]

Lomax continued,

> For this is the precise fate of those who threaten the nickel and dime numbers racket that rakes in millions of welfare dollars each year; this is the precise fate of those who threaten the millions reaped each year by white underworld czars who peddle dope as an antidote for despair.[85]

The Reverend King's commitment to nonviolence hardly mitigated the threat he posed to the Mafia's murderous empire.

On April 4, 1968, Dr. King was fatally shot in Memphis, Tennessee.[86] A massive manhunt led to the capture several weeks later of James Earl Ray,[87] a reputed narcotics and jewel smuggler,[88] who pleaded guilty to the slaying.[89] Ray acted alone, maintained attorney Percy Foreman at Ray's sentencing.[90] To support his claim, Foreman related that it had taken Ramsey Clark and J. Edgar Hoover "less than one day after the murder to conclude there was no conspiracy."[91] But Ray himself took issue with Foreman's pronouncement. "I can't agree with Mr. [Ramsey] Clark," Ray told the court.[92] "I don't want to add something on I haven't agreed to in the past."[93]

Ray, who of all people should have known, was not alone in this conclusion. His brother John was convinced there was a conspiracy.[94] Ray's first attorney, Arthur Hanes, said that there was "no question" in his mind that Ray did not act alone.[95] W. Preston Battle, the judge at Ray's trial,[96] and Senator James Eastland[97] also doubted that Ray had been a lone assassin. Moreover, Canadian police found it probable that Ray "had important, perhaps underworld accomplices helping him to make his escape through Canada," the *New York Times* reported.[98] And in 1978, the House Assassinations Committee concluded "there is a likelihood that James Earl Ray assassinated Dr. Martin Luther King as a result of a conspiracy."[99]

A Mob conspiracy, in particular, two sources suggest. On February 1, 1975, comedian-activist Dick Gregory told a Boston University audience that Dr. King had once called him from a hotel room:[100]

> I said, "what is it Martin," and he said, "could you explain to me what the Mafia is." And I did. And that was the only reason he was killed.[101]

Mafia culpability was also suggested in *The Two Kennedys*, an Italian documentary.[102] The film reported a rumor that the King murder was arranged by New Orleans Mafia boss Carlos Marcello as a favor to the Ku Klux Klan.[103]

The trail of the King case did in fact lead into Marcello's turf. On December 15, 1967, less than four months before the Memphis shooting, Ray and another man, Charles Stein, took a car trip from California to New Orleans[104]—the same city frequented by Oswald, Ruby, Ferrie and Brading in the months before the Kennedy assassination.[105] According to the House Assassinations Committee, Ray took the "possibly sinister"[106] trip with a specific and important objective,[107] accomplished it rapidly,[108] met with someone in New Orleans[109] and received money on the trip.[110] Ray himself admitted receiving $500 during this trip, but provided a dubious account of how he obtained it.[111] His brother John explained the apparent limit to Ray's candor:

> If my brother did kill King he did it for a lot of money—he never did anything if it wasn't for money—and those who paid him wouldn't want him sitting in a courtroom telling everything he knows.[112]

The underworld involvement of Ray's traveling companion, Charles Stein, provides a possible clue to whom Ray met in New Orleans. A 38-year-old former resident of that city,[113] Stein had touched key bases there during his criminal career. In the mid-1950s, he worked at several bars in the French Quarter, including Marie's Lounge, where he managed and ran dice tables.[114] In the early 1960s, he ran a prostitution ring that included his wife.[115] During the same period, he was also reputedly involved in selling narcotics[116]—a favorite Mafia activity in New Orleans, along with gambling and prostitution.[117] Later, in 1974, Stein was convicted of selling heroin in California.[118]

When Stein and Ray arrived in New Orleans on December 17, 1967, they drove to the Provincial Motel, where Ray checked in on Stein's recommendation.[119] According to William Sartor, an independent researcher, both Stein and Ray subsequently met with three men: Salvatore "Sam" DiPiazza, Dr. Lucas A. DiLeo and Salvadore La Charda.[120] Sartor alleged that DiPiazza and La Charda had direct ties to Carlos Marcello, and that all three were avid racists.[121] The site of the meeting was either the Provincial Motel, where Ray was staying, or Marcello's Town and Country Motel;[122] both were reputed underworld hangouts.[123]

When questioned by the House Assassinations Committee, Carlos Marcello, DiPiazza, DiLeo, Stein, and two of Sartor's reported sources denied his allegations;[124] La Charda could not be interviewed since he had "committed suicide in June 1968."[125] Yet the committee did confirm that DiPiazza was a bookmaker with reputed Marcello connections.[126] It also found that DiLeo, a practicing physician, "had a record for such minor offenses as disturbing the peace, resisting arrest, and assault."[127] And the committee could establish nothing about the whereabouts of DiPiazza, DiLeo or La Charda during mid-December 1967 to preclude the alleged meeting with Ray and Stein.[128]

The complicity of Marcello Mobsters in the murder of Martin Luther King was further suggested by a report out of Memphis, Tennessee. On April 8, 1968, John McFerren told the FBI of a remark he had overheard four days earlier, the day of King's assassination, at the Liberto, Liberto and Latch Produce Store.[129] According to McFerren, as the House Assassinations Committee summarized, company president Frank Liberto "indicated that his brother in New Orleans, La., was going to pay $5,000 to someone to kill a person on a balcony."[130] The Committee noted that Liberto did in fact have a brother, Salvatore, in New Orleans, who was indirectly linked to the Marcello clan.[131] And researcher William Sartor alleged that Frank Liberto himself was connected with organized crime figures in both Memphis and New Orleans.[132] Frank Liberto denied any involvement in or knowledge of Dr. King's murder, but admitted making disparaging remarks about King in the presence of his customers.[133]

In 1976, Ray's unsuccessful appeal of the King murder conviction was handled by attorney Bernard Fensterwald, Jr.[134] Fensterwald had served in the mid-1960s as chief counsel for the hearings on invasion of privacy chaired by Missouri Senator Edward Long.[135] As Life reported, Long initiated these hearings under the influence of his Teamster contacts, and used them "as an instrument to keep Jimmy Hoffa out of prison."[136]* In particular, during the Long probe, "Counsel Bernard Fensterwald, Jr. worked zealously to discredit federal [organized] crime investigators."[150] After his stint with the Long subcommittee, Fensterwald formed the Committee to Investigate Assassinations,[151] in which capacity he was charged with playing a disingenuous, Garrison-like role.[152]

/3/ The Assassination of Robert Kennedy

On the night of June 4, 1968, Senator Robert Kennedy was at the Ambassador Hotel in Los Angeles celebrating his decisive victories in two Democratic presidential primaries.[153] Shortly after midnight, Kennedy finished a speech to campaign workers, and was led out of the Embassy Room through the hotel pantry.[154] Suddenly, shots rang out; Kennedy and five bystanders were hit.[155] Kennedy fell to the floor, mortally wounded, his right hand clutched near a clip-on necktie.[156]

The assailant who held out his flashing gun, who drew the attention of dozens of witnesses,[157] was Sirhan Sirhan. And the man who wore the clip-on tie, pulled from his neck in Kennedy's dying grasp, was the assassin.

Robert Kennedy's notorious enemy. Marcus Aurelius counseled "careful inquiry in all matters of deliberation," never satisfaction "with appearances which first present themselves."[158] To follow this course in the Robert Kennedy murder case, however compelling the initial appearances are, leads once again to a suspect with motive, means and declared intention to kill.

---

*In 1964, ex-McCarthy aide Roy Cohn, a friend of J. Edgar Hoover,[137] joined forces with Teamster lobbyist Sid Zagri to seek Congressional support for the campaign to spring Jimmy Hoffa.[138] Out of this effort came a resolution calling for the investigation of the "persecution" of Hoffa.[139] It was introduced by U.S. Congressman Roland Libonati,[140] a Chicago Mafia ally who "not only represented the Syndicate but gave all appearances of being a Mafioso himself."[141] The resolution also called for a probe into a 1962 arrest of Dallas Bircher Edwin Walker and into the federal prosecution of Roy Cohn for perjury and obstruction of justice in connection with Cleveland Mob dealings.[142]

But Libonati's resolution came to naught when it was exposed as a carbon copy of a Teamster proposal.[143] The cry was then taken up by a friend of both Zagri and Cohn,[144] Senator Edward Long.[145] Chairman of the Senate Judiciary Committee, Long had obtained this post "with a large assist from Bobby Baker."[146] But Long's motivation became embarrassingly clear when in 1966, he joined convicted felon Jimmy Hoffa on the platform at a Teamster convention to deplore wiretapping and heap accolades on Hoffa.[147] Long's probe ultimately collapsed when he came under scrutiny by the Senate Ethics Committee for receiving $160,000 in questionable legal fees from sources affiliated with the Mob and Teamsters.[148] Long "repeatedly contradicted himself," *Life* reported, in trying to explain these fees.[149]

A list of Robert Kennedy's enemies during the 1960s is conspicuously topped by one person: Jimmy Hoffa. During the summer of 1962, as discussed earlier, Hoffa had outlined plans to assassinate the attorney general.[159] But Hoffa deferred to the presidential assassination plan previewed by his associates Marcello and Trafficante, which aborted the Kennedys' crime-fighting campaign and resolved the Mob's vendetta against them.[160] As for Robert Kennedy personally, Hoffa was content to gloat the day of the Dallas killing that his nemesis had become "just another lawyer."[161]

Over the next four years, the only reported plots against Robert Kennedy were initiated by Frank Chavez, the vicious boss of Puerto Rican Teamster Local 901.[162] During Kennedy's New York senatorial campaign of 1964, according to former aide Walter Sheridan, Chavez traveled to New York to kill Kennedy, but was dissuaded from going through with it.[163] Later, in March 1967, Chavez left San Juan for Washington, armed, after having sworn to kill Kennedy, Sheridan and witness Ed Partin if Hoffa went to prison.[164] Placed under surveillance, with police protection provided for his intended victims, Chavez did not follow through on his plan.[165]

But in 1968, when Robert Kennedy launched a promising campaign for the presidency, the situation required more than one thug's heroics. For the Mafia was not about to let its foremost antagonist reach the pinnacle of power to finish the job his brother's administration had left undone. Nor was it going to wait for the inconvenience of again penetrating a tight Secret Service cordon, when Kennedy could be hit on June 5 at the Ambassador Hotel with no police protection.[166] And the final green light to such an assassination plan would have been signaled by Kennedy's decisive primary victories that evening,[167] which left him the favorite for the presidency.[168]

Robert Kennedy posed a further threat to the Mob by his curiosity about his brother's death. As reported by William Turner and Jonn Christian in their book, *The Assassination of Robert F. Kennedy,* Kennedy had suspected from the beginning that "his archenemy Jimmy Hoffa might somehow have been responsible."[169] Robert Kennedy had, in fact, asked Assistant Secretary of Labor Daniel Moynihan to investigate this possibility.[170] In 1967, to explore the same issue, Kennedy sent his former press secretary, Edwin O. Guthman, to meet with Jim Garrison,[171] whose sinister connection with Carlos Marcello had not yet been exposed.[172] And on May 28, 1968, a week before his death, Kennedy spent two hours in Oxnard, California checking out a reported lead to his brother's death.[173]

By June 1968, the Mafia's plans for Robert Kennedy were in fact well under way. Quoting again from Turner and Christian, a recently released FBI document disclosed

> that a wealthy Southern California rancher who had ties to the
> ultraright Minutemen and detested RFK because of his support

of Cesar Chavez reportedly pledged $2,000 toward a $500,000 to $750,000 Mafia contract to kill the senator "in the event it appeared he could receive the Democratic nomination" for President.[174]

And Sirhan biographer Robert Blair Kaiser reported that

a fellow prisoner of Hoffa's in the Lewisburg, Pennsylvania Federal Penitentiary had told the FBI that he overheard Hoffa and his cronies talking in May, 1968, about a "contract to kill Bob Kennedy."[175]

One of these cronies may have been New York Mafia boss Carmine Galente, with whom Hoffa spoke frequently at Lewisburg.[176] Galente was the top boss of the prison's Mafia row,[177] and an ally of both Carlos Marcello and Santos Trafficante.[178]

The racetrack devotee. The Mafia's planned contract on Robert Kennedy would be academic, however, if Sirhan Sirhan had stood in with a timely, unassisted shooting. But an examination of Sirhan's background discounts the possibility that he acted alone.

Sirhan Bishara Sirhan, a Palestinian immigrant, claimed to have shot Kennedy because of the senator's support for Israel.[179] Yet Sirhan told an interviewer that he did not "identify with the Arabs politically or any other way."[180] Sirhan said that he did not go for Arab food, "their robes and all that bullshit," and that he was a Christian who could barely speak Arabic.[181] And curiously, Sirhan carried four hundred-dollar bills but no personal identification at the time of the shooting.[182] To Robert Houghton, chief of detectives of the Los Angeles Police Department, this suggested a pattern of "hired killer."[183]

Also fitting this pattern was Sirhan's compulsive racetrack gambling and his heavy losses, particularly in the months before the assassination.[184] And this pastime brought him into contact with a rather notorious crowd. Between 1965 and 1967, following in the footsteps of Jack Ruby,[185] Sirhan worked and hung out at the Santa Anita track,[186] a Syndicate meeting place.[187] Sirhan had also worked at the Del Mar Race Track,[188] which was frequented by some of the nation's most infamous racketeers.[189]

A particularly suspicious racing acquaintance of Sirhan was Frank Donneroummas, alias Henry Ramistella, of New Jersey,[190] whose rap sheet showed several arrests in New York and Miami.[191] Donneroummas knew Sirhan at the Santa Anita Race Track,[192] and in 1966 found him a job at the Corona Breeding Farm, where he was Sirhan's boss and close associate.[193] FBI agents attempted to question Donneroummas after the assassination, but it took them ten months to locate him.[194] And their desire to question him was far from idle, given the following passage in one of Sirhan's notebooks:

> happiness hppiness Dona Donaruma Donaruma Frank Donaruma pl please ple please pay to 5 please pay to the order of Sirhan Sirhan the amount of 5 . . .[195]

Two guns and 13 bullets. Did someone in fact hire Sirhan to kill Robert Kennedy? The question is intriguing, but is overshadowed by a surprising ballistic conclusion: the fatal shot to Robert Kennedy's head was not fired from Sirhan's gun.

Position of the murder weapon. Four shots struck Robert Kennedy from point-blank range.[196] This was the conclusion of both Los Angeles County Coroner Thomas Noguchi and police examiner DeWayne Wolfer, based on an autopsy examination of powder burns on Kennedy's body,[197] chemical tests performed on his jacket[198] and further ballistic tests.[199] In particular, Dr. Noguchi testified, the fatal bullet was fired with the gun tip within inches of Kennedy's right ear, and less than one inch from his head.[200] And a Los Angeles Police report concluded that "the muzzle of the weapon was held at a distance of between one and six inches from the coat at the time of all firings."[201]

But the forensically determined position of the Kennedy murder weapon was not the position of Sirhan's gun. In grand jury and trial testimony, many eyewitnesses fixed the closest distance between Sirhan's gun and Kennedy at roughly one yard;[202] not one witness reported this distance at less than two feet.[203] Furthermore, eyewitnesses uniformly reported that Sirhan fired at Kennedy from the front,[204] whereas the autopsy revealed that all shots struck him from behind, sharply below and to his right.[205]

Particularly adamant on Sirhan's position was Karl Uecker, assistant maitre d' at the Ambassador Hotel, who was the only person standing between Kennedy and Sirhan during the shooting.[206] In court testimony and subsequent interviews, Uecker positively asserted that Sirhan fired with his gun about two feet in front of Kennedy.[207] Uecker was also "a hundred percent sure" that he pushed Sirhan over the pantry steam table, completely out of point-blank range, just after the second shot.[208]

Bullet characteristics. The apparent difference in the positions of Sirhan's gun and the murder weapon perturbed William Harper,[209] a nationally respected West Coast criminologist.[210] And when Harper compared the bullet removed from Kennedy's neck with one removed from a bystander, he observed another critical disparity. Harper found that the two bullets differed distinctly in rifling angle and all other characteristics he checked,[211] and in his opinion "could not have been fired from the same gun."[212] He concluded that "two 22 calibre guns were involved in the assassination": one fired by Sirhan, wounding the five bystanders behind Kennedy, and the other fired at Kennedy from behind.[213] Forensic expert Herbert MacDonnell discovered another significant difference between the two bullets, and likewise concluded that they could not have been fired from the same weapon.[214]

Number of bullets fired. But the coup de grace to the lone assassin assumption came with a count of the number of bullets fired in the Ambassador Hotel kitchen. For Sirhan's eight-chamber revolver could have fired at most eight bullets.[215] And all eight were accounted for: two recovered from Senator Kennedy, five from wounded bystanders, and another, police reported, lost in the ceiling interspace.[216]

Yet additional bullets lodged in ceiling panels, a door divider and a doorjamb, were described by eyewitnesses.[217]* And a series of captioned FBI photographs taken at the Ambassador Hotel shortly after the shooting, released under the Freedom of Information Act in 1976,[223] clearly demonstrate that many more than eight bullets had been fired. As the FBI captioned, two of these photos show "two bullet holes, which are circled" in "the doorway leading into the kitchen."[224] Another photograph released by local authorities shows these same two bullet holes being examined and measured by Los Angeles County Coroner Thomas Noguchi.[225] A third FBI photograph shows, as captioned, a "close-up view of two bullet holes located in the center door frame inside kitchen serving area."[226] Two bullet holes and a bullet were reported in the same spot in affidavits by eyewitnesses Martin Patrusky[227] and Angelo DiPierro.[228]

More photographs, FBI notations and eyewitness accounts document that at least one more bullet was at the scene,[229] yielding a total of at least 13 bullets. At least five bullets, therefore, were not shot by Sirhan Sirhan. At least one additional gunman fired with Sirhan, accounting for the irregular bursts of sound heard by witnesses, like a string of firecrackers, rather than regularly spaced reports.[230] The evidence was well summarized by Vincent Bugliosi, the former Los Angeles district attorney who prosecuted the Charles Manson murders and who was active in the reexamination of the RFK case:[231]

> Gentlemen, the time for us to keep on looking for additional bullets in this case has passed. The time has come for us to start looking for the members of the firing squad that night.[232]

---

*Following persistent requests by researchers to examine the objects in question,[218] District Attorney Evelle Younger promised in June 1969 that "tons of information" in police possession would be "made available."[219] But nothing was forthcoming until 1975, when the Los Angeles Superior Court began a probe of ballistic irregularities in the case.[220] It was then that a Los Angeles Police spokesman disclosed that the ceiling panels and door parts had been destroyed by police on June 27, 1969[221]—two weeks after Younger's pledge.[222]

The second gunman. But the search for the star performer in the RFK hit squad is deadly straightforward. For the autopsy revealed that four closely grouped shots struck Kennedy at point-blank range from behind, sharply below and to the right.[233] And standing directly behind and right of Kennedy was security guard Thane Eugene Cesar, who dropped down with his gun drawn when Sirhan began firing.[234] Cesar best described his position and movements in 1969, before suspicions of a second gunman became publicized, in a filmed and tape-recorded interview with journalist Theodore Charach:

> **Cesar**: For some reason, I don't know why, I had a hold of his [Kennedy's] arm under his elbow here . . . his right arm. . . . And I was a little behind Bobby. . . . When the shots were fired, when I reached for my gun, and that's when I got knocked down. . . .
> **Charach**: Did you see other guys pull their guns after you pulled your gun. . . . in the kitchen?
> **Cesar**: No, I didn't see anyone else pull their guns in the kitchen area. . . . Except for myself. . . .
> **Charach**: How far did you have it out?
> **Cesar**: Oh, I had it out of my holster. I had it in my hand.[235]

The possibility that Cesar shot Kennedy accidentally was found highly unlikely by criminologist William Harper.[236] It was also ruled out by Cesar's response to Charach's subsequent question:

> **Charach**: Is there any chance that that gun could have gone off?
> **Cesar**: My gun?
> **Charach**: Yea.
> **Cesar**: [rapidly:] Ah, the only way it would've gone off is [if] I'd'v pulled the trigger because the hammer wasn't cocked. (Pause.) It would have taken more pressure, I would'a had to, I would'a had to wanna fire the gun. . . .[237]

And the fact that Cesar did fire his gun—the only gun in the exact position to inflict Kennedy's wounds—is demonstrated by the report of CBS News employee Donald Schulman, who was standing behind Kennedy and Cesar at the time of the assassination.[238] Moments after the shooting, still apparently stunned, Schulman provided the following account to radio reporter Jeff Brant:

> **Schulman**: A Caucasian gentlemen [Sirhan] stepped out and fired three times, the security guard [Cesar] hit Kennedy all

three times. Mr. Kennedy slumped to the floor. They carried him away. The security guard fired back.

Brant: I heard about six or seven shots in succession. Is this the security guard firing back?

Schulman: Yes, the man who stepped out fired three times at Kennedy, hit him all three times and the security guard then fired back ... hitting him. ...[239]

The same information was more coherently phrased in a broadcast on the Los Angeles CBS-TV affiliate minutes after the shooting:

Don Schulman, one of our KNXT employees, witnessed the shooting that we've been telling you about. Kennedy was walking toward the kitchen and was en route out of the ballroom; a man stepped out of a crowd and shot Kennedy; Kennedy's bodyguard fired back. ...[240]

A similar report appeared on June 6 in the Paris newspaper *France Soir*: "a bodyguard of Kennedy drew his gun, firing from the hip, as in a western."[241] And in an interview several months later with journalist Theodore Charach, Schulman confirmed that "the guard definitely pulled out his gun and fired."[242]

Although Cesar claimed that the gun he drew was a .38-caliber revolver,[243] it so happened that he also owned an H&R .22-caliber nine-shot revolver,[244] of the same caliber as Sirhan's pistol and the recovered bullets.[245] When questioned by police about this .22-caliber gun, Cesar said that he had sold it three months before the assassination.[246] Yet a bill of sale showed that Cesar sold it on September 6, 1968, three months *after* the assassination.[247] And when investigators tried to locate this gun in 1972, the purchaser reported that it had been stolen.[248]

But these irregularities concerning Cesar's .22-caliber revolver were not surprising. For Cesar's gun, and only Cesar's gun, was in position to pump four slugs point blank into Kennedy from behind, under cover of Sirhan's flashing pistol. Kennedy himself may have discerned this in his last moments of consciousness, as suggested by a telltale sign of struggle. For it was Cesar's necktie that was shown in photographs near the dying senator's right hand[249] and missing from Cesar's neck;[250] it was Cesar's necktie that Robert Kennedy ripped off before felled by the fatal head shot.[251]

More deaths, disappearances, assaults and threats. As researchers uncovered the evidence implicating Thane Eugene Cesar in Robert Kennedy's murder, an all-too-familar campaign of terror unfolded. In August 1971, the day before criminologist William Harper was scheduled to testify about the case, a bullet from a high-powered gun struck the car in which he was riding.[252] Cesar and CBS employee Don Schulman both disappeared in the early 1970s.[253] Wald Emerson, a financial backer of research on the case, received threatening phone calls.[254] The wife of attorney Godfrey Isaacs, who assisted the probe, died under mysterious circumstances.[255] Journalist Theodore Charach, a leading investigator of the case who witnessed RFK's shooting, was accosted with a gun and asked to hand over evidence.[256] His assistant, Betty Dryer, was knifed.[257] And further incidents were described by Charach:

> You see the hotel also had Mafia connections too. Mr. Gardner, who was in charge of security, he disappeared, and Cesar told me, "well we've taken care of him; you'll never get an interview with him." Now I don't know whether he's in the bottom of the Pacific Ocean, or where he is, but I haven't been able, you know, to locate him. And then another man, who was overall operations director, he committed suicide, and of course the files were destroyed, we found out, at the Ambassador Hotel.[258]

A Mafia contract. Of course, there is one organization for which this pattern of terror is routine. It was this combine of killers that repeatedly plotted to murder Robert Kennedy, that had killed his brother, and that would stop at nothing to keep another Kennedy from the White House. It was this same group that had in fact been tied to the Ambassador Hotel since the 1940s, when Mickey Cohen ran a major gambling operation there with some of its personnel.[259] And it was again the Mafia—as the final piece of the RFK case locks into place—that was linked to a last-minute stand-in for guard duty there: assassin Thane Eugene Cesar.

On the night of Robert Kennedy's murder, Cesar was assigned to the Ambassador Hotel by the Ace Guard Service,[260] a firm that had protected C. Arnholt Smith's U.S. National Bank.[261] But as disclosed to the author by Alex Bottus, a crime investigator from Chicago, Cesar was only carried by Ace as a temporary employee.[262] According to California State records, Bottus reported, Cesar "hadn't worked for months and months" for Ace before that night.[263] And Cesar was called in just a day and a half before the assassination to substitute at the Ambassador for a regular employee of the firm.[264]

Cesar's specialty in the field of crime, however, was not prevention. As disclosed to the author by Bottus, Cesar had been arrested several times in Tijuana, Mexico.[265] "And it was all fixed by none other than John Alessio"[266]—the California Mobster who had been a director of C. Arnholt Smith's conglomerate before the collapse of the U.S. National Bank.[267] Alessio, Cesar's criminal backer, was cited by the *New York Times* as "the most obvious example of Smith's connection to organized crime."[268] And Cesar's organized crime ties, Bottus reported, were demonstrated by "his whole track record."[269] "You trace him either through Missouri, Arkansas, and go down like I said into Chula Vista, you get down in University City, you get down into Tijuana, they all know about Cesar. And this guy's got connections like crazy."[270]

Replay of the Cermak assassination. And so we come full circle in the Mafia's contract on America. For recall that on February 15, 1933, Chicago Mayor Anton Cermak was shot together with several bystanders as Giuseppe Zangara stepped forward and fired his revolver.[271] Cermak, who died after accusing the Mob of the shooting,[272] had, like Robert Kennedy, aroused its wrath by intensive official action against it.[273] And Zangara, the conjectured victim of a Mafia squeeze play,[274] was like Sirhan a drifter who spent much of his time betting at race tracks.[275]

But most chillingly reminiscent of the Cermak slaying was the role of RFK assassin Thane Cesar. For according to noted sociologist Saul Alinsky, the way Cermak was killed had "been commonly known for many years in many circles in Chicago."[276] As quoted earlier from *The Bootleggers* by Kenneth Allsop,

> In the crowd near Zangara was another armed man—a Capone killer. In the flurry of shots six people were hit—but the bullet that struck Cermak was a .45, and not from the .32-calibre pistol used by Zangara, and was fired by the unknown Capone man who took advantage of the confusion to accomplish his mission.[277]

The supporting cast. With the murder of Robert Kennedy, another of America's noblest leaders joined the thousands felled by the Mafia's army of killers. But the Mob's murder machine functions only when greased by its nationwide network of corrupt officials,[278] and by the million-dollar lawyers who front its operations and arrange its fixes.[279] It is therefore appropriate to acknowledge the supporting cast in the RFK murder and other recent assassinations.

During the trial of Sirhan Sirhan, his defense lawyers repeatedly cut off prosecution testimony on the nature and position of Robert Kennedy's wounds.[280] And to avoid having the issue probed, chief defense counsel Grant Cooper magnanimously told the court he would stipulate that the fatal bullet to Kennedy's head was fired from Sirhan's gun.[281] Police expert DeWayne Wolfer later testified, however, that this point could not be positively determined.[282]

While Sirhan's trial was in progress, attorney Cooper also represented one of four codefendants of Mafioso Johnny Roselli in a gambling case.[283]

All five were accused and all but one eventually convicted of running a card cheating scam at the Friar's Club in Beverly Hills, where Frank Sinatra and Dean Martin had sponsored Roselli for membership.[284] And in 1969, Cooper himself was convicted of an accessory crime: the unauthorized possession of secret grand jury testimony against the five defendants.[285] Cooper admitted to the court that he had lied about where he got the transcripts, and refused to divulge their actual source.[286] It is pertinent to note that the Mafia uses leaked grand jury transcripts to prepare perjured testimony[287] and to determine the identities of witnesses who are subsequently murdered.[288]

As Cooper became increasingly preoccupied with underworld swindling and his own perjury, the burden of Sirhan's defense fell on co-counsel Russell Parsons.[289] Parsons had represented many Mob clients,[290] and had once been investigated himself for hoodlum connections by the chief counsel of the Senate rackets committee: Robert Kennedy.[291] Although Parsons viewed Robert Kennedy as "a dirty son of a bitch,"[292] he had warmer feelings toward California Mobster Mickey Cohen. Parsons had written a letter of reference for Cohen to Cleveland authorities, recommending that his criminal probation be terminated.[293] The disclosure of this letter brought a quick end to a campaign by Parsons to become mayor of Los Angeles.[294]

But the Mob involvements of Sirhan's attorneys were apparently routine qualifications on the assassination circuit. Recall, for example, that Melvin Belli, a lawyer for Jack Ruby,[295] was a friend of Mobster Mickey Cohen who lent the California hoodlum $3,000.[296] Belli had been brought into Ruby's case by Michael Shore,[297] a business partner and close contact of Chicago Mobster Irwin Weiner.[298] Edward Bennett Williams, who represented Malcolm X's assassin Talmadge Hayer,[299] had defended some of the nation's most notorious Mafia members and associates.[300] And Bernard Fensterwald, who represented Martin Luther King's accused assassin, James Earl Ray,[301] had "worked zealously to discredit federal [organized] crime investigators," as *Life* noted, in the Teamster-inspired eavesdropping hearings of Senator Edward Long.[302]

Rounding out Sirhan's legal team was the defense's chief investigator, Michael McCowan.[303] McCowan was a former Los Angeles policeman convicted of mail theft,[304] who resigned from the force after becoming linked to a massive real estate fraud in the San Fernando Valley.[305] His background was reminiscent of that of Albert DeLamielleure, the Detroit Police investigator of the Reuther shootings.[306] DeLamielleure had turned in his badge and joined the Teamsters after the hatching ground of the Mafia contract against Walter Reuther was reported to be a bar owned by DeLamielleure.[307] And not to be forgotten was another professed public protector, New Orleans District Attorney Jim Garrison, whose fraudulent JFK probe focused on everyone but his patron—New Orleans Mafia boss Carlos Marcello.[308]

Also pivotal in Sirhan's case was District Attorney Evelle Younger,[309] who unsuccessfully ran for the California governorship in 1978.[310] According to a 1979 report in the *Washington Monthly*,

> When Evelle Younger, the recently defeated Republican guber-
> natorial candidate in California, was asked during the campaign
> about well-documented charges that he was too friendly to the
> Mafia, he replied, according to Rolling Stone's Greil Marcus, "I
> never said I was tough on crime."[311]

Younger perhaps exhibited this philosophy by his repeated interventions to block examinations of conspiracy in the RFK case.[312] Also suspicious, as noted earlier, was the destruction of critical evidence in the case two weeks after Younger had pledged its release.[313]

A web of ties to the Mob and to both Kennedy murder cases is further spun by other, more successful candidates for the California governorship. The links of Jerry Brown, who defeated Younger, to Mobster Sidney Korshak were satirized in a 1979 series of Doonesbury cartoons;[314] that particular series was dropped by several major newspapers in California and Nevada.[315] An expert Mob fixer and media manipulator,[316] Korshak had supplied derogatory claims against a witness in an attempt to undermine evidence linking Carlos Marcello to the John Kennedy assassination.[317]

Edmund "Pat" Brown, Jerry's father, provided special treatment for Mobsters both before and after he governed in Sacramento. In 1949, as district attorney of San Francisco, Pat Brown mysteriously dropped a murder charge against Mafioso Sebastiano Nani.[318] And in 1977, Brown telegraphed a glowing recommendation for John Alessio,[319] Cesar's Mob backer, who was then under examination by the New Mexico State Racing Commission.[320]

Extending the web, Alessio contributed $26,000 to the 1968 presidential campaign of a one-time California gubernatorial candidate, Richard Nixon.[321] Among the many other Mob contributors to Nixon[322] was Mickey Cohen,[323] the old acquaintance of Jack Ruby,[324] who had been furnished a reference by Sirhan's attorney Russell Parsons.[325] Assisting Cohen in raising money for Nixon was Murray Chotiner,[326] the Mob attorney and fixer dubbed "the one that made Nixon,"[327] who once shared an office with Parsons.[328] Chotiner also managed campaigns for another California governor of subsequent national prominence: Earl Warren.[329]

The epilogue to *Contract on America* is over. The Mafia's contract on America, unfortunately, is not. Reinforced by a continuing influx of gangsters from Sicily,[330] the Mob's nationwide army of assassins continues to kill and brutalize American citizens. Wholesale Mob corruption continues to subvert and paralyze the nation's police, courts and government. The Mob's burgeoning plunder and financial infiltration is now at crisis proportions. A detailed review of this underworld activity is provided in Appendix 4; a final summary and prescription for ending it is offered next, in the conclusion.

Yet the challenge posed by this book's revelations is already quite clear. As for our martyred leaders, the Kennedys and others, will we continue to shroud them in cover-up? Or will we recognize the moral imperatives posed by their lives and deaths, and prepare a safer reception for their successors? And as for the Mafia's contract on America, will we write a continuing epilogue—or an epitaph?

The extraordinary thing about organized crime is that America has tolerated it for so long.

U.S. President's Commission on Law Enforcement and Administration of Justice, Task Force on Organized Crime[1]

Where there is only a choice between cowardice and violence, I would advise violence.

Mahatma Gandhi[2]

Conclusion

"Robbery, murder, and resistance to law have become so common as to cease causing surprise." So wrote President Chester A. Arthur in 1882,[3] referring to an infestation of Arizona by several outlaw gangs that held the territory in a "condition of terrorism."[4] The citizens were "so intimidated," noted Governor T. A. Tritle, "that few of them dare[d] express an opinion adverse to lawlessness and crime."[5] Law enforcement officers, too, were intimidated and overpowered by the outlaws,[6] and "seemed powerless to arrest them";[7] it was widely suspected that many officials were taking payoffs to ignore or even collaborate in their crimes.[8] In a request to Washington for military assistance to eradicate this gangland plague, Acting Governor John J. Gosper concluded, "We have within our borders a small army of outlaws well armed and fully able to cope with the ordinary civil power of our several counties."[9]

Responding to Gosper's request, on April 15, 1882, U.S. Attorney General Benjamin Harris Brewster affirmed that the president was "*expressedly authorized* to employ the military forces of the United States" against the Arizona gangs.[10] [Emphasis in original.] Brewster cited R.S. 5298,[11] which, as amended in 1956 to become title 10, section 332 of the U.S. Code, reads as follows:

> Whenever the President considers that unlawful obstructions, combinations, or assemblages, or rebellion against the authority of the United States, make it impracticable to enforce the

laws of the United States in any State or Territory by the ordinary course of judicial proceedings, he may call into Federal
service such of the militia of any State, and use such of the
armed forces, as he considers necessary to enforce those laws
or to suppress the rebellion.[12]

As a prerequisite to the use of troops under this statute, President Arthur
issued a proclamation calling upon the Arizona gangs to disperse.[13] An intensive campaign of enforcement by local authorities followed this proclamation, and within a year the outlaws were brought under control.[14]

President Arthur's intervention against the Arizona gangsters in 1882, as
specifically authorized by 10 U.S.C. 332, was fully grounded in Constitutional principle and precedent. The federal government is empowered to
use troops "to execute the laws of the union" and is enjoined to protect the
states against domestic violence under article I, section 8 and article IV,
section 4 of the U.S. Constitution. The Supreme Court underscored this
power in an 1879 ruling:

We hold it to be an incontrovertible principle that the Government of the United States may, by means of physical force,
exercised through its official agents, execute on every foot of
American soil the powers and functions that belong to it.[15]

In 1895, the Court reiterated that "the entire strength of the nation may be
used" to guarantee the Constitutional rights of American citizens.[16] Since
1794, in fact, when President George Washington used 13,000 troops to
crush an insurrection by whiskey producers,[17] military force has been used
to aid civil authorities on more than 100 occasions.[18]

Two recent examples of the application of such federal power were provided in 1962 and 1963, under the administration of John F. Kennedy. On
September 30, 1962, President Kennedy issued a proclamation and an executive order preliminary to deploying troops when Mississippi Governor
Ross Barnett vowed to obstruct the court-ordered registration of James
Meredith, a black, at the all-white University of Mississippi.[19] Kennedy finally called the Army into action when a squad of U.S. deputy marshals
preparing to escort Meredith to register was attacked by a mob of 2,500
with clubs, rocks, pipes, bricks, bottles, bats, firebombs and guns.[20] A year
later, Kennedy dispatched troops to bases near Birmingham, Alabama following the bombings of a black home and black hotel in that city.[21] President Kennedy acted in these two cases under title 10, sections 332 and 333
of the U.S. code.[22] Similar to section 332, the latter statute mandates the
use of federal troops to guarantee the rights and safety of American citizens when civil authorities are unable or unwilling to do so:

The President, by using the militia or the armed forces, or both, or by any other means, shall take such measures as he considers necessary to suppress, in a State, any insurrection, domestic violence, unlawful combination, or conspiracy, if it—

(1) so hinders the execution of the laws of that State, and of the United States within the State, that any part or class of its people is deprived of a right, privilege, immunity, or protection named in the Constitution and secured by law, and the constituted authorities of that State are unable, fail, or refuse to protect that right, privilege, or immunity, or to give that protection; or

(2) opposes or obstructs the execution of the laws of the United States or impedes the course of justice under those laws.[23]

At the same time that President Kennedy invoked these two statutes to protect American citizens in the South, they were strikingly applicable to another national threat. The Mafia, with its governing National Commission,[24] its nationwide network of execution squads,[25] its domestic membership of 5,000, structured along military lines, plus many additional thousands of underlings and associates,[26] surely qualified as "an unlawful combination, or conspiracy." With witnesses against it routinely murdered and intimidated,[27] judges, prosecutors and jurors bribed,[28] police forces rendered impotent by its payoffs,[29] and its criminal machinations virtually unchecked,[30] it was clearly "impracticable to enforce the laws of the United States" against it "by the course of ordinary judicial proceedings."

U.S. citizens, forced to pay dues to the Mafia's captive unions without commensurate benefits,[31] to pay inflated prices for its goods and services,[32] to suffer the overall terror and crime caused and promoted by Mob activities,[33] were certainly being "deprived of a right, privilege, immunity, or protection named in the Constitution and secured by law." State and local law enforcement authorities, overpowered by Mob wealth and muscle, and riddled with Mob corruption,[34] were obviously "unable, fail[ing], or refus[ing]" to provide these protections. In short, by its slaughter, intimidation, plunder and corruption, the Mafia was clearly "obstruct[ing] the execution of the laws of the United States" and "imped[ing] the course of justice." The conditions of title 10, sections 332 and 333, which mandated military protection of U.S. citizens in the absence of effective civil measures, were compellingly satisfied.

The need for some such extraordinary action to stop the Mob's murderous rampages was highlighted during October 1963 in the U.S. Senate hearings on organized crime and narcotics, which were coordinated by chief counsel Robert Kennedy. Tampa Police Chief Neil Brown, summarizing the feelings of other police officials, testified that it was

> almost impossible for the Police Department of the City of Tampa, or any other municipality, to cope effectively with the activities of a national or international crime syndicate such as these hearings show exists in the United States.[35]

Chicago Police Chief O. W. Wilson, former dean of the School of Criminology at the University of California, Berkeley,[36] declared:

> It is absurd and naive to assume that anything less than an all-out effort on the part of all echelons of government will produce results in the fight against organized crime. . . .
> Let us hope that we can develop a ground swell of public opinion demanding that this parasitical menace called Cosa Nostra, or by any other name, be eradicated.[37]

Chicago Police Deputy Superintendent Joseph F. Morris affirmed that "the Federal Government must assume the leadership in this all-out war on syndicated crime."[38] And Senator John McClellan, who chaired the subcommittee which conducted the hearings, summarized:

> The shocking narratives that we have heard here during these days of testimony generates, I think, an immediate sense of urgency. The conditions depicted here cannot be shrugged off. These thousands of skilled and confirmed professional criminals drain the strength of this Nation, both morally and economically. These conditions are not improving; they are getting worse and will continue to get worse until adequate steps are taken to combat and contain this national menace.[39]

Under the relentless leadership of Attorney General Robert Kennedy, supported fully by the President, the federal government was moving toward precisely such an "all-out war against syndicated crime." The way to a final crushing onslaught was cleared by Joseph Valachi's Senate testimony of October 1963, which outraged Americans;[40] Attorney General Kennedy pledged to intensify the government's sweeping anti-racketeering crusade,[41] and planned a "massive, frontal assault" on the Mob's Las Vegas base.[42] The rest has been told: Mafia assassination, cover-up, reversal of the Kennedys' policies; corruption, then collusion with the Mob under Johnson and Nixon; and finally, under Ford, Carter and Reagan, complacent tolerance by a battered American citizenry of this bloated and well-entrenched confederation of killers. In short, aborting government counterattack with a murderous coup, the Mafia made the frightening transition from overgrown outlaw gang to occupying army.

Today, through ironclad control of the Teamsters,[43] the nation's largest union, the Mafia has achieved its 1947 plan to "unionize every truckdriver in the Nation," so it could "bring industry to its knees, and even the Government."[44] And through similar tight control of the International Longshoremen's Association, concluded NBC News, the Mob "runs the docks in this country."[45] Its operating procedure on the waterfront is standard: "assault, organized theft, pilferage, extortion, kickbacks, loan-sharking, gambling, payroll padding, other criminal activities and even murder."[46] In effect, concluded NBC, "the Mafia and the Longshoremen's Union have been able to put their own tax on every item moving in or out of the ports they control."[47]

With the nation's roads and docks in its strangle hold, the Mafia's tentacles also reach out into its airports, as reported by *Harvard Business Review*: "Ground operations at international airports are at present permeated by the syndicate or by men under its control."[48] A case in point, as noted by Senator John McClellan, is the "mob takeover of the air freight trucking industry at Kennedy airport" in New York.[49] This conquest was achieved in the late 1960s, when every trucking company at the leading international airport capitulated to a Mob-controlled industry association and a captive Teamster local following strikes and extensive sabotage against the firms.[50] With this Mafia incursion came a wave of "trucking rackets, mail thefts, hijacking, flagrant pilferage, loansharking,"[51] and a hundred-fold increase in annual volume of cargo theft at the airport.[52] "Rampant Mob rule at Kennedy Airport," noted author Michael Dorman, "is typical of the underworld's role at airports across the country."[53]

In the construction field, another pivotal support system for the American economy, "the Mafia has taken over," as one union member put it.[54] Indicative of this Mafia influence was the unique background of the "labor troubleshooter" for the Gilbain Building Company, one of the world's largest construction firms.[55] The employee was Stephan Broccoli, alias "Peanuts the Dwarf," convicted three times for armed robbery, and placed on the Gilbain payroll by New England Mafia boss Raymond Patriarca.[56]

Also par for the course was a Pentagon construction contract in St. Louis, where "Mob controlled unions hold much of the available labor in a virtual hammerlock."[57] The contract was handled by Laborers Local 42, headed by Mob killer Lou Shoulders.[58] The project was finally completed, a year late, with a 200-percent, $14 million overrun, distributed mainly among "a small army of Mob soldiers, relatives and high-rankers," including a Syndicate arsonist, who turned up on the federal payroll.[59] Kickbacks, paychecks for "ghost workers," and on-site racketeering, as occurred on this contract,[60] are standard for construction work performed by Mob-dominated unions in many parts of the nation,[61] leading one New York underworld informer to comment, "And you wonder why it costs so much to put up a building?"[62]

From such bastions of Mafia influence as trucking, shipping and construction, and from such traditional activities as murder,[63] assault,[64] extortion,[65] arson,[66] gambling,[67] narcotics trafficking,[68] fencing of stolen goods,[69] pension fund fraud,[70] price-fixing,[71] political corruption,[72] sexual blackmail,[73] and subversion of the press,[74] the Mafia has branched out since the 1960s to such new or newly emphasized arenas as securities theft and fraud,[75] infiltration of banks and insurance companies,[76] promotion of rock concerts,[77] art theft,[78] bankruptcy fraud,[79] cigarette smuggling,[80] bootlegging of records and tapes,[81] counterfeiting of prescription drugs,[82] and dumping of toxic chemical wastes.[83]

Exemplifying such recent additions to the Mob's repertoire of crime is its infiltration of the health industry. According to officials in Dade County, Florida, the Miami Heart Institute is "a regular meeting place for a number of organized crime figures," such as Mafia don Sam DeCavalcante, who was monitored going there almost daily.[84] In Boston, ownership of the Kenmore Hospital was traced to Mafia underboss Jerry Angiulo;[85] an investigator "identified eight known bookies who entered the building in the course of a single afternoon."[86] Mafia defector Vincent Teresa remarked, "With what I knew about doctors on the Mob payroll in Boston, I wouldn't have gone near a Boston hospital if I was on my deathbed."[87]

In Chicago, an investigation of underworld Medicaid fraud was punctuated by five violent incidents.[88] Among these were the murders of two Mob-affiliated partners who owned a medical syndicate that had "a virtual monopoly over welfare medicine on the south and west sides."[89] A Chicago police spokesman asserted that underworld elements "control a lot of the pharmaceutical business and are probably heavy into Medicaid in Illinois."[90]

In New York City, as Jack Anderson reported, a federal grand jury "heard secret testimony that some mobsters have used fraud, extortion, arson, assault and other strong-arm tactics against Medicaid practitioners."[91] According to one doctor who was shot and wounded shortly after testifying, the Mob extorted monthly payments from owners of Medicaid clinics with threats of beatings and arson, together with promises of political assistance and protection from competition.[92] Its monthly take from some clinics reached several thousand dollars a month; other clinics were forced to use the services of Mob-controlled businesses.[93] Anderson also noted that "notorious mobsters like Meyer Lansky and Joe Colombo reportedly have been linked to nursing homes, hospitals, and clinical laboratories."[94]

Official estimates of the Mob's annual income in the United States "usually begin at $120 *billion*," *Newsweek* reported;[95] this is the cost of its countless such criminal operations. Yet the truly alarming threat to America now is the drain of untold billions more through what *Harvard Business Review* described as the "massive infiltration of the national economy by members of organized crime."[96] Mob control of 50,000 U.S. firms,[97] "hoodlum connections with some of the biggest banks in the country,"[98] $385 million siphoned off from the Teamsters pension fund,[99] the U.S. National Bank collapse and similar recent bank failures[100]—these are among the manifestations of an underworld financial incursion which, as Senator Charles Percy noted, "underpins the whole economy of the United States, virtually all private ownership."[101] With similar alarm, Congressman Claude Pepper pointed out "how extensively organized criminal elements have infiltrated the banking, securities and insurance industries";[102] he called this Mob influence "pervasive."[103]

The golden lining of such financial firms for the Mob is the opportunity they provide to draw cash against fraudulent or overvalued paper assets. Important accessories in this process are corrupt accountants and lawyers,[104] and, as described by one-time securities fence Edward Wuenche, Mob-controlled banks, whose top officers are merely "figureheads for organized crime."[105] These Syndicate fronts "don't make a move without first consulting someone else," Wuenche testified. "This has become more and more prevalent in the last 10 years. ... There are so many of them that it would really shake you in your boots."[106]

Illustrating this paper-to-cash transformation is the conversion of stolen stock certificates. Virtually impossible to sell, such certificates typically yield about 80 percent of their value in cash when used as collateral for loans.[107] Since discovering this stock conversion technique, the Mob has staged a blitzkrieg assault on Wall Street, bringing it control of some brokerage firms, cooperation of employees in others, and a ready supply of securities.[108] The tactics of penetration are standard: narcotics, vice, gambling and loansharking debts, terror, and murder.[109] The result is a booming trade in stolen securities, which, as a U.S. Senate chart outlined, the Mob controls from theft to distribution and conversion.[110]

The volume of losses from securities thefts has grown explosively, from $9.1 million in 1966 to $494 million in the first six months of 1971, as estimated by federal officials.[111] But the real shocker was the figure reported to the U.S. Senate in 1973 by Henry DuPont, chairman of the board of the Securities Validation Corporation.[112] DuPont estimated that the value of securities stolen or otherwise lost as of June 1973 was $50 *billion*—representing 4.8 percent of the value of all outstanding stocks.[113] Most banks are reluctant to check their securities portfolios, DuPont testified, explaining why:

We had one bank check a demand loan file, I believe, on one of
their smaller loans. . . . Sixty-nine out of the 70 certificates col-
lateralizing the demand loans were stolen securities.[115]*

The staggering extent of the Mafia's securities drain was also noted by Mob
defector Gerald Zelmanowitz: "There are so many bad securities right now
in the vaults and pledged against and inside corporate structures that to
expose them on your own would cause a downfall of half the brokerage
firms."[116]

Further illustrating the Mob's mammoth network of plunder are the affairs of Michele Sindona, who began his career in the late 1940s as a lawyer
and wartime trader in Sicily.[117] Within 20 years, displaying the magic touch
of a Mobster,[118] Sindona had become owner or director of American and
European firms worth billions of dollars.[119] Among his U.S. holdings was the
Franklin National Bank of New York, which was the nation's 19th largest
bank;[120] Sindona was chairman of the board and held a controlling interest.[121] Another major American firm interlocked with Sindona's financial
empire was the Gulf and Western Corporation.[122] In one transaction, Gulf
and Western purchased 15 million shares of *Societa General Immobiliare,*
an Italian conglomerate dominated by Sindona, and listed them on its
books at one-and-one-half times their market value.[123] Sindona, in turn,
purchased a Hollywood holding from the American conglomerate at double its assessed value.[124]†

---

*A further statistic suggests the extent of underworld penetration of the national
economy. The Internal Revenue Service recently reported that 40 percent of the
$125 billion of currency in circulation is in hundred-dollar bills, used mainly by
"those who need a highly liquid, anonymous form of wealth. . . . They include tax
evaders, drug traffickers, illegal gamblers, loan sharks, fences of stolen goods, and
corrupt politicians."[114]

† In a similar transaction with the Mob-linked[125] Resorts International corporation, the Securities and Exchange Commission alleged, Gulf and Western inflated
the value of a real estate property in the Bahamas by a factor of 12.[126] These suspicious dealings fit the pattern of overvaluation of holdings, irregular financial reporting and stock price manipulation that have characterized the conglomerate's
operations.[127] According to government sources, as the *New York Times* put it,
"many of these complex transactions had one thing in common: inflated appraisals
of real estate and stocks that were used by Gulf and Western to hide its losses and
also to help acquire assets from other companies whose value was subsequently
overstated."[128]

The final destination for Gulf and Western's paper profits may be organized
crime, some have suspected.[129] This is suggested by Mobster Sidney Korshak's close
involvement with the firm and its chairman, Charles Bludhorn,[130] the purchase of a
Mexican Mafia hideaway by its real estate subsidiary,[131] a questionable transaction
between that subsidiary and the Teamsters pension fund,[132] and alleged fraud in
Gulf and Western's own pension fund.[133] All federal charges of misconduct were
deemed "outrageous" by the firm's attorney: Edward Bennett Williams.[134]

Sindona's modus operandi was clarified in 1974 with the collapse of *Banca Privata Italiana* of Milan, the Franklin National Bank, and other banks he controlled.[135] The Italian government accused him of draining $225 million from the Milan bank,[136] while a 99-count U.S. federal indictment returned in 1979 charged him with stealing $45 million from the Franklin National Bank.[137] As the *Washington Post* reported, the U.S. indictment detailed

> the intricate steps by which Sindona allegedly looted the Milan banks he controlled to come up with the funds to buy Franklin National, then drained deposits from Franklin National to put funds back in his Italian institutions. All of the funds made the trip from Italy to the U.S. via Switzerland, most of the time through a Zurich bank that Sindona also controlled. . . .[138]

Sindona evaded U.S. prosecution through a faked kidnapping, which according to Assistant U.S. Attorney John Kenney, was staged in connection with organized crime figures.[139]

While the prime beneficiary of Sindona's transactions was undoubtedly the Mafia, the big loser was the Vatican. In the spring of 1969, Sindona had received a private audience with Pope Paul VI,[140] who had been seeking to reform the Church's financial administration by diversification of its assets.[141] By the time Sindona had kissed the papal ring and departed, the Pope had signed a document giving Sindona control over a large part of the Vatican's wealth.[142] And by January 1975, the Vatican had lost approximately $240 million from Sindona's financial manipulations.[143] Perturbed by these huge losses, and perhaps haunted by his meeting with Sindona, Pope Paul remarked in 1977, "perhaps only the hand of an oppressor can free Us and the Church from it all. Satan may overleap himself."[144]*

In August 1982, Banco Ambrosiano, Italy's largest private bank, was liquidated after "the apparent looting of $1.4 billion through that bank and sev-

---

*Pope Paul's successor, John Paul I, was not able to get to the bottom of the colossal Mafia scam, since he died 33 days after becoming pope, in October 1978, reportedly from a stroke.[145] A Vatican decree enacted in 1975 prohibited any autopsy on the body of a pope.[146] *Time* cited this decree as illustrative of how far the Church had come since an earlier age, when "so untimely a death might have stirred deep suspicions," even "talk that John Paul was poisoned."[147]

On May 13, 1981, Pope John Paul II was shot and critically wounded by Mehmet Ali Agca, a "cold professional killer."[148] Noting clear signs of help from others in Agca's escape from prison and travels through Europe before the shooting,[149] an Italian court concluded that the assassination attempt was part of a conspiracy, whose promoters or motives it could not identify:

> Agca was only the visible point of a conspiracy. . . . The menacing figure of Mehmet Ali Agca appeared suddenly in the crowd to carry out, with bureaucratic coldness, a mandate given him. . . .[150]

eral foreign subsidiaries."[151] According to investigators, the money was funneled from Italy to Luxembourg, back to Italy, then to Nicaragua, Peru, and
finally Panama, where it "seems to have disappeared."[152] Closely involved
in these manipulations was Archbishop Paul Marcinkus, the Vatican's chief
banker, who hails from Cicero, Illinois.[153] Marcinkus had chosen Michele
Sindona as his "trusted adviser,"[154] and is suspected of prior complicity
with New York Mafioso Vincent Rizzo in a $1 billion counterfeit securities
fraud.[155] He refused to tell what he knew about the Ambrosiano scam.[156]

The silence of other key figures in the affair was assured. Banco Ambrosiano President Roberto Calvi was found dead, "hanging off a bridge in
London."[157] Calvi's secretary "plunged to her death in Milan."[158] Roberto
Rosone, vice president of the bank, was luckier: he survived a murder attempt.[159] Five other individuals related to the Sindona and Ambrosiano
scandals have met violent deaths;[160] Sindona was indicted for one of these
murders.[161]

The collapse of the Franklin National Bank, the largest bank failure in the
United States,[162] and of Banco Ambrosiano, Italy's largest private bank,[163]
underscored the economic peril to both nations caused by the underworld's increasingly brazen machinations of plunder. In 1982, recognizing
the intolerable threat posed by the Mafia, the Italian government commissioned its senior antiterrorist policeman, General Carlo Dalla Chiesa, to investigate it.[164] On September 3, Dalla Chiesa and his wife were murdered by
gunshots fired at their car in Palermo, Sicily; a police escort was also
killed.[165] Italian Prime Minister Giovanni Spadolini blamed the Mafia for the
killings,[166] commenting:

> General Dalla Chiesa, who had made an immense contribution
> to the struggle against terrorism, has fallen at a moment when
> he was putting into action, with intelligence and courage, a
> battle plan against the Mafia terror.[167]

The prime minister called the murders "a mortal challenge launched by
the Mafia against the democratic state, a challenge that for some time has
turned into open warfare."[168]

Two decades ago, brothers John and Robert Kennedy, also with intelligence and courage, launched a battle plan against this vicious combine in
the United States. The Mafia murders of each posed, and continue to pose,
the same mortal challenge to this nation; they furthermore emphasize that
this murderous army's machinations have long since passed the point of
control by civil authorities. The time has come to pick up the Kennedys'
fallen torch, and to put an end to the continuing, century-long record of
human suffering and subjugation imposed by the Mob in America. The required action is clear—the same used by George Washington to crush the

Whiskey Rebellion, and by Chester Arthur against organized crime in Arizona: eradication of the Mafia with military force under title 10, sections 332 and 333 of the United States Code. The prerequisites for recall of troops are simple: a total end to the Mafia's crimes, to its strangle hold of terror, and to all of its operations.

For the United States to continue pretending to fight the Mafia with local police is ludicrous—as ludicrous as it would have been for the Pearl Harbor Police Force to have broadcast subpoenas to attacking Axis pilots on December 7, 1941. Indeed, a government that must hide or disguise citizens who wish to testify freely has forfeited its authority. A government that must concede major segments of the nation's political and economic structure to underworld control has surrendered its sovereignty. And until the government uses appropriate, Constitutionally mandated force* to crush the Mafia's brazen empire of crime, to stop its multimillion-dollar draining of America's urban ghettos and its multibillion-dollar plundering of America's financial institutions, no government program to fight crime or poverty, no economic juggling to reduce unemployment and inflation can hope to succeed.

Until such time as the government resumes the Kennedys' counterattack against the Mob, there is another way that each of us can fight back. The method is as Malcolm X had directed: "all-out war against organized crime in the community."[170] Specifically, I propose, effective immediately, a boycott of all Mafia-controlled enterprises and operations, with special focus on the Mafia-infested[171] casinos of Las Vegas and Atlantic City.† The moral imperative for participating may be best appreciated by its alternative. Take your next vacation, hold your next convention in Las Vegas or Atlantic City. There you can mingle with the scum of the earth, as your gambling losses support more Mafia crimes, from assassination to Medicaid fraud to toxic dumping.

If assassination and corruption abort every legitimate effort by Americans to eradicate the Mob, a third measure—a desperate, unfortunate, last

---

*It is interesting to note how, in recent decades, the same government officials—J. Edgar Hoover, Joseph McCarthy, and Richard Nixon—who failed to apply federal power appropriately to fight and investigate the Mafia's army of killers have channeled such power inappropriately against ideological dissidents.[169]

†Gambling itself is hardly evil; laws against it have only replicated the folly of Prohibition by diverting enormous potential tax revenues into the coffers of organized crime, and by transforming citizens into lawbreakers. It is pertinent to note that both George Washington and Thomas Jefferson wrote of personal winnings and losses from card games,[172] and that some of the nation's leading colleges, including Harvard and Yale, raised money through lotteries during the 18th and early 19th centuries.[173] With the Mob's current monopoly of gambling,[174] however, patronage of virtually any casino or bookmaker in the United States lines its coffers..

resort—is outlined by a precedent in New Orleans. On October 15, 1890, the city's police chief, David Hennessey, was wrapping up an investigation of Mafia dock racketeering when he was murdered by a salvo of shotgun blasts.[175] With fear overcome by public indignation, more than 60 witnesses came forward to testify, and 19 gangsters were indicted as principals or conspirators in the killing, including four identified at the scene of the crime.[176] The evidence was overwhelming, and newspapers viewed a guilty verdict as a foregone conclusion.[177] But following massive Mafia expenditures on the defense, suspicious prosecution maneuvers, plus bribery and intimidation of the jury,[178] all the accused were either acquitted or held over for further trial.[179]

The jury's verdict outraged the city, and on March 14, 1891, the day after it was announced, a protest rally was held with the encouragement of the mayor and two local newspapers.[180] It quickly turned into a roaring mob of eight thousand, which with "military precision" proceeded to hang eleven of the accused killers.[181]

The eradication of the Mafia is not the total answer, however, to the horrors chronicled here. For only by abandoning the ways of exploitation, manipulation and deception it has come to epitomize can we overcome the specter of this pathetic band of thugs and fulfill the promise of our martyred leaders.

Indeed, it is time that we Americans, descendants of pilgrims and prophets, follow our calling: to redeem the past with truth, to consecrate the present with courage, and to consummate the future with the moral vision upon which this nation was founded.

Appendix 1
Documents from the National Archives

This book relies on hundreds of government documents in the National Archives, some of which were published in the Warren Commission Hearings and Exhibits. To provide some feel for these documents, and for the way in which they were censored, the following are reproduced below:

1. An FBI report dated November 27, 1963 from the National Archives, Commission Document 84, pages 91–92. Note, as discussed in chapter 9, that Jack Ruby's reported close contact, "Joseph Cirello," is Dallas Mafia boss Joseph Civello.

2. The version of this FBI report published in the Warren Commission Hearings and Exhibits as Commission Exhibit 1536. Note that the published version is a photoreproduction of the first page of the original report, with the last three paragraphs blanked out.

3. The first and most significant page of a five-page FBI report dated December 7, 1963. It is from the National Archives, Commission Document 86, page 278. This page was omitted when the rest of this report was published in the Warren Commission Hearings and Exhibits as Commission Exhibit 1750.

FD-302 (Rev. 3-3-59)   FEDERAL BUREAU OF INVESTIGATION   C D

Date November 27, 1963

1

BOBEY GENE MOORE, 865 43rd Street, Oakland,
California, was interviewed at his home. He stated that
he desired to furnish information regarding JACK RUBY, who
he had known in Dallas, Texas. He stated that he had observed an interview on television with an associate of RUBY
in which the associate said that RUBY had no gangster connections. MOORE furnished the following information:

He was raised in Dallas, Texas, having been
born in that city on December 12, 1927. About 1951 or
1952, he was living at a rooming house at 1214 Poll Street,
Dallas. This house was at the rear of Hill's Liquor Store
at the corner of Ross Avenue and Bell Street. This liquor
store was a front for a bookie-type operation where bets
were taken on all types of athletic events and horse races.
It was operated by a man named HILL, first name unknown,
and his son. This gambling place was patronized by most
of the gambling element in Dallas and RUBY was a frequent
visitor. MOORE did not know whether or not RUBY was actually connected with the operation of the gambling place or
was merely a participant.

During that time MOORE was employed by Cirello
and LaMonte Italian Importing Company 3400 Ross Avenue.
MOORE suspected that his employers, JOSEPH CIRELLO and FRANK
LA MONTE, were engaged in racket activities because on occasion they would not allow him to open certain cartons containing cheese imported from Italy, although that was his
alleged job. It was his opinion, based on this, that they
might be importing narcotics. He had no additional information to substantiate this. RUBY was also a frequent visitor
and associate of CIRELLO and LA MONTE.

Two officers, CHARLIE SANSONE (PH), white, male,
American, about 40, a detective in the Dallas Police Department, and MARVIN BLUNT, a Texas State Policeman, were regular
patrons at Hill's Liquor Store and MOORE felt that they were
obviously either aware of the gambling action if they were
not actually involved.

Judge O'BRIEN, a Municipal Judge in Dallas, was
a friend of CIRELLO and LA MONTE and MOORE frequently put
hams and other food stuffs in O'BRIEN's car at their request.

on 11/26/63 at Oakland, California _____ File # DL 44-1639   SF 44-494

by Special Agent DONALD F. HALLAHAN &
THOMAS G. NG-CEB/ew/eah ___ 91 ___ Date dictated 11/27/63

This document contains neither recommendations nor conclusions of the FBI. It is the property of the FBI and is loaned to
your agency; it and its contents are not to be distributed outside your agency.

ST 44-404
DL 44-1639/e h

2

        RUBY was also friendly with PHIL BOSCO, owner
of the Gulf Service Station which was across the street
from Hill's Liquor Store, and MOORE felt that BOSCO was
also engaged in criminal activities in Dallas, although he
had no specific information to substantiate this.

        In about 195?, RUBY hired MOORE as a part-time
piano player and he played periodically after hours at the
Vegas Club from 1952 until 1956, when MOORE left Dallas
and moved to California. While at the Vegas Club, he saw
RUBY on numerous occasions with a revolver. RUBY was
friendly for awhile with CANDY BARR, a well-known Dallas
stripper. He is also well known to JIM JOHNSON, leader of
a quartet who played at the Vegas Club regularly from 1956
until January, 1963, when MOORE last visited Dallas.

        MOORE felt that from RUBY's association with
(FNU) HILL, CIRELLO, LA MONTE, and PHIL BOSCO that he was
connected with the underworld in Dallas.

        MOORE had no information regarding any connection
between RUBY and Dallas Police Officers. MOORE did not know
OSWALD and knew of no connection between RUBY and OSWALD.
He knew of no radical extremist views by RUBY or any racial
extremist views. He had no information concerning RUBY
being in California. He knew RUBY between approximately
1952 until 1956, when MOORE left Dallas and went to California.
He saw RUBY again previously on a visit to Dallas in January,
1963. He had no additional factual information.

FEDERAL BUREAU OF INVESTIGATION

Date __November 27, 1963__

1

     BOBBY GENE MOORE, 865 43rd Street, Oakland, California, was interviewed at his home. He stated that he desired to furnish information regarding JACK RUBY, who he had known in Dallas, Texas. He stated that he had observed an interview on television with an associate of RUBY in which the associate said that RUBY had no gangster connections. MOORE furnished the following information:

     He was raised in Dallas, Texas, having been born in that city on December 12, 1927. About 1951 or 1952, he was living at a rooming house at 1214 Boll Street, Dallas. This house was at the rear of Hill's Liquor Store at the corner of Ross Avenue and Boll Street. This liquor store was a front for a bookie-type operation where bets were taken on all types of athletic events and horse races. It was operated by a man named HILL, first name unknown, and his son. This gambling place was patronized by most of the gambling element in Dallas and RUBY was a frequent visitor. MOORE did not know whether or not RUBY was actually connected with the operation of the gambling place or was merely a participant.

on __11/26/63__ at __Oakland, California__ _____ File # __SF 44-494__
                                                          __DL 44-1639__

            DONALD F. HALLAHAN &
by Special Agent __THOMAS G. MC GEE/rcw/cah__ _____ Date dictated __11/27/63__

COMMISSION EXHIBIT No. 1536

Date ⸳⸳⸳⸳⸳⸳

WILLIAM B. ABADIE, who is employed at Scott
Instrument Company, 3734 West Slauson, Los Angeles,
California, was interviewed at his residence, 4820 West
Slauson, Los Angeles. At the inception of the interview
ABADIE advised that he had jumped bond in the amount of
$300. at Dallas, Texas; that this bond had been to cover
his release on a charge of DWI (Driving While Intoxicated).
He advised that he knew the Dallas Police Department would
be looking for him and wanted to know if he was going to
be arrested by the Agents. The Agents immediately informed
him that they wanted to interview him concerning his knowledge
and associations with JACK LEON RUBY, of Dallas, Texas. He
was further advised that this Office had no warrant for him
and no interest at this time in the local violation at Dallas.
He was advised that anything that he said would be voluntary,
that he did not have to be interviewed by the Agents or
furnish any information to them, that if he did it could be
used as evidence in a court of law, but that the subject of
the interview was entirely concerning his associations with
JACK RUBY. Mr. ABADIE then advised that he hardly knew RUBY
and was entirely willing to discuss anything concerning RUBY
with the Agents.

ABADIE first became acquainted by observation with
the man known as JACK LEON RUBY, whom, according to newspaper
accounts read by ABADIE, shot and killed LEE HARVEY OSWALD,
the alleged assassin of President JOHN F. KENNEDY. ABADIE
had never known RUBY prior to the early part of March, 1963,
at which time, after having been on an extended alcoholic binge,
ABADIE was hired by RUBY's Shop Foreman as a slot machine and
juke box mechanic. This employment continued for a period of
about seven weeks, ABADIE leaving at the end of this time to
try and locate his estranged wife.

ABADIE stated he had never even spoken to RUBY
or been spoken to by him. He advised that he did see RUBY
in the warehouse shop where he, ABADIE, was performing his
mechanics duties, but that he at no time had any discussions
with him socially or because of his employment. For the
most part his work was at the aforementioned warehouse.
However, on one occasion for a few days he "wrote tickets"
as a bookie in one of RUBY's establishments.

On __12/6/63____ at __Los Angeles, California___ File #Los Angeles 44-895_____

by __SA's WILLIAM N. HEARD and DOUGLAS J._____ Date dictated __12/7/63_____
                      KRAUTER/srb

                              278

Appendix 2
Profiles of the Apalachin 58

Following are profiles of the 58 persons apprehended by New York State Police at the 1957 Mafia convention in Apalachin, New York. Although names have changed and operations have expanded, the interlocking structure of this nation-wide criminal conspiracy remains intact. The information below is from U.S.-Senate, McClellan Labor Hearings, pp. 12194–201.

Alaimo, Dominick (Pittston, Penna.). Co-owner Jane Hogan Dress Co., Pittston. Committeeman for Local 8005, United Mine Workers of America. Arrests: robbery, suspicion, violation internal revenue laws.

Barbara, Joseph Mario, Sr. (Apalachin, N.Y.). Host at Apalachin meeting. President of Canada Dry Bottling Co. of Endicott, N.Y. Arrests: suspicion of murder (2), revolver, illegal acquisition of sugar.

Bonanno, Joseph (Brooklyn). Formerly in B and D Coat Co., manufacturers of women's coats. Arrests: grand larceny, revolver, conspiracy, violation of Wage and Hour Law.

Bonventre, John (Brooklyn). Reputed occupations: undertaker, cheese and oil business, Pinta Clothing Co., Levine and Bonventre, ladies' coat contractors, real estate of [sic] salesman for Joseph A. Bivana, Brooklyn, uncle of Joseph Bonanno.

Bufalino, Russell J. (Kingston, Penna.). Owner of Penn Drape and Curtain Co., Pittston, Pa. Arrests: criminally receiving stolen property (2).

Cannone, Ignatius (Endwell, N.Y.). Owns Nat's Place, Endicott, and Plaza Lounge, Endwell, N.Y. Two arrests for disorderly conduct. One for fighting in Endwell, the other for shooting dice in New York City.

Carlisi, Roy (Buffalo, N.Y.). Arrests: violation Internal Revenue Act. Indicted for 15 counts of contempt by Tiogo County Grand Jury February 27, 1958.

Castellano, Paul (Brooklyn). Possession dangerous weapon, robbery with violence. Brother-in-law of Carlo Gambino [who was] at Apalachin.

Cateno, Gerardo Vito (S. Orange, N.J.). Employee and stockholder Runyon Vending Sales Co., Newark. Arrests: 3 for gambling, robbery (2), grand larceny (truck), material witness in murder case, loitering, bribery of federal juror. Close associate of Longy Zwillman.

Chivi, Charles Salvatore (Palisade, N.J.). Officer of Automotive Conveying Co., in which Joe Adonis was his partner. No known criminal record.

Civello, Joseph Frances (Dallas, Tex.). Food and liquor importer. Arrests: murder, violation liquor law. Conspiracy of Harrison Act (2). Associate: John Ormento.

Colletti, James (Pueblo, Colo.). Owns Colorado Cheese Co., Pueblo. Arrests: receiving stolen goods, disorderly person.

Cucchiara, Frank (Watertown, Mass.). Treasurer of Purity Cheese Co. since 1938, Boston. Arrests: assault and battery, possession morphine and dynamite, lottery, conspiracy to set up lottery, grand larceny, sale of narcotics, forgery, possession of still (3), conspiracy to erect still.

D'Agostino, Dominick (Niagara Falls, N.Y.). Arrests: Buffalo-Harrison Act. Indicted April 8, 1958 on seven counts. Criminal contempt by Tioga County Grand Jury.

De Mooco, John Anthony (Shaker Heights, Ohio). Arrests: robbery, extortion, blackmail, investigation in bombing. Associate of John Scolish, also at Apalachin.

Desimone, Frank (Downey, Calif.). Former partner of Jack Dragna in Latin Importing Co.

Evola, Natale Joseph (Brooklyn). President-treasurer of Belmont Garment Delivery Co., and president of Amity Garment Co. Arrests: dangerous weapon, coercion. Presently under indictment with John Ormento and others in federal narcotics conspiracy.

Falcone, Joseph (Utica). Manager of Utica Retail Liquor Company. Brother, Salvatore, also at Apalachin. Arrest: violation Internal Revenue Liquor Tax.

Falcone, Salvatore (Utica and Miami). Operates grocery store in Miami. Arrests: violation Internal Revenue Liquor Tax.

Gambino, Carlo (Brooklyn). Associated with S.G.S. Associates, labor consultants. Arrests: grand larceny, violations Internal Revenue Act (still), several federal alcohol tax arrests. Brother-in-law of Paul Castellano, also at Apalachin.

Genovese, Michael James (Gibsonia, Pa.). Owner of Archie's Car Wash. Partner in L & G Amusement Co., Pa., coin-machines, with John La Rocca in 1956. Arrests: robbery, concealed weapon.

Genovese, Vito (Atlantic Highlands, N.J.). Ranked among top gangsters in the country.

Guarnieri, Anthony Frank, a.k.a. "Guv" (Johnson City, N.Y.). Vice president of Tri-Cities Dress Co., Inc., Binghamton, and president-treas. of Owego Textile Co., Owego. Arrests: possession fire arms, lottery, felonious assault.

Guccia, Bartolo (Endicott, N.Y.). Fish-peddler. Barbara is godfather to his children. Arrests: possession weapon (2), bank robbery, breaking & entering, bootlegging, murder—1st degree.

Ida, Joseph (Highland Park, N.J.). Automobile salesman. Associate of Mike Clemente and Rocco Pellegrino.

La Duca, James Vincent (Lewiston, N.Y.). Was sec.-treas. of Local 66, Hotel, Restaurant Employees, Buffalo. Associate of Steve & Anthony Maggadino, Roy Carlisi and John Montana.

Lagattuta, Samuel (Buffalo). Arrests: arson, murder investigation, dangerous weapon.

Larasso, Louis Anthony (Linden, N.J.). Was trustee of Local 394, Common Laborers & Hod Carriers.

Lombardozzi, Carmine (Brooklyn). Arrests: homicide, burglary, unlawful entry, disorderly conduct, abduction-rape, weapon, policy (3), common gambler.

Maggadino, Antonio (Niagara Falls). V.P. of Maggadino Funeral Home. Record (all in Italy): falsifying name on passport, clandestine activities, homicide, denounced for rape, robbery and murder.

Magliocco, Joseph (East Islip, N.Y.). Arrests: transporting wine, possession of gun and alcohol. Sole stockholder of Sunland Beverage Company; wholesale beer distributor.

Majuri, Frank Thomas (Elizabeth, N.J.). Was V.P. of Local 364, Hod Carriers and Common Laborers Union. Arrests: conspiracy to commit robbery, possession of liquor, violation ABC Act and contempt, illicit manufacture of alcohol with intent to sell, disorderly conduct, bookmaking.

Mancuso, Rosario (Utica, N.Y.). November 1953 elected president of Local 186, Hod Carriers and Common Laborers Union. Arrested 3/25/51 for assault with intent to commit murder.

Mannarino, Gabriel (New Kinsington, Pa.). Former owner, with brothers, of Sans Soucie, Havana, now owned by Louis Santos, also at Apalachin. Arrests: gambling, violation liquor laws, robbery, firearms act, lottery, obstructing justice. Owner of Nu-Ken Novelty Co. (slot and cigarette machines, juke boxes).

Miranda, Michele A. (Forest Hills, N.Y.). Close associate of Vito Genovese. Arrests: disorderly conduct, suspicious person (2), vagrancy (2), homicide (2). On federal intl. narcotics list #229.

Monachino, Patsy (Auburn, N.Y.). Partner with brother Sam in Super Beverage Company.

Monachino, Sam (Auburn, N.Y.). Partner with brother, Patsy, in Super Beverage Co., beer wholesalers and distributors. Visited Joe "Socks" Lanza at Auburn Prison.

Montana, John Charles (Buffalo). President of several companies and director, chairman, etc., of various civic associations. Associate of Maggadinos, La Duca.

Olivetto, Dominick (Camden, N.J.). Arrests: criminal registration (2), illicit alcohol. Associated with Forest Products, Almonesson, New Jersey.

Ormento, John "Big John" (New York). A prominent figure in 107th Street (NYC) narcotics circles. He was arrested together with Salvatore La Proto for the possession of two guns, one with silencer, concealed in a trap in an automobile. Has 3 narcotics convictions and is currently subject of nationwide manhunt in connection with a large narcotics conspiracy. Operates Long Island Trucking Co.

Osticco, James Anthony (Pittston, Pa.). Arrests: liquor law and conspiracy. Official of Medico Industries, Inc.

Profaci, Joseph (Brooklyn). Owner of Carmela Mia Packing Co. Numbers of arrests in Italy and United States. An old-time well established gangster.

Rao, Vincent (Yonkers, N.Y.). Real estate operator and owner. Arrests: grand larceny, possession of gun (2), violation Workmen's Compensation Act.

Rava, Armand (Brooklyn). Manager of New Comers Restaurant, Brooklyn. Arrests: extortion, policy, Internal Revenue law, vagrancy. Close contact with Albert Anastasia.

Riccobono, Joseph (Staten Island, N.Y.). Owns Christine Dresses and Toni Belle Dresses, Brooklyn. Arrests: weapon extortion and conspiracy.

Riela, Anthony (W. Orange, N.J.). Owns Airport Hotel, Newark. Arrests: Maintaining a nuisance and permitting prostitution on premises.

Rosata, Joseph (New York). Alias "Joe Palisades." Owner of two trucking companies in the garment industry. Arrested for homicide—gun.

Santos, Louis (Havana, Cuba). Real name Louis [Santos] Trafficante, Jr., who now operates Sans Souci gambling casino in Havana. His father has been boss of Tampa rackets for years.

Scalish, John (Cleveland, Ohio). Operates Buckeye Cigarette Co.—vending machines. Arrests: burglary, robbery(2).

Sciandra, Angelo Joseph (Pittston, Pa.). Associated with Dixie Frocks Co., Wyoming, Pa., and Claudia Frocks, New York City. Arrest: assault.

Sciortino, Patsy (Auburn, N.Y.). Associated with Diana Bleach Co., Auburn, N.Y. Arrest: violation of Immigration Act.

Scozzari, Simone (San Gabriel, Calif.). Arrests: suspicion bookmaking (2). Had $10,000 in cash and checks when picked up. He operates cigar stand at Venetian Athletic Club, Los Angeles.

Tornabe, Salvatore (New York City). (Deceased 12/30/57.) Beer salesman for Sunland Beverage Corp., owned by Joe Magliocco. Admitted sale of whiskey to federal agent in 1921.

(Trafficante, Santos, Jr. See Louis Santos.)

Turrigiano, Patsy (Endicott, N.Y.). Arrests: operating still. Associated with grocery store.

Valente, Costenze Peter (Rochester). At Apalachin meeting with brother Frank. They operate Valente Bros. Produce business in Rochester. Has operated restaurants in Pittsburgh.

Valente, Frank Joseph (Rochester). At Apalachin meeting with brother Costenze Peter Valente, and with whom he operates produce business in Rochester. Arrests: counterfeit money, forgery, blackmail, larceny, Internal Revenue laws, assault and battery to commit rape, robbery, murder (2), conspiracy to violate Selective Service Act.

Zicari, Emanuel (Endicott, N.Y.). Arrests: counterfeiting. Occupation: shoe worker.

Zito, Frank (Springfield, Ill.). Owner and operator of Modern Distributing Co.—juke boxes. Claims to be retired. Arrests: conspiracy to violate prohibition laws.

Appendix 3
Background on
Jack Ruby's Telephone Records

A telephone with unpublished number WH1–5601 was listed to Jack Ruby from November 1962 through November 1963 at his residence, 223 South Ewing Street, Apartment 207, Dallas.[1] A telephone with number RI7–2362 was listed from November 1959 through November 1963 to the Carousel Club, 1312½ Commerce Street, Dallas,[2] which was owned and operated by Ruby;[3] the phone was in Ruby's office.[4] A third telephone with number LA8–4775 was listed from March 1956 through November 1963 to the Vegas Club, 3508 Oak Lawn, Dallas, and to Jack Ruby.[5] But since the Vegas Club was managed by Ruby's sister Eva Grant,[6] and there is no indication that calls from that phone were placed by Ruby, the small number of long distance calls placed from that phone in the latter part of 1963[7] have been ignored.

Toll calls placed from Ruby's home phone (WH1–5601) and his Carousel phone (RI7–2362) are itemized in telephone company records subpoenaed by the FBI[8] and in some telephone bills found in Ruby's possessions.[9] Included are toll calls from Ruby's Carousel phone from January 17 through March 1 and April 10 through November 22, 1963, and toll calls from Ruby's home phone from May 7 through November 22, 1963.

There are several indications that virtually all of the out-of-state calls from both Ruby's home and Carousel phones were placed by Ruby. Ruby testified he "had numerous phone calls, long-distance calls, all over the country."[10] Many of the persons called from Ruby's home and Carousel phones reported that the party who placed the calls in question was Jack Ruby.[11] Neither Ruby's roommate,[12] George Senator, nor his Carousel Club live-in handyman,[13] Larry Crafard, recalled making any out-of-state calls from these phones.[14] In fact, only one call among those from these phones appears to have been placed by a party other than Jack Ruby.[15] And there are gaps in Ruby's telephone records[16] corresponding to three periods during which Ruby was away from Dallas: the New York-Chicago trip of August 4–6,[17] the New Orleans trip the week of June 5,[18] and a trip to Houston and Edna, Texas beginning on May 9.[19]

Appendix 4
Mafia Review: References by Subject

Contents

I. A Look at the Menace

1. Introduction *309*
2. Infiltration of the Food and Drug Industries *309*
3. The Worst Victims: the Poor and the Black *311*
4. Louisiana: the Mafia's Sovereign Domain *312*

II. General Description and History

5. Structure *314*
6. Modus Operandi *320*
7. Roots in Sicily *327*
8. Metastasis in America *328*

III. Criminal Operations

9. Gambling *329*
10. Loan Sharking *331*
11. Narcotics *332*
12. Extortion *332*
13. Securities Theft and Fraud *333*
14. Cargo Theft *335*
15. Other Activities *336*
16. The Mafia and Street Crime *341*

IV. Economic Penetration

17. Infiltration of Business *344*
18. Infiltration of Labor *351*
19. Estimated Annual Income *360*

V. Corruption of American Government

20. Scope and Methods of Corruption *360*
21. Police Corruption *363*

22.   Corruption and Assault of the Judicial Process   *369*
23.   Corruption of Local Government   *377*
24.   Corruption of State Government and State-Wide Networks of
         Corruption   *382*
25.   Corruption of Federal Government   *386*

26.   Subversion of the Press   *392*
27.   From the Redwood Forests to the Gulf Stream Waters   *395*

Appendix 4
Mafia Review: References by Subject

Following are highlights from selected references on the Mafia, grouped by subject. Citations beginning with the prefix "U.S.–" are abbreviations for government documents listed in the bibliography. Any phrase in quotes, unless tagged with a footnote or identified parenthetically, is from the first reference subsequently cited.

Most of the sources on the Mob cited in this appendix and throughout this book are dated in the 1960s and 1970s. The similarity in the material spanning these two decades is a consequence of historical context. The Mafia began its mass migration from Sicily to America in the late 1800s;[1] by 1890, a New Orleans grand jury could conclude, "the existence of a secret organization known as the Mafia has been established beyond doubt."[2] Over the last century, despite proclamations of its imminent demise after the 1931 conviction of Al Capone[3] and after the 1957 bust of the Apalachin Mafia convention,[4] its structure and character have changed little.

I. A LOOK AT THE MENACE

1. Introduction

1.1 "The Mob . . . it poisons us all." Photos show 24 bosses of Mafia families across the country; a cartoon depicts Mafia activities, including gambling, murder, loan sharking, corruption, narcotics, bankruptcy fraud, union embezzlement, extortion, strike-breaking, prostitution, and business infiltration. *Life*, September 1, 1967, pp. 15, 20–21.

1.2 Undermining the American economy and government. Cressey, *Theft of the Nation*, pp. 1–3.

1.3 Congressional action: a public law "to seek the eradication of organized crime." *U.S.–OC Control Act of 1970.*

2. Infiltration of the Food and Drug Industries

2.1 "Mafia war on the A&P." Several major food chains agreed to carry a Mafia-promoted detergent described by the FDA as "extremely dangerous, toxic, and hazardous"(B), but A&P refused. A&P, at the time the world's largest food retailer, was subsequently almost put "out of business on the East Coast" through $60 million in damage from arson and the murders of two grocery store managers.

A–*Reader's Digest*, July 1970, pp. 71–76; B–Dorman, *Payoff*, pp. 242–48; also, C–*Good Housekeeping*, August 1971, pp. 68ff.

2.2 "The Mafia in the Supermarket." *Newsday* (1971), reproduced in Gage, *Mafia, U.S.A.*, pp. 323–34.

2.3 Mafia infiltration of the legitimate drug industry. From $50 to $100 million annually in counterfeit drugs are distributed nationwide. Included are subpotent, contaminated, or totally inert facsimiles of lifesaving medicines. Operations are dominated by the Mob and characterized by traditional Mafia tactics. From the Congressional testimony of Margaret Kreig, an author who worked with FDA undercover investigators, in *U.S.–House, Federal Effort Against OC*, pp. 137–64.

2.4 "How the Mafia Drives Up Meat Prices. . . . it reeks—just reeks with rottenness." The Mafia adds $1 million a week to meat bills in the New York City area alone through labor racketeering. This is probably more profit than is made by the supplying farmers. *Farm Journal*, August 1972, pp. 18–19.

2.5 "How the Mafia Gets Its Cut. . . . as many as a hundred murders." The Mob was suspected in the killings of up to 100 food company employees. So stated Clarence Adamy, president of the National Association of Food Chains, in 1972 testimony before Congress. Adamy added, "A man from my staff disappeared on May 10, 1971, under the most peculiar circumstances." *Farm Journal*, September 1972, pp. 24, 48.

□□□□□□□□□□□□□□□□□□□□□□□□

The Mafia's heavy hand falls on key people. . . . Here is a chemist who is having financial trouble. Let him know how he can make a buck and then lean on him. . . .

A pharmacist does not like their pills? Then they offer to throw him down the cellar stairs or through his front window. . . .

"Joe's Truck Stop won't stock our Bennies? Break Joe's legs!" That has happened. . . .

Is it an exaggeration to talk of criminal takeover of segments of the legitimate drug industry when:

A major manufacturer sold only a few bottles of a leading drug in one of our largest cities because black-marketeers got there first?

At least one company has already been driven into bankruptcy because its most heavily advertised drug was counterfeited?

Countless pharmacies are forced out of business by unfair competition from unethical druggists who buy on the black market?

Mafia leaders from a number of states have little Apalachin-type "sit-downs" to discuss getting into chemicals and pharmaceuticals to avoid the heat of narcotics trafficking?

Hoodlum enforcers use muscle to persuade reluctant collaborators—and there is more than a whiff of suspicion that labor racketeers have engineered splendid drug-selling deals in various parts of the country by forcing union members to trade in pharmacies supplied and controlled by mob members?

Margaret Kreig, in *U.S.–House, Federal Effort Against OC*, pp. 148–49.
□□□□□□□□□□□□□□□□□□□□□□□□

2.6 Mafia extortion adds 15 percent to meat prices in New York. *New York Times*, May 9, 1972, p. 1.

2.7 Extortion and murder in St. Louis. Reid, *Grim Reapers*, pp. 73–74.

2.8 Mafia frankfurters from "carcasses of diseased cows, horses, and sheep." These were sold to supermarkets—no returns allowed—by a formerly reputable meat company infiltrated by the Mob. Gage, *The Mafia is not an Equal Opportunity Employer*, pp. 175–77.

3. The Worst Victims: the Poor and the Black

3.1 "How the Mafia Preys on the Poor." Narcotics, numbers racketeering and loan sharking drain and degrade the nation's urban ghettos. *Reader's Digest*, September 1970, pp. 49–55.

3.2 "Organized crime takes from the urban poor far more money than the government puts in." The New York State Joint Legislative Committee on Crime found that in 1968, organized crime extracted $343 million in narcotics and gambling revenues from New York City's three main slum areas. That was $70 million more than the state spent on welfare in those areas that year.

The quoted phrase was stated by Congressman Joseph McDade and appears in Cressey, *Theft of the Nation*, p. 196. The figures are from the *New York Times* (1970–71), reprinted in Gage, *The Mafia is not an Equal Opportunity Employer*, p. 150. These figures are also cited in *U.S.–House, OC Control*, p. 423.

3.3 "Cosa Nostra is comparable to an invading army." Wide-open gambling, narcotics, and vice operations directed by the Mafia frustrate federal anti-poverty programs and make law enforcement a mockery to ghetto youth. From a statement to Congress by sociologist Donald Cressey, in *U.S.–House, Criminal Justice Hearings*, pp. 446–51.

3.4 Pushing Mafia-imported dope to pay the Mafia loan shark to cover debts from Mafia controlled gambling. From the *New York Times* (1970–71), reprinted in Gage, *The Mafia is not an Equal Opportunity Employer*, pp. 149–61.

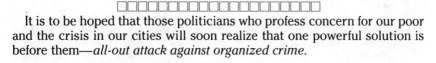

It is to be hoped that those politicians who profess concern for our poor and the crisis in our cities will soon realize that one powerful solution is before them—*all-out attack against organized crime.*

Eugene Methvin, Washington correspondent, *Reader's Digest*, September 1970, p. 55.

3.5 "We must declare all-out war on organized crime in our community." From a speech by Malcolm X, transcribed in *By Any Means Necessary*, pp. 50–51.

3.6 Organized crime: "the nightmare of the slum family." Martin Luther King, Jr., "Beyond the Los Angeles Riots: Next Stop, The North," *Saturday Review*, November 13, 1965, p. 34.

3.7 Addicts and pushers harassed; major narcotics suppliers ignored.
Congresswoman Shirley Chisholm, in *U.S.–House, Criminal Justice Hearings*, pp.
788–89.

3.8 Organized crime: "Raping the ghetto." The similar positions of Whitney
Young, Floyd McKissick, the Hughes Commission, and organized crime expert
Ralph Salerno. As summarized in the Congressional statement of Salerno in
U.S.–House, Criminal Justice Hearings, pp. 150, 163–65. Also see Cressey, *Theft of
the Nation*, pp. 275–77.

3.9 Mafia control of ghetto numbers rackets. From the testimony of Detroit
Police Chief George Edwards in *U.S.–Senate, OC and Narcotics Hearings*, pp.
412–15.

3.10 Corrupt policemen help the Mob eliminate black competition. Cressey, *Theft of the Nation*, pp. 197–99.

**3.11 The Mob opposes urban renewal in Mount Vernon: "more money out
of a Harlem than a Scarsdale."** Salerno and Tompkins, *Crime Confederation*, p.
377.

**3.12 "One part of the answer to improved conditions for the urban poor
must be a war on organized crime."** As concluded by Congressman Joseph Mc-
Dade, with supporting information, in a 1967 report on organized crime and the
poor, prepared by McDade and 22 Republican colleagues in the House. Cressey,
Theft of the Nation, pp. 196–97; Salerno and Tompkins, *Crime Confederation*, pp.
271–73.

4. Louisiana: the Mafia's Sovereign Domain

4.1 Carlos Marcello "controlled the State of Louisiana." *Life*, April 10, 1970,
p. 31, summarizing *Life*, September 8, 1967, pp. 94–97 and September 29, 1967, pp.
34–36.

4.2 Mob actions in Louisiana "are more flagrant than ever." Marcello's po-
litical control has been maintained, his economic penetration extended. *Life*,
April 10, 1970, pp. 31–36. See also Mollenhoff, *Strike Force*, pp. 164–65; Dorman,
Payoff, pp. 102–3, 115–17; Cook, *Two Dollar Bet*, p. 162.

4.3 Growth of the Mob in Louisiana: capitalizing on "Huey Long's welcome
to [Mafia boss Frank] Costello." *U.S.–Senate, Kefauver Report, Third Interim*, pp.
77–83, 89–90.

4.4 Carlos Marcello: from thug to Mafia boss. Statement of Aaron Kohn, director of the New Orleans Metropolitan Crime Commission, in *U.S.–Senate, Gambling and OC*, pp. 509–13.

4.5 Marcello's influence spans the United States. Marcello's nationwide influence is indicated by his control of organized crime in the Gulf Coast area,[5]
close ties in Dallas and other parts of Texas,[6] representation in Las Vegas,[7] former
interest in a Cuban casino,[8] control of a racing wire service in several states,[9]
nationwide phone contacts,[10] and attendance at the 1966 Mafia mini-conclave at
La Stella Restaurant in New York City.[11] Gambling warehouses in Louisiana, Missis-

sippi and Oklahoma,[12] a gambling book in Houston,[13] rock festivals in California,[14] and an extortion scheme in Indiana[15] were also linked to him. Marcello is currently considered the nation's top-ranking Mafia boss.[16]

a. How Louisiana's first family enriches its treasury

4.6 The Mob's annual income in New Orleans "runs to $1,114,000,000, making it by far the state's largest industry." Half of the Mob's income in New Orleans comes from wide-open illegal gambling operations; 14 Mob casinos in Gretta were visible in an aerial photograph. Bill Davidson, "Cosa Nostra's Wall Street," *Saturday Evening Post*, February 29, 1964, pp. 15ff.

4.7 Dun and Bradstreet estimates that 50 percent of New Orleans area hotels are financially backed by Marcello. From the *Wall Street Journal* (1968–70), reproduced in Gartner, *Crime and Business*, pp. 10–15.

4.8 Mafia business interests in Louisiana range from banks to whiskey distributorships, from bus lines to shrimpboat fleets, plus traditional illegal operations. Dorman, *Payoff*, pp. 100–101.

4.9 Marcello enterprises are "scattered through surrounding states and include thousands of acres of oil leases on federal land." Reid, *Grim Reapers*, pp. 152–53.

b. From corruption to political control

4.10 "They're all in deathly fear of Carlos Marcello because he's got the law, all the politicians in the state, right in his hip pocket." Teresa, *My Life in the Mafia*, p. 357.

4.11 A unique interview with Carlos Marcello and an aide. Rackets provided the main source of campaign funds in Louisiana and other Southern states. "We picked the candidates; we paid for their campaigns; we paid them off; we told them what to do. We even provided the poll-watchers and vote-counters." Dorman, *Payoff*, pp. 103–4, 109–10.

4.12 New York Mafia boss Frank Costello was received in New Orleans in 1955 by a police honor guard. From the testimony of Metropolitan Crime Commission Director Aaron Kohn in *U.S.–House, OC in Sports*, p. 886.

4.13 Jefferson Parish Police harass bar owners who don't buy Marcello jukeboxes. Cook, *Two Dollar Bet*, pp. 160–61; *Saturday Evening Post*, February 29, 1964, p. 16.

4.14 Marcello's criminal enterprise "required, and had, corrupt collusion of public officials at every critical level including police, sheriffs, justices of peace, prosecutors, mayors, governors, judges, councilmen, licensing authorities, state legislators and at least one member of Congress." Statement of Aaron Kohn in *U.S.–House, OC Control*, p. 433.

4.15 Ninety-eight percent of Louisiana legislators will accept bribes. Reported by Peter Hand, a former Mob-affiliated bookmaker, close friend of Governor Earl Long, and member of the Louisiana legislature for eight years. Cook, *Two Dollar Bet*, pp. 167–69.

4.16 A Mob gambler was convicted of bribery, then pardoned by Governor Earl Long, his graft money returned. Cook, *Two Dollar Bet*, p. 158; *U.S.–House, OC Control*, p. 435.

4.17 A "cozy relationship" between underworld figures and the New Orleans office of the Small Business Administration. This relationship "resulted in millions in Federal funds going to persons with known Mafia backgrounds and their associates." *New York Times*, February 28, 1974, p. 24.

II. GENERAL DESCRIPTION AND HISTORY

5. Structure

a. Conclusions of the U.S. government

5.1 Kefauver Committee, 1951: "There is a nationwide crime syndicate known as the Mafia." It controls the most lucrative rackets and resorts to murder, political influence, bribery and intimidation. *U.S.–Senate, Kefauver Report, Third Interim*, p. 150.

5.2 McClellan Committee, 1964: The Mafia "operates vast illegal enterprises that produce an annual income of many billions of dollars." It consists of separate families structured along military lines, and is run by a national commission. *U.S.–Senate, OC and Narcotics Report*, p. 117.

5.3 U.S.–Task Force on Organized Crime, 1967: The U.S. government "is being seriously challenged, if not threatened" by the Mob. The Mafia is comprised of approximately 5,000 members of Italian descent, grouped into 24 families, and is governed by a national commission. It works with large numbers of nonmember associates from all ethnic groups. It uses specialists in murder and corruption. *U.S.–Task Force Report*, pp. 1, 6–8.

5.4 U.S. Departments of Justice and Transportation, 1972: the Mafia's "existence, structure, activities, personnel . . . have been confirmed and reconfirmed beyond rational dispute." Confirmation of these facts and such terminology as "boss," "captain," "family," "soldier," and "commission" has been achieved "through interceptions of phone conversations and other oral communications at different times and places between [Mob] members and associates." *U.S.–Cargo Theft and OC*, p. 24.

b. Conclusions of individual commentators

5.5 Donald R. Cressey, member of the President's Commission on Law Enforcement and Administration of Justice: Mafia families, united under a national commission, control gambling, loan sharking, narcotics importation and wholesaling, and "own several state legislators and federal congressmen and other officials in the legislative, executive, and judicial branches of government at the local, state, and federal levels." Cressey, *Theft of the Nation*, pp. x-xi.

5.6 Charles Grutzner, *New York Times* reporter: Five thousand Mafia members in 24 families work with at least 50,000 associates. Grutzner, "How to Lock Out the Mafia," *Harvard Business Review*, March-April 1970, p. 47.

5.7 Senator John McClellan: "Never ... has organized crime had greater adverse impact and widespread control over the social, political, and economic lives of our citizens and institutions than it does today." *U.S.–House, OC Control*, p. 86.

5.8 Ralph Salerno, retired New York Police expert on organized crime: "There is a national criminal conspiratorial organization within the United States whose members refer to as La Cosa Nostra." Families contain these leadership positions: capo (boss), sottocapo (underboss), consiglieri (counselor), and caporegime (captain). An ordinary member is called a soldier, a made man or a button man. "Other terms for the organization or its individual families, often used by outsiders, are the Mafia, the organization, the clique, the boys, the office, the arm.... They engage in political activity to an inordinate degree." *U.S.–House, Assassination Hearings, JFK*, vol. 5, pp. 427–28.

5.9 Aaron Kohn, director of the New Orleans Metropolitan Crime Commission: Although directed by "only 3,000 to 5,000 hard-core members," the Cosa Nostra "burdens, frightens and, in one way or another, victimizes everyone in the United States." *U.S.–House, OC Control*, pp. 437–38.

5.10 Nicholas Gage, New York Times reporter: The Mafia consists of 5,000 full-fledged members in 26 families based in 21 metropolitan areas across the United States. Gage, *Mafia, U.S.A.*, p. 16.

c. Conclusions of law enforcement agencies

5.11 Findings of a New Orleans grand jury in 1890 upon indictment of 19 Mafia gangsters for the murder of Police Chief David Hennessey: "The existence of a secret organization known as the Mafia has been established beyond doubt." Sondern, *Brotherhood of Evil*, pp. 58–62; Reid, *Grim Reapers*, pp. 146–50.

5.12 William J. Duffy, director of the Intelligence Division of the Chicago Police Department: The Mafia is "aggressively engaged in attempts to subvert the process of government by well-organized endeavors"; it is "dedicated to commit murder and other acts of violence." *U.S.–Senate, OC and Narcotics Hearings*, pp. 506–8.

5.13 Tampa, Florida Police Chief Neil Brown: "It is our considered conclusion that the Mafia exists in Tampa, that it controls most illegal gambling in Tampa and central Florida, and that its members have interstate and international ties to other Mafia groups." This conclusion is "based upon personal knowledge, criminal records, surveillance reports, personal histories, familial relationships, statistical analyses, reports from confidential informants, information from Federal and local law enforcement agencies, and other customary police intelligence sources." *U.S.–Senate, OC and Narcotics Hearings*, p. 522.

5.14 A 1961 Kansas City grand jury report: "It is an indisputable fact that the professional criminals in Kansas City are highly organized. This criminal group is ruled by an 'inner circle' commonly called 'the syndicate.' The 'syndicate' functions like a board of directors, formulating policy and giving orders to the other members. ... Based on sworn testimony it is the belief of this jury that the Kansas City 'syndicate' is probably connected with the Mafia or Black Hand Society.

"Beginning in Kansas City in the early 1900's there was a small group of thugs, mostly of foreign descent, who started by preying upon members of their own national group. By means of threats of arson, bombing, beatings and murder, this parasitical element established a flourishing extortion racket. . . . Based on sworn testimony presented to this jury, it now seems apparent that sometime in 1953 a 'deal' was made between the 'syndicate' and certain members of the Kansas City, Missouri, Police Department which led to the 'syndicate' being permitted to operate a number of gambling and after-hours liquor establishments, control prostitution, and fence stolen merchandise in Kansas City."

From a 1961 Kansas City grand jury report, reproduced in Tyler, *Organized Crime in America*, pp. 296–98.

□□□□□□□□□□□□□□□□□□□□□□□□

The Affiant has learned through numerous conversations with other Agents of the FBI and through a comprehensive review of confidential information furnished by reliable informants to Agents of the FBI in Cleveland, Ohio, and elsewhere, that there exists within the United States an organized crime conspiracy which is exclusively Italian. Geographical areas of the United States are apportioned to the members of this conspiracy for the conduct of illegal activities. Within this organized criminal conspiracy there are "families" in charge of certain criminal activity in each geographical area. Each "family" is headed by a "capo" or boss[;] the second in command is the "sotto-capo" or underboss. A "consiglieri" or counselor is typically an elder member who serves as an adviser. Various members of the "family" are controlled by an individual referred to as a "caporegima" or captain, who is responsible to the capo. The said criminal organization in the United States is controlled by a policy group known as the "commission." The "commission" members are actually the various bosses of the "families." This criminal organization is engaged in the conduct of gambling, loan sharking, extortion, murder, labor racketeering, and other violations of federal and state law.

> From an affidavit filed by FBI agent E. Michael Kahoe on December 27, 1977 in an Ohio Court, in connection with a case involving organized crime. *U.S.–House, Assassination Hearings, JFK*, vol. 5, p. 389.

□□□□□□□□□□□□□□□□□□□□□□□□

5.15 Detroit Police Chief George Edwards: Chief Edwards named 66 members and 18 associates of the Detroit Mafia family, and described its organizational structure, blood and marriage interrelationships, criminal arrests and convictions, and connection to the nationwide Mafia organization. He presented a chart of its infiltration into 98 businesses, histories of gambling, prostitution, and narcotics cases involving several of its members, and synopses of 69 gangland murders committed in the Detroit area. *U.S.–Senate, OC and Narcotics Hearings*, pp. 400ff.

5.16 Charts of 11 Mafia families from the 1963–64 Senate Organized Crime and Narcotics Hearings. Included were charts of five families in New York City and of families in Chicago, Detroit, Tampa, Rhode Island, Boston, and

Buffalo, New York. Charts gave the names, aliases, FBI numbers, photos, and criminal activity codes of known family members. They were prepared using information from local police files, the FBI, the Federal Bureau of Narcotics, the testimony of Joseph Valachi, and other sources. The average number of arrests for each of the 356 identified members of the five New York families was seven. *U.S.-Senate, OC and Narcotics Hearings*, pp. 259, 410, 508, 522, 550, 580, 652.

d. Information from electronic surveillance

5.17 The Taglianetti Airtels: publicly released transcripts of FBI eavesdropping on the Mafia's Rhode Island headquarters between 1962 and 1965. These voluminous transcripts, released in connection with the tax evasion trial of Louis Taglianetti, provide a detailed, inside look at Mafia operations. They confirmed the existence of Mafia families, formal members, a military chain of command ("boss," "caporegime," "soldier," etc.), and the governing national commission. They also provided evidence of diverse criminal activities, including infiltration of business, corruption of high ranking officials (the state attorney general, for one), and a dozen murders performed under the orders of boss Raymond Patriarca. One point: all types of crime in his territory, including robberies, hijackings, kidnapping, thefts, and arson, were cleared with Patriarca. Cressey, *Theft of the Nation*, pp. 120–26; *Life*, September 1, 1967, p. 44.

5.18 The "DeCavalcante Tapes": 2,000 pages of publicly released transcripts of FBI surveillance of New Jersey Mafia hangouts between 1961 and 1965. Detailed descriptions of Mafia operations. Mollenhoff, *Strike Force*, chapter 2; *Newsweek*, June 23, 1969, pp. 37–38; *Life*, September 1, 1967, p. 44–45.

5.19 The "Gold Bug": from a police bug in a Mafia base of operations in Brooklyn, New York, in the early 1970s. It yielded 300 miles of taped conversations, plus 36,000 feet of color movie film and 54,000 photographs. The bug recorded the visits of 100 New York policemen and deals involving arson, assault, auto theft, bookmaking, burglaries, coercion, corruption, counterfeiting, extortion, forgery, hijacking, insurance frauds, labor racketeering, loan sharking, narcotics sales, policy, possession and sale of weapons, receiving stolen property, and robbery. *Time*, October 30, 1972, pp. 26, 28.

5.20 FBI electronic surveillance. The House Assassinations Committee released numerous segments from FBI surveillance of the Mob during the early 1960s. Two excerpts are quoted below.
Buffalo Mafia boss Stefano Magaddino to members of his Family on June 3, 1963, about the FBI: "They know everybody's name. They know who's Boss. They know who is on the Commission. ... The FBI said, 'What was your caporegime doing here?' ... To Carlo Gambino they said 'This is your underboss, this is your caporegime, this is your consiglieri.'"
Detroit Mafia Captain Anthony Zerilla to Nick Ditta on December 4, 1963: "You are a friend of ours [a Mafia member] and you belong to my Regime. If I tell you to jump off a 20-story building, you jump off and you jump off any time I tell you to." *U.S.-House, Assassination Hearings, JFK*, vol. 5, pp. 424–26, see pp. 437–53.

5.21 Several other publicized transcripts of electronic surveillance of Mafia operations. See *U.S.-Senate, Kefauver Hearings*, vol. 5, pp. 1175–87; *Life*, August 9, 1968, pp. 20–27; *Life*, May 30, 1969, pp. 45–47; Dorman, *Payoff*, pp. 45–49; *Saturday Evening Post*, November 9, 1963, p. 20.

e. Information from Mob defectors

5.22 Inside information spanning 50 years, from Mobsters Tony Notaro, Nicola Gentile, Joseph Valachi, and Joseph Luparelli. Gage, *Mafia, U.S.A.*, pp. 15–16; see also *U.S.–House, Assassination Appendix, JFK*, vol. 9, p. 44.

5.23 The testimony of Tony Notaro. During his lengthy testimony in 1918, Notaro described his initiation into the Mafia. Gage, *The Mafia is not an Equal Opportunity Employer*, pp. 31–32.

5.24 The confessions of Sicilian Mafioso Dr. Melchiorre Allegra. Obtained by Italian authorities in 1937, they were discovered and published by *L'Ora* in 1962. Allegra described the structure and modus operandi of the Mafia, and the high positions in society of its members. He also recounted his initiation into the organization. Cook, *Secret Rulers*, pp. 59–61.

5.25 The memoirs of Sicilian Mafioso Nicola Gentile. Written during the 1950s, these were supported by the subsequent testimony of Joseph Valachi. Gage, *The Mafia is not an Equal Opportunity Employer*, pp. 32–33.

5.26 Information provided in 1945 by Mafia associate Charles Wall. Wall was forced to accept Mafioso Santos Trafficante, Sr. as a partner in his large-scale gambling operations after three Mafia murder attempts. Wall described the structure of the Mafia and its tremendous power in the United States. Related by Tampa Police Chief Neil G. Brown in *U.S.–Senate, OC and Narcotics Hearings*, pp. 531–33.

5.27 The testimony of Joseph Valachi. In appearances before the U.S. Senate in the fall of 1963 (see section 5.1 of text), Mafia defector Joseph Valachi provided extensive information about the organization. Included were "detailed accounts of approximately three dozen murders that were directly linked with Mafia activities, and police officials specifically corroborated his information in dates, locations, and circumstances." *U.S.–Senate, OC and Narcotics Report*, pp. 12–13, 118–19; see Valachi's testimony in *U.S.–Senate, OC and Narcotics Hearings*, i.e., pp. 180–84.

5.28 An exhaustive description of the Mafia from a former top-ranking insider, Vincent Teresa. Teresa was the number-three man in the New England Mafia organization. He operated throughout the East Coast, the Caribbean, and Europe, and was one of the Mob's leading moneymakers. When he defected in 1970 and testified in Senate hearings and court trials, he became perhaps the most important single source of information on the Mob. His remarks are often cited in this volume. See, for example, Teresa's testimony in *U.S.–Senate, OC and Stolen Securities, 1971*, pp. 777–78; and his memoirs, *My Life in the Mafia*, pp. 1, 86–89, 216–17.

5.29 The Senate testimony of Mob money-mover Michael Raymond (appearing under the name "George White"). Raymond worked for Peter LaPlaca, a New Jersey Mafia boss, who told Raymond he had bodies "planted like potatoes in New Jersey." Raymond explained how in one deal, Mobsters from another family planned to relieve him of $500,000 in stocks and then kill him, until he mentioned his connection to LaPlaca. Carmine Lombardozzi, a Gambino Family captain who attended the Apalachin Mafia conclave,[17] later said to Raymond, "why didn't you tell us? I was going to drink your blood," adding "other charming euphemisms."

Raymond, like Vincent Teresa and several other witnesses against the Mob quoted in this volume,[18] testified under a grant of immunity from U.S. District Court Judge John Sirica. *U.S.-Senate, OC and Stolen Securities, 1971*, pp. 637, 656–64, 956, 1245–46.

5.30 Information to prosecutors and newsmen from former Detroit Mafia Lieutenant Eugene Ayotte. Love nests and bodies in concrete were among the subjects covered in his disclosures. *Chicago Daily News*, September 17, 1974; Jack Anderson, "Stories of Mafia Operations in Detroit Area Business," *Detroit Free Press*, September 19, 1974.

5.31 The Senate testimony of Robert Cudak and James Schaeffer. Cudak and Schaeffer were airport mail thieves who dealt frequently with the Mob. They noted that organized crime is controlled by the Mafia, and described a Mafia "sit-down." *U.S.-Senate, OC and Stolen Securities, 1971*, pp. 224–25, 228–29, 584–85.

5.32 The House testimony of Joseph Barboza, former killer for the New England Patriarca Mafia Family. Bookmaking in Massachusetts operates "like a big wagon wheel with Patriarca in the center." Excerpts from Barboza's testimony are quoted at several points in this appendix. *U.S.-House, OC in Sports*, pp. 764, 731.

f. Mafia conclaves

5.33 Cleveland, 1928. Police stumbled upon a meeting of 21 Mafiosi in a Cleveland hotel, several of whom later became top bosses. Cook, *Secret Rulers*, p. 77; Salerno and Tompkins, *Crime Confederation*, p. 278.

5.34 Atlantic City, 1929. Informants described a large meeting of Mobsters from cities across the Eastern United States, including such notables as Frank Costello, Lucky Luciano, Frank Nitti, and Al Capone. Cook, *Secret Rulers*, pp. 77–79.

▢▢▢▢▢▢▢▢▢▢▢▢▢▢▢▢▢▢▢▢

When you go on a thing like that [a Mafia initiation ceremony], they bring you in front of the family. You sit down and take the oath. Then you're officially made. . . .

I remember when [Colombo Family underboss Joseph Yackovelli] was made. . . . The family boss and the consigliere and all the captains were there. It was supposed to be secret, but everyone in the neighborhood knew about it.

> Colombo Family member Joseph Luparelli, who defected and became a government witness in 1972, in Meskil, *Luparelli Tapes*, pp. 80–81, 123.

▢▢▢▢▢▢▢▢▢▢▢▢▢▢▢▢▢▢▢▢

5.35 Apalachin, New York, 1957. In November 1957, New York State Police arrested 58 persons from across the country meeting at the estate of Joseph Barbara in Apalachin, New York. Most were identified Mafia members and several were top national bosses. Fifty had arrest records, 35 had convictions, 22 were involved in labor-management relations, and most were active in business enterprises. Roughly half of the arrested delegates were related by blood or marriage.

Salerno and Tompkins, *Crime Confederation*, pp. 297–99; Kennedy, *Enemy Within*, pp. 228–29; McClellan, *Crime Without Punishment*, pp. 119–21; Sondern, *Brotherhood of Evil*, pp. 35–37; Tyler, *Organized Crime in America*, pp. 23–27; *U.S.–Senate, McClellan Labor Hearings*, pp. 12194–201, vol. 32 exhibit 5; *U.S.–House Assassination Appendix, JFK*, vol. 9, pp. 7–9; see Appendix 2 of this book.

5.36 Forest Hills, New York, 1966. On September 22, 13 men sitting around a table at La Stella Restaurant in Forest Hills, New York were arrested. They were Carlo Gambino, boss of the Gambino Family; Carlos Marcello, boss of New Orleans; Santos Trafficante, Jr., boss of Tampa, Florida; Anthony Corollo and Frank Gagliano of the Marcello Family; Joseph N. Gallo, caporegima in the Gambino Family; Anthony Carillo, soldier in the Genovese Family; Aniello Dellacroce, caporegima in the Gambino Family; Joseph Marcello, Jr., member of the Marcello Family; Dominick Alongi, soldier in the Genovese Family; Thomas Eboli, acting boss of the Genovese Family; Joseph Colombo, boss of the Colombo Family; and Michael Miranda, consiglieri in the Genovese Family. Reid, *Grim Reapers*, pp. 329, 158–59.

g. Mafia response to criminal charges: the Fifth Amendment

5.37 The consistent use of the Fifth Amendment by Mobsters in Congressional testimony. McClellan, *Crime Without Punishment*, pp. 132–37. For other examples, see *U.S.–Senate, McClellan Labor Hearings*, p. 14035; *U.S.–House, OC in Sports*, pp. 970–72, 1496.

6. Modus Operandi

a. Murder and violence

6.1 "The ultimate solution to everything is to kill somebody." The ability "to commit murder and other acts of violence without compunction" is the "one single characteristic which is most responsible for the success and continuity" of the Syndicate. From the testimony of former Chicago Police Intelligence Director William Duffy in *U.S.–Senate, OC and Narcotics Hearings*, pp. 512–13. The title phrase is from testimony by Mob defector Michael Raymond ("George White") in *U.S.–Senate, OC and Stolen Securities, 1971*, p. 672.

6.2 The testimony of defected Mob killer Joseph Barboza, formerly "the most feared rackets enforcer in New England." Barboza gave details of several murders he committed for New England Mafia boss Raymond Patriarca, naming his victims and describing the methods used. In some cases he got the contract through channels: "Peter Lemoine was the one who gave me the contract, and I got the ok from [underboss] Henry Tameleo, who subsequently got all the final ok's from Raymond Patriarca." In other cases he got "the ok to kill people" directly from Patriarca. Barboza also related how he severely beat a candidate for office in the baker's union in Boston whom the Mob did not want to run. Barboza "left him in a heap, a bloody heap in the middle of the street." *U.S.–House, OC in Sports*, pp. 731–34, 740–41, 767–69.

6.3 Comments of Mafia defector Vincent Teresa. Each Mafia family "has its own assassination squads who are available for lend-lease assignments." Teresa described several Mob murders in which hit men were imported from one Mafia family to perform a job for another. He also discussed the various side activities of Mob hit squads, such as selling machine guns, hand grenades, and mines. One killer mentioned by Teresa was "Ice Pick Barney" of "Anastasia's Old Murder, Inc.," who would puncture his victims through the ear with an ice pick, leaving them to die of what would be ruled a cerebral hemorrhage. Teresa, *My Life in the Mafia*, chapter 17, especially pp. 180–87.

□□□□□□□□□□□□□□□□□□□□□
From the 1971 hearings of the Permanent Investigations Subcommittee of the Senate Government Operations Committee, in *U.S.–Senate, OC and Stolen Securities, 1971*, pp. 633–35, 616:

Mr. Gallinaro [Committee investigator]: Information received from law enforcement intelligence agencies states that Gregory Scarpa is a member of the Joseph Colombo crime family in Brooklyn, N.Y. . . .

Scarpa is involved in gambling, policy, and fencing stolen property. He has met on a frequent basis with alleged LCN [Cosa Nostra] members of the Colombo family, including Joseph Colombo himself, at the Cantalupo Realty Co., located at 1434 86th Street, Brooklyn, N.Y.

Chairman McClellan: Do you want to deny whether you met with Colombo?

Mr. Scarpa: I respectfully decline to answer the question, Senator, on the ground it may tend to incriminate me.

Chairman McClellan: Proceed.

Mr. Gallinaro: Scarpa has taken the fifth amendment before the Federal grand jury in the Eastern District of New York, to all questions concerning the Colombo crime family in the past. . . .

Chairman McClellan: You mentioned two people were killed. . . . They were killed after testifying where?

Mr. Gallinaro: Before a grand jury in the City of New York. . . . Richard [LoCicero], after he testified, was stabbed 100 times and killed. . . . [The other murdered man, Richard's uncle, was a "very close associate" of Scarpa.]

Chairman McClellan: There is some information that frequently witnesses are disposed of, prospective witnesses, in this fashion by the organized crime elements. Would you have any information about that that you would care to tell us, Mr. Scarpa.

Mr. Scarpa: No, Senator.

Chairman McClellan: You don't have any information? Or do you?

Mr. Scarpa: I respectfully decline to answer the question, Senator, on the ground that it may tend to incriminate me. . . .

Senator Percy: Do you consider yourself a "made man" [full-fledged member] in Mob circles?

Mr. Scarpa: I respectfully decline to answer the question, Senator, on the ground it may tend to incriminate me. . . .

Senator Gurney: . . . I did notice that you were laughing uproariously at the exchange I had on [dumping Mob counterfeit money at] the church bazaar. Were you listening at that time?

Mr. Scarpa: I respectfully decline to answer the question, Senator, on the ground it may tend to incriminate me.

□□□□□□□□□□□□□□□□□□□□□□□□

6.4 A Mafia hit squad on tape. The conversation of Chicago Mobsters John Cerone, Fiore Buccieri, Dave Yaras, and others was picked up by an FBI bug while they were in Miami to kill Chicago union boss and political bigwig Frank Esposito. They discussed plans for killing Esposito and reminisced about their previous contracts, including the sadistic murder of FBI informant William Jackson. The FBI bug saved Esposito's life. Excerpts from the transcripts of a February 11, 1962 conversation of the Mob hit squad in *Life*, May 30, 1968, pp. 45–47; Demaris, *Captive City*, pp. 60–63.

6.5 The Mafia murder of a government witness, disguised by rape and robbery. In 1970, Sol Landie furnished information to authorities on the gambling activities of Kansas City, Missouri Mafia boss Nick Civella and other local Mafia figures, leading to an indictment against Civella and associates on October 22. One month later, four young men robbed Landie's house, shot him dead, and then raped his wife. Three men were arrested for the murder, and they confessed that it was a contract killing; "they had received instructions through intermediaries to make it appear that robbery was the motive for the murder." Mob associate Tony Lee, who assigned the contract, was convicted of murder. *U.S.–House, Assassination Report*, p. 163; *U.S.–House, Assassination Appendix, JFK*, vol. 9, pp. 51–52; Mollenhoff, *Strike Force*, pp. 150–52, 237.

6.6 The arrangements for a typical Mob contract. A Mob murder is usually a methodical job, performed by a coordinated team of specialists. Up to 15 gunmen, drivers, spotters, and other backup personnel, plus several cars, are used on some jobs. Tyler, *Organized Crime in America*, pp. 229–31; Meskil, *Luparelli Tapes*, p. 13, passim, *U.S.–House, Assassination Appendix*, vol. 9, pp. 44–47.

6.7 The efficient disposal of bodies was a frequent topic of conversation in the DeCavalcante tapes (these tapes were recordings of FBI surveillance of Mafia hangouts in New Jersey during 1961–65). One idea discussed was a pulverizing device capable of turning a human body into a "meatball." *Time*, June 20, 1969, pp. 22–23.

6.8 Joseph Valachi: "You are there for that purpose." Valachi testified how he performed several murder contracts for the Mob without pay as part of the obligations of membership. *U.S.–Senate, OC and Narcotics Hearings*, pp. 192–93.

6.9 The murder of Detroit radio commentator Gerald Buckley. In 1930 Buckley was shot to death after he "had threatened to reveal the identity of the gangland's overlords and their connections with city government." Indicted were four men including Mafiosi Joe Bommarito and Pete Licavoli, the latter of whom fled the state until his three codefendants had been acquitted. Police later found the gun used to kill Buckley at the home of Mafioso "Cockeyed Joe" Catalanotte. From the testimony of Detroit Police Chief George Edwards in *U.S.–Senate, OC and Narcotics Hearings*, pp. 428–29; see also Reid, *Grim Reapers*, p. 76.

6.10 "A trail of murder from Tampa to San Francisco": several cases of Mafia murders in various American cities were described by the Kefauver Committee. In one case, government witness Carl Carramusa was shot to death in front of his 15-year-old daughter in Chicago, "where he had gone to escape retribution by the Mafia." The killing occurred three years after his testimony in a Kansas City narcotics trial. The Kefauver Committee concluded that it had been performed by

Chicago Mobsters "on orders from the Kansas City group." Government witness Thomas Buffa was likewise killed after he fled to California. *U.S.–Kefauver Report, Third Interim,* pp. 38, 148–49.

6.11 "Let's take Joey's share." Airport mail thief Robert Cudak testified that in one $125,000 deal, Mafioso[19] Billy Ricchiuti suggested that the two increase their share by setting a murder contract on Cudak's partner Joe Russo. *U.S.–Senate, OC and Stolen Securities, 1971,* pp. 227–28.

6.12 The acid blinding of noted labor columnist Victor Riesel. Mafioso[20] Johnny Dioguardi escaped a conviction for this crime after a prosecution witness refused to testify, but he was later sentenced to two years in prison on an extortion charge. According to U.S. Attorney Paul Williams, the man who splashed the acid on Riesel, Abraham Telvi, was paid $500 and subsequently murdered on Dioguardi's orders. Reid, *Grim Reapers,* p. 174; *U.S.–House, Assassination Appendix, JFK,* vol. 9, pp. 47–49.

6.13 The shooting of New York Mob boss Joseph Colombo. Colombo irked the conservative Mob leadership by drawing attention to the Mafia in a ludicrous campaign which portrayed it as "a myth." The farce was rudely shattered at one of his rallies in New York's Columbus Circle in 1971, when he was gunned down by an assailant who was shot to death immediately afterwards. Colombo was taken to the hospital, whose corridors were ringed with Mafia guards in an "almost surrealistic parody"(B) of a scene from *The Godfather.* A–Dorman, *Payoff,* pp. 276–86; B–*Time* (1971) reprinted in Gage, *Mafia, U.S.A.,* pp. 179–87; C–*U.S.–House, Assassination Appendix, JFK,* vol. 9, pp. 50–51.

6.14 The murder of New York Mafia boss Joseph Gallo. Mafia defector Joseph Luparelli testified that the 1972 murder of Gallo was ordered by Colombo Family boss Vincent Aloi, and Luparelli described how it was carried out. Aloi was convicted of perjury in connection with the Gallo killing. Luparelli, a former bodyguard and driver for Colombo Family underboss Joseph Yackovelli, also related how prior to the killing of Gallo, Yackovelli tried to set a trap for Gallo and Gallo underling John Cutrone. Yackovelli gave these instructions to Mafia intermediary Nick Bianco: "tell him [Cutrone] I'm willing to sit down with him and Joe Gallo. Tell him to ask Gallo to please come. Promise him nothing will happen. . . . When Gallo comes there, I want you to kill him. . . . If anybody gets in front of the gun, shoot through them."
Meskil, *Luparelli Tapes,* pp. 235, see also 209–47; *New York Times,* June 21, 1973, p. 18; June 27, 1973, p. 57.

6.15 Specialists from New England. "So feared are the New England Mafia specialists in violence that Mafia families in other cities frequently send for the Boston or Providence boys to do their dirtiest work." For example, the FBI learned that Jackie Nazarian of Providence was assigned to kill New York Mafia underboss Albert Anastasia; Nazarian gunned him down in 1957 in a barber's chair in a Manhattan hotel. Anastasia was the founder of "Murder, Incorporated," a Mafia hit squad which itself exported killers out of town. Another New Englander, Joe Puzzangara, is often assigned to out-of-state bombing contracts. Bill Davidson, "The Mafia: How It Bleeds New England." *Saturday Evening Post,* November 18, 1967, p. 28; see Teresa, *My Life in the Mafia,* p. 178.

6.16 The murder of Ferdinand Boccia. Mafia boss Vito Genovese assigned a contract to a friend of the intended victim and then lined up an assassin to take care of the killer. Maas, *Valachi Papers*, pp. 155–56.

6.17 "Kill your wife." Joseph Yackovelli, New York Colombo Family underboss, told Family member Joseph Luparelli, as Luparelli later related: "You shouldn't be with your kids so much. You're not paying attention to Our Thing." He then said to Luparelli, "Your wife is a cancer to you. I want you to cut her out of your life. I want you to kill her." It was this order and the suspicion engendered in Yackovelli when Luparelli refused to carry it out that led to Luparelli's defection. In a similar case, related by Vincent Teresa, New England Mafia boss Raymond Patriarca ordered old-time Mafioso Joe Medica to murder Medica's son, who had stolen $200,000 from a Mafia-controlled finance company. Meskil, *Luparelli Tapes*, pp. 212–13; Teresa, *My Life in the Mafia*, pp. 97–98.

6.18 The abortive contract on Joseph Barboza. Vincent Teresa described how, on orders from New England Mafia underboss Henry Tameleo, he procured weapons from the New Jersey Mob and joined a hit squad which prepared to kill Barboza. The contract plans also called for the murder of Guy Frizzi, an associate of Barboza who was delegated to set him up. When Barboza got wind of the plan, Tameleo wanted Teresa to assure Barboza that everything was okay, explaining to Teresa that they would later "whack him when he least expect[ed] it." Teresa, *My Life in the Mafia*, pp. 245–47.

6.19 Between 1919 and 1963, 976 gangland-type slayings were charted in Chicago. Of these, just two were cleared by the arrest and conviction of the killers. "These executions were usually committed by hired guns often imported from other cities for this specific purpose." From the testimony of Chicago Police Chief O. W. Wilson in *U.S.–OC and Narcotics Hearings*, p. 487.

6.20 The recent murders of four Mob defectors under federal protection and more than a dozen murders of FBI informants. Between 1971 and 1977, four Mob defectors under federal protection were murdered, while six others died unnatural deaths as the apparent result of corruption in the witness protection program. Between 1976 and 1977, almost 20 FBI informants were murdered, when their covers were blown by FBI agents. *Newsweek*, November 28, 1977, p. 66; NBC Evening News, "Segment 3," December 16, 1977.

6.21 A special Mafia hit squad murders 20 victims. In 1977 Gino Gallina, a Manhattan district attorney who became a Mob attorney, was killed gangland style in Greenwich Village. Gallina had testified to a Newark grand jury about a Mafia hit squad armed with .22 caliber automatics complete with silencers. This squad had murdered at least 20 persons in the last two years, including six FBI informants and witnesses. Federal officials think that a leak from the grand jury led to Gallina's slaying; other leaks from government files and court records have led to similar murders. *Time*, November 21, 1977, p. 39.

b. Various other methods of operation

6.22 Information from the Dallas bribe case. Dallas Police Sheriff Steve Guthrie and Lt. George Butler feigned cooperation with Chicago Mobster Paul Roland Jones and Mafioso Pat Manno in negotiations for Mob takeover of Dallas rackets, while the lengthy conversations were taped by police (see chapter 7 of text). Among the matters discussed by the Mobsters in the 1946 negotiations, as related in the testimony of Lt. Butler before the Kefauver and McClellan Committees, were the following:

The takeover of local gambling operations. Organizing "every truckdriver in the Nation" to be able to "bring industry to its knees, and even the Government." An offer to buy narcotics from police in any large haul. Union extortion. The takeover of the nationwide wire service. An offer to Sheriff Guthrie of huge payoffs, and letters of recommendation from "some pretty important people in this country" to support his reelection campaign.

"The coin-machine business was theirs." The Syndicate operates "from coast to coast, and in Canada and Spain." Help is available from the Mob to visiting members in any large city in the nation. *U.S.–Senate, Kefauver Hearings*, vol. 5, pp. 1175–87; *U.S.–Senate, McClellan Labor Hearings*, pp. 12519–26.

6.23 Philosophy behind the methods. The Mafioso "believes he has the right to steal, corrupt, even murder." Reid, *Grim Reapers*, pp. 1–2.

6.24 Recruitment and training. Convicts and college graduates. *U.S.–Task Force Report*, pp. 55–56.

6.25 Counterintelligence. Salerno and Tompkins, *Crime Confederation*, pp. 172–73.

6.26 Silence and insulation. Orders are given through intermediaries; "each man is a wall protecting the next guy higher up." Teresa, *My Life in the Mafia*, pp. 87–88.

6.27 Mafia "licenses" to unaffiliated allies. In New England, where the resident Mafia family is relatively small, "non-Mafia allies hold Mafia 'licenses'" to be bookies, loan sharks or fences. The Mafia takes 25 to 40 percent of the receipts. Some allies have Mafia licenses for whole territories. The aging town of Somerville, Massachusetts, is the haven of Howie Winter, the last of the Irish gang leaders who once ran the Boston underworld. "Winter pays tribute regularly to Angiulo's men"; they meet in the Nautical Cafe, a Boston night club. Bill Davidson, "The Mafia: How it Bleeds New England," *Saturday Evening Post*, November 18, 1967, p. 28.

6.28 Feigning illness to evade the law. Both Al Capone and Meyer Lansky pleaded serious or terminal illness in the 1920s to duck grand jury subpoenas. The Taglianetti airtels revealed that New England Mafioso[21] Louis Taglianetti was "considering feigning a heart attack in order to postpone his tax case." Doctors on the hook with the Mob sometimes cooperate. Mollenhoff, *Strike Force*, p. 122; Gage, *The Mafia is not an Equal Opportunity Employer*, pp. 59–60; Teresa, *My Life in the Mafia*, p. 192; Allsop, *The Bootleggers*, p. 321.

6.29 Mafia treatment of nonmember employees. "They bleed you dry and ... when your mind and body aren't any use to them—they throw you out and have you killed." Testimony of Mob defector Patsy Lepera in *U.S.–OC and Stolen Securities, 1973*, pp. 453–54, 470.

6.30 Dirty tricks, Watergate style. A New York Mafioso hired blacks and Puerto Ricans to build white backlash against a referendum to authorize a new race track in Secaucus, New Jersey. The hired men passed out leaflets in support of the referendum stating that it would "bring full integration to Secaucus," and went door to door trying to rent rooms as future track employees. The referendum was defeated. Salerno and Tompkins, *Crime Confederation*, pp. 267–68.

6.31 Framing the FBI. New Jersey Mobsters obtained copies of classified FBI documents concerning a loan sharking case and attempted to implicate the FBI in illegal activities. *Newark* [N.J.] *Star Ledger*, August 8, 1974, p. 1.

6.32 Anti-Mafia prosecutors were fired, threatened and libeled in New Jersey. Several New Jersey district attorneys suffered political setbacks, including dismissal, when they vigorously prosecuted the Mafia. In the 1960s, when U. S. Attorney Frederick Lacey was securing indictments and convictions against top New Jersey Mafiosi and politicians, his family was threatened and he was smeared with absurd charges of Communist collaboration. "Is the power of organized crime in America now so great that any man who tries to stand up to it must expect to become the victim of threats, lies and vilification?" Fred Cook, "New Jersey: The State of Mafia," *Nation*, May 11, 1970, pp. 560–63, 574.

6.33 Maintaining Family traditions. On July 20, 1973, two men dropped off a third man at the emergency room door of Wyckoff Heights Hospital. He was "clad only in charred shorts and burned over 90 percent of his body." Moments before, the Vic Construction Company six blocks away had burst into flame after an explosion. The fire marshal's office called it arson. The burned man, who later died of his injuries, was Leonard Vario, the 23-year-old son of New York Mafia boss Paul Vario. *New York Times*, October 11, 1973, p. 12.

6.34 Laundering money through foreign banks. Cash from Mafia illegal activities, such as narcotics or loan sharking, is funneled into banks in Switzerland, the Bahamas, and other foreign countries, and returned as loans. This hides Mafia income from law enforcement authorities and the IRS. Foreign banks are also used to facilitate such illegal transactions as sales of stolen stocks. And the Mob has gone a step further in its foreign bank dealings, notes former U.S. Attorney Robert Morgenthau: "Today, numerous banks in Switzerland and the Bahamas are owned and controlled not only by Americans, but in some cases by American hoodlums closely linked to loansharking, gambling rackets, and other illegal businesses." Dorman, *Payoff*, pp. 255–58; testimony of former Mob money-mover Gerald Zelmanowitz in *U.S.–Senate, OC and Stolen Securities, 1973*, pp. 73–74.

6.35 A Mafioso's prayer. When Chicago Mafioso Sam DeStefano was troubled, reported informant Charles Crimaldi, he would kneel down and "smash his fists against the floor in frustration and rage. The drool would pour from his mouth in streams. . . . His gravelly voice would become a croak so guttural that his words were barely comprehensible." He would then pray to the devil: "What are you doin' to me? How come you bring me, Sam, all this heat? I'm your fuckin' disciple. You put me where I am. How can you do this thing and cause me all this goddamned heat—all this fuckin' agitation. What do you want me to do? Kill somebody? Can't you tell me in another way instead of handin' me all this fuckin' aggravation?" John Kidner, *Crimaldi: Contract Killer* (Washington, D.C.: Acropolis Books, 1976), pp. 134–35.

c. Public relations and the affectation of respectability

6.36 Polite demeanor characterized a Mafia hit man. Gage, *Mafia, U.S.A.*, p. 21.

6.37 Aping an upstanding citizen. Gifts to charity and a professional public relations firm were used to bolster a Mobster's image. Dorman, *Payoff*, p. 276; Cressey, *Theft of the Nation*, p. 274.

6.38 Buffalo, New York "Man of the Year," prominent in business and politics, was exposed as Mafia member. John Montana, a one-time Buffalo City Councilman, owner of the largest taxicab company in western New York State and member of civic and fraternal organizations, was one of those arrested at the Apalachin Mafia conclave in 1957. He was found to be a lieutenant in the Buffalo Magaddino Family, with close ties to several area Mafia figures. Joseph Valachi, who knew Magaddino well, confirmed this in his Congressional testimony. *U.S.-Senate, OC and Narcotics Hearings*, pp. 591–92, 196, 299.

6.39 The glad hand. "The Mafia front men are characterized by the smile, the glad hand, the tuxedo and the ticket to the charity ball. But the basic Mafia tools are still money, murder, and corruption." From the testimony of Detroit Police Chief George Edwards in *U.S.-Senate, OC and Narcotics Hearings*, pp. 400–401.

7. Roots in Sicily

7.1 Origins of the Mafia. "The taproots of the criminal organization known as the Mafia lie deep in the troubled history of the island of Sicily, which was overrun by invaders and conquerors for almost 2,000 years." During this period, Sicilian slave labor enriched a succession of foreign powers, including the Romans, Normans, Germans, French, Aragonese, Spaniards and Bourbons. The last stretch of brutality was imposed by the Inquisition, which disbanded in Sicily at the end of the 18th century. Under the direction of Sicilian barons, Sicilians were tortured and stripped of their property for a variety of vaguely defined offenses or philosophical positions. The Duke of Merindaceli, the Spanish Viceroy, wrote: "It would take a year to describe the things they do. Unheard of things—the most hideous and frightful enormities."(B)

"The precise origins and development of the secret criminal society on the island are uncertain, but it is probable that the Mafia came into being to fight the excesses of absentee feudal landlords in their harsh treatment of the peasantry on the island. Historians who have traced the growth of the organization from medieval times into the modern era are generally agreed that the Mafia was conceived in rebellion against Sicily's conquerors. In modern times, the Sicilian Mafia has almost entirely lost its ancient aura of revolutionary and patriotic lawlessness and has become primarily a criminal combine specializing in fraud and extortion, among other crimes." A–*U.S.-Senate, OC and Narcotics Report*, p. 5; B–Gage, *Mafia, U.S.A.*, pp. 65–67.

7.2 From Robin Hoods to hoods. A tradition of revenge and silence was developed under foreign oppression. By 1945 the Mafia had become the worst oppressor of the peasants. The Mafia imposed its own tax on all forms of agriculture, industry, and commerce. It virtually replaced the police department. It secured the election of puppet candidates through rigged balloting. It took over the manufacture of religious relics to make huge profits from facsimiles. Lewis, *The Honored Society*, reprinted in Gage, *Mafia, U.S.A.*, pp. 67–77.

7.3 No subtlety in its approach. Scores of political and trade union leaders in Sicily have been murdered by the Mafia. Eighteen bystanders were wounded in 1944 when the Mafia fired into the crowd at an anti-Mob political rally. A Mafia-backed political candidate declared, "I am a friend of the Mafia." A Mafia physician poisoned a murder witness. Mafiosi bombed facilities of a leading Sicilian newspaper. Pantaleone, *Mafia and Politics*, pp. 73, 88, 115–16, 127, 202–6.

7.4 The Mafia in Sicily in the 1920s. It "dominated and controlled the whole social life . . . in big cities and in small centres, . . . forced its way into every kind of business, and got its way by means of threats and intimidation." From a January 19, 1931 report of the Procurator-General of Palermo, reprinted in Cook, *Secret Rulers*, p. 55.

7.5 The Mafia in Sicily in the 1960s. "The Mafia doctor got all the patients" and the "Mafia advocate had all the briefs he could handle." The Mafia got the government contracts and arranged the elections of members of Parliament. Lewis, *The Honored Society*, p. 84; Luigi Barzini, *The Italians* (New York: Atheneum, 1964), pp. 259–60.

7.6 The Mafia in Sicily in the 1970s. The Mafia has managed to "survive and prosper" in changing times with its standard techniques "including terror, extortion and bribery." In Palermo, "there's good reason to believe that not a single traffic light goes up these days without its ok." Mafia operations have been extended to the mainland; Mafia hit men are sent from Sicily to the mainland and vice versa. Close ties and "mutual dependence" exist between the Mafia and the ruling Christian Democratic Party, as documented in a 270-page 1971 report by the Italian Parliament. *Newsweek*, October 23, 1972, p. 58; July 26, 1971, p. 38.

7.7 Wholesale slaughter. The Mafia's chief foe in Italy was executed in broad daylight. Judge Cesare Terranova, age 58, was caught in Palermo's rush-hour traffic on September 24, 1979, when two men opened fire on his car. His murderers fled, "having demonstrated publicly the fate that awaited those who dared oppose them." Terranova "had an encyclopedic knowledge of the connections between the Mafia and politicians, the police, judges, Government officials, the nobility, the Vatican, and captains of industry. . . ." He was about to have been given more power when he was murdered.

Other Mafia victims in 1979 alone included the provincial secretary for the Christian Democrats in Palermo, the vice commandant of Palermo's police force, the chief of Palermo's strike force against narcotics, the investigator of Italy's largest bank failure, "in which the Mafia was believed heavily involved," and a police colonel who had sent dozens of Mafiosi to jail. Italian murder victims of the Mafia in the 1970s, according to police estimates, number at least 1,000.

Klaus Schwidrowski, "Italy's Mafia Blight," *Die Zeit* (Hamburg), translated and reprinted in *World Press Review*, March 1980, p. 56.

8. Metastasis in America

8.1 Black-Hand extortion letters and dock racketeering at the turn of the 20th century. Investigation of these led to the Mafia murders of New Orleans Police Chief David Hennessey in 1890 and of New York Police Lieutenant Joseph Petrosino in 1909. Sondern, *Brotherhood of Evil*, pp. 56–65; Reid, *Grim Reapers*, pp. 146–50.

8.2 Description of the Mafia in the early 1900s from the memoirs of Mafioso Nicola Gentile. Gage, *The Mafia is not an Equal Opportunity Employer*, pp. 32–35; Messick and Goldblatt, *The Mobs and the Mafia*, pp. 7–9.

8.3 The Capone era: an example of Mafia operations in the 1920s and 1930s. "All restraints were lifted." Dozens of citizens were murdered, including a newspaper reporter and assistant state's attorney William McSwiggin. The homes of Senator Beneen and political candidate John Swanton were bombed. From the testimony of Joseph Morris, Chicago Deputy Superintendent of Police, in *U.S.–Senate, OC and Narcotics Hearings*, pp. 502–3.

8.4 Post-Prohibition adjustments. "The underworld turned to industry, labor, and real estate." From "servant" to "master" in labor relations. Tyler, *Organized Crime in America*, pp. 152–53.

8.5 The birth of a unified nationwide organization. The "Castellammarese war" of 1930–31 between Mafia factions was ended with a mass meeting in New York. Presiding was boss Salvatore Maranzano, who laid out a national structure which unified the various Mafia gangs in America. Maas, *Valachi Papers*, pp. 104–7; *Time*, August 22, 1969, p. 19; *U.S.–House, Assassination Appendix, JFK*, vol. 9, pp. 5–6.

III. CRIMINAL OPERATIONS

9. Gambling

9.1 "The meat and potatoes of the Mafia." Gage, *Mafia, U.S.A.*, pp. 17–18.

9.2 A Massachusetts crime commission found that state residents spent more on gambling than on food. A 1957 Commission report, which focused on organized crime's corruption of police, found that in 1954, the state's illegal gambling turnover was $2 billion, almost double its food sales. Cook, *Two Dollar Bet*, pp. 6–7.

a. Mafia control of gambling

9.3 Mafia members "control all but a tiny part of the illegal gambling in the United States." Those illegal betting and lottery operations "they do not own they control, or provide with essential services." Cressey, *Theft of the Nation*, pp. xi, 75; *U.S.–Task Force Report*, pp. 2–3.

9.4 The Mob controls bookmakers through its hold on the nationwide racing information wire service. In 1951, the Kefauver Committee reported: "The apparent control by the Capone mob of the wire services to bookmakers . . . provides a stranglehold over large bookmaking operations. To the extent that the Capone crime syndicate controls the wire service, it is in that proportionate measure a partner of every bookmaker of consequence in the country." *U.S.–Senate, Kefauver Report, Second Interim*, p. 11, see pp. 15–25.

9.5 "Office" protection is mandatory—for a 50 percent cut. From the testimony of defected New England Mob killer Joseph Barboza in *U.S.–House, OC in Sports*, p. 751.

9.6 Kefauver Committee findings: "The committee was repeatedly struck by the magnitude of the gambling business and by the pattern of domination in this business by an interlocking group of gangsters, racketeers, and hoodlums." *U.S.–Senate, Kefauver Report, Third Interim*, p. 90.

9.7 Independent gambling operations are eliminated. Carlton O'Brien ran a bookie network in Rhode Island independent of Mafia boss Raymond Patriarca.

"O'Brien's bookies were held up, bookie parlors wrecked, and telephone lines pulled out, bookmakers slugged and robbed." Finally, in 1951, O'Brien was murdered by a shotgun blast. From the testimony of Col. Walter E. Stone, superintendent of the Rhode Island State Police, in *U.S.–Senate, OC and Narcotics Hearings*, p. 552.

b. Improving the odds

9.8 A Mafia-licensed Detroit numbers operation was "completely crooked." Winning numbers were changed when heavily bet. From the testimony of Detroit Police Chief George Edwards in *U.S.–Senate, OC and Narcotics Hearings*, pp. 412–415.

9.9 Rigging the number in New York City. The winning number of a Mob-controlled New York numbers game was based on the daily volume of the Cincinnati Clearinghouse. Police wiretaps and a confession of the clearinghouse secretary revealed that this figure was adjusted daily by the secretary for a $1,000-a-month payoff to match the number least heavily bet. Tyler, *Organized Crime in America*, pp. 274–81.

c. Examples of Mob-controlled bookmaking, casino, and numbers operations

9.10 Anatomy of a bookmaking ring. Vincent Teresa testified about a small Massachusetts bookmaking ring employing 60 to 70 agents which he once operated with Mobster[22] Robert Visconti. The ring, which was run with an okay from Mafia boss Patriarca, layoffs to the Mob and payoffs to police, grossed about $5 million per year. *U.S.–Senate, OC and Stolen Securities, 1971*, pp. 814–15.

9.11 The Mob's Las Vegas casino operations. They are characterized by concealed ownerships and millions of dollars skimmed annually, transported to Swiss banks by international couriers. *Life*, September 8, 1967, pp. 98–100.

9.12 The numbers racket: bleeding the poor. A majority of the adult residents in New York's and Chicago's major slum areas play Mob-controlled numbers games. A New York State committee found that the average resident bet $150 to $250 a year; Malcolm X reported that he used to bet up to $15 to $20 per day. Gage, *The Mafia is not an Equal Opportunity Employer*, pp. 150–51; *U.S.–Senate, Kefauver Report, Third Interim*, p. 56; Eugene Methvin, "How the Mafia Preys on the Poor," *Reader's Digest*, September 1970, pp. 51–52; Malcolm X, *The Autobiography of Malcolm X*, pp. 84–85.

9.13 A booming business in industrial plants and office buildings. In Washington, D.C., for example, elevator operators, car pool drivers, and messengers often double as numbers runners and bookies in federal buildings "not excluding the FBI section of the Department of Justice." The IRS has conducted gambling raids on government buildings including the Pentagon. King, *Gambling and Organized Crime*, p. 29; Cook, *Two Dollar Bet*, p. 129; Tyler, *Organized Crime in America*, pp. 262–63.

9.14 How the Mob took over numbers operations in New York. "They 'persuaded' people with lead pipes, wet cement, baseball bats, brass knuckles, fists, feet, and blackjacks." Malcolm X, *The Autobiography of Malcolm X*, p. 87; *The New York Post* (1960), reprinted in Tyler, *Organized Crime in America*, pp. 260–74.

□□□□□□□□□□□□□□□□□□□□□□

Gambling is the single most important activity for organized crime. They control it all over the country and all over the world. . . . From it comes the corrupt politicians and policemen, the bribes and the payoffs, and sometimes murder. . . .

There is no bookmaker that can do business by himself; he couldn't survive. The mob would turn him over to the police, give him a few beatings, or even kill him if he's real stubborn. He has to go with them, because they run everything.

. . . There isn't one casino in the world, outside of the Communist countries, that doesn't have the mob involved in some way. . . . As an example of how the mob's control stretches everywhere, I can tell you about George Raft's Colony Sportsmen's Club in London. . . . Dino Cellini is involved in that club and so is Meyer Lansky. I know, because I ran gambling junkets, and we couldn't put a junket in there without their ok. It's the same at Paradise Island in the Bahamas. . . .

When you lose $50,000 in London on credit, you don't come home and send the money to London. You pay Cellini and Meyer Lansky.

> Mafia defector Vincent Teresa, in *U.S.-Senate, OC and Stolen Securities, 1971*, pp. 813–14.

□□□□□□□□□□□□□□□□□□□□□□□□□

10. Loan Sharking

10.1 Loans at exorbitant interest—the borrower's body is collateral. Small loans are characteristically made at "six for five," or 20 percent interest *per week*. Larger loans are made at lower rates. *Time*, August 22, 1969, p. 20; *Reader's Digest*, September 1970, p. 52.

10.2 Loan shark victims often turn to crime. "He gets in deep, and he can't pay, and they beat him up. He gets out of the hospital, and they beat him up again. Then he either turns to crime to get the money—say he is a truckdriver and starts hijacking trucks, or else he runs away. He leaves his wife and his kids and his home and runs away." From the testimony of Mafia defector Vincent Teresa in *U.S.-Senate, OC and Stolen Securities, 1971*, p. 815.

10.3 Case studies of Mafia loan sharking transactions. The "objective is to take every dime the borrower can lay his hands on." Threats and beatings often drive victims to crime or force them to become inside men for the Mob in a variety of crimes. Cressey, *Theft of the Nation*, pp. 78–91.

10.4 Mafia loan sharking exposed by testimony in a 1966 Illinois state investigation. Victims became caught in an unending nightmare of threats, beatings, and murders. "They may torture you, squeeze you—that's what it is—they squeeze you until there's no juice left. It destroys a man." Demaris, *Captive City*, pp. 50–59.

10.5 The testimony of former Mob loan shark collector Louis Mastriana. Mastriana told the Senate how he collected loans in the Washington, D.C. area for New Jersey Mafioso[23] Charlie Tourine. "I would give them a week to pay. Then if he didn't pay, you whacked them ... break his head." *U.S.–Senate, OC and Stolen Securities, 1973*, pp. 167, 138–39.

10.6 Two-thirds of murders and maimings in New England involve Mafia loan shark victims. Charles Rogovin, the Massachusetts Attorney General's expert on organized crime, stated that "all other Mafia families" usually "stop short of killing, on the theory that a dead man can't pay. But not here. They're totally ruthless about loansharking debts. Two-thirds of the murders and maimings in New England involve people who have surrendered the collateral of their bodies to the loansharks." Reid, *Grim Reapers*, p. 67.

□□□□□□□□□□□□□□□□□□□□□□□□□

If a man is three weeks late in his vigorish [interest payments], he gets a broken arm or leg. If he's six to eight weeks late, he has an accident. We fix the brakes of his car or we run him off the road, or we blow up his house or his business. Sometimes we go to his house and beat up his wife, or we break a leg on his kid on his way home from school. If the guy owes more than $15,000, or if he's arrogant about falling behind in his vigorish, he gets death.

> As described to an undercover agent by Phil Waggenheim, enforcer for Mafia loan shark Larry Baioni. Quoted in Davidson, "The Mafia: How it Bleeds New England," *Saturday Evening Post*, November 18, 1967, p. 29.

□□□□□□□□□□□□□□□□□□□□□□□□

11. Narcotics

11.1 Mafia control of most U.S. heroin traffic was reported by the Federal Bureau of Narcotics in 1963 and 1969. *U.S.–Senate OC and Narcotics Report*, p. 56; *U.S.–House, Criminal Justice Hearings*, p. 333.

11.2 Non-Mob elements are moving into high-risk street sale of narcotics. "But the fact is that the Mafia is still bankrolling the drug traffic and pocketing most of the profits." Gage, *Mafia, U.S.A.*, p. 17.

11.3 New York Mafia boss Carmine Galente expanded narcotics operations in the mid-1970s. *Time*, May 16, 1977, p. 36.

11.4 The Mafia reaps additional profits through fencing operations. Addicts spend about $2 billion a year on heroin, most of which is raised by stealing. The goods stolen to buy the drugs are usually taken from homes and stores in slum neighborhoods, and are often converted into cash (at 20 percent of value) through Mob fencing networks. Gage, *The Mafia is not an Equal Opportunity Employer*, pp. 158–59, 164–65.

12. Extortion

12.1 Self-proclaimed business partners. Cressey, *Theft of the Nation*, pp. 103–105.

12.2 Shaking down Boston area bars not owned by the Mob. Notorious killer Joseph Barboza and his men "would go into these places and tear the joints apart. They'd bust up a few people, break the furniture, smash the bar, and storm out." Soon, 20 clubs were doling out $1,000 a month each to keep Barboza in check. Barboza and his men got 25 percent of this money while three top New England Mafiosi, Raymond Patriarca, Henry Tameleo, and Vincent Teresa, split the other 75 percent. As described by Teresa and Barboza, who both became government witnesses, in Teresa, *My Life in the Mafia*, pp. 116–17; and *U.S.–House, OC in Sports*, pp. 745–47.

12.3 "A reverse twist of the old Black Hand technique." Detroit Mafioso Santo Perrone first bombed his victim with a small explosive device, then demanded extortion money. From the testimony of Detroit Police Criminal Intelligence Director Vince Piersante in *U.S.–Senate, OC and Narcotics Hearings*, p. 476.

13. Securities Theft and Fraud

13.1 Volume of thefts: from $9.1 million in 1966 to $50 billion in 1973. Wall Street and government estimates of securities thefts show an astronomical increase: $9.1 million in 1966,[24] $37 million in 1967,[25] $400 million in 1969 and 1970,[26] and $494 million in the first six months of 1971.[27] But the real shocker was the figure for 1973, as presented in the Senate's Organized Crime and Stolen Securities hearings. Henry DuPont, chairman of the board of the Securities Validation Corporation, estimated from a data base of 10 percent (in dollar value) of U.S. securities that the value of securities stolen or otherwise lost as of June 1973 was $50 billion, or 4.8 percent of all outstanding stocks. *U.S.–Senate, OC and Stolen Securities, 1973*, pp. 9–11, 20, 35, 42–43.

a. Mafia control of securities thefts

13.2 Organized crime elements "control the theft, distribution and conversion" of stolen securities. This conclusion is noted on a government chart showing the "Pattern of Organized Crime Perpetration of Thefts and Conversion of Securities." It was prepared by the Senate Government Operations Committee. Following is an excerpt, with punctuation modified: "Factors Involved in Thefts: 1. Direct Infiltration By The Mob; 2. Persons Under Pressure to Steal Securities [through] A. Gambling Debts, B. Loansharking Debts, C. Narcotics Addiction, D. Strong Arm; 3. Thieves Who Depend On Mob For Conversion." The Senate chart similarly outlined Mob conversion and distribution of stocks. *U.S.–Senate, OC and Stolen Securities, 1971*, pp. 62–63.

13.3 The Mobsters "came to Wall Street with their same 'bag of tricks,' and . . . were more than able to breach the flimsy fortress of Wall Street security." From the testimony of New York Assistant District Attorney Murray Gross in *U.S.–Senate, OC and Stolen Securities, 1971*, pp. 72–77, 90–91.

13.4 Control through terror. "Utilizing terror as their usual practice, utilizing all of their normal techniques, they control the production of counterfeit securities, they control the theft of the securities. . . . On the street, and it has been known for years, they [Mobsters] look to get [securities] runners and customers, men on juice [in debt to loansharks]. They look to get them with girls. They look to get them with narcotics, any way they can, to control the situation." From the testimony of Michael Raymond, a financial operator who worked closely with the Mafia, in *U.S.–Senate, OC and Stolen Securities, 1971*, p. 681; for background on Raymond, see pp. 659–64, 956, 1245–46.

☐☐☐☐☐☐☐☐☐☐☐☐☐☐☐☐☐☐☐☐☐☐
House Crime Committee Chairman Claude Pepper, opening the
Committee's 1971–72 hearings on worthless securities, in
U.S.–House, OC and Worthless Securities, pp. 1–2:

This is the first of a series of hearings designed to show how extensively
organized criminal elements have infiltrated the banking, securities, and
insurance industries. The evidence uncovered thus far shows that important racketeers have combined with lawyers and accountants in develop-
ing schemes which have defrauded the general public as well as companies
in the banking, securities, and insurance industries of hundreds of millions
of dollars each year.
    ... The tremendous amounts of money they are able to amass ... en-
ables them to facilitate their operations by offering substantial bribes to
bank presidents, insurance company executives, and stock brokerage management. ...
    These individuals move across State lines—from coast to coast and in-
ternationally—bankrupting small banks, insurance companies and stock
brokerage institutions. Local law enforcement is entirely inadequate to
cope with a scheme which is planned in California, prepared in New Jersey,
and executed in Ohio. ...
    In addition to the bribery of banking and securities officials, these crimi-
nals are associated with corrupt lawyers and accountants. Evidence developed during our investigation shows that corrupt lawyers have been able
to bribe judges in order to obtain preferential treatment. ... This disclosure demonstrates the pervasive influence of organized crime in our State
courts.

☐☐☐☐☐☐☐☐☐☐☐☐☐☐☐☐☐☐☐☐☐☐☐☐

**13.5 "The major portion of stolen securities" is controlled by organized
crime.** When asked by Senator Gurney "how to get at the organized crime people
who run the show," Mr. Wuenche suggested, "if you started a program of rounding
these people up from the top to the bottom eventually you might make a big
dent." From the testimony of Edward Wuenche, former Mob securities fence, in
U.S.–Senate, OC and Stolen Securities, 1971, pp. 868–69; background on Wuenche
in pp. 842–46.

13.6 The Mafia's role in the stolen securities business: "it is total." Stocks
stolen-to-order within 24 hours. From the testimony of Patsy Lepera, former Mob
securities fence, in *U.S.–Senate, OC and Stolen Securities, 1973,* pp. 474–75; background in 389–90.

**b. Cases of Mob securities thefts and racketeering activities on Wall
Street**

13.7 The Wall Street connection. A Mafia-controlled international stolen securities ring was uncovered by police. Twenty-five persons, including Genovese
Family member Vincent Rizzo and other high-level Mobsters, were indicted on
"charges ranging from narcotics smuggling to extortion to attempted murder."
Newsweek, July 23, 1973, pp. 62–63.

13.8 A witness was murdered after the robbery of "a fortune in negotiable securities." A securities messenger, a nephew of a Mafioso, was robbed. He subsequently testified several times before the grand jury looking into whether the robbery was staged. During the investigation, "the messenger's corpse was found, covered with stab wounds." Grutzner, "How to Lock Out the Mafia," *Harvard Business Review*, March-April 1970, p. 56.

13.9 The theft and nationwide distribution of $21 million in securities stolen in 1968 from a mail pouch at New York's JFK airport. The theft was committed by Mafioso[28] William Ricchiuti and Mob associate[29] James Schaeffer. The principle fences were Gus Cangiano and Anthony Garafola, both Mafia members.[30] Within two years, securities from the pouch turned up in San Diego, Houston, Miami, Oklahoma City, Phoenix, Los Angeles, Boston, Mexico City, Chicago, New York, Toronto, and other cities. Also in that period, two associates of Cangiano and another man linked to the 1968 JFK theft were murdered (Cangiano invoked the Fifth Amendment when questioned about the murder[31]). From the testimony of U.S. Chief Postal Inspector William J. Cotter in *U.S.-Senate, OC and Stolen Securities, 1971*, pp. 108–19, 247–49, 611–12.

13.10 Mobsters "have obtained control of established financial houses . . . [and] sold millions of dollars in worthless or near-worthless stocks to gullible victims the nation over." Sylvia Porter, "On Wall Street," *New York Post*, August 3–7, 1959, reprinted in Tyler, *Organized Crime in America*, pp. 298–302.

13.11 Selling millions in worthless stocks at securities firms owned by the Gambino Family. Meskil, *Don Carlo*, pp. 191–92; Cook, *Secret Rulers*, pp. 363–65.

14. Cargo Theft

14.1 Exerpts from the U.S. government publication *Cargo Theft and Organized Crime*. Cargo theft is increasing at an alarming rate—it amounted to more than $2 billion in 1972—causing major economic dislocations. Losses are passed on to consumers. The increase in crime costs "has outpaced any corresponding increase in tonnage or revenue."

"Organized crime has a direct hand in the *execution* of cargo thefts, in *the distribution* of this cargo . . . and *in the actual consumption* of the stolen goods through the businesses it owns or otherwise controls." The Mafia "is the inner core of organized crime." Up to 80 percent of the thefts are committed by employees, often enlisted through Mob loan sharking activities, threats, and Mob-union collusion.

Guards are "frightened away" from stopping thefts. "Attempts to control theft on the waterfront have frequently resulted in personal injury through 'accidents' or direct assaults." "More portwatchmen were apprehended for stealing cargo . . . than they—the portwatchmen force—apprehended."

"What would alleviate the cargo theft problem is to break up organized crime." *U.S.-Cargo Theft and OC*, pp. 5–11, 15–19, 23–29.

14.2 Hijackings are arranged by the Mob, from staged "holdup" to disposition of the goods. "Most so-called hijacks with guns never happened that way. It was all set up before by the Mob." The truck driver, often in debt to the Mob, turns over his cargo to "some fringe punk" lined up to handle the theft. The Mob disposes of the goods and gets "the lion's share" of the profits. From the comments of Mafia defector Vincent Teresa in *My Life in the Mafia*, pp. 134–39.

14.3 "The mob takeover of the air freight trucking industry at Kennedy Airport, N.Y. . . . annual thefts jumped 100-fold in 5 years, from $45,000 to 4.5 million." The Mob gained control of the union, Teamster Local 295, and the industry association, the National Association for Air Freight (NAAF), handling air freight at JFK Airport. It then pressured trucking companies at JFK to join the NAAF, sign contracts with Local 295, and obey its dictates. Companies were induced to comply by Teamsters strikes and extensive sabotage.

"Trucking rackets, mail thefts, hijacking, flagrant pilferage, loansharking, illegal gambling and other crimes are still flourishing at JFK, gangland's Open City."(B) Cargo is stolen with the help of cargo handlers, truckers, and even U.S. Customs employees on the Mob payroll, who are often hooked by loan sharking debts. "Rampant Mob rule at Kennedy Airport is typical of the underworld's role at airports across the country."(C)

A–Senator John McClellan, from testimony in *U.S.–House, OC Control*, p. 87; B–Meskil, *Don Carlo*, pp. 154–59; C–Dorman, *Payoff*, pp. 272–76.

14.4 The nation's biggest armed robbery. In December 1978, $5,850,000 in cash and jewelry was seized from a Lufthansa cargo facility at Kennedy Airport. According to *Time*, members of the Mafia Family of the late Tommy Lucchese probably masterminded the crime. Officials think that the Mob secured the cooperation of airline employees "by the time-honored method of inducing them to gamble, pressuring them to pay up, loaning them money at exorbitant rates, and, finally, pointing out that they could cancel their debts by helping out with the heist." The FBI suspects that the loot was laundered "through a maze of Mafia business channels." *Time*, March 5, 1979, p. 23.

Most of the drivers and a lot of the warehousemen are gamblers. They lose their salaries at Mob card and dice games, and the games are usually rigged. They get in a hole, and they start borrowing from the loansharks. Then you have them. They can never get even, never pay off all they owe, because the juice mounts up. That's when you start the squeeze. They have a choice. Broken legs or arms, a threat against the family, or provide us with information on truckloads of goods they're hauling.

Vincent Teresa, in *My Life in the Mafia*, p. 138.

15. Other Activities

a. Pornography and vice

15.1 "The Mafia now dominates the manufacture and distribution of pornographic books, magazines and movies." Volume of business: $2.2 billion a year. "The Mafia: Big, Bad and Booming," *Time*, May 16, 1977, pp. 33–34.

15.2 "The Gambino Mafia Family has a large interest in the child pornography business." The Mafia is moving back into prostitution. Genovese Family members allegedly control many nude bars in New York where girls are recruited for prostitution. *Time*, November 28, 1977, p. 23.

15.3 The Mafia takeover of the pornography industry is marked by traditional methods: terror, intimidation and murder. Ralph Blumenthal and Nicholas Gage, "Crime 'Families' Taking Control of Pornography," *New York Times*, December 10, 1972, pp. 1, 82; George Denison, "Smut: The Mafia's Newest Racket," *Reader's Digest*, December 1971, pp. 157–60.

15.4 The report of former Mafia operative James Barrett. Barrett, who worked for the Mafia in pornography ventures, became an FBI undercover informant and later a government witness. He reported that through muscle and payoffs to police and politicians, the Mafia ensures that no pornography enters any city in the United States without some payment to the local family. The Mob, he summarized, "has an iron grip on the smut industry." James Barrett, "Inside the Mob's Smut Rackets," *Reader's Digest*, December 1973, p. 128.

15.5 The Mafia-supplied prostitute "almost invariably is in league with the electronically equipped extortionist." Police estimate that the take from sex-blackmail is far more than that from the prostitution itself. Federal agents raided one Chicago sex-blackmail ring directed by Mafia associate[32] Dominic Galiano in which "victims were drugged, robbed and shaken down for five-figure payoffs." Indictments were handed down against two Mobsters and seven associates in a similar ring in Detroit. In New York, police found a concealed television monitor and tape recording facilities in a massage parlor in the Mob-infested midtown vice district. Demaris, *Captive City*, pp. 96–97; *Time*, May 16, 1977, p. 35; *New York Times*, August 27, 1972, p. 1.

b. Rigged sporting events

15.6 "Banana" races in New England. "There was hardly a race track in New England where the mob didn't put the fix in at one time or another. . . . The races were so crooked you couldn't get them into the ground with a corkscrew." Vincent Teresa, *My Life in the Mafia*, pp. 152–63.

15.7 Mobsters "control" horse racing. Fixes were always placed with Mob consent. An estimated 60 percent of race horses in America are owned by Mobsters through fronts. Loan sharking debts, drugs, women, and bribes are routinely used by the Mob to hook jockeys into cooperating in fixes. From the testimony of Bobby Byrne, a former top horse racing fixer well connected with the Patriarca and Gambino families, who operated at tracks across the country, in *U.S.–House, OC in Sports*, pp. 1086–87, 1123, 1127–28, 1131–33, 1136, background pp. 1083ff., 1117.

15.8 Mafia approval was needed to cash counterfeit twin double tickets at New York's Roosevelt Raceway. From the testimony of Nassau County, N.Y. District Attorney William Cahn in *U.S.–House, OC in Sports*, p. 1025.

15.9 Mafia boss Raymond Patriarca was connected with Scarborough Downs, the Berkshires, and "owned about fifty percent of the horses that ran in New England." So Mob defector Joseph Barboza learned from Mob sources, including New England Mafia underboss[33] Henry Tamello. Barboza named three persons who fronted ownership of horses for the Mafia. From Barboza's testimony in *U.S.–House, OC in Sports*, pp. 750–51.

15.10 Contacts between Mobsters and half the Boston Patriots football team. "Half" the team frequented Arthur's Farm, a vegetable store, Mafia meeting place, and outlet for stolen merchandise in Revere, Massachusetts. Team members bought merchandise and associated with the Mobsters who hung out there. Reported in *Life*, September 8, 1967, p. 93, and also by Vincent Teresa in *My Life in the Mafia*, p. 143. Mob defector Joseph Barboza reported one occasion when Babe Parilli (quarterbacking for the Patriots) and Gene Conley (playing for the Celtics) met with Mafia underboss Henry Tamello at the Ebb Tide, after which "Tamello came out and said, 'Take the Lakers with four points.'" *U.S.–House, OC in Sports*, pp. 738–39; See also *Saturday Evening Post*, November 18, 1967, p. 29.

☐☐☐☐☐☐☐☐☐☐☐☐☐☐☐☐☐☐☐☐☐

[A jockey] owed a $1,500 tab in the Ebb Tide [a Mafia hangout]. He owed it to Richard Castucci. He [Mafia underboss Henry Tamello] said, "Bring him in and start to pressure him . . . and I will come in there and I will stop you. Don't hurt him, but just really come on strong."

So I went in there and said, "You owe $1,500. . . ." I pulled out a knife and put it at his throat and said I was going to slice it. And Henry came in and said, "What's this? What's going on? . . ." Henry Tamello says, "I want to pay for him. I am telling you, don't bother this kid any more. . . ."

I walked out of the cloakroom. Henry Tamello stayed there with the jockey maybe 15–20 minutes, and he came out, and he had a jockey that was going to pull horses for him.

> Defected New England Mob killer Joseph Barboza, in *U.S.–House, OC in Sports*, pp. 737–38. (Barboza testified that Tamello used a similar technique on other jockeys [ibid., p. 753].)

☐☐☐☐☐☐☐☐☐☐☐☐☐☐☐☐☐☐☐☐☐

15.11 "A full squad of hoods, including a Cosa Nostra boss, was operating in Joe Namath's night club." The criminals, including Mafiosi Carmine Tramunti, Carmine Persico, and Thomas Mancuso, worked gambling operations from phones in the club. Namath continued to associate with the hoods even after a federal agent revealed their identities. In 1969, when the gangster infestation of Bachelor's III was disclosed by football commissioner Pete Rozelle, Namath threatened to quit the Jets rather than sell the night club. *Life*, June 20, 1969, pp. 22ff.

15.12 Personal and business contacts were reported between Mobsters and players on the New Orleans Saints football team. In addition, federal officials proved the Mob "had attempted to influence, through payments of money to players," the scores of four L.S.U. football games in September and October 1966. From the testimony of New Orleans Metropolitan Crime Commission Director Aaron Kohn, *U.S.–House, OC in Sports*, pp. 953–55.

15.13 Top lightweight boxer Frank DePaula was shot by his Mafia friends. DePaula was friendly with New Jersey Mafia boss Joseph Zicarelli and was a regular at Namath's Bachelor's III bar. When DePaula was indicted with his manager for an $80,000 dock theft and interrogated by federal agents, the Mafia suspected he talked and ordered him hit. DePaula recovered from the bullets in his back and arm; "Mafia insiders were surprised that the slaying had been fumbled." *Newsweek*, June 8, 1970, pp. 67–68.

c. The music business

15.14 The Mafia moves in on "Rare Earth" and "Three Dog Night." After its first album sold two million copies in 1969, the rock group "Rare Earth" faced declining fortunes in the 1970s. And then, with ready cash, entered Joe Ullo: a reputed Mob enforcer from New York who had moved into the rock music business. By 1976, reported NBC, Ullo was boasting to associates that he "had taken over a hidden interest" in Rare Earth, by providing "Mob money and Mob muscle" to take care of their debts. The members of the group said "all they knew was that their manager was making deals with people who carry guns."

In 1978, noted NBC, Ullo was arrested "for the murder of former basketball star Jack Molinas—and police say members of Rare Earth are lucky no one got hurt." But it was a different story with Ullo's involvement in "Three Dog Night." The group's accountant "was shot in the arm and paralyzed in what police believe was a dispute over control of Three Dog Night."

NBC News, "Segment 3," May 7, 1979.

15.15 "Payola and the Mob." A federal investigation of "payola, sex, drugs, and organized crime in the recording industry" began when Pasquale Falcone, a Mafia-connected talent manager for three Columbia artists, was indicted for heroin trafficking. "Sources close to the investigation say that at least one Columbia artist was driven into Falcone's stable with the help of Mafia muscle." *Newsweek,* July 30, 1973, p. 62.

15.16 "Payoffs to some disc jockeys, the use of threats by Mafiosi to keep performers in line and the use of drugs as payola." *New York Times,* June 15, 1973, p. 31.

15.17 The Mob is heavily involved in promoting rock concerts. The "Super Bowl of Rock" in Chicago featured some of the biggest rock stars and sold more than $2 million in tickets. According to NBC, "A federal grand jury is now investigating allegations that the Mob ran these concerts." Mobsters were suspected of paying city officials to get exclusive use of Soldier Field for concerts, booking rock stars through fronts, and forcing up ticket prices—"all part of a huge Mob scheme to make big money in the rock concert business." Terry Bruner, of the Chicago Better Government Association, noted, "This kind of thing goes on all over the country." NBC News, "Segment 3," May 8, 1979.

15.18 A hidden interest of New Jersey Mafia boss Angelo DeCarlo in Roulette Records and the Four Seasons singing group. From the testimony of defected Mob money-mover Gerald Zelmanowitz, in *U.S.–Senate, OC and Stolen Securities, 1973,* p. 60.

15.19 A gangland murder, two bombings characterize "organized crime's growing role" in the illegal bootleg tape cassette industry. Of $600 million spent on tape recordings in America in 1972, $200 million went for pirated tapes. *Chicago Tribune,* May 22, 1973, p. 10; *Newsweek,* July 30, 1973, p. 62; and *New York Times,* June 15, 1973, p. 31.

15.20 "The Mafia has become one of the biggest producers of records and tapes in this country." In November 1978, FBI agents raided 23 warehouses of a counterfeit tape operation run by New York's Colombo Mafia Family. This network was just part of the Mob's massive bootleg record and tape operations, whose volume is approaching the $4 billion annual sales of the legitimate recording industry. For example, RSO Records sold 23 million copies of the sound track from the movie, "Saturday Night Fever." According to NBC, however, "Federal investigators say Mob counterfeits made and sold at least that many." The bootleg copies were virtually identical to the originals, but the recording artists got no royalties from their sales. One undercover agent in the Mob's record business said, "I don't think there's a store in the country you can go into and not find some counterfeit product on a given day." NBC News, "Segment 3," May 9, 1979.

d. Miscellaneous

15.21 Dumping truckloads of toxic chemical wastes in the New England countryside. The chemical industry produces large quantities of toxic and radioactive waste material that can cause severe illness, birth defects, or death, sometimes even in trace amounts. The U.S. Environmental Protection Agency requires that these wastes be disposed only in carefully controlled dumping sites. With large profits at stake, however, the Mob has established less exacting procedures.

"With the aid and precision of organized crime, authorities say, gypsy truckers are hauling toxic chemicals from factories in the mid-Atlantic and Western States and illegally dumping the hazardous waste in the woods and farmland of Northern New England. ... Their trucks loaded with rusting, often leaky drums of solvents, cyanide solutions, pesticides and acids, the truckers operate with apparent immunity. ... It is common talk among truckers that the brokers represent organized crime. They say that those who question turn up with broken arms or collarbones." Noted Dennis Roberts, Rhode Island's attorney general, "It's clear to us that the shipping is being arranged by people with organized-crime involvement."

One illegal Mob dumping operation in Elizabeth, New Jersey, came to light in April 1980, when sixty thousand 55-gallon drums of toxic chemicals exploded. Only favorable winds kept huge clouds of toxic smoke from floating over New York City. The poisonous mess has still not been totally cleaned up. *Albuquerque Journal*, March 17, 1980, p. C11; *Newsweek*, January 5, 1981, pp. 35, 39.

15.22 Mafia control of fuel distribution in parts of New England and sales of stolen gasoline in New York City. *Hartford Courant*, January 22, 1974; *Time*, December 10, 1973, p. 34.

15.23 The Mafia is "siphoning off as much as $50 million a year" from cigarette smuggling. Reid, *Grim Reapers*, p. 44; *U.S.–Cargo Theft and OC*, p. 39.

15.24 The Mob is active in the multimillion dollar "chop shop" business. Late-model cars are stolen on order and cut up for parts. NBC Evening News, "Segment 3," January 19, 1978.

15.25 Counterfeiting and credit card fraud. Counterfeit securities, passports, postage stamps, drivers' licenses and money are printed by Mafia experts in any quantity members can use. Millions of dollars in counterfeit bills are routinely passed. Credit cards are counterfeited, stolen from the mail, or obtained from inside sources at credit card companies. Cards are used for airline tickets, hotel and restaurant bills, loans, jewelry, clothing, tires, and for cars that are rented and then stolen. From the testimony of Mafia defector Vincent Teresa in *U.S.–Senate, OC and Stolen Securities, 1971*, pp. 808–13, also see p. 142.

15.26 Defrauding the Veterans Administration. Boston underworld figures "rented" veterans' names or addresses to receive fraudulent benefits. Two men involved in the scheme were slain gangland style. It was believed that "many veterans were denied benefits, even though they were eligible, because of the widespread fraud." *Boston Globe*, August 17, 1974, p. 1; August 16, 1974, p. 1.

15.27 Fencing stolen art. In 1976, Detroit Mafioso Peter Licavoli was convicted in Tucson for trying to sell a stolen 400-year-old painting for $80,000 to an FBI agent working undercover. Until then, officials had assumed Licavoli had retired in Arizona to operate an art gallery. NBC Evening News, "Segment 3," March 13, 1978.

15.28 A partial list of Mob activities. "The list of organized crime's activities would include gambling, usury, bribery, perjury, fraud, extortion, kidnapping, murder, labor racketeering, forgery, counterfeiting, narcotics, burglary, hijacking, fencing, monopoly, prostitution, terrorism, and tax evasion, among many others." It was noted that "the predominant group and inner core of organized crime" is the Mafia. *U.S.–Cargo Theft and OC*, pp. 23, 25.

16. The Mafia and Street Crime

16.1 "Almost every bit of crime we study has some link to organized crime." Statement of Milton Rector, director of the National Council on Crime and Delinquency, in *Time*, August 22, 1969, p. 18. See similar statements by Congressman Richard Poff, Senator John McClellan and Congressman Joseph McDade in *U.S.–House, OC Control*, pp. 80, 86, 594.

16.2 Mob corruption nullified law enforcement. "Cosa Nostra's ability to flout the law makes preachment of law and order a joke" to the urban poor. Police busy collecting payoffs cannot effectively stop any kind of crime. *Time*, August 22, 1969, p. 18; *New Republic*, July 18, 1970, p. 13; *U.S.–House, Criminal Justice Hearings*, p. 150; Maas, *Serpico*, passim.

□□□□□□□□□□□□□□□□□□□□□□□

Drug addiction turns your little sister into a prostitute before she gets into her teens; makes a criminal out of your little brother before he gets in his teens. . . .

When a person is a drug addict, he's not the criminal; he's a victim of the criminal. The criminal is the man downtown who brings this drug into the country.

Malcolm X, from a speech transcribed in *By Any Means Necessary*, pp. 50–51.
□□□□□□□□□□□□□□□□□□□□□□□

a. Mob heroin promotes crime

16.3 Half of street crime in large Eastern cities is committed by heroin addicts. As estimated by Congressman Joseph McDade, by authorities in the District of Columbia, and by New York Police organized crime expert Ralph Salerno. The drugs are supplied by organized crime (see section 11). *U.S.–House, OC Control*, pp. 594, 423; *U.S.–House, Criminal Justice Hearings*, p. 158.

16.4 $5 billion in stolen goods per year supports heroin addiction in New York City alone. Most of the victims of the robberies and thefts are inner city residents and stores. *Reader's Digest*, September 1970, pp. 50–51.

16.5 Mob narcotics, gambling, and loan sharking are behind much crime. Hearst newspapers (March 1970) reprinted in *U.S.–House, OC Control*, pp. 423–24.

b. Mafia directs robberies, burglaries and thefts

16.6 "All types of crime" in the New England territory of Mafia boss Raymond Patriarca "are cleared by Patriarca." Among them are "bank robberies, hijackings, arson, jewel thefts and kidnapping." From the Taglianetti airtels, as summarized in *Life*, September 1, 1967, p. 44. (The FBI bug in Patriarca's office allowed police to thwart repeated murder attempts against two gangsters out of favor with Patriarca. Within two years after the bug was removed as a result of Johnson Administration orders, both men were murdered—one in Providence and the other in Miami.)[34]

16.7 The Mob is "responsible for much crime against property—burglary, automobile theft, bank robbery, arson." Salerno and Tompkins, *Crime Confederation*, p. 93.

16.8 The Mob lines up the market, assembles a burglary crew. Mafia defector Joseph Luparelli described how he operated during his apprentice years as a burglar. "On most of the jobs, we already had the stuff sold before we took it. Usually a businessman would contact a made guy [Mafia member] and say he wanted a certain type of merchandise, like wool cloth or machine parts. A deal would be made on the price. Then the made guy would put a crew together and send them out to get the stuff. He'd tell them where to go and what they'd find there." Meskil, *Luparelli Tapes*, p. 42.

16.9 A Mafia-backed burglary ring brutally murdered the daughter of Senator Charles Percy during a robbery of the Percy home. One morning in 1966, Charles H. Percy, then candidate for senator, was awakened by his wife's screams. He then entered the bedroom of his 21-year-old daughter Valerie and found her "agonizingly near death—her face, chest and stomach mutilated by stab wounds." By 1973, authorities were "all but certain" that Valerie Percy's murderers were members of a Mafia-backed band of thieves that flourished nationwide from 1965 to 1967. The gang, which operated with "almost military precision," would forward two-thirds of its take to the Mafia in return for planning expertise and the fencing of stolen merchandise. *Time*, December 10, 1973, p. 29.

16.10 The Mafia financed preparations and fenced the $1.5 million take for the 1962 mail robbery in Plymouth, Massachusetts. Mafia underboss Jerry Angiulo lent Billy Aggie $8,000 for planning and equipment for the robbery. As in several other jobs by the gang, Angiulo fenced the loot; i.e., he paid unmarked cash (in this instance 80 cents on the dollar) for the money, and then stashed away those bills that were traceable. According to information received by the federal government, the money "disappeared into Boston Mafia loan-shark operations within two days after the robbery."(B) A–Vincent Teresa, *My Life in the Mafia*, pp. 68–71; B–Bill Davidson, "The Mafia: How it Bleeds New England," *Saturday Evening Post*, November 18, 1967, p. 29.

16.11 A Mafioso stole $475,000 in furs: the store went bankrupt. New England Mafia defector Vincent Teresa described how, while perpetrating sophisticated multimillion dollar stolen stock schemes, he was always out for an easy score. In two burglaries of the same furrier on Boylston Street in Boston, Teresa and criminal associates stole $475,000 in furs, for which they received $100,000 in cash from Mafia underboss Henry Tameleo. Earlier, Teresa had twice burglarized a high-volume supermarket across from a night club he owned, netting $31,000. Teresa, *My Life in the Mafia*, pp. 102–3.

16.12 New York Mafia boss Carlo Gambino was arrested for conspiring to commit a $6 million armored-car robbery. The plan was foiled when a leader of the robbery gang was arrested for a similar crime in Boston. Mollenhoff, *Strike Force*, p. 234.

16.13 Twelve Mob-tied criminals were convicted of stealing $1 million in goods in four truck hijackings. *U.S.–Cargo Theft and OC*, p. 38.

16.14 One hundred murders and five robberies were charged in a November 1973 indictment to ten members of a New Jersey Mafia gang. The gang, associated with the Genovese Family, coupled robberies with traditional gambling and narcotics operations, including "the manufacture and distribution of cocaine and heroin." The murder victims included rivals, disloyal associates, suspected police informants, and potential prosecution witnesses. "The gang used bribery and threats of violence to influence jurors and witnesses." *New York Times*, November 30, 1973, pp. 1, 41.

c. The Mob's fencing network

16.15 One hundred million dollars from airport mail robberies were fenced with the Mob; the Mob got 85 percent of the take. Robert Cudak testified that between December 1967 and September 1970, he and his partners committed 125 mail thefts, stealing about $100 million in stocks, bonds, jewelry, cash, furs, and other items. This was confirmed by one of his partners, James Schaeffer, and by post office figures which showed that $34 million was lost in just 14 of the thefts. Both Cudak and Schaeffer testified that the fences to whom they passed the goods were always affiliated with the Mob, and that they received from the fences at most 15 percent of the value of the goods.

Cudak reported that the most important of his partners in the thefts was Mobster William Ricchiuti, and that a gang led by Mobster Anthony Capucci was also active in airport mail thefts. Cudak testified that his thefts would not have been profitable without the Mob fences with whom he dealt. *U.S.–Senate, OC and Stolen Securities, 1971*, pp. 210–17, 227, 230–31, 246–47, 250–54, 565–70.

16.16 Mob fences in action. In one Mob-engineered theft, a load of coffee was hijacked in New York at 4:30 p.m. and on sale at a supermarket by 5:15 p.m. the same day. One Mob fence operating in New York, Mike Jace, dealt in "silver bars, cash, credit cards, securities, jewels, rare coins, art treasures, and trailer loads of cigarettes, liquor, razor blades, furs, 'you name it.'" In monitored phone conversations, he discussed sales of driver's licenses, 3,800 airline tickets, 500,000 acres of land and a $500,000 diamond, and he inquired about the progress of a $340,000 cargo theft two days before it occurred.

During one conversation involving a casino transaction, Jace explained that the Mafia families appoint bosses "like a government." "The only ones other than [those with a certain ethnic background] who can get involved with them is one who gains their respect." *U.S.–Cargo Theft and OC*, pp. 38–42.

IV. ECONOMIC PENETRATION

17. Infiltration of Business

17.1 "The rodents in charcoal suits." "The Mafia muscles its way into thriving businesses, milks their assets, and then drives them into bankruptcy. Thousands of working men and women are forced to settle for starvation wages under sweetheart contracts between unions and companies dominated by the Mob. Insurance rates rise because of thefts, frauds, and acts of violence committed by the Mafia to wipe out competition and advance its supposedly legitimate business interests. And consumers suffer when the Mob gains a business monopoly and boosts prices as high as the traffic will bear."(B) A–Cook, *Secret Rulers*, p. 2; B–Dorman, *Payoff*, p. 238.

a. Extent of infiltration

17.2 Organized crime "owns or has decision-making influence in 50,000 commercial or industrial companies," including two multinational conglomerates. Grutzner, "How to Lock Out the Mafia," *Harvard Business Review*, March-April 1970, p. 49; *U.S.–Cargo Theft and OC*, pp. 28–29.

17.3 "Seventy separate types of businesses into which countless hoodlums had infiltrated." They were listed by the Kefauver Committee in 1951: "Advertising, amusement industry, awnings, automobiles, bakeries, ballrooms, banking, baseball, bonding, ... shipping, slot machines, steel, surplus property, tailoring, television manufacturing and sales, textiles, theaters (stage and movies), trucking, transportation, unions, and washing machines." Kefauver, *Crime in America*, reprinted in Tyler, *Organized Crime in America*, p. 292.

17.4 The Boston area: The Mafia owns "25 or 30 percent" of motels and restaurants. "They have their fingers in just about everything." From the testimony of Vincent Teresa in *U.S.–Senate, OC and Stolen Securities, 1971*, p. 816; also see Davidson, "The Mafia: How it Bleeds New England," *Saturday Evening Post*, November 18, 1967, p. 29.

17.5 Pennsylvania: "More than 375 major businesses," including a large defense contractor, "are controlled by the Mob." Medico Industries, a multimillion-dollar corporation in Luzerne County, received a $3.9 million Pentagon contract to produce 600,000 warheads for use in Vietnam. Company president Phillip Medico was described by northeastern Pennsylvania Mafia boss Russell Bufalino, in an FBI-recorded conversation, as a capo in his Mafia family. Bufalino was also an associate of company general manager William Medico, and "frequently visited the Medico offices."(B) A third Medico official, James Osticco, was a delegate to the 1957 Apalachin Mafia convention(C). Peter Maggio, a captain in the Angelo Bruno Family, was "a partner in Michael's Dairies, Inc., one of the largest dairy companies in Philadelphia." Michael's Dairies received contracts to provide milk to two military bases, and three other companies owned by Philadelphia Mafia figures received sizable government contracts.

A–Dorman, *Payoff*, pp. 254–55; B–*Time*, March 6, 1978, p. 21; C–*U.S.–Senate, McClellan Labor Hearings*, p. 12199.

17.6 New York: "In every kind of business." The businesses controlled by the Gambino Family include "insurance and real estate companies, a labor relations firm, construction, fuel oil distribution, dress factories." Private garbage disposal throughout New York City and several suburban areas is reportedly controlled by the Gambino Family, too. Meskil, *Don Carlo*, pp. 59–60.

17.7 Detroit: 100 Mafia-controlled businesses named in a chart prepared for the U.S. Senate by the Detroit Police. Businesses "owned, infiltrated, or influenced" by the Mafia, whose names and addresses were listed, include a 960-acre motel and restaurant complex and four other motels; several bars, restaurants, bakeries, car washes and food companies; the Hazel Park Race Track, 23 dry cleaning shops, a barber college and barber supply company; steel, aluminum, metal finishing and nickel surplus companies; extensive real estate holdings, including the Chrysler Office Building in Detroit and several properties in Arizona, Canada and Chicago; and construction, trucking, insurance, vending, concrete paving, die casting, cold storage, oil, linen, bus, and printing companies. *U.S.–Senate, OC and Narcotics Hearings*, p. 472.

☐☐☐☐☐☐☐☐☐☐☐☐☐☐☐☐☐☐☐☐☐☐☐

Mob defector Patsy Lepera described how a fraudulent financial statement based on stolen securities was used by some contractors who "belong[ed] to" Philadelphia Mafia boss Angelo Bruno. From Lepera and Goodman, *Memories of a Scam Man*, pp. 82–83:

What these apartment house guys do shows you how the mob operates. First, they borrow $200,000 on the statement, which of course is phony to begin with. Then they steal $100,000 right off the top and whack it up. With the rest, they break ground, put the footing in. It looks great—but they're murdering the subcontractors. They're not paying them. A subcontractor's got fifty coming ... they give him ten. He's hooked. They're paying off the inspectors. The inspector comes around, collects, reports back to the mortgage company everything is going along perfect. They borrow another $200,000 cash. They steal some of that and deduct the interest from their taxes. They ain't paying the subcontractors. Who are the subcontractors going to sue—Angelo Bruno? They're afraid they'll get put away. Most of the subcontractors who worked on those buildings went out of business...

Now you go to a legitimate buyer to sell this thing. ... These buildings are easy to sell. These buildings will make money, if they stay up.

☐☐☐☐☐☐☐☐☐☐☐☐☐☐☐☐☐☐☐☐☐☐☐

17.8 Chicago: "There are few types of businesses or industries that have not been touched at one time or another by organized crime investments." Among the long list of business fields in which underworld figures were reported operating are food manufacturing, steel, oil, dairy, stock brokerage, banking, real estate, and insurance. Names and addresses of a number of businesses controlled by the Chicago crime syndicate were listed. "In whatever activity organized crime engages, legitimate or illicit, its method of operation is the same—the maintenance of a monopoly through extortion and violence or imposing the fear of violence." From a 1960 report by the Chicago Crime Commission; quoted in Allsop, *The Bootleggers*, p. xiv.

17.9 Mob money movers are "constantly searching for new areas" to sink burgeoning profits. Grutzner, "How to Lock Out the Mafia," *Harvard Business Review,* March-April 1970, p. 49.

b. Methods of infiltration and operation

17.10 "Thievery is their way. Their executives are extortionists. Some of their salesmen are killers." Mob business operations are intricate, international in scope, but true-blue Mafia in character. Skimming receipts to avoid taxes is common. *Life,* September 8, 1967, p. 98.

17.11 "They take their habits with them wherever they go." "If things don't go right off the bat, they want to break somebody's head. ... Or they will put a gun to your head and say 'Here, sign this. Here is a buck. That makes it legal.'" From the testimony of Mafia defector Vincent Teresa in *U.S.–Senate, OC and Stolen Securities, 1971,* p. 837.

17.12 Failure of store owners to rent Mafia vending machines in New England "resulted in the wrecking of the store, fixtures, and bodily harm." The legitimate business people who were thus intimidated declined out of fear to testify against the Mafia hoodlums. From the testimony of Col. Walter E. Stone, Superintendent of the Rhode Island State Police, in *U.S.–OC and Narcotics Hearings,* p. 552.

17.13 Some Mob business practices described by the U.S. Chamber of Commerce. "Included among these methods are the forcing of businessmen to join 'dummy' or fraudulent associations; the use of planned bankruptcy to make fast profits and leave legitimate creditors 'high and dry'; the establishment of gambling operations within plants and elsewhere; the infiltration of labor unions and the formation of phony labor organizations as a means to intimidate legitimate businesses; the lending of money at extortionate rates (loansharking); the use of all types of practices—violent and otherwise—to reduce competition and secure monopoly in a given field (through threats, bribes, arson, personal and property assaults, etc.); and the illegal use of stocks, bonds, and cards." *U.S.–House, OC Control,* pp. 409–10.

17.14 Cash "being put into constructive purposes. . . . made them crazy." Defected Mob money mover Michael Raymond testified how the Mafia pressured him to milk the assets of one successful company for a few hundred thousand dollars in immediate gain, when millions could have been earned legitimately. And top Mafia defector Vincent Teresa provided an inside view into such thinking with his description of the attempted bust-out of a night club: "the night club was making money, but it was strictly a grind, and who needs a grind when there's easy money to be made?"(B) A–*U.S.–OC and Stolen Securities, 1971,* pp. 656–64, background pp. 637, 956, 1245–46; B–Teresa, *My Life in the Mafia,* p. 102.

17.15 A medical center in Florida and a Mafia-owned hospital in Boston serve as Mob meeting places. *Saturday Evening Post,* November 18, 1967, p. 29; *U.S.–OC and Stolen Securities, 1971,* p. 816; NBC Evening News, "Segment 3," December 12, 1977.

17.16 Business enterprises "serve a double function for the Mafia." Cleaners "are handy for over-the-counter bookie and loan-shark operations." A resort has buildings that can hold hijacked goods. "What better laboratory for making LSD ... than the back room of a late-hours Boston drugstore near three college campuses where customers abound?" Davidson, "The Mafia: How it Bleeds New England," *Saturday Evening Post*, November 18, 1967, p. 29.

17.17 "The dollar sign is stained . . . with blood." Kefauver, *Crime in America*, reprinted in Tyler, *Organized Crime in America*, p. 293.

17.18 Drain the assets and leave the shell to the public. From the testimony of Mob-connected securities fence Edward Wuenche in *U.S.–Senate, OC and Stolen Securities, 1971*, pp. 880–81.

17.19 Using captive unions to take over businesses. Meskil, *Don Carlo*, p. 21.

17.20 A loan shark debt leads to a silent partner. Cressey, *Theft of the Nation*, pp. 102–3.

17.21 "Once brought under the Mob's umbrella, a business almost always ceases to operate legitimately." From kickbacks to arson and murder. "The Mafia v. America," *Time*, August 22, 1969, p. 21.

17.22 Case studies of Mafia business methods. Several cases of Mafia infiltration, takeover, and draining of multimillion dollar businesses are described in detail. For example, the Mafia took over and bankrupted the Progressive Drug Company of New York, a formerly reputable $10 million-a-year wholesale business. It accomplished this using Twentieth Century Industries, a large conglomerate which owned drug, plastics, metals, mining, and soft-drink companies. The conglomerate was deeply involved with the Mafia, with Gambino Family underboss Aniello Dellacroce on its payroll;[35] its vice president took the Fifth Amendment when questioned by the New York State Investigation Commission. The first step in the Mafia takeover of Progressive was a switch in its labor contract from a reputable AFL-CIO union to a Teamsters local.

There can "no longer be any doubt in the minds of perceptive business executives that there has been a massive infiltration of the national economy by members of organized crime."

Grutzner, "How to Lock Out the Mafia," *Harvard Business Review*, March-April 1970, pp. 45–58; see Dorman, *Payoff*, p. 253.

c. Examples of Mob infiltration: banking and finance

17.23 The "pervasive influence of organized crime in the banking and securities industries." As noted by House Crime Committee Chairman Claude Pepper, who also pointed out "how extensively organized criminal elements have infiltrated the banking, securities and insurance industries." *U.S.–House, OC and Worthless Securities*, pp. 1, 242.

17.24 A rash of bank collapses in the 1960s, plus the nation's three largest bank failures in the 1970s, were caused by Mob infiltration and draining (see section 16.2 of text). Cook, *Secret Rulers*, pp. 367; Jeff Gerth, address at *The Politics of Conspiracy*, workshop on organized crime (Boston University, George Sherman Union, East Ballroom), February 1, 1975, tape-recorded by author; *New York Times*, September 10, 1973, pp. 1ff.

17.25 "Hoodlum connections with some of the biggest banks in the country" were noted by former House Banking Committee Chairman Wright Patman. Representative Patman added that "criminal control of banks is widespread. It reaches from New York to Miami to Chicago, and even to some small towns. I would say there are dozens of banks influenced or owned by hoodlums." Cook, *Secret Rulers*, pp. 367–68.

17.26 Draining banks instead of robbing them. Reid, *Grim Reapers*, p. 21.

17.27 Hundreds of depositors lost their savings in the collapse of a Louisiana Loan and Thrift Company. "About one third of the deposits had been loaned to, or through, organized crime enterprises." In 1970, federal prosecution was pending against Louisiana Attorney General Jack Gremillion, State Representative Salvatore Anzelmo, and others, who were charged with fraudulent acts contributing to the bankruptcy. *U.S.–House, OC Control*, p. 431.

17.28 "Substantial infiltration of the banking, brokerage, insurance, and other financial communities by many persons who are directly or indirectly connected with organized crime." Details were reported from first-hand experience in the 122-page testimony of Michael Raymond, a defected Mob money mover. Raymond described numerous instances in which Mob financial transactions were aided by corrupt judges, police, and regulatory personnel. *U.S.–Senate, OC and Stolen Securities, 1971*, pp. 636–757, especially 712–13, 734–37; background, pp. 637–38, 659–64, 956, 1245–46.

17.29 "Hoodlum infiltration into the loan and bonding business." *U.S.–Senate, Kefauver Report, Third Interim*, p. 178.

17.30 Top Mobster Meyer Lansky took steps in 1968 to form a Miami stock exchange. Ex-Washington lobbyist Robert Winter-Berger described how he was paid $500 to do some research for the project, which was being handled by his associate, Mob-tied Washington lobbyist Nathan Voloshen. Winter-Berger learned that Voloshen "had met with Lansky at least three times to discuss the project," and that his fee had been paid by Lansky. Winter-Berger, *Washington Payoff*, pp. 130–31.

17.31 Organized crime works with several New York banks. From the testimony of New York Assistant District Attorney Murray Gross in *U.S.–OC and Stolen Securities, 1971*, pp. 96–97.

17.32 Heavy loans and overdrafts for Mobsters were coupled with political influence and interest-free government accounts in a bank in Brooklyn, N.Y. Waller, *Swiss Bank Connection*, pp. 140–43.

17.33 The numerous benefits derived by the Mob from controlling a bank. Dorman, *Payoff*, p. 260; Grutzner, "How to Lock Out the Mafia," *Harvard Business Review*, March-April 1970, p. 51.

17.34 A friendly banker. New York Mobsters[36] Lou Shomberg and Stanley Polley "could reach in any direction that they wanted. Polley set up a loan for me at Bankers Trust Co. It took me 15 minutes to walk in and walk out with $50,000. ... It was a hook loan. The banker belonged to me." From the testimony of defected

Mob money mover Michael Raymond in *U.S.–Senate, OC and Stolen Securities, 1971*, p. 665.

17.35 Mob penetration of the financial industry "underpins the whole economy of the United States, virtually all private ownership." As noted by Senator Charles Percy, who also commented, "as the mob moves in and extends its tentacles ... you get a reaction of terror, of intimidation, of extortion and murder." *U.S.–Senate, OC and Stolen Securities, 1971*, p. 737.

d. Examples of Mob infiltration: trucking, garbage collection, and garment manufacture in New York

17.36 The remarkable success of the Ross Trucking Company. The Ross Trucking Company, whose underworld connections were suspected by a member of the New York Waterfront Commission, hauls half the bananas imported into the New York area—despite its "exorbitant" rates and the lack of protective insulation in its trucks. Some jobbers questioned about the arrangement complained about being forced to use Ross, while others refused to comment or expressed fear of discussing the subject. From a series of articles by Stanley Penn in the *Wall Street Journal* (1969), reprinted in Gage, *Mafia, U.S.A.*, pp. 340–43.

17.37 "The destroyers move into your town." "Dangerously unsound buildings or highways or vehicles," at "outrageously high costs" characterize city contracts obtained by Mafia-controlled businesses. An example: garbage collection in Mount Vernon, New York. Gage, "How Organized Crime Invades the Home," *Good Housekeeping*, August 1971, pp. 68ff.

17.38 Murdering to monopoly. Two companies were competing for the multimillion dollar garbage removal business of New York's Westchester county. One was Rex Carting Company, a reputable firm which had a labor agreement with Teamsters Local 456, a legitimate union run by Everett Doyle and John Acropolis. The other was Westchester Carting Company, which was operated by Mafia soldier[37] Nick Ratteni, who spent 7½ years at Sing Sing Prison, and by Joey Surprise, also a Sing Sing alumnus, with several arrests and a reversed first-degree murder conviction. Westchester Carting had a labor contract with Teamsters Local 27, run by Secretary-Treasurer Joe Parisi, a Mobster with 11 arrests and one rape conviction, and Bernard Adelstein, with five arrests and a reversed extortion conviction.
Westchester Carting Company expanded its operations as "businessmen were threatened, equipment of competitors was burned and destroyed, and reluctant store keepers were picketed." In 1952 at a Teamster convention, legitimate union leader Acropolis was threatened by Mobster Parisi. "Three weeks after the convention, Acropolis was shot to death as he opened the door to his house. A month later, Rex Carting sold out to Westchester Carting, which now had monopoly control of the garbage removal business in Westchester County." Robert F. Kennedy, *The Enemy Within*, pp. 230–32.

17.39 "Customers ended up footing the bill." A leading dress manufacturer found its existence threatened by hijackings and sabotage when it refused to use a trucking firm owned by one of Mafia boss Thomas Lucchese's relatives. When the dress company finally switched to the recommended firm, its troubles stopped but its trucking costs rose 10 percent. The increase was passed on to consumers. Gage, "How Organized Crime Invades the Home," *Good Housekeeping*, August 1971, p. 118.

17.40 A Mafia interest in 20 percent of firms in the New York garment industry. "The first choice a New York dress manufacturer has to make, outside the high fashion field, is whether he wants a racketeer as a partner, creditor or competitor. No matter which way he turns, he will probably have a racketeer as his trucker." Mafia garment firms characteristically pay low wages to workers, often blacks and Puerto Ricans in nonunion shops. Hutchinson, *Imperfect Union*, pp. 91–92.

e. Bankruptcy fraud

17.41 At least 200 Mob bankruptcy frauds are discovered each year, "each leaving up to 250 creditors holding the bag." Total debts in each case "usually run upward of $200,000." Dorman, *Payoff*, pp. 238–39.

17.42 Six bust-outs by Vincent Teresa: "We took manufacturers and insurance companies for more than five million bucks." Teresa and underworld partners would first set up a company, fronted by someone with a good credit rating, and lease a store or large building. The company would build up a credit line by ordering and paying for merchandise, then place huge orders a few months before Christmas. They would sell as much of this merchandise as they could, then surreptitiously send all the remaining goods to a fence. All that was left were a few broken toys, crates, or appliances they hauled in from a junk pile. Then they would "hire a torch, a good arsonist." After the building burned, they would "collect the insurance and declare bankruptcy."

Teresa used this technique on Auction City in Somerville, Massachusetts, and on Joseph's Department Store in Boston, the latter a five-story building before it was torched. From these bust-outs, as well as from every one of Teresa's operations, New England Mafia boss Raymond Patriarca and underboss Henry Tameleo got a percentage of the proceeds. Teresa, *My Life in the Mafia*, pp. 99–101.

17.43 The bust-out of Murray Packing Co. The Mafia muscled into the prosperous family meat business when the owners borrowed from a finance company that proved to be a Gambino Family loan shark operation. In eight days the Mafia siphoned $745,000 out of the company, and it soon went into bankruptcy, leaving $1.3 million in debts. Grutzner, "How to Lock Out the Mafia," *Harvard Business Review*, March-April 1970, p. 53; Dorman, *Payoff*, pp. 239–41.

17.44 Fifteen underworld figures, including three Mafia captains, were arrested by the FBI in a bankruptcy fraud operation in the Detroit-Toledo area. Mollenhoff, *Strike Force*, p. 234.

17.45 Five reputed Mob figures, including a cousin of Carlo Gambino, were arrested in a New York bust-out scheme. The same five men had been indicted five months earlier in an almost identical case. *New York Times*, August 22, 1973, p. 17.

17.46 Some operations of the versatile king of scam, Chicago Mafioso Phil Alderisio. Among the incidents tied to Alderisio and associates were a $600,000 scam of an auto dealership and a $1 million fire that destroyed the Fullerton Metals Company. Four Alderisio associates were convicted of a $50,000 scam of Vogue Credit Jewelers, based on the testimony of one witness, Joseph Polito. He was murdered by four shotgun blasts on March 7, 1967. Demaris, *Captive City* , pp. 80–83.

**17.47 "About a half-billion dollars a year goes to Cosa Nostra as profits"
from bankruptcy frauds.** More individual cases are described. Cressey, *Theft of
the Nation*, pp. 105–6.

18. Infiltration of Labor

**18.1 The Mafia "kept cropping up in almost every investigation that was
made into improper activities in labor and management."** Of the 58 delegates apprehended at the 1957 Mafia conclave at Apalachin, 23 "were directly connected with labor unions or with labor-management bargaining groups." John Mc-
Clellan, *Crime Without Punishment*, p. 116.

18.2 "Control through strictly muscle." Mob defector Louis Mastriana, who
was president of one union in New Jersey and ran another "paper" local, testified
that he knew of few unions "that are not controlled by the [crime] families." When
asked to explain how the Mafia controlled unions, he explained: "You got a goon
squad. A lot of people want to go home at night but they don't want to go home all
busted up." When asked by Senator Huddleston, "Do you mean this is still going
on?" Mastriana replied, "Of course it goes on. It goes on every day." *U.S.–Senate, OC
and Stolen Securities, 1973*, p. 168.

18.3 Methods of extortion and embezzlement using labor unions. Paper
locals, sweetheart contracts, extortion through threat of labor strike, and embezzlement of union funds are basic Mob labor practices. Cressey, *Theft of the Nation*,
pp. 95–99.

**18.4 "Underworld infiltration into labor-management affairs . . . a
shocking pattern across the country."** The Mob is "increasing its effort to seize
control of legitimate businesses and unions," leading to "monopoly control" in
some industries. Robert Kennedy, *The Enemy Within*, pp. 228–29.

18.5 The Mob's entry into the labor field. In the early 1930s, the Syndicate's
income was sharply reduced by the repeal of Prohibition and the Depression,
while some of the "biggest and most solvent treasuries in the world were in the
labor unions." The Capone gang, with years of experience in supplying thugs to
break strikes for employers, turned its attention to the unions. The Syndicate began applying "steamroller pressure": murders and bombings were used to take
over unions and capture their treasuries. By 1932, as Chicago Crime Commission
President Frank Loesch reported, the Chicago Mob controlled or extracted tribute
from two-thirds of all Chicago area unions, while the AFL conceded that 28 of its
Chicago locals were dominated by the underworld. From *The Stolen Years*, by ex-
Chicago gangster Roger Touhy and Ray Brennan, reprinted in Tyler, *Organized
Crime in America*, pp. 193–95; also Hutchinson, *Imperfect Union*, pp. 116–17.

a. The construction unions

**18.6 Extracting millions of Pentagon dollars through a Mafia-controlled
union.** During the late 1960s, a Pentagon construction contract in St. Louis was
handled by the Mafia-controlled Laborers Local 42. At the time, the local was led
by Lou Shoulders, a Mob killer who was himself murdered gangland-style in 1972.
Among those who turned up on the government payroll were "a small army of
Mob soldiers, relatives and high-rankers," some of whom actually showed up at

the construction site—to run gambling operations, shake down workers for kick-backs, and instill terror into project supervisors. Millions of dollars were si-phoned off in phony overtime payments and paychecks to ghost workers.

One of those who drew $8,000 in a four-month period was Mike Trupiano, a nephew of St. Louis Mafia boss Tony Giardano, who had been arrested for bur-glary and brandishing a deadly weapon. Trupiano, who never came close to the plant while under surveillance during a five workday period, later became busi-ness agent of Laborers Local 110, with a fat salary and expense account. Over a dozen other named Mafia members and associates were on the payroll, including "a Syndicate arsonist," Joseph Scalise. Not surprisingly, the cost of the Pentagon contract came to $22 million, almost triple the original estimate.

The Mafia-controlled Laborers Local 42 also had jurisdiction over the construc-tion of a St. Louis bridge. This job, too, was characterized by terror and inflated costs: two union officials who protested the arrangements were brutally beaten, and one union member was murdered on the construction site. Indeed, St. Louis unions in general have been plagued with racketeering, "in which the Mafia domi-nated crime syndicate has played the major role. Mob-controlled unions hold much of the available labor in a virtual hammerlock." It was thus not surprising that the 25 to 50 percent productivity at the Pentagon project was shrugged off by Army brass as "typical of the St. Louis area."

Denny Walsh, "The Mob: It Racks Up Overtime on a Government Payroll," *Life*, February 14, 1969, pp. 52–56; for background on Local 42 boss Lou Shoulders see "Shoulders Bid $7,000 on Contract to Kill," *St. Louis Post Dispatch*, March 1, 1974.

☐☐☐☐☐☐☐☐☐☐☐☐☐☐☐☐☐☐☐☐☐☐☐☐

Glimco, Joseph Paul [profile of a Mafia labor leader]

Record dates back to 1923, more than 38 arrests: disorderly conduct, va-grancy, assault with auto, . . . armed robbery, assault with gun with intent to murder, murder. Prime suspect in at least 4 murders. . . . Tried for murder in 1928 after a deathbed statement by victim, acquitted. A 17-count indict-ment for violations of Taft-Hartley Act was dismissed by Federal Judge Mi-chael L. Igoe in August 1965. Convictions: larceny, . . . conspiracy to violate the Volstead Act. . . . Citizenship granted in 1943 by Federal Judge Michael L. Igoe after State Representative Andrew A. Euzzino had subject's police record destroyed. Took Fifth 80 times before Kefauver Committee, and 152 times before McClellan Committee. . . .

Modus Operandi: The Syndicate's top labor czar; boss of at least 15 Teamster locals; a power in the jukebox and coin machine industry, and a hidden owner of a wide variety of legitimate enterprises—a front for top Syndicate bosses, who in turn uses fronts. A Mafia don with a reputation as a vicious and brutal gangster who enforces his edicts with violence and murder.

Ovid Demaris, *Captive City*, pp. 342–43.
☐☐☐☐☐☐☐☐☐☐☐☐☐☐☐☐☐☐☐☐☐☐☐☐

18.7 Extorting $35,000 from a New Jersey contractor. Mafia boss Nick Del-more offered labor relations assistance to developers of a large apartment com-plex. "Within weeks, pickets from a Cosa Nostra-controlled union had shut down the entire project." The developers then paid $35,000 to Delmore and his Mafia partner, Sam DeCavalcante, to settle the strike. William Schulz, "The Mob's Grip in New Jersey," *Reader's Digest*, February 1971, p. 113.

18.8 Pervasive Mafia extortion in New Jersey construction. The DeCavalcante tapes bore out the boast of New Jersey Mafia boss Sam DeCavalcante that no new apartment units were built in his territory without his approval. DeCavalcante, in cooperation with construction unions and the Teamsters, would guarantee labor peace for a hefty fee, permitting builders to save $1,000 a unit through the use of nonunion workers. As one union leader told DeCavalcante, "Right now the picture is ideal for you, Sam. . . . I told the guy he's gotta be one hundred percent union. . . . I got the pickets ready and everything. . . . He knows if he doesn't go your way, he's gotta go one hundred percent." DeCavalcante associate Gaetano Vastola explained, "When I sit down with the boss [the builder] I tell him how much it's gonna cost him in welfare, hospitalization and all that. . . . [I'll say] 'It's gonna cost one hundred thousand dollars a year. Let's cut it in half, and forget about it.'" Not content with shaking down contractors, DeCavalcante and his associates also formed their own union—Warehousemen's Local 242—to pocket the $5 a month in dues paid by the members. Mollenhoff, *Strike Force*, pp. 8–18.

18.9 Description of a New York Mafia union leader's operations. Bobbie Cervone was business agent of Mason Tenders Local 13, which the New York State Investigation Commission identified as Mob-dominated. Cervone was also a Mafia associate and loan shark, who was questioned in a number of murders and arrested three times but never convicted.

Cervone's union operation was described by a former Mob associate, Vincent Siciliano, who had worked in the union. Cervone drew an official salary of $175 per week from the union but owned a Rolls-Royce, a Cadillac, houses in Long Island and Florida, a couple million dollars in a Swiss bank account, and several million dollars in assets in the U. S. Much of this loot came from his union's welfare funds. Collecting 8 percent of his members' salaries, Cervone amassed $1 million a year in welfare payments. Little of this was ever disbursed to the membership. Siciliano explained, "If one of the union members get hurt or something, Bobbie can just make a deal—maybe throw in a few bucks for the doctor. Who is the guy going to kick to? He could end up dead instead of sick if he tried."

"Do you think that *people* build all those buildings around New York? *Ghosts* build most of them—that's people who just aren't." [Emphasis in original.] Whenever contractors hired workers from Cervone's Mason Tenders Union, the steward would record workers who were not there, sometimes more "ghosts" than workers; the paychecks went to Cervone. "The contractor expects this. He already has raised his prices to take care of it. . . . And you wonder why it costs so much to put up a building? Besides all of this, every time a guy wants to build, he also has to pay something straight out to Bobbie."

Cervone made additional income from "concession money," a cut from bookmaking, loan sharking, prostitution, and dope operations on construction sites under his jurisdiction. This income covered large bribes, which secured him top political and police connections. Cervone was eventually suspended from the union post when his racketeering involvements were publicized. But "he never for a second lost control"; his replacement was his former chauffeur.

Vincent Siciliano, *Unless They Kill Me First*, pp. 123, 134–37. See also *Newsweek*, January 5, 1981, p. 37.

18.10 A Mafia representative serves as labor troubleshooter for one of the world's largest construction firms. Stephen Broccoli, alias "Peanuts the Dwarf," was shop steward for Local 251 of the Laborers Union in Providence. He was also employed by the Gilbain Building Company, "one of the largest construction companies in the world," where he acted as an intermediary between labor and management. Broccoli had been convicted three times for armed robbery and according to information from Rhode Island police, was placed on the Gilbain payroll by New England Mafia boss Raymond Patriarca. From the testimony of Colonel Walter Stone, Superintendent of Rhode Island State Police, in *U.S.–Senate, OC and Narcotics Hearings*, p. 557.

18.11 The International Union of Operating Engineers is plagued with multimillion dollar embezzlement, undemocratic management, violence, and murder; its leadership is allied with the Mafia. The McClellan Committee reported that "literally millions of dollars have vanished from the IUOE treasury, often reappearing in the form of improved living standards for union bigwigs." The Committee described kickbacks, collusion with employers, and sweetheart contracts, some officials owning the very companies with which they negotiated. It found rule by intimidation and violence, with little democratic control by the 280,000 members. And the Committee reported connections and joint extortion ventures between International president William Maloney and Chicago Mobsters. The situation was summed up by Dennis Ziegler, who led a dissident movement which was subjected to armed violence by Maloney and Teamster-Syndicate figures. Ziegler noted the union's reputation of "being dominated and controlled by the worst forms of racketeers, hoodlums, and murderers in America." He was later murdered after having received a death threat from Maloney. Hutchinson, *Imperfect Union*, pp. 189–94.

18.12 "The hidden wiring that links politicians, trade union leaders and the crime syndicate." In the early 1960s, *Chicago Tribune* reporter George Bliss wrote a Pulitzer Prize-winning series on the Chicago Metropolitan Sanitary District. He wrote that through faking time sheets, padding payrolls, inflating wage scales, kicking back insurance money, and rigging contracts and real estate leases, Mob-connected employees were bilking Chicago taxpayers of "at least $5 million a year." Richard B. Ogilvie, then candidate for sheriff, charged that the district was "a rest home and haven for relatives and friends of the Chicago crime syndicate," and listed 36 district workers connected to the Mob. A new district superintendent, appointed in the heat of the scandal, then probed deeper and committed what the *Chicago Daily News* termed "the unforgivable political sin": exposing "some of the hidden wiring that links politicians, trade union leaders and the crime syndicate." A few hours after the superintendent asked for evidence in his probe, he started his car and escaped death only when four sticks of dynamite "failed to detonate because a wire had slipped off a spark plug."

One item investigated was a $3 million sewer, built under a contract questionably awarded to a construction firm reputed to have close ties to the Mob. Because of "serious construction defects," the sewer caused $5 million in damages to a nearby water treatment facility and had to be replaced. Demaris, *Captive City*, pp. 207–13.

18.13 "The Mafia and its associates inside labor": "looting some pension funds, terrorizing officials, rank-and-filers and employers alike, shaking down contractors and extorting millions of dollars annually." Covering a conference of federal officials from strike forces against organized crime, noted labor columnist Victor Riesel wrote: "it was reported that anyone looking too closely at some New York construction unions would get 'a bullet in the back. ...' Despite gory killings and car bombings of St. Louis pipefitters (plumbers) union local 562, 'the racketeering surface hasn't been scratched there. ...' national AFL-CIO construction union chiefs ... can't control many of their locals. Frequently, trustees aren't put in because there are few men who'll dare attempt to take over a Mafia-controlled local union until there is a conviction."

Riesel declared that the time has come to confront racketeers "from New York with its complex construction unions to Mafiosi now surveying 'open' cities reaching from Atlanta to Los Angeles." *New Orleans Times Picayune*, September 27, 1973, p. 11.

18.14 Terrorism in the building trades. A sickening barrage of dynamitings, arson, vicious beatings, and murders against nonunion contractors was related in a four-part series in *Reader's Digest*. Cases from across the country were described, representative of "172 separate instances of violence, vandalism and similar harassment" against contractors reported in 1972 alone. The violence allowed the racketeer-infested unions to continue "wholesale shakedowns of the contractors, while stealing from and cheating their own members." As one union member explained, "it is a standing phrase in construction work that the Mafia has taken over, thus the violence—and the kickbacks and bullying systems so obvious to the workers."

Charles Stevenson, *Reader's Digest*, June 1973, pp. 89–94; July 1973, pp. 79–83; August 1973, pp. 153–57; December 1973, pp. 85–90.

b. Restaurant workers' unions

18.15 The Mafia takeover of both the unions and business association in the restaurant field in Chicago; 124 bombings and arsons by 1965. "Goon squads smashed windows, slugged owners and patrons with baseball bats, slashed tires, dumped sugar in gasoline tanks, tossed stinkbombs, set fires and planted black-powder and dynamite bombs, and when everything else failed, resorted to murder." In sweetheart contracts arranged by the unions—one of which was operated by a Mafia lieutenant without even the pretext of a front—everyone but the workers benefited. After a new epidemic of bombing and arson in the early 1960s, the *Chicago Daily News* declared that the risk to Chicagoans had "passed the point of toleration," while the *American* deemed the situation an emergency. Demaris, *Captive City*, pp. 22–29; McClellan, *Crime Without Punishment*, pp. 138–46.

18.16 Mafia "paper" unions in New York. Mafia representatives "organized" New York restaurants using intimidation, picketing, and sabotage. Restaurant owners or employees paid monthly union "dues" without receiving union cards, union scale wages or any benefits whatsoever. From the *Wall Street Journal* (1968–70), reprinted in Gartner, *Crime and Business*, pp. 194–96.

c. The International Longshoremen's Association

18.17 The "Mob runs the docks in this country." The International Longshoremen's Association (ILA) is run by the Genovese, Gambino, and Marcello Mafia families. One International vice president, Tony Scotto, is a captain in the Gambino Family; Scotto took the Fifth Amendment when asked in 1970 by New York State's joint legislative committee on crime whether he was a member of the Mafia.[38] He was convicted on a federal racketeering count in 1979.[39] Through the cooperation of ILA officials, the Mob carries out massive systematic hijackings at U.S. docks. "In effect, the Mafia and the Longshoremen's Union have been able to put their own tax on every item moving in or out of the ports they control." NBC Evening News, "Segment 3," September 6, 1977 and September 7, 1977.

18.18 "In the upper echelons there is an amalgamation" between the Mafia, Teamsters, and ILA. As stated in 1967 by Henry Peterson, then chief of the Justice Department's organized crime and racketeering section. Reid, *Grim Reapers*, p. 275.

18.19 Mafia control of New York docks in the 1940s and 1950s. A special waterfront investigation by the Brooklyn district attorney's office in 1940 revealed that Mafia boss Albert Anastasia "had been stealing hundreds of thousands of dollars from unions" and that there had been "crimes of extortion, larceny of union funds, destruction of union books and falsification of new ones, kickbacks in wages for the benefit of racketeers." And the New York State Crime Commission, after an investigation in the early 1950s that logged 4,000 interviews and 30,000 pages of testimony, found that "at least thirty percent of officials of the ILA longshore locals have police records. . . . Through their powers as union officials, they place their confederates in key positions on the docks, shake down steamship and stevedoring companies by threats of work stoppages, operate the lucrative public loading business, and carry on such activities as pilferage, loan-sharking and gambling."

The membership was found to be "virtually disenfranchised." The Commission cited 22 ILA hiring bosses who participated in or encouraged "assault, organized theft, pilferage, extortion, kickbacks, loan-sharking, gambling, payroll padding, other criminal activities and even murder." The Commission named a number of Mobsters behind the criminal network at the New York docks, and noted that the steady deterioration of the competitive position of the New York port was due mostly to "criminal or quasi-criminal practices."

U.S.–Senate, Kefauver Report, Third Interim, pp. 130–32; Hutchinson, *Imperfect Union*, pp. 98–107.

18.20 Mafia control of New York docks in the 1960s and 1970s. Despite changes in leadership and image, the Mafia still maintains ironclad control of the New York and New Jersey docks and the area ILA locals. *Life*, September 8, 1967, pp. 101–3; Meskil, *Don Carlo*, pp. 159–66.

18.21 Port Newark is "a flat Cosa Nostra concession." Gambling, loan sharking, and cargo theft are rampant. *Life*, September 8, 1967, p. 103; *Reader's Digest*, February 1971, p. 113.

18.22 The ILA, like the Teamsters, was ousted from the AFL for infestation by "gangsters, racketeers and thugs." In 1953, the ILA was expelled by the AFL, which reported that the ILA "has permitted gangsters, racketeers and thugs to fasten themselves to the body of its organizations, infecting it with corruption and destroying its integrity, its effectiveness and its trade-union character." Hutchinson, *Imperfect Union*, p. 297.

(Note: The Teamsters Union, at its top levels, functions essentially as a "mob subsidiary."[40] Since Mafia-Teamster ties have been amply treated in several books and the news media, and a review of these connections would occupy a volume in itself, they are not discussed here. Several references in the preceding 24 chapters, however, should be adequate to demonstrate the closeness of this relationship.)

d. Motion picture and theatrical workers' unions

18.23 Convictions were secured against Chicago Mafia members and associates in the 1940s for multimillion dollar labor extortion in the motion picture industry. After Chicago Mobsters captured one local of the International Alliance of Theatre Stage Employees (IATSE), they decided to take control of the International. So in 1934, top Syndicate figures and their gunmen descended upon the International's convention in Louisville, and Mob front George Browne was elected president without one dissenting vote. The Mob then persuaded the Hollywood studios to give the IATSE jurisdiction over its employees by closing every theatre from St. Louis to Chicago.

With the entire motion picture industry now in the Mob's grip, Mob representative Willie Bioff contacted industry spokesman Nicholas Schenck, president of Loew's, and demanded $2 million against the threat of a nationwide strike. A deal was arranged in which major studios would pay the Mob $50,000 a year, minor companies $25,000; the payments were to continue indefinitely. But federal investigators uncovered the scheme and sent several Chicago Mafia members and associates to prison. From the essay "Crime on the Labor Front" by Malcolm Johnson (1950), reprinted in Tyler, *Organized Crime in America*, pp. 199–205; also see Hutchinson, *Imperfect Union*, pp. 134–37.

Note: According to investigative reporter Jeff Gerth, "the movie industry since the 1930s has been controlled by organized crime."[41] For current material on Mob-Hollywood connections see *New York Times*, June 27, 1976, p. 20; *New York Times Magazine*, December 26, 1976, pp. 18ff; *Public Affairs Series Special Report 13: The Mafia Today* (Los Angeles: Knight Publishing, 1977), pp. 54–61.

18.24 A 72-year-old projectionist opposing a syndicate union boss was murdered. In 1960, Herman Posner, a 72-year-old projectionist, attempted to lead a rebel movement in the Mafia-controlled IATSE Chicago Local 110. But Posner was knifed to death a few days before he was to turn over to federal investigators evidence of shakedowns and kickbacks. His killers fled with the evidence. "Posner's murder was the seventh in the bloody history of the union." Demaris, *Captive City*, p. 35.

e. Coin machine workers' unions

18.25 The McClellan Committee uncovered "permeation of racket figures" in coin machine unions and businesses in 13 states. "Every new witness brought familiar names and stories of familiar methods—intimidation and violence." John McClellan, *Crime Without Punishment*, pp. 212–14; see also Hutchinson, *Imperfect Union*, pp. 211–13.

18.26 The Teamsters used standard tactics to capture coin machine locals from the International Brotherhood of Electrical Workers (IBEW). Teamsters Local 396, led by convicted perjurer[42] Frank Matula, began raiding IBEW coin machine locations in California. In response, members of IBEW Local 1052 picketed Teamster headquarters in Los Angeles, and one Local 1052 official told the McClellan Committee what happened: "We put twenty-one men on the first day. The next day Teamsters put an equal number in behind each one of our pickets with spikes in their shoes. They ripped our men's legs and sent most of them to the hospital."

When the same IBEW official later tried to organize coin machine operators in San Diego, Mobster Frank Bompensiero demanded 50 percent of the local's income. After the official refused to comply, he was viciously assaulted and man-handled. Also related are several other cases of assault, sabotage, and murder directed against persons and companies that resisted Mob control in the coin machine field.

Hutchinson, *Imperfect Union*, pp. 224–25, 212–18; Kennedy, *The Enemy Within*, pp. 239–40.

□□□□□□□□□□□□□□□□□□□□□□□

[New York Mafioso[43]] Joey Gallo was a labor-management racketeer and chief suspect in a murder where the victim was shot so many times in the head that facial recognition was impossible. Down in my office before he testified [in the McClellan labor hearings], we asked him about his part in it and received a giggle and a shrug in reply.

The Gallo brothers had formed their own International union. . . . Milton Green testified to the way their union was operated. Green was a jukebox distributor who opposed his association's signing up with the Gallo-DeGrandis local, feeling it was dominated by gangsters. He went to a meeting and voiced his opposition, even though he had been warned to keep quiet. His objections were overruled. He described what happened on his way home: "They came out with steel bars and they split my skull open for me and I was taken to the hospital."

When he appeared before the Committee, seven months later, Milton Green was a thin, wan, pathetic figure, still without full use of his faculties. He will never completely recover.

Robert Kennedy, *The Enemy Within*, pp. 238–39.

□□□□□□□□□□□□□□□□□□□□□□□

18.27 Operators were forced to buy Mob-counterfeited records and promote "Syndicate-owned" singers on Mob jukeboxes. Hutchinson, *Imperfect Union*, p. 217; Kennedy, *The Enemy Within*, pp. 242–43.

18.28 A coin machine union servicing non-Mob pinball machines was harassed by the prosecutor and police in Lake County, Indiana. John Testo, the coin machine union leader, told the McClellan Committee that prosecutor Metro Holovachka ordered him to stop his union activities, warning him: "Listen, I am going to get something on you. I am going to put you in jail." Police selectively raided non-Mob machines until they were removed, or removed the machines themselves. Syndicate machines were then installed, which were ignored by the police. The clear indication of official corruption was reinforced by Holovachka's subsequent tax evasion conviction, based on unreported earnings four times his official salary whose source he refused to divulge.

Testo's independent union went out of business. As Robert Kennedy commented, when Mobsters need a labor union they create one, and "when they feel it is more beneficial they put a labor organization out of existence." Hutchinson, *Imperfect Union*, pp. 218–219; see Kennedy, *The Enemy Within*, pp. 242–43; McClellan, *Crime Without Punishment*, p. 289.

f. Unions in New York and surrounding states

18.29 Unskilled workers are exploited by sweetheart contracts and embezzlement of union funds. In one case discussed, the New York State Investigating Commission exposed the workings of a New York local of the Laborers International union. Electronic surveillance revealed that it was controlled by a Mafia soldier on orders from Carlo Gambino. "Union members, under sweetheart contracts, were forced to work for wages below union scale." The welfare and pension funds were so thoroughly plundered that they went bankrupt. Union stewards ran loan sharking and gambling on job sites. "Mafia rule was enforced with threats, shootings, even bombings." In factories under the jurisdiction of other Mafia unions, employees worked for poverty wages in substandard conditions. Methvin, "How the Mafia Preys on the Poor," *Reader's Digest,* September 1970, p. 53; Kennedy, *The Enemy Within,* pp. 215–16.

18.30 Mafia labor czar Frank Costello gave New Yorkers a puppet show. Costello was asked by the night manager of a Manhattan hotel to avoid using the hotel's steam baths. The next day, not one waiter, custodian, maid, or elevator operator came to work at the hotel. Within hours, the hotel's manager was "frantically begging him to return." Gage, *Mafia, U.S.A.*, p. 19.

18.31 Mafioso[44] Johnny Dio straightened out any union problems. "Senator, I had a dress shop, a negligee and dress contract, on Prospect Avenue. I never belonged in any union. If I got in trouble, any union organizer came around, all I had to do was call up John Dio or Tommy Dio and all my troubles were straightened out." From the testimony of Mafia defector Joseph Valachi in *U.S.–Senate, OC and Narcotics Hearings,* p. 227.

18.32 The S.G.S. labor relations firm was hired by leading New York businesses; the "G" stood for Mafia boss Carlo Gambino. When service and maintenance men struck the Chrysler Building in 1960, the owners hired Gambino's S.G.S. Associates. The strike was soon settled after armed goons arrived in Cadillacs and ran the elevators. Grutzner, "How to Lock Out the Mafia," *Harvard Business Review,* March-April 1970, pp. 53–54. Similar services rendered by Gambino Family underboss[45] Carmine Lombardozzi are described in Kennedy, *The Enemy Within,* pp. 229–30.

18.33 The traditional mix of labor racketeering, business infiltration, illegal activities and corruption in Camden County, New Jersey. Camden County prosecutor Thomas Shusted charged that up to 25 county businesses and unions were infiltrated by organized crime. Shusted noted that organized crime could not operate in the county "without, at least, the tacit cooperation of certain police and civilian officials." One Camden County Police detective sergeant summarized the Mafia's interest in unions this way: "It's the control of people, control for many uses. Not only do they collect dues, they can recruit men for sharking, gambling, muscle, shakedowns." *Philadelphia Inquirer,* January 22, 1974.

18.34 Profile of a New York Mafia labor boss. Tony "Ducks" Corallo, a caporegime in the New York Lucchese Family,[46] controlled five Teamster locals and locals of such other unions as the Toy and Novelty Workers Union, the Painters and Decorators Union, the Food Handlers Union, the Conduit Workers Union, and the United Textile Workers. Workers in many of Corallo's unions were victimized by sweetheart contracts, substandard wages and poor working conditions. Corallo served six months in prison on a narcotics violation, and was described by a New York Police official as involved in "gambling, labor racketeering, extortion, strongarm and murder."(B) During 1963 Senate rackets hearings, he invoked the Fifth

Amendment 120 times. A–Dorman, *Payoff*, pp. 76–77; B–*U.S.–Senate, OC and Narcotics Hearings*, pp. 282–83.

18.35 Goons, bombs, embezzlement, and extortion in Mafia-controlled unions in New Jersey. As usual, everyone benefited but the captive members of the Mafia-controlled unions. Schulz, "The Mob's Grip on New Jersey," *Reader's Digest*, February 1971, p. 113.

19. Estimated Annual Income

In 1981, *Newsweek* reported that official estimates of the Mob's annual income "usually begin at $120 billion."[47] The following additional estimates are listed by source, year, and annual amount (figures in parentheses represent value in 1980 dollars, adjusted for inflation using the consumer price index): Congressman Dante, B. Fascell, former Chairman of the Legal and Monetary Affairs Subcommittee of the House Committee on Government Operations, 1969, "at least $60 billion" ($138 billion);[48] organized crime expert, Ralph Salerno, 1969, at least $40 billion ($92 billion);[49] journalist Stanley Penn, in the *Wall Street Journal*, 1969, "as much as $50 billion" ($115 billion);[50] Congressman Robert McClory, 1970, "between $50 to $60 billion" ($108 billion to $130 billion);[51] *Time*, 1977, "at least $48 billion" ($71 billion).[52] Experts in Chicago and New Orleans estimated in 1964 that the Mob's combined annual income in just those two cities was $3.1 billion ($8.4 billion).[53]

Time magazine estimated that fully half of the Mob's huge annual income is realized as profit[54]—money pocketed by Mafia members and top associates. The rest goes mainly to lower level functionaries and outside assistants: a bookie or numbers runner,[55] a truck driver who sets up a hijacking,[56] a Wall Street clerk who pilfers stock certificates,[57] a businessman who fronts a bankruptcy fraud,[58] or a nonmember associate who assaults and murders for the Mafia.[59] One of the Mob's largest expenses goes toward corruption of police and politicians at all levels of government. In expert estimates and case studies in several U.S. cities, the percentage of Mob income paid out in bribes has been found to average at least 15 percent.[60] Applying that percentage to a conservative income estimate of $100 billion per year yields an annual corruption expenditure of $15 billion.[61]

V. CORRUPTION OF AMERICAN GOVERNMENT

20. Scope and Methods of Corruption

20.1 "Organized crime is, in the vernacular, taking us over." U.S. Attorney Frederick B. Lacey, commenting on Mob corruption in New Jersey, quoted in Dorman, *Payoff*, p. 53.

20.2 The Mafia has "locked a strangle hold on American politics." Mafia political operations "tear at the fabric of American society" to an extent "greater than ever before in our history." Dorman, *Payoff*, pp. 13–14.

20.3 The Mob cannot operate without corruption. Former Mob money mover Michael Raymond: "There is no area in organized crime that can operate without the duplicity of the police, the agencies involved. I have had enormous experience in the area. I have seen it. ... [for example] there is no numbers operation in the world that can operate without police protection. It doesn't exist. Anyone who tells you that is lying." *U.S.–Senate, OC and Stolen Securities, 1971*, pp. 670–71.

20.4 "A war on organized crime is inseparable from a war on political corruption. In this fact may lie hidden the reason why it is so difficult for political leadership to wage a comprehensive war on organized crime—for to do so would be to risk severe political consequences." From a 1967 report by 23 Republican members of the U.S. House of Representatives, quoted in Cressey, *Theft of the Nation*, p. 275.

a. Some methods of corruption

20.5 Each Mafia family has at least one specialist in corruption who "bribes, buys, intimidates, threatens, negotiates, and sweet-talks himself into a relationship with police, public officials, and anyone else who might help 'family' members maintain immunity from arrest, prosecution, and punishment." Cressey, *Theft of the Nation*, p. 250.

□□□□□□□□□□□□□□□□□□□□□□

At the heart of every successful gangster's operation is the Fix—the working arrangement with key police and elected officials and business and union executives. ... It can be accomplished by putting in fear, through means as unsubtle as a crack over the head, an arm broken by twisting, an implied disclosure of family skeletons, a hoarse voice on the phone, a timely murder. It can be accomplished by campaign "contributions" or by outright bribes. It can be attained through employment of public relations counsels. ... It can be helped immeasurably with cheap devices like easy "loans" to a reporter whose tastes outrun his income.

Life, September 1, 1967, p. 22.

□□□□□□□□□□□□□□□□□□□□□□

20.6 An anti-Mob candidate for sheriff in Newport, Kentucky was drugged, put to bed with a stripper, arrested by cooperative police. The residents of Newport, Kentucky became fed up with the wide-open gambling and vice operations in their city, "recognized the relation of crime to politics, and decided the only chance for reform was to elect some honest officials." Ex-football star George Ratterman was persuaded to run for sheriff, and despite the frame against him, which city residents did not swallow, was elected in 1961. Soon after Ratterman took office, as Attorney General Robert Kennedy reported, gambling "virtually ceased" in Newport. Hank Messick and Burt Goldblatt, *The Mobs and the Mafia* (New York: Ballantine, 1972), pp. 184–87.

20.7 Sexual blackmail used to help lure a politician to Hollywood. A Mob corrupter described how one captive politician became excessively greedy and had to be removed from office. "Some of our guys wanted to put out a 'contract' on him, but I persuaded them that knocking him off would just bring us more heat than we could afford. ... I had created him and now I had to eliminate him."

The corrupter played on the politician's secret desire to be a movie star, with the help of a leading actor and Mobster with a secret interest in a movie studio. To blackmail the actor into cooperating, a party was arranged for the actor and politician which was "stocked with whores" and wired with "a half-dozen hidden microphones." The politician "bit like a fish on a worm ... resigned from office, packed his stuff and left. ... We picked out another guy we could control and elected him to the vacant office." Dorman, *Payoff*, pp. 91–93.

20.8 Hooking a policeman or official through minor bribes and favors.
One official who ignored the criminal record of a Mafia soldier in a liquor license application was threatened with exposure of that transaction if he did not approve other licenses for the Mob. Soon, the official was deeply involved in corruption. He was discovered and indicted, but he was murdered before the trial began. Another compromised officeholder related, "I forgot that those gangsters are animals. When I gave them my hand, they began nibbling at my fingertips. Before I knew it, they had swallowed my arm and were gnawing on my shoulders." Cressey, *Theft of the Nation*, pp. 288–89.

20.9 Getting out the vote for a Mob candidate. To elect their chosen slate of candidates, some New York Mobsters offered a free play on the numbers to all neighborhood residents who voted, and provided Mob-employed chauffeurs and baby sitters to assist the voters. A record turnout resulted and the Mob candidates were elected. Dorman, *Payoff*, p. 15.

20.10 The systematic use of politics by a Mafia underboss. New England Mafia underboss Henry Tameleo "used politics to get the things [boss Raymond] Patriarca wanted. He could reach out to a governor's office or a police precinct or a city council or a state legislature, even a congressman to get the things the mob needed." Teresa, *My Life in the Mafia*, p. 81.

☐☐☐☐☐☐☐☐☐☐☐☐☐☐☐☐☐☐☐

Let's say, for example, you have a judge or a senator along on your junket, and plenty of them went on mine. You arrange for him to be with a hooker, to get a blow job in the suite you've rented. At the same time, the place is set up so that you can get pictures and tape recordings of what is going on. Then, when one of your people gets in trouble with the law, or the mob needs votes on a bill they want passed, a copy of that photograph or tape recording is sent to him.

> Vincent Teresa, who ran gambling junkets to casinos in Las Vegas and abroad, *My Life in the Mafia*, p. 232.

☐☐☐☐☐☐☐☐☐☐☐☐☐☐☐☐☐☐☐

20.11 The transcript of a bribe offer from a Chicago Mafioso to a policeman. A Chicago Mafioso, Joseph Aiuppa, and a former Cook County sheriff's vice squad commander tried to persuade Detective Donald Shaw to provide a loophole for an indicted Mafia underling in a bribery case. Shaw, however, wore a small transmitter and the conversation was recorded by officers in a nearby parked car. Aiuppa assured Shaw that he was an upstanding citizen being wrongly harassed by an out-of-town guy—"like all those Negroes and demonstrators"—and that Shaw would be stupid not to bend the law for him. Aiuppa promised Shaw $2,000 to establish a loophole in the bribery case, plus $100 a month for regular information on gambling raids. Aiuppa also promised to arrange set-up raids for Shaw, and never to involve him in an embarrassing situation. "If you walked into a place and saw me there and your superior said, 'Pinch him,' I never even met you. Go ahead and pinch me. I go along with the show." Dorman, *Payoff*, pp. 45–49.

20.12 "Official cover-up: A flagrant case in point." *Life* magazine noted that cover-up inevitably accompanies Mob corruption. One example *Life* cited was the censored report on organized crime by President Johnson's crime commission (*U.S.–Task Force Report*). Among the suppressed items, from a section by Notre Dame Professor G. Robert Blakey:

"The success of the Chicago group [of the Mob] has been primarily attributable to its ability to corrupt the law enforcement processes, including police officials and members of the judiciary. . . .

"Control, sometimes direct, has been exercised over local, state and federal officials and representatives. Men have been told when to run or not run for office or how to vote or not to vote on legislative issues or [for judges] how to decide motions to suppress evidence or judgments of acquittal." *Life*, September 8, 1967, p. 103.

21. Police Corruption

21.1 Police corruption, almost always tied to Mob-controlled illegal gambling, has been uncovered again and again throughout the country. The New York City Police Department, the oldest in the nation, has been repeatedly rocked by major scandals involving massive firings, resignations, and reorganizations. Such scandals have occurred in the early 1930s, 1950, 1959, 1964, and 1971, each involving gambling or other Mob-controlled operations. Similar scandals have shaken police departments in cities throughout the country, including Albany, Atlanta, Baltimore, Chicago, Denver, Detroit, Kansas City, Louisville, New Orleans, Newark, Philadelphia, Reading, Reno, San Francisco, and Seattle. Maas, *Serpico*, pp. 11, 137–40, 299–302, passim; Methvin, "How Organized Crime Corrupts Our Law Enforcers," *Reader's Digest*, January 1972, pp. 85–89.

21.2 The Kefauver Committee "received evidence of corruption of law enforcement officers and connivance with criminal gangs in every city in which it held hearings." *U.S.–Senate, Kefauver Report, Third Interim*, p. 184.

21.3 Illegal gambling cannot exist without police corruption—the Massachusetts Crime Commission. The Commission reported in 1957 that "it seems to have been a universal finding by crime survey commissions that organized illegal gambling could not exist within a community without the knowledge and protection of the local police. For all practical purposes, that is a fair statement. . . . The existence of an illegal gambling operation is as apparent as any other type of retail business." The Commission concluded that police corruption was made possible largely by the connection between racketeers and politicians. Cook, *Two Dollar Bet*, pp. 7–8.

21.4 Organized crime cannot operate without police protection—Malcolm X. "Wherever you have organized crime, that type of crime cannot exist other than with the consent of the police, the knowledge of the police and the co-operation of the police. You'll agree that you can't run a number in your neighborhood. . . . A prostitute can't turn a trick on the block. . . . A man can't push drugs anywhere along the avenue without the police knowing it. And they pay off the police so they will not get arrested. I know what I'm talking about—I used to be out there." Malcolm X noted, "The police are all right. . . . there's some good ones and some bad ones. But they usually send the bad ones to Harlem." From a speech by Malcolm X, transcribed in *By Any Means Necessary*, p. 50.

21.5 A Yale University study showed that one out of five policemen "was observed in a criminal violation." The 1966 study monitored the actions of 597 policemen selected at random in Boston, New York, and Washington, D.C. Twenty percent of the policemen committed crimes, *even though they knew they were being watched*, including "actual theft, receiving protection payoffs, and accepting money to alter sworn testimony." Maas, *Serpico*, pp. 138–39.

21.6 The rookie policeman is faced with a climate of corruption. After a 1971 investigation of police corruption in New York City, the Knapp Commission concluded that "the underlying problem is that the climate is inhospitable to attempts to uncover acts of corruption and protective of those who are corrupt. The rookie is faced with the situation where it is easier for him to become corrupt than to remain honest." Defected Mob killer Joseph Barboza described the situation this way: "Every other cop is taking money, and a new police officer gets on the force and his partner is taking money, his zeal kind of leaves him, and then, also, probably because of the low pay. The enticement of big money. "(B) A–Methvin, "How Organized Crime Corrupts Our Law Enforcers," *Reader's Digest*, January 1972, p. 88; B–*U.S.–House, OC in Sports*, p. 765.

21.7 The Mob got data from a national police intelligence association. The Law Enforcement Intelligence Unit, established to exchange information on crime among local police departments, has been plagued with leaks to the Mob since its inception in 1956. Its Pueblo, Colorado chapter was expelled in 1960 for passing sensitive intelligence to the underworld and its Denver and Kansas City chapters were expelled in ensuing years on corruption charges. In 1966, a former Dallas policeman stole a photocopy of an FBI file on the Mafia. In September 1978, the Las Vegas chapter was thrown out when FBI wiretaps revealed that an intelligence specialist with the Las Vegas police had leaked information to reputed Mobsters. *Washington Post*, November 24, 1978, pp. A1, A8.

a. Chicago

21.8 "Corruption Behind the Swinging Clubs. Walker Report: Chicago Cops Rioted; Life Report: Mob Payoffs to Police." Summarizing the Walker Report, *Life* magazine noted that during the 1968 Democratic Convention, several Chicago police units "simply dissolved in violent gangs and attacked protesters, press and bystanders indiscriminately" in "what can only be called a police riot." *Life* concluded that discipline under pressure requires trust and morale. "And it is clear that such trust and morale could not exist in Chicago, where an important section of the police structure, from patrolman to high rank in headquarters, has been—and is today—seriously corrupted by payoffs and favors from the Mob."

Following are highlights from this lengthy *Life* magazine report:

Chicago Police Captain William Duffy, head of the intelligence division, was a "superb cop" of "national stature in law enforcement." In September 1964 Duffy led a raid by police and FBI agents on a numbers operation. Police found a list of payoffs containing names and badge numbers of 469 Chicago policemen in three districts. Police headquarters took no action.

In January 1968, Duffy's men and federal officials raided a numbers operation run by Mob racketeers. In this raid of "one of a score" of Mob numbers operations in Chicago, "ice lists" were confiscated, as reproduced in *Life*, showing payoffs to police "in 10 of Chicago's 21 police districts." Also shown were 38 special payments, supplementing standard-scale graft, to individual policemen for extra services. Again no action was taken on the graft. Six weeks after a Mob gambling boss boasted publicly that "we got a promise that Duffy will go," Captain Duffy was relieved of his command of the intelligence division and transferred.

In 1963, the U.S. Justice Department filed an 18-page report which "named 29 policemen alleged to be trafficking with or taking payoffs from the Mob." Nothing was done about the charges and most of the 29, including six with high positions, were still on the force in 1968. One on the list, Lt. Paul Quinn, was a top Chicago police liaison to City Hall in 1968.

A number of policemen actually worked for the Mob. One detective talked almost daily with a Mafia killer, Phil Alderisio, and moonlighted for Alderisio by tapping the phones of bookies suspected of cheating the Mob. And gambling boss Angelo Volpe kept another detective as a confidant and occasional chauffeur-bodyguard. As *Life* summarized, "there is a climate around Chicago police in which organized crime thrives like jungle shrubbery."

Sandy Smith, "Corruption Behind the Swinging Clubs," *Life*, December 6, 1968, pp. 35–43; see also Demaris, *Captive City*, pp. 233–320, for dozens of similar cases.

21.9 A policeman suspended for service to a Mobster became chief of police of a Chicago suburb. When Rocco Salvatore was tried for a speeding violation in 1966, Melrose Park Police Sergeant Dominic Cimino attested to Salvatore's fine character and told the court that Salvatore needed his driver's license for his business. Cimino was later temporarily suspended from the Melrose Park Force when it surfaced that Salvatore's "business" was acting as chauffeur and bodyguard for Chicago Mafioso[62] Sam Battaglia. But in 1967, Dominic Cimino became chief of police of Melrose Park. Shortly afterward, reports surfaced that Cimino often met with Charles (Chuck) Nicoletti, a Mob enforcer and terrorist. "News accounts related that Chief Cimino was observed conferring with Nicoletti almost daily." Cressey, *Theft of the Nation*, pp. 262–63.

21.10 Comments of an informant on the Chicago Police Force. "The going rate for promotions to sergeant today [in the Chicago Police Force] runs around $3,000 to $5,000—depends on how much they think they can take off the man." Lieutenancies cost about $10,000 and captaincies at least $15,000. The bribes are usually paid by sponsors in "the Party or the Outfit [Mafia]."

The informant cited the case of "an Outfit hood by the name of Mike Glitta, who owns the Shore club on North Clark Street." His brother-in-law, Vince Serritella, became a police sergeant, "and Glitta bragged it cost him five grand." Glitta intended to have Serritella assigned to the state's attorney's office where he could be of maximum service to Glitta. The informant mentioned other cases of Outfit-connected cops. "Believe me, there are a lot of sleepers in the department. I mean policemen who are Outfit connected, hoodlum related."

The informant noted that some police captains ask Mobsters for tips to make an arrest. The Mobsters "give them a stick-up team or something that's not Outfit connected. Or they'll pinch some free-lancing whore or knock over a little Negro-operated policy wheel."

From a lengthy interview with an unnamed informant on the Chicago Police Force, transcribed in Demaris, *Captive City*, pp. 257–61.

b. Detroit

21.11 "The continual brazen effort of the Mafia to secure their immunity from law enforcement by direct briberies of police officials." Detroit Police Chief George Edwards related several examples of this effort. He also noted that in

1939 "we saw the former mayor of the city of Detroit, the former prosecuting attorney, the former sheriff, the former superintendent of police, and roughly 250 police officers all go to jail for the acceptance of graft in order to let gambling operate in the city of Detroit." *U.S.–Senate, OC and Narcotics Hearings*, pp. 402–5.

21.12 Six of Detroit's top 12 policemen were found on a Mafia bribe list. In 1965, agents under Detective Vince Piersante arrested a Mafia member in the act of giving a Detroit cop his monthly payoff. Piersante confiscated a notebook showing bribes to 134 Detroit policemen, including six of the top 12 members of the force. The arrested Mafioso was sentenced to just 60 days in prison of a possible five-year term. But Piersante "was hounded by his superiors with reprisals ranging from an attempt to frame him on a charge of stealing seized property to harassment and transfers of his men." In 1971 federal and local law enforcement officials arrested 151 persons, including 16 Detroit policemen, for participating in illegal gambling. *Reader's Digest*, January 1972, p. 86.

c. Philadelphia

21.13 A Pennsylvania crime commission reported in 1974 that "police corruption in Philadelphia is ongoing, widespread, systematic, and occurring at all levels of the police department." In every police district and every rank, from patrolman to inspector, corruption was found. Gamblers, racketeers, prostitutes, and night club owners often paid off the police, as detailed in the report. More than 400 policemen were identified as having received cash, goods, meals or sex. Raymond C. Brecht, "Gamblers Pay and Flourish, Probers Find," *Philadelphia Evening Bulletin*, March 10, 1974.

d. Boston, Providence and other New England cities

21.14 "Crooked cops were the mainstay of the New England Mob." Mafia defector Vincent Teresa reported that overall police protection was handled by New England Mafia underboss[63] Jerry Angiulo, who claimed he could control 300 of Boston's 360-odd detectives. Providence, Rhode Island boss Raymond Patriarca "had half the city on his payroll."

Teresa related how in several New England cities, dozens of cops would go into Mob hangouts "to get their presents and their envelopes at Christmas time." Teresa described how he cultivated one particular Boston policeman, who for "a G-note" ($1,000) ignored $160,000 in stolen furs in Teresa's possession, and for $2,500 blocked a police investigation of $50,000 in fraudulent bank loans. The policeman fed Teresa information regularly and performed similar favors in exchange for payoffs.

"There were so many cops on the mob's pad, it's really hard to remember them all." When a policeman gave the Mafia a hard time, Patriarca would call Angiulo, who would get in touch with one of the high-ranking officers on the pad. Soon the policeman would be transferred to another district where he would be out of the Mob's way.

"People have got to understand that there are lots of Reveres, lots of Bostons in this country." Policemen are on the take, Teresa noted, because they don't earn much and get disillusioned when they see the politicians taking and judges dismissing cases they've slaved over. "It don't take long for a cop to get the message. Everyone's making money and he isn't, so he just joins the parade."

Teresa, *My Life in the Mafia*, pp. 146–51.

e. Columbus, Ohio

21.15 Corrupt police frustrate, impede, and arrest federal officers conducting a gambling investigation. Assistant Attorney General Will Wilson described flagrant gambling-related corruption and misbehavior among the leadership and most of the officers of the Columbus Police vice squad. Senator John McClellan noted that "the Mafia can operate successfully on the scale that it does, only because of the connivance and incompetence of key law enforcement personnel." *U.S.–House, OC Control*, pp. 88–89.

f. New York City

21.16 The pad: payoffs as systematic as paychecks in every one of New York's 80 police precincts. In a series of speeches to Congress in 1960, preacher-politician Adam Clayton Powell charged that the Mob was wiping out black numbers operators in Harlem, detailed the mechanics of Mob-police payoffs, and pinpointed some specific numbers games and persons involved. Monthly payoffs for one typical numbers game ran as follows (punctuation changed from original list format): "Division-$420, Borough Headquarters-$275, Police Commissioner-$275, 1st Deputy Commissioner-$275, Chief Inspector-$275 [these categories referred to departments and not necessarily to individuals]. Precinct: Captain-$50, 23 sergeants at $10-$230, 8 lieutenants-$260, uniformed officers on post $192, radio cars (2 shifts)-$192. Detective squad: 33 detectives-$330, Detective Lieutenant-$50, Detective Sergeant-$25. Total: $2,749."

In 1960, the same year that Powell publicized the situation in Harlem, the *New York Post* published a series of investigative reports on the numbers game which furnished a monthly breakdown of payoffs similar to that described by Powell. The *Post* reported that there were 90 numbers spots in a single section of Harlem, each of which paid off about $2,500 a month, yielding an annual police payoff of $2,500,000 in just that one Harlem area from numbers alone. The *Post* concluded that the numbers racket was controlled by "call them what you like—the East Harlem Mob, the Syndicate, the Mafia." And it quoted one expert source who noted "there are 80 precincts in New York City, and in all my experience in all five boroughs, I have not found a single one in which a Pad for policy isn't maintained in one form or another."

Cook, *Two Dollar Bet*, pp. 134–36; Ted Poston, "The Numbers Racket," *New York Post* (1960) reprinted in Tyler, *Organized Crime in America*, pp. 260–71. The same systematic and pervasive corruption was described from first-hand experience by the heroic New York policeman, Frank Serpico, in Maas, *Serpico*, passim.

21.17 Mobster Stanley Polley "had enormous contact with the Police Department in New York, with political figures." Defected Mob money mover Michael Raymond testified about one of his former associates, Stanley Polley, a fixer for the Mob. "When I met Stanley and as the relationship developed, I had met many high police officials in New York. I sat in front of more police stations in New York waiting for Stanley to come out than I even knew existed. ... This was virtually a nightly occurrence. At all odd hours of the morning we would meet with high police officials. I have been witness to conversations with high police officials involving many, shall we say, breaches of security in the police world." *U.S.–Senate, OC and Stolen Securities, 1971*, p. 649.

21.18 A 1972 investigation of a police gambling unit in Brooklyn revealed that "70 percent of the police in the special unit were taking payments

from organized-crime gamblers." In 1973, 16 policemen were convicted in the Brooklyn Supreme Court of accepting "protection money from gamblers linked to organized crime." Payoffs averaged more than $10,000 per year.(B) A–Gage, *Mafia, U.S.A.*, p. 14; B–*New York Times*, June 10, 1973, p. 43; see also Meskil, *Luparelli Tapes*, p. 168.
(See chapter 10 of text for material on police corruption in Dallas.)

g. Beyond malfeasance: cases of Mob-police criminal complicity

21.19 "The creeping paralysis of law enforcement" from gambling-tied corruption "contributes to a breakdown in connection with other fields of crime." It was also noted that "wherever organized criminal gangs are entrenched in a particular community and have been given the green light to operate, it is not unusual to see the forces of law enforcement being used against their competitors, while protected operations are left alone." Such selective enforcement was found in New York, Miami, and Los Angeles, forcing one bookmaking syndicate in Miami "to capitulate to the demands of the Accardo-Guzik-Fischetti crime syndicate." *U.S.–Senate, Kefauver Report, Third Interim*, p. 182.

21.20 A New York policeman made dumdum bullets for the Mafia to kill federal "stool pigeons." A New York policeman agreed to make "dumdum bullets" for a Mafia soldier, knowing that they would be used to kill federal informants. A transcript of a bugged conversation between the Mafioso and policeman provides details of the arrangement. After the policeman promised to supply bullets which would make a hole "you can put your fist through," the Mafioso informed him that they would be used to shoot federal informers: "Nobody else. Only stool pigeons. I mean, like, the cops like stool pigeons when they go, especially if they're federal stool pigeons, right?" Cressey, *Theft of the Nation*, pp. 191–93.

21.21 "Involvement in corruption by dozens of Indianapolis policemen . . . has led some members in the department to criminal activities." The *Indianapolis Star*, the FBI, and a federal organized crime strike force investigated widespread corruption among Indianapolis police. A murder and a car bombing shortly after the *Star*'s disclosures were believed linked to the investigation. *New York Times*, March 4, 1974, p. 19.

21.22 "Some officials bend over backwards to help their Mafia friends." A sheriff in Florida some years ago furnished "special policing" for some illegal gambling casinos; the sheriff "even deputized the men who drove the armored cars carrying the casino's profits to the bank." Gage, *Mafia, U.S.A.*, p. 269.

21.23 New York policemen were charged in the disappearance of $70 million worth of confiscated heroin and cocaine. State special prosecutor Maurice Nadjari charged that "less than 10" policemen planned it, "and then solicited the underworld for aid" in selling the 400 pounds of narcotics. Fifty-seven pounds of heroin were from the "French Connection" case. *New York Times*, October 15, 1973, p. 41.

21.24 Two Baltimore policemen were suspended in connection with the disappearance of 248 bags of heroin. The narcotic theft scandal broke during an investigation of illegal gambling payoffs which led to the indictments of six city policemen. *New York Times*, January 28, 1973, p. 39, June 15, 1973, p. 13.

21.25 The Chicago Police in the Capone era: A private army for the underworld. It was officially estimated that in 1923, 60 percent of Chicago policemen were engaged in bootlegging, "not in connivance, but actually." Allsop, *The Bootleggers*, p. 17.

21.26 The Chicago Police today: Regularly committing every crime, including Mafia-directed murder. "Policemen still regularly commit burglary, robbery, felonious assault, bribery, auto theft, extortion, larceny, brutality and murder. They still moonlight for the Syndicate as procurers, narcotics peddlers, bootleggers, collectors and assassins. Cases are made against policemen in nearly all these categories monthly. In the majority of the incidents, they are exonerated by the courts and continue on the police payroll."

One case, which led to what Intelligence Division Chief William Duffy described as "the first crime-syndicate murder conviction in my memory," involved four Chicago policemen who were also members of a Syndicate narcotics ring. One member of that ring, Chicago Policeman Thomas N. Durso, was convicted with Syndicate terrorist Michael Gargano of the murder of federal narcotics informant Anthony Moschiano. Durso and Gargano were each sentenced to 100 to 150 years in prison. Demaris, *Captive City*, pp. 65–68, 264–65.

22. Corruption and Assault of the Judicial Process

22.1 Some standard Mob judicial procedures. Bribe the police and the district attorney. "Get to the witnesses"; some "can be intimidated, some can be bought, and some must be liquidated." Hit the jury with "the usual round of bribes and threats." Provide unlimited funds for the best lawyers. If all else fails, arrange soft jobs, special treatment, and financial support for Mobsters sent to prison. Tyler, *Organized Crime in America*, pp. 231–33.

□□□□□□□□□□□□□□□□□□□□□□□
You and I know what the problem is. They buy off the judge, they buy off the prosecutor, they buy off the sheriff, and they buy off the law enforcement officers locally, directly or indirectly.

Senator Henry Jackson, in *U.S.–Senate, Gambling and OC*, p. 31.
□□□□□□□□□□□□□□□□□□□□□□□

a. Intimidation and murder of witnesses

22.2 Prosecutions against the Mob have too often failed "because essential witnesses have been killed, bribed or intimidated into forgetfulness." "In connection with a prosecution for embezzlement of union funds, based upon a Teamsters-Mafia alliance in Kansas City, key federal witness Robert Williams had to be preserved by shipping him to the Canal Zone in 1962." In the same case, "one of the codefendants was Floyd Hayes, who was convicted and then became a cooperative government witness. He made a series of statements to prosecutors about unsolved syndicate crimes which had extended over many years. . . . his cooperation surfaced as a witness in a perjury trial. About six weeks later he was murdered. Five or more prosecutions died with him." From the statement of New Orleans Metropolitan Crime Commission Director Aaron Kohn in *U.S.–House, OC Control*, pp. 430–31.

22.3 Twenty-two observers, no witnesses in a Mob murder in Providence. Jackie Nazarian, an assassin for New England Mafia boss Raymond Patriarca, murdered George Baletto in the Bella Napoli Cafe in Providence. Of the 22 patrons there, one man, an ex-boxer named Eddie Hannan, considered testifying but he was garroted by Nazarian and left in a dump. Reid, *Grim Reapers*, p. 66.

22.4 Mob slayings are difficult to solve primarily because of reluctance of witnesses to furnish information to law enforcement officials. From the testimony of Tampa Police Chief Neil Brown in *U.S.–Senate, OC and Narcotics Hearings*, p. 536.

b. Corruption of judges and prosecutors

22.5 Extensive Mob corruption in the nation's largest court system. A federal report named 16 circuit court judges in the Cook County, Illinois judiciary who had "at one time or another been contacted by various representatives of the crime syndicate to handle specific cases." The report found that the Mob routinely used its political clout to assign its cases to such judges. Specifically, it noted that 90 percent of all cases in one year involving arrests in Loop strip joints were brought before five judges, who handed down "very few, if any," guilty verdicts.

One blatant example was the trial of George Ammirati, the 45-year-old son of a former Mob boss, who described himself to police as a "self-employed bookie" and boasted of his top Syndicate contacts. On December 3, 1962, Ammirati shot a man who tried to disarm him in a barroom brawl. Ammirati followed his victim outside, and fired a second, fatal shot into his back. Ammirati then hired an attorney specializing in Mob clientele, "which automatically assured him of a dozen continuances in the quest for a sympathetic judge."

The case was finally heard before Judge George B. Weiss, who dispensed with a jury at Ammirati's request, tried the case in one day, and dismissed the charges of murder and voluntary manslaughter. Judge Weiss found Ammirati guilty of only involuntary manslaughter, carrying a one-to-ten year prison term, and suspended his sentence to just 90 days in jail plus five years probation. The judge defended his decision to newsmen by claiming that Ammirati was "a good family man" and that the shots "were on the accidental side."
Demaris, *Captive City*, pp. 296–98.

22.6 a. The judicial and political connections of Colombo Family members Joseph Yackovelli and Carmine Persico. Yackovelli and Persico "had a lot of connections with politicians and judges." Persico's contacts included both state and federal judges. Reported by Mafia defector Joseph Luparelli in Meskil, *Luparelli Tapes*, p. 217.

22.6 b. A Mobster killed a black couple at a party before 30 guests; Yackovelli and Persico secured his freedom. Charles Shepard and his common law wife, Shirley Green, were hired to serve at a New Year's Eve party at the Wayne, New Jersey home of Mobster Joseph (Fatty) Russo. During the party, Shepard angered Russo by drinking and dancing with one of the guests. Russo then got his gun and fired six shots into Shepard. Shirley Green "was screaming and fighting to get out of there but a couple of guys held on to her. Fatty went back upstairs and reloaded. Then he came down and shot her too." The bodies were found in a roadside snow bank on the morning of January 1, 1971.

Russo later went to Colombo Family underboss Joseph Yackovelli for assistance, as described by their mutual associate, Joseph Luparelli, who was present during the conversation. Yackovelli told Russo, "I know the chief of police out there" and "probably could get in touch with the judge. But it would cost you." Russo said he would "go as high as a hundred thousand dollars." Yackovelli then discussed the matter with another Colombo Family member, Carmine Persico, assuring Persico "the guy's all right. He just blew his top and killed two blacks." Persico told Yackovelli, "We'll see what we can do."

In Russo's December 1971 trial, one of the 30 guests at the party gave an eyewitness account of both murders. But the trial was aborted when Passaic County Court Judge Louis Schwartz dismissed the jurors after 15 hours of deliberations, claiming that they were exhausted. In June 1972 Russo was again tried, and Judge Schwartz again declared a mistrial, explaining that one of the jurors felt ill and that the two alternate jurors said they had discussed the case. Russo totally escaped punishment for the two murders.

Meskil, *Luparelli Tapes*, pp. 217–23.

22.6 c. Yackovelli and Persico were indicted for obstruction of justice; then freed through suspicious judicial maneuvers. Colombo Family members Joseph Yackovelli and Carmine Persico, along with Joseph Russo and Carmine DiMase, were indicted for conspiracy to thwart the Shepard-Green murder prosecution of Russo. On September 24, 1973, Federal Judge John Bartels, presiding over the trial of Persico and Russo, made the unusual request that the press refuse to report the backgrounds of the defendants. The next day, after the press ignored the order, Judge Bartels "declared a mistrial . . . dismissed the jury and began trying the case himself." One week later, Judge Bartels dismissed the indictment against all four defendants. *New York Times,* September 25, 1973, p. 24; September 26, 1973, p. 43; October 3, 1973, p. 50.

22.7 New York Mafia boss Thomas Lucchese "was for many years a patron of a number of public officials in New York City." Twenty-two judges were guests of Lucchese in just two of the many charity dinners he attended. And the tables were turned on one occasion when Lucchese's hotel tab was picked up by an assistant U.S. attorney, Armand Chankalian. Reid, *Grim Reapers*, p. 41.

22.8 New York State Supreme Court Justice Dominic Rinaldi investigated for alleged judicial misconduct in "wrist-slapping" sentences to Mafia hoodlums. The New York State special prosecutor's office investigated the cases of Lucchese captain Paul Vario, who received a $250 fine from Rinaldi on a bribery conviction, instead of the maximum sentence of a year in jail, and of Mafia associate Salvatore Agro, who received only a suspended sentence on charges connected with a million-dollar swindle. Rinaldi also gave a conditional discharge to a narcotics dealer who had a long criminal record and had violated parole by continuing to sell narcotics. The New York State Committee on Crime found that this conditional discharge was "illegal" and resulted in "no punishment whatsoever" for the narcotics trafficking conviction. Assistant District Attorney Edward Panzarella, who prosecuted the Agro case and appeared to approve of Rinaldi's sentence, "later resigned in a controversy over an alleged failure to prosecute another drug case." *New York Times,* November 13, 1973, pp. 1, 36.

22.9 A line to a federal judge. Defected Mob money-mover Gerald Zelmanowitz testified, "I was in Florida with [New Jersey Mafioso[64]] Ray DeCarlo and [John

V.] Kenney, another gentleman from New Jersey, now currently in prison, or I believe he has been released since then. He was head of the Democratic Party in Union County, N.J." Zelmanowitz related that a call was made in his presence to a federal judge, who in this instance refused to perform the favor asked, stating that "it is too hot a potato for me to touch." Zelmanowitz advised, however, that at other times the judge had been "cooperative with Mr. Kenney and Mr. DeCarlo." *U.S.–Senate, OC and Stolen Securities, 1973*, p. 99.

22.10 Widespread Mob Corruption in New York Courts. The New York Joint Legislative Committee on Crime documented cases of court fixes, political interference in Mob trials, and leniency towards racketeers by many judges. The corruption was described to the committee by several witnesses, who wore hoods to hide their identities. One testified that Mafia superiors had told him there would be no problem if he were arrested in Brooklyn, because "we got judges on the payroll that can straighten it out one-two-three."

The criminal record of New York Mafia enforcer Dominick "Mimi" Scialo exemplified this corrupt pattern. "Since 1944, Scialo has been arrested fourteen times on charges ranging from felonious assault and rape to first degree murder. But he has never been sent to jail." In Scialo's murder case, the Mafioso and accomplices were accused of beating two young men to death with snow-tire chains. Scialo had previously hired the victims—Bartholomew Garafalo, age 18, and Alexander Menditto, age 19—to torch a dance hall in Boston. In his hospital bed, before he died, Menditto signed a police statement implicating Scialo. Based on this and other evidence, Scialo was charged for the murders. But later, "Menditto's deathbed statement was said to have mysteriously disappeared from the district attorney's office. The charges were then dismissed."

Michael Dorman, *Payoff*, pp. 122–24.

22.11 A Mobster's diary contained names of top Chicago Mafiosi and "an impressive list of assistant prosecutors, defense attorneys, judges and police captains." Leo Foreman was a multiple ex-convict who headed LeFore Insurance Company. He used the company as a front for a loan sharking operation which specialized in bankrolling criminals to finance burglaries, robberies and hijackings. In May 1963, Foreman accompanied his close associate, Chicago Mafia underboss Sam DeStefano, to a municipal court trial of DeStefano. The trial was judged by Cecil C. Smith, who was also a long-time friend of Foreman. Judge Smith had in fact been master of ceremonies at a "business" dinner given by Foreman, which was attended by another judge and several Chicago area police chiefs.

In late 1963, Foreman was found dead in a car trunk of knife and bullet wounds. He had told police, "If you find me in a trunk, DeStefano is the man who put me there." Foreman's diary was found to contain the names of DeStefano and fellow Mafioso[65] Anthony Accardo, along with those of several assistant prosecutors, defense attorneys, judges, and police captains. Judge Smith, one of those named in Foreman's diary, admitted accepting kickbacks and resigned in January 1964.

Demaris, *Captive City*, pp. 299–302.

22.12 New York State Supreme Court Justice Thomas Aurelio thanked Mafia boss Frank Costello profusely for obtaining the judgeship for him. Aurelio added, "I want to assure you of my loyalty for all you have done. It's undying." Costello told Aurelio, "When I tell you something is in the bag, you can rest assured." Although the wiretap of the conversation was made public and investigated by a grand jury, Aurelio retained his Supreme Court position. Dorman, *Payoff*, p. 122; or see *U.S.–Senate, Kefauver Report, Third Interim*, p. 122.

22.13 Flagrant misconduct on behalf of the Mob by a top Arizona judge.
U.S. District Court Judge Walter E. Craig, a former president of the American Bar Association, had a reputation for exceptional leniency in cases involving organized crime. In one case, for example, Judge Craig dismissed a tax evasion charge against a gambler whom Craig admitted having known for many years. And Judge Craig was criticized for the light sentences and unusually low bonds he granted to a man with a long criminal record and two others accused of sizable narcotics operations.

When questioned about his conduct, Craig protested, with perhaps unintentional irony, "I don't remember individual cases. These cases go through here like money through a slot machine." Craig also proclaimed, "I don't know of any organized crime in Arizona."

In 1972 Judge Craig presided over the murder conspiracy trial of Joe Bonanno, Jr., son of the top Mafia boss. Five of Bonanno's codefendants had already pleaded guilty to various charges. When the intended murder victim testified against Bonanno, as juror Robert Clark later described, Judge Craig had "incredulous looks" on his face and made gestures indicating disbelief. Clark noted that "his conduct was anything but impartial" and "his reaction to various witnesses and their testimony left little doubt as to what he thought of them." U.S. Attorney Ann Bowen, who prosecuted the case, charged that during her presentation, Judge Craig buried his face in his hands, openly laughed, mimicked one government witness in a falsetto voice, and "generally ridiculed her entire presentation by rolling his eyes and gesturing."

In May of 1972, the jury convicted Bonanno of conspiracy to murder as charged. After the verdict, a window of the gas station owned by the jury foreman was shot out. Another juror's car was struck by a truck which careened out of control; the truck was found to have been stolen and the driver was never located. And six weeks after the verdict, Judge Craig overturned the conviction, claiming that the jury might have reached its decision unjustly because of Bonanno's participation in a shakedown attempt. The jury was "flabbergasted" by Craig's reversal, reported foreman Jerry Boyd. Another juror stated that Craig's speculations concerning how the jury reached its verdict were "as slanderous as they are false," and petitioned for Craig's impeachment.

Craig's behavior, however, was not unique in Arizona judicial circles. One former State Supreme Court justice furnished a liquor license reference for an associate of Detroit-based Mafioso[66] Pete Licavoli. Another state judge, who socialized with a Phoenix bookmaker, was believed to have met several underworld figures at a restaurant and discussed drug importation. Former State Attorney General Gary Nelson, who became a state appellate judge, was under a federal probe concerning his conduct in office. And Arizona authorities investigated an attorney tied to Mafioso Pete Licavoli suspected of high level narcotics dealings, along with another lawyer believed to be providing cover for a major heroin supplier.

From the Investigative Reports and Editors (IRE) series on organized crime in Arizona, *Albuquerque Journal*, April 3, 1977, pp. A1, A6.

22.14 The Mob coaches a captive judge on responding to corruption charges. An FBI bug placed in Chicago First Ward Democratic headquarters, a hangout for Chicago gangsters, recorded a conversation between Illinois Circuit Judge Pasqual Sorrentino and Pat Marcy, "a friend of the Chicago LCN [La Cosa Nostra] family." When Judge Sorrentino asked Marcy what to reply if questioned by federal agents about his associations with gangsters, Marcy responded: "Stand on your dignity. Don't answer those questions. Tell them they're trying to embarrass you. Stay on the offensive." "The Mafia v. America," *Time*, August 22, 1969, p. 19.

22.15 A Brooklyn law firm arranges fixes for the Mob in the adjoining district attorney's office. Defected Mob money-mover Gerald Zelmanowitz testified how he personally was involved in a $5,000 bribe, "distributed among the various people in the district attorney's office," that blocked the prosecution of a criminal with three prior convictions. Zelmanowitz also related how the D.A.'s chief investigator, Walter Bookbinder, was given a new Buick from a dealership owned by Mafia boss Joseph Colombo for delaying a subpoena to Colombo. Zelmanowitz noted several other similar occurrences. *U.S.–Senate, OC and Stolen Securities, 1973*, pp. 87–88.

22.16 New York Federal Judge Mark Constantino made strange errors which freed defendants. For example, two of Judge Constantino's actions, described by government lawyers as "unbelievable" and "incomprehensible," aborted prosecutions of an alleged narcotics dealer and two men accused of receiving stolen goods. In another case, Judge Constantino directed the City of New York to sell a piece of land to a realtor for $1.5 million instead of the $2.5 million the land was worth, and subsequently entered into a business deal with the realtor. But Constantino's actions were not surprising, given a *New York Times* report that he had been picked up and questioned by police while talking with a reputed case-fixer in a hangout of the Colombo Mafia Family. The fixer was a judge who had resigned after New York State hearings disclosed that he had acted as an intermediary for the Mob. *New York Times*, July 6, 1973, pp. 1, 38; July 10, 1973, p. 32.

22.17 "The best judge that money can buy." In 1971, New York State brought criminal charges against State Supreme Court Judge Mitchell D. Schweitzer, who retired with the charges pending. This ended his years of blatant misconduct on behalf of Mob defendants. Mob defector Michael Raymond testified, for example, how he paid Schweitzer $50,000 through an intermediary for a light sentence and easy probation terms in a grand larceny case. During the trial, Judge Schweitzer met with defendant Raymond in his chambers and told him, "nobody in this court has any intention of hurting you."(B)

In another case, described by ex-Washington lobbyist Robert Winter-Berger, Schweitzer allowed Massachusetts Mobster Manuel Bello to go free in a securities theft case. Winter-Berger had been to dinner with Schweitzer, Bello's lawyer and notorious Washington fixer Nathan Voloshen a week before Bello's hearing. On another occasion, Winter-Berger observed Voloshen hand an envelope to Schweitzer, telling the judge, "This is what I promised you."(C)

When former Mobster Raymond was asked by Senator Charles Percy whether Judge Schweitzer was "the best judge that money can buy," Raymond responded, "I agree with you 100 percent." Raymond added that Stanley Polley, a fixer "well connected with organized crime," had "often made the statement to me that there was no judge sitting in New York that he couldn't reach." Raymond also testified in a Massachusetts court that he had arranged, through an intermediary, to pay $35,000 to Massachusetts Superior Court judges Edward J. Desaulnier, Jr. and Vincent R. Brogna to obtain a suspended sentence in a fraud case.

A–*U.S.–Senate, OC and Stolen Securities, 1971*, pp. 647–54; B–Dorman, *Payoff*, pp. 200–202; C–Winter-Berger, *Washington Payoff*, pp. 120, 124–30.

c. Criminal lawyers and lawyer criminals

22.18 Some techniques of Mob lawyers. "The courtroom antics of Mob mouthpieces are more often staged than spontaneous. Witnesses experience lapses in memory, policemen make reversible slip-of-the-tongue errors, prosecutors ignore valuable evidence, judges rule improperly, and jurors are bribed, intimidated or just plain hate to commit their childhood heroes to prison." In one case, for example, a lawyer worked out a small change in the story of the arresting officer, which would justify acquittal on a legal technicality. The lawyer could hardly have failed to realize that the policeman would be bribed to incorporate this change. Demaris, *Captive City*, p. 308; Cressey, *Theft of the Nation*, pp. 255–57.

22.19 Arguing the Mob's case in Congress. Attorney Charles Bellows was former chairman of the criminal law section of the American Bar Association. In 1970, he appeared before the House Judiciary Committee to oppose the Organized Crime Control Act. That bill provided highly effective measures to fight the Mob, and was passed later that year.

Bellows claimed that the bill would "infringe upon constitutional rights," potentially a genuine concern. But other code phrases of Mob lobbyists, expressed by Bellows in their glaring absurdity, left little doubt as to his stance. Bellows spoke of organized crime as hypothetical; when asked if there is "a syndicate operation in the Chicago area," he replied "I am really trying to be honest with you—I am not pulling any punches—there probably is." Bellows, in the classic tradition of Mob corruption, told the Committee that more important than legislation against organized crime was combatting "crime on the streets." He claimed he saw "very little relationship" between the two.

Then, to the astonished queries of Congressmen at the hearing, Bellows suggested that the proposed legislation was not really necessary, based on his experience in Chicago, because of progress already achieved in that city. Bellows asserted that the federal government was doing a "marvelous job" in prosecuting organized crime cases in Chicago, with "99.9 [percent] convictions of those charged with what might be called 'organized crime.'" He added that the Chicago city administration was "unusually clean." In fact, as Congressman Richard Poff pointed out to Bellows, between 1960 and 1969, only 3.5 percent of American Cosa Nostra members were convicted of any federal crime. And in 1965, U.S. Attorney General Nicholas Katzenbach had noted that "we have made less progress in Chicago than anywhere" in prosecuting organized crime cases.[67] (ABA president-elect Edward Wright appeared before the House Judiciary Committee following Bellows to represent the ABA and register its "unqualified" support of the proposed anti-Mob legislation.) *U.S.–House, OC Control*, pp. 441, 446–53, 538.

22.20 A Syndicate lawyer orchestrated perjury, bribed a juror. Richard Gorman, a former Chicago policeman and federal prosecutor, specialized in defending Syndicate figures against federal raps. An expert on legal loopholes, Gorman once freed a client in a tax evasion case by arguing that the $900,000 in question was embezzled from the Laundry Workers Union and therefore not taxable income; Gorman charged his $15,000 fee to the Laundry Workers Union.

In 1959, Gorman defended Mobster Gerald Covelli in a hijacking case which ended in a hung jury when one member, Robert Saporito, held out against conviction. Covelli later became a government witness and testified that Gorman had instructed him to lie, had rehearsed the perjury with him, and had shown him a list of jury members with Saporito's name marked with an X. Saporito confessed to accepting the bribe offered via his brother Michael, who was on the Chicago Police force. "The boys have approached me on this," Michael told his brother. Michael was in fact promised a promotion to the police narcotics detail by his Mob sponsor in return for his intercession. In 1962, Gorman, Chicago Mafioso[68] Joseph DiVarco, and Charles Hudson were indicted by a federal grand jury for jury tampering. The outcome of the case was classic. The Saporitos' bond was posted by a cousin of Chicago Mafioso[69] John Cerone. Robert was given only a suspended sentence after pleading no contest; Michael disappeared and was presumed murdered. Gerald Covelli, the Mob defendant turned witness, was killed when a bomb exploded in his car in 1967 in Encino, California. And after the notoriously corrupt federal judge Michael Igoe appeared as character witness for Gorman, Gorman and the other defendants were acquitted. Gorman, however, was later convicted and sentenced to two years in prison for income-tax evasion. Demaris, *Captive City*, pp. 309–16.

d. Accommodating the few who get sent to prison

22.21 Royal treatment for Mobsters in jail. The Mob's influence helps secure the most comfortable facilities, quick parole, and special privileges for members in jail, while dependents receive weekly cash payments. Not atypical was the case of Chicago Mafioso Sam DeStefano, moved by court order in 1968 from an Illinois penitentiary to a hospital for surgery. "Three weeks later it was discovered that he was operating a loanshark business from his guarded room and enjoying fine foods, vintage wines, card games with underworld friends, and visits from women." Salerno and Tompkins, *Crime Confederation*, p. 183.

22.22 Carrying the power of the organization behind bars. From James D. Horan, *The Mob's Man*, reproduced in Tyler, *Organized Crime in America*, pp. 237–44.

e. The end result: corruption neutralizes law enforcement

22.23 In 1965, 5116 adults were arrested for gambling felonies in New York State; four were sent to prison. In 1966, .3 percent of those arrested on gambling charges were convicted. Salerno and Tompkins, *Crime Confederation*, pp. 164–65.

22.24 "Years of dedicated investigation nullified." Judges often give light sentences to Mobsters "because of corruption, political considerations or lack of knowledge." In Pennsylvania, for example, Mafia corrupter Walter Plopi gave a $300 bribe to a state senator while being tape-recorded with the senator's consent. Plopi asked the senator to influence a prosecutor to ignore gambling violations, promising $2,000 a month to the prosecutor, plus $200,000 a year. Plopi also promised the senator 50 percent of the gambling profits, and money for any political campaigns "if you really want to play ball on a county-wide basis." Plopi could have received a year in jail for the corruption conviction. But he was fined only $250—and then reimbursed his $300 bribe.

In New York, John Lombardozzi, brother of a Gambino Family captain, drew no jail term on convictions for smuggling and bankruptcy fraud. Lombardozzi also received far less than the maximum sentences in convictions for assaulting an FBI agent, whose skull he fractured with Mafia accomplices, and for the theft of more than $1 million in securities.

In Chicago, the FBI and federal prosecutors spent four years to convict Mafioso Joey Glimco on a union extortion charge. Yet Glimco, with 36 previous arrests on charges including robbery and murder, got only a $40,000 fine instead of a possible four years in jail. Assistant U.S. Attorney David Shippers commented, "When Glimco got a kiss and went free, it was devastating to us all."

In Boston, Mafia underboss Jerry Angiulo was convicted of assaulting a federal officer. "FBI agents, electronically monitoring boss Patriarca's headquarters, recorded how Angiulo discussed his pending prosecution in detail, plotting to defeat it by procuring a blind man to perjure himself and establish an alibi, then getting a second 'standup' witness to lie that he, too, saw the phantom encounter." Angiulo got only 30 days in jail out of a possible three year sentence. Other similar cases are cited.

John McClellan, "Weak Link in Our War on the Mafia." *Reader's Digest*, April 6, 1970, reprinted in *U.S.–House, OC Control*, pp. 111–13.

23. Corruption of Local Government

23.1 "A Two-Faced Crime Fight in St. Louis: Both the mayor and his new crime commissioner have personal ties to the underworld." A yearlong investigation by *Life* disclosed that "Mayor Cervantes himself has business and personal ties with the gangsters that operate in his city. Any real drive against organized crime in St. Louis could start with a number of the mayor's own associates."

The new crime commissioner, Morris Shenker, was one of the Mob's leading lawyers in the U.S. His relations with prominent hoodlums went "far beyond mere legal representation. ... Shenker, in fact, would have to do little more than tell what he already knows about organized crime to go a long way toward breaking its back in St. Louis and several other places as well."

As an example of Mayor Cervantes' Mob ties, *Life* magazine cited Tony Sansone, "the man closest to Cervantes, as friend, business associate, campaign manager and unofficial but forceful influence around city hall." Sansone is also Cervantes' liaison with the Mafia and the Syrian Mob "that coexists these days as an 'ally by treaty' with the Sicilian Mafia family headed by Anthony Giardano." In December 1964, two days before Cervantes announced his candidacy for mayor, he met with Sansone and the late Syrian Mob leader Jimmy Michaels to plan campaign strategy at a Mob-controlled business incorporated by Shenker. Three months later, after Cervantes had won the primary, Sansone, Michaels, and Mafia boss Giardano met at the same place to discuss his prospects for the general election.

Denny Walsh, "A Two-Faced Crime Fight in St. Louis," *Life*, May 29, 1970, pp. 25–31.

23.2 How the Mob ran Reading, Pennsylvania in the 1950s and early 1960s. The Mob's complete control of the city government and wide-open rackets operations were detailed in a 19-page study included as an appendix to the 1967 U.S. Task Force Report on Organized Crime. Mob control was broken in the mid-1960s, at least temporarily, when the mayor and rackets boss were convicted of extortion, several other city figures jailed, and a reform administration elected. John A. Gardiner, "Wincanton: The Politics of Corruption," *U.S.–Task Force Report*, appendix B, pp. 61–79. See also Dorman, *Payoff*, pp. 18–32, which identifies some whose names were fictionalized in the Gardiner report, and identifies the specific Mafia families involved.

23.3 A Kansas City political boss was also a Mafia member. Charles Binaggio, the leader of the First Ward Democratic Club in Kansas City, Missouri, was described as a "Democratic political boss" and "the successor to Pendergast as the political power in Kansas City";(A) a "powerful political leader" who could control an important segment of the Democratic vote in the city.(B) He was also described, by Chicago Crime Commission Director Virgil Peterson, as "the gambling boss and lord of the underworld in Kansas City, Missouri."(C) Charles Gargotta, his political crony, was distinguished by 39 arrests on charges from burglary to murder. Binaggio and Gargotta were both described in the Senate Kefauver Report as "believed to be members of the Mafia."(B) The dual affiliations of the two men were dramatized in 1950, when both were slain gangland-style in a political clubhouse.

The situation changed little in the Kansas City area after 15 years, as noted in 1966 by a county commissioner running for reelection. He declared that the national crime syndicate "controls some county officials and it considers the county government its bastion. The issue in this election is whether the people rule or the Mafia rules."(D)

A–Mollenhoff, *Strike Force*, pp. 78–81; B–*U.S.–Senate, Kefauver Report, Third Interim*, pp. 37–38, 185–86; C–*U.S.–Senate, Kefauver Hearings*, vol. 2, p. 184; D–Cressey, *Theft of the Nation*, pp. 263–64.

☐☐☐☐☐☐☐☐☐☐☐☐☐☐☐☐☐☐☐☐☐☐☐

Chairman Pepper: What are the reasons why local officials in areas where mob operations are carried on over a period of years, are unable to break up the mob and protect the community and other people against their operations? Why is it that they are not able to do it?

Mr. Barboza [defected New England Mob killer]: Well, they don't really want to. In other words, they are getting money from them. . . .

From *U.S.–House, OC in Sports*, p. 760.
☐☐☐☐☐☐☐☐☐☐☐☐☐☐☐☐☐☐☐☐☐☐☐

23.4 Two mayors refuse Mob bribes. Mayor Richard Hatcher of Gary, Indiana, disclosed that the Mob offered him $100,000 to withdraw from a Democratic primary contest against the machine candidate. It then offered him the same amount after the election for an "understanding" to permit gambling and other rackets. Meanwhile, the forces of Hatcher's predecessor, who was jailed for income-tax evasion, started to undermine the reform program. Hatcher asked Gary citizens to resist "a machine which bought votes wholesale and stole the rest; a machine which exploited blacks and Latins and ignored their just demands; a machine greased with the millions which float from rackets, gambling, and prostitution."

In Newark, "even after Mayor Hugh Addonizio was convicted in an extortion conspiracy and defeated at the polls, the greedy Mafia overlords tried to perpetuate their empire."(B) Shortly after reform Mayor Kenneth Gibson took office in 1970, he revealed in outrage how he had been offered $15,000 to appoint a particular police director and encouraged to follow the former practice of pocketing 10 percent of monies on all city contracts.

A–Dorman, *Payoff*, pp. 32–33; B–Methvin, "How Organized Crime Corrupts Our Law Enforcers," *Reader's Digest*, January 1972, p. 87.

23.5 Chicago in the Capone era: Mafia control of government. In 1931, Albert R. Brunker of the Chicago Civic Safety Committee stated that "there are six thousand city, State and Federal officials in Capone's pay," and "eighty per cent of Chicago's magistrates and judges are criminals."(A) Representative was James Adduci, who was described by the press as a "hoodlum," "gangster," "vice monger," "West Side gambler," and "notorious member of the murderous Capone gang." Adduci "was arrested eighteen times between 1920 and 1934—the year he was first elected to the state legislature."(B) A–Allsop, *The Bootleggers*, pp. 314–15; B–Demaris, *Captive City*, p. 173.

23.6 Chicago in recent years: venal and pervasive Mafia corruption. In 1962, an internal FBI document noted "the almost complete influence and control of politicians, police, and even courts in the Chicago area by the underworld."(E) *Life* Magazine observed that in Chicago, "the connection between the Mob and the politicians remains extensive and arrogant." Below are a few examples.

When *Life* investigated the situation in 1967, Mafia boss Sam Giancana and his lieutenants were "firmly in control of both the Democratic and the Republican political organizations in Chicago's famous First Ward." That ward includes City Hall, the Cook County court house, the federal court house, police headquarters, the Chicago Stock Exchange and Board of Trade, the city's largest office buildings and hotels, and its commercial center. Giancana's main liaison with the First Ward politicians was Pat Marcy, secretary of the First Ward Democratic organization, who previously served a prison term for bank robbery.

Chicago's city treasurer in 1967 was Marshall Korshak, brother of powerful Mafia representative[70] Sidney Korshak. Treasurer Marshall Korshak had "an especially warm relationship" with Giancana lieutenant Gus Alex, and was listed on an apartment application as the employer of Alex.

"La Cosa Nostra exerts major influence in a dozen Chicago wards and dictates the votes of as many as 15 state legislators. . . . The Mob opposes anticrime bills in the state legislature, forces gangsters onto the payroll of Mayor Richard Daley's Chicago machine, and corrupts the city police department."(B) Richard Cain, former chief investigator for the Cook County Sheriff's office, once gave lie detector tests to five robbery suspects. He "was not after the guilty man but in search of the FBI informant among the five. The tipster, Guy Menolia, Jr., was subsequently murdered."(B) Cain later became a "chauffeur and courier" to Chicago Mafia boss Sam Giancana. Eventually he became an FBI informant, and "admitted that he had worked covertly for Giancana and been on his payroll while he was a member of the Chicago Police Department from 1956–60, director of a private intelligence agency from 1960–62, and chief investigator for the Cook County Sheriff's Office from 1962–64."(E)

Boss of Chicago's 24th Ward, Ben Lewis was praised by the late Mayor Richard Daley as a "superior alderman."(D) A secret federal report differed: "Advised in 1961 that Ben Lewis . . . is Lenny Patrick's boy and that he does not do anything without Patrick's O.K. Anyone who operates a book in the 24th Ward is required to give Patrick 50 percent. . . . Advised that Patrick could not be stopped in his gambling and other illicit activities since he was backed politically by [Chicago politicians] Jake Arvey, Sidney Deutsch and Arthur X. Elrod."(C) Lenny Patrick was a top Syndicate killer.[71] Patrick's captive alderman, Ben Lewis, was later slain gangland-style at his political headquarters.

A former assistant U.S. attorney general who headed the Justice Department's Organized Crime Section reported on the fate of federal agents sent to investigate Mafia-political ties in Chicago. "We had a great deal of evidence of payoffs to protect syndicate gambling and other rackets. The Mob had connections all the way to the top—at the Chicago City Hall, the Illinois State House, and in Congress."(D) According to the official, who resigned in protest over the handling of the probe, it was impeded at every turn by Chicago officials, staff members of the local U.S. attorney, federal judges, and finally called off on direct orders from the White House.

A–*Life*, September 1, 1967, pp. 42b-43; B–*Time*, August 22, 1969, pp. 18–19; C–Demaris, *Captive City*, pp. 151–53, 168–69; D–Dorman, *Payoff*, pp. 52–53; E–*U.S.–House, Assassination Appendix, JFK*, vol. 9, pp. 14–15; vol. 10, p. 172.

□□□□□□□□□□□□□□□□□□□□□□□

Organized criminal activities are run in our big cities by professional criminals with long arrest records and with well-documented criminal reputations but who remain immune from prosecution and punishment. . . .

One example of many in the minutes of this committee is the prosecution of Charles Gargotta for the murder of a deputy sheriff in Kansas City. There were 29 continuances before the case finally came to trial. It is alleged that the gun with which the deputy sheriff was killed was switched by Kansas City police officers, so that ballistics tests were made on the wrong gun. Gargotta was acquitted of the homicide charge although he had been practically caught in the act. However, he was convicted of the illegal possession of a gun, sentenced to a minimum term, and released promptly. Eventually, over the protest of the police department, he was pardoned by the Governor.

U.S.–Senate, Kefauver Report, Second Interim, p. 8.

□□□□□□□□□□□□□□□□□□□□□□□□

23.7 Pervasive Mafia corruption in New York City in the 1940s and 1950s. The Kefauver Committee detailed the tremendous influence of the Mafia, especially of Genovese Family boss Frank Costello and underboss[72] Joe ("Adonis") Doto, on New York City government in the 1940s. The Committee reported for example, that Mayor William O'Dwyer was "intimate" with "close friends" of Mafia bosses Costello and Doto. It concluded that O'Dwyer had failed to take "effective action against the top echelons of the gambling, narcotics, water-front, murder or bookmaking rackets," and in fact had "impeded promising investigations of such rackets."(A)

Representative of O'Dwyer's conduct was his prosecution of the Murder, Inc. case during his term as New York District Attorney between 1942 and 1946. A grand jury investigated his conduct, and strongly condemned O'Dwyer for allowing Mafia boss Albert Anastasia and six other bosses of the Brooklyn Mob hit squad to escape indictment. The Kefauver Committee found that O'Dwyer had "not prosecuted Anastasia nor had he even sought an indictment against him" during the 20 months witness Abe Reles could have testified against Anastasia in a murder case. The prosecution's case then collapsed when Reles was found dead below the window of his hotel room, where he was being guarded by six New York policemen. Mafia defector Joseph Valachi later implicated New York boss Vito Genovese in the Reles killing.

Frank Bals, the supervisor of Reles's six police guards, was promoted to a high police position when O'Dwyer became mayor. Another man instrumental in the obstruction of the Murder, Inc. prosecution was "O'Dwyer's man Friday," James Moran, who "ordered the wanted cards against Anastasia and two of his ace killers, Dandy Jack Parisi and Tony Romeo, removed from police files and destroyed." When O'Dwyer became mayor, "he made Moran a deputy fire commissioner and, shortly before his resignation, gave him a life job as commissioner of the board of water supply."(A) Moran was "subsequently sent to prison for running a $500,000-a-year extortion racket in New York's Fire Department."(C)

A–*U.S.–Senate, Kefauver Report, Third Interim*, pp. 121–44; B–*U.S.–Senate, OC and Narcotics Hearings*, p. 118; C–Cook, *Secret Rulers*, pp. 110–13, 149; see also Sondern, *Brotherhood of Evil*, pp. 176–77.

23.8 The same situation in the 1950s and 1960s. In the mid-1950s, New York Mayor Vincent R. Impelitteri fired several top city officials after it was disclosed that they and other Tammany Hall politicians had met with members of the Genovese Mafia Family. "The mayor himself was shortly embarrassed when it was found that he had met with Thomas Lucchese, head of another Cosa Nostra group, shortly before a new police commissioner was to be appointed."

Corruption in the 1960s was exemplified by the activities of Lucchese Family caporegime Tony "Ducks" Corallo. In 1961, Corallo, a New York State Supreme Court Justice and a U.S. Attorney were each sentenced to two years in prison. The conviction arose from a bribe by Corallo to the two high officials to free a Mob associate in a bankruptcy fraud case. After his prison stay, Corallo went back to work by extending an exorbitant interest loan to James Marcus, Mayor Lindsay's water commissioner. Marcus was steered to Corallo by Daniel Motto, an ex-convict and a top official in the Bakery and Confectionary Workers Union. Once on the hook, Marcus was forced to award an $835,000 city reservoir drainage contract to a scandal-ridden firm, which in turn gave kickbacks to Corallo, Marcus, Motto, and another individual. Mafia lieutenant Corallo, Tammany Hall boss Carmine DeSapio, and Water Commissioner Marcus were each sentenced to jail after the reservoir contract and similar deals were exposed. The trial was marked by a plot to murder the chief prosecution witness. Fortunately, this political penetration by the Mafia was discovered before another scheme to extort $5 million on a $100 million contract for a nuclear power plant could be realized.

Salerno and Tompkins, *Crime Confederation*, p. 254; Dorman, *Payoff*, pp. 77–91; Gage, *Mafia, U.S.A.*, pp. 271–90.

☐☐☐☐☐☐☐☐☐☐☐☐☐☐☐☐☐☐

The crime problem in the Miami area . . . has existed here for decades. Since the days of Al Capone, crime if not welcomed has been tolerated.

In order to exist, crime has corrupted our public life. Not only public officials have cooperated with the mob, but many of our businessmen have been associated in syndicate activity. . . .

Recently we had an election on Miami Beach. More than half the candidates running had criminal arrest records. A candidate for mayor had just been acquitted on a grand larceny charge. An incumbent city councilman had just escaped a bribery charge. . . .

Under the circumstances it isn't surprising that there should also be an increase in such nonorganized crime fields as juvenile delinquency and crime on the streets. When organized crime creates a climate of cynicism, of disrespect for law and justice, it is sure to be recognized by the young, by the petty hood. Indeed, much of the discontent on the part of our young people today stems from the fact that they recognize the hypocrisy of our generation which pays lip service only to the ideals of justice.

. . . I assure you, the public will respond to an intelligent, fearless, aggressive investigation that penetrates beyond the appearance of things and gets to the reality.

Bayard Strell, president of the Miami Beach Taxpayers Association, from a statement in *U.S.–House, Crime in America*, pp. 403–4.
☐☐☐☐☐☐☐☐☐☐☐☐☐☐☐☐☐☐☐

23.9 An Iowa Mobster makes friends in high places. Luigi Fratto, alias Lew Farrell, whose record included 20 arrests and convictions, became the Chicago Mafia's ambassador to Iowa in 1939. While he continued his involvement in illegal gambling, shakedowns and counterfeiting, Fratto cultivated and exploited the friendship of top-ranking politicians and law enforcement officials in Iowa. Among Fratto's many friends was Judge Edwin Moore, who wrote a letter praising Fratto as a reference for a liquor permit. A few months later, Judge Moore dropped an illegal gambling charge against Fratto. Moore later became Chief Justice of the Iowa Supreme Court.

Journalist Clark Mollenhoff, of the *Des Moines Register*, described how Fratto and his associates could reverse IRS decisions at the highest levels. Mollenhoff also "watched the tentacles of Lew Farrell reach into the Des Moines Police Department to promote his friends; into the Sheriff's Office for a gun permit; into the Prosecutor's Office to kill a criminal indictment; into the local courts to manipulate decisions on evidence; and into the state political arena." Fratto was also close with top Teamster officials, including Jimmy Hoffa and the notorious goon Barney Baker.

Mollenhoff, *Strike Force*, pp. 34–54.

24. Corruption of State Government and State-Wide Networks of Corruption

a. New Jersey

24.1 Mafia domination of New Jersey government. Mafia control of political figures at every level—from police chiefs, judges and mayors, to political party leaders, a congressman and a governor—has been exposed in dozens of court convictions and in a 2,000 page transcript of FBI electronic surveillance of Mafia hangouts. A good sampling of such information, which is too extensive to summarize adequately in this short review, is provided in the following sources: *Newsweek*, June 23, 1969, p. 37, January 19, 1970, p. 23; Dorman, *Payoff*, pp. 53–74; William Schulz, "the Mob's Grip on New Jersey," *Reader's Digest*, February 1971, pp. 111–15; Fred Cook, "New Jersey: The State of Mafia," *Nation*, May 11, 1970, pp. 560–74. State official William Brennan summarized, "organized crime in New Jersey manages to work its way into . . . almost every area of our society except the church."[73]

b. Massachusetts and Rhode Island

24.2 Excerpts from the Taglianetti Airtels (publicly released FBI summaries of electronic surveillance of Mafia headquarters in Providence, Rhode Island). When a murderer was identified by a witness, "a payoff of $5000.00 was necessary to 'square the rap away.' $5000.00 was furnished to a Lt. Dunn (phonetic) for this purpose and the charge was dropped. The individual was released. . . . (10/26/64)

". . . Joe Modica, Boston, Mass. contacted [Mafia boss] Patriarca specifically concerning the Berkshire Downs Race Track in which Raymond Patriarca allegedly has a financial interest. Patriarca told Modica to contact his friend who is allegedly extremely close to Attorney General Edward W. Brooke of Massachusetts and have him arrange to release the $100,000 bond that is being held by the Massachusetts Court in connection with civil suits that have been heard in Massachusetts courts. (1/25/65)

"[Mafia underboss] Henry Tameleo advised he contacted George Kattar and reiterated to Kattar that in order to operate he 'must have the State.' Kattar told him that he has arranged to pay off the State Police and that he would furnish Tameleo

the identities and the amounts paid to individual members of the State Police. ... (1/28/65)"
Providence Journal, May 20, 1967, quoted in Cressey, *Theft of the Nation*, pp. 269–70.

24.3 The New England Mafia Family's "impressive list of allies among the area's politicians." Informants say that a high-ranking state official, a court administrator, a police chief, two licensing officials, and several powerful state legislators are all "in the bag." Such officials grease the Mob's path: ignoring its crime, allowing its bars and clubs to stay open late, giving its trials to lenient judges, and arranging pardons and paroles for its convicts.

In 1963, FBI agents observed Mafia boss Patriarca meet with the high-ranking state official in the parking lot of a Boston hospital. Patriarca later commented on the FBI surveillance of the meeting, his words picked up by an FBI bug in his office. Patriarca stated that he had contacted the official to obtain the parole of two of his lieutenants, Leo Santaniello and Larry Baioni, who had been convicted of loan sharking extortion.

The Taglianetti Airtels also revealed that the Mafia had tried to present $100,000 bribes to Massachusetts ex-Lieutenant Governor Francis Bellotti during his campaigns for governor and attorney general in the mid-1960s. When Bellotti refused the bribes, the Mob countered by spreading the word that he *had* accepted them; "these rumors were a major factor in Democrat Bellotti's defeat in both campaigns."

Bill Davidson, "The Mafia, How It Bleeds New England," *Saturday Evening Post*, November 18, 1967, p. 28.

24.4 A pardon for Patriarca. In 1938, budding Mafioso Raymond Patriarca was sentenced to five years in jail for burglary, a sentence to be served concurrently with convictions for armed robbery and arson. After serving just 84 days in jail, however, he was given a full pardon by the Massachusetts governor on the advice of Executive Councilor Daniel Coakley. Coakley was later impeached after a state commission concluded that he had used "deceit and fraud" in pressing the pardon. Reid, *Grim Reapers*, pp. 63–64.

c. Illinois

24.5 Eulogies marred by $800,000 in cash. When Illinois Secretary of State Paul Powell died in 1970, he was given a funeral befitting a state politician of the greatest stature, with flowery homage from leaders of both political parties. The accolades ended, however, when it was discovered that Powell had accumulated an estate of $3 million including $800,000 in cash found in shoe boxes, envelopes, a closet and an office safe. Powell's salary had never exceeded $30,000 a year in the 36 years he had held state office. Federal and state agents discovered "that one of the chief sources of his riches was an alliance with Illinois gambling interests." Demonstrating this alliance, for example, Powell had once issued a special unlisted license plate to Chicago Mafia boss Sam Giancana. Dorman, *Payoff*, pp. 136–37.

d. California

24.6 "Mr. Big" in California. The Kefauver Committee Report devoted several pages to the activities of lobbyist Adrian Samish, who it said could "safely be called 'Mr. Big' in California," and whose power "nearly defie[d] description." The

Committee found that while Samish acted as a corrupt intermediary between liquor interests, state legislators, and other parties, he had visits and phone contacts with several Mobsters and Mob-owned businesses across the country. His diverse contacts included ties to both Meyer Lansky and J. Edgar Hoover.[74]

The Kefauver Report found it "even more incredible" that such disclosures about Samish's corrupt activities had been made in a 1938 report of the California legislature, which "strangely enough ... was almost immediately expunged from the record." Copies disappeared "to the extent that the report became a virtual collector's item." In that report, Samish was quoted as saying, "I am the governor of the legislature, to hell with the Governor of the State." Samish served 26 months in prison for income-tax evasion in the late 1950s, only to resume his previous activities upon release.

U.S.–Senate, Kefauver Report, Third Interim, pp. 100–106; Reid, *Grim Reapers,* pp. 177–81.

24.7 A district attorney dropped a murder indictment against a Mafioso, became governor. Nick DeJohn was a member of the Chicago Mob delegation involved in the Dallas bribe attempt.[75] In 1947, he was murdered. After a diligent investigation by two San Francisco police inspectors, Frank Ahern and Thomas Cahill, three men were indicted for the murder: New York Colombo Family Mafioso[76] Sebastiano Nani, convicted narcotics dealer Leonard Calamia, and Scappatora Abati. At the conclusion of the murder trial, the jury spent more than 30 hours considering the verdict. But the district attorney then dropped the charges against the three men, assuring Ahern and Cahill that it would be legally advantageous to do so and reinstate charges at a later date. No subsequent charges, however, were ever pressed. And the district attorney, Edmund "Pat" Brown, later became Governor of California.

In 1977, then ex-Governor Brown got another chance to demonstrate his loyalties. John Alessio was a convicted felon, described by federal agents as a member of organized crime.[77] Alessio and relatives were being scrutinized by the New Mexico state racing commission in connection with a race track license. During the investigation, Brown sent a telegram to the commission proclaiming that he had, as governor of California, "met Mr. John Alessio" and his relatives under scrutiny, and had found them "very helpful in many matters affecting our state." Brown declared he had "no hesitation in recommending them."

Paragraphs respectively from Reid, *Grim Reapers,* pp. 202–4; *Albuquerque Journal,* March 9, 1977, p. 1.

e. New York

24.8 Bipartisan Mafia corruption. On May 22, 1972, Chairman Claude Pepper opened the House Crime Committee's investigation of "organized crime and public corruption activities relating to the racing industry" in New York. As Pepper outlined, "Testimony will be adduced of underworld interests and official corruption in relation to the issuance of a license for the Canandaigua or Fingerlakes Racetrack in upstate New York. ... In addition, testimony will show that certain persons resorted to bribery, subornation of perjury, perjury, and an abortive murder plot in an effort to thwart a grand jury investigation [of] these activities." Testimony did indeed establish that payoffs of hundreds of thousands of dollars were given to officials, including both the Democratic and Republican Party chairmen of New York State. *U.S.–House, OC in Sports,* pp. 551, 613–22.

f. Ohio

24.9 "The Governor and the Mobster": commutation of a murder sentence. Mafia boss Thomas "Yonnie" Licavoli had engaged in bootlegging, gambling, and extortion, deserted the Navy, and killed for the Mob. In 1934, he and four underlings were convicted of murdering three men and a woman, and were sentenced to life imprisonment. During his term in prison, his record was "outrageously bad." He received regular visits from Mafia members and associates, such as Teamster boss Jimmy Hoffa; he continued to run Toledo numbers rackets from prison; and he received special favors which led to the firing of two wardens and the resignation of another. Licavoli, in fact, became "the prison's 'inside boss,' banking an internal numbers game, heading a narcotics and liquor ring, and receiving special food."

For more than a decade it was common knowledge among the underworld and police that anyone who helped Licavoli out of prison would receive $250,000 from a "spring Yonnie" fund. Indeed, one former governor acknowledged that overtures had been made to him to consider Licavoli's case, while another reported repeated attempts to bribe him to commute the Mobster's sentence. In 1969, "the underworld grapevine began humming with the word that the [Spring Yonnie] fund had risen to $300,000—and that Yonnie would be released shortly." The pivotal official was now Ohio Governor James Rhodes, whose "financial shenanigans," detailed by *Life* magazine, culminated in IRS claims against Rhodes for more than $100,000 in tax interest and penalties on unreported income. In January 1969, everything fell into place when Governor Rhodes commuted the sentence of Mafia boss Licavoli. Rhodes refused to answer questions or comment on *Life* magazine's story about the commutation.

Denny Walsh, "The Governor and the Mobster," *Life*, May 2, 1969, pp. 28–32A; *U.S.–Senate, OC and Narcotics Hearings*, p. 425.

g. Pennsylvania

24.10 "A long history of gubernatorial pardons to Syndicate racketeers." The Pennsylvania State Crime Commission issued a report detailing gubernatorial pardons and other official actions in behalf of Mobsters. It reported that Governor John Fine pardoned Mafia boss John S. LaRocca for crimes of larceny, operating a lottery, and receiving stolen goods, and back-dated the pardon to thwart federal deportation proceedings against LaRocca. Fine also pardoned Mafia caporegime Joseph Rosa for crimes including bombing and illegal entry.

Governor George Earle pardoned Mafia members Luigi Quaranta and Joseph Luciano for crimes of murder and robbery. Governor James Duff pardoned Mafia caporegime Nicholas Piccolo in a robbery case. He also pardoned Frank Palermo, a Mafia member notorious in the professional boxing world, for crimes of aggravated assault and battery and operating a lottery. The pardon enabled Palermo to get a boxing manager's license; he was later convicted of interstate extortion involving boxing rackets. Four other gubernatorial pardons were granted to other organized crime figures.

The commission report also named dozens of Pennsylvania officials who appeared as character witnesses on behalf of Mafia members and associates, including judges, top police officials, a congressman, a mayor, a state representative, and several city councilmen. The Pennsylvania Crime Commission noted the result of such actions by Pennsylvania officials on the judicial system: "Whether through bribery, political influence, or subtle manipulation of its processes, the

criminal justice system has operated more to the advantage of the racketeer than for justice and the safety of society."
Dorman, *Payoff*, pp. 118–21.

25. Corruption of Federal Government

25.1 Leading organized crime expert Ralph Salerno estimates that the votes of about 25 Congressmen can be delivered by Mob pressure. "Others say that estimate is far too low."(B) A–"The Mafia v. America," *Time*, August 22, 1969, p. 19; B–Dorman, *Payoff*, p. 178.

25.2 A prominent Congressman was a "tool and collaborator of a Cosa Nostra gang lord." Cornelius Gallagher was a prominent representative of New Jersey's 13th District in Congress between 1958 and 1972. Lyndon Johnson considered him a possible running mate. He served as the second-ranking Democrat on a House subcommittee that investigated organized crime in the late 1960s, in which position he disparaged efforts against the Mafia.

Using wiretaps suppressed for years by the LBJ Justice Department, *Life* magazine exposed regular contacts between Gallagher and New Jersey Mafia boss Joe Zicarelli. *Life* presented excerpts from the transcripts of several such conversations, citing the place and date of each call. Gallagher's dealings with the Mafia boss encompassed everything from fixes of local police to Caribbean politics to bogus cancer cures.

On June 21, 1960, for example, Zicarelli called Gallagher at his unlisted law office phone. The Mafia boss complained to the Congressman that Bayonne police had staked out key stations of his gambling network, and that his business was being disrupted by a top police official. Gallagher replied, "O.K. Let me get hold of him right now." In a conversation a few hours later, Gallagher told Zicarelli, "I got hold of a friend who said [the police official] was jumping. I got hold of the little guy in Jersey City and told him to reach out for him." In a conversation of June 22, Gallagher told Zicarelli that his request to call off the state police from Zicarelli's gambling operations "has already been taken care of." On June 25, Gallagher reported to Zicarelli that he had "laced into" the Bayonne police over Zicarelli's complaint. And a few days later in Washington, Gallagher quickly left the House floor to answer a telephone call from Zicarelli.

When Gallagher denied the reported contacts with Zicarelli in a pre-publication interview, his attorney suggested that *Life* "test its sense of fairness" by having Gallagher take a lie detector test. But Gallagher quickly cut in: "Hey, let me say something. I don't believe in lie detector tests. They're snake oil." After publication, Gallagher "never bothered to sue *Life* for its disclosures about him."(B) Yet Gallagher retained his positions on two House committees, including the one which conducted hearings on organized crime, for three years after the *Life* disclosures.[78] (In contrast, in 1973, 27 out of 30 members of an Italian parliamentary anti-Mafia commission "resigned to protest the membership on the commission of Giovanni Matta, a Christian Democratic deputy who ha[d] been linked to the Mafia."(C))

In the early 1970s, Gallagher served a 17-month prison term for tax evasion.(D)

A–Sackett, Smith and Lambert, "The Congressman and the Hoodlum," *Life*, August 9, 1968, pp. 20–26; B–*Time*, August 22, 1969; C–*Washington Post*, January 19, 1973, p. A22; D–*Washington Post*, May 2, 1982, p. A7.

25.3 Top-secret Justice Department information was leaked to the Mafia. "Among political favors rendered by paid-for officials to Cosa Nostra are the passing along of information that comes over their desks, and the sending up of storm signals whenever official action against the Mob is threatened." In 1962, for example, a top-secret list of gangsters compiled by the Justice Department turned up in a Chicago office used by Mafiosi Sam Giancana and Gus Alex.

In 1977 and 1978, the FBI conducted a massive investigation of waterfront corruption. The investigation revealed that the International Longshoremen's Association is controlled by the Genovese, Gambino, and Marcello Mafia families and that it has extorted multimillion dollar payments from shipping company executives. Among the sources of information were an undercover agent who served as a courier for such payoffs, and a shipping company executive who became a government witness. Another source was a court-approved bug of the office of top ILA official Anthony Scotto, who was identified in a 1969 Justice Department report as a captain in the Gambino Mafia Family.[79] The FBI, via the same bug, then learned to its astonishment that Scotto's men had gotten hold of secret FBI reports summarizing the information from the bug. The leak caused the convening of "one of the largest Mafia gatherings since the celebrated Apalachin, N.Y. meeting." More than 20 prominent Mafiosi met in Miami to discuss underworld business and consider ways to undermine the FBI probe.

Time magazine reported another use made by the Mafia of secret government documents. In 1977, a gangland slaying silenced Gino Gallina. He had been testifying before a Newark grand jury on Mafia executions of informants and potential witnesses against the Mob. "Federal officials blame his slaying on a leak from the grand jury; leaks from secret Government files and sealed court records have led to the deaths of other informants."(D) Also, several times during the 1960s and 1970s, as discussed in entry 21.7, corrupt police officials have leaked federal intelligence on the Mob to underworld figures.

A–*Life*, September 1, 1967, p. 43; B–*Time*, March 20, 1978, p. 19; C–NBC Evening News, "Segment 3," September 6, 1977 and September 7, 1977; D–*Time*, November 21, 1977, p. 39; E–*Washington Post*, November 24, 1978, pp. A1, A9.

25.4 A Congressman from Illinois "not only represented the Syndicate but gave all appearances of being a Mafioso himself." Roland Libonati went beyond even the norms of Illinois politics by posing for a photograph with Al Capone at a baseball game, and by dubbing Mafiosi Tony Accardo and Paul DeLucia (alias Ricca) "charitable" and "patriotic" fellows. Other notorious Chicago Mobsters were among 20 gangsters and politicians bagged in a police raid of Libonati's campaign headquarters in 1931. The Kefauver Report offered this assessment of his political leanings: "Roland Libonati, Democratic State Senator from the West Side, and a close associate of Capone's, spearheaded the opposition to the reform [anti-racketeering] legislation proposed by the Chicago Crime Commission and Governor Stevenson and backed by the bar."(B)

Libonati maintained this record as a U.S. Congressman between 1958 and 1964. Federal agents monitoring visits to Washington, D.C. of Murray Humphreys, a Chicago Mafia associate,[80] reported several contacts during the early 1960s between Humphreys and Libonati. Humphreys, "the master fixer of the Chicago Mob, . . . frequently delivered messages and packages to Libonati and other members of the Illinois Congressional Delegation."(C) Another contact of Humphreys' was Illinois Congressman Thomas O'Brien, who earned the nickname "Blind Tom" O'Brien while Cook County Sheriff. It was O'Brien who sponsored Libonati in a successful "vigorous behind-the-scene movement" to place Libonati on the powerful House Judiciary Committee.

On August 24, 1960, according to a federal informant, Libonati visited Chicago Mafioso[81] Paul DeLucia at the U.S. Penitentiary at Terre Haute, Indiana. When DeLucia and Libonati met, there was "a disgusting display of affection with hugging and kissing."(E) A secret federal report noted that in November of 1960, "Humphreys was apparently in frequent communication and personal contact with Congressman Libonati . . . to expedite the early release of Paul DeLucia" from prison.

On October 23, 1962, as monitored by an FBI bug, Libonati spoke with Pat Marcy, a "Giancana political underling," and John D'Arco, another political stooge of the Mafia boss. Libonati's words, as quoted by the House Assassinations Committee, again demonstrated his total subservience to the Mob: "Last time you guys built me up to 98,000 votes, and the other guy to 23,000. Who ran against me last time?" Libonati also discussed Robert Kennedy: "I killed six of his bills. That wiretapping bill, the intimidating informers bill."(E) Before Libonati left office in 1964, he distinguished himself by introducing a bill to prevent federal agents from keeping gangsters under surveillance.

A–Demaris, *Captive City,* pp. 142–50; B–*U.S.–Senate, Kefauver Report, Third Interim,* p. 59; C–*Life,* September 1, 1967, pp. 42B–43; D–Dorman, *Payoff,* pp. 178–83; E–*U.S.–House, Assassination Appendix, JFK,* vol. 9, pp. 22–25.

25.5 Libonati's successor: current Congressman Frank Annunzio. In 1963, Libonati announced that he would not seek reelection. A secret federal report assessed the situation: "Congressman Roland V. Libonati stepped down on orders from Sam Giancana. . . . Giancana has already selected Frank Annunzio to replace Libonati. Annunzio will follow dictate of Mob." It appeared that Giancana wanted someone whose subservience to the Mafia was less obvious; another secret federal report had stated: "Advised in February, 1962 that Sam Giancana has emphatically instructed his associates and lieutenants not to call 'these politicians' or meet them at their houses. . . . because if they [the Mob] lost these men they 'were dead.' Among the individuals indicated by Giancana were Frank Annunzio. . . ."

Annunzio demonstrated his loyalty to Giancana by retaining Libonati's top congressional aide, Anthony P. Tisci, with a hefty hike in salary. A son-in-law of Chicago Mafia boss Sam Giancana, Tisci resided in Giancana's Oak Park mansion between 1959 and 1963. Tisci also represented Giancana in court while on the Congressional payroll. Annunzio refused to fire Tisci even after Tisci took the Fifth Amendment in three appearances in 1965 before a federal grand jury investigating organized crime in Chicago. Seven weeks after Tisci finally resigned under pressure, he was bagged by St. Louis Police in a raid of what was believed to be a high-level Mob conclave. Also picked up in the St. Louis raid was Mobster-politician[82] John D'Arco—a partner in a Chicago insurance business with Congressman Annunzio.

Demaris, *Captive City,* pp. 144–45, 147–51; Dorman, *Payoff,* pp. 182–84; *Life,* September 1, 1967, pp. 42B-43.

25.6 Hundreds of private bills are introduced in Congress to aid the Mob. "Hundreds of private bills have been slid through at the tail end of congressional sessions to forestall deportation proceedings against Syndicate men who entered the country illegally or who made false statements on their naturalization applications." Salerno and Tompkins, *Crime Confederation,* pp. 250–51.

25.7 Prominent guests at a West Coast Syndicate retreat. Moe Dalitz is a leading Mafia associate and the founder of La Costa Country Club, a "Mafia watering hole" whose membership list includes Mobsters from across the country.[83] Massive surveillance of La Costa by local and federal law enforcement officers disclosed numerous prominent politicians and judges freeloading at La Costa, with Moe Dalitz footing the bill. They included "a prominent United States Senator from the East Coast, known in politics as an ardent liberal, a Federal Court appeals judge from Washington, D.C., and a member of the State Supreme Court of Nevada." Noyes, *Legacy of Doubt*, pp. 243–44.

25.8 The "Flood-Medico-Bufalino triangle." U.S. Congressman Daniel Flood of Pennsylvania was investigated "by at least eight separate U.S. Attorney's offices" and appeared headed for a federal indictment with "175 possible cases" pending against him. According to former aide Stephen Elko, who testified against Flood, he was "Congress's most successful 'muscler', an official who used his considerable influence to direct federal contracts to people and companies that said 'thank you' in cash."

The first instance of Flood's questionable conduct cited in *Time* magazine's "Floodgate" article centered around the "Flood-Medico-Bufalino triangle." Medico Industries was a large Pennsylvania corporation that received a $3.9 million Pentagon contract to produce 600,000 warheads for use in Vietnam. Northeastern Pennsylvania Mafia boss Russell Bufalino, who frequented Medico's offices, was an associate of company general manager William Medico. And according to FBI intelligence, company President Phillip Medico was "a capo (chief) in his Mafia family." *Time* reported that "the FBI discovered more than a decade ago that Flood steered Government business to the Medicos and traveled often on their company jet."

Time, March 6, 1978, p. 21; Dorman, *Payoff*, pp. 254–55.

25.9 No trouble from the Securities and Exchange Commission. "During both the Red-O-Lier deal and the Wavetronics deal [when] we were skirmishing constantly with the Securities and Exchange Commission, [Mobster[84]] Stanley Polley seemed to be able to handle any problems with the SEC without trouble. He claimed that he was able to reach anybody and pay the appropriate amount to reduce the pressure on us." From the testimony of defected Mob money mover Michael Raymond in *U.S.–Senate, OC and Stolen Securities, 1971*, p. 669.

25.10 A prominent Senate aide was convicted of attempting to fix a Mafia business fraud indictment. On November 19, 1970, a federal grand jury indicted three Mafia leaders, three Mafia associates and ten others in a fraud case involving a Florida investment company. The defendants were charged with taking over the company through threats and beatings and then jacking up the price of shares to artificially high selling levels to make huge profits. Before their trial, Robert Carson, chief aide to U.S. Senator Hiram Fong and president of the U.S. Senate Staff Club, was indicted and subsequently convicted of what federal officials termed "a brazen attempt to corrupt the administration of criminal justice" in attempting to fix the Mafia fraud case. Dorman, *Payoff*, pp. 202–11.

25.11 "We can do anything in Washington—anything short of murder." Nat Voloshen was a close associate of several top Mob figures and Washington lobbyists. His record of contacts and dealings illustrates a mind-boggling morass of Mafia corruption.

Some of Voloshen's activities were exposed in 1970 when he was indicted with Martin Sweig, chief aide to House Speaker John McCormack. They were charged with perjury and conspiracy to misuse McCormack's office for the benefit of Voloshen's clients—including several members and associates of the Mafia. Sweig was convicted of perjury, acquitted on the conspiracy count, and sentenced to two-and-a-half years in prison; Voloshen pleaded guilty.

Among the alleged actions of the pair was a call by Sweig to New York State Parole Board Chairman Russell Oswald, as Oswald testified at Sweig's trial. Sweig asked Oswald to release Voloshen's client Manuel Bello, a close criminal associate of Mafia boss Raymond Patriarca. Trial testimony also established that Sweig had intervened with federal officials on behalf of another imprisoned Voloshen client, New York Lucchese Family member[85] Salvatore Granello. When Speaker McCormack was called to the witness stand, he professed ignorance of the activities of Sweig and Voloshen, explaining, "I'm not an inquiring fellow." But McCormack admitted that he was a long-time friend of Voloshen, whom he generally saw once or twice a week.

As Congressman Gerald Ford told a lobbyist in 1967, noting the difficulty of investigating Voloshen's gangland connections, "You can only go so far on the man and then the walls of protection come down before you can really get at him."(B) Indeed, it appears that the Sweig-Voloshen indictment merely scratched the surface of their activities. Robert Winter-Berger, a former Washington lobbyist and associate of Voloshen, wrote of his first-hand observations of the corrupter at work. Winter-Berger reported that he often heard McCormack tell Voloshen's clients, "Nat can take care of that for you. Nat's my dear friend and I will do anything I can for him."(B) Winter-Berger described how he once heard Voloshen and Sweig discuss the $2,500 a month "rent" Voloshen paid McCormack for use of his office. He related, "Twice I saw [New York Mafia boss Frank] Costello with Nathan Voloshen in House Speaker McCormack's offices."(B)

Winter-Berger described Voloshen's ties with other members of Congress, too. In October 1968, he accompanied Voloshen to a fund raising party at the Overseas Press Club in New York for Congressman John Rooney, the chairman of one House committee and ranking member of another. During the party, Winter-Berger saw Voloshen hand Rooney a white envelope, which Winter-Berger had watched Voloshen stuff with twenty $100 bills before the party. Voloshen told Rooney, "John, as you know, it isn't the first and it won't be the last." Rooney replied, "Nat, anything you want is yours. You're a dear, dear friend. I'm proud to know you."(B) (It was this same Congressman Rooney who requested and received petty "dirt" on a political opponent from FBI Director J. Edgar Hoover, as revealed in FBI memos released in 1978.)[86] Winter-Berger noted that Voloshen, in addition to being close to Congressman McCormack and Rooney, "was also the vest-pocket lobbyist-friend of House Majority Leader Carl Albert; House Majority Whip Hale Boggs; former Representative James Roosevelt of California; and former Representative Adam Clayton Powell of New York."(B)

A–Dorman, *Payoff*, pp. 189–97; B–Winter-Berger, *Washington Payoff*, pp. 50–51, 105–14.

25.12 The Voloshen-Sweig-McCormack combine, the Parvin-Dohrmann case, and a U.S. Supreme Court justice.

The stock of the Parvin-Dohrmann Company, a conglomerate, was enjoying a meteoric rise. But on May 5, 1969, it was suspended from trading by the Securities and Exchange Commission because of suspected illegal stock manipulation and underworld connections. As summarized by the *New York Times*, it was then suggested that Parvin-Dohrmann enlist Mob lobbyist Nathan M. Voloshen. Working with Martin Sweig, Speaker McCormack's top aide, Voloshen arranged a meeting between Parvin-Dohrmann officials and Hamer T. Budge, chairman of the Securities and Exchange Commission. Sidney Korshak, Parvin-Dohrmann's counsel, saw to it that Parvin-Dohrmann paid Voloshen $50,000 for his assistance.

On May 12, 1969, six days after the meeting, the injunction against trading Parvin-Dohrmann stock was lifted. Two weeks later, Washington lobbyist Robert Winter-Berger went to McCormack's Washington office to meet Voloshen. Winter-Berger saw McCormack hold an envelope and tell Voloshen: "Many thanks for this, Nat. I appreciate it. I will salt it away. Glad you succeeded with Hamer Budge. Let me know if Martin [Sweig] can be of any further help to you."(B) The next day, Winter-Berger learned from Voloshen that $15,000 of Voloshen's $50,000 fee had gone to McCormack and $10,000 to Sweig.

The Parvin-Dohrmann company had been the subject of other federal probes. Suggestive of Mafia ties were the company's investments in Las Vegas hotels linked to the Mob and Teamsters, and its mysterious multimillion dollar transactions with Swiss banks. Also under federal scrutiny were the Parvin Foundation and Albert Parvin, a key figure in both the company and foundation. Specifically, journalist Clark Mollenhoff summarized, a 1971 federal indictment of Meyer Lansky alleged that a $200,000 "finder's fee" paid to Lansky was actually "part of the Hotel Flamingo conspiracy involving the Albert Parvin Foundation."(C) And "according to the indictment, Albert Parvin . . . was believed by the Internal Revenue Service, the FBI, and Strike Force lawyers Mike DeFeo and Robert Thaller to be a front for the Lansky group."(C)

Given the reputed connections of Albert Parvin and his enterprises, it came as a shock to many when it was disclosed that Supreme Court Justice William Douglas had received over $100,000 during the 1960s as president of the Parvin Foundation. A number of Congressmen called for Douglas's impeachment; "the arrangement looked too much like an indirect payoff to the High Court Justice as a reward for opinions that coincided with the mob's best interests."(C) The Parvin-Douglas connection became yet more suspicious in 1976 after the *New York Times* published a four-part series on Mob attorney Sidney Korshak, which confirmed the major Mob influence in the Parvin-Dohrmann company. After acquiring sealed SEC records under the Freedom of Information Act, the *Times* concluded that Korshak, one of the most powerful Mobsters in America, had "dominated the affairs of the Parvin-Dohrmann corporation in the late 1960's."(A) The *Times* reported that corporate chairman Delbert Coleman had served merely as a front for Korshak and was excluded from at least one important company meeting which Korshak attended. And the *Times* disclosed a secret Parvin-Dohrmann payment of $500,000 to Korshak—a payment not disclosed to shareholders in violation of SEC rules—for Korshak's role in the company purchase of the Las Vegas Stardust Hotel and Casino. "Federal officials concluded that it was Mr. Korshak's influence with organized crime figures rather than the extent of his activity that earned him his high fee."(A)

A–Seymour Hersh, in collaboration with Jeff Gerth, "Major Corporations Seek Korshak's Labor Advice," *New York Times*, June 29, 1976, pp. 1, 16; B–Winter-Berger, *Washington Payoff*, pp. 77–79; C–Mollenhoff, *Strike Force*, pp. 90–91, 189–92, 195–96.

25.13 Letters of recommendation for a notorious Mob killer from two powerful Illinois congressmen. William Dawson was an influential congressman from Illinois, chairman of the House Committee on Government Operations and vice chairman of the Democratic National Committee. Once a lawyer specializing in underworld clients, Dawson was also featured prominently in a 1954 federal investigation of illegal gambling. The investigation revealed that several calls were placed to Dawson's unlisted Washington number from telephones used by the Chicago Mob.

Gus Alex was one of the most notorious of Chicago Mob figures, a "ruthless, vicious killer" and "political fixer and power behind First Ward politicians." His "record dates back to 1930, [including] more than 25 arrests: fugitive, bribery, assault with intent to kill, manslaughter, kidnapping; prime suspect in at least 6 murders—two gave deathbed statements naming Alex as their slayer, 3 received death threats from Alex shortly before their murder."

In 1967, Chicago newspapers reported that both Congressman Will Dawson and Senator Everett Dirksen had written letters to the Swiss government on Alex's behalf, even though the Chicago Police had identified him to the McCellan Committee as a "non-member associate" of the Mafia. The Swiss considered Alex an undesirable and had banned him, but his representatives in Congress were trying to persuade them otherwise. Senator Dirksen claimed that his letter for Alex was handled as "a routine matter" by his staff. Congressman Dawson stated that he had known Alex for many years and "never knew him to do anything wrong."(B)

A–Demaris, *Captive City*, pp. 170–72, 324–25; B–Salerno and Tompkins, *Crime Confederation*, pp. 249–50.

Also see the main text for the Mob contacts and dealings of LBJ's secretary Bobby Baker (sections 17.7 and 17.8), presidents Lyndon Johnson (section 16.1) and Richard Nixon (section 16.2), and Senators Russell Long (chapter 9, Frank Caracci) and Edward Long (section 24.2).

☐☐☐☐☐☐☐☐☐☐☐☐☐☐☐☐☐☐

George Jackson rotted in jail for nearly a decade for heisting $70. Jimmy Hoffa cops a million, bribes juries, runs with the most dangerous gangsters in America and, thanks to the intervention of his good friend Dick Nixon, does an easy five. This, after the parole board had rejected Hoffa's appeal three times in a row.

> Budd Schulberg, from the introduction to *The Fall and Rise of Jimmy Hoffa* by Walter Sheridan.

☐☐☐☐☐☐☐☐☐☐☐☐☐☐☐☐☐☐☐

26. Subversion of the Press

26.1 Planting and suppressing newspaper stories. "A Fix ... can be attained through employment of public relations counsels who stress things like the good name of a city or the amount of money donated to charity by Mob enterprises, or who plant in newspaper columns evidences of the charm, wit and good connections of key mobsters as they are seen about the spots where expensive people gather. It can be helped immeasurably with cheap devices like easy 'loans' to a reporter whose tastes outrun his income. ...

"It is a matter of particular pride to [Mafia boss] Giancana and his boys that they are firmly in control of both the Democratic and the Republican political organizations in Chicago's famous First Ward. ... [C]ertain journalists are part and parcel of the First Ward Fix. The First Ward Democratic organization, if it serves the gangsters needs, can—and on occasion does—swing enough influence in city rooms to get a story killed or softened to the point where it is almost an apology." *Life*, September 1, 1967, pp. 22, 42B.

26.2 Information about a top Mob figure was consistently suppressed. In June 1976, the *New York Times* ran a four-part series on attorney Sidney Korshak. It described him as "the most important link between organized crime and legitimate business," and one of the most powerful Syndicate figures in the Country. Korshak's "name has come up in at least 20 investigations of organized crime."

His clout in the outfit was indicated one day in 1961, when Korshak arrived unexpectedly at the Riviera Hotel in Las Vegas; Teamster boss Jimmy Hoffa was thrown out of the hotel's presidential suite and moved to smaller quarters to make room for Korshak.

The *Times* found that in Chicago—Korshak's nurturing ground—the papers repeatedly lauded him for his charitable activities and mentioned him in gossip columns. But there has been no real reporting on him, and articles always skirted his underworld ties "with such vague phrases as 'wheeler-dealer' and 'mystery man.'" One veteran Chicago reporter cited two instances when top editors deleted unpleasant references to Korshak. The reporter noted, "You couldn't get a story about him in the paper." And "a former close Korshak friend recalled that he often heard Mr. Korshak boast that he was able to influence the *Chicago Tribune* to soften or tone down stories about him."

Seymour Hersh, in collaboration with Jeff Gerth, series on Sidney Korshak, *New York Times*, June 27, 1976-June 30, 1976; information on press coverage in June 30, 1976, p. 14.

26.3 A weekend "you won't forget." Pulitzer Prize-winning journalist Clark Mollenhoff had covered Iowa Mobster Luigi Fratto (alias Lew Farrell) and associates as a police reporter on the *Des Moines Register*. Mollenhoff wrote that they had displayed "a fondness for newsmen and police, and had a special interest in college athletes and sports writers. Lew even offered to pick up the tab for me for a weekend 'you won't forget' in St. Louis or Chicago. I am sure now that I never would have forgotten that weekend; I wouldn't have been permitted to do so." Mollenhoff, *Strike Force*, p. 39.

26.4 Corruption of reporters by the Teamsters. The McClellan Committee learned during its late-1950s labor probe that "Teamsters Union money had contaminated a few reporters, a few columnists, a few feature writers. We found that in a number of cases Hoffa's union had paid cash or given gifts or 'expenses' to get favorable press coverage." Robert Kennedy, *The Enemy Within*, p. 226.

26.5 A leading syndicated columnist was reportedly on the Mob payroll. "The Mob had on its payroll one of the nation's best-known syndicated newspaper columnists—who secretly lobbied in Washington on behalf of racket interests. Every six months, racketeers throughout the country set aside one day's take from slot and pinball machines and delivered it to the columnist—half in cash and half in a check to his favorite charitable foundation." From information furnished by Jack Halfen, a Texas Mobster and political fixer, reported in Dorman, *Payoff*, p. 156.

26.6 A Mob boss bans the word "Mafia." Joseph Colombo was boss of a New York Mafia family and a member of the Mafia National Commission.[87] In 1970, he formed the Italian-American Civil Rights League, thereby performing, as *New York Magazine* commented, "a feat of traditional 17th-century Sicilian sleight of hand," making "allies of his own victims." The absurdity of the Mafia's public relations campaign was highlighted when Colombo was gunned down at a League rally in 1971.[88] Yet the League succeeded in pressuring Attorney General John Mitchell to ban the words "Mafia" and "Cosa Nostra" from all Justice Department and FBI reports; several governors and other officials followed suit. League officials also managed to convince "Godfather" producer Al Ruddy to delete all references to the Mafia and Cosa Nostra from the film, and to donate revenues from the movie's premier performance to the League. A League-orchestrated campaign featuring "close to 100 letters of protest ... from Senators, Congressmen and New York State Legislators"(B) had failed to stop production of the movie.

Perhaps most disturbing, however, was the censorship Mafia boss Colombo's organization exerted over the press. In 1970, after League members led by Colombo's son Anthony picketed the *New York Times*, the newspaper stopped using the words "Mafia" and "Cosa Nostra." The next day's issue referred to a notorious Mafioso as a "reputed member of organized crime." When New York City's *Staten Island Advance* refused to comply with Colombo's censorship or to cancel a series of articles on local Mobsters, the League picketed the Advance building and attempted to stop the newspaper's deliveries. One delivery truck carrying 10,000 papers "was forced off the road and set afire by four Colombo goons who pulled the driver and a circulation manager out of the truck and beat them with tire irons."(C)

A–Meskil, *Don Carlo*, pp. 203–4; B–*Time*, March 13, 1972, p. 57; C–Meskil, *Luparelli Tapes*, pp. 154–55; D–Dorman, *Payoff*, p. 281.

□□□□□□□□□□□□□□□□□□□□□□□□

Under any just and fair system of government it would seem that his [Robert Kennedy's] persecution of Hoffa should cease, since the only "crime" that Hoffa seems to be guilty of is that he will not knuckle under to the Kennedys and give them slavish obedience. . . . The fight of James Hoffa against the Kennedys is becoming the fight of all Americans who want to stay free men and women.

> William Loeb, in a front page editorial in the *Manchester Union Leader*, May 13, 1963, quoted in Sheridan, *Fall and Rise of Jimmy Hoffa*, p. 280. A year after the editorial appeared, Hoffa was convicted of jury tampering and defrauding the Teamster pension fund of $2 million;[89] five weeks earlier, the *Manchester Union Leader* had received a $500,000 loan from the Teamsters pension fund.[90]

□□□□□□□□□□□□□□□□□□□□□□□□□

26.7 A movie on the Mob that never appeared. One of the most powerful books ever written about the Mob was Robert Kennedy's 1960 best seller, *The Enemy Within*. The book summarized the wholesale Mafia extortion, embezzlement, and violence in the labor movement revealed in the McClellan Committee hearings. On the prompting of Attorney General Kennedy, Budd Schulberg wrote a motion picture script based on the book, to be produced by Jerry Wald of 20th Century Fox, "who alone had the courage to produce it."

But Jerry Wald died suddenly. The new studio head refused to handle it after a labor tough walked into his office and threatened to prevent delivery of prints to theaters if the movie were ever produced. As Schulberg related, "there have been ever-increasing ties between the Mob and some of the film studios and, of course, those studios rejected it out of hand." Schulberg then attended a meeting with several interested Columbia executives, but that studio turned it down after everyone at the meeting received an implicitly threatening letter from Mob-Teamster lawyer William Bufalino. When Schulberg tried to produce the film himself with Robert Kennedy's encouragement, one film star initially phoned Schulberg to say he loved the script. Schulberg related, he "then came to my house drunk to tell me he was afraid he might be killed if he did it."

From Budd Schulberg's introduction to *The Fall and Rise of Jimmy Hoffa* by Walter Sheridan.

26.8 Mob-Teamster shakedowns of several major newspapers. As Robert Kennedy summarized, "in a series of hearings [of the McClellan Committee] beginning in May 1959, . . . it was disclosed that associates of Mr. Hoffa had practiced shakedowns on management people engaged in newspaper distribution. The papers were: The *New York Times*, the New York *Daily Mirror*, the Detroit *Times*, the Pittsburgh *Sun-Telegraph*, and the *American Weekly*." Senator McClellan wrote that the Committee hearings revealed "gangster infiltration and dominance of the newspaper and magazine distribution business" in New York City during the 1950s, and "reported payoffs made to union officials by news publications who sought union peace by yielding to shakedowns and extortion."(B) Senator McClellan commented, "once more the venal coalition was revealed: hoodlums, collusive management, and union leaders, all working together."(B)

A–Kennedy, *The Enemy Within*, pp. 220–26; B–McClellan, *Crime Without Punishment*, p. 215; C–Hutchinson, *Imperfect Union*, pp. 274–76.

26.9 Murder and corruption in Arizona. Don Bolles, an Arizona reporter, was nominated for a Pulitzer Prize in 1965 and named the state's "Newsman of the Year" in 1974. In June 1976, Bolles set out to pursue a lead on his main investigative interest—Mob ties to business and politics. But when Bolles turned the ignition of his car, he was mutilated by the blast of a bomb planted under the floorboard. Before he died, Bolles told firemen "they finally got me—the Mafia."(D)

The Mob's timing was bad, however, for the bombing occurred just one week before the national meeting in Indianapolis of the Investigative Reporters and Editors Group (IRE). In response to the murder of Bolles, the IRE sent 36 reporters to Arizona under the direction of Pulitzer Prize winners Bob Greene and Dick Cady. The IRE sought to complete Bolles' work through an intensive investigation of organized crime in that state.

In a 23-part newspaper series that appeared nationwide in March and April 1977, the IRE exposed the pervasive influence of the Mob in Arizona. It detailed the penetration in Arizona's businesses, courts, and political establishment of more than 200 representatives of Mafia families from New York, Boston, Detroit, St. Louis, Chicago, Cleveland, and other cities. And it reported that three of the state's leading political figures "have dominated Phoenix and much of Arizona while maintaining friendships and other alliances with Mob figures."(B)

Investigative Reporters and Editors Inc., Phoenix Project (IRE series), *Albuquerque Journal*, March 13 through April 3, 1977, especially A–March 13, p. A1; B–March 14, p. A1; C–March 15, pp. A1, A6. Also D–*Newsweek*, June 14, 1976, pp. 83–84; E–*New York Times*, March 17, 1977, p. A26; F–Reid and Demaris, *The Green Felt Jungle*, pp. 47, 50, 51.

27. From the Redwood Forests to the Gulf Stream Waters

Following are miscellaneous references grouped alphabetically by state, concluding with a brief selection of sources on Mafia activities outside the United States.

27.1 Alabama: Liquor profits. The Mob has been "making a fortune" in liquor distribution in Alabama. Dorman, *Payoff*, pp. 124–25.

27.2 Alaska: A piece of the oil pipeline action. The well-paid, free-spending workers on the Alaska pipeline represented a golden opportunity for the Mob. Salvatore Spinelli and Jerome Max Pasley, who are associated with Arizona Mafia boss Joseph Bonanno, quickly moved in. "Today, Bonanno's influence is strong in that state." IRE series on organized crime in Arizona, *Albuquerque Journal*, March 27, 1977, p. A4; also see Grutzner, "How to Lock Out the Mafia," *Harvard Business Review*, March-April 1970, p. 58.

27.3 Arizona: Mafia infestation. "Organized crime is staging a blitzkrieg invasion of Phoenix, Tucson and other Arizona cities. . . . There is a historic and continuing relationship between underworld chieftains and leading power-brokers of both the Republican and Democratic parties." Former U.S. Attorney William Smitherman commented, organized crime "has Arizona by the throat." IRE series on organized crime, *Albuquerque Journal*, March 13, 1977, pp. A1, A4; also see succeeding articles, from March 14, 1977 to April 2, 1977.

27.4 Arkansas: A Mob gambling center in Hot Springs. Hot Springs over the years has served as a meeting place for such top Mafia figures as Al Capone and Frank Costello. Dorman, *Payoff*, pp. 36–37.

27.5 California, northern: "infiltration of crime into state business." An investigator for the State Department of Consumer Affairs was offered bribes and threatened to lay off an investigation of a Mob-infiltrated San Francisco Bay area employment agency. He continued the probe and then, following a break-in at his office, was "beaten to a pulp" outside a San Francisco restaurant. State Consumer Affairs Director John Kehoe noted, "profits from prostitution, gambling and other rackets are being 'laundered' in seemingly legitimate businesses." *Los Angeles Times*, October 19, 1973, p. 3.

27.6 California, southern: "The Mafia . . . has zeroed in." While advance elements of the Mob settled into Los Angeles, Orange and San Diego counties, Mafia bosses from Chicago, New York, Detroit and Las Vegas secretly convened and sent underlings scurrying about with messages and money. A seven count federal indictment against 12 Southern California Mafia members and associates revealed "a widespread pattern of extortion, loansharking and racketeering."(B)
A–Bill Hazlett, "Mafia Infiltrates Southland with Men and Money," *Los Angeles Times*, June 1, 1973, pp. 1, 18, 19; B–Hazlett, "12 Indicted Here in Crackdown on Mafia," *Los Angeles Times*, July 10, 1974, pp. 1, 19.

27.7 Colorado: Mafia operations for decades. Chicago Crime Commission Director Virgil Peterson described Mob gambling activities and business ventures in Blend, Canon City, Central City, Colorado Springs, Denver, Pueblo, and Trinidad, Colorado. Peterson named several Mafia members and associates from Kansas City, Los Angeles, and New York as well as local Mobsters who were involved in Colorado operations. *U.S.–Senate, Kefauver Hearings*, vol. 2, pp. 186–87.

27.8 Florida: "An expanding base of operations" for 14 of the 24 Mafia families. Extensive Mafia operations and real estate interests throughout the state are detailed by state and federal officials. *U.S.–House, Crime in America*, pp. 192–93, 317–56; *Life*, October 24, 1969, p. 62; Reid, *Grim Reapers*, p. 102; *U.S.–Senate, Kefauver Report, Third Interim*, pp. 30–36, 63–67.

27.9 Georgia: "11 Mafia families are represented." "Mafia racketeers from across the country are moving into Atlanta in increasing numbers" from cities across the nation. They move into gambling, drugs, liquor, prostitution, real estate, and commercial businesses. Mobsters have taken over "office buildings and night clubs, real estate, auto leasing and other ventures." Francis Kent, "Mafia Moving Into Atlanta—City Called 'Peach' Ripe for Picking." *Los Angeles Times*, July 1, 1974, p. 14; also see *Atlanta Journal*, March 22, 1974.

27.10 Illinois (Chicago): "A city in the grip of the Mob." "The situation today is nearly the same as it was . . . even in 1930, at the height of Al Capone's reign of terror. . . . The Syndicate is so solidly entrenched there and so monolithic in structure that it is almost impossible to root out. It has worked its way into nearly every facet of the life of the city. . . . you may be doing business with the Syndicate when you subscribe to a diaper service, hire a scavenging firm to haul your garbage away, buy a neon sign, park your car in a downtown garage, purchase bread in a supermarket, order a carpet, contract for plumbing work, get airline tickets through a travel agency, take out a loan at a bank or even go to the polls to vote." Bill Davidson, "How the Mob Controls Chicago." *Saturday Evening Post*, November 9, 1963, pp. 17–27.

27.11 Michigan: Mafia business interests. The *Detroit Free Press* revealed that Mafia boss Vincent Meli "apparently runs" J&J Cartage Company, one of Detroit's largest steel cartage companies. *Detroit Free Press*, April 11, 1974; see also "When the Mafia Takes Over a City; Detroit," *U.S. News and World Report*, October 21, 1963, p. 6.

27.12 Mississippi: Mob contracts "all over the state." One major Mob corrupter says he makes "as much money in Mississippi and Alabama as [he does] anywhere else." As an indication of his involvements there, he showed a business card that lists him as a construction company official in Jackson, Mississippi. Dorman, *Payoff*, p. 124.

27.13 Missouri: Mafia stronghold in Kansas City. *U.S.–Kefauver Hearings*, vol. 2, pp. 185–86; Tyler, *Organized Crime in America*, pp. 296–98.

27.14 Nevada: "In some cases . . . top Mob leaders have dominated both gambling and political operations." Pierre La Fitte, an undercover investigator hired by the *Las Vegas Sun*, impersonated a big-time racketeer and was able to bribe county and state officials to secure protection for his pretended operations. In a tape-recorded conversation with Lt. Governor and Democratic national committeeman Clifford Jones, La Fitte, using the name Louis Tabet, told Jones he'd "taken care of the county" and named several county officials whom he had agreed to pay off. Jones replied, "You're with the right people. I talk for the state. Louie Wiener, my [law] partner, takes care of the legal end of the deals and the finances." Tabet asked Jones for help in obtaining a gambling license, despite his admitted criminal record ("a few things when I was young—a little narcotics, bootlegging, murder, manslaughter"). When assured that Tabet had no recent convictions, Jones told him, "you're all right, but not until after the first of the year when [Gubernatorial candidate Vail] Pittman takes office."

Following the *Las Vegas Sun*'s exposure of the exploits of "Louis Tabet," Jones resigned his position as Democratic national committeeman, but not as lieutenant governor. Jones, who held interests in three Las Vegas casinos, later became

involved with LBJ aide Bobby Baker in negotiations for gambling casinos in the Caribbean.
Dorman, *Payoff*, pp. 139–44.

27.15 New England states: Vicious and prosperous Mafia operations. The Mob owns "diaper services, linen services, auto agencies, car-repair firms, drugstores and garbage collecting firms. ... It controls numerous night clubs, bars and restaurants—ranging from dives ... to some of the finest gourmet eating places in New England. The mob owns, or has owned, cemeteries, dude ranches, a New Hampshire ski resort and a country club north of Boston." Bill Davidson, "The Mafia: How it Bleeds New England," *Saturday Evening Post*, November 18, 1967, pp. 27–31; also see *U.S.–House, OC in Sports*, pp. 764–65.

27.16 New Jersey: Versatile goons. DeCavalcante Family Mafioso Gaetano Vastola has a number of business interests in neighboring New York, including a leading booking agency for entertainment figures, and was convicted of extorting $500,000 from a rug company in Georgia. Genovese Family member Anthony Russo, after organizing bookmaking and loan sharking operations in the North Jersey Shore area, became owner of a number of construction firms, secured extensive horse racing interests, was hired as a labor consultant by two large resort hotels, and served a 3–5 year prison sentence for perjury. Mafia associate Michael Stavola, with convictions for assaulting an officer and bribery, owns or is the principal in more than 40 corporations "involved in road materials and construction, contracting equipment, condominium apartments, horseracing, refuse collection, landfill, beach clubs, soft drinks, and real estate. He does business in New Jersey, New York, Florida, Pennsylvania, Delaware, and owns a farm in Maine." From the testimony of New Jersey Police Captain William Baum in *U.S.–House, OC in Sports*, pp. 570–76.

27.17 New York: gambling, robbery, perjury, and extortion. After a series of raids in upstate New York and Scranton, Pennsylvania, indictments on these charges were handed down against northeastern Pennsylvania Mafia boss Russell Bufalino, 15 underlings and 8 others, three of whom were already in prison for possession of incendiary devices. Bufalino and his associates were also charged with conspiring to assault two competitors of a Mob cigarette vending firm in Binghamton, New York which, not surprisingly, gained monopoly control of business in that area. According to affidavits by Mafia defector Joseph Zito, who was held in protective custody, Mob henchmen beat one competitor over the head with baseball bats. *New York Times*, April 22, 1973, p. 30; May 1, 1973, p. 46; May 6, 1973, p. 51.

27.18 Ohio: A Mafia reign of terror in Youngstown. During the 1950s and early 1960s, friction between rival Mob factions in Youngstown, Ohio resulted in 81 gangland bombings and several murders. A settlement was imposed following a November 8, 1959 meeting of 150 Mafia dons in a Worcester, Massachusetts hotel, as was reported by Massachusetts Attorney General Edward McCormack, yet rivalries persisted. This was brought home to Youngstown residents on November 22, 1962, when a bomb exploded in the car of Mafia boss Charles Cavallaro, killing him and his 11-year-old son Thomas, and crippling his 12-year-old son Charles, Jr.

The violence finally led voters to oust Mayor Frank Franko, an unfrocked judge and disbarred lawyer, for a reform administration. But after 40 years in which the underworld had "controlled politics, the police, and sometimes even the courts," traditions died hard. Police Chief William Golden, who had substituted merit for graft as a basis for promotions and had tripled the city's gambling arrests, found dynamite fuses wired to his car. Mobster Joey Naples, who was caught with gambling slips, stolen goods, and an arsenal of weapons at his home, almost escaped conviction when incriminating evidence was stolen right out of the courtroom. Finally, Naples' conviction was reversed when his lawyer raised a technical point concerning a search warrant and, to everyone's surprise, prosecutor John Cianflona agreed to the defense motion. Cianflona, an assistant Ohio attorney general, was fired for this action by State Attorney General William Saxbe, who suggested that a $20,000 slush fund to spring Naples may have contributed to the reversal.

Cook, *Secret Rulers*, pp. 26–54; Dorman, *Payoff*, pp. 94–96.

27.19 Wisconsin: "The Mafia has several footholds in Wisconsin businesses." The Grande Cheese Company was a large Mob-owned firm in Leroy, Wisconsin, founded in 1941 by Chicago Mafia boss Ross Prio. In 1973, it became the beneficiary of a $2.5 million industrial revenue bond issue voted in illegal and secret sessions of the town's board of supervisors.

In Forrestville, Wisconsin, associates of the New York Gambino Mafia Family bought their way into the Badger State Cheese Company. By 1977, eight months after the Mafia took over, Badger Cheese was bankrupt. The new owners skipped town with the company's assets, leaving a debt of more than $500,000 to the dairy farmers who supplied milk to the plant. "Fifty-five people lost their jobs. One bank is out $200,000 in loans to Gambino and his associates. And the economy of a small town was hurt badly. ... The dairy farmers around here now know what it's like to do business with the Mob."(B)

A–Madison, Wisconsin *Capital Times*, February 4, 1974; B–NBC Evening News, "Segment 3," December 13, 1977. NBC also reported that the Mob has a virtual monopoly on cheese sold to pizzerias on the East Coast; it supplies the cheese at inflated prices.

27.20 Mafia tentacles around the world. Following are a scattering of references to Mafia activities and dealings outside the United States. Australia: Bob Wiedrich, "Aussies are wary of Mafia Invasion," *Chicago Tribune*, September 18, 1973, p. 14; Salerno and Tompkins, *Crime Confederation*, p. 385. The Bahamas: Reid, *Grim Reapers*, pp. 125–45; Salerno and Tompkins, pp. 385–87. Brazil: Reid, pp. 281–82. Canada: Salerno and Tompkins, p. 285. Dominican Republic: *Life*, September 8, 1967, p. 101. Great Britain: Salerno and Tompkins, pp. 382–83. Haiti: Teresa, *My Life in the Mafia*, pp. 222–30; Salerno and Tompkins, pp. 386–87. Italy: see section 7. For general information on international Mob activity, see Messick, *Syndicate Abroad*.

27.21 A series of indictments typify the Mafia's worldwide activities. Nineteen federal and state indictments were handed down against 25 persons, including high-ranking Mobsters. Among the crimes charged were narcotics smuggling, extortion, loan sharking, sale and distribution of counterfeit money and airline tickets, and attempted murder. The alleged principals in this web of crime were Mafiosi Matteo DiLorenzo and Vincent Rizzo, of New York's Genovese Family. DiLorenzo reputedly controls criminal activities at Kennedy International Airport in New York City.

"The indictments ... talk of threats and beatings, of people being thrown through windows and men traveling thousands of miles to make payments for drugs and other items. ... They tell of deals in Buffalo, Las Vegas, New York, Argentina, Chile and Japan, of smuggling counterfeit money into the United States from Canada and then distributing the bills throughout the United States and into Japan and South America. . . ." Among the crimes charged was the attempted murder by two Genovese Family members of a boy, whom they beat up, breaking his skull, and then tossed out a window, for no apparent reason. The indictments reveal "a complex narcotics smuggling operation throughout Latin America." They describe "a number of incidents involving loan-sharking, extortion, and threat of bodily harm." *New York Times*, December 8, 1972, pp. 1, 90.

□□□□□□□□□□□□□□□□□□□□□□

Mafia-controlled companies having branches in Latin America and interests in Europe serve as conduits for the outflow of profits from illicit operations in the United States. Some of the funds go to the smugglers of raw opium from the Near East; some to the refiners of heroin in France and Italy; others to coded accounts in Swiss Banks whence some of the money comes back, through U.S. Banks, in the form of untraceable investments in major American corporations or equally untraceable "loans" to the very underworld bosses who started the funds on their roundabout journey.

Charles Grutzner, "How to Lock Out the Mafia," *Harvard Business Review,* March-April 1970, p. 51.
□□□□□□□□□□□□□□□□□□□□□

Appendix 5
A Conversation Between Alex Bottus, Theodore Charach, and the Author

The conversation transcribed below took place on Sunday afternoon, February 2, 1975, during a conference, "The Politics of Conspiracy," at Boston University, Sherman Student Center Conference Auditorium, in Boston. It was tape-recorded by the author, and the tape is in his possession. Background on the information discussed is provided in section 24.3 of the text. Some segments of the conversation of little significance have been omitted from this transcript, as denoted by ellipses. Theodore Charach is a leading investigator of the Robert Kennedy assassination, and Alex Bottus is an investigator of crime and corruption from Chicago.

Bottus: Cesar [inaudible] at the last minute was put in as a temporary guard. He replaced another guy that was supposed to be the guard. And within a day and a half, he replaced the real man that was supposed to be the guard just because he was on this payroll as a temporary employee of this security guard outfit.

Charach: He was called at the last moment.

Bottus: That's right.

Charach: And that's why he [inaudible]. He was called at the last moment, that is true, so that's very interesting.

Bottus: Now listen to me—

Charach: Why was he called at the last moment?

Bottus: To do the job. To do the job.

Charach: He received a call at the last moment. Now why did they have him replaced?

Bottus: No, no, he didn't get the call. He was all set up. You had a guard that was supposed to be there at the Ambassador, right? That guard—

Charach: But there could have been several guards. Kennedy could have gone through another door and—

Bottus: I'm using him as one example—

Charach: Because that's what happened.

Bottus: I'm telling you this security guard outfit has to file reports with your state [California], and they have to show their daily roster of the regular men who are on duty, their payroll, this and this and everything else, right?

Charach: Um-hum.

Bottus: And they also have to show their temporary personnel. You find out when the last date was that Cesar worked for this security guard firm before that night. He hadn't worked for months and months for this security firm; he was carried as a temporary employee.

Charach: I know that. This part is true.

Bottus: Okay, now.

Charach: And that's his out, saying that he was just called at the last minute.

Bottus: Bullshit.

Charach: But he got divorced, immediately—his wife might have known something, so did Meridan; Meridan escaped to the Las Vegas area.

Bottus: Then you go check the police records down in Tijuana, how many times Cesar got arrested down there, and it was all fixed by none other than John Alessio.

Charach: Well then, he went—

Bottus: Go check it out in the Tijuana Police records.

Charach: He was arrested?

Bottus: Sure. He's always down there. He's fighting, he's a very argumentative-type guy. He's a fighter, he got in a fight with Marines.

Charach: Yea, he's supposed to be a goldbricker that will do anything for money. I had it checked through Lockheed, through the public relations, that's what they told me. . . .

Scheim: Excuse me, I'm very interested in this.

Bottus: All right.

Scheim: Do you mind if I'm recording this, or do you want me to shut it off?

Bottus: Well what were you going to ask me?

Scheim: I just want to know what specific ties does he have with organized crime. I'm very interested in this whole business.

Bottus: Well, his ties with organized crime—

Scheim: Cesar, Cesar.

Bottus: Yea, Cesar. They're identified by the very detective firm that he works for.

Scheim: Okay, what—I didn't quite catch that.

Bottus: Well, they've been cited a number of times.

Scheim: Which firm, what's the name of the firm?

Bottus: I can't remember the name now because you're asking me what I dug into, what, six, seven years ago, and gave up on.

Scheim: So Cesar's firm is connected with Alessio and—

Bottus: Right, they were the same firm that protected the bank that went under under C. Arnholt Smith. John Alessio and—they were sent away and the papers covered up because it was Mob connections, the Mob's layoff bookie man being on the board of directors with C. Arnholt Smith. . . .

Scheim: Are there any other ties aside from working for that detective agency? In terms of his arrest record—

Bottus: Well, his whole track record. You trace him either through Missouri, Arkansas, and go down like I said into Chula Vista, you get down into University City, you get down into Tijuana, they all know about Cesar. And this guy's got connections like crazy. And he's gotten in trouble with his gun both on duty and off duty, none of that shit was brought out.

[The author then questioned Bottus concerning the background of his disclosures.]

Bottus: I got a tip to follow up on a lead to see when this guard got on duty, all right? And then I put someone on it, and the Bobby Kennedy thing then had about

30 people jump in on it, we had more than all our own hell busting loose inside of Chicago at that time, so I just pulled back my tracks. That was the little bit of information I had. I was surprised Tad didn't have it.

   Scheim: The thing is, it's the obvious—just the most obvious suspect.
   Bottus: Sure. . . .

Appendix 6
Additional Underworld Contacts
of Jack Ruby

Bobby Joe Chapman was a Dallas bookmaker who reportedly operated in partnership with James Dolan,[1] a notorious Mafia associate.[2] Chapman was one of 11 men arrested by the FBI on January 18, 1972 in a series of gambling raids in Dallas.[3] An envelope marked "The Dallas Cowboys Football Club," containing $10,000 in $100 bills, was returned to Chapman after charges against the 11 men were dropped "to protect confidential informants."[4]

Contacts with Ruby. On December 13, 1963, Chapman told the FBI that he had known Ruby for "about ten or twelve years."[5] The notation "Bobby Chapman, DA4–4139" was found on a slip of paper with four other names in Ruby's auto.[6]

An FBI report described **James Henry Dolan** as one of the two most notorious hoodlums in Dallas.[7] Currently residing in Atlanta Federal Penitentiary,[8] Dolan boasts an arrest record spanning seven states, with convictions for operating a racetrack swindle, impersonating a federal officer, violating parole, possessing burglary tools, and arson.[9] Although his record does not reflect the judicial immunity given a ranking organized crime figure, his roster of associates includes Mob heavies Santos Trafficante, Nofio Pecora, Irwin Weiner, James Fratianno, Russell D. Matthews, and Eugene Hale Brading.[10] From 1958 to 1961, Dolan served as the Dallas representative of the American Guild of Variety Artists (AGVA), a union representing night club entertainers.[11]

Contacts with Ruby. Dolan saw Ruby frequently during his term as Dallas AGVA representative.[12] Dolan and Ruby even produced one musical together, which they expropriated from a musician in Dolan's AGVA membership.[13] Dolan also met Jack Ruby in Dallas about two months before the assassination.[14]

Joseph Locurto, alias Joseph Bonds,[15] had a criminal record dating back to 1930.[16] It shows six arrests in three states on charges including assault to murder, attempted grand larceny, rape, and sodomy, with a conviction and jail sentence on the last charge.[17]

Contacts with Ruby. Joseph Locurto and Jack Ruby were partners in the Vegas Club in the early 1950s and were close associates between 1948 and 1954, according to Ruby, Locurto, and other sources.[18]

Isadore Max Miller, whose name appeared on the Seidband list of Dallas gamblers,[19] was a principal in one of Dallas' three most important bookmaking operations.[20] Among the men Miller hired as collectors were hoodlums Russell D. Matthews and James Dolan.[21] Although Miller had been engaged in illicit gambling operations since the 1930s,[22] he was first convicted in 1965, on federal gambling charges.[23]

Contacts with Ruby. Miller told the FBI that he had known Jack Ruby since 1949.[24] Both his name and his brother's (Dave L. Miller) were found among Ruby's personal effects.[25]

Meyer Panitz made a full swing in the Mob-dominated[26] gambling circuit, from bookmaker[27] to box man in Dallas crap games for Lewis McWillie;[28] then from employee of the Capri Hotel in Cuba,[29] in which Santos Trafficante held a major interest,[30] to box man in the Lansky-owned[31] Thunderbird Hotel in Las Vegas.[32] Panitz was "a very close friend" of Mobster Lewis McWillie.[33]

Contacts with Ruby. Panitz told the FBI he was a "good friend of Ruby's" from 1947 to 1958, when Panitz lived in Dallas.[34] McWillie concurred that Panitz was a "close friend" of Ruby.[35] In the summer of 1959, Panitz met Ruby in Miami on two occasions.[36] These meetings were arranged as a result of a phone call to Panitz from McWillie in Cuba.[37] Panitz told the FBI he called Ruby in mid-1963 "while passing through Dallas, Texas."[38]

Johnny Ross Patrono owned a Dallas liquor store[39] and operated a night club.[40] He was also a bookmaker,[41] reportedly in partnership with Bobby Chapman and James Dolan.[42]

Contacts with Ruby. In an FBI interview of December 18, 1963, Patrono said that he had "known Jack Ruby for about seven or eight years," and had once received a $500 loan from him.[43] Joseph Campisi and another witness described Patrono as a friend of Ruby.[44] Patrono told the FBI that he visited Ruby at the Carousel Club "about the middle of November, 1963."[45]

The FBI identified **Jack Yanover** and Pasquale Stella as co-owners of the Dream Lounge in Cicero, Illinois,[46] a strip joint and gambling operation run by Chicago hoodlums.[47] Ruby's sister Eva Grant testified that Yanover had "upped himself from racketeering" to a position with the American Guild of Variety Artists in Chicago.[48] But given the widespread collusion between this union and the Mob, exposed in 1962 Senate hearings,[49] it is more likely that Yanover's position represented a rise in, rather than out of, racketeering.

Contacts with Ruby. Telephone records show an 11-minute call placed on May 12, 1963 from the Carousel Club to the Dream Lounge in Cicero, Illinois.[50] Since Ruby's brother Hyman[51] and his sister Eva Grant[52] reported that they knew Yanover, it appears that this call was from Ruby to Yanover.

Appendix 7
Reports on Ruby by
"State and Federal officials"

Considered in chapter 6 were amazing statements by the Warren Commission claiming denials of Ruby's Mob connections by "virtually all of Ruby's Chicago friends" and by "numerous persons." Of similar character was the following Commission assertion: "Both State and Federal officials have indicated that Ruby was not affiliated with organized crime activity."[1] When the evidence is examined, this claim proves equally flimsy.

One of the state officials cited by the Warren Commission was Charles Batchelor, assistant chief of the Dallas Police, whose pertinent statement was that "Ruby's operation has not been a troublesome one for the Dallas Police Department."[2] Indeed, as already shown, Ruby's operations and other Syndicate activities were quite rewarding to much of the force. But this reflected mainly on the Dallas Police, as Batchelor's further assertion that "the crime and vice problem in Dallas was not a substantial one"[3] reflected mainly on his own judgment or integrity.

The other state reference cited by the Commission was William F. Alexander, a Dallas assistant district attorney,[4] whose signed Carousel pass card was found among Ruby's possessions,[5] and who spoke with Ruby the day before the assassination.[6] Alexander told the FBI that he didn't know of any connection between Ruby and the underworld.[7] If there was such a connection, he believed that "it would have come to the attention of his office."[8] This is remarkably similar to a statement of Dallas Police Detective E. E. Carlson concerning Ruby's ties to hoodlum Joseph Locurto, alias Joseph Bonds.[9] Detective Carlson advised the FBI he knew "more about Ruby than any other officer in the Dallas Police Department," and asserted that

> he [knew] of no association whatever between Bonds and Ruby and [felt] certain if there was such an association, he, Carlson, would be aware of it.[10]

Yet Bonds and Ruby were business partners and close associates until Bonds left Dallas in 1954;[11] this relationship was reported by Ruby,[12] Bonds,[13] and several other witnesses.[14] So much for the cited state officials.

The remaining references provided for the quoted Commission assertion were two federal sources which discussed the clientele of Ruby's Carousel Club.[15] An

FBI report asserted that the Carousel was not "frequented by any known criminal element."[16] And FBI Director J. Edgar Hoover testified that it "wasn't any so-called 'joint. . . .' It was just another night-club."[17]

Although hardly relevant to the issue of Ruby's criminal affiliation,[18] Hoover's observation was quite correct. The Carousel Club certainly was no joint (unlike one of Ruby's earlier clubs, the Silver Spur—a Mob hangout[19] where "you could get exonerated for murder easier than you could for burglary"[20]). The Carousel was a classy establishment, where prostitution dates ran $100 a night.[21] Its patrons were generally well-dressed, as was customer Lewis McWillie, who could pass for "a doctor or a lawyer."[22] Visitors to the Carousel were not unmannerly, two-bit thugs, but prominent underworld figures: including McWillie,[23] a Mob "gambler and murderer";[24] James Dolan,[25] one of the most notorious hoodlums in Dallas;[26] Joseph Campisi,[27] a Mobster close to the Marcellos;[28] Paul Roland Jones,[29] a Chicago Mob liaison convicted of murder;[30] and other Syndicate men from across the country who dropped in to see Ruby.[31]

Notes

Abbreviations and Conventions

Edem., short for *eisdem* (the same, plural), refers to the same sources cited in the note preceding the one in question. It is analogous to *ibid.*, but applicable to several cited sources.

Citations with the prefix "*U.S.–*" are abbreviations for government documents, as listed in the bibliography. Citations that omit the author's first name also generally refer to sources listed in the bibliography.

The standard conventions used in this volume for citing material released by the Warren Commission are best demonstrated by the following examples:

> "CD 123" refers to Commission Document 123 in the collection on the assassination of President Kennedy in the National Archives. National Archives documents are generally cited only when they are omitted or not reproduced faithfully in the published 26-volume Hearings and Exhibits.
>
> "23H 99" refers to volume 23, page 99 in the Hearings and Exhibits.
>
> "CE 1234" refers to Commission Exhibit 1234 in the Hearings and Exhibits.
>
> Citations of the form "Smith Exhibit 8" refer to exhibits categorized by name in volumes 19–21 of the Hearings and Exhibits.
>
> "WR 99" refers to page 99 of the Warren Commission Report.
>
> Complete titles and publication information for the Warren Commission materials are listed in the bibliography under *U.S.–Warren Commission.*

"JFK microfilm" refers to *Files of Evidence Connected With the Investigation of the Assassination of President John F. Kennedy* (Washington, D.C.: Microcard Editions, 1967). It is a collection of 21 volumes of documents from the Texas Attorney General's investigation of the JFK assassination. A copy is held in the Library of Congress rare book collection, catalog number E842.9.F47.

Material released by the House Assassinations Committee is cited as follows:

> "HAH 3H 99" refers to volume 3, page 99 of the House Assassinations Committee hearings on the assassination of President Kennedy, or of the appendix to those hearings (volumes 1–5 comprise the hearings, 6–12 the appendix).
>
> "HAH-MLK 13H 99" refers to volume 13, page 99 of the appendix to the House Assassinations Committee hearings on the assassination of Martin Luther King.
>
> "HAR 99" refers to page 99 of the House Assassinations Committee Report.
>
> Complete titles and publication information for the House Assassinations Committee materials are listed in the bibliography under *U.S.–House, Assassinations.*

Introduction

1. Jack Newfield, *Robert Kennedy: A Memoir* (New York: Dutton, 1969), p. 57.
2. Buchanan, *Who Killed Kennedy?* (London: Secker and Warburg, 1964), pp. 136–37; see Buchanan (New York: Putnam, 1964), p. 150, for date and author of this statement.
3. Buchanan, British edition, p. 130.
4. Ibid., p. 139.
5. Ibid., pp. 137–38.
6. Buchanan, British edition, pp. 137–39, cf. American ed., especially pp. 151–53, which begin and end as the text surrounding the deleted portion. Ironically preserved was a passing allusion to Groussard's thesis, with the promise that it would be "examined in detail a little later" (American ed., p. 131; British ed., p. 120).
7. Buchanan, British edition, pp. 140–41, cf. American ed., especially pp. 151–53, which begin and end as the text surrounding the deleted portion.
8. Buchanan, British edition, p. 135; American ed., p. 152.
9. Buchanan, British edition, p. 24; American ed., p. 25.
10. Buchanan, British edition, p. 26; American ed., p. 26.
11. Buchanan, British edition, p. 137; see American ed., p. 150.
12. Buchanan, American edition, p. 151.
13. WR 790; See section 6.4.
14. See section 6.4.
15. See chapter 9, Joseph Francis Civello; see also Appendix 1.
16. See Appendix 4.
17. See section 5 of Appendix 4.
18. See chapter 4.
19. HAR 161; see HAR 169, 173, 176; chapters 2 and 17.
20. See chapter 4.
21. Chiefly new material is presented in part III, which shows that the murder of Oswald was a conspiracy, and in part V, which links the Mob and Jack Ruby to the assassination of President Kennedy through an analysis of activities and contacts between May and November 1963 and of the alibis offered to cover them. Part I and chapter 15, in contrast, review well-known information. The remainder of the book presents some new evidence and ties together other evidence which has been covered in a wide scattering of sources.

Chapter 1
Precedents

1. Salerno and Tompkins, *The Crime Confederation*, p. 72.
2. A 1961 Kansas City grand jury report, reprinted in Tyler, ed., *Organized Crime in America*, p. 297.
3. See chapter 4.
4. Lyle, *The Dry and Lawless Years*, p. 254. See also Demaris, *Captive City*, pp. 116–19; Gottfried, *Boss Cermak of Chicago*, pp. 318–19; Lyle, pp. 261, 265.
5. Allsop, *The Bootleggers*, p. 219; Lyle, p. 265; Demaris, p. 118; Gottfried, p. 319.
6. Lyle, p. 265; see also Allsop, p. 170.
7. Allsop, pp. 216–20; Demaris, pp. 116–19; Kobler, *Capone*, p. 322; Lyle, pp. 318–19.
8. Expressed during the 1931 Chicago mayoral campaign by Democratic candidate Cermak to

Republican contender John H. Lyle, quoted by Lyle in *The Dry and Lawless Years*, p. 260.
9. Gottfried, p. 320; Lyle, p. 261.
10. Edem.
11. Allsop, pp. 219–20; Demaris, p. 118; Gottfried, p. 319; Lyle, pp. 265–66.
12. Demaris, p. 121; Gottfried, pp. 320–21.
13. Demaris, p. 119; Gottfried, pp. 320–21.
14. Demaris, p. 119; Gottfried, pp. 320–21; Lyle, p. 264.
15. Gottfried, pp. 320, 424.
16. Allsop, p. 220; Demaris, pp. 119–20; Kobler, p. 322.
17. Edem.
18. Edem.
19. Demaris, p. 120; Gottfried, pp. 318, 321–22.
20. Edem.
21. Demaris, p. 121.
22. WR 463.
23. Ibid.
24. Demaris, p. 120.
25. Ibid., p. 121.
26. Ibid.
27. Ibid.
28. Lyle, p. 267.
29. Demaris, p. 120.
30. Ibid., p. 111.
31. Ibid., p. 120.
32. Ibid.
33. Lyle, p. 267; Gottfried, pp. 320, 424.
34. Lyle, p. 268.
35. Ibid., pp. 254, 258–61; Allsop, p. 216.
36. Lyle, p. 21.
37. Kobler, p. 322; Allsop, pp. 170, 220; Demaris, pp. 119–22.
38. Demaris, p. 121; Gottfried, p. 321.
39. Gottfried, p. 326; Demaris, p. 121.
40. Kobler, p. 322.
41. Allsop, pp. 168–69.
42. Ibid., pp. 168–70.
43. Ibid., pp. 169–70.
44. Ibid., p. 170.
45. See section 4.1.
46. The quoted phrase and several examples of such practices are furnished in Siciliano, *Unless They Kill Me First*, pp. 123, 134–36; see also section 18 of Appendix 4.
47. Sources at the U.S. Department of Labor estimated that at least $385 million has been lost through Mob-tied loans by the Teamster Central States Pension Fund (Brill, *The Teamsters*, pp. 252–55).
48. *New York Times*, May 9, 1972; see Wennblom, "How the Mafia Drives Up Meat Prices," *Farm Journal*, August 1972, pp. 18–19.
49. Walsh, "The Mob: It Racks Up Overtime on a Government Payroll," *Life*, February 15, 1969, pp. 52–56.
50. As quoted by Herbert Hill in "Thieves in the House of Labor," *Nation*, June 27, 1981, p. 793.
51. Ibid., see also section 18 of Appendix 4.
52. Stevenson, series on construction union terrorism in *Reader's Digest*, July 1973, p. 81.
53. Ibid.
54. Ibid.
55. Ibid.
56. *Philadelphia Inquirer*, January 22, 1974, p. C1.
57. Stevenson, *Reader's Digest*, June 1973, pp. 89–94, July 1973, pp. 79–83, December 1973, pp. 85–90.
58. Stevenson, *Reader's Digest*, December 1973, p. 88.
59. Wennblom, "How the Mafia Gets Its Cut," *Farm Journal*, September 1972, p. 24.

60. Ibid.
61. Ibid.
62. Ibid.
63. See, for example, Kennedy, *The Enemy Within*; Sheridan, *The Fall and Rise of Jimmy Hoffa*; Mollenhoff, *Tentacles of Power*; Brill, *The Teamsters*; and Moldea, *The Hoffa Wars*.
64. Washington, D.C. *Daily Rag*, July 27, 1973, pp. 3–4; *Los Angeles Free Press*, June 29, 1973, pp. 6ff.
65. Edem.
66. Edem.
67. Edem.
68. Washington, D.C. *Daily Rag*, July 27, 1973, p. 4.
69. Ibid.
70. *Newsweek*, May 21, 1973, p. 82.
71. Ibid.
72. Roger Touhy and Ray Brennan, *The Stolen Years*, in Tyler, ed., *Organized Crime in America*, pp. 193–95; Hutchinson, *The Imperfect Union*, pp. 116–17; see section 18 of Appendix 4.
73. Cormier and Eaton, *Reuther*, pp. 13–17.
74. Gould and Hickok, *Walter Reuther: Labor's Rugged Individualist*, pp. 46–48, 384.
75. Ibid., pp. 61–63.
76. Ibid., p. 339; Cormier and Eaton, p. 391.
77. Cormier and Eaton, p. vii.
78. Ibid., p. 276.
79. Ibid., p. 342.
80. Gould and Hickok, pp. 135–37, see also p. 139.
81. Ibid., p. 134; Cook, *Walter Reuther*, p. 101; see also Reid, *The Grim Reapers*, p. 76.
82. Gould and Hickok, pp. 97, 134.
83. *U.S.–Senate, Kefauver Report, Third Interim*, p. 73.
84. *U.S.–Senate, OC and Narcotics Hearings*, p. 248, Chart A.
85. *U.S.–Senate, Kefauver Report, Third Interim*, p. 73; Cook, *The Secret Rulers*, p. 122.
86. Cormier and Eaton, pp. 128–29; Gould and Hickok, p. 139.
87. Gould and Hickok, pp. 254–56.
88. *Business Week*, August 21, 1948, pp. 92–94.
89. Ibid.
90. *U.S.–Senate, Kefauver Report, Third Interim*, p. 71.
91. Ibid.
92. Gould and Hickok, p. 256.
93. Cormier and Eaton, p. 255; Cook, *Walter Reuther*, p. 167; Gould and Hickok, p. 261.
94. Cook, *Walter Reuther*, p. 167; Gould and Hickok, p. 263.
95. Cook, *Walter Reuther*, p. 167.
96. Gould and Hickok, p. 269.
97. Ibid.
98. *Business Week*, August 21, 1948, p. 92.
99. Gould and Hickok, p. 256.
100. Cormier and Eaton, pp. 262–66.
101. Ibid., p. 262.
102. Ibid., pp. 266, 252.
103. *U.S.–Senate, OC and Narcotics Report*, p. 40.
104. Gould and Hickok, p. 271; Cormier and Eaton, pp. 262–63.
105. Gould and Hickok, p. 272.
106. Cormier and Eaton, pp. 263–64; *U.S.–Senate, Kefauver Report, Third Interim*, p. 74.
107. Cormier and Eaton, pp. 263–64; *U.S.–Senate, Kefauver Report, Third Interim*, pp. 74–75.
108. Edem.
109. Edem.
110. *U.S.–Senate, Kefauver Report, Third Interim*, pp. 74–75.
111. Ibid., p. 75; Cormier and Eaton, pp. 263–64.
112. *U.S.–Senate, Kefauver Report, Third Interim*, p. 75.
113. Cormier and Eaton, pp. 262, 264; Gould and Hickok, pp. 271–72; *U.S.–Senate, Kefauver Report, Third Interim*, p. 76.
114. *U.S.–Senate, Kefauver Report, Third Interim*, pp. 74–76; Cormier and Eaton, p. 264.
115. *U.S.–Senate, Kefauver Report, Third Interim*, p. 76.
116. Ibid.
117. Ibid.
118. Ibid.
119. Cormier and Eaton, p. 275.
120. Ibid., pp. 274–75.
121. Ibid., p. 267; Gould and Hickok, p. 272.
122. Cormier and Eaton, p. 263.
123. Ibid., p. 267.
124. Ibid.
125. See section 5.4.
126. Cormier and Eaton, pp. 267, 271.
127. Ibid., p. 267.
128. Ibid., p. 269.
129. Ibid.; Gould and Hickok, p. 274.
130. Cormier and Eaton, p. 269.
131. Ibid., p. 274.
132. Gould and Hickok, p. 320.
133. Kennedy, *The Enemy Within*, p. 281; Cormier and Eaton, p. 266.
134. Kennedy, *The Enemy Within*, p. 281.
135. Gould and Hickok, p. 271.
136. Cormier and Eaton, p. 270.
137. Ibid.; Gould and Hickok, p. 275.
138. Cormier and Eaton, p. 270.
139. *U.S.–Senate, OC and Narcotics Hearings*, p. 410, Exhibit No. 18.
140. Cormier and Eaton, pp. 270–71.
141. Reported in the *New York Times*, January 10, 1954, and the *Detroit News* January 9, 1954, as cited in Cormier and Eaton, p. 272.
142. Cormier and Eaton, pp. 272–73.
143. *U.S.–Senate, OC and Narcotics Hearings*, p. 404.
144. Ibid., p. 405.
145. See entry 21.12 of Appendix 4.
146. Cormier and Eaton, p. 273; Gould and Hickok, pp. 276–77.
147. *U.S.–Senate, Kefauver Report, Third Interim*, p. 128; see entry 23.7 of Appendix 4 and section 14.5 of text.
148. Cook, *Walter Reuther*, p. 173.
149. Hutchinson, p. 313.
150. Ibid., p. 314; *U.S.–Senate, OC and Narcotics Hearings*, pp. 479–80.
151. Hutchinson, p. 314; Demaris, p. 31; see also Hutchinson, pp. 156–59.
152. Demaris, pp. 30–31; Hutchinson, pp. 156–59.
153. The UAW-AFL was renamed the Allied Industrial Workers of America in 1956 (Hutchinson, p. 314).
154. *U.S.–Senate, OC and Narcotics Hearings*, p. 479; Demaris, pp. 30–31.
155. *U.S.–Senate, OC and Narcotics Hearings*, p. 479; Demaris, pp. 30, 33.
156. Demaris, pp. 30–32; *U.S.–Senate, OC and Narcotics Hearings*, p. 479.
157. Demaris, pp. 30–31.
158. Ibid., p. 31.
159. *U.S.–Senate, OC and Narcotics Hearings*, p. 479.
160. Ibid.; Demaris, p. 31.
161. *U.S.–Senate, OC and Narcotics Hearings*, pp. 479–80.
162. Ibid.; Demaris, pp. 32–33.
163. *U.S.–Senate, OC and Narcotics Hearings*, p. 480.

164. Demaris, p. 33; *U.S.–Senate, OC and Narcotics Hearings*, p. 487; Navasky, *Kennedy Justice*, p. 47.
165. Demaris, p. 31.
166. Ibid., p. 32.
167. Ibid., pp. 31–32.
168. See chapter 4.
169. Anslinger, *The Protectors*, p. 216.

Part I
Assassins at Large

1. WR 1–2.
2. WR 2, 4.
3. WR 3.
4. WR 3. The Warren Commission described the location of President Kennedy's first wound as the "back of his neck" (WR 3, 19), mandated by its infamous single bullet theory. Actually, according to eyewitness accounts of the autopsy and several items of physical evidence, the wound was in the shoulder, several inches below the neckline (see Thompson, *Six Seconds in Dallas*, pp. 40–51). Both the bullet holes in the president's clothing (5H 59–60; see Thompson, pp. 48, 222–23) and Commission photos depicting "the point where the bullet entered" (WR 97, 102–3) show the wound location in the shoulder, well below the neckline.
5. WR 4.
6. WR 6–7.
7. WR 8–9.
8. *New York Times*, November 24, 1963, p. 1; WR 8–9, 16–19.
9. WR 17.
10. WR 17, 219.
11. WR 17–18.
12. Kantor Exhibit 3, p. 366.
13. *U.S.–Senate, Intelligence Report, JFK Assassination*, p. 32.
14. Ibid., p. 33.
15. Ibid., p. 23.
16. Ibid.
17. WR ix.
18. WR v.
19. *U.S.–Senate, Intelligence Report, JFK Assassination*, pp. 34–35, see also p. 23. The quoted phrase is from *Time*, December 13, 1963, p. 26.
20. WR vii, 18–22, 374.
21. Among the best such books are *Accessories After the Fact* by Sylvia Meagher; *Inquest* by Edward J. Epstein; *Six Seconds in Dallas* by Josiah Thompson; *Forgive My Grief* by Penn Jones; and *Rush to Judgment* by Mark Lane (although Lane's subsequent Jonestown involvement may appear questionable, this book is well-documented and presents many valid criticisms of the Commission's case). For articles, see the literature review by U.S. Representative Thomas Kupferman, 89th Congress, 2nd session, September 28, 1966, *Congressional Record*, vol. 118, pp. 24160–61. Also Cyril Wecht, "JFK Assassination: 'A Prolonged and Willful Cover-up,'" *Modern Medicine*, October 28, 1974, pp. 40X–40FF.
22. *New Times*, August 8, 1975, p. 32; *Life*, October 7, 1966, p. 38.
23. *Time*, January 10, 1977, p. 17. A 1978 Harris Poll reported a similar finding (*Washington Post*, December 4, 1978, p. A7).
24. Statement of Representative Thomas Kupferman, 89th Congress, 2nd session, September 28, 1966, *Congressional Record*, vol. 118, p. 24157.

25. HAR 9–10.
26. HAH 5H 553–695.

Chapter 2
Crossfire in Dealey Plaza

1. WR 71.
2. HAR 1.
3. HAH 1H 40; WR 48.
4. Edem.
5. Figure 1 is derived from topographical maps (Thompson, *Six Seconds in Dallas*, pp. 252–53; HAH 5H 562) and aerial photographs (Thompson, front endpaper; HAH 5H 501, WR 33) of Dealey Plaza, and from a figure published by the House Assassinations Committee (HAH 8H 29). The map and photograph in Thompson (pp. 252–53, front endpaper) are particularly clear, and should be checked concerning matters of placement not apparent in the diagram. The scale of the diagram is determined from Thompson, pp. 252–53, 275.
6. Manchester, *Death of a President*, p. 154.
7. Holland Exhibit D; 6H 239–45.
8. Holland Exhibit D; 6H 243–44; Thompson, p. 115; see figure 1 and note 5.
9. Edem.
10. Holland Exhibit D.
11. 6H 243–44.
12. Filmed and tape-recorded interview of Dodd by Mark Lane, Decatur, Texas, March 24, 1966, cited in Lane, *Rush to Judgment*, pp. 40, 420.
13. CE 1422.
14. CE 2003, p. 41.
15. Tape-recorded interview of Murphy by Stewart Galanor, Dallas, May 6, 1966, cited in Lane, pp. 40, 420.
16. CE 1416; filmed and tape-recorded interview of Simmons by Lane, Mesquite, Texas, March 28, 1966, cited in Lane, pp. 40, 420.
17. Tape-recorded interview of Winborn by Stewart Galanor, Dallas, May 5, 1966, cited in Lane, pp. 40, 420.
18. CE 1422.
19. Tape-recorded interview of Holland by Josiah Thompson, November 30, 1966, cited in Thompson, p. 138.
20. Thompson, p. 138.
21. Meagher, *Accessories After the Fact*, p. 19n; HAH 1H 138; see HAR 503–8 for the nonconspiracy stance of Congressman Sawyer, who raised this point.
22. HAH 7H 373; see also HAH 12H 24–25; HAH 1H 138.
23. Thompson, pp. 252–53; HAH 8H 21, 173. Note that each uncircled number on the Thompson map represents the frame on the Zapruder film which was taken when President Kennedy was at the designated location. Note also that the last shot was fired at about the time that Zapruder frame 313 was filmed (HAH 5H 722), and that the Zapruder film ran at 18.3 frames per second (WR 97; *New York Times*, December 8, 1966, p. 40; see Thompson, pp. 293–94).
24. *Texas Observer*, December 13, 1963, cited in Lane, pp. 44, 421.
25. Ibid.; CD 205, cited in Thompson, p. 124. Smith indicated that he searched directly behind the picket fence (7H 535; see aerial photograph in Thompson, front endpaper).
26. 7H 535.
27. 6H 244; tape-recorded interview of Holland by Thompson, November 30, 1966, cited in

Thompson, pp. 121–22; filmed and tape-recorded interview of Holland by Lane, Dallas, March 23, 1966, cited in Lane, pp. 34–35, 419; filmed and tape-recorded interview of Simmons by Lane, Mesquite, Texas, March 28, 1966, cited in Lane, pp. 34, 419; tape-recorded interview of Dodd by Lane, March 24, 1966, cited in Thompson, pp. 122, 138.
28. For location, see 6H 245–46; also see diagram by Holland in Thompson, p. 123.
29. 6H 246.
30. 6H 245–46.
31. 6H 246.
32. Filmed and tape-recorded interview of Simmons by Lane, Mesquite, Texas, March 23, 1966, cited in Lane, pp. 34, 419.
33. Tape-recorded interview of Dodd by Lane, March 24, 1966, cited in Thompson, pp. 122, 138.
34. HAR 87–91, 605–6; HAH 8H 139–41; Thompson, p. 25; Lane, p. 39, see pp. 399–402.
35. CE 2003, p. 45; CE 1431; see Thompson, Appendix A.
36. CE 2003, p. 45; see also Thompson, p. 126.
37. CE 1431; CE 2003, p. 43.
38. 24H 520; see Thompson, Appendix A.
39. *Dallas Morning News*, November 23, 1963, section 1, p. 3.
40. See Thompson, Appendix A.
41. Thompson, p. 193. See photographs in HAH 5H 507, 632; Thompson, pp. 103, 126, Appendix A.
42. 17H 461, see p. 492.
43. Ibid.
44. 19H 515.
45. Reports: 2H 181; 6H 244, 246–47, 288; 19H 502, 508, 514, 528, 530, 540; CE 1421. Photographs: Thompson, pp. 100, 119; HAH 5H 507. Note that the grassy knoll was almost deserted before the shots were fired (Thompson, pp. 186, 188).
46. 6H 247, 288, 294; CE 1416, 1417; see HAH 5H 507–8.
47. 6H 288.
48. HAH 5H 505–6; CE 1421.
49. 2H 181; 6H 288.
50. 19H 516; CD 5, cited in Thompson, p. 119; 19H 514, 530.
51. CD 5, quoted in Thompson, p. 119.
52. Ibid.
53. 7H 109.
54. Ibid.
55. 7H 107.
56. 6H 284–86; WR 72–73.
57. 6H 285.
58. 6H 285–86.
59. Ibid.
60. 6H 286.
61. 6H 287; tape-recorded interview of Bowers by Lane, Arlington, Texas, March 31, 1966, cited in Lane, pp. 30–31, 418. See Thompson, front endpaper and pp. 115, 121, for position.
62. Tape-recorded interview of Bowers by Lane, Arlington, Texas, March 31, 1966, cited in Lane, pp. 31, 418.
63. 6H 288; Tape-recorded interview of Bowers by Lane, Arlington, Texas, March 31, 1966, cited in Lane, pp. 32, 418.
64. 19H 492.
65. Ibid.
66. Filmed and tape-recorded interview of Price by Lane, Dallas, March 27, 1966, cited in Lane, pp. 32–33, 419.
67. 7H 535.
68. Ibid.
69. CD 3, p. 44; CE 1024; WR 52; see Meagher, p. 25.

70. Thompson, pp. xv-xvii, 6–10, 273–74.
71. Thompson, pp. 115–29. The preceding discussion of these points in the text was greatly influenced by Thompson's presentation of the evidence.
72. Thompson, pp. 115–29.
73. Ibid., pp. 82–86, 120–23.
74. Ibid., pp. 83–85; 6H 243–45.
75. Thompson, pp. 120–21; 6H 243–45. Holland indicated that the smoke moved out from the fence corner toward the grassy knoll (edem.), as it would have with the 15 mile-per-hour wind blowing from the west at that time (HAH 8H 21, 173). In Holland's November 22 affidavit, the shot at which the smoke appeared, which sounded like a firecracker, is reported as the first shot (Holland Exhibit D, see 6H 245). But this designation may be an error attributable to the excited atmosphere Friday afternoon in which the affidavit was prepared and signed (edem.).
76. Thompson, p. 121. The westerly direction is implicit in his description; see the photograph of Holland's view in Thompson, p. 121 and the map in Thompson, pp. 252–53.
77. Thompson, p. 122.
78. Ibid.
79. Ibid.
80. Ibid., pp. 194–95.
81. Ibid., p. 195.
82. Ibid.
83. HAR 66–67; HAH 2H 16–17, 107–10; HAH 5H 637.
84. Edem.
85. HAH 8H 5, 11.
86. HAH 5H 638; see HAR 67.
87. HAH 8H 70–74; WR 48–49.
88. HAR 66.
89. HAR 66–67; HAH 2H 17; HAH 5H 644, 674–75.
90. HAR 69, 72.
91. HAH 5H 555, 644; HAR 69.
92. HAR 67–72; HAH 2H 17–105.
93. HAH 5H 690, 723; HAH 8H 49–50; HAR 68.
94. HAH 5H 690; HAH 8H 49–50; HAR 79.
95. HAR 68–69.
96. HAH 2H 94; HAR 72.
97. HAR 72, 69; HAH 5H 593; HAH 8H 4.
98. HAH 8H 6–10; HAH 5H 557–58; HAR 72–73.
99. HAR 73; HAH 5H 673.
100. HAH 5H 555–72. Within a "coincidence window" of plus or minus .001 seconds, 10 of the 12 computed echo spikes appeared on the dictabelt. The remaining two also appeared, but below the noise threshold selected (HAR 73–74; HAH 8H 10, 26–32; HAH 5H 569–70, 586). The shape of each recorded echo spike was the mirror image of the shape of the muzzle blast spike, further demonstrating that the recorded spikes were the echo pattern of a gunshot (HAH 5H 581).
101. See HAR 68–69.
102. HAH 5H 555–615.
103. HAH 5H 556, 583; see HAR 74; HAH 8H 32.
104. HAH 5H 593.
105. HAH 5H 672–74.
106. HAR 71; HAH 2H 64–67, 70; see HAH 2H 49, 89.
107. The officer was H. B. McLain (HAH 5H 617–41). For the motorcycle position, see HAR 76; HAH 8H 29; HAH 5H 616–17, 628–30, 636–37, 717. For the relative position of the microphone on the motorcycle, see HAR 74; HAH 5H 582, 618, 631. See also HAH 5H 630, 636–37; HAH 8H 11 for confirmation of other implicit predictions about the microphone.

108. HAH 5H 171; HAR 74–75. The detected supersonic shock waves did not rule out pistol fire, since both pistols and pistol ammunition were available in 1963 to fire supersonic bullets (HAH 5H 614, 574). The House Assassinations Committee also determined, from test firings, that pistols could be fired virtually as accurately as rifles over the short range from the grassy knoll to the presidential limousine at the time of the third shot (HAH 5H 614).
109. HAH 8H 29. A radius of error of approximately five feet was associated with this placement (ibid., HAH 5H 570).
110. Thompson, pp. 121–22; see text above.
111. See figure 1 and note 5 above.
112. Edem.
113. WR 3.
114. HAR 1.
115. HAR 97.
116. See, for example, HAR 79–83; Thompson, pp. 82–111; HAH 6H 298–302; Washington Post, June 18, 1979, pp. A1, A6, June 19, 1979, p. A2, June 29, 1979, p. A3; New York Times, August 27, 1972, pp. 1, 57.
117. See Thompson, pp. 86–90; the left rearward snap is clear in a viewing of the film.
118. 2H 141; see WR 104; 6H 290, 292, 294–95; 7H 518; Thompson, pp. 86–102. The calculations presented in HAH 1H 412–14 are of little relevance, since they are based on a bullet fired from a Mannlicher-Carcano rifle. A high-powered, larger caliber rifle would fire a bullet with much greater momentum. The "jet-effect" theory (HAH 1H 428–42) is totally negated by the observed left-rearward motion of the bulk of the impact debris. Other explanations are equally dubious (see Thompson, pp. 90–94).
119. Thompson, p. 100.
120. HAH 5H 690; HAH 8H 49–50; HAR 79.
121. HAH 5H 690, 723; HAR 79, 83. There is a .01 second discrepancy between the interval of 1.66 seconds cited in the House Assassinations Report (p. 83) and the figure of 1.65 seconds calculated from the data which is presented in the hearings (HAH 5H 723). Actually, based on the tape speed correction factor of 1.043 used by Weiss and Aschkenasy (HAH 8H 27), the interval is 1.64 seconds. With the transmitting microphone approaching the Depository Building at about 11 miles per hour (HAR 73), however, the actual firing interval would be about .01 seconds greater than the time interval between the recorded sounds of the first and second shots.
122. 3H 403–7, 443–46; WR 97, 106.
123. HAH 12H 3–6; Thompson, pp. 235–40.
124. The House Assassinations Committee proposed that Oswald could have fired at the recorded speed using the rifle's iron sights, rather than the telescopic scope used in the tests for the Commission (HAR 83; HAH 8H 185). But the basis of the Committee's conjecture was merely a "preliminary" test, with a rifle other than Oswald's, in which the minimum firing interval achieved using iron sights was 1.9 seconds (HAH 8H 183–85; HAH 2H105–7; HAH 5H 615–16; see HAR 483–84). Firing intervals below 1.65 seconds were achieved only when the rifle was "point aimed"—i.e., pointed toward the target using neither scope nor sights (HAH 8H 185). This firing technique would be suitable for a Saturday night shoot-out, but hardly for a precise shot at a moving

target from a six-story elevation.
125. HAH 6H 121–25; Thompson, p. 34; Model and Groden, JFK: The Case for Conspiracy, pp. 143–44.
126. HAH 6H 122, 123.
127. HAH 6H 124.
128. Ibid.
129. See photos in HAH 6H 122.
130. HAH 6H 123.
131. HAH 6H 125.
132. John Sparrow, After the Assassination: A Positive Appraisal of the Warren Report (New York: Chilmark Press, 1967), p. 39, see p. 10.
133. Turner and Christian, The Assassination of Robert F. Kennedy, p. 215.

Chapter 3
A Telltale Trail of Murder

1. U.S.-Senate, OC and Stolen Securities, 1971, p. 672. Raymond testified under the name "George White" (p. 956).
2. Ibid., p. 637.
3. HAH 5H 345.
4. Dorman, Payoff, pp. 58–59.
5. Ibid.
6. Ibid.
7. Ibid.
8. Ibid.
9. Ibid.
10. See Appendix 4 for many other similar examples.
11. See the introduction.
12. CE 2887.
13. Ibid.
14. CE 2887.
15. See part II.
16. Midlothian (Texas) Mirror, June 3, 1965, reprinted in Jones, Forgive My Grief, vol. I, p. 5.
17. Ibid.; see also Joachim Joesten, Oswald: The Truth (London: P. Dawney, 1967), pp. 124–26.
18. JFK microfilm, vol. I, p. 394; National Archives, entry 45, Ruby-Oswald chronology, p. 861.
19. San Francisco Chronicle, April 24, 1964, p. 9; Jones, vol. I, p. 6.
20. Edem.
21. Jones, vol. I, p. 6.
22. Dallas Times Herald, September 22, 1964, cited in Lane, Rush to Judgment, p. 284; Jones, vol. I, p. 6.
23. Jones, vol. II, p. 13.
24. Ibid., pp. 8–9.
25. New York Times, March 29, 1965, p. 33; Jones, vol. I, p. 6.
26. Jones, vol. I, p. 6.
27. Ibid.
28. 14H 256–57.
29. Ibid.
30. See text below.
31. Jones, vol. II, pp. 12–13.
32. Joesten, Oswald: Assassin or Fall Guy?, p. 102.
33. Ruby stated in his medical interview, "I did like Dorothy Kilgallen until she wrote a column saying I was a gangster so I don't like her now" (JFK microfilm, vol. 5, p. D24).
34. Jones, vol. II, p. 13.
35. Ibid.
36. Ibid.
37. WR 363.
38. New York Times, February 23, 1967, p. 22; CE 2882.
39. New York Times, February 23, 1967, p. 22; Jones, vol. I, p. 8; Jones, vol. II, p. 2.
40. New York Times, February 23, 1967, p. 22.

41. Ibid.
42. Ibid.
43. Ibid.
44. Ibid.
45. Ibid.
46. Ibid.
47. Jones, vol. II, p. 2.
48. *New York Times*, February 23, 1967, p. 22.
49. Ibid.
50. HAH 10H 199.
51. Ibid.
52. Ibid.
53. "The Bizarre Deaths Following JFK's Murder," *Argosy*, March 1977, p. 52; Jones, vol. II, p. 22; HAH 10H 199–204.
54. HAH 10H 200–203.
55. Ibid., p. 200.
56. Ibid., pp. 200–201.
57. Ibid., p. 199.
58. Ibid.
59. 6H 284.
60. See chapter 2.
61. Filmed and tape-recorded interview with Mark Lane, cited in Lane, p. 32; see chapter 2.
62. Reprinted in Jones, vol. II, p. 27.
63. Ibid.
64. Ibid.
65. See end of chapter 9 and section 18.3.
66. 14H 355–56.
67. Ibid.
68. 14H 356.
69. Sybil Leek and Bert Sager, *The Assassination Chain* (New York: Corwin, 1976), p. 207.
70. WR 165.
71. Ibid.; see WR 172; HAH 12H 41.
72. HAR 59–60; HAH 12H 41.
73. HAR 60n.
74. WR 20.
75. See Meagher, *Accessories After the Fact*, chapter 13; Lane, chapters 14–15.
76. WR 167–68.
77. 3H 310.
78. Ibid.
79. 3H 310–11.
80. 3H 311.
81. WR 167.
82. WR 169–71.
83. WR 171.
84. Ibid.
85. CE 2523.
86. CE 2589.
87. Ibid.
88. Ibid.
89. 11H 438.
90. CE 2589.
91. 11H 437.
92. CE 2589.
93. Ibid.
94. Ibid.
95. CE 2587.
96. 11H 434–42.
97. CE 2587; 11H 438–40.
98. CE 2587.
99. 11H 441.
100. 11H 442.
101. CE 2587; 11H 441–42.
102. 11H 435.
103. See index to Warren Report; *New Leader*, October 12, 1964, p. 9.
104. Filmed and tape-recorded interview of Clemons by Lane, Dallas, March 23, 1966, cited in Lane, pp. 193–94.
105. Lane, p. 194.
106. 21H 139; 24H 7.

107. Lane interview, March 23, 1966, cited in Lane, p. 280.
108. Ibid.
109. WR 252.
110. 2H 261, 294.
111. 2H 261.
112. WR 166; 2H 347; see Lane, p. 193.
113. 3H 335.
114. 2H 256.
115. *Fort Worth Star Telegram*, December 19, 1965, cited in Lane, p. 333; Jones, vol. II, p. 12.
116. As noted by Chief Justice Warren during Ruby's testimony (5H 205–6). According to Seth Kantor in *Who Was Jack Ruby?* (p. 12), Dallas probate records fix the date of Mc-Lane's death at March 16, 1960. Kantor reports that McLane was riding in a taxi with a 32-year-old woman when his cab "was rammed by another car, which disappeared into the night. McLane was killed on the spot. No one else was hurt."
117. 5H 205–6; see HAH 9H 185.
118. Peter Dale Scott, *The Dallas Conspiracy* (unpublished manuscript), chapter VI, p. 22; or see Kantor, p. 12.
119. Edem. Background information on Alfred McLane, Santo Sorge, Rimrock International, and other participants in the Dallas meeting described is provided in Kantor, p. 12.
120. *U.S.–Senate, OC and Narcotics Hearings*, p. 997.
121. 10H 352.
122. 10H 353–54.
123. 10H 353.
124. Ibid.
125. 10H 353–55; 26H 451.
126. Edem.
127. Edem.
128. 26H 577, 682–83.
129. 10H 340–51, 355; 26H 685, 702; WR 321.
130. CE 3091, 3092.
131. 10H 354; 26H 685.
132. WR 321.
133. Ibid.
134. See Lane, chapter 27; Anson, *"They've Killed the President!"*, chapter 7.
135. As cited in Lane, p. 333.
136. *San Francisco Chronicle*, November 18, 1973, p. 8A; Jones, vol. II, p. 37.
137. Edem.
138. 6H 260–73.
139. Ibid.; 23H 817; see Noyes, *Legacy of Doubt*, pp. 84–94.
140. Noyes, p. 84.
141. Ibid.
142. Ibid.
143. HAH 12H 18.
144. WR 282.
145. For example, see indices in the Warren Report, Meagher and Anson.
146. *Albuquerque Tribune*, March 30, 1977.
147. Ibid.
148. Meagher, pp. 293–302; Jones, vols. I-III.

Chapter 4
The Why and the Wherewithal

1. Anson, *"They've Killed the President!"*, p. 327.
2. Kennedy, *The Enemy Within*, p. 18.
3. Ibid.
4. Ibid., p. 16.
5. Ibid., pp. 15–16.
6. Ibid., passim.
7. Ibid.

8. Mollenhoff, *Strike Force*, p. 3.
9. Navasky, *Kennedy Justice*, pp. 44–46; Anslinger, *The Protectors*, pp. 214–15.
10. See section 17.6.
11. Navasky, p. 72, see pp. 47, 62–63; see also HAH 9H 31–35.
12. Navasky, pp. 62–63.
13. Ibid., p. 48.
14. Anslinger, *The Protectors*, pp. 215–16.
15. Navasky, p. 53; Salerno and Tompkins, *The Crime Confederation*, p. 308.
16. Navasky, p. 55.
17. One hundred sixty racketeering convictions in the first half of 1963 versus 35 in the first half of 1960, as reported by Robert Kennedy in "Robert Kennedy Defines the Menace," *New York Times Magazine*, October 13, 1963, p. 106. See also HAH 9H 11–43, especially p. 21.
18. "Robert Kennedy Defines the Menace." *New York Times Magazine*, October 13, 1963, p. 106.
19. *U.S.–Senate, OC and Narcotics Hearings*, pp. 181–83.
20. See section 5e of Appendix 4.
21. Salerno and Tompkins, pp. 311, 315–16; HAH 9H 37–39; HAH 5H 449–53.
22. Salerno and Tompkins, pp. 311, 315–16; *U.S.–Senate, OC and Narcotics Report*, p. 118; see Valachi testimony in *U.S.–Senate, OC and Narcotics Hearings*.
23. Reid, *The Grim Reapers*, p. 162.
24. Anson, p. 317.
25. McClellan, *Crime Without Punishment*, p. 282.
26. Ibid.
27. Navasky, p. 50.
28. Ibid., p. 51.
29. Sheridan, *The Fall and Rise of Jimmy Hoffa*, p. 300.
30. HAH 5H 448.
31. Ibid.
32. HAH 5H 437–38, 440, 447.
33. HAH 5H 443.
34. HAH 5H 446.
35. Ibid.
36. Jack Anderson, "The Life and Trials of Carlos Marcello," *Parade*, August 10, 1980, pp. 4–5; HAH 5H 416.
37. "The Mafia: Big, Bad and Booming," *Time*, May 16, 1977, pp. 32ff.
38. HAH 9H 65–66.
39. HAH 9H 66, 69; Noyes, *Legacy of Doubt*, p. 143; *U.S.–House, OC Control*, p. 412; Jack Anderson, "The Life and Trials of Carlos Marcello," *Parade*, August 10, 1980, pp. 4–5.
40. HAH 9H 61, 64–65.
41. Davidson, "New Orleans: Cosa Nostra's Wall Street," *Saturday Evening Post*, February 29, 1964, p. 15.
42. *U.S.–House, OC Control*, p. 433.
43. Chandler, "The 'Little Man' is Bigger Than Ever," *Life*, April 10, 1970, p. 31; see also "The Mob," *Life*, September 8, 1967, pp. 94ff; *Life*, September 29, 1967, pp. 34ff.
44. Lawson, "Carnival of Crime," *Wall Street Journal*, January 12, 1970, p. 1.
45. Noyes, pp. 142–44.
46. Reid and Demaris, *The Green Felt Jungle*, pp. 85, 88, 91.
47. Reid, *The Grim Reapers*, p. 160; Dorman, *Payoff*, p. 100.
48. Meskil, *Don Carlo*, p. 137.
49. *Dallas Morning News*, March 28, 29, 30, and 31, 1973, p. A1.
50. *Houston Post*, April 20, 1975, p. 2A; *U.S.–Senate, Kefauver Report, Third Interim*, p. 82;

51. See chapter 9, Joseph Campisi and Joseph Francis Civello.
52. HAH 9H 62.
53. Ibid.; Reid, *The Grim Reapers*, p. 151.
54. HAH 9H 62.
55. Ibid.
56. HAH 9H 63.
57. *U.S.–Senate, McClellan Labor Hearings*, pp. 17265–67; HAH 9H 64; Mollenhoff, *Strike Force*, p. 159.
58. HAH 9H 63; Mollenhoff, *Strike Force*, p. 159.
59. HAH 9H 63. The case was still pending in 1979 (ibid.).
60. HAH 9H 69–70.
61. HAH 9H 71–72; Reid, *The Grim Reapers*, pp. 151–53; Mollenhoff, *Strike Force*, p. 159. Marcello's lawyers had fabricated records listing that country as his birth place to minimize inconvenience to him in the event of such action to deport him (Reid, *The Grim Reapers*, p. 152; HAH 9H 72).
62. HAR 169.
63. HAH 9H 74; Mollenhoff, *Strike Force*, p. 160.
64. HAH 9H 74.
65. Ibid.
66. HAH 9H 74–75; Mollenhoff, *Strike Force*, pp. 160–61.
67. See section 22a and entries 22.18, 22.20 of Appendix 4; Sheridan, p. 7.
68. *New Orleans Times Picayune*, November 23, 1963, p. 1; HAH 9H 74.
69. Reid, *The Grim Reapers*, pp. 160–62; HAH 9H 75.
70. HAH 9H 81–84.
71. HAH 9H 77, 80–82.
72. HAH 9H 80–82, 85.
73. Reid, *The Grim Reapers*, pp. 160–61; HAH 9H 75.
74. Reid, *The Grim Reapers*, pp. 161–62.
75. HAH 9H 82.
76. HAH 9H 82–83.
77. HAH 9H 83.
78. HAH 9H 77; "New President" instead of "new President" in the source.
79. HAH 9H 82–83.
80. HAH 9H 83.
81. Ibid.; Reid, *The Grim Reapers*, p. 162.
82. HAH 9H 83.
83. HAH 9H 84.
84. Ibid.
85. HAR 9H 69–70.
86. Ibid.
87. HAH 9H 84.
88. Ibid.
89. HAH 9H 104.
90. CD 75, p. 287.
91. HAH 9H 81.
92. HAH 9H 76.
93. HAH 9H 83, 85.
94. HAH 9H 80–81, 85.
95. HAH 9H 82–83.
96. HAH 9H 83.
97. Ibid.
98. Reid, *The Grim Reapers*, p. 300; Moldea, *The Hoffa Wars*, pp. 178–79.
99. Reid, *The Grim Reapers*, pp. 93, 95, 115, 290; HAR 152; McCoy, *The Politics of Heroin in Southeast Asia*, p. 27.
100. Reid, *The Grim Reapers*, pp. 93, 95, 115, 132.
101. *U.S.–Senate, McClellan Labor Hearings*, pp.

12194–12201 (see "Louis Santos" on p. 12200);
see entry 5.35 of Appendix 4 and Appendix 2
for background on the Apalachin convention.
102. Reid, *The Grim Reapers*, pp. 158, 329; HAH 9H
66–67.
103. Edem.
104. HAH 5H 295, see 257–58; see also Crile, "The
Mafia, the CIA, and Castro," *Washington Post*,
May 16, 1976, p. C1.
105. HAR 152, 173.
106. HAR 173; Moldea, p. 352; Scott, *Crime and
Cover-Up*, p. 21.
107. Reid, *The Grim Reapers*, p. 300.
108. See section 15.6.
109. HAH 5H 441.
110. HAR 173.
111. Crile, "The Mafia, the CIA, and Castro," *Washington Post*, May 16, 1976, p. C4.
112. Ibid.
113. Ibid.
114. Ibid.
115. Ibid.
116. Ibid.
117. Ibid.
118. Ibid.
119. *New York Times*, March 17, 1977, p. A23.
120. Ibid.
121. Ibid.
122. HAR 173.
123. HAH 5H 345–48, 373–77.
124. HAH 5H 304–5.
125. HAH 5H 305.
126. HAR 174; HAH 5H 323, 345.
127. HAH 5H 306.
128. HAH 5H 314, 317–20; HAR 174.
129. HAH 5H 317.
130. HAH 5H 319.
131. See, for example, Kennedy, *The Enemy Within*;
Sheridan, *The Fall and Rise of Jimmy Hoffa*;
Mollenhoff, *Tentacles of Power*; Moldea, *The
Hoffa Wars*, and Brill *The Teamsters*.
132. Anson, p. 325.
133. *Time*, August 25, 1975, p. 55; Brill, pp. 248–57;
see Anson, pp. 317–25.
134. Moldea, pp. 5–6.
135. Ibid., p. 178; *Life*, September 29, 1967, p. 34;
"The Mob," part 1, *Life*, September 1, 1967, p.
22.
136. Moldea, p. 169.
137. HAR 176.
138. Sheridan, p. 300.
139. HAR 176; Moldea, pp. 148–49.
140. Edem.
141. Moldea, p. 149.
142. Ibid., p. 148.
143. Sheridan, pp. 224–25, 227, 229–45, 247–51, 257;
Moldea, p. 142. Partin was found credible by a
jury which convicted Hoffa on a jury tampering charge in 1964 (Moldea, pp. 171–73).
144. *New York Times*, April 12, 1964, pp. 1, 35; HAR
176; Sheridan, p. 217.
145. Sheridan, pp. 216–17; HAR 176; Moldea, p. 148.
146. Sheridan, p. 217.
147. Ibid.
148. Ibid.; see Benjamin Bradlee, *Conversations
With Kennedy*, pp. 124–27.
149. Moldea, p. 149.
150. Sheridan, p. 7.
151. HAR 176–77.
152. HAR 176; Moldea, p. 148.
153. HAR 176.
154. Ibid.
155. Moldea, pp. 5–6.
156. HAH 9H 77, 82–83.

157. Moldea, p. 150.
158. Ibid.
159. Ibid.
160. HAR 176; Sheridan, p. 217.
161. HAR 176.
162. Brill, p. 374.
163. Teresa, *My Life in the Mafia*, p. vii; Vincent Teresa, *Vinnie Teresa's Mafia* (Garden City, N.Y.:
Doubleday, 1975), p. 39.
164. Teresa (this and subsequent references are to
My Life in the Mafia), p. 180; Tyler, ed., *Organized Crime in America*, comments by Tyler
on p. 229; *U.S.–Senate, OC and Narcotics Hearings*, pp. 192–93; see section 6a of Appendix 4.
165. Teresa, p. 182.
166. Ibid., p. 180.
167. Ibid., p. 186; HAR 163.
168. Mollenhoff, *Strike Force*, p. 151; HAH 9H 51–53.
169. *New York Times*, June 21, 1973, p. 18.
170. See section 6a of Appendix 4.
171. Teresa, p. 182.
172. Maas, *The Valachi Papers*, pp. 155–57.
173. *U.S.–Senate, OC and Narcotics Hearings*, pp.
428–29.
174. *Newsweek*, June 14, 1976, pp. 83–84.
175. Reid and Demaris, pp. 71–72.
176. See section 1.2.
177. Salerno and Tompkins, p. 388; "The Mob," part
2, *Life*, September 8, 1967, p. 101.
178. See section 6a of Appendix 4.
179. *U.S.–Senate, OC and Narcotics Hearings*, p.
487; Navasky, p. 47.
180. Charles Rogovin, former Massachusetts Attorney General's expert on organized crime,
stated that the New England Mafia family is
"totally ruthless about loan-shark debts. Two
thirds of the murders and maimings in New
England involve people who have surrendered
the collateral of their bodies to the loansharks." As quoted in Reid, *The Grim Reapers*,
p. 67.
181. Teresa, pp. 180, 182.
182. Ibid., p. 180.
183. Ibid., pp. 179–80, 183–86.
184. Ibid., p. 183.
185. Rogers, "The Persecution of Clay Shaw," *Look*,
August 26, 1969, p. 56.
186. HAR 161, 169, 173, 176.

Chapter 5
Four Suspects

1. Noyes, *Legacy of Doubt*, p. 160.
2. HAH 10H 107.
3. HAH 10H 109, 112.
4. Noyes, p. 128.
5. HAH 10H 126–27.
6. *New Orleans States Item*, April 25, 1967, cited
in Anson, *"They've Killed the President!"*, p.
124. The address of Banister's office was 531
Lafayette Street, which was a side entrance to
544 Camp Street, as noted in *Plot or Politics?*
by Rosemary James and Jack Wardlow (New
Orleans: Pelican, 1967), p. 116.
7. HAH 10H 111, 127.
8. Rogers, "The Persecution of Clay Shaw," *Look*,
August 26, 1969, p. 56.
9. Ibid.; HAH 10H 111–12; HAR 143–45, 170.
10. Rogers, "The Persecution of Clay Shaw," *Look*,
August 26, 1969, p. 56.
11. Ibid.; HAH 10H 112; *Los Angeles Times*, September 4, 1970; Noyes, pp. 144–45.
12. HAH 10H 112.
13. HAH 10H 12; see text below.

14. HAH 10H 132.
15. HAH 9H 113–14.
16. HAR 142.
17. HAH 10H 132; HAR 142–43; HAH 4H 482.
18. HAH 10H 130.
19. Ibid.
20. CD 75, pp. 216–18, 309; HAH 10H 112–13, 130; HAR 143.
21. HAH 10H 112, 129–30.
22. HAH 10H 130; see also HAH 10H 121–22.
23. HAH 10H 112, 129–30, 135n.
24. HAH 10H 130.
25. HAH 10H 112.
26. HAR 145.
27. Ibid.; Noyes, p. 126.
28. CD 75, p. 199; HAH 10H 107, 111.
29. CD 75, p. 199; HAR 170.
30. CD 75, p. 199.
31. HAH 10H 113, 114.
32. CD 75, p. 220; HAH 10H 114.
33. HAH 9H 70–71.
34. Ibid.; see *U.S.–House, OC in Sports*, p. 970.
35. HAH 10H 114, note 5.
36. HAH 10H 114; CD 75, p. 220.
37. CD 75, p. 288; Rogers, "The Persecution of Clay Shaw," *Look*, August 26, 1969, p. 56.
38. Edem.; HAH 10H 113; Anson, p. 106.
39. Anson, p. 106.
40. Ibid.; CD 75, p. 288.
41. CD 75, p. 287.
42. CD 75, p. 221.
43. Noyes, pp. 131–32.
44. HAH 10H 113.
45. CD 75, p. 291.
46. HAH 10H 113.
47. HAH 10H 113; Marcello's ownership of the Ala-motel was reported in Paris Flammonde, *The Kennedy Conspiracy* (New York: Meredith, 1969), p. 28.
48. CD 75, p. 287; HAH 10H 112.
49. CD 75, p. 287.
50. CD 75, p. 307.
51. Ibid.
52. HAH 10H 113, 122; Rogers, "The Persecution of Clay Shaw," *Look*, August 26, 1969, p. 56.
53. CD 75, p. 291.
54. Rogers, "The Persecution of Clay Shaw," *Look*, August 26, 1969, p. 56.
55. *U.S.–House, OC in Sports*, pp. 967, 971–72.
56. CD 75, p. 292.
57. HAR 171; see section 4.3.
58. WR 670, 711, 731, 736, 738.
59. WR 191; see Lane, *Rush to Judgment*, pp. 123–24.
60. WR 375–76, 422–23.
61. See, for example, Meagher, *Accessories After the Fact*.
62. Kantor Exhibit 3, p. 366.
63. HAH 10H 123.
64. Ibid.
65. WR 406–7, 375–76.
66. HAH 10H 132; HAR 180; HAH 4H 482.
67. HAH 10H 3.
68. WR 290–92.
69. HAR 170; see CD 75, p. 160.
70. HAR 170.
71. HAR 170; see CD 75, p. 160.
72. HAH 9H 96–99, see p. 116.
73. HAR 170; HAH 9H 95, 116.
74. HAH 9H 99.
75. HAR 170.
76. CE 1920; CD 302, p. 194.
77. CD 75, p. 167; WR 670–80; HAH 9H 95.
78. National Archives, entry 45, Ruby-Oswald

79. chronology, p. 615; see CD 75, p. 159; WR 728.
79. WR 728.
80. National Archives, entry 45, Ruby-Oswald chronology, p. 633.
81. HAR 170.
82. HAH 9H 93.
83. HAH 9H 94.
84. HAH 9H 115–16.
85. Ibid.
86. HAH 9H 115.
87. See section 4b of Appendix 4.
88. See section 21a of Appendix 4.
89. HAH 9H 117.
90. Thompson, *Six Seconds in Dallas*, pp. 129–33.
91. Ibid., pp. 132–33.
92. Ibid., p. 193n.
93. As described in a tape-recorded interview of the family of retired Air Force Major Phillip Willis with Dr. Josiah Thompson, November 29, 1966, cited in Thompson, pp. 132, 139. For background of Willis, see Model and Groden, *JFK: The Case for Conspiracy*, p. 143.
94. Edem.
95. 20H 499; see Thompson, pp. 132, 139.
96. Thompson, p. 132.
97. Decker Exhibit 5323, pp. 469, 527.
98. Ibid.
99. Ibid.
100. Ibid.
101. Ibid.
102. Ibid.; see Noyes, pp. 20–23.
103. Decker Exhibit 5323, pp. 469, 527.
104. Noyes, p. 27.
105. Ibid., p. 28.
106. Ibid., p. 29.
107. Ibid., pp. 24, 80.
108. Ibid., pp. 26–39.
109. Ibid., pp. 37–39.
110. Ibid., pp. 27, 30, 72.
111. Ibid., pp. 30, 38.
112. Houghton, *Special Unit Senator*, p. 158.
113. Noyes, p. 47.
114. Noyes, pp. 47–48.
115. Reid, *The Grim Reapers*, pp. 181, 191–92.
116. Ibid., p. 184; Noyes, p. 56.
117. Reid, *The Grim Reapers*, p. 299; Noyes, pp. 56–57.
118. Noyes, pp. 48, 57.
119. Ibid., pp. 28–29.
120. Ibid., pp. 39, 40, 58.
121. Ibid., p. 33.
122. Ibid., p. 72.
123. Ibid., p. 73.
124. Ibid.
125. Ibid., p. 74.
126. Ibid., p. 73.
127. Ibid., p. 79.
128. Ibid., pp. 71–72, 81.
129. Ibid.
130. Ibid., p. 72.
131. Ibid., pp. 72–73, see p. 75.
132. Ibid.
133. Ibid., pp. 65–66, 72–73.
134. Ibid., p. 75.
135. Ibid.
136. Ibid.
137. Ibid., pp. 157–58.
138. Ibid., p. 158.
139. Ibid.
140. Ibid.
141. See review of assassination commentary by Representative Thomas Kupferman, 89th Congress, 2nd session, September 28, 1966, *Congressional Record*, vol. 118, pp. 24160–61.

142. Thompson, *Six Seconds in Dallas* (published in 1967); see chapter 2 of this volume.

143. Statement of Representative Thomas Kupferman, 89th Congress, 2nd session, September 28, 1966, *Congressional Record*, vol. 118, pp. 24157–59.

144. *New Times*, August 8, 1975, p. 32; *Life*, October 7, 1966, p. 38.

145. Louis Harris Poll, reported in the *Washington Post*, October 3, 1966, p. A21, and the *New York Post*, October 3, 1966, p. 4.

146. Edem.

147. Anson, pp. 105, 119, 301.

148. Anson, chapter 4; Noyes, chapter 8; Garrison interview and background, *Playboy*, October 1967, pp. 59ff.

149. Rogers, "The Persecution of Clay Shaw," *Look*, August 26, 1969, pp. 54–55; *New York Times*, February 23, 1967, p. 22; Noyes, pp. 105, 109–10; *Playboy*, October 1967, p. 59.

150. Edem.

151. Anson, p. 119.

152. Anson, pp. 110–12; Epstein, *Counterplot*, pp. 67–69.

153. Anson, pp. 113–14; *Playboy*, October 1967, p. 59.

154. Edem.

155. Anson, pp. 121–22; Rogers, "The Persecution of Clay Shaw," *Look*, August 26, 1969, pp. 53, 55.

156. Anson, pp. 107–8; Noyes, p. 107; Rogers, "The Persecution of Clay Shaw," *Look*, August 26, 1969, p. 55.

157. Rogers, "The Persecution of Clay Shaw," *Look*, August 26, 1969, p. 53.

158. Sheridan, *The Fall and Rise of Jimmy Hoffa*, p. 416.

159. *Newsweek*, May 15, 1967, pp. 36–40.

160. *New York Times*, June 12, 1967, p. 1.

161. Rogers, "The Persecution of Clay Shaw," *Look*, August 26, 1969, pp. 53ff.

162. James Phelan, "Rush to Judgment in New Orleans," *Saturday Evening Post*, August 26, 1969.

163. *The JFK Conspiracy: The Case of Jim Garrison*, NBC, June 19, 1967, cited in Sheridan, p. 420.

164. Epstein, *Counterplot*; see also Anson, chapter 4 and Noyes, chapters 7–8.

165. As cited in notes 159–64.

166. *Newsweek*, May 16, 1967, pp. 35–40.

167. *New York Times*, June 12, 1967, p. 1.

168. Epstein, *Counterplot*, pp. 50, 57.

169. Garrison interview, *Playboy*, October 1967, pp. 59ff.; Epstein, *Counterplot*, p. 71; Noyes, p. 105.

170. Rogers, "The Persecution of Clay Shaw," *Look*, August 26, 1969, p. 56; Noyes, p. 106.

171. Garrison interview, *Playboy*, October 1967, p. 174.

172. Ibid.

173. 14H 330–64.

174. 14H 334, 353–55; see CE 3061, p. 627.

175. Rogers, "The Persecution of Clay Shaw," *Look*, August 26, 1969, p. 56; Noyes, p. 106.

176. Rogers, "The Persecution of Clay Shaw," *Look*, August 26, 1969, p. 56.

177. Ibid.; *Life*, September 29, 1967, p. 35.

178. James R. Phelan, "The Vice Man Cometh," *Saturday Evening Post*, June 8, 1963, p. 71.

179. *Life*, September 29, 1967, p. 36.

180. Ibid.

181. Ibid.

182. Sheridan, p. 417.

183. "The Mob," part 2, *Life*, September 8, 1967, p. 96.

184. Sheridan, p. 417.

185. "The Mob," part 2, *Life*, September 8, 1967, pp. 94–95.

186. Ibid.

187. *Life*, September 29, 1967, p. 35.

188. Chandler, "The 'Little Man' is Bigger Than Ever," *Life*, April 10, 1970, p. 33.

189. Noyes, p. 106.

190. Sheridan, p. 417; *Playboy*, October 1967, p. 60.

191. Sheridan, p. 417.

192. Chandler, in *Life*, April 10, 1970, p. 33.

193. Ibid.

194. Ibid.

195. *New York Times*, August 20, 1973, p. 15; see *New York Times Index*, 1973, pp. 856–57.

196. *New York Times*, September 28, 1973, p. 30.

197. *New York Times*, August 20, 1973, p. 15.

198. *New York Times*, September 7, 1973, p. 15; see *New York Times Index*, 1973, pp. 856–57.

199. *New York Times*, September 28, 1973, p. 30.

200. *New York Times*, September 21, 1973, p. 25.

201. Mollenhoff, *Strike Force*, pp. 160–61; see section 4.3.

202. Rogers, "The Persecution of Clay Shaw," *Look*, August 26, 1969, p. 58.

203. Ibid.

204. Ibid., pp. 54, 56, 58.

205. Ibid., p. 58.

206. Ibid., pp. 54, 56.

207. Ibid., p. 58.

208. Ibid.

209. Ibid.

210. Testimony of Aaron Kohn in *U.S.–House, OC Control*, pp. 429–30.

211. Ibid.; Sheridan, p. 432; *Life*, September 29, 1967, p. 34.

212. *U.S.–House, OC Control*, pp. 429–30.

213. Ibid., pp. 410–38; Lawson, "Carnival of Crime," *Wall Street Journal*, January 12, 1970, p. 1; "The Mob," part 2, *Life*, September 8, 1967, p. 94; Rogers, "The Persecution of Clay Shaw," *Look*, August 26, 1969, p. 56; NBC Evening News, September 7, 1977.

214. Salerno and Tompkins, *The Crime Confederation*, p. 290.

215. Ibid., p. 291n.

216. Ibid.

217. Anson, pp. 125–28; Reid, *The Grim Reapers*, p. 162.

218. Anson, pp. 105, 119, 301.

219. Noyes, pp. 95–103, 159–61.

220. Ibid., p. 97.

221. Noyes, pp. 97–103.

222. Noyes, pp. 102–3, 161.

223. "The Mob," part 1, *Life*, September 1, 1967, p. 22; Sheridan, chapter 12.

224. Sheridan, pp. 411–12, see pp. 415, 427, 429, 457 for similar actions by Gill in the spring-Hoffa campaign.

225. Sheridan, pp. 411–12.

226. Ibid., p. 423.

227. Ibid.

228. Ibid., p. 411.

229. See chapter 9, Frank Caracci.

230. Ibid.

231. *Playboy*, October 1967, p. 60.

232. Garrison's statement in *Playboy*, October 1967, pp. 60, 74; James A. Autry, "The Garrison Investigation: How and Why It Began," *New Orleans*, April 1967, p. 8; Rogers, "The Persecution of Clay Shaw," *Look*, August 26, 1969., p. 54.

233. Garrison, *Heritage of Stone*, p. 8.

234. Reid, pp. 162–63.

Part II
Mob Fixer in Dallas

1. *New York Times*, quoted in *U.S.–House, Criminal Justice Hearings*, p. 149; for further background on Salerno, see *U.S.–Senate, OC and Narcotics Hearings*, pp. 121–22.
2. HAH 5H 427–28.
3. Sondern, *Brotherhood of Evil*, p. 60.
4. *U.S.–Cargo Theft and OC*, p. 24.
5. See section 5 of Appendix 4.
6. See section 5g of Appendix 4.
7. See entry 26.6 of Appendix 4.

Chapter 6
Jack Ruby in Chicago:
Molding of a Mobster

1. Stated at "The Politics of Conspiracy," conference at Boston University, workshop on organized crime, George Sherman Student Center, February 1, 1975, tape-recorded by author.
2. WR 780.
3. Ibid.
4. WR 781–83; C. Ray Hall Exhibit 3, p. 12.
5. CE 1288; CE 2980, p. 6; 15H 20–21; 14H 409.
6. CE 1288.
7. Ibid.
8. Ibid.
9. CE 1289.
10. 14H 409–10; CE 1289; CE 2980, p. 6; CE 1208.
11. WR 789; CE 1289; CE 1208.
12. CE 1289; Landesco, *Organized Crime in Chicago*, p. 173; Allsop, *The Bootleggers*, p. 71.
13. Landesco, p. 173; Kobler, *Capone*, pp. 80, 98.
14. 14H 409–10.
15. CE 1288.
16. Ibid.
17. Ibid.
18. CE 1258.
19. Ibid.
20. Ibid.
21. CE 1247.
22. Ibid.
23. Ibid.
24. *U.S.–Senate, OC and Narcotics Report*, p. 37; Reid, *The Grim Reapers*, p. 326.
25. *Newsweek*, August 15, 1977, p. 22.
26. 14H 533–34; JFK microfilm, vol. 5, p. D26.
27. JFK microfilm, vol. 5, p. D26.
28. WR 785.
29. CE 1217.
30. WR 786–87; C. Ray Hall Exhibit 3, p. 13.
31. *U.S.–Senate, Kefauver Hearings*, part 5, pp. 391, 399–400.
32. C. Ray Hall Exhibit 3, p. 13; CE 2980.
33. CE 2328; 14H 458.
34. CE 2328.
35. CE 1753; CE 1242.
36. CE 1289.
37. WR 788.
38. JFK microfilm, vol. 5, pp. R2–3.
39. CE 1293; CE 1321; C. Ray Hall Exhibit 1.
40. CE 1279.
41. Ibid.
42. JFK microfilm, vol. 5, p. D19.
43. WR 785.
44. Ibid.; 14H 470.
45. See chapter 9, Paul Roland Jones.
46. CE 1184; see chapter 9, Paul Roland Jones.
47. CE 1184.

48. Model and Groden, *JFK: The Case for Conspiracy*, p. 243.
49. CE 1292.
50. December 9, 1939, p. 1.
51. CE 1184.
52. Sheridan, *The Fall and Rise of Jimmy Hoffa*, pp. 15–16; Kennedy, *The Enemy Within*, p. 87; WR 788.
53. WR 788; CE 1289; CE 1236; see text below.
54. CE 1289.
55. 14H 445.
56. *U.S.–Senate, McClellan Labor Hearings*, pp. 16082–87; Kennedy, *The Enemy Within*, pp. 87–89.
57. Sheridan, p. 15; CE 2980; Kennedy, *The Enemy Within*, p. 87.
58. *New York Times*, November 26, 1963, p. 15.
59. *U.S.–Senate, McClellan Labor Hearings*, pp. 16086–87.
60. CE 1293.
61. *New York Times*, interview with Dorfman, November 26, 1963, p. 15.
62. JFK microfilm, vol. 5, pp. R2–3; Ruby told his medical interviewer that he was held there overnight (ibid., p. D26).
63. CE 1202.
64. JFK microfilm, vol. 5, p. R3.
65. Demaris, pp. 189, 340, 350, 352.
66. Ibid., p. 259.
67. Tampa: *U.S.–Senate, Kefauver Report, Third Interim*, p. 65. New York: Cook, *A Two-Dollar Bet Means Murder*, p. 132; *U.S.–Senate, Kefauver Report, Third Interim*, p. 129. Miami: Salerno and Tompkins, *The Crime Confederation*, pp. 287–88. Cleveland: Reid, *Mickey Cohen: Mobster*, p. 42.
68. JFK microfilm, vol. 5, p. D19; C. Ray Hall Exhibit 1.
69. CE 1279.
70. WR 788.
71. CE 1236.
72. CE 1236; WR 788.
73. CE 1236.
74. JFK microfilm, vol. 5, pp. R2–3; CE 1235.
75. CE 1321.
76. Ibid.
77. See selections in Tyler, ed., *Organized Crime in America*, pp. 189–97.
78. *U.S.–Senate, McClellan Labor Hearings*, pp. 14011–17.
79. Ibid., pp. 14016, 14022.
80. Ibid.
81. Moldea, *The Hoffa Wars*, p. 7; Brill, *The Teamsters*, chapter 6; Sheridan, pp. 16–17.
82. See section 18 of Appendix 4.
83. *Newsweek*, May 18, 1981, p. 95; see also *Reader's Digest*, January 1977, p. 56; Moldea, p. 414.
84. *Reader's Digest*, January 1977, p. 54; Moldea, p. 414.
85. *Reader's Digest*, January 1977, p. 56; see Moldea, pp. 413–14.
86. *Reader's Digest*, January 1977, p. 54.
87. Ibid.
88. *Reader's Digest*, January 1977, pp. 56–57; Moldea, pp. 415–17.
89. Moldea, pp. 415–16.
90. C. Ray Hall Exhibit 3, p. 13; 14H 370, 442.
91. WR 788–91; C. Ray Hall Exhibit 3, p. 13; 14H 370, 442.
92. CE 1184.
93. Ibid.
94. CE 1193.
95. Ibid.
96. Demaris, p. 84.

97. Ibid., p. 85.
98. CE 1240.
99. Ibid.
100. Landesco, pp. 33, 173–74.
101. CE 1240.
102. Ibid.
103. Ibid.
104. CE 1277.
105. Ibid.
106. CE 1245.
107. CE 1505.
108. *U.S.–Senate, OC and Narcotics Report*, p. 37; Reid, *The Grim Reapers*, p. 326.
109. CE 1247.
110. CE 1211, 1212, 1321.
111. CE 1211.
112. CE 1321.
113. Ibid.
114. CE 1210.
115. *U.S.–Senate, AGVA Hearings*, p. 208; CE 1212.
116. CE 1212.
117. Ibid.
118. Ibid.
119. Ibid.
120. CE 1262.
121. Ibid.
122. CE 1277, 1245, 1240.
123. CE 1213, 1758, 1517.
124. WR 790.
125. CE 1287.
126. 15H 22.
127. CE 1201.
128. Ibid.
129. CD 1193, p. 89.
130. WR 790.
131. WR 779–92.
132. WR 790.
133. CE 1321.
134. CE 1210.
135. CE 1212; see *U.S.–Senate, AGVA Hearings*, p. 208.
136. CE 1321, 1210, 1212.
137. CE 1202.
138. *U.S.–Senate, OC and Narcotics Report*, p. 37; Demaris, p. 349.
139. *U.S.–Senate, OC and Narcotics Report*, p. 37.
140. Demaris, p. 349.
141. CE 1246.
142. CE 1193.
143. CE 1201; 15H 22.
144. CE 1241, 1203, 1242, 1288, 1289.
145. CE 1200; C. Ray Hall Exhibit 3, p. 13.
146. WR 801.
147. CE 1748.
148. See chapter 9, Joseph Campisi.
149. CE 2322.
150. CE 1229.
151. 14H 14–15; CD 84, p. 152; CE 1322, pp. 727, 773; CE 1567; 14H 13–14; CD 722, pp. 3–5.
152. See section 10.6, displayed footnote.
153. CE 1543.
154. Ibid., p. 195.

Chapter 7
The Mob and Jack Ruby Move to Dallas

1. Cook, *The Secret Rulers*, p. 2.
2. Dorman, *Payoff*, pp. 151–62.
3. Reid and Demaris, *The Green Felt Jungle*, pp. 184–211.
4. *U.S.–Senate, Kefauver Hearings*, part 2, p. 193; see also Reid and Demaris, pp. 184–211.
5. CE 1251.
6. Ibid.
7. Reid, *The Grim Reapers*, pp. 73–74.
8. Ibid., pp. 74–75.
9. *U.S.–Senate, Kefauver Hearings*, part 2, pp. 184–86.
10. Ibid., vol. 5, pp. 1175–87.
11. *U.S.–Senate, McClellan Labor Hearings*, pp. 12519–27.
12. Ibid., p. 12520.
13. Hutchinson, *The Imperfect Union*, pp. 207–10.
14. Ibid., p. 414.
15. *U.S.–Senate, McClellan Labor Hearings*, p. 12778.
16. *U.S.–Senate, OC and Narcotics Hearings*, p. 508.
17. Joe Demma and Tom Renner, "The Mafia in the Supermarket," *Newsday* (1971), reprinted in Gage, *Mafia, U.S.A.*, pp. 326–27.
18. Ibid.
19. Ibid.
20. *U.S.–Senate, McClellan Labor Hearings*, pp. 12520–23.
21. Ibid., p. 12523.
22. Ibid., pp. 12523–26.
23. *U.S.–Senate, Kefauver Hearings*, part 5, pp. 1181–87.
24. Ibid., pp. 1179–81.
25. CE 1184.
26. *U.S.–Senate, McClellan Labor Hearings*, p. 12524.
27. Ibid.
28. *U.S.–Senate, Kefauver Hearings*, part 5, pp. 1180–81.
29. Ibid.
30. Ibid.
31. Dorman, *Payoff*, p. 155.
32. *U.S.–Senate, Kefauver Hearings*, part 5, p. 1178.
33. Ibid., p. 1181.
34. Ibid., pp. 1182–83.
35. Ibid., p. 1183.
36. Ibid., pp. 1182–86.
37. WR 792–93.
38. CE 1251.
39. Ibid.
40. WR 793.
41. HAH 9H 524; HAH 9H 519.
42. CE 2416.
43. WR 793.
44. HAH 9H 520, 1154.
45. CE 1265.
46. HAH 9H 157, see 518 for date of last negotiation session.
47. HAH 9H 157.
48. CE 2002, p. 13.
49. CE 2249, p. 41.
50. CE 2887.
51. CE 1321.
52. *U.S.–Senate, McClellan Labor Hearings*, pp. 12520–21.
53. Viorst, "The Mafia, the CIA, and the Kennedy Assassination," *Washingtonian*, November 1975, p. 116.
54. Anthony Summers, *Conspiracy* (New York: McGraw-Hill, 1980), p. 458.
55. CE 1184.
56. CE 1184, 1300.
57. CE 1184.
58. Ibid.
59. Ibid.
60. CE 1251.
61. *U.S.–Senate, McClellan Labor Hearings*, p. 12520.

62. Ibid.
63. *U.S.–Senate, OC and Narcotics Hearings*, p. 1098.
64. *U.S.–Senate, McClellan Labor Hearings*, p. 12196.
65. Salerno and Tompkins, *The Crime Confederation*, p. 323.
66. WR 793.
67. Ibid.
68. C. Ray Hall Exhibit 1; C. Ray Hall Exhibit 3, p. 14.
69. CE 1265; WR 793.
70. JFK microfilm, vol. 5, p. D20.
71. WR 794; C. Ray Hall Exhibit 1; C. Ray Hall Exhibit 3, p. 14.
72. WR 794.
73. JFK microfilm, vol. 5, p. D20; C. Ray Hall Exhibit 1; C. Ray Hall Exhibit 3, p. 14; WR 799.
74. CE 1228.
75. Ibid.
76. JFK microfilm, vol. 5, p. D26.
77. CE 1228.
78. Ibid.; CD 1102c (identifies "Bonds" as Locurto).
79. CD 1102c; WR 794.
80. WR 794.
81. Ibid.
82. WR 795; C. Ray Hall Exhibit 2.
83. Edem.
84. Edem.
85. Edem.
86. WR 799; JFK microfilm, vol. 5, pp. D20–26.

Chapter 8
Jack Ruby's Criminal Activities

1. *U.S.–House, OC Control*, p. 437.
2. See section 11 of Appendix 4.
3. See section 10 of Appendix 4.
4. See section 16c of Appendix 4.
5. See entry 15.25 of Appendix 4.
6. See section 12 of Appendix 4.
7. See section 15a of Appendix 4.
8. See section 13 of Appendix 4.
9. "The Gambino family has a large interest in the child pornography business," as reported in *Time*, November 28, 1977, p. 23.
10. See entry 15.23 of Appendix 4.
11. See section 17e of Appendix 4.
12. See section 14 of Appendix 4.
13. See entry 2.3 of Appendix 4.
14. Gage, *Mafia, U.S.A.*, pp. 17–18; Cressey, *Theft of the Nation*, pp. 74–75; see section 9 of Appendix 4.
15. *New York Times*, April 24, 1969, p. 30; *U.S.–Task Force Report*, p. 3; see entry 9.2 and section 19 of Appendix 4.
16. See section 9a of Appendix 4.
17. CE 1693.
18. Ibid.
19. Ibid.
20. CD 86, p. 278.
21. Ibid.
22. Ibid.
23. Ibid.
24. Ibid.
25. Ibid.
26. Ibid.
27. CE 1750.
28. CD 86, p. 278.
29. Ibid.
30. CD 86, pp. 278–82.
31. CD 86, p. 278.
32. Ibid.

33. CE 1763.
34. Ibid.
35. Ibid.
36. Ibid.
37. CD 4, p. 366; CD 86, pp. 248–49; CE 2980; see CE 1693.
38. CE 1763.
39. CE 1227, 1251, 2822; 15H 432; see section 8.3.
40. CE 1753.
41. Ibid.
42. Ibid.
43. Ibid.
44. HAH 5H 70–71, 170; HAH 9H 428.
45. CE 1753.
46. CE 2980.
47. CE 1708.
48. CE 2980.
49. *U.S.–Senate, Kefauver Hearings*, part 5, p. 1177.
50. CE 1761.
51. Ibid.
52. Ibid.
53. Ibid.
54. CE 1762.
55. Ibid.
56. Ibid.
57. Ibid.
58. Ibid.
59. CE 2980; CE 1240; CE 1708.
60. See chapter 9, Joseph Francis Civello.
61. CE 1761.
62. CE 1251.
63. CE 1763.
64. CE 1606; 15H 625–26. The cited interpretation of this transaction is supported by the conflict between the accounts of Larry Meyers (15H 625–26) and Dale (CE 1606) concerning this payment, and by the fact that Meyers, although married (15H 621), traveled to Dallas on another occasion with a woman he described as "a rather dumb but accommodating broad" (CE 2267).
65. CE 2822.
66. Ibid.
67. CE 1227.
68. 15H 432.
69. CD 86, p. 278.
70. CE 1763.
71. CE 1753.
72. CE 1761.
73. CE 1762.
74. CE 2822.
75. These include Carlos Malone in Louisville, Kentucky (CE 1559); Bobby Gene Moore in Oakland, California (CD 84, p. 91); Blaney Mack Johnson in Atlanta (CE 3063); and Nancy Perrin Rich in Hanover, Massachusetts (14H 331).
76. See sections 6.3, 6.4.
77. See chapters 12, 13, 21.
78. CE 1772.
79. Ibid.
80. Crafard Exhibit 5226; 15H 224; CE 1549; CE 1507; CE 1322, pp. 738, 746, note razor blades.
81. CE 1762.
82. Razor blades: Teresa, *My Life in the Mafia*, p. 135. Pornographic materials: see section 15a of Appendix 4.

Chapter 9
Jack Ruby's
Underworld Contacts

1. *U.S.–Senate, OC and Stolen Securities, 1973*, p. 453.
2. Ibid., p. 389.
3. Mollenhoff, *Strike Force*, p. 54.
4. Kennedy, *The Enemy Within*, p. 91.
5. Sheridan, *The Fall and Rise of Jimmy Hoffa*, p. 194.
6. Sheridan, p. 20; HAH 9H 276; *U.S.–Senate, McClellan Labor Hearings*, pp. 14059–61.
7. Kennedy, *The Enemy Within*, p. 91.
8. Ibid., pp. 91–92.
9. *U.S.–Senate, McClellan Labor Hearings*, pp. 14052–53.
10. Ibid., pp. 14059–61; HAH 9H 274.
11. Sheridan, p. 21.
12. Hutchinson, *The Imperfect Union*, p. 247.
13. Ibid.; HAH 9H 274–75.
14. Mollenhoff, *Strike Force*, p. 54.
15. Kennedy, *The Enemy Within*, p. 91.
16. CE 2331.
17. HAH 9H 274.
18. *U.S.–Senate, McClellan Labor Hearings*, pp. 14047–48, 14080; Hutchinson, p. 248; HAH 9H 274–76.
19. CE 2303.
20. Ibid.
21. CE 1322, p. 738.
22. HAH 9H 1146.
23. HAR 171; HAH 9H 335–36; JFK microfilm, vol. 5, p. G12; *Houston Post*, April 20, 1975, p. 2A.
24. HAH 9H 392.
25. *U.S.–Senate, McClellan Labor Hearings*, p. 12196; *U.S.–Senate, OC and Narcotics Hearings*, p. 1098.
26. HAH 9H 1146.
27. HAH 9H 336.
28. HAH 9H 335, 412.
29. HAH 9H 336.
30. Ibid.
31. HAH 9H 335.
32. Ibid.
33. *Houston Post*, April 20, 1975, p. 2A.
34. Ibid.; HAH 9H 392–97.
35. *Houston Post*, April 20, 1975, p. 2A.
36. HAH 9H 396.
37. *Houston Post*, April 20, 1975, p. 2A.
38. HAH 9H 392–97.
39. JFK microfilm, vol. 5, p. G12.
40. CD 106, p. 89.
41. CE 2259.
42. HAH 9H 343–48, 355–62, 366–67, 382–87.
43. HAH 9H 359.
44. CE 2259; CE 1748; see HAH 9H 336.
45. CE 2259.
46. CD 86, pp. 138–39.
47. CE 2259.
48. HAH 9H 363–64, 374.
49. *U.S.–House, OC Control*, p. 430.
50. Chandler, "The 'Little Man' is Bigger Than Ever," *Life*, April 10, 1970, p. 33.
51. Lawson, "Carnival of Crime," *Wall Street Journal*, January 12, 1970, p. 18.
52. Chandler, in *Life*, April 10, 1970, p. 31.
53. Ibid., p. 33; *Houston Post*, April 20, 1975, p. 2A.
54. Edem.
55. Edem.
56. Chandler, in *Life*, April 10, 1970, p. 33.

57. Ibid., pp. 33–34; Sheridan, pp. 458–59.
58. Chandler, in *Life*, April 10, 1970, pp. 33–34; Sheridan, pp. 458–59.
59. Chandler, in *Life*, April 10, 1970, pp. 33–34.
60. Ibid., p. 33.
61. *New York Times*, February 28, 1974, p. 24.
62. Chandler, in *Life*, April 10, 1970, pp. 33–34.
63. *Houston Post*, April 20, 1975.
64. Chandler, in *Life*, April 10, 1970, p. 34.
65. HAH 9H 72; Marcello has successfully fought deportation for more than 25 years, spending more money in the process than in any other such case in American history (HAH 9H 63).
66. Chandler, in *Life*, April 10, 1970, p. 34.
67. Sheridan, pp. 408, 411, 424–25, 427–28, 433, 458–59, 465–66, 482–83, 492, 505. For background on the campaign to spring Hoffa, see *Life*, September 29, 1967, pp. 34ff; "The Mob," part 1, *Life*, September 1, 1967, p. 22; Sheridan, passim.
68. Chandler, in *Life*, April 10, 1970, p. 34.
69. Ibid.
70. *U.S.–House, OC in Sports*, p. 954.
71. Ibid.
72. Ibid.
73. Ibid.
74. Ibid.
75. Ibid.
76. Ibid., p. 949.
77. See chapter 19.
78. Sheridan, pp. 202, 274, 356, 406–8; Moldea, *The Hoffa Wars*, p. 151; *U.S.–Senate, McClellan Labor Hearings*, p. 16642.
79. Sheridan, pp. 406–7; Moldea, p. 151.
80. Reid and Demaris, *The Green Felt Jungle*, pp. 104–5; Moldea, p. 151.
81. Edem.
82. Sheridan, p. 356.
83. Sheridan, pp. 406–8; see section 24.3.
84. Sheridan, p. 408.
85. CD 86, p. 558; Reid and Demaris, p. 104.
86. CD 86, p. 558.
87. Ibid.
88. Moldea, p. 163.
89. Ibid., pp. 163–64; Scott, *Crime and Cover-Up*, pp. 45–46.
90. Moldea, p. 112; Brill, *The Teamsters*, p. 131.
91. Sheridan, p. 282; Mollenhoff, *Strike Force*, p. 225.
92. Moldea, p. 417; NBC Evening News, "Segment 3," June 14, 1978.
93. See section 6.2.
94. *U.S.–Senate, OC and Narcotics Hearings*, p. 1098; *U.S.–Senate, Kefauver Report, Third Interim*, p. 82; "The Mob," part 1, *Life*, September 1, 1967, p. 20.
95. *U.S.–Senate, McClellan Labor Hearings*, p. 12195; *U.S.–Senate, OC and Narcotics Hearings*, p. 1098.
96. *Houston Post*, April 20, 1975, p. 2A.
97. *U.S.–Senate, OC and Narcotics Hearings*, p. 1098; *U.S.–Senate, McClellan Labor Hearings*, p. 12196.
98. *Houston Post*, April 20, 1975.
99. *U.S.–Senate, Kefauver Report, Third Interim*, p. 82.
100. CD 302, p. 16.
101. See chapter 9, Joseph Campisi.
102. CD 84, pp. 91–92.
103. Ibid.
104. Ibid.
105. Compare CD 84, pp. 91–92, with Golz, *Dallas Morning News*, April 26, 1972, p. D1. See also CE 1506, 1585, 1618, 1652, 1757, 1758 concern-

ing the friendship between Ruby and "Candy Barr" which Moore reported.
106. CD 84, p. 91.
107. Ibid.
108. Golz, *Dallas Morning News*, April 26, 1972, p. D1; see HAH 9H 390.
109. Sondern, *Brotherhood of Evil*, p. 240.
110. U.S.–Senate, OC and Narcotics Hearings, p. 1098.
111. CD 84, p. 91.
112. CD 302, p. 30.
113. CD 84, pp. 91–92.
114. CD 84, p. 92.
115. WR 801.
116. Kennedy, *The Enemy Within*, p. 250; see Reid, *Mickey Cohen: Mobster*.
117. Reid, *Mickey Cohen: Mobster*, passim; see section 16.2.
118. Reid, *Mickey Cohen: Mobster*, pp. 158, 161, 217–20.
119. CE 1757.
120. CE 1228.
121. CE 1506, 1585, 1618, 1652, 1757, 1758.
122. Reid, *Mickey Cohen: Mobster*, pp. 86–87; CE 1757; Kantor, *Who Was Jack Ruby?*, p. 21.
123. Reid, *Mickey Cohen: Mobster*, pp. 86–87; Kantor, p. 21.
124. 14H 446.
125. 14H 445.
126. Ibid.
127. 14H 444.
128. See chapter 9, Lewis J. McWillie, Lenny Patrick and Dave Yaras.
129. Hersh, *New York Times*, June 27–30, 1976.
130. Ibid., June 27, 1976, p. 1.
131. Ibid., June 27, 1976, p. 20.
132. Ibid., June 28, 1976, p. 1.
133. Ibid., June 27, 1976, p. 20.
134. Ibid., June 29, 1976, p. 16.
135. 5H 200; CE 1765.
136. CE 2308; CE 1322, p. 742.
137. CE 2284.
138. Ibid.
139. CD 1144, pp. 5–6.
140. Ibid.
141. Kantor, p. 22.
142. CE 2243, 2284.
143. Edem; 5H 185–86.
144. CE 2303.
145. CE 2243, 2284; see section 23.1.
146. U.S.–Senate, Kefauver Hearings, part 5, pp. 1175–87; U.S.–Senate, McClellan Labor Hearings, pp. 12519–27; see section 7.1.
147. U.S.–Senate, Kefauver Hearings, part 5, p. 1177; U.S.–Senate, McClellan Labor Hearings, p. 12520.
148. Edem.
149. Edem.; HAH 9H 513.
150. U.S.–Senate, Kefauver Hearings, part 5, p. 1177.
151. CE 1184; HAH 9H 514–18.
152. CE 1184; HAH 5H 518.
153. U.S.–Senate, Kefauver Hearings, part 5, p. 1177; CE 1184.
154. CE 1184.
155. CE 1184, 1300.
156. Edem.
157. CE 1184, 1708, 2980.
158. CE 1184, 1300.
159. HAH 9H 527.
160. CE 2989; HAH 9H 525; *New York Times*, January 4, 1959, p. 6.
161. HAH 9H 527–30.
162. *Dallas Morning News*, January 12, 1974, p. 1.

163. Ibid.
164. HAH 9H 525.
165. HAR 173; HAH 9H 529, 380–81.
166. HAH 9H 528–29.
167. HAH 9H 529.
168. CE 2988; CE 1748; CE 1752; CD 86, p. 147.
169. CE 2303; CE 2989.
170. CE 1693.
171. CD 686d, p. 2.
172. U.S.–Senate, Kefauver Hearings, part 2, p. 193; Reid and Demaris, pp. 184–85, 187.
173. CE 1692.
174. Reid and Demaris, p. 188; U.S.–Senate, OC and Narcotics Hearings, p. 891.
175. Edem.
176. CE 1692, 1693, 1184; U.S.–Senate, Kefauver Hearings, part 2, p. 194; 14H 445.
177. CE 1692, 1184; U.S.–Senate, Kefauver Hearings, part 2, p. 194.
178. 14H 445.
179. CE 1693.
180. CE 1691; CE 1697, p. 1; HAH 5H 3.
181. U.S.–Senate, OC and Narcotics Hearings, p. 569; Scott, "From Dallas to Watergate," in Blumenthal and Yazijian, ed., *Government by Gunplay*, p. 126; *New York Times*, January 4, 1959, p. 6; Anson, p. 309.
182. CE 1691; CE 1697, p. 1.
183. *Life*, March 10, 1958, p. 33; HAH 5H 161.
184. CD 686d, p. 2.
185. CE 1690, 1691, 1697; see section 15.2.
186. HAH 5H 19–20.
187. CE 1692; HAH 5H 3.
188. Wallace Turner, *Gambler's Money*, pp. 159–65, 295; Demaris, *Captive City*, p. 11.
189. CE 1692, 1544.
190. Reid, *The Grim Reapers*, p. 75.
191. Wallace Turner, pp. 240–42.
192. CE 1692; CE 1697, p. 4.
193. HAH 5H 4.
194. Wallace Turner, p. 127.
195. CE 1692; CE 1697, p. 4.
196. HAH 5H 18.
197. 5H 201; JFK microfilm, vol. 5, p. D31; CE 1697, p. 1; HAH 4H 549–50; CE 1655.
198. CE 1697, p. 1; C. Ray Hall Exhibit 3, p. 15; 5H 201.
199. 5H 201.
200. CD 5, pp. 413–14; CE 1697, p. 4; HAH 5H 33.
201. See sections 20.1, 20.2.
202. Sheridan, p. 292.
203. *Time*, December 10, 1973, p. 30.
204. HAH 4H 566.
205. CE 2303; CD 360, p. 149; HAH 4H 566.
206. U.S.–Senate, OC and Narcotics Report, p. 37; HAH 9H 943–48.
207. Edem.
208. Demaris, pp. 348–49.
209. Ibid.
210. HAH 9H 948, 945; Demaris, pp. 348–49.
211. HAH 9H 942; Demaris, p. 169.
212. HAH 9H 942.
213. HAH 9H 948; HAH 4H 567.
214. Reid, *The Grim Reapers*, p. 292.
215. HAH 9H 948.
216. Demaris, pp. 348–49.
217. CE 1202.
218. Ibid.
219. 14H 445; see 15H 29, HAH 4H 567.
220. U.S.–House, OC Control, pp. 416, 434.
221. HAH 4H 565.
222. *New York Times*, February 28, 1974, p. 24.
223. CE 2303; CD 84, pp. 131–32; U.S.–House, OC Control, p. 434; see section 19.2.

224. HAR 155; HAH 4H 565; see Appendix 3.
225. Reid, *The Grim Reapers*, pp. 188, 299.
226. Ibid., p. 299.
227. Ibid., pp. 216, 258–59.
228. See entry 18.23 of Appendix 4.
229. *U.S.–Senate, Intelligence Report, Foreign Assassinations*, pp. 75–77; HAH 10H 151.
230. HAH 10H 186.
231. Malone, "The Secret Life of Jack Ruby," *New Times*, January 23, 1978, p. 51.
232. Ibid.
233. Malone, "The Secret Life of Jack Ruby," *New Times*, January 23, 1978, p. 47; WR 786–87.
234. Malone, p. 51.
235. *Chicago Tribune*, April 22, 1973, p. 5; HAH 9H 1040.
236. HAH 9H 1040–42.
237. *Washington Post*, April 6, 1978, p. VA19.
238. HAH 9H 1040.
239. Demaris, pp. 64, 324.
240. HAH 4H 564; HAH 9H 1041–42; *Chicago Tribune*, April 22, 1973, p. 5.
241. HAH 9H 1041–42.
242. HAH 9H 1042.
243. Ibid.
244. Sheridan, pp. 137–38; HAH 9H 1041.
245. HAH 9H 1041.
246. Sheridan, p. 364.
247. HAH 9H 1042.
248. HAH 9H 1040–41.
249. See chapter 18.
250. HAH 9H 1042.
251. HAH 9H 1041.
252. Sheridan, pp. 137–38.
253. Ibid.
254. *New York Times*, February 20, 1974, p. 14; *Boston Globe*, January 3, 1974, p. 31; Brill, pp. 219–28; see also *Chicago Tribune*, April 22, 1973, p. 5; HAH 9H 1041.
255. Edem.
256. Brill, pp. 252–55.
257. HAH 9H 1041; see Brill, pp. 223–28; *Wall Street Journal*, July 24, 1975; Investigative Reporters and Editors Inc., Phoenix Project (IRE series), *Albuquerque Journal*, March 15, 1977, pp. 1, 14.
258. HAH 9H 1043.
259. CE 2303.
260. CD 84, p. 229.
261. See section 21.3.
262. HAH 9H 948, 961.
263. *U.S.–Senate, OC and Narcotics Report*, p. 37.
264. Demaris, p. 354.
265. Ibid.; HAH 4H 567.
266. *Life*, May 30, 1969, pp. 45–47.
267. Ibid.
268. Ibid.
269. Moldea, pp. 178–79.
270. Ibid., p. 155.
271. Ibid., pp. 123–24; *U.S.–Senate, McClellan Labor Hearings*, pp. 7416, 12522.
272. Moldea, p. 124.
273. Marcello: Meskil, *Don Carlo*, p. 137. Trafficante and Roselli: *U.S.–Senate, Intelligence Report, Foreign Assassinations*, pp. 75–77; HAH 10H 151. Hoffa: Moldea, pp. 122–23. Ruby: see chapter 18. Matthews: CE 2989; HAH 9H 525; *New York Times*, January 14, 1959, p. 6. McWillie: see chapter 9, Lewis J. McWillie. Patrick: HAH 9H 948. Weiner: HAH 9H 1042.
274. *U.S.–Senate, McClellan Labor Hearings*, p. 12522; Moldea, p. 124.
275. Moldea, pp. 124, 42.
276. HAH 4H 567.

277. *U.S.–Senate, Kefauver Report, Third Interim*, pp. 150–60; *U.S.–Senate, Kefauver Report, Second Interim*, pp. 11, 16–17; see also section 9a of Appendix 4.
278. *U.S.–Senate, Kefauver Report, Third Interim*, pp. 153, 155, 81.
279. Ibid., pp. 154–55.
280. *U.S.–Senate, McClellan Labor Hearings*, pp. 12524–25.
281. *U.S.–Senate, Kefauver Report, Third Interim*, p. 155; *U.S.–Senate, Kefauver Hearings*, part 2, p. 189.
282. Reid and Demaris, p. 25.
283. *U.S.–Senate, McClellan Labor Hearings*, p. 12525.
284. Demaris, pp. 130, 354.
285. Ibid.
286. Reid and Demaris, pp. 71–72.
287. Ibid.
288. Ibid.
289. Ibid.; *U.S.–Senate, OC and Narcotics Hearings*, p. 504.
290. Demaris, p. 130.
291. CE 1268.
292. Ibid.
293. Ibid.
294. CE 2303; see chapter 9, Barney Baker, and section 20.3.
295. CE 2332.
296. Ibid.
297. Ibid.
298. CE 1559.
299. Ibid.
300. Ibid.
301. Ibid.
302. Ibid.
303. Ibid.
304. 14H 340–41.
305. CE 3061, p. 627.
306. Ibid.
307. 14H 354.
308. 14H 353–55. For example, pursuing this line of questioning, counsel asks, "and you came to the conclusion, then, that Vito Genovese were involved in this matter." (14H 355).
309. 14H 359; see next chapter.

Chapter 10
Jack Ruby and the Dallas Police

1. Dorman, *Payoff*, p. 13.
2. *U.S.–Senate, Gambling and OC*, p. 31.
3. See part V and section 19 of Appendix 4.
4. See section 21 of Appendix 4.
5. Quoted by Fred Cook in *Two Dollar Bet Means Murder*, p. 7.
6. Rufus King, *Gambling and Organized Crime*, p. 28.
7. See section 21 of Appendix 4.
8. Reid and Demaris, *The Green Felt Jungle*, pp. 187, 197.
9. CE 1754; HAH 9H 527–28.
10. *Dallas Morning News*, March 29, 1974.
11. CD 1102d.
12. *Dallas Morning News*, January 12, 1974.
13. HAH 9H 529.
14. Demaris, *Captive City*, pp. 257–61.
15. Ibid., pp. 264–65.
16. Smith, "Corruption Behind the Swinging Clubs," *Life*, December 6, 1968, pp. 35–43.
17. Ibid., p. 42.
18. CE 1693; 14H 445; CE 1692; CE 1184; HAH 5H 20–23.

19. *Dallas Morning News*, April 26, 1972, p. D1.
20. Ibid.
21. HAH 9H 517.
22. Reid and Demaris, chapter 10; *U.S.–Senate, Kefauver Hearings*, part 2, p. 193; HAH 9H 530.
23. HAH 9H 517.
24. Ibid.
25. HAH 9H 527.
26. HAH 9H 412.
27. WR 43.
28. WR 209.
29. CD86, pp. 138–39; WR 809; note that Decker was the Dallas County Sheriff and that Ruby was in the Dallas County jail.
30. CE 1697.
31. WR 801.
32. CE 1535.
33. 14H 603.
34. CE 1592.
35. CE 1467.
36. CE 1228.
37. CE 1615.
38. CE 1632.
39. CE 1624.
40. CE 1659.
41. CE 1735.
42. WR 801.
43. Ibid.
44. CE 1322, p. 750.
45. CE 1322, p. 748.
46. CE 1322, p. 741.
47. CE 1322, p. 735.
48. CE 1322, p. 736.
49. JFK microfilm, vol. 5, pp. R35–38.
50. Ibid.
51. Ibid.
52. Ibid.
53. JFK microfilm, vol. 5, p. R32.
54. Demaris, p. 115.
55. JFK microfilm, vol. 5, p. R32.
56. CE 1636.
57. CE 1515.
58. CE 1659.
59. CE 1657.
60. CE 1649.
61. CE 1646, 1615, 1632.
62. CE 1659.
63. 14H 341.
64. Ibid.
65. CE 1505.
66. CE 1624, 1632, 1636, 1696; JFK microfilm, vol. 5, pp. C7–9.
67. CE 1515.
68. CE 1659.
69. Ibid.
70. Ibid.
71. Ibid.
72. CE 1652.
73. CE 1646.
74. Ibid.
75. CE 1696.
76. CD 5, pp. 413–14.
77. Alice Nichols Exhibit 5355; CE 1227; CE 2887; C. Ray Hall Exhibit 3, p. 16; CE 1745; Sam Ruby Exhibit 1; CE 2392; CD 84, p. 106.
78. CD 302, pp. 128–29.
79. CE 1612.
80. CE 1184; *Dallas Times Herald*, November 25, 1963, p. 24A; *Austin* (Texas) *American*, November 25, 1963, p. 8; CE 2980.
81. WR 804–5.
82. CE 1184, p. 29; *Austin* (Texas) *American*, November 25, 1963, p. 8; *Dallas Morning News*, November 25, 1963, section 4, p. 1; CE 1543; CE 1651; CD 104, p. 64.
83. CE 1756.
84. CE 1300.
85. CE 1684.
86. CE 1561.
87. CE 2980, p. 4.
88. CE 1672.
89. Ibid.
90. Ibid.
91. CE 1672.
92. CD 4, p. 533.
93. Ibid.
94. 14H 343.
95. 14H 358.
96. Ibid.
97. CE 1543.
98. CE 1207.
99. CE 1528.
100. Ibid.
101. Ibid.
102. CE 1518.
103. CE 2980.
104. CE 1608; CE 1528.
105. CE 1608.
106. JFK microfilm, vol. 5, p. D25.
107. CE 1610.
108. Ibid.
109. CE 1611, 1612.
110. JFK microfilm, vol. 5, p. B1.
111. CE 1517.
112. CE 1515.
113. See sections 12.2, 23.3.
114. 14H 359.
115. CD 4, p. 529. Al Bright, who reported this assertion by Ryan, also reported Ryan had told him that Ruby was friendly with Jimmy Hoffa (ibid.); Ryan denied this too (CE 1229). Supporting Bright, however, is a recent statement by Hoffa's son, James Hoffa, Jr.: "I think my dad knew Jack Ruby, but from what I understand, he [Ruby] was the kind of guy everybody knew. So what?" (Anthony Summers, *Conspiracy* [New York: McGraw-Hill, 1980], p. 472).
116. CE 1229.
117. Crafard Exhibit 5226; CD 84, p. 152; CE 1322, pp. 727, 773; CE 1567; CD 722, pp. 3–5; 14H 14–15; 13H 370–71; CE 2322.
118. CE 2322.
119. 15H 418.
120. Ibid.
121. Ibid.
122. CE 2322; 13H 370–71.
123. CD 722, p. 3.
124. CE 1753.
125. CE 1750.
126. CE 1763.
127. See section 20a of Appendix 4.

Chapter 11
Jack Ruby, Mobster

1. *Time*, December 19, 1977, pp. 18, 23.
2. HAH 3H 494.
3. See section 6.4.
4. WR 802–6.
5. CE 1322, pp. 725–26; Rossi Exhibit 1.
6. CE 1672.
7. CE 1184; *Dallas Times Herald*, November 25, 1963, p. 24A; *Austin* (Texas) *American*, November 25, 1963, p. 8; CE 2980.
8. CE 1322, pp. 746–47.
9. CD 86, pp. 279–80.
10. 14H 605–7, 611–12; 14H 602.
11. 14H 617.
12. CD 86, pp. 278–80.

13. CE 1505.
14. CE 1753.
15. C. Ray Hall Exhibit 3, p. 16; CE 1772; CD 86, p. 273.
16. 13H 428.
17. JFK microfilm, vol. 5, p. B10.
18. 13H 318.
19. CE 1469.
20. CE 1322, p. 754. The first page was evidently included since the copy bore a mailing label (ibid.).
21. *Wall Street Journal*, November 18, 1963, p. 1.
22. CE 1322, p. 755.
23. *New York Mirror*, September 8, 1963, p. 11.
24. Ibid.
25. *Dallas Morning News*, November 25, 1963, p. 7.
26. CE 1322, pp. 762–63.
27. CE 1322, pp. 725–26.
28. CE 2417, p. 260.
29. CE 1567.
30. CD 86, p. 486.
31. CD 86, p. 488.
32. 15H 477–78.
33. CE 1271; CE 1237.
34. Demaris, *Captive City*, p. 119.
35. CE 1318.
36. WR 788.
37. WR 798–99.
38. Messick, *Lansky*, p. 182.
39. Ibid.
40. "The Mafia v. America," *Time*, August 22, 1969, pp. 21–22.
41. Messick, *Lansky*, pp. 222–23, 253–54.
42. Ibid., pp. 180–83.
43. Teresa, pp. 125–26.
44. Ibid., p. 130.
45. Reid, *The Grim Reapers*, p. 151.
46. WR 355.
47. CD 86, p. 486.
48. CD 86, p. 488.
49. CE 1322, pp. 732, 757.
50. 13H 213; CD 4, p. 612.
51. C. Ray Hall Exhibit 3, p. 16; CD 86, p. 488.
52. C. Ray Hall Exhibit 3, p. 16; CE 1753.
53. CE 1753.
54. Ibid.
55. CE 1625–27.
56. CE 1584, 1753; C. Ray Hall Exhibit 3, p. 16.
57. CE 1772; C. Ray Hall Exhibit 3, p. 16.
58. CE 1559.
59. CE 1586, 1588–89, 1600–1601; CD 86, p. 459.
60. CE 1521–26; CD 84, pp. 131, 219–20.
61. CE 3063; CE 3065; see section 18.1.
62. C. Ray Hall Exhibit 3, p. 15; 15H 201, 205; CE 1697, pp. 1–2; see section 18.2.
63. Sam Yaras: *U.S.-Senate, McClellan Labor Hearings*, p. 12522; CE 1268.
64. Nick DeJohn, Paul Labriola and Jimmy Weinberg: *U.S.-Senate, McClellan Labor Hearings*, p. 12524.
65. Danny Lardino: ibid., p. 12526. Marcus Lipsky: ibid., p. 12520; Demaris, p. 245. Paul Roland Jones: CE 1184.
66. CE 1251.
67. *U.S.-Senate, OC and Narcotics Hearings*, p. 1098; *U.S.-Senate, McClellan Labor Hearings*, p. 12196.
68. CE 1708; CE 2980; See section 8.2.
69. CE 1761.
70. See section 9 of Appendix 4.
71. Reid, *The Grim Reapers*, chapters 2–5; see section 5 of Appendix 4.
72. Messick, *Lansky*, passim; Reid, *The Grim Reapers*, pp. 223–24; Reid, *Mickey Cohen: Mobster*,

passim; George Carpozi, Jr., *Bugsy* (New York: Pinnacle, 1973), passim.
73. See section 5 of Appendix 4.
74. Teresa, pp. 216–17; see Messick, *Lansky*.
75. Teresa, pp. 216–17.
76. Reid, *The Grim Reapers*, p. 316.
77. Teresa, foreword by Thomas Renner, pp. v-vi.
78. Ibid., pp. 216–19.
79. Ibid., p. 217.
80. 14H 566.

Part III
Murder
on Cue

1. WR 208, 16.
2. WR 354, 357.
3. WR 354.
4. 13H 204–5.
5. 5H 199.
6. 13H 211–12.
7. CE 2298.
8. WR 354, 357.
9. Ibid.
10. WR 209–16.
11. Ibid.
12. Ibid.
13. 13H 7, 17; WR 216; 4H 233.
14. 13H 28–29.
15. 13H 17.
16. WR 216.
17. C. Ray Hall Exhibit 2; C. Ray Hall Exhibit 3; 5H 181–213.
18. CE 2298.
19. WR 354, 357.
20. Ibid.
21. 5H 206.

Chapter 12
Perjury and Suspicious
Activities

1. Buchanan, *Who Killed Kennedy?*, British edition, p. 25.
2. C. Ray Hall Exhibit 2; C. Ray Hall Exhibit 3; 5H 181–213; see text below.
3. 5H 184–85; C. Ray Hall Exhibit 3, p. 4.
4. 5H 207; C. Ray Hall Exhibit 3, p. 5.
5. Kantor Exhibit 7.
6. Kantor Exhibit 8.
7. 15H 71–96.
8. Kantor Exhibit 7, 8; 15H 71–96.
9. 15H 72.
10. Kantor Exhibit 8.
11. 15H 88; see also Kantor Exhibit 8.
12. 15H 392–94.
13. WR 336–37.
14. WR 336. See 15H 419 and CE 1518, Ruby's traffic violation record, concerning the Warren Commission's conjecture, "it is likely that congested traffic conditions on November 22 would have extended the driving time"(WR 336). See section 13.2 concerning the credibility of the testimony of Andrew Armstrong (13H 331–32) and Karen Carlin (13H 208–9) placing Ruby at the Carousel Club for the 1:45 p.m. call to the Carlin residence (CE 2303, p. 27). Also see 13H 305–6, 314, 333–34 concerning Armstrong's general credibility and chapter 13 concerning Karen Carlin's general credibility.
15. WR 336.

16. Kantor Exhibit 7.
17. HAR 158.
18. HAR 158–59.
19. WR 340–42.
20. Ibid.; 5H 188–89. Ruby later explained that he had gone to the police station that night to get the unlisted "hot line" number of the newsroom at radio station KLIF, so he could bring sandwiches to the employees there (5H 187–88; C. Ray Hall Exhibit 3, p. 6). Yet that telephone number (RI7–9319) appeared on two lists found on Ruby after he shot Oswald (CE 1322; pp. 727, 729; see 15H 437, Dowe Exhibit 1 for an identification of that number). On both, the number was followed by several names and phone numbers of people whom Ruby had contacted before November 22. In particular, in the first list (CE 2308; CE 1322, p. 729), following the KLIF entry were the name and Minneapolis address of Smokey Turner, whom Ruby called in Minneapolis on November 16 (CE 2302), and the name and address of Connie Trammel, whom he saw on November 21 (CE 2270). In the second list (CE 1322, pp. 729–30), following the KLIF entry were the names and numbers of Joe Severeign, Frank Goldstein and Irv Mazzei, whom Ruby called at the listed numbers respectively on July 18 (CE 2308; CE 1322, p. 729), November 12 (CE 2303), and November 9 (CE 2303), 1963.
21. Eberhardt Exhibit 5026.
22. 13H 187; Eberhardt Exhibit 5026.
23. 15H 615.
24. Ibid.
25. Ibid.
26. Robertson Exhibit 1.
27. 15H 348–51.
28. Ibid.
29. CE 2249, p. 14.
30. Jenkins Exhibit 1; National Archives, entry 45, Ruby-Oswald chronology, pp. 844–47.
31. CE 2276.
32. JFK microfilm, vol. 5, p. D28.
33. 15H 588–89.
34. Ibid.
35. 15H 356–57.
36. Ibid.
37. CE 2326.
38. CE 2327.
39. National Archives, entry 45, Ruby-Oswald chronology, pp. 844–47.
40. 5H 187–88; C. Ray Hall Exhibit 3, pp. 5–10.
41. Robertson Exhibit 2.
42. 15H 487–88.
43. 15H 257.
44. 15H 477–78.
45. C. Ray Hall Exhibit 3, p. 12.
46. 5H 185.
47. C. Ray Hall Exhibit 2, p. 14.
48. 5H 198.
49. C. Ray Hall Exhibit 2, pp. 14–15.
50. Ibid.
51. Ibid.; 5H 198–99.
52. HAR 158.
53. *Newsweek*, March 27, 1967, p. 21; HAR 158.
54. CE 1753.
55. Ibid.
56. CE 1245.
57. CE 1184.
58. 5H 198.
59. Ibid.
60. 14H 564.
61. Ibid.
62. Ibid.

63. 14H 567.
64. CE 2161.
65. C. Ray Hall Exhibit 3, p. 8.
66. Ibid.
67. Ruby testified that he came into KLIF with disc jockey Russ Knight (5H 190; C. Ray Hall Exhibit 3, p. 8). This account was confirmed by KLIF employee Glenn Duncan, who testified that he saw Ruby enter the newsroom with Knight (15H 486). Yet Knight testified that Ruby arrived at KLIF about 15 or 20 minutes after Knight, and that Knight was with Glenn Duncan when Ruby came in (15H 256–57). Still another KLIF employee reported that he was the one who let Ruby into the station (McCurdy Exhibit 1; 15H 532).
68. 15H 365–66.
69. 15H 529–30. Also note that Pappas testified that he spent all of his time at KLIF in the newsroom (15H 366), and three KLIF employees placed Ruby in the newsroom during most of his visit (15H 257–58, 261, 486, 529–30; see also 5H 190).
70. 15H 257–58, 261.
71. 15H 364–65.
72. 15H 365.
73. C. Ray Hall Exhibit 1; HAH 5H 87, 172.
74. C. Ray Hall Exhibit 1; HAH 5H 172; Sheridan, *The Fall and Rise of Jimmy Hoffa*, p. 503.
75. 5H 187.
76. 5H 188.
77. Sheridan, p. 503; for background on Smith see Sheridan, p. 492.
78. CE 1322, pp. 727, 730, 735–37, 771; Andrew Armstrong Exhibit 5305-K.
79. 15H 530 (the number was DA1–0467).
80. CE 1322, p. 727.
81. CE 1322, p. 730.
82. Ibid.
83. CE 2980, p. 12.
84. C. Ray Hall Exhibit 3, p. 8.
85. 5H 194.
86. 14H 631, 633, 646–48.
87. Ibid.
88. 14H 646–48.
89. Ibid.
90. 14H 631, 633, 646–48.
91. CE 2418.
92. Ibid.
93. 5H 191.
94. 5H 191, 193.
95. 15H 257, 259.
96. 5H 193.
97. CE 2318.
98. 14H 631.
99. Ibid.
100. 14H 632.
101. CE 2418.
102. Ibid.
103. 5H 191.
104. 14H 631–33, 648–49, 5H 191.
105. 14H 648.
106. 14H 649.
107. 14H 633.
108. CE 2318.
109. 5H 191.
110. 14H 632.
111. 14H,648.
112. 15H 364–65; see section 12.5.
113. 14H 631–33.
114. CE 2418.
115. 14H 627–28, 642; 15H 215; CE 2318.
116. 14H 629–30.
117. Ibid.

118. Ibid.
119. 14H 645–46.
120. Ibid.
121. 14H 630–31 vs. 14H 646; 14H 635 vs. 14H 649.
122. 14H 635, 645, 649.
123. 14H 635, 649.
124. C. Ray Hall Exhibit 3, p. 5.
125. 14H 636–37.
126. Ibid.
127. 14H 650.
128. 14H 650–51.
129. 14H 635–36, 650.
130. 15H 214; 14H 653.
131. 14H 653.
132. 15H 214.
133. Ibid.
134. 15H 653; 14H 634.
135. 14H 637.
136. 14H 626, 642, 653.
137. C. Ray Hall Exhibit 3, p. 8; 5H 193.
138. C. Ray Hall Exhibit 3, pp. 8–9; Crafard Exhibit 5226; 5H 203; 13H 463–66, 504; 14H 219, 220, 324.
139. C. Ray Hall Exhibit 3, p. 8.
140. As cited in note 138.
141. 14H 219–20 vs. 13H 463–66, 504, and Crafard Exhibit 5226; 13H 251–52 vs. 13H 463 and Crafard Exhibit 5226.
142. C. Ray Hall Exhibit 3, pp. 8–9; 5H 203; 14H 324.
143. 14H 233; Senator Exhibit 5401, p. 3.
144. Senator Exhibit 5401, p. 3.
145. Senator Exhibit 5400.
146. 14H 300–303.
147. Ibid.
148. CE 1322, p. 725.
149. Senator Exhibit 5401.
150. CD 360, p. 132; JFK microfilm, vol. 5, p. R83; National Archives, entry 45, Ruby-Oswald chronology, p. 851.
151. Reid and Demaris, *The Green Felt Jungle*, p. 188; also note the employment at the Southland Hotel of Mobsters Lester Binion and Lewis McWillie (CE 1692).
152. Reid and Demaris, p. 188.
153. WR 371–72.
154. HAH 9H 985–88.
155. 14H 256; 14H 256–57.
156. 14H 257.
157. Ibid.
158. CE 3024, p. 5.
159. Ibid., p. 6.
160. Jones, *Forgive My Grief*, vol. I, p. 5.
161. 14H 256–59.
162. 13H 468–69; 14H 39–40; Crafard Exhibit 5226.
163. Crafard Exhibit 5226.
164. 5H 206.
165. 13H 17, 28–29.
166. CE 2341.
167. Ibid.
168. 15H 490–91.
169. Ibid.
170. Ibid.
171. 15H 433–34.
172. Ibid.
173. See section 12.5.
174. Dowe Exhibits 1, 2; 15H 432–34.
175. Dowe Exhibit 2.
176. 15H 432.
177. 15H 491.
178. 15H 397–98.
179. CE 2302, p. 15; WR 358, 795.
180. 15H 397–98.
181. 15H 398–99.
182. 15H 399.

183. Ibid.
184. 15H 402.
185. C. Ray Hall Exhibit 3, pp. 11–12; C. Ray Hall Exhibit 2, p. 16.
186. C. Ray Hall Exhibit 3, p. 7; WR 356–57.
187. C. Ray Hall Exhibit 2, p. 16.
188. C. Ray Hall Exhibit 3, p. 7.
189. 5H 205.
190. 5H 207–8.
191. 13H 311–12, 343–44; 14H 83–85; 14H 147; Wright Exhibit 1; CE 1623.

Chapter 13
Premeditation and Conspiracy

1. 14H 567.
2. 15H 620.
3. See section 13.2.
4. WR 353.
5. 13H 206–7.
6. See section 8.3.
7. 15H 216; JFK microfilm, vol. 5, pp. B9, B17, D30.
8. 13H 206.
9. 15H 619–20.
10. Ibid.
11. Ibid.
12. Ibid.
13. Ibid.
14. JFK microfilm, vol. 5, p. B17.
15. 15H 660.
16. Sybil Leek and Bert Sager, *The Assassination Chain* (New York: Corwin, 1976), p. 206; "Houston Hotel" in the source.
17. CD 722, p. 7.
18. 13H 202.
19. JFK microfilm, vol. 5, p. D30.
20. JFK microfilm, vol. 5, p. B17.
21. Ibid.; CE 2313, p. 264.
22. 15H 427.
23. 15H 216.
24. Ibid.
25. CE 2313.
26. 15H 642–43.
27. CD 722, p. 7.
28. 15H 642–44.
29. 15H 643.
30. Ibid.
31. 15H 643–47.
32. 15H 646; 13H 209.
33. 15H 643–44; see WR 42 concerning JFK trip to Houston.
34. 15H 642–43.
35. 15H 643–44.
36. CE 2313.
37. Ibid.
38. 5H 661.
39. HAH 1H 55–56.
40. See text below.
41. 13H 209.
42. 13H 209–10.
43. Ibid.
44. Ibid.
45. 13H 210–11; 15H 663.
46. Edem.
47. CE 2303, p. 245.
48. 13H 208; Armstrong Exhibit 5310G.
49. 13H 208.
50. 13H 209.
51. Armstrong Exhibit 5310G.
52. Ibid.
53. Ibid.; WR 337.
54. 13H 505.
55. 13H 333.
56. Ibid.

57. Ibid.
58. 13H 334.
59. 13H 209.
60. Ibid.
61. 15H 653; 15H 421–22.
62. Karen Carlin Exhibit 5318.
63. Ibid.
64. 15H 421–23.
65. 13H 210, 245–46; 15H 651; CE 2334.
66. CE 2334.
67. ibid.
68. Ibid.
69. 13H 247.
70. 13H 246.
71. 15H 423.
72. 15H 421–24, 653.
73. 15H 423–24.
74. 15H 423.
75. Ibid.
76. C. Ray Hall Exhibit 3, p. 10.
77. 13H 209.
78. 13H 333.
79. 15H 335.
80. 15H 423.
81. Ibid.
82. C. Ray Hall Exhibit 2, p. 13.
83. 15H 423.
84. 15H 411, 424.
85. WR 358.
86. See section 12.9.
87. 15H 335.
88. 13H 248.
89. 13H 244–45, 249.
90. 15H 335.
91. Ibid.
92. 15H 335; 14H 455–46.
93. 15H 335.
94. Ibid.
95. CE 2298. The phone numbers, respectively, were JE4–8525 and WH1–5601.
96. 13H 204–5, 211–12; 5H 199.
97. C. Ray Hall Exhibit 3, pp. 10–11; 5H 199.
98. Edem.
99. 14H 236–40.
100. Senator Exhibit 5401, pp. 3–4.
101. See section 12.7.
102. 14H 300–303.
103. Ibid.
104. 13H 292–95.
105. 13H 293.
106. Ibid.
107. 13H 295.
108. As noted in 13H 295.
109. 13H 256–58.
110. Ibid.
111. Ibid.
112. 13H 279–84.
113. Ibid.
114. 13H 282.
115. 13H 283.
116. Ibid.
117. CD 85, pp. 501, 517.
118. CD 85, p. 502.
119. Ibid.
120. WR 352.
121. I.e., WR 62–64, 143–46, 166–71.
122. WR 352.
123. 15H 488.
124. 15H 508.
125. CE 2415. Ruby apparently discarded his overcoat in the late morning, when the temperature reached 48 degrees (ibid.).
126. WR 352.
127. Ibid.
128. See chapter 12.
129. WR 371–72.
130. WR 353.
131. CE 3072. See Meagher, *Accessories After The Fact*, pp. 449–51.
132. 12H 75–79.
133. Ibid.
134. Ibid. For example, Revill introduced the matter of Rushing's visit with the remark, "by the way, he rode up on the elevator with Jack Ruby" (ibid.).
135. 12H 75–79.
136. Meagher, *Accessories After the Fact*, p. 452.
137. 13H 230–31.
138. Ibid.
139. Ibid.
140. 13H 231.
141. Ibid.
142. CE 2002, p. 73.
143. Ibid.
144. CD 85, p. 271.
145. Ibid.
146. Ibid.
147. ABC-TV newsreel no. 9145, Dallas, November 24, 1963, cited by Mark Lane in *Rush to Judgment*, p. 216.
148. CD 85, p. 480.
149. CD 85, p. 484.
150. Ibid.
151. CD 85, p. 483.
152. CD 84, p. 88.
153. Ibid.
154. Ibid.
155. 15H 350–51; CE 2249, p. 14; see section 12.2.
156. CD 84, p. 89.
157. WR 43.
158. WR 209.
159. CD 86, pp. 138–39; WR 809; note that Decker was the Dallas County Sheriff and that Ruby was in the Dallas County jail.
160. HAH 9H 517.
161. HAH 9H 412, 527.
162. See section 12.6.
163. Ibid.
164. 5H 206.
165. 14H 567.

Chapter 14
The Startling Testimony
of Jack Ruby

1. 5H 190.
2. 5H 194.
3. 5H 196.
4. 5H 211.
5. CE 1528.
6. *U.S.–Senate, Kefauver Hearings*, part 5, p. 1177; *U.S.–Senate, McClellan Labor Hearings*, p. 12520.
7. See chapter 9, Dave Yaras.
8. John Kaplan and Jon Waltz, *The Trial of Jack Ruby* (New York: Macmillan, 1965), p. 20.
9. See section 22 of Appendix 4.
10. C. Ray Hall Exhibit 2.
11. Ibid.
12. Ibid.
13. Ibid.
14. C. Ray Hall Exhibit 3.
15. Meagher, *Accessories After the Fact*, p. 452.
16. 5H 190, 197.
17. 5H 181.
18. 5H 183–91, 193–94, 197–200; C. Ray Hall Exhibit 3.

19. 5H 182.
20. 5H 182–91, 193–94, 197–200.
21. 5H 207.
22. Ibid.
23. 5H 185.
24. 5H 192.
25. 5H 198.
26. 5H 199.
27. 5H 190.
28. Ibid.
29. Ibid.
30. 5H 191.
31. 5H 192.
32. 5H 194, see p. 193.
33. 5H 194.
34. Ibid.
35. Ibid.
36. C. Ray Hall Exhibit 3.
37. Kennedy, *The Enemy Within*, p. 250; see Reid, *Mickey Cohen: Mobster.*
38. Reid, *Mickey Cohen: Mobster*, p. 103.
39. Ibid.
40. Gary Wills and Ovid Demaris, *Jack Ruby* (New York: New American Library, 1968), p. 68.
41. Reid, *Mickey Cohen: Mobster*, pp. 86–87; Kantor, *Who Was Jack Ruby?*, p. 21.
42. CE 1506, 1585, 1618, 1652, 1757, 1758.
43. HAH 9H 1051, 1073–74, 1078, 1061, 1044; 14H 473, 400–403.
44. CE 1507.
45. HAH 9H 1050, 1078, 1044; CE 1507.
46. 5H 194.
47. 5H 195.
48. Ibid.
49. 5H 195–96.
50. 5H 196–97.
51. 5H 198.
52. 5H 209–13.
53. 5H 208.
54. 5H 210–13; see also 14H 531, 546.
55. 5H 210.
56. 5H 211–13.
57. HAH 10H 201.
58. HAH 10H 199.
59. CD 86, p. 558; see chapter 9, Frank Chavez.
60. CD 86, p. 558.
61. See section 3.9.
62. Ibid.
63. See section 3.5.
64. Ibid.
65. See section 3.1.
66. Ibid.
67. 14H 256–57; see sections 3.1 and 12.7.
68. See sections 12.6, 12.7, and 13.1.
69. 15H 619–20.
70. See section 13.1.
71. *U.S.–Senate, Kefauver Report, Third Interim*, p. 128; see entry 23.7 of Appendix 4.
72. Reid, *The Grim Reapers*, pp. 32–33; see section 15.3.
73. Pantaleone, *The Mafia and Politics*, pp. 155–57.
74. *Newsweek*, November 28, 1977, p. 66.
75. NBC Evening News, "Segment 3," December 16, 1977.
76. CD 86, p. 138.
77. HAH 9H 517.
78. *Houston Post*, April 20, 1975; see chapter 9, Joseph Campisi.
79. CE 2259; CD 86, pp. 138–39.
80. See chapter 17.
81. 5H 181, 190, 197.
82. 5H 192, 197, 210.
83. 5H 192.
84. 5H 196–97.

85. CE 2980.
86. Ibid.
87. Ibid.
88. Ibid.
89. Ibid.
90. See chapter 20.
91. See chapter 19.
92. 5H 181–213.
93. 5H 193–98.
94. See WR 345–52.
95. WR 345–52.
96. 5H 198.
97. 5H 181–213.
98. 5H 190, 192, 193.
99. 5H 197.
100. 5H 194–95.
101. 5H 198.
102. Ibid.
103. 5H 199.
104. Ibid.
105. 5H 196.
106. Ibid.
107. 5H 197.
108. HAH 3H 622.
109. George O'Toole, "The Assassination Tapes," *Penthouse*, June 1973, pp. 45ff.
110. Ibid.
111. Ibid.
112. *TV Guide*, April 8, 1978, p. A5.
113. O'Toole, *Penthouse*, June 1973, pp. 45ff.
114. Ibid.
115. Ibid.
116. Ibid.
117. Ibid.
118. 5H 212.
119. 5H 181, 182, 190, 191, 193, 196, 211–13.
120. 5H 211.
121. 5H 212.
122. 5H 213.
123. 5H 212.
124. CE 2728.
125. Ibid.
126. CE 3062, 3061.
127. CE 2728.
128. Meagher, pp. 452–53.
129. CE 2729.
130. CE 2730.
131. WR 808.
132. Ibid.
133. Ibid.
134. Ibid.
135. 14H 504.
136. 5H 181.
137. HAR 159.
138. 14H 565–67.
139. 14H 567.
140. See sections 12.4 and 14.5.
141. 5H 206.
142. 14H 543.
143. Ibid.
144. 14H 548.
145. 14H 565.
146. Ibid.
147. 14H 566.
148. Ibid.
149. Meagher, pp. 452–53.
150. Ibid.
151. Sylvia Meagher, *Subject Index to the Warren Report and Hearings and Exhibits* (New York: Scarecrow Press, 1966).
152. Meagher, *Accessories After the Fact*, pp. 452–53.
153. Ibid.
154. Ibid.
155. Ibid.

156. 14H 565.
157. 14H 566.
158. 14H 543.
159. 5H 211.
160. 14H 566.

Part IV
Pilgrims and Pirates

1. G. Robert Blakey and Richard N. Billings, "An Expert's Theory," *Parade*, November 16, 1980, pp. 5–6; Carl Oglesby and Jeff Goldberg, "Did the Mob Kill Kennedy," *Washington Post*, February 25, 1979, pp. B1, B4; "Hints of the Mob," *Newsweek*, October 9, 1978, pp. 44, 47; William Scott Malone, "The Secret Life of Jack Ruby," *New Times*, January 23, 1978, pp. 46–51; *Time*, January 10, 1977, p. 17; George Crile III, "The Mafia, the CIA, and Castro," *Washington Post*, May 16, 1976, pp. C1, C4; Milton Viorst, "The Mafia, the CIA, and the Kennedy Assassination," *Washingtonian*, November 1975, pp. 113–18; Robert Anson, *"They've Killed the President!"*, pp. 327–28; Peter Noyes, *Legacy of Doubt*, pp. 222–28; Dan Moldea, *The Hoffa Wars*, chapter 8.
2. "The religious and civic life of the [Massachusetts Bay] Colony was governed by the Mosaic laws. . . . The Old Testament was their Book of Laws, Moses was their law giver, and the ministers were the interpreters of these laws" (Walter A. Powell, *The Pilgrims and Their Religious, Intellectual and Civic Life* [Wilmington, Delaware: Walter Powell, 1923], pp. 183, 189–90). The Pilgrims saw themselves battling evil forces as did Israel in the Bible, observed Robert Bartlett in *The Faith of the Pilgrims* (New York: United Church Press, 1978), p. 53. "England was their oppressor, like Egypt. King James was their pharaoh, and the Atlantic Ocean was their Red Sea. New England was to be their Canaan, they hoped and prayed" (ibid.). The leaders of Massachusetts Bay viewed their colony as a "Zion in the wilderness," related the *Encyclopaedia Britannica* (15th ed., 1981, vol. 18, p. 948).
3. Lev. 19:18. Note that the Hebrew word for neighbor is the same as used in Exodus 11:2, referring to an Egyptian neighbor; the commandment is thus not restricted to someone of the same nationality and religion. This commandment was stressed as central by two great Jewish teachers: Hillel (Talmud, Shab. 31a) and Jesus (Matt. 22:35–40; all quotations from the New Testament are from the New International Version).
4. Lev. 19:2.
5. Concerning the deification of the Caesars, see Haim Cohn, *The Trial and Death of Jesus*, (New York: Ktav, 1977), p. 4; Solomon Grayzel, *A History of the Jews* (New York: New American Library, 1968), p. 152; Tacitus, pp. 273–74. See also Suetonius, *The Twelve Caesars*, translated by Robert Graves (New York: Penguin, 1979), chapter subtitles; and Joseph Klausner, *From Jesus to Paul*, translated by William Stinespring (New York: Macmillan, 1943), pp. 109–12.
6. Grayzel, pp. 152, 156–69; Chaim Potok, *Wanderings* (New York: Knopf, 1978), pp. 203–21; Cohn, pp. 2–20.
7. Edem.; Cohn, p. 220; Josephus, *The Jewish War*, translated by G. A. Williamson (New York: Penguin, 1969), pp. 12, 314–15, 364. With the Jewish political revolutionaries, noted the German historian Emil Schurer, were associated religious zealots. "Advancing the claim of a divine mission, they roused the people to a wild enthusiasm" for "that freedom which consisted in casting off the Roman yoke and setting up the kingdom of God." The Roman governor Felix "recognized clearly enough the dangerous tendency of the movement, and invariably broke in upon all such undertakings with the sword" (Schurer, *A History of the Jewish People in the Time of Jesus* [New York, Schocken Books, 1961, first published in English in 1886 by T. & T. Clark, Edinburgh], pp. 230–31). When one such Jew, an Egyptian, gathered several thousand followers in the wilderness, promising a miraculous redemption from Rome, Felix sent troops to slaughter and scatter the band (ibid., p. 231). Another who proclaimed himself a prophet, Theudas, marched a multitude of followers to the Jordan River, which he promised to part by his word. The aftermath of the miracle would be rebellion against Rome—at least that was how Fadus, the Roman governor, viewed it. Fadus sent troops to attack the throng, Theudas was decapitated, and his head was carried off to Jerusalem as a sign of the Romans' victory (ibid., p. 225; see also p. 162). Both incidents occurred in the middle of the first century.
8. Josephus, pp. 12, 314–15, 364; Cohn, pp. 220–21; Schurer, pp. 162, 227–28, 267. Christians were later persecuted in like manner by the empire.
9. When asked what commandment is most important, Jesus replied that the foremost is "Hear, O Israel, the Lord our God, the Lord is one; love the Lord your God with all your heart and with all your soul and with all your mind and with all your strength" (Mark 12:28–34, quoting Deut. 6:4–5). Note that Jesus drew a clear distinction between himself and God (Luke 18:18–19; Mark 10:17–18; Mark 13:32; Matt. 24:36; Matt. 12:31–32), and that the term "Son of God" and analogues were often applied metaphorically to human beings in both Jewish (Ps. 89:20–27; Deut. 14:1; Isa. 1:2) and Christian (Matt. 6:6–9; Rom. 8:14–16; Rom. 9:4; Gal. 3:26; Gal. 4:6–7; Acts 17:28–29) writings. On the other hand, humans becoming gods, gods taking human forms and gods coupling with humans were standard pagan themes (Klausner, *From Jesus to Paul*, chapter 3; see Acts 14:11–13; Acts 28:6), especially prevalent in Roman mythology (H. W. Household, *Rome, Republic and Empire*, vol. 1 [London: J. M. Dent and Sons, 1936], pp. 2, 11–15).
10. Although Jesus extended his love to all peoples (Matt. 24:14) and castigated his own (Matt. 15:7–9, 23:1–39), in the tradition of the prophets, he also exhibited a strong degree of national identification (Mark 7:26–27; Matt. 6:7, 10:5–6, 18:17, 20:34). See also Joseph Klausner, *Jesus of Nazareth*, translated by Herbert Danby (New York, Macmillan, 1925), pp. 9, 76, 94–95, 363–68.
11. Since before Jesus's time, Jews have viewed the messiah as both a spiritual redeemer and a physical liberator—a descendant of David, the greatest sovereign Jewish king, who would free the Jews from foreign oppression. Although Jesus's view of his messianic mission was not completely traditional, it is doubtful that Caesar's minions were cognizant of the

differences. Indeed, the crime for which Jesus was charged by Pilate was being "king of the Jews" (Matt. 27:11; Mark 15:2; Luke 23:3), which was tantamount to high treason under the Roman code *Lex Julia maiestatis* (Cohn, pp. 170–74). Also, the *titulus* Pilate ordered inscribed on Jesus's cross, proclaiming his crime, was "Jesus of Nazareth, the King of the Jews" (John 19:19). In *The Twelve Caesars* (p. 170), Suetonius records a contemporaneous incident in which a Roman slave was to be brutally punished for theft on the order of Emperor Caligula and paraded around at a public gathering "displaying a placard in explanation of his punishment." Later, the Spanish Inquisition followed the same custom: each prisoner to be executed bore a placard with his name, birthplace, and offense (Martin A. Cohen, *The Martyr* [Philadelphia: Jewish Publication Society, 1973], pp. 174, 255).

12. In drawing historical conclusions from the New Testament accounts of Jesus's murder, the following points are crucial. First, the high priests of the time were Roman puppets, held in contempt by the Jewish masses. A Jewish ballad expressing hate for the Boethusean high priests, including Ananus of the Gospels, is recorded in the Talmud (Pesahim 57a; T. Menahot 13:21; see Klausner, *Jesus of Nazareth*, p. 337). The Talmud also recorded how the Roman procurator used to reappoint a new high priest every year because of the bribes he could extract from candidates for the position (Yoma 8b; see Klausner, *Jesus of Nazareth*, pp. 151–52, 161–63, 168). Second, the multitudes of Jesus's followers (Mark 3:8–9, 20, 32, 6:33–34) were Jews; the events described in connection with these followers took place in Palestine, as did all events in the life of Jesus. Third, Governor Pontius Pilate was reputed for "acts of corruption, insults, rapine, outrages on the people, arrogance, repeated murders of innocent victims, and constant and most galling savagery" (as portrayed by Philo in *Legatio ad Gaium*, quoted in Cohn, p. 15; see also Cohn, pp. 7–17; Klausner, *Jesus of Nazareth*, pp. 163–64, 348). Finally, the New Testament was compiled under the watchful eyes of the Roman Empire, whose capital prohibition against sedition was still in force.

13. Some of America's founding fathers perceived that corruptions had been superimposed upon the supreme spirituality of Jesus's teachings. Benjamin Franklin wrote, "As to Jesus of Nazareth, . . . I think the system of morals and his religion, as he left them to us, the best the world ever saw or is likely to see; but I apprehend it has received various corrupt changes, and I have, with most of the present dissenters in England, some doubts as to his divinity" (Norman Cousins, ed., *In God We Trust* [New York: Harper, 1958], p. 19). Of biblical biographies of Jesus, Thomas Jefferson wrote that "sublime ideas of the Supreme Being, aphorisms, and precepts of the purest morality and benevolence" are intermixed with "superstitions, fanaticisms, and fabrications" (Ibid., pp. 152–53, see pp. 149, 128–29).

14. See section 7 of Appendix 4.
15. Reid, *Grim Reapers*, p. 6.
16. See section 8 of Appendix 4.
17. See section 18 of Appendix 4.
18. Noyes, *Legacy of Doubt*, p. 34; Demaris, *Cap-*

tive City, pp. 61–63; *Los Angeles Times*, May 31, 1973, p. 22.
19. See section 17c of Appendix 4.
20. See section 25 of Appendix 4 and chapter 16.

Chapter 15
The Cuban Coalition

1. Anson, *"They've Killed the President!"*, p. 327.
2. See sections 1.2 (the Reuther shooting) and 15.3; see also section 15.2.
3. Scott, "From Dallas to Watergate," in Blumenthal and Yazijian, ed., *Government by Gunplay*, p. 114; HAH 10H 7–8.
4. Wise and Ross, *The Invisible Government*, pp. 35–36, 185.
5. Ibid., p. 36.
6. Ibid., pp. 39, 67–70.
7. Ibid., pp. 67–70, 188–89.
8. HAH 10H 3, 9; Anson, pp. 269–70, 278.
9. Cited in Anson, p. 269.
10. Wise and Ross, pp. 184–86.
11. Taylor Branch and George Crile III, "The Kennedy Vendetta," *Harper's*, August 1975, p. 50; see also HAH 1H 6.
12. Harry Ransom, "Containing Central Intelligence," *New Republic*, December 11, 1965, p. 13, cited in Scott, "The Death of Kennedy and the Vietnam War," in Blumenthal and Yazijian, p. 166.
13. HAH 1H 7; HAH 10H 12; Wise and Ross, 297–98; Khrushchev, *Khrushchev Remembers*, p. 553.
14. HAH 10H 3, 12–13; Anson, p. 265.
15. HAH 10H 13; Scott, "The Death of Kennedy and the Vietnam War," in Blumenthal and Yazijian, p. 161.
16. Anson, p. 270.
17. *U.S.–Senate, Intelligence Report, Foreign Assassinations*, pp. 173–74; *U.S.–Senate, Intelligence Report, JFK Assassination*, p. 20; William Attwood, *The Reds and the Blacks* (London: Hutchinson, 1967), pp. 142–44.
18. Schlesinger, Jr., *A Thousand Days*, pp. 959, 962–63; see also HAH 1H 8.
19. Schlesinger, Jr., *A Thousand Days*, pp. 972–73.
20. Ibid., pp. 900–901; see also HAH 1H 7.
21. Scott, "The Death of Kennedy and the Vietnam War," in Blumenthal and Yazijian, p. 159.
22. Ibid.
23. Schlesinger, Jr., *A Thousand Days*, p. 920.
24. *Business Week*, November 23, 1963, p. 41; Scott, "The Death of Kennedy and the Vietnam War," in Blumenthal and Yazijian, p. 159.
25. Scott, "The Death of Kennedy and the Vietnam War," in Blumenthal and Yazijian, p. 159.
26. *Business Week*, November 23, 1963, p. 41.
27. Anson, p. 16.
28. Dorman, *Payoff*, pp. 254–55.
29. Ibid.
30. Ibid.
31. *Time*, March 6, 1978, p. 21.
32. Ibid.
33. See "James Osticco" in *U.S.–Senate, McClellan Labor Hearings*, p. 12199.
34. *Time*, March 6, 1978, p. 21.
35. Ibid.
36. Ibid.
37. Joesten, *Oswald, Assassin or Fall Guy?*, p. 149.
38. O'Donnell and Powers, *Johnny We Hardly Knew Ye*, p. 16.
39. *Public Papers of the Presidents*, John F. Kennedy, 1963 (U.S. Government Printing Office, 1964), pp. 759–60.

40. Ibid.
41. Ibid., p. 828.
42. Scott, "The Death of Kennedy and the Vietnam War," in Blumenthal and Yazijian, pp. 153–54.
43. Manchester, *Death of a President*, p. 46.
44. Ibid.
45. Joachim Joesten, *The Case Against Lyndon Johnson in the Assassination of President Kennedy* (Munich: Dreischstr. 5, Selbstverlag, 1967), p. 9.
46. UPI, Dallas, December 20, 1963, cited in Joesten, *Oswald: Assassin or Fall Guy?*, p. 150.
47. Ibid.
48. WR 298.
49. Ibid.
50. WR 292–97.
51. WR 296–97.
52. HAH 5H 258, 295–96.
53. Ibid., p. 296.
54. Ibid.
55. Ibid.
56. Ibid.
57. *Life*, March 10, 1958, pp. 32ff; Jack Anderson, *Parade*, April 28, 1963, pp. 4–5; *New York Times*, January 4, 1959, p. 6; Salerno and Tompkins, *The Crime Confederation*, p. 386; Anson, p. 313.
58. Meskil, *Don Carlo*, p. 137.
59. Moldea, *The Hoffa Wars*, p. 87.
60. *The Two Kennedys*, an Italian documentary film, shown at the Orson Welles Theatre, Cambridge, Mass., March 14, 1976.
61. Moldea, pp. 122–23.
62. See Dorman, *Payoff*, p. 101; see also Moldea, p. 122.
63. Crile, "The Mafia, the CIA, and Castro," *Washington Post*, May 16, 1976, p. C4; Anson, pp. 312–13; see also Moldea, p. 122.
64. Moldea, pp. 122–23.
65. Anson, pp. 312–13; Crile, "The Mafia, the CIA, and Castro," *Washington Post*, May 16, 1976, pp. C1, C4.
66. HAH 5H 296; *Time*, March 2, 1959, pp. 22, 25; Malone, "The Secret Life of Jack Ruby," *New Times*, January 23, 1978, pp. 47–50; Jack Anderson, "How Castro Double-Crossed the Gambling Syndicate," *Parade*, April 28, 1963, pp. 4–5.
67. Anson, pp. 312–13; HAH 10H 156; Scott, "From Dallas to Watergate," in Blumenthal and Yazijian, pp. 126–27; Malone, "The Secret Life of Jack Ruby," *New Times*, January 23, 1978, p. 48.
68. Edem.
69. Malone, "The Secret Life of Jack Ruby," *New Times*, January 23, 1978, p. 49; see HAH 10H 156–57, 176.
70. HAH 5H 296; Crile, "The Mafia, the CIA, and Castro," *Washington Post*, May 16, 1976, pp. C1, C4; Anson, p. 313.
71. Malone, "The Secret Life of Jack Ruby," *New Times*, January 23, 1978, p. 48.
72. Anderson, *Parade*, April 28, 1963, p. 4.
73. As cited in Anson, p. 313.
74. *New York Times*, January 4, 1959, p. 6.
75. Anderson, *Parade*, April 28, 1963, p. 4.
76. Ibid.
77. See section 15.4.
78. Miles Copeland, *Without Cloak or Dagger* (New York: Simon and Schuster, 1974), p. 235, cited in Anson, p. 291.
79. Thomas Sciacca, *Luciano* (New York: Pinnacle Books, 1975), p. 180, cited in Anson, p. 291.
80. Anson, pp. 291–92; Frederic Sondern, *The Brotherhood of Evil*, reprinted in Gage, *Mafia,*

U.S.A., pp. 154–57; see Rodney Campbell, *The Luciano Project* (New York: McGraw-Hill, 1977).
81. Edem.
82. McCoy, *The Politics of Heroin in Southeast Asia*, pp. 23–27; Anson, pp. 238, 292, 308–9.
83. Edem.
84. McCoy, p. 24; see pp. 7–8, 16, 23–28, 31.
85. Sondern, *Brotherhood of Evil*, in Gage, *Mafia, U.S.A.*, pp. 155–56; see Campbell, *The Luciano Project*.
86. Reid, *The Grim Reapers*, pp. 30, 32.
87. Meskil, *Don Carlo*, p. 77; Reid, *The Grim Reapers*, p. 30; Frank J. Prial, "Vito Genovese—Power to Spare," in Gage, *Mafia, U.S.A.*, pp. 166–67.
88. Prial, in Gage, *Mafia, U.S.A.*, pp. 166–67.
89. *U.S.–Senate, McClellan Labor Hearings*, pp. 12411–12, 12417; Reid, *The Grim Reapers*, p. 30.
90. McCoy, pp. 22–23; Reid, *The Grim Reapers*, p. 31.
91. Prial, in Gage, *Mafia, U.S.A.*, p. 167; Reid, *The Grim Reapers*, p. 32.
92. Reid, *The Grim Reapers*, p. 31; Meskil, *Don Carlo*, p. 77; Prial, in Gage, *Mafia, U.S.A.*, p. 167; Pantaleone, *The Mafia and Politics*, p. 63.
93. Reid, *The Grim Reapers*, p. 31.
94. Ibid., p. 32.
95. Ibid.; Prial, in Gage, *Mafia, U.S.A.*, p. 167; Meskil, *Don Carlo*, p. 77.
96. Meskil, *Don Carlo*, p. 77; Prial, in Gage, *Mafia, U.S.A.*, pp. 167–68.
97. *U.S.–Senate, McClellan Labor Hearings*, pp. 12367, 12412; Reid, *The Grim Reapers*, p. 32.
98. *U.S.–Senate, McClellan Labor Hearings*, pp. 12367–68, 12412; Reid, *The Grim Reapers*, p. 33; Meskil, *Don Carlo*, p. 77.
99. McCoy, pp. 7, 22–23; see text below.
100. McCoy, pp. 19–20; Salerno and Tompkins, pp. 276–77.
101. McCoy, pp. 20–21; Pantaleone, pp. 52–58.
102. McCoy, p. 22; Pantaleone, p. 53.
103. Harry L. Coles and Albert K. Weinberg, *United States Army in World War II. Civil Affairs: Soldiers become Governors* (Washington, D.C.: Office of the Chief of Military History, Department of the Army, U.S. Government Printing Office, 1964), p. 210.
104. Pantaleone, p. 52.
105. See section 7 of Appendix 4.
106. Wise and Ross, pp. 94–95.
107. McCoy, pp. 30–31; see below.
108. Anson, p. 326; McCoy, p. 31.
109. McCoy, pp. 31, 44–46; Anson, p. 293.
110. McCoy, pp. 44–45; Anson, p. 293.
111. McCoy, pp. 45–47; Anson, p. 293.
112. *New York Times*, March 10, 1975, p. 49.
113. Anson, pp. 295–96.
114. Anson, pp. 296–97.
115. HAH 10H 10–15, 151, 157, 170–71; *U.S.–Senate, Intelligence Report, Foreign Assassinations*, pp. 71–90, 257; *U.S.–Senate, Intelligence Report, JFK Assassination*, pp. 2, 99; Scott, "The Death of Kennedy and the Vietnam War," in Blumenthal and Yazijian, pp. 161–65.
116. HAH 10H 157, 170–71; Anson, p. 313; Scott, *Crime and Cover-Up*, pp. 16–17; Malone, "The Secret Life of Jack Ruby," *New Times*, January 23, 1978, p. 49.
117. *U.S.–Senate, Intelligence Report, JFK Assassination*, p. 100; Scott, "The Death of Kennedy and the Vietnam War," in Blumenthal and Yazijian, p. 164; Anson, pp. 268, 313.

118. Scott, "From Dallas to Watergate," in Blumenthal and Yazijian, p. 117; Scott, "The Death of Kennedy and the Vietnam War," in Blumenthal and Yazijian, p. 161; HAH 10H 13.
119. Hans Tanner, *Counter-Revolutionary Agent* (London: G. T. Foulis, 1972), p. 127.
120. HAH 10H 95–101.
121. *U.S.–Senate, Intelligence Report, Foreign Assassinations*, pp. 71–85, 97; *U.S.–Senate, Intelligence Report, JFK Assassination*, pp. 99–104; HAH 10H 151–57, 161–89.
122. *U.S.–Senate, Intelligence Report, Foreign Assassinations*, p. 92.
123. Ibid., pp. 74, 94–97; *U.S.–Senate, Intelligence Report, JFK Assassination*, p. 99; Moldea, p. 128.
124. HAH 10H 176; Malone, "The Secret Life of Jack Ruby," *New Times*, January 23, 1978, p. 49; Gage, *The Mafia is not an Equal Opportunity Employer*, p. 78; Anson, pp. 298, 313.
125. HAH 10H 171, see pp. 156–57.
126. HAH 10H 151–52; *U.S.–Senate, Intelligence Report, Foreign Assassinations*, pp. 74–82.
127. HAH 10H 151–52; *U.S.–Senate, Intelligence Report, Foreign Assassinations*, pp. 82–86.
128. *U.S.–Senate, Intelligence Report, Foreign Assassinations*, p. 71.
129. Ibid.
130. Ibid., pp. 74–85; Scott, *Crime and Cover-Up*, p. 22; HAH 10H 166–67.
131. Scott, *Crime and Cover-Up*, p. 22.
132. *U.S.–Senate, Intelligence Report, Foreign Assassinations*, pp. 75–77; HAH 10H 151.
133. See section 20.3.
134. HAH 10H 154; Jack Anderson's column, *Albuquerque Journal*, September 7, 1976 (reprinted in HAH 10H 159–60).
135. Edem. Former LBJ staff member Leo Janos wrote in the *Atlantic Monthly*, July 1973, that LBJ had proposed such a theory.
136. HAH 10H 164–66, 181–82.
137. "Dousing a Popular Theory," *Time*, October 2, 1978, p. 22; Vivian Cadden, "The Murder of President Kennedy," *McCall's*, March 1977, p. 172; Anson, pp. 260–65; Kirby Jones, "Unlikely Assassin," *New Republic*, July 3, 1976, pp. 5–6; Viorst, "The Mafia, the CIA, and the Kennedy Assassination," *Washingtonian*, November 1975, p. 118.
138. *U.S.–Senate, Intelligence Report, Foreign Assassinations*, p. 71n.
139. Ibid., pp. 74–75, 92; *U.S.–Senate, Intelligence Report, JFK Assassination*, p. 99.
140. *U.S.–Senate, Intelligence Report, Foreign Assassinations*, pp. 151–52; HAH 10H 187; Tad Szulc, "Cuba on our Mind," *Esquire*, February 1974; *New York Times*, March 10, 1975.
141. *Time*, December 19, 1977, p. 23.
142. HAH 10H 3.
143. Schlesinger, Jr., *A Thousand Days*, p. 1029; HAH 3H 184–85.
144. Anson, pp. 262–65.
145. Khrushchev, pp. 507–8, 555, 557.
146. Anson, pp. 263–64.
147. *U.S.–Senate, Intelligence Report, Foreign Assassinations*, pp. 173–74; *U.S.–Senate, Intelligence Report, JFK Assassination*, p. 20; HAH 10H 165.
148. *U.S.–Senate, Intelligence Report, Foreign Assassinations*, p. 174; HAH 3H 184–92.
149. HAH 10H 165–66, 182.
150. Anson, pp. 264–65. Castro gave what *Time* Magazine called "eloquent testimony" against the theory that he was behind the JFK killing

in a 4½ hour April 1978 interview with members of the House Assassinations Committee (*Time*, October 2, 1978, p. 22). See also Kirby Jones, "Unlikely Assassin," *New Republic*, July 3, 1976, pp. 5–6; and HAH 10H 164–65.
151. See section 4.1.
152. See section 15.1.
153. Anson, p. 272; Vivian Cadden, "The Murder of President Kennedy," *McCall's*, March 1977, p. 172; Viorst, "The Mafia, the CIA, and the Kennedy Assassination," *Washingtonian*, November 1975, p. 114.
154. HAH 10H 3, 13; Scott, "From Dallas to Watergate," in Blumenthal and Yazijian, p. 117; Scott, "The Death of Kennedy and the Vietnam War," in Blumenthal and Yazijian, p. 161.
155. Anson, p. 325.
156. Ibid., p. iv.
157. Ibid., p. 325.
158. Ibid., pp. 293–94. See also McCoy, chapters 3–7; and Viorst, "The Mafia, the CIA, and the Kennedy Assassination," *Washingtonian*, November 1975, p. 114.
159. McCoy, p. 213.
160. Ibid.
161. Ibid.
162. Ibid., pp. 215–16.
163. Ibid., p. 216; see Moldea, p. 352.
164. Anson, pp. 293–94; McCoy, p. 248.
165. Anson, p. 294; McCoy, p. 211.
166. McCoy, pp. 152, 156, 163, 167–74, 187–90, 199–205, 213.
167. Ibid., pp. 171–72, 218–19.
168. Anson, p. 294.
169. Jeremiah O'Leary, "Haig Probe: Did Nixon Get Cash From Asia?" *Washington Star*, December 5, 1976, p. A11.
170. Ibid.
171. McCoy, pp. 186–87.
172. Ibid.; O'Leary, *Washington Star*, December 5, 1976, p. A11.
173. O'Leary, *Washington Star*, December 5, 1976, p. A11.
174. Ibid.

Chapter 16
Post-Assassination Policy

1. *Ramparts*, May 1968, p. 27.
2. *U.S.–Senate, OC and Stolen Securities, 1971*, p. 670.
3. Scott, "The Death of Kennedy and the Vietnam War," in Blumenthal and Yazijian, ed., *Government by Gunplay*, p. 152.
4. Tom Wicker, *JFK and LBJ: The Influence of Personality on Politics* (New York: William Morrow, 1968), pp. 183–85; Alfred Steinberg, *Sam Johnson's Boy* (New York: Macmillan, 1968), pp. 760–61.
5. See excerpts reprinted in Scott, "The Death of Kennedy and the Vietnam War," in Blumenthal and Yazijian, pp. 170–81.
6. Ibid., p. 156; see pp. 152–87 and reprints from and references to the Pentagon Papers in this source.
7. Ibid., p. 156.
8. Ibid., p. 157.
9. Ibid.
10. Ibid., pp. 167–68.
11. Tad Szulc, *Compulsive Spy* (New York: Viking, 1974), pp. 96–98.
12. Anson, *"They've Killed the President!"*, p. 325.
13. Scott, "The Death of Kennedy and the Vietnam War," in Blumenthal and Yazijian, p. 168.

14. Anson, p. 325; Scott, "The Death of Kennedy and the Vietnam War," in Blumenthal and Yazijian, p. 168.
15. "The Mob," part 2, *Life*, September 8, 1967, p. 101.
16. Ibid.
17. Ibid.
18. *New York Times*, December 15, 1963 and August 19, 1964, as cited by Joesten in *The Case Against Lyndon B. Johnson in the Assassination of President Kennedy* (Munich: Dreischstr. 5, Selbstverlag, 1967), pp. 6–8, 12–13.
19. William Turner, *Hoover's FBI*, p. 97; Scott, *Crime and Cover-Up*, p. 11.
20. Sheridan, *The Fall and Rise of Jimmy Hoffa*, p. 506.
21. Robert G. Sherill, "Portrait of a Super-Patriot," in *Nation*, February 24, 1964.
22. *New York Times*, August 19, 1964, quoted by Joesten in *The Case Against Lyndon Johnson*, pp. 12–13.
23. Cressey, *Theft of the Nation*, p. 196.
24. Ibid.
25. Navasky, *Kennedy Justice*, p. 49n; Salerno and Tompkins, *The Crime Confederation*, pp. 271–73; Mollenhoff, *Strike Force*, pp. 5–6.
26. Navasky, p. 49n; see also HAH 9H 21.
27. Dorman, "LBJ and the Racketeers," *Ramparts*, May 1968, p. 28 (most of the information in this article is also furnished in chapter 7 of Dorman's book, *Payoff*). Dorman developed an unusual knack for cultivating Mobsters and obtained selective information on their political dealings during his ten years as a reporter for the *Houston Press*, his subsequent term with *Newsday* and his work as an author (*Ramparts*, May 1968). Dorman secured a unique on-the-record interview with Mafia boss Carlos Marcello (*Payoff*, pp. 103–4, 109–10), assisted federal investigators in the Hoffa case (*Payoff*, pp. 151, 229), assisted a New York State organized crime probe (*Payoff*, p. 226), and testified as an expert witness before a Texas grand jury investigating organized crime (*Payoff*, p. vii).
28. Ibid., p. 27.
29. Ibid.
30. Ibid.
31. Ibid., pp. 28–30.
32. Ibid.
33. Ibid., p. 30.
34. Ibid., p. 34.
35. Ibid.
36. Ibid.
37. *U.S.–Senate, Kefauver Report, Third Interim.*
38. Dorman, *Ramparts*, May 1968, p. 34.
39. Ibid., pp. 30, 34.
40. Ibid., p. 34.
41. Sheridan, pp. 380–81.
42. Ibid.
43. Ibid.
44. Ibid.
45. Ibid., p. 7.
46. Ibid., p. 381.
47. Ibid.
48. Ibid., p. 478.
49. *New York Times*, November 18, 1972, p. 1.
50. Sheridan, p. 478.
51. Sheridan, pp. 408, 411, 424–25, 427–28, 433, 458–59, 465–66, 482–83, 492, 505.
52. Chandler, "The 'Little Man' is Bigger Than Ever," *Life*, April 10, 1970, p. 34.
53. *Newsweek*, August 8, 1977, p. 27; Messick, *Secret File*, pp. 257–58.
54. Edem.
55. *Newsweek*, August 8, 1977, p. 27.
56. Ibid.
57. Ibid.; Messick, *Secret File*, pp. 257–58.
58. *Newsweek*, August 8, 1977, p. 27.
59. Ibid.
60. Robert A. Caro, *The Years of Lyndon Johnson*, excerpts from the *Atlantic Monthly*, October 1981, p. 44.
61. Ibid., p 43.
62. *New York Times*, January 28, 1973, p. 43.
63. Winter-Berger, *The Washington Payoff*, p. 54; Reid, *The Grim Reapers*, p. 133.
64. Mollenhoff, *Strike Force*, pp. 104–5, 186; Reid, *The Grim Reapers*, pp. 133–45; Dorman, *Payoff*, pp. 143–48; Winter-Berger, p. 68; Anson, pp. 323–24; see sections 17.7 and 17.8.
65. Reid, *The Grim Reapers*, p. 133.
66. Winter-Berger, pp. 61–66.
67. Carl Oglesby, "Presidential Assassination and the Closing of the Frontier," in Blumenthal and Yazijian, p. 194.
68. Ibid., pp. 194–95. See also Scott, "From Dallas to Watergate," in Blumenthal and Yazijian, pp. 128–29; Moldea, pp. 104–6.
69. Scott, "From Dallas to Watergate," in Blumenthal and Yazijian, p. 114; see also Moldea, *The Hoffa Wars*, p. 127; Oglesby and Goldberg, "Did the Mob Kill Kennedy?" *Washington Post*, February 25, 1979, p. B1.
70. Oglesby, in Blumenthal and Yazijian, p. 194.
71. Gerth, in Blumenthal and Yazijian, p. 151.
72. The close Nixon-Rebozo relationship is well known; i.e., see Gerth, in Blumenthal and Yazijian, pp. 139–40.
73. Moldea, p. 105.
74. Scott, "From Dallas to Watergate," in Blumenthal and Yazijian, p. 128; Gerth, in Blumenthal and Yazijian, p. 142; Moldea, p. 105; *U.S.–Senate, OC and Narcotics Hearings*, p. 1049.
75. *New York Times*, January 21, 1974, p. 18.
76. Messick, *Lansky*, p. 192; Waller, *The Swiss Bank Connection*, pp. 145–46.
77. Reid, *The Grim Reapers*, pp. 119–23, 139–40; Waller, pp. 123–35; Hank Messick and Burt Goldblatt, *The Mobs and the Mafia*, pp. 195–96; Gerth, in Blumenthal and Yazijian, pp. 137–39.
78. Gerth, in Blumenthal and Yazijian, p. 140.
79. *New York Times*, January 21, 1974, p. 1.
80. Gerth, in Blumenthal and Yazijian, p. 139; Waller, pp. 132–33.
81. *Life*, February 3, 1967, pp. 68–69.
82. Waller, p. 133; Gerth, p. 138.
83. *New York Times*, January 21, 1974, p. 18.
84. Gerth, in Blumenthal and Yazijian, pp. 137–39, 141–47; Scott, "From Dallas to Watergate," in Blumenthal and Yazijian, pp. 128–29; Moldea, pp. 104–6.
85. *New York Times*, September 10, 1973, pp. 1, 28.
86. Ibid., p. 28.
87. Jeff Gerth, statement at "The Politics of Conspiracy," conference at Boston University, workshop on organized crime, George Sherman Student Center, February 1, 1975, tape-recorded by author.
88. *New York Times*, September 10, 1973, p. 28.
89. Ibid., pp. 1, 28.
90. Ibid.
91. Ibid., p. 28.
92. Ibid.
93. Ibid.
94. Ibid.
95. Gerth, in Blumenthal and Yazijian, p. 149.
96. Gerth, in Blumenthal and Yazijian, p. 148.

97. Jeff Gerth, statement at "The Politics of Conspiracy," conference at Boston University, workshop on organized crime, George Sherman Student Center, February 1, 1975, tape-recorded by author.
98. Cook, *The Secret Rulers*, p. 367.
99. Ibid.
100. Ibid.
101. Ibid.
102. *U.S.–House, OC and Worthless Securities*, p. 1.
103. Ibid., p. 242.
104. As cited in note 97; see sections 13 and 17c of Appendix 4.
105. Sheridan, p. 465; Waller, p. 126; Gerth, in Blumenthal and Yazijian, p. 135; Moldea, pp. 103–5.
106. Waller, p. 126; Moldea, p. 104; Gerth, in Blumenthal and Yazijian, p. 135.
107. Sheridan, p. 508.
108. Waller, p. 127; Moldea, p. 104.
109. Moldea, p. 104.
110. Waller, p. 126.
111. Moldea, pp. 104–5, 260–61.
112. Sheridan, pp. 465, 493, 504.
113. Ibid., pp. 408, 492.
114. Noyes, *Legacy of Doubt*, p. 142.
115. Sheridan, pp. 408–11, 430, 465, 492–94, 496, 498–504, 508, 511, 513–14, 520, 525, 526, 535.
116. Sheridan, passim.
117. "The Mob," part 1, *Life*, September 1, 1967, p. 22.
118. Sheridan, pp. 408–11, 430, 465, 492–94, 496, 498–504, 508, 511, 513–14, 520, 525, 526, 535.
119. Sheridan, pp. 8–9, 521.
120. Moldea, p. 261.
121. Sheridan, p. 9.
122. Ibid., p. 7.
123. *New York Times*, December 24, 1971, p. 24.
124. *Los Angeles Times*, June 1, 1973, section II, p. 6.
125. Noyes, p. 34.
126. Moldea, pp. 316–17; Brill, *The Teamsters*, pp. 102–4.
127. Edem.; see Reid, *The Grim Reapers*, p. 287 for identification of Accardo.
128. Moldea, p. 317; Brill, p. 103.
129. Edem.
130. Edem.
131. Moldea, p. 317.
132. Ibid.; Brill, pp. 103–4.
133. Moldea, p. 317.
134. Ibid.; see also Noyes, p. 244 concerning Chotiner's presence there on another occasion.
135. Moldea, p. 318.
136. Ibid.; Brill, p. 104.
137. Edem.
138. *New York Times*, April 30, 1973, p. 30.
139. Ibid.
140. *Chicago Tribune*, April 29, 1973, p. 6.
141. Gerth, in Blumenthal and Yazijian, p. 150; Dorman, *Payoff*, pp. 205–11.
142. Clark Mollenhoff, *Game Plan for Disaster* (New York: Norton, 1976), pp. 192–93, 329–30; Brill, p. 104; *Arizona Republic*, March 21, 1977, p. A7.
143. Brill, p. 104; *Arizona Republic*, March 21, 1977, p. A7; *Washington Post*, April 16, 1981, pp. A1, A13.
144. *Washington Post*, April 15, 1981, p. A10, April 16, 1981, pp. A1, A13; *Arizona Republic*, March 21, 1977, p. A7.
145. *Time*, August 8, 1977, p. 28; see also Moldea, p. 320; Brill, pp. 64, 105.
146. *Time*, August 8, 1977, p. 28.
147. Moldea, pp. 112, 417; Brill, p. 131; NBC Evening News, "Segment 3," June 14, 1978; *New York Times*, May 30, 1980, p. B2.
148. *Time*, August 8, 1977, p. 28.
149. Ibid.; Moldea, p. 7; Brill, chapter 6.
150. Moldea, p. 7.
151. *Time*, August 8, 1977, p. 28.
152. As summarized in Moldea, p. 319.
153. *Time*, August 8, 1977, p. 28.
154. Ibid.
155. Ibid. Indeed, as *Time* noted, hotel records showed that Provenzano's courier was in Las Vegas on January 6, while Colson's calendar showed that Colson spoke to Fitzsimmons on January 8.
156. Moldea, p. 320.
157. Quoted in Gerth, in Blumenthal and Yazijian, pp. 131–32.
158. *Time*, August 8, 1977, p. 28.
159. Ibid.
160. White House Transcripts, March 21, 1973, 10:12 - 11:15 a.m., cited in Moldea, pp. 318–19, 432; also quoted in *Time*, August 8, 1977, p. 28 (there are minor discrepancies between the two sources).
161. Ibid.
162. Ibid.
163. Moldea, p. 319.
164. Ibid.
165. *New York Times*, September 24, 1981, p. D26.
166. Ibid.
167. Mickey Cohen, *Mickey Cohen: In My Own Words* (Englewood Cliffs, N.J.: Prentice-Hall, 1975), p. 223.
168. Ibid.
169. Moldea, pp. 108, 260.
170. Ibid.
171. HAR 176; Moldea, pp. 142–43; Sheridan, pp. 224–25, 247–51, 257.
172. HAR 176; Moldea, pp. 172–73; Sheridan, p. 217.
173. Jeremiah O'Leary, "Haig Probe: Did Nixon Get Cash From Asia?" *Washington Star*, December 5, 1976, p. A11; see Moldea, pp. 351–52.
174. Moldea, p. 352.
175. As cited in Gerth, in Blumenthal and Yazijian, p. 130.
176. Ibid.
177. *Newsweek*, December 29, 1980, p. 19; *Albuquerque Journal*, March 19, 1980, p. B3; Ovid Demaris, *The Last Mafioso* (New York: Times Books, 1981), p. 363.
178. *Newsweek*, December 29, 1980, p. 19.
179. Gerth, in Blumenthal and Yazijian, p. 130; for Provenzano's background, see Moldea, pp. 112, 417; Brill, p. 131; NBC Evening News, "Segment 3," June 14, 1978; *New York Times*, May 30, 1980, p. B2.
180. Mollenhoff, *Strike Force*, pp. 29–30.
181. Ibid., p. 32.
182. Ibid., p. 32.
183. Ibid.
184. Ibid., pp. 32–33.
185. Ibid., p. 29.
186. Ibid., p. 30.
187. Ibid.
188. Ibid.
189. *New York Times*, July 6, 1973, p. 20.
190. Ibid.
191. Mollenhoff, *Strike Force*, pp. 30, 33.
192. Ibid., chapter 2.
193. *Newsweek*, June 23, 1969, pp. 37–38.
194. Ibid.
195. Mollenhoff, *Strike Force*, pp. 29–34, 144.
196. *New York Times*, July 6, 1973, p. 20; July 20, 1973, p. 13.

197. *Facts on File*, 1977, pp. 637–38, 658, 728–29.
198. Ibid.
199. Mollenhoff, *Strike Force*, p. 122; Allsop, *The Bootleggers*, p. 321; Gage, *The Mafia is not an Equal Opportunity Employer*, pp. 59–60; Vincent Teresa, *Vinnie Teresa's Mafia* (Garden City, N.Y.: Doubleday, 1975), pp. 128–32; see Teresa's *My Life in the Mafia*, p. 192.
200. Pantaleone, *The Mafia and Politics*, p. 59.
201. *New York Times*, July 6, 1973, p. 1, July 20, 1973, p. 13.
202. *Newsweek*, July 16, 1973, p. 19.
203. *New York Times*, July 20, 1973, p. 13.
204. Ibid.
205. Ibid.
206. *New York Times*, July 6, 1973, p. 1.
207. *New York Times*, August 9, 1973, p. 75, July 6, 1973, p. 20.
208. *Washington Post*, July 6, 1973, p. A4.
209. *U.S.–Senate, OC and Stolen Securities, 1973*, pp. 80–84.
210. Ibid., p. 284.
211. Ibid., p. 85.
212. Ibid., pp. 85, 87.
213. Ibid., p. 86.
214. Ibid., p. 122.
215. *Newsweek*, November 28, 1977, p. 66.
216. Ibid. Almost 20 Mob informants were killed in 1976 and 1977, as reported on NBC Evening News, "Segment 3," December 16, 1977; see also *Time*, November 21, 1977, p. 39.
217. *Newsweek*, November 28, 1977, p. 66.
218. Ibid.
219. Oglesby, in Blumenthal and Yazijian, p. 194.
220. As cited in *U.S.–House, Criminal Justice Hearings*, p. 149.
221. *Time*, August 22, 1969, p. 19.
222. Salerno and Tompkins, p. 250.
223. NBC Evening News, "Segment 3," December 13, 1977.
224. *New York Times*, December 8, 1972, p. 90.
225. Meskil, *Don Carlo*, p. 253.
226. Teresa, *My Life in the Mafia*, p. 355.
227. Ibid.
228. Ibid.
229. Meskil, *Don Carlo*, p. 249.
230. Ibid., p. 250.
231. Ibid.
232. NBC Evening News, "Segment 3," December 13, 1977.
233. NBC Evening News, "Segment 3," December 16, 1977.
234. "The Mob," part 2, *Life*, September 8, 1967, p. 103.

Chapter 17
The Warren Commission Cover-Up

1. Tacitus, *The Histories*, translated by Kenneth Wellesley (New York: Penguin, 1964), p. 38.
2. Feuerlicht, *Justice Crucified*, pp. 269, 339–59, 374–75, 410.
3. Ibid., pp. 374–75, 380–81, 409.
4. *Boston Herald*, August 9, 1927, cited in Feuerlicht, p. 380.
5. *New York Times*, August 8, 1927, p. 16.
6. *New York World*, August 8, 1927.
7. Feuerlicht, pp. 358–59.
8. Ibid., p. 409.
9. Felix Frankfurter, *The Case of Sacco and Vanzetti* (New York: Grosset and Dunlap, 1962), passim.
10. *Boston Globe*, July 19, 1977, p. 3, July 20, 1977, pp. 1, 6.
11. Edem.
12. Teresa, *My Life in the Mafia*, pp. 43, 45; Feuerlicht, p. 316.
13. Teresa, p. 45; Feuerlicht, p. 318; Francis Russell, *Tragedy in Dedham* (New York: McGraw-Hill, 1962), pp. 288–89.
14. Ehrmann, *The Case That Will Not Die*, pp. 412–13.
15. Ibid., pp. 404–49, 23, 43–44, 191–94, 399–400; Ehrmann, *The Untried Case*, chapter 5; Feuerlicht, pp. 312–22.
16. Teresa, pp. 45–46.
17. Ibid., pp. 43, 45.
18. Ibid., p. 45.
19. Ibid., p. 46.
20. *U.S.–Senate, Intelligence Report, JFK Assassination*, p. 32.
21. Ibid., p. 33.
22. Ibid., p. 23.
23. Ibid. When asked by Congress fifteen years later why he had so hastily issued these rash pronouncements, Katzenbach's reply underscored the absence of any satisfactory explanation: "Because, very simply, if that was the conclusion that the FBI was going to come to, then the public had to be satisfied that that was the correct conclusion" (HAH 3H 652).
24. *U.S.–Senate, Intelligence Report, JFK Assassination*, p. 34, see p. 23.
25. Ibid., pp. 34–35.
26. *Time*, December 13, 1963, p. 26.
27. Ibid.
28. *Washington Post*, June 24, 1976, p. A1.
29. HAH 5H 475.
30. Wise and Ross, *The Invisbile Government*, p. 186.
31. Warren Commission Executive Transcript, December 5, 1963, cited in Anson, *"They've Killed the President!"*, pp. 41, 368.
32. *U.S.–Senate, Intelligence Report, JFK Assassination*, pp. 67–68, 70.
33. Ibid., pp. 74–75.
34. John D. Weaver, *Warren: The Man, the Court, the Era* (Boston: Little, 1967), p. 302; Epstein, *Inquest*, pp. 20–21.
35. Epstein, *Inquest*, pp. 20–21.
36. Ibid., pp. 13–14, xiii.
37. Warren Commission Executive Session Transcript, January 27, 1964, p. 171, cited in Scott, *Crime and Cover-Up*, p. 4, and excerpted in *The Assassinations*, edited by Peter Dale Scott, Paul L. Hoch and Russell Statler (New York: Vintage Books, 1976), p. 138.
38. Ibid.
39. Epstein, *Inquest*, pp. 81–84.
40. The Warren Commission based its investigation largely on the FBI summary report of December 9, 1963 (WR xi, see *U.S.–Senate, Intelligence Report, JFK Assassination*, p. 46), which affirmed Hoover's immediately drawn conclusion that Oswald was the lone assassin (*U.S.–Senate, Intelligence Report, JFK Assassination*, pp. 32–35).
41. Weaver, p. 302.
42. Ibid.
43. *Facts on File*, 1974, pp. 634–36, 939–40.
44. HAH 3H 472.
45. *U.S.–Senate, Intelligence Report, JFK Assassination*, passim; HAR, passim.
46. *Time*, December 19, 1977, p. 23.
47. *Time*, February 4, 1974, p. 13.
48. Ibid.

49. WR 98, 105–6; Thompson, *Six Seconds in Dallas*, chapters 3 and 4.
50. WR 97, 193–94; 3H 403–7.
51. WR 3, 19, 105–7.
52. CD 5, quoted in Thompson, pp. 40–41.
53. CD 7, quoted in Epstein, *Inquest*, pp. 169–70.
54. National Archives, FBI summary report of December 9, 1963, reproduced in part in Epstein, *Inquest*, p. 149.
55. National Archives, FBI supplemental report of January 13, 1964, reproduced in part in Epstein, *Inquest*, p. 162.
56. National Archives, Presidential Commission Administrative Records, J. Lee Rankin, December 1963 to March 1964, cited in Thompson, p. 45; see CD 7, quoted in Epstein, *Inquest*, pp. 169–70.
57. As cited in notes 52, 54 and 55.
58. 5H 59–60; CE 393–94; see Thompson, pp. 48–50, 201–2, 214, 222–23.
59. WR 3.
60. See Thompson, pp. 222–23, 281.
61. WR 18, 94–95.
62. 17H 49; 4H 121; see photos in Thompson, pp. 151–52.
63. WR 56, 92–93; 2H 375–76; 4H 113, 120, 125; 6H 111; CE 392.
64. 2H 374–76, 382; Note that Colonel Finck stated that this bullet could not have inflicted the wound on Governor Connally's wrist (2H 382), whereas the Warren Commission reported that "ballistic experiments and medical findings established that the missile which passed through the Governor's wrist and penetrated his thigh had first traversed his chest" (WR 94).
65. Thompson, pp. 152–54.
66. 5H 79–82; WR 582–84; CE 856, 857; see Thompson, pp. 151–52.
67. WR 109.
68. WR 582; see WR 56, 92–94; Thompson, p. 283.
69. WR 582.
70. Ibid.
71. WR 92.
72. Epstein, *Inquest*, p. 109.
73. Ibid., pp. 111–20, quoted phrase on p. 119.
74. Ibid., pp. 77–78.
75. 1H 1–264.
76. Epstein, *Inquest*, p. 78.
77. See, for example, Anson, chapters 6–7.
78. See part II and chapter 4.
79. WR 663; see also WR 785, 801.
80. HAH 3H 494.
81. *Time*, December 19, 1977, p. 18.
82. For example: CD 75, p. 491 (Caracci); CD 686d (McWillie); CD 86, p. 558 (Chavez); CD 4, p. 366 (association with Dallas gambling circle); CD 1193, p. 89 (offer of numbers job); CD 1102c (Joe Bonds); CD 84, p. 229 (Weiner); CD 4, p. 529 (Teamsters).
83. CD 86, pp. 278–82, cf. CE 1750; CD 1144, cf. CE 2284; see Appendix 1.
84. CD 84, pp. 91–92, cf. CE 1536; see Appendix 1.
85. WR 790.
86. *U.S.–Senate, OC and Narcotics Report*, p. 37; Demaris, *Captive City*, p. 349; see section 6.4.
87. See section 6.4.
88. See section 22 of Appendix 4.
89. IRE series, *Albuquerque Journal*, April 3, 1977, p. A6.
90. Ibid.
91. Ibid.
92. Ibid., pp. A1, A6.
93. Ibid.

94. Ibid., p. A6.
95. Ibid.
96. Ibid.
97. Ibid.
98. Ibid.
99. See section 22 of Appendix 4.
100. IRE series, *Albuquerque Journal*, April 3, 1977, p. A1; WR xiv.
101. WR xiv-xv.
102. HAH 5H 453.
103. See section 26 of Appendix 4.
104. See entries 6.12, 26.6, 26.7 and xxx of Appendix 4.
105. See entry 26.8 of Appendix 4.
106. See entries 26.1, 26.2, 26.6, 26.7 of Appendix 4; see text below.
107. See entries 26.1, 26.2 and the Loeb quotation following in Appendix 4.
108. Kennedy, *The Enemy Within*, p. 226.
109. HAH 5H 172; Sheridan, *The Fall and Rise of Jimmy Hoffa*, p. 503.
110. C. Ray Hall Exhibit 1; HAH 5H 87.
111. See section 12.5.
112. 5H 187.
113. Sheridan, p. 503.
114. HAH 5H 29, 87, 172; see also CE 1322, p. 767.
115. HAH 5H 29, 87, 172.
116. HAH 5H 26–27, 120; HAH 9H 544.
117. HAH 5H 30, 169.
118. HAH 5H 27–30, 120, 170, 172.
119. HAH 9H 378.
120. HAH 9H 544.
121. HAH 5H 120, 169.
122. HAH 5H 28, 168.
123. HAH 9H 378.
124. *Houston Post*, April 20, 1975, p. 2A.
125. HAH 9H 378.
126. HAH 5H 169.
127. HAH 5H 168, 170.
128. HAH 5H 168.
129. HAH 9H 168–69.
130. HAH 9H 167–69.
131. HAH 5H 120–25.
132. CE 1697; HAH 5H 125–29, 133–34.
133. HAH 9H 168–69; HAH 5H 173. Zoppi claimed that he never checked his 1973 story with McWillie, which Committee interviewers found "very surprising" (HAH 5H 170–71).
134. Hersh, "The Contrasting Lives of Sidney R. Korshak," *New York Times*, June 27, 1976, p. 20.
135. Ibid., June 30, 1976, p. 14.
136. Ibid.
137. Ibid.
138. "The Mob," part 1, *Life*, September 1, 1967, p. 42B.
139. *Washington Star*, July 12, 1979, p. 1.
140. Ibid.
141. Ibid.
142. Ibid.
143. See section 4.3.
144. Reid, *The Grim Reapers*, pp. 160–62; HAH 9H 75–76.
145. HAH 9H 77.
146. HAH 9H 78.
147. Ibid.
148. Ibid.
149. HAH 9H 86.
150. HAH 9H 79.
151. HAH 9H 86.
152. HAH 9H 78, 85, 86.
153. HAH 9H 85.
154. HAH 9H 79, 85–86.
155. Ibid.
156. HAH 9H 78.

157. HAH 9H 85.
158. *U.S.–Senate, Intelligence Report, JFK Assassination*, p. 33.
159. Ibid., pp. 34, 35, 46.
160. Ibid., pp. 5, 47.
161. HAH 3H 489.
162. *U.S.–Senate, Intelligence Report, JFK Assassination*, p. 5, see p. 47.
163. Salerno and Tompkins, *The Crime Confederation*, p. 306.
164. Ibid., pp. 306–7; William Turner, *Hoover's FBI*, pp. 44, 59, 167, 177–85; Navasky, *Kennedy Justice*, pp. 44–45; Viorst, "The Mafia, the CIA, and the Kennedy Assassination," *Washingtonian*, November 1975, pp. 113–14; William Turner, "Crime is Too Big for the FBI," *Nation*, November 8, 1965, pp. 322–28; NBC Evening News, "Segment 3," December 16, 1977; HAH 3H 460; Hank Messick, "The Schenely Chapter," *Nation*, April 5, 1971, pp. 428–31; Schlesinger, Jr., *Robert Kennedy and his Times*, pp. 283–86, 288, 289.
165. William Turner, *Hoover's FBI*, p. 79.
166. *Time*, December 22, 1975, pp. 19–20.
167. William Turner, *Hoover's FBI*, p. 79.
168. *Life*, May 26, 1967, p. 28; Messick, *Secret File*, pp. 350–51.
169. Edem.
170. *Time*, December 12, 1977, p. 90.
171. For example, of the 58 individuals apprehended at the 1957 Mafia convention in Apalachin, New York, 50 had been arrested and 35 had been convicted of various crimes (*U.S.–Senate, McClellan Labor Hearings*, vol. 32, Exhibit 5). The average number of arrests of the members of the five New York Mafia families was determined to be 6.6 (*U.S.–Senate, OC and Narcotics Hearings*, p. 259). In *Vinnie Teresa's Mafia* (p. 39), Mafia defector Teresa noted "you admit to being a member of the Mafia, then you're admitting you're a killer because that's the only way you get to be a member."
172. As cited in note 164.
173. Navasky, pp. 44–45; Salerno and Tompkins, pp. 306–7; see also HAH 3H 460.
174. Edem.
175. Navasky, p. 44.
176. William Turner, *Hoover's FBI*, pp. 177–85; Salerno and Tompkins, pp. 306–7.
177. Navasky, pp. 44–45; William Turner, *Hoover's FBI*, pp. 19, 44, 59, 167, 177–85.
178. Navasky, pp. 44–46.
179. Ibid., pp. 45–46.
180. IRE series, *Albuquerque Journal*, March 19, 1977, pp. A1, A9.
181. Ibid., pp. A1, A9.
182. Ibid., p. A9.
183. William Turner, *Hoover's FBI*, pp. 80–81, 97; Jack Anderson, *San Francisco Chronicle*, December 31, 1970, p. 25.
184. William Turner, *Hoover's FBI*, p. 97.
185. Ibid.
186. Scott, *Crime and Cover-Up*, pp. 11, 34–35, 38; Reid, *The Grim Reapers*, pp. 141–42.
187. *U.S.–Senate, Bobby Baker Hearings*, pp. 1864–67.
188. Navasky, p. 30.
189. Fred Cook, *The FBI Nobody Knows* (New York: Pyramid, 1964), p. 240.
190. Jack Anderson, *San Francisco Chronicle*, December 31, 1970, p. 25.
191. William Turner, *Hoover's FBI*, p. 80; Dorman, *Payoff*, pp. 212–14, 220, 223, 231–32, 235–36;

Messick, "The Schenely Chapter," *Nation*, April 5, 1971, pp. 428–31. For background on Joe Fusco, Alfred Hart, and their liquor companies, see Reid, *The Grim Reapers*, p. 254; Demaris, p. 224; and *U.S.–Senate, Kefauver Hearings*, part 5, p. 539.
192. For Costello's background, see *U.S.–Senate, Kefauver Report, Third Interim*, pp. 111–24; Reid, *The Grim Reapers*, pp. 10–11; *U.S.–Senate, OC and Narcotics Hearings*, p. 652, chart B.
193. *Time*, December 22, 1975, p. 20.
194. Schlesinger, Jr., *Robert Kennedy and his Times*, p. 286n.
195. *Time*, December 22, 1975, p. 14.
196. Ibid.; William Turner, *Hoover's FBI*, p. 96.
197. *Time*, December 22, 1975, p. 20; Joseph Nocera, "The Art of the Leak," *Washington Monthly*, July-August, 1979, p. 25.
198. *Newsweek*, July 9, 1979, p. 35.
199. HAH 3H 646.
200. *Newsweek*, July 9, 1979, pp. 35–36.
201. *Time*, December 22, 1975, pp. 15–16.
202. *U.S.–Senate, Intelligence Report, JFK Assassination*, see notes on pp. 23, 33, 34, 41, 46–48, 50–55.
203. *Newsweek*, July 9, 1979, p. 35.
204. *U.S.–Senate, Intelligence Report, JFK Assassination*, pp. 33–34.
205. Ibid., p. 34.
206. WR ix.
207. *U.S.–Senate, Intelligence Report, JFK Assassination*, pp. 23, 33.
208. Robert A. Caro, *The Years of Lyndon Johnson*, excerpts from the *Atlantic Monthly*, October 1981, p. 44, see p. 63; see also section 16.1.
209. Caro, p. 42.
210. Ibid.
211. Ibid.
212. Ibid.
213. "The Mob," part 2, *Life*, September 8, 1967, p. 103.
214. Winter-Berger, pp. 53–54.
215. Ibid.
216. Ibid., pp. 58, 60.
217. Ibid., p. 54; Reid, *The Grim Reapers*, p. 133; Mollenhoff, *Strike Force*, p. 82.
218. Winter-Berger, p. 61.
219. Ibid., p. 69; Mollenhoff, *Strike Force*, p. 115.
220. Mollenhoff, *Strike Force*, pp. 102–5, 186; Reid, *The Grim Reapers*, pp. 133–45; Dorman, *Payoff*, pp. 143–48; Winter-Berger, p. 68.
221. Anson, p. 324.
222. Winter-Berger, p. 68.
223. William Turner, *Hoover's FBI*, p. 185; Mollenhoff, *Strike Force*, p. 5.
224. Winter-Berger, pp. 61–66.
225. Ibid., pp. 15–17.
226. Ibid., passim; Dorman, *Payoff*, pp. 189–97.
227. Dorman, *Payoff*, p. 194; see entries 25.11, 25.12 of Appendix 4.
228. Winter-Berger, pp. 61–66.
229. Ibid., p. 62.
230. Ibid., pp. 62–63.
231. Ibid., p. 65.
232. Ibid.
233. Ibid., pp. 65–66.
234. See entries 25.11 and 25.12 of Appendix 4.
235. Reid, *The Grim Reapers*, pp. 125, 133–40.
236. Ibid., pp. 140–42.
237. Ibid.
238. Reid, *The Grim Reapers*, p. 141.
239. Mollenhoff, *Strike Force*, pp. 6, 110.
240. Ibid., p. 110.
241. Ibid., pp. 117–18.

242. Ibid., pp. 110, 112–13.
243. Mollenhoff, *Strike Force*, p. 113.
244. Ibid.
245. Demaris, p. 14.
246. Ibid., pp. 77, 324.
247. *Life*, May 30, 1969, p. 45.
248. National Archives, Texas Supplemental Report, November 26, 1963; also see Mollenhoff, *Strike Force*, p. 6.
249. *U.S.–House, OC and Worthless Securities*, p. 3.
250. Ibid., pp. 119, 207–9, 226.
251. Ibid., pp. 3, 193, 223.
252. For other examples, see Grutzner, "How to Lock Out the Mafia," *Harvard Business Review*, March-April 1970, pp. 45–48; and section 17 of Appendix 4.
253. *U.S.–House, OC and Worthless Securities*, pp. 3, 193–94, 223–25.
254. Ibid., p. 193.
255. Ibid., pp. 197, 224.
256. Ibid., pp. 193, 224.
257. Ibid., pp. 223–24, 242.
258. Ibid., p. 224; see Teresa, *My Life in the Mafia*, p. 239, and quotation after entry 15.10 in Appendix 4 for description of feigned Mob "good guy, bad guy" routines.
259. *U.S.–House, OC and Worthless Securities*, p. 224.
260. Ibid., pp. 2–3.
261. Ibid., p. 2. Among those involved were Genovese Family loan shark (Gage, *Mafia, U.S.A.*, pp. 326, 364) John Masiello; "Murder, Inc." enforcer (*U.S.–House, OC and Worthless Securities*, p. 154) "Trigger Abe" Chapman; and John Battaglia, an associate of California Mafioso Jimmy Fratianno (Reid, *The Grim Reapers*, pp. 175, 191). Badalamente took the Fifth Amendment on all substantive questions at his appearance before the committee (*U.S.–House, OC and Worthless Securities*, pp. 207–9).
262. *U.S.–House, OC and Worthless Securities*, pp. 1–2, 9–26, 27–35, 242.
263. Ibid., p. 242.
264. Ibid.
265. Tacitus, *The Histories*, translated by Kenneth Wellesley (New York: Penguin, 1964), p. 38.
266. Dorman, *Payoff*, p. 13.
267. See, for example, Kennedy, *The Enemy Within*; Sheridan, *The Fall and Rise of Jimmy Hoffa*; Mollenhoff, *Tentacles of Power*; Brill, *The Teamsters*; Moldea, *The Hoffa Wars*; and sections 1.2, 6.2.
268. See section 25 of Appendix 4 and chapter 9, Frank Caracci.
269. See section 20.2, displayed footnote; section 15c of Appendix 4; Gage, *The Mafia is not an Equal Opportunity Employer*, pp. 98–116.
270. See sections 13 and 17c of Appendix 4.
271. See section 15e of Appendix 4.
272. See section 2 of Appendix 4.
273. Ibid.
274. See entry 15.2 of Appendix 4; Malcolm X, *By Any Means Necessary*, p. 50; quotation by Charles Kenyatta in section 24.1.
275. See section 6a of Appendix 4.
276. See sections 14, 18a and 18c of Appendix 4.
277. See sections 21 and 22 of Appendix 4.
278. See part IV of Appendix 4.
279. See section 2 of Appendix 4.
280. Noyes, *Legacy of Doubt*, p. 34; Demaris, *Captive City*, pp. 61–63; *Los Angeles Times*, May 31, 1973, p. 22; see section 2 of Appendix 4.
281. See entry 17.15 of Appendix 4 and Teresa, pp. 192, 336.

282. HAH 9H 1041–42; *Miami Herald*, March 3, 1978, p. 7A; *Washington Post*, April 6, 1978, p. VA19.

Chapter 18
Jack Ruby and the Cuban Coalition

1. Malone, "The Secret Life of Jack Ruby," *New Times*, January 23, 1978, p. 47.
2. HAH 9H 162.
3. CE 3063.
4. Ibid.
5. Reid, *The Grim Reapers*, pp. 11, 92; *U.S.–Senate, McClellan Labor Hearings*, p. 14060.
6. CE 3063.
7. Ibid.
8. HAH 10H 161; Malone, "The Secret Life of Jack Ruby," *New Times*, January 23, 1978, pp. 47–48.
9. Malone, "The Secret Life of Jack Ruby," *New Times*, January 23, 1978, p. 48.
10. CE 3065.
11. Ibid.
12. Ibid.
13. Ibid.
14. Ibid.
15. Ibid.
16. WR 788.
17. CE 3065.
18. Ibid.
19. Ibid.
20. Ibid.
21. Ibid.
22. Ibid.
23. Ibid.
24. Ibid.
25. Ibid.
26. Ibid.
27. Malone, "The Secret Life of Jack Ruby," *New Times*, January 23, 1978, p. 48.
28. Ibid.
29. Ibid.
30. Jack Anderson, *Parade*, April 28, 1963, p. 5; Malone, "The Secret Life of Jack Ruby," *New Times*, January 23, 1978, pp. 47–48; see section 15.2.
31. Anderson, *Parade*, April 28, 1963, pp. 4–5; *Time*, March 2, 1959, pp. 22, 25; Malone, "The Secret Life of Jack Ruby," *New Times*, January 23, 1978, pp. 48–50; see section 15.2.
32. Edem.
33. C. Ray Hall Exhibit 3, p. 15.
34. 5H 202.
35. CE 1688.
36. CE 1688–89; HAH 9H 178.
37. CE 1689; see HAH 9H 178.
38. CE 1689.
39. Ibid.
40. Ibid.
41. Ibid.
42. Ibid.
43. Ibid.
44. Ibid.
45. Ibid.
46. Ibid. When questioned by the House Assassinations Committee in 1976, McKeown confirmed the essential features of this account, although he provided several new details which appeared confused and inconsistent (HAH 9H 180–82). Given the consistent initial accounts of McKeown, Ruby and Deputy Sheriff Ayo, however, a contact between Ruby and McKeown concerning some Cuban dealing appears well established.

47. CE 2980.
48. Ibid.
49. CE 3063.
50. C. Ray Hall Exhibit 3, p. 15; 5H 201, 205.
51. CE 1697, pp. 1–2.
52. 5H 201.
53. C. Ray Hall Exhibit 3, p. 15.
54. CE 1691; CE 1697, p. 1.
55. *U.S.–Senate, OC and Narcotics Hearings*, p. 569; Scott, "From Dallas to Watergate," in Blumenthal and Yazijian, ed., *Government by Gunplay*, p. 126; Anson, *"They've Killed the President!"*, p. 309; *New York Times*, January 4, 1959, p. 6.
56. See chapter 9, Lewis J. McWillie.
57. CD 686d, p. 2.
58. 5H 201, 205, 207, 208; C. Ray Hall Exhibit 3, p. 15; See also CE 1697, pp. 1–2 and HAH 9H 164.
59. HAH 9H 172.
60. CE 1442–43; HAH 9H 175.
61. CE 1773–74.
62. CE 1773.
63. HAH 9H 162.
64. CE 2329.
65. HAH 9H 175.
66. HAR 151; see also HAH 9H 176.
67. CE 1440; see HAH 9H 159, 161.
68. JFK microfilm, vol. 5, p. D47.
69. WR 798–99.
70. JFK microfilm, vol. 5, p. G5.
71. CD 84, p. 215.
72. Ibid.
73. Ibid.; see chapter 9, Lewis J. McWillie.
74. HAR 152; see also HAH 9H 177.
75. HAR 152.
76. HAH 9H 172–73; HAR 153.
77. HAR 152.
78. Malone, "The Secret Life of Jack Ruby," *New Times*, January 23, 1978, p. 51.
79. HAH 9H 166–67; HAH 5H 162–65.
80. HAH 5H 167; see also HAH 5H 147 and Malone, "The Secret Life of Jack Ruby," *New Times*, January 23, 1978, p. 50.
81. HAR 153; HAH 9H 173–74, 169–70.
82. HAR 153.
83. HAH 9H 164.
84. HAR 173.
85. Malone, "The Secret Life of Jack Ruby," *New Times*, January 23, 1978, p. 50.
86. Ibid.
87. HAH 9H 173; HAR 153.
88. Malone, "The Secret Life of Jack Ruby," *New Times*, January 23, 1978, p. 49; *Time*, March 2, 1959, pp. 22, 25; Anderson, *Parade*, April 28, 1963, pp. 4–5.
89. CE 1690; CE 1697, p. 1.
90. CE 2988; see chapter 9, Russell D. Matthews.
91. 5H 201.
92. HAH 10H 10; see sections 15.2, 15.4.
93. 14H 330–64; see also CE 3061.
94. WR 369.
95. WR 663.
96. WR 801.
97. See section 17.5.
98. CE 3058–62.
99. 14H 360–61; CE 3061, pp. 629–31; CE 3059, p. 618.
100. CE 3059, p. 618.
101. Ibid.; CE 3061, p. 631; CE 1517.
102. *U.S.–Senate, Kefauver Hearings*, part 2, p. 193; CE 1517.
103. CE 3061, p. 630.
104. CE 3059, pp. 624–25.
105. CE 3059, p. 619; cf. CE 3061, p. 630.
106. CE 3059, p. 619.
107. CE 3060, p. 627.
108. CE 3058, p. 615.
109. Ibid.
110. Ibid.
111. Ibid.
112. Ibid.
113. CE 3061, p. 627.
114. CE 3061, pp. 628, 630, 633.
115. 14H 330–64.
116. 14H 340–41.
117. Reid, *The Grim Reapers*, p. 167.
118. 14H 333–34.
119. 14H 334–35, 345.
120. 14H 340–41.
121. CE 3059, p. 618.
122. 14H 336, 340.
123. 14H 345–49. For identification of Dave Cherry, see 14H 360–61; CE 3059, p. 618; CE 3061, pp. 629–31.
124. 14H 345–48.
125. 14H 348–49.
126. 14H 349.
127. 14H 349–50.
128. Ibid.
129. 14H 353.
130. 14H 353.
131. 14H 354.
132. 14H 355.
133. HAH 10H 10; Anson, pp. 257–60, 313; Moldea, *The Hoffa Wars*, pp. 126–33.
134. CE 1322, p. 725.
135. See section 12.7.
136. CE 1322, p. 730.
137. C. Ray Hall Exhibit 3, p. 8; 5H 203.
138. CE 1322, p. 730.
139. CE 2980, pp. 9, 12.
140. CE 2980, p. 13.
141. Joachim Joesten, *The Case Against Lyndon Johnson in the Assassination of President Kennedy* (Munich: Dreischstr. 5, Selbstverlag, 1967), p. 9.
142. WR 296; see section 15.1.
143. HAH 9H 532.
144. Ibid.
145. See chapter 9, Russell D. Matthews.
146. CE 1753.
147. HAH 5H 170; HAH 9H 428.
148. HAH 5H 70–71; CE 1546. Although McWillie reported in 1978 that he was "almost positive" that he met Ruby after the Top of the Hill club closed (HAH 5H 71), McWillie told the FBI in 1963 that Ruby had visited that club (CE 1546).
149. CE 2980, p. 13.
150. CE 1322, pp. 734, 754, 757.
151. See section 23.3.

Part V
A Mafia Contract

1. *Newsweek*, November 28, 1977, p. 63; Schlesinger, Jr., *Robert Kennedy and His Times*, p. 371.
2. *Newsweek*, November 28, 1977, p. 63.
3. Ibid.
4. Ibid.
5. Ibid.; he was sentenced to life imprisonment (ibid.).

Chapter 19
Contacts with the
Marcello Family

1. *U.S.–Senate, OC and Stolen Securities, 1973,* pp. 120–21.
2. *U.S.–Senate, McClellan Labor Hearings,* p. 17264.
3. See section 4.3.
4. HAH 9H 69; see section 4.3.
5. Reid, *The Grim Reapers,* pp. 151–53; Mollenhoff, *Strike Force,* p. 159; see section 4.3.
6. Mollenhoff, *Strike Force,* p. 160; see section 4.3.
7. *U.S.–Senate, OC and Stolen Securities, 1971,* p. 672.
8. Reid, *The Grim Reapers,* pp. 160–62.
9. HAH 9H 81–84; see section 4.3.
10. HAH 9H 82; see section 4.3.
11. Edem.
12. Reid, *The Grim Reapers,* p. 162; HAH 9H 83.
13. National Archives, entry 45, Ruby-Oswald chronology, p. 519.
14. CE 2308; JFK microfilm, vol. 5, p. T16.
15. Reid, *The Grim Reapers,* p. 155; Lawson, "Carnival of Crime," *Wall Street Journal,* January 12, 1970, p. 1; "The Mob," part 2, *Life,* September 8, 1967, p. 95.
16. Edem.
17. CE 2309; JFK microfilm, vol. 5, p. T11.
18. CE 1524–26.
19. CE 1525, 1526; CD 86, p. 487.
20. *U.S.–House, OC in Sports,* p. 949.
21. Edem.
22. See chapter 9, Frank Caracci.
23. CD 84, pp. 131–32.
24. CD 84, p. 233.
25. CE 1244; CE 1581–83; CE 2308–9; JFK microfilm, vol. 5, p. T16. Note that area codes cited in CE 1244 and CE 1581 are incorrect; e.g., the number of the Bull-Pen in Arlington, Texas, 275–4891, which Ruby called frequently (see CE 2303) is prefixed with area code 807, which corresponds to Ontario, Canada. The call to 523–0930 is presumably to the Old French Opera House, a New Orleans bar with that number (JFK microfilm, vol. 5, p. T16), since Ruby called that number often that summer (CE 2308–9) and since he called another New Orleans number on August 4 (CE 2309).
26. CD 4, p. 666; CD 86, p. 487.
27. CD 4, p. 666.
28. CD 86, p. 487.
29. CD 4, p. 666.
30. CD 84, pp. 131–32.
31. CE 2309; CD 84, p. 132.
32. *U.S.–House, OC Control,* p. 434; HAH 4H 565.
33. HAH 4H 565.
34. Ibid.
35. *U.S.–House, OC Control,* pp. 416, 434; *New York Times,* February 28, 1974, p. 24; Sheridan, *The Fall and Rise of Jimmy Hoffa,* p. 492.
36. *U.S.–House, OC Control,* p. 416.
37. HAH 4H 565.
38. Ibid.; see note 30.
39. CE 1521; CE 1523; CE 1526; CE 1561; CD 84, p. 219; CD 4, p. 666.
40. Edem. Jada was employed at the Sho-Bar at the time of Ruby's early June visit, according to Sho-Bar managers Nick Graffagnini (CE 1526) and Henry Morici (CD 84, p. 219) and

other witnesses (CE 1521, 1522, 1524, 1525); Morici reported that Jada's engagement there ran from April 5 to June 12, 1963 (CD 4, p. 663). But Paul Cascio, who worked just across from the Sho-Bar, told the FBI that at the time of Ruby's visit Jada was "a dancing girl at the 500 Club" (CE 1523). And Jada, who described Ruby's early June visit in some detail (CE 1561), stated only that she had been associated with her husband, Joseph Conforto "in the operation of a strip tease club known as 'Madame Francine's' " which closed in June 1963 (CE 1561).
41. CE 1561.
42. CE 1244.
43. 14H 639.
44. 5H 200; C. Ray Hall Exhibit 3, p. 16; see section 18.2.
45. See chapter 21.
46. CD 4, p. 666; CE 1526; CE 1521; CE 1561; CE 1523; CD 84, p. 219.
47. CD 84, pp. 131–32; CD 86, pp. 445, 486–89; CD 223, p. 136; JFK microfilm, vol. 5, pp. T9–18; CE 2303, 2308, 2309.
48. See section 6.3.
49. As cited in note 47.
50. CD 84, pp. 131–32.
51. Warren Report index.
52. 15H 795 (index to the hearings); 14H 57.
53. CD 84, pp. 131–32.
54. CD 86, p. 486.
55. CD 86, p. 487; CD 84, p. 131.
56. JFK microfilm, vol. 5, p. T16.
57. CE 1561.
58. CD 223, p. 136.
59. JFK microfilm, vol. 5, p. T11; CE 2303, p. 242.
60. CD 84, pp. 131–32.
61. CE 1524; CE 1522.
62. CE 1526.
63. CD 4, p. 666.
64. CE 1561.
65. As cited in note 47.
66. CD 84, pp. 131–32.
67. 14H 455; WR 803.
68. HAH 9H 13–14, 38.
69. HAH 9H 29.
70. HAH 4H 565.
71. CD 84, pp. 131–32; CD 223, p. 136.
72. CD 84, pp. 131–32; CE 2303, 2309.
73. It is interesting to observe that on both August 4 and October 30, the dates of these contacts, Ruby had telephone contact with other New Orleans numbers which were attributed to "Harold Tannenbaum" (CE 2303, 2309, CD 86, p. 445; CD 84, pp. 131–32).
74. HAH 4H 565.
75. CD 84, p. 131.
76. CD 75, p. 491.
77. Ibid.
78. Ibid.
79. CD 4, p. 666.
80. Ibid.
81. CE 2302, 2303.
82. CE 1322, p. 771.
83. CD 4, p. 666.
84. *U.S.–House, OC Control,* p. 430.
85. *U.S.–House, OC in Sports,* p. 949.
86. See section 23.5.

Chapter 20
Meeting Mobsters and
Teamsters

1. Teresa, *My Life in the Mafia*, p. 345.
2. Crile, "The Mafia, the CIA, and Castro," *Washington Post*, May 16, 1976, p. C4; see section 4.4.
3. See section 4.5.
4. Moldea, *The Hoffa Wars*, p. 150.
5. National Archives, entry 45, Ruby-Oswald chronology, p. 519.
6. Ruby's home phone number was WH1–5601; the Carousel Club RI7–2362. See Appendix 3 for a discussion of those telephone records.
7. CE 2308 (the number called was 523–9468); JFK microfilm, vol. 5, p. T16; Reid, *The Grim Reapers*, p. 155; Lawson, "Carnival of Crime," *Wall Street Journal*, January 12, 1970, p. 1.
8. CD 5, pp. 413–14.
9. Ibid.
10. 14H 542–43, 567.
11. 14H 543.
12. HAH 5H 33; see also CE 1697, p. 4.
13. More detailed background on McWillie and other Ruby contacts is provided in chapter 9.
14. CE 1693.
15. Wallace Turner, *Gambler's Money*, p. 127; Reid and Demaris, *The Green Felt Jungle*, pp. 141, 147.
16. CE 2309 (735–4111); JFK microfilm, vol. 5, p. T12; CD 722, p. 6.
17. CE 1692; CE 1697, p. 4.
18. CE 1697, pp. 4–5; CD 86, p. 474.
19. 14H 459.
20. CE 2309 (652–9658); JFK microfilm, vol. 5, p. T12; CD 84, p. 229.
21. CD 84, p. 229.
22. 15H 28–29; 14H 445 (both Hyman and Eva reported that they knew Jack Yanover).
23. CD 84, p. 229; see Appendix 6, Jack Yanover.
24. WR 28.
25. CE 2308 (523–0930); JFK microfilm, vol. 5, p. T16; CD 84, p. 233.
26. CE 1522, 1524–26; see section 19.1.
27. CE 1525, 1526; CD 86, p. 487.
28. Kantor, *Who Was Jack Ruby?*, p. 20.
29. Ibid.
30. Ibid.; see JFK microfilm, vol. 5, p. T10; CD 86, p. 542.
31. CE 2309 (275–4321); JFK microfilm, vol. 5, p. T10; CD 86, p. 542.
32. CE 2309 (523–9468); JFK microfilm, vol. 5, p. T11; Reid, *The Grim Reapers*, p. 155; Lawson, "Carnival of Crime," *Wall Street Journal*, January 12, 1970, p. 1.
33. CE 2309; JFK microfilm, vol. 5, p. T10; CD 86, p. 542.
34. Edem (523–0930). JFK microfilm lists the date of the call as June 15.
35. Edem.; CE 2308; JFK microfilm, vol. 5, p. T16.
36. CE 2309 (735–4303); JFK microfilm, vol. 5, p. T12; CD 722, p. 6.
37. CE 2308, 2309 (523–0930); JFK microfilm, vol. 5, pp. 11, 16.
38. CE 2308 (274–0043); JFK microfilm, vol. 5, pp. T16–17; CE 1507.
39. Edem (466–8211).
40. CE 1507.
41. See chapter 9, Irwin Weiner.
42. HAH 9H 1050, 1078.
43. 14H 473.
44. 14H 130.
45. 15H 432.
46. See section 12.5.
47. See section 17.5.
48. See section 18d of Appendix 4.
49. "The Politics of Conspiracy," conference at Boston University, workshop on organized crime, George Sherman Student Center, February 1, 1975, tape-recorded by author.
50. See section 15c of Appendix 4.
51. Hersh, "The Contrasting Lives of Sidney R. Korshak," *New York Times*, June 27, 1976, pp. 1, 20.
52. Ibid., p. 20.
53. Ibid., June 29, 1976, pp. 1, 16.
54. Ibid.
55. Gage, *The Mafia is not an Equal Opportunity Employer*, pp. 98–116; *Newsweek*, July 31, 1972, pp. 21–22; *Newsweek*, January 19, 1970, p. 23; *U.S.–House, OC in Sports*, p. 752.
56. CE 2309 (735–4111); JFK microfilm, vol. 5, p. T12; CD 722, p. 6.
57. See notes 17–19.
58. CE 2308 (464–4785); JFK microfilm, vol. 5, p. T16; CE 1544.
59. CE 2309 (271–9722); JFK microfilm, vol. 5, p. T13; CE 1544.
60. CE 1544; Wallace Turner, pp. 240–41.
61. CE 1544, 1545.
62. Wallace Turner, pp. 240–41.
63. Sheridan, *The Fall and Rise of Jimmy Hoffa*, pp. 7, 361–62.
64. Wallace Turner, pp. 240–42.
65. CE 2308 (735–4111); JFK microfilm, vol. 5, p. T17; CD 722, p. 6.
66. See notes 17–19.
67. CD 84 (242–5431), pp. 131–32.
68. HAH 4H 565.
69. CE 2308 (247–4915); JFK microfilm, vol. 5, p. T16; CE 1261.
70. CE 1261; CE 1288.
71. CE 1288; Kantor, pp. 92, 98.
72. CE 1322, p. 741.
73. National Archives, entry 45, Ruby-Oswald chronology, p. 622.
74. CE 1581.
75. CD 106, p. 259.
76. Ibid.
77. National Archives, entry 45, Ruby-Oswald chronology, p. 622.
78. HAH 9H 251.
79. C. Ray Hall Exhibit 3, p. 16.
80. CE 1244.
81. CE 1288.
82. Ibid.
83. Allsop, *The Bootleggers*, pp. 61–64, 88–90.
84. CE 1288.
85. CE 1581 (523–0930); CD 84, p. 233. Note that area codes cited in CE 1244 and CE 1581 are incorrect; e.g., the number of the Bull-Pen in Arlington, Texas, 275–4891, which Ruby called frequently (see CE 2303) is prefixed with area code 807, which corresponds to Ontario, Canada. The call to 523–0930 is presumably to the Old French Opera House, a New Orleans bar with that number (JFK microfilm, vol. 5, p. T16), since Ruby called that number this summer (CE 2308–9) and since he called another New Orleans number on August 4 (CE 2309).
86. CE 1581; CE 1507.
87. 5H 200.
88. CE 1765.
89. Ibid.
90. Hersh, *New York Times*, June 29, 1976, p. 16.

91. Ibid., June 27, 1976, p. 20.
92. Ibid., June 29, 1976, p. 16.
93. 14H 446.
94. See chapter 9, Joseph Glaser.
95. CE 1581; CE 1507.
96. CE 1581.
97. C. Ray Hall Exhibit 3, p. 16.
98. An FBI chronology reports that Cheryl Aston saw Ruby at Henrici's Restaurant around the first or second week in August and was subsequently called by Ruby (CD 86, p. 488). Ruby's toll records show a 34-minute call on August 7 from Ruby's home phone to the Chicago number 631–1489, listed to Dewey Aston (CE 2308 JFK microfilm, vol. 5, p. T17).
99. Kobler, *Capone*, pp. 184, 191–92; *U.S.–Senate, McClellan Labor Hearings*, p. 13921.
100. Edem.; Demaris, p. 128–29.
101. Patronage at Henrici's: *U.S.–Senate, McClellan Labor Hearings*, pp. 13915, 13921. Background, including more than 40 arrests in Chicago: ibid., pp. 13900–922; Sheridan, p. 57.
102. Patronage at Henrici's: *U.S.–Senate, McClellan Labor Hearings*, pp. 13915, 13921. Background, including Marchesi's invocation of the Fifth Amendment when asked if he was a member of the Mafia: ibid., pp. 13915, 14034–36, 14080; Kennedy, *The Enemy Within*, p. 92.
103. CE 2308 (582–7700); JFK microfilm, vol. 5, p. T16; CE 1322, p. 742.
104. CE 2308 (735–4111); JFK microfilm, vol. 5, p. T17; CD 722, p. 6 (JFK microfilm does not list the August 22 call).
105. CE 1697, pp. 4–5; CD 86, p. 474.
106. CE 1693.
107. CE 2308 (274–0043); JFK microfilm, vol. 5, p. T17; CE 1507.
108. CE 2308, 2309; JFK microfilm, vol. 5, pp. T9–18; CD 86, pp. 488–89.
109. *Dallas Morning News*, September 26, 1963, p. 1. National Archives, entry 45, Ruby-Oswald chronology, pp. 667ff.
110. CE 2303, 2309.
111. CE 1322, pp. 758–59, 764–66.
112. CE 2302, 2308; compare with CE 2303, 2309.
113. CE 2303 (661–3753); CE 2989.
114. CE 2989; HAH 9H 545–46.
115. See chapter 9, Russell D. Matthews.
116. CE 2989.
117. HAH 9H 527.
118. HAR 173; HAH 9H 529.
119. HAH 9H 529.
120. HAH 9H 528, 529, 531.
121. CD 75, p. 491; see section 19.4.
122. Edem.
123. See chapter 9, Frank Caracci.
124. Malone, "The Secret Life of Jack Ruby," *New Times*, January 23, 1978, p. 51.
125. *U.S.–Senate, Intelligence Report, Foreign Assassinations*, pp. 75–77; HAH 10H 151.
126. Malone, "The Secret Life of Jack Ruby," *New Times*, January 23, 1978, p. 51.
127. Jack Anderson, *Albuquerque Journal*, September 8, 1976; Jack Anderson, *Washington Post*, January 3, 1979, p. B15.
128. Malone, "The Secret Life of Jack Ruby," *New Times*, January 23, 1978, p. 51.
129. Jack Anderson, *Albuquerque Journal*, September 8, 1976.
130. Ibid.; HAH 10H 155, 186; Moldea, *The Hoffa Wars*, p. 433.
131. Moldea, p. 433.
132. G. Robert Blakey and Richard N. Billings, "An Expert's Theory," *Parade*, November 16, 1980, p. 6.

133. Ibid.; Brashler, *The Don*, pp. 321–23; HAH 10H 155, 186.
134. Brashler, p. 324.
135. HAH 10H 186.
136. CE 2302 (956–2687); CE 1507.
137. CE 2303 (743–6865); see section 21.3.
138. See chapter 9, Irwin Weiner.
139. Ibid.
140. Ibid.
141. CD 84, p. 229.
142. See section 21.3.
143. HAH 9H 1069, 1071.
144. HAH 9H 1055–56, 1061, 1069.
145. HAH 9H 1056.
146. 15H 29; see below and chapter 9, Irwin Weiner, for a definitive identification of this Chicago bail bondsman as Weiner.
147. CE 1202.
148. 14H 445; HAH 4H 567. Ruby's telephone records show no calls to numbers listed to Patrick (CE 2302, 2303, 2308, 2309; JFK microfilm, vol. 5, pp. T9–18), but he could have called Patrick collect, or from a pay phone, or at any of the six Chicago numbers shown in his phone logs not listed to relatives: 236–5561, 728–4031, 427–3172, 652–9658, 631–1489, or 743–6865.
149. See chapter 9, Lenny Patrick.
150. Demaris, *Captive City*, pp. 348–49.
151. CE 2303 (272–9836—a second home number).
152. CE 2309 (242–5431); CD 84, p. 132; *U.S.–House, OC Control*, p. 434; HAH 4H 565.
153. CE 2303 (274–0043).
154. Crafard Exhibit 5226; C. Ray Hall Exhibit 3, p. 3; 25H 318.
155. 14H 8.
156. Ibid.; see 14H 1–2 and Armstrong Exhibit 5308.
157. 14H 8. Ruby's telephone records show five calls to that Fort Worth number between September 24 and November 5. See CE 2302, 2303, 2308.
158. CE 2303.
159. CE 2331.
160. CE 2331; HAH 9H 274; see chapter 9, Barney Baker.
161. HAH 9H 276; Moldea, p. 118.
162. CE 2303 (532–2561).
163. CD 360, p. 149; HAH 4H 566.
164. Sheridan, p. 292; *Time*, December 10, 1973, p. 30.
165. HAH 4H 566.
166. CE 2303.
167. CE 2332.
168. Lepera, *Memoirs of a Scam Man*, pp. 80–81.
169. See section 15b of Appendix 4.
170. *Life*, May 30, 1969, p. 46.
171. Ibid.
172. CE 2303 (587–7674); CE 2328.
173. CE 2328.
174. Ibid.
175. CE 1748.
176. CE 1692–93; 14H 445.
177. 14H 445.
178. HAH 9H 432.
179. CD 1144.

Chapter 21
The Collapse of the Mob's Assassination Alibi

1. Sackett, Smith and Lambert, "The Congressman and the Hoodlum," *Life*, August 9, 1968, p. 23.

2. See entry 16.9 of Appendix 4.
3. See entry 22.6 of Appendix 4.
4. See entry 6.5 of Appendix 4.
5. See sections 13–16 of Appendix 4.
6. See section 16c of Appendix 4.
7. Cressey, *Theft of the Nation*, p. 288.
8. *Life*, August 9, 1968, p. 22; Cressey, p. 288.
9. *Life*, August 9, 1968, p. 20; see entry 25.2 of Appendix 4.
10. See Appendix 2 and entry 5.35 of Appendix 4.
11. Salerno and Tompkins, *The Crime Confederation*, p. 299; HAH 9H 7–10.
12. *U.S.–Senate, McClellan Labor Hearings,* vol. 32, exhibits 4–5.
13. Ibid.
14. See section 5 of Appendix 4.
15. Sondern, *The Brotherhood of Evil*, p. 35.
16. Ibid., p. 37.
17. Ibid.
18. Ibid., pp. 37–38.
19. Ibid., pp. 38–39; *U.S.–Senate, McClellan Labor Hearings*, pp. 12297–310.
20. Edem.
21. Edem.
22. John McClellan, "Weak Link in Our War on the Mafia," *Reader's Digest*, April 6, 1970, reprinted in *U.S.–House, OC Control*, p. 113.
23. Cressey, p. 212.
24. Ibid.
25. Ibid.
26. Ibid., pp. 212–13.
27. Chronicled in *The Fall and Rise of Jimmy Hoffa* by Walter Sheridan. For Marcello's role, see *Life*, September 1, 1967, p. 34.
28. Sheridan, p. 7.
29. Ibid., p. 390.
30. Ibid.
31. Ibid., pp. 390–91.
32. Ibid., p. 391.
33. See sections 6.3 and 19.3 and chapters 12–13.
34. 5H 200.
35. Ibid.; see section 21.2 below.
36. See section 21.3 below.
37. See text below.
38. *U.S.–Senate, AGVA Hearings.*
39. Ibid., pp. 629–30.
40. Ibid., p. 94.
41. Ibid., p. 213.
42. See section 18 of Appendix 4.
43. *U.S.–Senate, AGVA Hearings*, p. 101.
44. Ibid., pp. 209–10.
45. Ibid., p. 630.
46. Ibid., pp. 587–88.
47. Ibid., p. 214.
48. Ibid., pp. 92–93.
49. Ibid., pp. 19–20.
50. Sheridan, pp. 210, 258; see also Kennedy, *The Enemy Within*, pp. 44–51.
51. *U.S.–Senate, AGVA Hearings*, pp. 3–4, 22–24.
52. HAH 9H 200.
53. HAH 9H 419, 1147.
54. HAH 9H 419.
55. HAH 9H 418–21.
56. HAH 9H 422–23.
57. HAH 9H 420.
58. HAH 9H 421.
59. HAH 9H 418.
60. HAH 9H 425.
61. HAH 9H 419.
62. HAH 9H 419–20.
63. Ibid.
64. HAH 9H 425, 428–29.
65. CE 1475.
66. HAH 9H 420–21.

67. HAH 9H 422.
68. CE 2303, 2308; CE 1543; CE 1322, p. 728.
69. CE 1543, p. 1.
70. CD 84, p. 229; 15H 29.
71. CD 84, p. 229.
72. CE 2309; JFK microfilm, vol. 5, p. T12; CD 84, p. 229.
73. 15H 28–29; 14H 460.
74. CE 2302; JFK microfilm, vol. 5, p. T17; CE 1322, p. 727; CE 2323.
75. CE 2323; 15H 217.
76. CE 2323.
77. 15H 217.
78. Ibid.
79. CE 2308, 2309; JFK microfilm, vol. 5, pp. T13, T16.
80. HAH 5H 171.
81. CE 2302, 2303; CE 1562.
82. 5H 200.
83. CE 1582.
84. CE 1244; see section 20.2.
85. CE 1244.
86. See section 20.2.
87. CE 1765.
88. CE 1543.
89. CE 1562.
90. See section 20.2.
91. WR 797; 15H 248, 212.
92. 15H 248, 415.
93. 15H 211–12.
94. 14H 459; 15H 211–12, 415; 5H 200.
95. CE 1543; 5H 200; 15H 212, 248–49.
96. CE 1543.
97. 15H 415; 5H 200; CE 1507; CE 1543; 15H 212–13; CE 1562; HAH 9H 463, 1048.
98. 15H 212–13, 415; 5H 200; CE 1543.
99. CE 1562; 5H 200; HAH 5H 172; HAH 9H 297–98, 465; CE 1507.
100. CE 1562; CE 1543; 15H 211–12; 5H 200.
101. 5H 200.
102. 14H 605; 15H 415; 15H 248.
103. HAH 9H 245, 348, 351, 405; 13H 322–23; 15H 192–93, 212, 220, 249, 415–16.
104. See note 97.
105. HAH 9H 245; 13H 322–23; 15H 249.
106. CE 1543; 15H 212.
107. 15H 248.
108. 15H 249, 415.
109. 15H 248.
110. See chapter 8.
111. CE 1322, p. 726.
112. See chapter 10.
113. See section 20.3.
114. Crafard Exhibit 5226; 13H 502; 15H 416; see beginning of chapter 23.
115. 15H 416.
116. HAH 9H 206.
117. HAH 9H 244–47.
118. HAH 9H 242, 247–48.
119. See section 8.3.
120. 15H 208; CE 1648; CE 1505; 15H 199.
121. HAH 9H 230–31.
122. 15H 211, 208.
123. CE 1517; CE 1543; 15H 210; CD 4, p. 533; 14H 343; HAH 9H 424.
124. *U.S.–Senate, AGVA Hearings*, pp. 629–30, 160.
125. 15H 208.
126. 15H 213.
127. 15H 208.
128. HAR 156; HAH 9H 426; 14H 601–2.
129. HAH 9H 424, 426.
130. CD 4, p. 533.
131. 15H 410.
132. 14H 605.

133. 14H 607.
134. 14H 605–7.
135. 14H 602.
136. 14H 605.
137. 14H 606.
138. 14H 605–8.
139. HAH 9H 1075.
140. CE 2331.
141. Ibid.
142. CE 2303.
143. HAH 9H 297–305.
144. HAH 9H 297, 298; HAH 9H 300–301, 304–5.
145. HAH 9H 298.
146. CE 2284.
147. CE 2243.
148. 5H 200.
149. CE 1244.
150. CE 1544.
151. Ibid.
152. CD 84, p. 229.
153. HAH 9H 1043.
154. Moldea, p. 155.
155. HAH 9H 1043.
156. Ibid.; HAH 9H 1047.
157. HAH 9H 1048.
158. HAR 155; HAH 9H 1049, 1075, 1077.
159. HAR 155.
160. CE 1697.
161. See chapter 9, Lewis J. McWillie.
162. CD 360, p. 149.
163. See chapter 9, Murray W. "Dusty" Miller.
164. CE 1507.
165. HAH 9H 1050, 1053, 1078.
166. CE 2328.
167. Ibid.
168. CE 1765.
169. See chapter 9, Joseph Glaser.
170. HAH 5H 171–72.
171. CE 1543, 1562, 2323; see also 15H 213.
172. CE 2323.
173. CE 1543.
174. CE 1562.
175. HAR 156n.

Chapter 22
Jack Ruby, Lee Oswald
and Officer J. D. Tippit

1. *U.S.–House, OC Control*, p. 86.
2. Kennedy, *The Enemy Within*, p. 253.
3. See references cited in footnote 1134 in WR 845, and those listed in *Subject Index to the Warren Report and Hearings and Exhibits*, by Sylvia Meagher (New York: Scarecrow, 1966), p. 82.
4. CE 2249, p. 41.
5. *Dallas Morning News*, November 25, 1963, p. 6.
6. Ibid.
7. Crowe Exhibit 1.
8. 15H 111.
9. 15H 105–6, 111.
10. See section 3.6.
11. See sections 3.1, 12.7, 13.3.
12. CD 1193, p. 205.
13. CE 2995, pp. 500–503.
14. Ibid., pp. 500, 505.
15. Ibid., pp. 504–5.
16. Ibid.
17. Ibid., pp. 500–501, 505; CD 1193, pp. 205, 209.
18. CE 2995, p. 505.
19. Ibid., p. 504.
20. Ibid., p. 503.
21. Ibid.; 15H 110.

22. CE 2995, p. 503.
23. 15H 110.
24. CE 2995, p. 502.
25. 15H 620.
26. Ibid.; 15H 658–59; 13H 219.
27. 15H 658–59.
28. CE 2821.
29. Ibid.
30. Ibid.
31. Ibid.
32. Ibid.
33. Jones, *Forgive My Grief*, vol. I, p. 54.
34. CE 2821.
35. CE 2821, p. 568, cf. 572.
36. CE 2821, pp. 259–60.
37. WR 736–37; see below.
38. See text below.
39. CE 2821.
40. WR 731, 736–37.
41. CE 2821.
42. Ibid.
43. Ibid.
44. Ibid.
45. Ibid.
46. Kantor Exhibit 3, p. 366.
47. CE 3149.
48. Ibid.
49. Ibid.
50. See section 23.1.
51. CE 3149.
52. 13H 214–15.
53. CE 3149.
54. Ibid.
55. CE 2821.
56. CE 3149.
57. Ibid.
58. Ibid.
59. Ibid.
60. Ibid.
61. Ibid., p. 272.
62. CE 3149.
63. Ibid.
64. 14H 107.
65. CE 3149.
66. 14H 107–8.
67. 5H 194, 196; see sections 14.3 and 14.4.
68. See chapter 14.
69. 14H 531.
70. 14H 546.
71. 14H 542, 557, 567.
72. Ibid.
73. 14H 557.
74. 14H 542, 557, 567.
75. 14H 557.
76. Ibid.
77. 14H 542, 557, 567.
78. 1H 152–53, 237–38.
79. 1H 153.
80. 1H 152–53, 237–38.
81. 1H 238.
82. Ibid.
83. 1H 153.
84. 1H 237–38; WR 364.
85. Edem.
86. WR 364.
87. Ibid.
88. *Washington Post*, June 24, 1976, p. A1; see section 17.2.
89. Ralph Haber, "How We Remember What We See," *Scientific American*, May 1970 (vol. 223), p. 104.
90. Ibid.
91. CD 223, p. 366.
92. Ibid.

93. Ibid.
94. Ibid.
95. Ibid.
96. Ibid., pp. 366–67.
97. Ibid.
98. Ibid., p. 366.
99. WR 614.
100. CD 223, p. 367; cf. WR 614.
101. JFK microfilm, vol. 5, p. L1.
102. Ibid.
103. CD 86, p. 526; JFK microfilm, vol. 5, p. L1.
104. Crafard Exhibit 5226.
105. CE 2403.
106. WR 126; CE 3002.
107. Karen Carlin Exhibit 5318.
108. CD 223, p. 366.
109. CE 3002; WR 126.
110. C. Ray Hall Exhibit 3, p. 3; 5H 183.
111. See section 3.8.
112. See section 3.6.
113. HAR 59–60.
114. Ibid.
115. Ibid.
116. CD 84, p. 89.
117. Ibid.
118. CE 1763.
119. 19H 101–2; CE 2430.
120. CE 2430.
121. *New York Herald Tribune*, December 5, 1963, quoted by Joachim Joesten in *Oswald: Assassin or Fall Guy?*, p. 111.
122. 14H 486.
123. CE 2987.
124. Filmed and tape-recorded interview with Mark Lane, April 3, 1966, reported in Lane, pp. 253–54.
125. Ibid.
126. Ibid.
127. Ibid.
128. CE 1222.
129. Ibid.
130. CE 1615.
131. 2H 58–61; see Lane, p. 249.
132. Edem.
133. 5H 504–9; WR 293–95.
134. CE 2430.
135. 25H 530. Crafard was not present at the Carousel Club on November 14, 1963 (25H 530). This did not stop the Warren Commission from pointing out that he "had no recollection of a Tippit, Weissman, and Ruby meeting" (WR 368), which reportedly occurred on that date.
136. 13H 498–99; 13H 333–34.
137. 15H 655.
138. 5H 203.
139. Ibid.
140. 5H 204.
141. Ibid.
142. Ibid.
143. 5H 203–4.
144. 5H 204.

Chapter 23
The Mafia Killed President Kennedy

1. *Newsweek*, July 30, 1979, p. 38.
2. *U.S.–House, Crime in America*, p. 360.
3. See section 20.3.
4. 15H 406.
5. 15H 416.
6. Crafard Exhibit 5226; C. Ray Hall Exhibit 3, p. 3; 25H 318.
7. Crafard Exhibit 5226.
8. Ibid.
9. 13H 502.
10. 13H 424.
11. CE 1184; see CE 1300.
12. Edem.
13. CE 1300.
14. See chapter 9, Paul Roland Jones.
15. Ibid.
16. CD 1144.
17. CD 722, p. 8.
18. HAH 9H 486.
19. Kantor, *Who Was Jack Ruby?*, p. 22.
20. HAH 9H 485.
21. CE 2284. See also CE 2243; HAH 9H 454, 461.
22. CE 2284.
23. HAH 9H 458.
24. HAH 9H 458–59.
25. HAH 9H 459.
26. Ibid.
27. 5H 185.
28. HAH 9H 462.
29. Ibid.
30. 5H 185.
31. CE 2284.
32. CE 2243.
33. CE 2284.
34. CE 2243; CE 2284.
35. Edem.
36. CE 2303 (the number was 935–1082); 5H 185.
37. CE 2379; C. Ray Hall Exhibit 3, p. 2; Crafard Exhibit 5226, p. 356; see 13H 245.
38. CD 86, pp. 366–67.
39. CE 2397.
40. Tortoriello was co-owner of the J. C. Adams Construction Company (CD 86, p. 256; see also 9H 349). J. C. Adams, in turn, had been a partner of Lester "Benny" Binion (CE 1692), the one-time rackets boss of Dallas (Reid and Demaris, *The Green Felt Jungle*, chapter 10; *U.S.–Senate, Kefauver Hearings*, part 2, p. 193; HAH 9H 530), in an enterprise which had employed Mobster Lewis McWillie (CE 1692). Adams was an associate of both Ruby (HAH 9H 349; CE 1322, p. 750) and Mafioso Joseph Campisi (HAH 9H 349).
41. HAH 9H 348–50, 353.
42. CD 86, pp. 256–57; Jada was the stage name of Janet Conforto.
43. CD 302, p. 20; CD 86, p. 366.
44. CE 2397; see Reid, *The Grim Reapers*, p. 292.
45. CD 302, p. 20.
46. CD 302, p. 41.
47. CD 302, p. 20.
48. CD 302, p. 20.
49. Ibid.
50. CD 86, p. 367; CD 302, p. 20.
51. CE 2396.
52. CD 302, p. 41.
53. CD 86, p. 366.
54. CD 86, p. 367.
55. CE 2396; see CD 302, p. 41.
56. CE 2396.
57. Armstrong Exhibits 5300A-F. The subject is identified as Gloria Fillmon through the accounts of Larry Crafard (13H 493–94, 14H 70) and Gloria Fillmon (CE 2379).
58. Crafard Exhibit 5226, p. 356; CE 2379.
59. See note 37.
60. See section 19.3.
61. CD 86, pp. 256–57; HAH 9H 349.
62. CD 302, p. 20.
63. Ibid.
64. Ibid.

65. Ibid.
66. C. Ray Hall Exhibit 3, pp. 2–3.
67. CE 2270, 2888.
68. C. Ray Hall Exhibit 3, p. 3.
69. Ibid.
70. CE 2980; see CE 2400.
71. CE 2980, p. 13.
72. See section 18.4.
73. Joachim Joesten, *The Case Against Lyndon Johnson in the Assassination of President Kennedy* (Munich: Dreischstr. 5, Selbstverlag, 1967), p. 9.
74. WR 296; see section 15.1.
75. CE 2002, p. 90.
76. Ibid.
77. Ibid.
78. CE 2245; CD 86, p. 495.
79. Edem.
80. Noyes, *Legacy of Doubt*, p. 71.
81. Ibid., pp. 58–59.
82. Ibid., pp. 28–29, 39, 40, 58.
83. Ibid., pp. 71–72.
84. Ibid., p. 72.
85. Ibid., pp. 65–66, 72–73, 75.
86. Ibid., p. 75.
87. Ibid.
88. CE 2399.
89. Ibid.
90. CE 2270. Ruby subsequently specified that he attended to his downtown business in the late morning (C. Ray Hall Exhibit 3, pp. 2–3), and other witnesses saw him in that area between 11 a.m. and noon (CE 2265; CE 2002, p. 160).
91. CE 2399.
92. Ibid.
93. CE 2322.
94. Ibid.
95. CE 2399.
96. CE 2303. Telephone records for Ruby's home phone show one call that day at 6:40 p.m. to the Bull-Pen restaurant in nearby Arlington, Texas (CE 2302). That establishment, called frequently from Ruby's phones during the fall of 1963 (CE 2302, 2303), was operated by Ralph Paul (CE 2302), a night club partner of Ruby (WR 795) and an acquaintance of Ruby's roommate, George Senator (14H 284). Although Senator did not recall calling Paul from his home phone, he testified that he did place calls to Paul at the Bull-Pen and did occasionally use his home phone for local calls (14H 298, 284); thus Senator may have placed that 6:40 p.m. call. Note that Ruby said he was in the Carousel Club on November 21 from the afternoon until about 9:30 p.m. (C. Ray Hall Exhibit 3, p. 3). Thus, attributing that call to Ruby would fit his alibi no better than it would fit the reports of the Houston witnesses described in the text below.
97. CE 2384; CD 86, p. 496.
98. CE 2303 (the number was 729–0891).
99. CE 2302, 2303.
100. CE 2399.
101. Ibid.
102. Ibid.
103. Ibid.
104. Ibid.
105. Ibid.
106. Ibid.
107. Ibid.
108. CD 86, p. 496; see also CE 2384.
109. CE 1518.
110. CE 2399.
111. Ibid.
112. Ibid.
113. Secret Service Agent Elmer Moore reported simply, "Ruby has no noticeable facial scars" (CE2399). In light of the poor quality of his investigation of Ruby's activities of November 21 (ibid., see above), and his questionable role in assisting Ruby's presentation of his alibi (see section 14.1), this simple assertion does not preclude a faint scar observable in the background of a heavy beard growth.
114. From the transcript of Jack Ruby's trial, March 10, 1964, reprinted in *Trauma*, vol. 6, no. 4 (1964), p. 67.
115. Ibid.
116. Ibid.
117. JFK microfilm, vol. 5, p. D17.
118. Ibid.
119. JFK microfilm, vol. 5, p. G5.
120. CE 2399.
121. Ibid.
122. Ibid.
123. Ibid.
124. Ibid.
125. Ibid.; C. Ray Hall Exhibit 2.
126. CE 2399.
127. Ibid.
128. Ibid.
129. See section 13.1.
130. 13H 498–99; 13H 333–34.
131. 15H 642–43.
132. CD 722, p. 7.
133. Karen Carlin Exhibit 5318.
134. 15H 643–44.
135. See section 13.1.
136. C. Ray Hall Exhibit 3, p. 3; 5H 183; CE 2259; CE 2274; CE 2344; CD 360, p. 130.
137. *Houston Post*, April 20, 1975, p. 2A.
138. CE 2259, 2274; HAH 9H 335.
139. See chapter 9, Joseph Campisi.
140. HAH 9H 363–64, 374.
141. CE 2259.
142. *Dallas Morning News*, March 18, 1973, p. 53.
143. CE 2266–68; CD 86, p. 496.
144. CE 2266–68; HAH 9H 807.
145. CD 86, p. 531; CE 2267.
146. Decker Exhibit 5323, pp. 469, 527.
147. CE 2267; 15H 620–39; HAH 9H 805–941.
148. CE 2267.
149. CE 2266.
150. CD 86, pp. 527–28.
151. Ibid.; 15H 624–25; HAH 9H 806; see section 8.3.
152. CD 86, p. 527.
153. CE 2267; 15H 622–23.
154. See chapter 21.
155. 15H 667.
156. 15H 339–40.
157. 15H 806–7, 899–905; CE 2267; 15H 631–36.
158. Friday: 15H 630; HAH 9H 879. Sunday: Meyers testified that he heard about the Oswald shooting while driving to McKinney, Texas "early Sunday morning" before a 10 a.m. golf date in Sherman, at least 30 miles further (HAH 9H 878, 914–16). But Ruby shot Oswald at 11:21 a.m. (WR 219). See also HAH 9H 807; CE 2267.
159. CD 223, p. 366.
160. Ibid.
161. Ibid.
162. Ibid.
163. Ibid.
164. CD 223, pp. 366–67; JFK microfilm, vol. 5, p. L1.
165. CE 1019, p. 668.
166. CE 1020, pp. 679, 682–90; 2H 68, 143; see WR 43–45.

167. CE 1020, pp. 682–90.
168. CE 1020, p. 679.
169. CE 1020, pp. 682, 683, 685, 687, 690.
170. CE 1020, pp. 671, 694–95, 702; see 14H 422.
171. CE 1020, p. 694.
172. Ibid.
173. CD 86, p. 271.
174. 15H 660.
175. JFK microfilm, vol. 5, p. B14. Note that Carlin was a prostitute (JFK microfilm, vol. 5, p. B9; see section 13.1).
176. HAH 5H 46–49, 58, see pp. 20–21; CE 1693.
177. 15H 422, see 430.
178. 15H 422.
179. Hansen Exhibit 1. Hansen was not sure whether the incident occurred on November 22 or the day before, but believed it occurred on November 22 (15H 449); this is the date reported in National Archives, entry 45, Ruby-Oswald chronology, p. 840.
180. Hansen Exhibit 1; 15H 442.
181. Hansen Exhibit 1.
182. HAH 5H 168, 170; see section 17.5.
183. C. Ray Hall Exhibit 3, p. 4; 5H 183; HAH 5H 170.
184. HAH 5H 170.
185. 5H 183; C. Ray Hall Exhibit 3, p. 4.
186. See section 17.5.
187. HAH 5H 170.
188. C. Ray Hall Exhibit 3, p. 4.
189. 5H 183.
190. C. Ray Hall Exhibit 3, p. 4; 5H 183–84. Note that President Kennedy was shot at 12:30 (WR 48).
191. C. Ray Hall Exhibit 3, p. 4; 5H 183–84.
192. WR 32, 34; the Dallas Morning News Building is at Houston and Young streets.
193. C. Ray Hall Exhibit 2, p. 14.
194. CE 1322, p. 754.
195. 14H 564.
196. National Archives, entry 45, Ruby-Oswald chronology, p. 841.
197. 14H 564.
198. Thompson, *Six Seconds in Dallas*, chapter 3; Epstein, *Inquest*, chapter 3.
199. WR 52.
200. WR 50–52.
201. See section 23.5.
202. See chapter 2.
203. See section 5.3.
204. Ibid.
205. Ibid.
206. Ibid.
207. HAH 9H 413.
208. HAH 9H 363–64, 374; CE 2259.
209. CE 2259; CD 86, pp. 138–39.
210. See section 12.1.
211. See section 22.6.
212. WR 6–7.
213. See section 12.6.
214. See section 12.2.
215. See chapter 13.
216. See chapter 3.
217. 14H 567.
218. 15H 619–20.
219. 15H 620.
220. 15H 660.
221. Ibid.
222. Sybil Leek and Bert Sager, *The Assassination Chain* (New York: Corwin, 1976), p. 206. See also JFK microfilm, vol. 5, pp. B15–16; in light of other events, Carlin's period of absence may not be so easily explainable.
223. See chapter 4.
224. See chapter 14.
225. See section 14.6.

226. 5H 198; see section 14.1.
227. 5H 206; see section 14.8.
228. 14H 543, 548, 565–66.
229. 14H 542, 557, 567.
230. 14H 543, 548.
231. 14H 566.
232. Buchanan, *Who Killed Kennedy?* (London: Secker and Warburg, 1964), pp. 130, 137–39.

Chapter 24
Epilogue

1. Gaia Servadio, *Mafioso* (New York: Stein and Day, 1976), p. 279.
2. Notes to *Sicily in Music and Song* (London: Argo Record Company, 1965), No. ZFB 71; Pantaleone, *The Mafia and Politics*, pp. 205–6.
3. Pantaleone, pp. 205–6.
4. *New York Times*, reprinted in Gage, *The Mafia is not an Equal Opportunity Employer*, p. 150; Eugene Methvin, "How the Mafia Preys on the Poor," *Reader's Digest*, September 1970, p. 55; Harry Kelly, Hearst newspapers, March 1970, reprinted in *U.S.-House, OC Control*, p. 423.
5. Edem.
6. *New York Times*, reprinted in Gage, *The Mafia is not an Equal Opportunity Employer*, p. 150.
7. Methvin, "How the Mafia Preys on the Poor," *Reader's Digest*, September 1970, p. 50.
8. Cressey, *Theft of the Nation*, p. 196.
9. *U.S.-House, Criminal Justice Hearings*, p. 163.
10. Methvin, "How the Mafia Preys on the Poor," *Reader's Digest*, September 1970, p. 50.
11. Ibid., p. 54; *U.S.-House, Criminal Justice Hearings*, p. 163; Salerno and Tompkins, *The Crime Confederation*, p. 360.
12. *U.S.-House, Criminal Justice Hearings*, p. 150.
13. *Report of the National Advisory Commission on Civil Disorders* (New York: Dutton, 1968), see summary and index. The report did state, without explanation, the token observation that "the Mafia was reputed to control much of the organized crime" in Newark (ibid., p. 59).
14. G. Robert Blakey and Richard N. Billings, *The Plot to Kill the President* (New York: New York Times Books, 1981), p. 181.
15. Ibid.; see entry 22.19 of Appendix 4.
16. Blakey and Billings, p. 181; *Newsweek*, April 30, 1973, p. 41.
17. Malcolm X, *The Autobiography of Malcolm X*, p. 84.
18. Ibid., pp. 84–85.
19. Ibid., p. 216.
20. Ibid., p. 221.
21. Peter Goldman, *The Death and Life of Malcolm X*, p. 82.
22. Malcolm X, *The Autobiography of Malcolm X*, p. 221.
23. From a speech by Malcolm X at the founding rally of the Organization of Afro-American Unity, transcribed in Malcolm X, *By Any Means Necessary*, pp. 50–51.
24. Goldman, pp. 273–74; epilogue by Alex Haley in Malcolm X, *The Autobiography of Malcolm X*, pp. 434–35.
25. Edem.
26. Goldman, pp. 274–76; epilogue by Alex Haley in Malcolm X, *The Autobiography of Malcolm X*, pp. 436–37.
27. Edem.
28. Goldman, pp. 289–92.
29. Epilogue by Alex Haley in Malcolm X, *The Autobiography of Malcolm X*, p. 441; Goldman, pp. 291–92.

30. Goldman, p. 293; epilogue by Alex Haley in Malcolm X, *The Autobiography of Malcolm X*, p. 448.
31. Goldman, pp. 358–59.
32. Ibid., p. 349.
33. Ibid., p. 288; *New York Times*, February 23, 1965, p. 20.
34. Goldman, pp. 288, 335, 370.
35. Ibid., p. 310.
36. Ibid., p. 329.
37. Ibid.
38. Ibid., pp. 304, 310–11, 321.
39. Ibid., pp. 304, 321–22.
40. Ibid., p. 304.
41. Ibid.
42. Ibid., pp. 304–5, 323.
43. Ibid., p. 324.
44. Ibid., pp. 331, 333.
45. Ibid., p. 311.
46. Ibid., p. 331.
47. Ibid.
48. Ibid., p. 329.
49. Ibid., p. 329.
50. Ibid.
51. Ibid., pp. 313–14.
52. Ibid., p. 313.
53. Ibid., pp. 315–17.
54. Ibid., p. 315.
55. Ibid., p. 316.
56. Ibid.
57. Ibid., p. 317.
58. Ibid.
59. Ibid.
60. Ibid.
61. Ibid., p. 349.
62. Ibid.
63. Ibid., pp. 350–53.
64. Teresa, *My Life in the Mafia*, p. 178; Brill, *The Teamsters*, pp. 131, 139–40, 69–70; see entries 6.16, 6.18 of Appendix 4.
65. See initial segment of chapter 21.
66. See entries 21.26, 22.6, 22.13 and other entries in part V of Appendix 4.
67. Malcolm X, *By Any Means Necessary*, p. 51.
68. Allan Morrison, *Ebony*, October 1965, pp. 138–39; see James Farmer, *Freedom When?* (New York: Random House, 1965), p. 100.
69. Goldman, p. 367n, 373–74.
70. Ibid.
71. Mollenhoff, *Strike Force*, p. 113.
72. Demaris, *Captive City*, p. 14.
73. Mollenhoff, *Strike Force*, p. 113.
74. Ibid., pp. 112–13.
75. Demaris, pp. 64, 324.
76. *Life*, May 30, 1969, p. 45.
77. Scott, *Crime and Cover-Up*, p. 22.
78. Messick, *Secret File*, pp. 348–49.
79. Ibid.
80. Frank Hercules, "To Live in Harlem," *National Geographic*, February 1977, p. 201.
81. Ibid.
82. From a speech of Martin Luther King on August 28, 1963 in Washington, D.C., in *A Treasury of the World's Great Speeches*, edited by Houston Peterson, p. 839.
83. Martin Luther King, Jr., "Beyond the Los Angeles Riots. Next Stop: The North," *Saturday Review*, November 13, 1965, p. 34.
84. Louis Lomax, *To Kill a Black Man*, p. 165.
85. Ibid.
86. Mark Lane and Dick Gregory, *Code Name Zorro* (New York: Pocket Books, 1977), chapter 18.
87. *New York Times*, March 11, 1969, pp. 1, 16.

88. Ibid.
89. Ibid.
90. Ibid.
91. Ibid.
92. Ibid.
93. Ibid.
94. *New York Times*, March 14, 1969, p. 10.
95. *New York Times*, March 13, 1969, p. 22.
96. *New York Times*, March 17, 1969, p. 23.
97. *New York Times*, March 13, 1969, p. 22.
98. *New York Times*, June 11 and 13, 1978.
99. *Washington Post*, December 31, 1978, p. A1.
100. "The Politics of Conspiracy," conference at Boston University, general session, Morse Auditorium, February 1, 1975, tape-recorded by author.
101. Ibid.
102. *The Two Kennedys*, shown at Orson Welles Theater, Cambridge, Mass., March 14, 1976.
103. Ibid.
104. HAH-MLK 13H 267–68.
105. See chapters 5 and 19.
106. HAR 334.
107. HAH-MLK 13H 268, 274, 275, 278.
108. HAH-MLK 13H 275, 278.
109. Ibid.; HAR 353.
110. HAH-MLK 13H 278; HAR 353.
111. HAR 352, 305–6; see HAH-MLK 13H 272.
112. HAR 332.
113. HAH-MLK 13H 268.
114. HAH-MLK 13H 269–70.
115. HAH-MLK 13H 270.
116. HAH-MLK 13H 280–81.
117. *U.S.–House, OC Control*, pp. 416–17.
118. HAH-MLK 13H 280.
119. HAH-MLK 13H 268, 273.
120. HAR 387–88; names spelled as determined correct by the House Assassinations Committee.
121. HAR 387–88.
122. Ibid.; see HAH-MLK 13H 276–77.
123. HAR 387.
124. HAR 388.
125. Ibid.
126. Ibid.
127. Ibid.
128. Ibid.
129. HAR 385–86.
130. HAR 386.
131. Ibid.
132. Ibid.
133. Ibid.
134. Lane and Gregory, *Code Name Zorro*, pp. 301–2.
135. William Lambert, "Strange Help-Hoffa Campaign of the U.S. Senator from Missouri," *Life*, May 26, 1967, pp. 26ff.
136. Ibid.; see also William Lambert, "A Deeper Debt of Gratitude to the Mob," *Life*, November 10, 1967, pp. 38–38B.
137. William Turner, *Hoover's FBI*, p. 79.
138. Lambert, *Life*, May 26, 1967, p. 28.
139. Demaris, pp. 149–50; Messick, *Secret File*, pp. 349–50.
140. Edem.
141. Demaris, p. 143; see entry 25.4 of Appendix 4.
142. Messick, *Secret File*, p. 350; Lambert, *Life*, May 26, 1967, p. 28.
143. Demaris, pp. 149–50; Messick, *Secret File*, pp. 349–50.
144. Lambert, *Life*, May 26, 1967, pp. 28–29.
145. Ibid., pp. 26ff.
146. Ibid., p. 27.
147. Ibid., pp. 26–27. Long conveniently ignored the

fact that Hoffa himself was one of electronic snooping's "most widely known practitioners" (ibid., p. 27).

148. Lambert, *Life*, November 10, 1967, pp. 38–38B; see also Lambert, *Life*, May 26, 1967, pp. 26ff.
149. Lambert, *Life*, November 10, 1967, p. 38.
150. Lambert, *Life*, May 26, 1967, p. 28.
151. New York *Village Voice*, March 8, 1973, pp. 5ff.
152. Michael Canfield and Alan Weberman, *Coup d'Etat in America* (New York: Third Press, 1975), pp. 2, 123; statement by Theodore Charach at "The Politics of Conspiracy," conference at Boston University, general session, Morse Auditorium, February 1, 1975, tape-recorded by author.
153. Kaiser, *"RFK Must Die!"*, pp. 15–27; *New York Times*, June 5, 1968, p. 1.
154. Turner and Christian, *The Assassination of Robert F. Kennedy*, pp. xiii-xiv.
155. Ibid., p. 178.
156. Kaiser, p. 29; Turner and Christian, p. xiv. The photo of Kennedy with the necktie near his right hand was widely published, for example, in the *Los Angeles Herald Examiner*, "extra," June 6, 1968, p. 1; and Turner and Christian, photo section, p. 3.
157. Kaiser, pp. 26–30, Appendix A.
158. Aurelius, *The Meditations of Marcus Aurelius*, I.16.
159. See section 4.5 and Moldea, *The Hoffa Wars*, p. 150.
160. See chapter 4.
161. Sheridan, *The Fall and Rise of Jimmy Hoffa*, p. 300.
162. See chapter 9, Frank Chavez.
163. Sheridan, p. 407.
164. Ibid., pp. 406–8.
165. Ibid.
166. Turner and Christian, p. 54.
167. *New York Times*, June 5, 1968, p. 1.
168. Turner and Christian, p. xiii.
169. Ibid., p. 26.
170. Ibid.
171. Ibid., p. 27.
172. See section 5.4.
173. Noyes, *Legacy of Doubt*, pp. 232–35; Turner and Christian, p. 27.
174. Turner and Christian, p. 320.
175. Kaiser, p. 469.
176. Moldea, pp. 187, 256–58, 262; Teresa, pp. 4, 301, 307–9.
177. Teresa, pp. 4, 299.
178. Moldea, p. 187.
179. Kaiser, p. 176.
180. Ibid.
181. Ibid.
182. Houghton, *Special Unit Senator*, pp. 5–7, 89.
183. Ibid., p. 89.
184. Kaiser, pp. 209, 216–17; Turner and Christian, pp. 108–9.
185. WR 786–87.
186. Kaiser, pp. 205, 209; Godfrey Janson, *Why Robert Kennedy Was Killed* (New York: Third Press, 1970), p. 126; Turner and Christian, p. 216.
187. *U.S.–Senate, Kefauver Hearings*, part 5, pp. 391, 399–400.
188. Houghton, p. 191.
189. Jack Anderson's column, *San Francisco Chronicle*, December 31, 1970, p. 25.
190. Kaiser, p. 537; Turner and Christian, p. 220.
191. Turner and Christian, p. 220.
192. Ibid.
193. Kaiser, pp. 206, 322; Turner and Christian, p. 220.

194. Kaiser, p. 537.
195. Turner and Christian, p. 220.
196. Betsy Langman and Alexander Cockburn, "Sirhan's Gun," *Harper's*, January 1975, p. 18; Turner and Christian, pp. 162, 376, 379; Lowenstein, "The Murder of Robert Kennedy," *Saturday Review*, February 19, 1977, pp. 6–17.
197. Langman and Cockburn, "Sirhan's Gun," *Harper's*, January 1975, p. 18; Turner and Christian, p. 376.
198. A Los Angeles Police report dated July 8, 1968, reproduced in Turner and Christian, p. 376.
199. Langman and Cockburn, "Sirhan's Gun," *Harper's*, January 1975, p. 18.
200. Ibid.; Turner and Christian, p. 162.
201. A Los Angeles Police report dated July 8, 1968, reproduced in Turner and Christian, p. 376.
202. Lowenstein, "The Murder of Robert Kennedy," *Saturday Review*, February 19, 1977, pp. 6–7; Langman and Cockburn, "Sirhan's Gun," *Harper's*, January 1975, pp. 18–20; Turner and Christian, p. 162.
203. Langman and Cockburn, "Sirhan's Gun," *Harper's*, January 1975, pp. 18–20; Turner and Christian, p. 162.
204. Turner and Christian, p. 162.
205. Langman and Cockburn, "Sirhan's Gun," *Harper's*, January 1975 p. 18; Turner and Christian, p. 162; Lowenstein, "The Murder of Robert Kennedy," *Saturday Review*, February 19, 1977, p. 6; William Harper affidavit, December 28, 1970, reproduced in Turner and Christian, pp. 378–81.
206. Lowenstein, "The Murder of Robert Kennedy," *Saturday Review*, February 19, 1977, p. 8.
207. Filmed and tape recorded interview of Uecker by Theodore Charach in the film *The Second Gun*, shown at Boston University on February 1, 1975; Lowenstein, "The Murder of Robert Kennedy," *Saturday Review*, February 19, 1977, p. 8.
208. Edem.
209. William Harper affidavit, December 28, 1970, reproduced in Turner and Christian, pp. 378–81.
210. Turner and Christian, p. 158.
211. William Harper affidavit, December 28, 1970, reproduced in Turner and Christian, pp. 378–81.
212. Ibid.
213. Ibid.
214. Langman and Cockburn, "Sirhan's Gun," *Harper's*, January 1975, p. 26.
215. Turner and Christian, p. 178; Lowenstein, "The Murder of Robert Kennedy," *Saturday Review*, February 19, 1977, pp. 7–8.
216. Edem.
217. Turner and Christian, pp. 177–91.
218. Lowenstein, "The Murder of Robert Kennedy," *Saturday Review*, February 19, 1977, pp. 8–9.
219. Ibid., p. 9.
220. Turner and Christian, p. 172.
221. Ibid., p. 178.
222. Lowenstein, "The Murder of Robert Kennedy," *Saturday Review*, February 19, 1977, p. 10.
223. "Charts and photographs showing layout of Ambassador Hotel area where shooting occurred," series E, reproduced in Turner and Christian, photo section, p. 12; see Turner and Christian, p. 186.
224. Edem.
225. As reproduced in Turner and Christian, photo section, p. 11; see Turner and Christian, Exhibit 2, p. 347.

226. As cited in note 223.
227. Turner and Christian, Exhibit 4, pp. 350–51.
228. Ibid., Exhibit 3, pp. 348–49.
229. As cited in note 223; also Turner and Christian, pp. 178–81, 345–46, photo section p. 10.
230. Turner and Christian, pp. 187–88.
231. Ibid., pp. 9–10, 175–77, 241–44; Lowenstein, "The Murder of Robert Kennedy," *Saturday Review*, February 19, 1977, p. 9.
232. Turner and Christian, p. 191.
233. William Harper affidavit, December 28, 1970, reproduced in Turner and Christian, pp. 378–81; Langman and Cockburn, "Sirhan's Gun," *Harper's*, January 1975, p. 18; Turner and Christian, p. 162; Lowenstein, "The Murder of Robert Kennedy," *Saturday Review*, February 19, 1977, p. 6.
234. Filmed and tape-recorded interview of Cesar by Charach in the movie *The Second Gun*, shown at Boston University on February 1, 1975; Turner and Christian, pp. 165–68; Kaiser, p. 26.
235. Cesar interview in *The Second Gun*.
236. William Harper affidavit, December 28, 1970, reproduced in Turner and Christian, pp. 378–81.
237. Cesar interview in *The Second Gun*.
238. Turner and Christian, p. 161.
239. Ibid., pp. 161–62.
240. KNXT newscast, June 5, 1968, played in *The Second Gun*.
241. *France Soir*, June 6, 1968, p. 8 ("Un garde du corps de Kennedy, dégaine à son tour, fait feu de la hanche, comme dans un western").
242. Recorded in *The Second Gun*.
243. Turner and Christian, p. 165.
244. Ibid., pp. 165–66; *The Second Gun*.
245. Edem.
246. Turner and Christian, p. 166.
247. Ibid.; *The Second Gun*.
248. Turner and Christian, pp. 166–67.
249. *Los Angeles Herald Examiner*, "extra," June 6, 1968, p. 1, reproduced in Turner and Christian, photo section, p. 3.
250. Turner and Christian, photo section, p. 2.
251. Turner and Christian, p. 167.
252. Ibid., pp. 157–58.
253. Statement of Charach at "The Politics of Conspiracy," conference at Boston University, workshop on the RFK assassination, George Sherman Student Center, February 2, 1975, tape-recorded by author.
254. Ibid.
255. Ibid.
256. Ibid.
257. Ibid.
258. Ibid.
259. Reid, *Mickey Cohen: Mobster*, pp. 185–86.
260. Turner and Christian, p. 165.
261. Statement of Alex Bottus, as transcribed in Appendix 5.
262. Ibid.
263. Ibid.
264. Ibid.
265. Ibid.
266. Ibid.
267. Walsh, *New York Times*, September 10, 1973, p. 28; see section 16.2.
268. Edem.
269. Statement of Alex Bottus, as transcribed in Appendix 5.
270. Ibid.
271. See section 1.1.
272. Ibid.
273. Ibid.
274. Demaris, p. 120; see section 1.1.
275. Lyle, p. 267; Demaris, p. 120.
276. Allsop, *The Bootleggers*, pp. 169–70.
277. Ibid., p. 170.
278. See part V of Appendix 4.
279. See section 22c of Appendix 4.
280. Turner and Christian, pp. 163–64; also as reported by Charach in *The Second Gun*.
281. Cooper declared, "We will stipulate that these fragments did come from Senator Kennedy. We will further stipulate they came from the gun." As reported by Theodore Charach in *The Second Gun*.
282. A few moments after Cooper's stipulation, Wolfer testified, "Because of the damage, I cannot say positively that it was fired from that gun, that is Sirhan's gun." As reported by Charach in *The Second Gun*.
283. Reid, *The Grim Reapers*, pp. 187, 189–91; *New York Times*, January 7, 1969, p. 25; Kaiser, p. 229.
284. Edem.
285. *New York Times*, September 24, 1969, p. 41, August 26, 1969, p. 20, January 7, 1969, p. 25.
286. Edem.
287. Dorman, *Payoff*, pp. 47–49.
288. *Time*, November 21, 1977, p. 39.
289. Kaiser, pp. 229, 244–45.
290. Noyes, p. 238; Kaiser, p. 245.
291. Noyes, p. 238; Kaiser, p. 241.
292. Kaiser, p. 241.
293. Noyes, p. 238.
294. Ibid.
295. C. Ray Hall Exhibit 3, p. 2.
296. Reid, *Mickey Cohen: Mobster*, p. 103.
297. 14H 400–403, 473; HAH 9H 1044, 1050–51, 1061, 1073–74, 1078.
298. HAH 9H 1050, 1053, 1078.
299. Goldman, pp. 367n, 373–74.
300. See section 24.1.
301. Lane and Gregory, *Code Name Zorro*, pp. 301–2.
302. Lambert, *Life*, May 26, 1967, p. 28.
303. Houghton, p. 157.
304. Noyes, p. 238.
305. Ibid.; Houghton, p. 157.
306. See section 1.2.
307. Ibid.
308. See section 5.4.
309. Turner and Christian, pp. 109, 114–18.
310. Ibid., p. 116.
311. *Washington Monthly*, February 29, 1979, p. 7.
312. Turner and Christian, pp. 115–18, 152, 314–15.
313. See the displayed footnote earlier in this section.
314. *Washington Star*, July 12, 1979, p. 1.
315. Ibid.
316. See section 17.5.
317. Ibid.
318. Reid, *The Grim Reapers*, pp. 203–4; see entry 24.7 of Appendix 4. Nani is identified as a Mafia member in *U.S.–Senate, OC and Narcotics Hearings*, p. 308, chart D.
319. *Albuquerque Journal*, March 9, 1977, p. 1.
320. Ibid.
321. Gerth, "Richard M. Nixon and Organized Crime," in Blumenthal and Yazijian, p. 149.
322. See section 16.2.
323. Mickey Cohen, *Mickey Cohen: In My Own Words* (Englewood Cliffs, N.J.: Prentice-Hall, 1975), p. 233, cited in Moldea, p. 104.
324. See chapter 9, Mickey Cohen.
325. Noyes, p. 238.

326. Cohen, p. 233, cited in Moldea, p. 104.
327. Sheridan, p. 508; see section 16.2.
328. Kaiser, p. 241.
329. Moldea, p. 104.
330. See section 16.3, displayed footnote.

Conclusion

1. *U.S.–Task Force Report*, p. 24.
2. Quoted by Arthur Waskow in *The Freedom Seder* (Washington, D.C.: Micah Press, 1969), p. 52.
3. H.R. Exec. Doc. No. 188, 47th Cong., 1st Sess., serial set 2030 (1882), p. 1.
4. H.R. Exec. Doc. No. 1, 47th Cong., 1st Sess., serial set 2018 (1881), p. 917; H.R. Exec. Doc. No. 1, 48th Cong., 1st Sess., serial set 2191 (1883), p. 514; H.R. Exec. Doc. No. 58, 47th Cong., 1st Sess., serial set 2027 (1882), pp. 2–3; H.R. Exec. Doc. No. 188 (1882), pp. 1–3.
5. H.R. Exec. Doc. No. 188 (1882), pp. 1–2; H.R. Exec. Doc. No. 1 (1883), p. 514.
6. H.R. Exec. Doc. No. 188 (1882), pp. 1, 3; H.R. Exec. Doc. No. 58 (1882), p. 2; H.R. Exec. Doc. No. 1 (1881), p. 917.
7. H.R. Exec. Doc. No. 1 (1883), p. 514; H.R. Exec. Doc. No. 1 (1881), p. 921.
8. H.R. Exec. Doc. No. 188 (1882), p. 2; H.R. Exec. Doc. No. 58 (1882), pp. 2–3; 17 Op. Atty. Gen. 334 (1882).
9. H.R. Exec. Doc. No. 1 (1881), p. 921.
10. 17 Op. Atty. Gen 335 (1882).
11. 17 Op. Atty. Gen 334 (1882).
12. 10 U.S.C. 332 (1956). The original statute specified "land and naval forces of the United States" instead of "armed forces"; the other revisions are clarifications in wording which do not significantly alter the meaning.
13. 17 Op. Atty. Gen 335 (1882); H.R. Exec. Doc. No. 1 (1883), p. 514.
14. H.R. Exec. Doc. No. 1 (1883), p. 514.
15. *Ex parte Siebold*, 100 U.S. 371, 395 (1879).
16. *In re Debs*, 158 U.S. 564, 582 (1895).
17. *Encyclopaedia Britannica*, 15th ed., 1982, vol. 10, p. 649; Frederick B. Wiener, "Martial Law Today," *American Bar Association Journal*, August 1969, p. 730.
18. *Dictionary of American History* (New York: Charles Scribner's Sons, 1976), vol. 4, p. 341. Also, since 1794, more than 30 proclamations of dispersal have been issued (Wiener, "Martial Law Today," p. 730).
19. Schlesinger, Jr., *Robert Kennedy and His Times*, pp. 341–45; Theodore C. Sorensen, *Kennedy* (New York: Harper & Row, 1965), pp. 483–84.
20. Sorensen, *Kennedy*, p. 486; Schlesinger, Jr., *Robert Kennedy and His Times*, pp. 346–47.
21. Sorensen, *Kennedy*, p. 491.
22. Proc. No. 3497, September 30, 1962, 27 Fed. Reg. 9681; Exec. Order No. 11053, September 30, 1962, 27 Fed. Reg. 9693; *Alabama v. United States*, 373 U.S. 545 (1963).
23. 10 U.S.C. 333 (1956). The statute concludes with the following additional, rather technical, sentence: "In any situation covered by clause (1), the State shall be considered to have denied the equal protection of the laws secured by the Constitution."
24. HAH 5H 427; see section 5 of Appendix 4.
25. See section 4.6 of the text and section 6 of Appendix 4.
26. See section 5 of Appendix 4.

27. See sections 6 and 22a of Appendix 4.
28. See section 22 of Appendix 4, and the beginning of chapter 21.
29. See section 21 of Appendix 4.
30. See Part III of Appendix 4.
31. See section 18 of Appendix 4.
32. See section 17 of Appendix 4.
33. See sections 6 and 16 of Appendix 4.
34. See sections 20–24 of Appendix 4.
35. *U.S.–Senate, OC and Narcotics Hearings*, p. 538.
36. Ibid., p. 485.
37. Ibid., pp. 490, 497.
38. Ibid., p. 505.
39. Ibid., p. 615.
40. Salerno and Tompkins, pp. 311, 315–16; *U.S.–Senate, OC and Narcotics Report*, p. 118; see Valachi testimony in *U.S.–Senate, OC and Narcotics Hearings*, pp. 78–395.
41. Reid, *The Grim Reapers*, p. 162.
42. Anson, p. 317.
43. See, for example, Kennedy, *The Enemy Within*; Sheridan, *The Fall and Rise of Jimmy Hoffa*; Mollenhoff, *Tentacles of Power*; Brill, *The Teamsters*; and Moldea, *The Hoffa Wars*.
44. *U.S.–Senate, McClellan Labor Hearings*, p. 12524; see the beginning of chapter 7.
45. NBC Evening News, "Segment 3," September 7, 1977; see section 18c of Appendix 4.
46. See entry 18.19 of Appendix 4.
47. NBC Evening News, "Segment 3," September 7, 1977.
48. Grutzner, "How to Lock Out the Mafia," *Harvard Business Review*, March-April 1970, p. 58.
49. *U.S.–House, OC Control*, p. 87.
50. See entry 14.3 of Appendix 4.
51. Meskil, *Don Carlo*, pp. 154–59.
52. *U.S.–House, OC Control*, p. 87.
53. Dorman, *Payoff*, p. 272.
54. Stevenson, *Reader's Digest*, December 1973, p. 88.
55. See entry 18.10 of Appendix 4.
56. Ibid.; *U.S. Senate, OC and Narcotics Hearings*, pp. 624–25.
57. *Life*, February 14, 1969, p. 52; see entry 18.6 of Appendix 4.
58. *Life*, February 14, 1969, pp. 52–56; see entry 18.6 of Appendix 4.
59. Edem.
60. Edem.
61. See section 18a of Appendix 4.
62. Siciliano, *Unless They Kill Me First*, p. 136; see entry 18.9 of Appendix 4.
63. See section 6 of Appendix 4.
64. Ibid.
65. See section 12 of Appendix 4.
66. See section 17e of Appendix 4.
67. See section 9 of Appendix 4.
68. See section 11 of Appendix 4.
69. See section 16c of Appendix 4.
70. See section 18 of Appendix 4 and section 1.2 of text.
71. See section 17 of Appendix 4.
72. See part V of Appendix 4.
73. See sections 15a and 20a of Appendix 4.
74. See section 26 of Appendix 4.
75. See section 13 of Appendix 4.
76. See section 17c of Appendix 4; see below.
77. See section 15c of Appendix 4.
78. See entry 15.27 of Appendix 4.
79. See section 17e of Appendix 4.
80. See entry 15.23 of Appendix 4.
81. See entry 15.20 of Appendix 4.
82. See section 2 of Appendix 4.

83. See entry 15.21 of Appendix 4.
84. NBC Evening News, "Segment 3," December 12, 1977.
85. Davidson, "The Mafia: How It Bleeds New England," *Saturday Evening Post*, November 18, 1967, p. 29; *U.S.–Senate, OC and Stolen Securities, 1971*, p. 816.
86. Davidson, "The Mafia: How It Bleeds New England," *Saturday Evening Post*, November 18, 1967, p. 29.
87. Teresa, "My Life in the Mafia," p. 336, see p. 192.
88. Jack Anderson, "Medicaid Inquiry Hit by Violence," *Washington Post*, April 6, 1978, p. VA19.
89. Ibid.
90. Ibid.
91. Jack Anderson, "The Mob Taps Into Medicaid," *Miami Herald*, March 3, 1978, p. 7A.
92. Ibid.
93. Ibid.
94. Ibid.
95. "The New Mafia," *Newsweek*, January 5, 1981, p. 40; see section 19 of Appendix 4.
96. Grutzner, "How to Lock Out the Mafia," *Harvard Business Review*, March-April 1970, p. 58.
97. Ibid., p. 49.
98. Cook, *Secret Rulers*, p. 367.
99. Sources at the U.S. Department of Labor estimated that at least $385 million has been lost through Mob-tied loans by the Teamster Central States Pension Fund (Brill, *The Teamsters*, pp. 252–55).
100. See section 16.2, *C. Arnholt Smith and the U.S. National Bank.*
101. *U.S.–Senate, OC and Stolen Securities, 1971*, p. 737.
102. *U.S.–House, OC and Worthless Securities*, p. 1.
103. Ibid., p. 242.
104. Ibid., pp. 1–2; *U.S.–Senate, OC and Stolen Securities, 1971*, p. 862; *U.S.–Senate, OC and Stolen Securities, 1973*, p. 475; see section 13 of Appendix 4.
105. *U.S.–Senate, OC and Stolen Securities, 1971*, pp. 863, 869–70; *U.S.–House, OC and Worthless Securities*, pp. 1–2; *U.S.–Senate, OC and Stolen Securities, 1973*, p. 475; see section 17c of Appendix 4.
106. *U.S.–Senate, OC and Stolen Securities, 1971*, p. 863.
107. Ibid., pp. 74–75, 843–47, 862–63; Teresa, "My Life in the Mafia," pp. 265–272.
108. See section 13 of Appendix 4.
109. Ibid.
110. See entry 13.2 and section 13a of Appendix 4.
111. *U.S.–Senate, OC and Stolen Securities, 1971*, pp. 72, 1248–49; see entry 13.1 of Appendix 4.
112. *U.S.–Senate, OC and Stolen Securities, 1973*, p. 9.
113. Ibid, pp. 9–11, 20, 34–35.
114. *Washington Post*, August 30, 1982, p. 14.
115. *U.S.–Senate, OC and Stolen Securities, 1973*, pp. 42–43.
116. Ibid., p. 104.
117. Malachi Martin, *The Final Conclave* (New York: Pocket Books, 1978), p. 32.
118. Sindona's suspected links to the Mafia are mentioned in *Newsweek*, October 29, 1979, p. 38, and *The Denver Post*, March 5, 1980, p. 7. The special advantages enjoyed by Mafia-tied businessmen in Italy are discussed in section 7 of Appendix 4.
119. Martin, pp. 32–34; *Washington Post*, March 25, 1979, pp. H1, H4.
120. *Washington Post*, March 25, 1979, p. H1.

121. *Miami Herald*, March 5, 1980, p. 22A.
122. Gulf and Western's chairman, Charles Bludhorn, was on the board of directors of *Societa Generala Immobiliare* (Martin, p. 33), an Italian conglomerate dominated by Sindona (*New York Times*, July 24, 1977, p. 34).
123. Seymour M. Hersh, with Jeff Gerth, "SEC Presses Wide Investigation of Gulf and Western Conglomerate," *New York Times*, July 24, 1977, p. 34.
124. Ibid.
125. Reid, *The Grim Reapers*, pp. 119–23, 139–40; Waller, pp. 123–35; Hank Messick and Burt Goldblatt, *The Mobs and the Mafia*, pp. 195–96; Gerth, in Blumenthal and Yazijian, pp. 137–39.
126. *Washington Post*, November 27, 1979, p. A12.
127. Hersh, *New York Times*, July 24, 1977, pp. 1, 34; *Washington Post*, November 27, 1979, pp. A1, A12.
128. Hersh, *New York Times*, July 24, 1977, p. 34.
129. Jeff Gerth, statement at "The Politics of Conspiracy," conference at Boston University, workshop on organized crime, George Sherman Student Center, February 1, 1975, tape-recorded by author; *Time*, July 18, 1977, p. 71; see also *New Yorker*, October 20, 1975, p. 6.
130. Seymour M. Hersh, with Jeff Gerth, "Major Corporations Seek Korshak's Labor Advice," *New York Times*, June 29, 1976, pp. 1, 16.
131. Ibid., p. 16.
132. Ibid.
133. *Washington Post*, November 27, 1979, p. A12.
134. Ibid., p. 1.
135. Martin, *The Final Conclave*, p. 35.
136. *Washington Post*, March 25, 1979, pp. H1, H14.
137. Ibid.; *Newsweek*, October 29, 1979, p. 38.
138. *Washington Post*, March 25, 1979, p. H1.
139. *Denver Post*, March 5, 1980, p. 7.; *Newsweek*, October 29, 1979, p. 38.
140. Martin, pp. 28–29, 33.
141. Ibid., pp. 28–29, 33.
142. Ibid., pp. 28–29, 33.
143. Ibid., pp. 35, 71.
144. Ibid., pp. 35–36.
145. *Time*, October 9, 1978, p. 68. Earlier in 1978, a source familiar with the Vatican had predicted that the Sindona scandal would be an issue in the selection of Pope Paul's successor (Martin, pp. 71, 173–74, 239, 368).
146. *Time*, October 9, 1978, p. 79.
147. Ibid.
148. *Washington Post*, May 21, 1981, p. A29.
149. *New York Times*, September 25, 1981, p. A3; see *Washington Post*, May 21, 1981, p. A29.
150. *New York Times*, September 25, 1981, p. A3.
151. *Newsweek*, August 16, 1982, pp. 48–49.
152. Ibid.; *Washington Post*, July 10, 1982, pp. B6, B7.
153. *Washington Post*, July 10, 1982, p. B6; *Newsweek*, August 16, 1982, pp. 48–49.
154. *Washington Post*, July 10, 1982, p. B6; *Newsweek*, August 16, 1982, p. 49.
155. *Newsweek*, September 13, 1982, pp. 62, 65, August 16, 1982, p. 49, July 23, 1973, pp. 62–63; see entry 13.7 of Appendix 4.
156. *Washington Post*, July 10, 1982, p. B6.
157. Ibid.
158. Ibid.
159. Ibid.
160. *Newsweek*, September 13, 1982, pp. 62, 65.
161. Ibid., p. 65.
162. *Washington Post*, March 25, 1979, p. H1.
163. *Newsweek*, August 16, 1982, p. 48.
164. *Washington Post*, September 4, 1982, p. A24.

165. Ibid.
166. Ibid.
167. Ibid.
168. Ibid.
169. See sections 16.2, 17.6.
170. From a speech by Malcolm X at the founding rally of the Organization of Afro-American Unity, transcribed in Malcolm X, *By Any Means Necessary*, pp. 50–51.
171. "Las Vegas and Atlantic City are more like Mafia colonies than autonomous urban communities," noted *Public Affairs Series Special Report #13: The Mafia Today* (Los Angeles: Knight Publishing, 1977), p. 23. See also section 9 of Appendix 4.
172. Henry Chafetz, *Play the Devil: A History of Gambling in the United States from 1492 to 1950* (New York: Potter, 1960), pp. 29, 31.
173. Ibid., pp. 20–27.
174. See section 9 of Appendix 4.
175. Sondern, *Brotherhood of Evil*, pp. 58–59; Reid, *Grim Reapers*, pp. 146–47.
176. Sondern, pp. 59–60; Reid, p. 147.
177. Sondern, p. 60.
178. Sondern, p. 60; Reid, pp. 147–48.
179. Reid, pp. 147–48; Sondern, p. 60.
180. Reid, p. 148; Sondern, p. 61.
181. Reid, pp. 148–49; Sondern, pp. 61–62.

Appendix 3
Background on Jack Ruby's Telephone Records

1. CE 2302, p. 237; C. Ray Hall Exhibit 1.
2. CE 2303, p. 241; C. Ray Hall Exhibit 1.
3. C. Ray Hall Exhibit 1; WR 795.
4. 13H 454–55.
5. CE 2305.
6. WR 794.
7. CE 2305; CE 2309, p. 255.
8. CE 2302, 2303, 2308, 2309; JFK microfilm, vol. 5, pp. T9–18.
9. CE 1322, pp. 746, 758–59, 764–66.
10. 14H 543.
11. See chapter 20.
12. WR 344.
13. WR 333.
14. 14H 298, 13H 500.
15. One party called from Ruby's home telephone on July 21, 1963 is identified as a friend of George Senator (JFK microfilm, vol. 5, p. T16), Ruby's roommate. Senator did not move into Ruby's apartment, however, until November 1, 1963 (CD 722, p. 2).
16. CE 2302, 2303, 2308, 2309; JFK microfilm, vol. 5, pp. T9–18.
17. See section 20.2.
18. CE 1521–26; CD 4, p. 663; see sections 19.1 and 19.2.
19. CD 86, p. 486.

Appendix 4
Mafia Review: References by Subject

1. *Time*, May 16, 1977, p. 32; Reid, *The Grim Reapers*, p. 6..
2. Sondern, *Brotherhood of Evil*, pp. 58–62; Reid, *The Grim Reapers*, pp. 146–50.
3. Salerno and Tompkins, *The Crime Confederation*, p. 280.
4. *New York Times*, May 25, 1959, p. 1.
5. Lawson, "Carnival of Crime," *Wall Street Journal*, January 12, 1970, p. 1; *U.S.–Senate, Gambling and OC*, p. 509.
6. *Dallas Morning News*, March 28, 29, 31, 1973, p. A1.
7. "The Mob," part 2, *Life*, September 8, 1967, p. 94; *Life*, September 29, 1967, p. 35; Chandler, "The 'Little Man' is Bigger Than Ever," *Life*, April 10, 1970, p. 33. Also Reid and Demaris, *The Green Felt Jungle*, pp. 85, 88, 91.
8. Meskil, *Don Carlo*, p. 137.
9. Dorman, *Payoff*, p. 100.
10. *U.S.–Senate, Kefauver Report, Third Interim*, pp. 82–83.
11. Reid, *The Grim Reapers*, pp. 158–59, 329.
12. Chandler, in *Life*, April 10, 1970, p. 34.
13. Ibid., p. 33.
14. Noyes, *Legacy of Doubt*, p. 142.
15. Reid, *The Grim Reapers*, p. 160.
16. Noyes, p. 143; *U.S.–House, OC Control*, p. 412.
17. *U.S.–Senate, OC and Narcotics Hearings*, p. 652, chart C; Kennedy, *The Enemy Within*, pp. 229–30.
18. *U.S.–Senate, OC and Stolen Securities, 1971*, pp. 637, 772–73, 841.
19. Ibid., pp. 326, 267, 315, 317, 569.
20. *U.S.–Senate, OC and Narcotics Hearings*, p. 652, chart F.
21. Ibid., p. 551; Teresa, *My Life in the Mafia*, p. 254.
22. *U.S.–Senate, OC and Stolen Securities, 1971*, p. 814.
23. *U.S.–Senate, OC and Narcotics Hearings*, p. 652, chart B.
24. *U.S.–Senate, OC and Stolen Securities, 1971*, p. 72.
25. Ibid.
26. Ibid., p. 8.
27. Ibid., pp. 1248–49.
28. Ibid., pp. 326, 267, 315, 317, 569.
29. Ibid., p. 271.
30. Ibid., pp. 225–26, 281–82, 285–86.
31. Ibid., pp. 284–85.
32. Demaris, *Captive City*, p. 81.
33. *U.S.–Senate, OC and Narcotics Hearings*, p. 550, Exhibit no. 53.
34. *Life*, September 1, 1967, p. 44; Mollenhoff, *Strike Force*, p. 119.
35. Dorman, *Payoff*, pp. 252–54.
36. *U.S.–Senate, OC and Stolen Securities, 1971*, pp. 647, 662–63.
37. *U.S.–Senate, OC and Narcotics Hearings*, p. 248, chart A.
38. Meskil, *Don Carlo*, pp. 163–64.
39. *Washington Post*, November 16, 1979, p. A16; *Newsweek*, November 26, 1979, p. 94.
40. Anson, *"They've Killed the President!"*, p. 325.
41. "The Politics of Conspiracy," conference at Boston University, workshop on organized crime, George Sherman Student Center, February 1, 1975, tape-recorded by author.
42. Kennedy, *The Enemy Within*, p. 309.
43. *U.S.–Senate, OC and Narcotics Hearings*, p. 652, chart D; Gage, *Mafia, U.S.A.*, pp. 183–86, 382–85.
44. *U.S.–Senate, OC and Narcotics Hearings*, p. 652, chart F.
45. Ibid., chart C.
46. Ibid., p. 274, chart B.
47. "The New Mafia," *Newsweek*, January 5, 1981, p. 40.
48. Grutzner, "How to Lock Out the Mafia," *Harvard Business Review*, March-April 1970, p. 49.

49. Salerno and Tompkins, *The Crime Confederation*, p. 225.
50. As reprinted in Gage, *Mafia, U.S.A.*, p. 336.
51. *U.S.–House, OC Control*, p. 449.
52. *Time*, May 16, 1977, p. 33.
53. Bill Davidson, "New Orleans: Cosa Nostra's Wall Street," *Saturday Evening Post*, February 29, 1964, pp. 15ff.
54. *Time*, May 16, 1977, p. 33.
55. *U.S.–Senate, Gambling and OC*, p. 84.
56. See section 14 of this appendix.
57. See section 13 of this appendix.
58. See section 17e of this appendix.
59. See section 6a of this appendix.
60. *U.S.–Senate, Gambling and OC*, p. 84; Rufus King, *Gambling and Organized Crime*, pp. 33–34; *U.S.–Senate, Kefauver Report, Third Interim*, p. 95; Cook, *The Secret Rulers*, pp. 23–24; Allsop, *The Bootleggers*, p. xv; Ted Poston, "The Numbers Racket," *New York Post*, February 29-March 10, 1960, reprinted in Tyler, ed., *Organized Crime in America*, p. 264; Hutchinson, *The Imperfect Union*, p. 113; *U.S.–Senate, Kefauver Hearings*, part 5, pp. 1179–80; Dorman, *Payoff*, p. 154.
61. In 1960, Milton Wessel, former head of the U.S. Attorney General's special committee on organized crime, estimated annual graft from nationwide illegal gambling at $4.5 billion (Cook, *A Two-Dollar Bet Means Murder*, pp. 9–11), or $12.8 billion in 1980 dollars.
62. Mollenhoff, *Strike Force*, p. 231.
63. *U.S.–Senate, OC and Narcotics Hearings*, p. 550, Exhibit no. 53.
64. Mollenhoff, *Strike Force*, pp. 7, 29.
65. *U.S.–Senate, OC and Narcotics Hearings*, p. 508, Exhibit no. 39.
66. Reid, *The Grim Reapers*, pp. 75–78.
67. Demaris, p. 233.
68. *U.S.–Senate, OC and Narcotics Hearings*, p. 508, Exhibit no. 39.
69. Ibid.
70. *New York Times*, June 27–30, 1976, pp. 1ff.
71. Demaris, pp. 348–49.
72. *U.S.–Senate, OC and Narcotics Hearings*, pp. 248, chart A, 652, chart B.
73. Thomas Hage, "New Jersey—The Friendly State," in Gage, *Mafia, U.S.A.*, p. 307.
74. Waller, *The Swiss Bank Connection*, p. 126.
75. *U.S.–Senate, McClellan Labor Hearings*, pp. 12521, 12524.
76. *U.S.–Senate, OC and Narcotics Hearings*, p. 308, chart D.
77. Denny Walsh, "Banker Friend of Nixon is Target of U.S. Inquiry," *New York Times*, September 10, 1973, p. 28.
78. "The Mafia v. America," *Time*, August 22, 1969, p. 19; *Congressional Directory*, 1972, pp. 109, 292.
79. On November 15, 1979, Scotto was convicted of racketeering in a $300,000 shakedown of waterfront businessmen (*Washington Post*, November 16, 1979, p. A16; *Newsweek*, November 26, 1979, p. 94).
80. *U.S.–Senate, OC and Narcotics Hearings*, p. 508, Exhibit no. 40.
81. Ibid., Exhibit no. 39.
82. Demaris, pp. 62–63, 139–42, 151–65, 185, 251–52, 296; "The Mob," part 1, *Life*, September 1, 1967, pp. 42B-43.
83. Noyes, pp. 34, 240–44.
84. *U.S.–Senate, OC and Stolen Securities, 1971*, pp. 647, 669.

85. *U.S.–Senate, OC and Narcotics Hearings*, p. 274, chart B.
86. NBC Evening News, "Segment 3," June 1, 1978.
87. "The Mob," part 1, *Life*, September 1, 1967, pp. 18–21; Reid, *The Grim Reapers*, pp. 37–39.
88. *Time* (1971), in Gage, *Mafia, U.S.A.*, pp. 179–80; see entry 6.13.
89. Sheridan, *The Fall and Rise of Jimmy Hoffa*, p. 7.
90. Ibid., p. 280.

Appendix 6
Additional Underworld Contacts of Jack Ruby

1. HAH 9H 385, 419; *Dallas Morning News*, March 28, 1974, p. 1A.
2. See text below.
3. *Dallas Morning News*, March 28, 1974.
4. Ibid.
5. CD 104, p. 64. Joseph Campisi also reported that Chapman was acquainted with Ruby (CE 1748).
6. CE 1322, p. 742.
7. HAH 9H 419.
8. HAH 9H 425.
9. HAH 9H 418–21.
10. HAH 9H 422–24.
11. HAH 9H 418, 425.
12. CE 1475.
13. 14H 601–2; HAR 156; HAH 9H 423.
14. CE 1475.
15. CD 1102c; CE 1504.
16. CD 1102c; CE 1504; WR 794.
17. Edem.
18. C. Ray Hall Exhibit 1; CE 1227; 14H 112; CE 1228, 1504, 1764; WR 794.
19. CE 1693.
20. HAH 9H 527–28.
21. Ibid.
22. CD 1102d; CE 1692, 1754.
23. *Dallas Morning News*, March 29, 1974.
24. CE 1755.
25. CE 1755; CE 1322, p. 734. (Dave L. Miller Exhibit 1 and 15H 454 establish that Isadore and Dave L. Miller are brothers).
26. See section 9a of Appendix 4.
27. HAH 5H 115.
28. Ibid.
29. Ibid.
30. HAH 5H 161.
31. Wallace Turner, p. 127.
32. CD 84, p. 106.
33. HAH 5H 114.
34. CD 84, p. 106.
35. HAH 5H 115.
36. HAH 5H 223.
37. Ibid.; HAR 152.
38. CD 84, p. 106.
39. CE 1752.
40. CD 105, p. 135.
41. HAH 9H 382–83, 419; CE 1748; Alice Nichols Exhibit 5355; CD 4, p. 289; 14H 123.
42. HAH 9H 419.
43. CD 105, p. 135.
44. HAH 9H 359; see CE 1748 and CE 1752.
45. CD 105, p. 135.
46. CD 84, p. 229.
47. Ibid.
48. 14H 445.
49. *U.S.–Senate, AGVA Hearings*, summarized in pp. 629–31.

50. JFK microfilm, vol. 5, p. T12; CD 84, p. 229.
51. 15H 28–29.
52. 14H 445.

Appendix 7
Reports on Ruby by
"State and Federal Officials"

1. WR 801.
2. CE 1353.
3. Ibid.
4. CE 1628.
5. CE 1322, pp. 735–36. The FBI report describing
   these cards states that each bore the signa-
   ture of the name listed (CE 1322, p. 736), and
   Alexander's name was listed (CE 1322, p. 735).
   A microfilm of the actual cards reveals a
   signed card for each name listed, except that
   Alexander's card is curiously missing (JFK microfilm, vol. 5, pp. R13–28).
6. WR 334.
7. CE 1628.
8. Ibid.
9. CD 1102c.
10. CE 1180.
11. WR 794–95, 801.
12. C. Ray Hall Exhibit 1.
13. CE 1227.
14. 14H 112; CE 1228; CE 1504; CE 1764.
15. 5H 103; CE 1760.
16. CE 1760.
17. 5H 103.
18. Several exclusive night clubs and restaurants
    are owned and operated by the Mafia; exam-
    ples are reported in *U.S.–Senate, OC and Sto-
    len Securities, 1971*, p. 816; Teresa, *My Life in
    the Mafia*, pp. 119–20; Davidson, "The Mafia:
    How It Bleeds New England," *Saturday Eve-
    ning Post*, November 18, 1967, p. 29.
19. CE 1265; WR 793.
20. JFK microfilm, vol. 5, p. D20.
21. CE 2822; see section 8.3.
22. 14H 445.
23. 5H 205.
24. CE 1693.
25. CE 1475.
26. See Appendix 6, James Henry Dolan.
27. HAH 9H 355.
28. See chapter 9, Joseph Campisi.
29. CE 1184; CE 1300.
30. See chapter 9, Paul Roland Jones.
31. CE 3061; 14H 354.

Selected Bibliography

Following is a list of the most important references cited. U.S. Government documents are grouped separately after books and articles, alphabetically ordered by abbreviations designated for convenient cross-reference.

Allsop, Kenneth. *The Bootleggers: The Story of Chicago's Prohibition Era.* New Rochelle, N.Y.: Arlington House, 1968.

Anslinger, Harry J., and Oursler, Will. *The Murderers: The Story of the Narcotics Gangs.* New York: Farrar, Straus, and Cudahy, 1961.

————, with Gregory, J. Dennis. *The Protectors: The Heroic Story of the Narcotics Agents, Citizens, and Officials in Their Unending, Unsung Battles Against Organized Crime in America and Abroad.* New York: Farrar, Straus, 1964.

Anson, Robert Sam. *"They've Killed the President!": The Search for the Murderers of John F. Kennedy.* New York: Bantam, 1975.

Blumenthal, Sid, and Yazijian, Harvey, ed. *Government By Gunplay: Assassination Conspiracy Theories from Dallas to Today.* New York: New American Library, Signet, 1976.

Brashler, William. *The Don: The Life and Death of Sam Giancana.* New York: Harper & Row, 1977.

Brill, Steven. *The Teamsters.* New York: Simon and Schuster, 1978.

Buchanan, Thomas G. *Who Killed Kennedy?* London: Secker & Warburg, 1964.

————. *Who Killed Kennedy?* New York: Putnam, 1964 (substantially different from the Secker & Warburg edition).

Chandler, David. "The 'Little Man' is Bigger Than Ever." *Life,* April 10, 1970, pp. 31–36.

Cook, Fred J. *The Secret Rulers: Criminal Syndicates and How They Control the U.S. Underworld.* New York: Duell, Sloan and Pearce, 1966.

————. *A Two-Dollar Bet Means Murder.* New York: Dial, 1961.

————. *Walter Reuther: Building the House of Labor.* Chicago: Encyclopaedia Britannica Press, 1963.

Cormier, Frank, and Eaton, William J. *Reuther.* Englewood Cliffs, N.J.: Prentice-Hall, 1970.

Cressey, Donald R. *Theft of the Nation: The Structure and Operations of Organized Crime in America.* New York: Harper & Row, Harper Colophon Books, 1969.

Crile, George, III. "The Mafia, the CIA, and Castro." *Washington Post*, May 16, 1976, pp. C1, C4.

Davidson, Bill. "How the Mob Controls Chicago." *Saturday Evening Post*, November 9, 1963, pp. 17–27.

———. "The Mafia: How It Bleeds New England." *Saturday Evening Post*, November 18, 1967, pp. 27–31.

———. "New Orleans: Cosa Nostra's Wall Street." *Saturday Evening Post*, February 29, 1964, pp. 15–21.

Demaris, Ovid. *Captive City*. New York: Lyle Stuart, 1969.

Denison, George. "Smut: The Mafia's Newest Racket." *Reader's Digest*, December 1971, pp. 157–60.

Dorman, Michael. "LBJ and the Racketeers." *Ramparts*, May 1968, pp. 26–35.

———. *Payoff*. New York: Berkley, 1972.

Ehrmann, Herbert B. *The Case That Will Not Die: Commonwealth vs. Sacco and Vanzetti*. Boston: Little, Brown, 1969.

———. *The Untried Case: The Sacco-Vanzetti Case and the Morelli Gang*. 2d ed. New York: Vanguard, 1960.

Epstein, Edward Jay. *Counterplot*. New York: Viking, 1969.

———. *Inquest: The Warren Commission and the Establishment of Truth*. New York: Viking, Bantam, 1966.

Feuerlicht, Roberta S. *Justice Crucified: The Story of Sacco and Vanzetti*. New York: McGraw-Hill, 1977.

Files of Evidence Connected With the Investigation of the Assassination of President John F. Kennedy (official documents from the Texas Attorney General's investigation of the JFK assassination), 1963–64. In the Library of Congress rare book collection. Also on microfilm, Washington, D.C.: Microcard Editions, 1967.

Gage, Nicholas. "How Organized Crime Invades the Home." *Good Housekeeping*, August 1971, pp. 68ff.

———. *The Mafia is not an Equal Opportunity Employer*. New York: Dell, 1971.

———, ed. *Mafia, U.S.A.* Chicago: Playboy Press, 1972.

Gartner, Michael, comp. *Crime and Business: What You Should Know About the Infiltration of Crime into Business—and of Business into Crime* (selections from the *Wall Street Journal*, 1968–70). Princeton: Dow Jones Books, 1971.

Gerth, Jeff. "Richard M. Nixon and Organized Crime." In *Government By Gunplay*, edited by Sid Blumenthal and Harvey Yazijian, pp. 130–51. New York: New American Library, Signet, 1976.

Goldman, Peter. *The Death and Life of Malcolm X*. New York: Harper & Row, 1973.

Gottfried, Alex. *Boss Cermak of Chicago: A Study of Political Leadership*. Seattle: University of Washington Press, 1962.

Gould, Jean, and Hickok, Lorena. *Walter Reuther: Labor's Rugged Individualist*. New York: Dodd, Mead, 1972.

Grutzner, Charles. "How to Lock Out the Mafia." *Harvard Business Review*, March-April 1970, pp. 45–58.

Hersh, Seymour M., with Gerth, Jeff. "The Contrasting Lives of Sidney R. Korshak." Four-part series. *New York Times*, June 27–30, 1976.

Hilsman, Roger. *To Move a Nation: The Politics of Foreign Policy in the Administration of John F. Kennedy*. Garden City, N.Y.: Doubleday, 1967.

Houghton, Robert A., with Taylor, Theodore. *Special Unit Senator: The Investigation of the Assassination of Senator Robert F. Kennedy*. New York: Random House, 1970.

Hutchinson, John. *The Imperfect Union: A History of Corruption in American Trade Unions*. New York: Dutton, 1970.

Investigative Reporters and Editors Inc., Phoenix Project. Report on organized crime in Arizona. *Albuquerque Journal*, March 13–April 2, 1977.

Joesten, Joachim. *Oswald: Assassin or Fall Guy?* New York: Marzani & Munsell, 1964.

Jones, Penn, Jr. *Forgive My Grief: A Critical Review of the Warren Commission Report on the Assassination of President John F. Kennedy*, vols. I and II. Midlothian, Texas: *Midlothian Mirror*, 1966–67.

Kaiser, Robert Blair. *"R.F.K. Must Die!": A History of the Robert Kennedy Assassination and its Aftermath*. New York: Dutton, 1970.

Kantor, Seth. *Who was Jack Ruby?* New York: Everest House, 1978.

Kefauver, Estes. *Crime in America*. Garden City, N.Y.: Doubleday, 1951.

Kennedy, Robert F. *The Enemy Within*. New York: Popular Library, 1960.

———. "Robert Kennedy Defines the Menace." *New York Times Magazine*, October 13, 1963, pp. 15ff.

King, Martin Luther, Jr. "Beyond the Los Angeles Riots. Next Stop: The North." *Saturday Review*, November 13, 1965, pp. 33ff.

King, Rufus. *Gambling and Organized Crime*. Washington, D.C.: Public Affairs Press, 1969.

Kobler, John. *Capone: The Life and World of Al Capone*. New York: Putnam, 1971.

Khrushchev, Nikita S. *Khrushchev Remembers*. Translated and edited by Strobe Talbott. New York: Little, Brown; Bantam, 1971.

Lambert, William. "A Deeper Debt of Gratitude to the Mob." *Life*, November 10, 1967, pp. 38–38B.

———. "Strange Help-Hoffa Campaign of the U.S. Senator from Missouri." *Life*, May 26, 1967, pp. 26ff.

Landesco, John. *Organized Crime in Chicago*. Chicago: University of Chicago Press, 1968.

Lane, Mark. *Rush to Judgment: A Critique of the Warren Commission's Inquiry into the Murders of President John F. Kennedy, Officer J. D. Tippit and Lee Harvey Oswald*. New York: Holt, Rinehart & Winston, 1966.

Langman, Betsy, and Cockburn, Alexander. "Sirhan's Gun: Further Inquiries into the Assassination of Robert F. Kennedy." *Harper's*, January 1975, pp. 16–27.

Lawson, Herbert G. "Carnival of Crime." *Wall Street Journal*, January 12, 1970, p. 1.

Lepera, Patsy A., and Goodman, Walter. *Memoirs of a Scam Man: The Life and Deals of Patsy Anthony Lepera*. New York: Farrar, Straus, and Giroux, 1974.

Lewis, Norman. *The Honored Society: A Searching Look at the Mafia*. New York: Putnam, 1964.

Lomax, Louis E. *To Kill a Black Man*. Los Angeles: Holloway House, 1968.

Lowenstein, Allard K. "The Murder of Robert Kennedy." *Saturday Review*, February 19, 1977, pp. 6–17.

Lyle, John H. *The Dry and Lawless Years*. Englewood Cliffs, N.J.: Prentice-Hall, 1960.

McClellan, John L. *Crime Without Punishment*. New York: Duell, Sloan and Pearce, 1962.

McCoy, Alfred W., with Read, Cathleen B., and Adams, Leonard P., II. *The Politics of Heroin in Southeast Asia*. New York: Harper & Row, 1972.

Maas, Peter. *Serpico*. New York: Bantam, 1974.

———. *The Valachi Papers*. New York: Bantam, 1969.

"The Mafia: Big, Bad and Booming." *Time*, May 16, 1977, pp. 32–42.

"The Mafia v. America." *Time*, August 22, 1969, pp. 17–27.

Malone, William Scott. "The Secret Life of Jack Ruby." *New Times*, January 23, 1978, pp. 46–51.

Manchester, William R. *The Death of a President: November 20–November 25, 1963*. New York: Harper & Row, 1967.

Marchetti, Victor, and Marks, John D. *The CIA and the Cult of Intelligence*. New York: Dell, 1974.

Meagher, Sylvia. *Accessories After the Fact: The Warren Commission, the Authorities, and the Report*. Indianapolis: Bobbs-Merrill, 1967.

Meskil, Paul S. *Don Carlo: Boss of Bosses*. New York: Popular Library, 1973.

———. *The Luparelli Tapes: The True Story of the Mafia Hitman Who Contracted to Kill Both Joey Gallo and His Own Wife*. Chicago: Playboy Press, 1976.

Messick, Hank. *Lansky*. 2d rev. ed. New York: Berkley, Berkley Medallion, 1973.

———. *Secret File*. New York: Putnam, 1969.

———. *Syndicate Abroad*. New York: Macmillan, 1969.

Methvin, Eugene H. "How Organized Crime Corrupts Our Law Enforcers." *Reader's Digest*, January 1972, pp. 85–89.

———. "How the Mafia Preys on the Poor." *Reader's Digest*, September 1970, pp. 49–55.

———. "Mafia War on the A&P." *Reader's Digest*, July 1970, pp. 71–76.

"The Mob." *Life*, part 1, September 1, 1967, pp. 15–21; part 2, September 8, 1967, pp. 91–104.

Model, F. Peter, and Groden, Robert J. F. *JFK: The Case for Conspiracy*. New York: Manor Books, 1976.

Moldea, Dan E. *The Hoffa Wars: Teamsters, Rebels, Politicians and the Mob*. New York: Paddington, 1978.

Mollenhoff, Clark R. *Strike Force: Organized Crime and the Government*. Englewood Cliffs, N.J.: Prentice-Hall, 1972.

———. *Tentacles of Power: The Story of Jimmy Hoffa*. Cleveland: World Publishing, 1965.

Navasky, Victor S. *Kennedy Justice*. New York: Atheneum, 1971.

Noyes, Peter. *Legacy of Doubt*. New York: Pinnacle, 1973.

O'Donnell, Kenneth P., and Powers, David F. *"Johnny, We Hardly Knew Ye": Memories of John Fitzgerald Kennedy*. Boston: Little, Brown, 1972.

Oglesby, Carl, and Goldberg, Jeff. "Did the Mob Kill Kennedy?" *Washington Post*, February 25, 1979, pp. B1, B4.

Pantaleone, Michele. *The Mafia and Politics*. New York: Coward-McCann, 1966.

Peterson, Houston, ed. *A Treasury of the World's Great Speeches*. Rev. and enl. ed. New York: Simon and Schuster, 1965.

Ransom, Harry H. "Containing Central Intelligence." *New Republic*, December 11, 1965, pp. 12–15.

Reid, Ed. *The Grim Reapers: The Anatomy of Organized Crime in America*. New York: Henry Regnery, Bantam, 1970.

———. *Mickey Cohen: Mobster*. New York: Pinnacle, 1973.

———, and Demaris, Ovid. *The Green Felt Jungle*. New York: Trident, 1963.

Rogers, Warren. "The Persecution of Clay Shaw: How One Man Ruined Another and Subverted Our Legal System." *Look*, August 26, 1969, pp. 53–60.

Sackett, Russell; Smith, Sandy; and Lambert, William. "The Congressman and the Hoodlum." *Life*, August 9, 1968, pp. 20–27.

Salerno, Ralph, and Tompkins, John S. *The Crime Confederation: Cosa Nostra and Allied Operations in Organized Crime*. Garden City, N.Y.: Doubleday, 1969.

Salinger, Pierre. *With Kennedy*. Garden City, N.Y.: Doubleday, 1966.

Schlesinger, Arthur M., Jr. *A Thousand Days: John F. Kennedy in the White House*. Boston: Houghton Mifflin, 1965.

———. *Robert Kennedy and His Times*. New York: Ballantine, 1979.

Schulz, William. "The Mob's Grip on New Jersey." *Reader's Digest*, February 1971, pp. 111–15.

Scott, Peter Dale. *Crime and Cover-Up: The CIA, the Mafia and the Dallas-Watergate Connection*. Berkeley: Westworks, 1977.

———. "The Death of Kennedy and the Vietnam War." In *Government by Gunplay*, edited by Sid Blumenthal and Harvey Yazijian, pp. 152–87. New York: New American Library, Signet, 1976.

————. "From Dallas to Watergate." In *Government By Gunplay*, edited by Sid Blumenthal and Harvey Yazijian, pp. 113–29. New York: New American Library, Signet, 1976.

Sheridan, Walter. *The Fall and Rise of Jimmy Hoffa*. New York: Saturday Review Press, 1972.

Siciliano, Vincent. *Unless They Kill Me First*. New York: Hawthorn, 1970.

Smith, Sandy. "Corruption Behind the Swinging Clubs." *Life*, December 6, 1968, pp. 35–43.

Sondern, Frederic J. *Brotherhood of Evil: The Mafia*. New York: Farrar, Straus, and Cudahy, 1959.

Stevenson, Charles. "The Tyranny of Terrorism in the Building Trades, Special Report, Installment no. 1." *Reader's Digest*, June 1973, pp. 89–94.

Teresa, Vincent, with Renner, Thomas C. *My Life in the Mafia*. Garden City, N.Y.: Doubleday, 1973.

Thompson, Josiah. *Six Seconds in Dallas: A Micro-Study of the Kennedy Assassination*. New York: B. Geis Assoc., dist. by Random House, 1967.

Turner, Wallace. *Gambler's Money: The New Force in American Life*. Boston: Houghton Mifflin, 1965.

Turner, William W. "Crime is Too Big for the FBI." *Nation*, November 8, 1965, pp. 322–28.

————. *Hoover's FBI: The Men and the Myth*. Los Angeles: Sherbourne, 1970.

————, and Christian, Jonn G. *The Assassination of Robert F. Kennedy: The Conspiracy and the Cover-up, 1968–1978*. New York: Random House, 1978.

Tyler, Gus, ed. *Organized Crime in America: A Book of Readings*. Ann Arbor: University of Michigan Press, Ann Arbor Paperbacks, 1967.

Viorst, Milton. "The Mafia, the CIA, and the Kennedy Assassination." *Washingtonian*, November 1975, pp. 113–18.

Waller, Leslie. *The Swiss Bank Connection*. New York: New American Library, Signet, 1972.

Walsh, Denny. "The Governor and the Mobster." *Life*, May 2, 1969, pp. 28–32A.

————. "The Mob: It Racks Up Overtime on a Government Payroll." *Life*, February 14, 1969, pp. 52–56.

————. "The Mayor, the Mob and the Lawyer." *Life*, May 29, 1970, pp. 24–31.

Wennblom, Ralph D. "How the Mafia Drives Up Meat Prices." *Farm Journal*, August 1972, pp. 18–19.

————. "How the Mafia Gets Its Cut." *Farm Journal*, September 1972, pp. 24–26.

Winter-Berger, Robert N. *The Washington Payoff: An Insider's View of Corruption in Government*. New York: Dell, 1972.

Wise, David, and Ross, Thomas B. *The Invisible Government*. New York: Random House, Vintage Books, 1974.

X, Malcolm, with Haley, Alex. *The Autobiography of Malcolm X*. New York: Grove, 1966.

X, Malcolm. *By Any Means Necessary: Speeches, Interviews and a Letter by Malcolm X*. Edited by George Breitman. New York: Pathfinder, 1970.

U.S. Government Documents
listed by abbreviations used in citations

U.S.–Cargo Theft and OC: U.S. Department of Justice. Law Enforcement Assistance Administration. *Cargo Theft and Organized Crime: Desk-Book for Management and Law Enforcement*. DOT P 5200.6. Washington, D.C., 1972. TD1.8:C19/3.

U.S.–House, Assassination Appendix, JFK: U.S. Congress. House. Select Committee on Assassinations. *Investigation of the Assassination of President John F. Kennedy: Appendix to Hearings Before the Select Committee on Assassinations*. Hearings pursuant to H.R. 222 and H.R. 433, 95th Congress, and H.R. 49, 96th Congress. March 1979. 95th Congress, 2d Session. (Vols. 6–12.)

U.S.–House, Assassination Appendix, MLK: U.S. Congress. House. Select Committee on Assassinations. *Investigation of the Assassination of Martin Luther King, Jr.: Appendix to Hearings Before the Select Committee on Assassinations*. Hearings pursuant to H.R. 222 and H.R. 433, 95th Congress, and H.R. 49, 96th Congress. March 1979. 95th Congress, 2d Session. (Vol. 13.)

U.S.–House, Assassination Hearings, JFK: U.S. Congress. House. Select Committee on Assassinations. *Investigation of the Assassination of President John F. Kennedy*. Hearings pursuant to H.R. 222 and H.R. 433, 95th Congress, and H.R. 49, 96th Congress. September 6–December 29, 1978. 95th Congress, 2d Session. (Vols. 1–5.)

U.S.–House, Assassination Report: U.S. Congress. House. Select Committee on Assassinations. *Report of the Select Committee on Assassinations: Findings and Recommendations*. Report pursuant to H.R. 222 and H.R. 433, 95th Congress, and H.R. 49, 96th Congress. March 29, 1979. 95th Congress, 2d Session. H. Rpt. 95–1828, part 2.

U.S.–House, Crime in America: U.S. Congress. House. Select Committee on Crime. *Crime in America: Aspects of Organized Crime, Court Delay, and Juvenile Justice*. Hearings pursuant to H.R. 17. December 4–8, 1969. 91st Congress, 1st Session. Y4.C86/3:C86/6.

U.S.–House, Criminal Justice Hearings: U.S. Congress. House. Select Committee on Crime. *The Improvement and Reform of Law Enforcement and Criminal Justice in the United States*. Hearings pursuant to H.R. 17. July 28–September 18, 1969. 91st Congress, 1st Session. Y4.C86/3:L41.

U.S.–House, Federal Effort Against OC: U.S. Congress. House. Committee on Government Operations. *The Federal Effort Against Organized Crime: Hearings Before a Subcommittee of the Committee on Government Operations*. June 13, 20, and 27, 1967. 90th Congress, 1st Session. Y4.G74/7:C86/2/pt. 2.

U.S.–House, OC and Worthless Securities: U.S. Congress. House. Select Committee on Crime. *Organized Crime: Techniques for Converting Worthless Securities into Cash*. Hearings. December 7–9, 1971. 1972. 92d Congress, 1st Session. Y4.C86/3:C86/8.

U.S.–House, OC Control: U.S. Congress. House. Committee on the Judiciary. Subcommittee Number Five. *Organized Crime Control*. Hearings pursuant to S. 30 and related proposals. May 20–August 5, 1970. 91st Congress, 2d Session. Y4.J89/1:91–27.

U.S.–House, OC in Sports: U.S. Congress. House. Select Committee on Crime. *Organized Crime in Sports (racing)*. Hearings. May 9–July 27, 1972. 1973. 92d Congress, 2d Session. Y4.C86/3:C86/15/pts. 1–4.

U.S.–OC Control Act of 1970: *Organized Crime Control Act of 1970*. Pursuant to S. 30. October 15, 1970. 91st Congress, 2d Session. Public Law No. 91–452.

U.S.–Senate, AGVA Hearings: U.S. Congress. Senate. Committee on Government Operations. Permanent Subcommittee on Investigations. *American Guild of Variety Artists*. Hearings pursuant to S. 250. June 20–26, 1962. 87th Congress, 2d Session. Y4.G74/6:Am3/pt. 2.

U.S.–Senate, Bobby Baker Hearings: U.S. Congress. Senate. Committee on Rules and Administration. *Financial or Business Interests of Officers or Employees of the Senate*. Hearings pursuant to S. 212 and S. 221. February 19–26, 1964. 88th Congress, 1st and 2d Sessions. Y4.R86/2:F49/pt. 14.

U.S.–Senate, Gambling and OC: U.S. Congress. Senate. Committee on Government Operations. Permanent Subcommittee on Investigations. *Gambling and Organized Crime*. Hearings pursuant to S. 69. August 22–25, 1961. 87th Congress, 1st Session. Y4.G74/6:G14/pt. 1.

U.S.–Senate, Intelligence Report, Foreign Assassinations: U.S. Congress. Senate. Select Committee to Study Governmental Operations with Respect to Intelligence Activities. *Alleged Assassination Plots Involving Foreign Leaders: Interim Report*. November 20, 1975. 94th Congress, 1st Session. S. Rpt. 94–465.

U.S.–Senate, Intelligence Report, JFK Assassination: U.S. Congress. Senate. Select Committee to Study Governmental Operations with Respect to Intelligence Activities. *Final Report, Book Five, The Investigation of the Assassination of President John F. Kennedy: Performance of the Intelligence Agencies*. 1976. 94th Congress, 2d Session. S. Rpt. 94–755.

U.S.–Senate, Kefauver Hearings: U.S. Congress. Senate. Special Committee to Investigate Organized Crime in Interstate Commerce. *Investigation of Organized Crime in Interstate Commerce*. Hearings pursuant to S. 202 and S. 129. May 26, 1950–August 7, 1951. 81st Congress, 2d Session, and 82d Congress, 1st Session. Y4.C86/2:C86/pts. 1–19.

U.S.–Senate, Kefauver Report, Second Interim: U.S. Congress. Senate. Special Committee to Investigate Organized Crime in Interstate Commerce. *Second Interim Report*. Pursuant to S. 202. February 28, 1951. 82d Congress, 1st Session. S. Rpt. 82–141. *U.S.–Senate, Kefauver Report, Third Interim*: U.S. Congress. Senate. Special Committee to Investigate Organized Crime in Interstate Commerce. *Third Interim Report*. Pursuant to S. 202. May 1, 1951. 82d Congress, 1st Session. S. Rpt. 82–307.

U.S.–Senate, McClellan Labor Hearings: U.S. Congress. Senate. Select Committee on Improper Activities in the Labor or Management Field. *Investigation of Improper Activities in the Labor or Management Field*. Hearings pursuant to S. 74 and S. 221, 85th Congress, and S. 44, 86th Congress. February 26, 1957–September 9, 1959. 85th Congress, 1st and 2d Sessions, and 86th Congress, 1st Session. Y4.Im:7:L11/pts. 1–58.

U.S.–Senate, OC and Narcotics Hearings: U.S. Congress. Senate. Committee on Government Operations. Permanent Subcommittee on Investigations. *Organized Crime and Illicit Traffic in Narcotics*. Hearings pursuant to S. 17 and S. 278. September 25, 1963–July 30, 1964. 88th Congress, 1st and 2d Sessions. Y4.G74/6:C86/pts. 1–4.

U.S.–Senate, OC and Narcotics Report: U.S. Congress. Senate. Committee on Government Operations. Permanent Subcommittee on Investigations. *Organized Crime and Illicit Traffic in Narcotics*. March 4, 1965. 89th Congress, 1st Session. S. Rpt. 89–72.

U.S.–Senate, OC and Stolen Securities, 1971: U.S. Congress. Senate. Committee on Government Operations. Permanent Subcommittee on Investigations. *Organized Crime, Stolen Securities*. Hearings pursuant to sec. 4 of S. 31. April 27–August 4, 1971. 92d Congress, 1st Session. Y4.G74/6:C86/2/pts. 1–4.

U.S.–Senate, OC and Stolen Securities, 1973: U.S. Congress. Senate. Committee on Government Operations. Permanent Subcommittee on Investigations. *Organized Crime, Securities Thefts and Frauds* (Second Series). Hearings pursuant to sec. 4 of S. 46. June 29 and July 13, 1973. 93d Congress, 1st Session. Y4.G74/6:C86/2/973/pt. 1.

U.S.–Task Force Report: U.S. President's Commission on Law Enforcement and Administration of Justice. Task Force on Organized Crime. *Task Force Report: Organized Crime*. Washington, D.C. 1967. Pr36.8:L41/Or3.

U.S.–Warren Commission Hearings and Exhibits: U.S. President's Commission on the Assassination of President John F. Kennedy. *Investigation of the Assassination of President John F. Kennedy*. Hearings pursuant to Executive Order 11130 and S.J. Res. 137, 88th Congress. Washington, D.C., 1964. Pr36.8:K38/H35/v. 1–26.

U.S.–Warren Commission Report: U.S. President's Commission on the Assassination of President John F. Kennedy. *Report of the President's Commission on the Assassination of President John F. Kennedy*. Washington, D.C. 1964. Pr36.8:K38/R29.

Index

A&P Tea Co., 309
Aase, Jean, 259
Abadie, William, 80, 82–83, 105, 107, 301
Abati, Scappatora, 384
Accardo, Anthony, 15, 174, 372, 387
Ace Guard Service, 280
Acoustical Society of America, 24
Acropolis, John, 349
Adams, Joey, 233
Adamy, Clarence, 9, 310
Addonizio, Hugh, 28, 378
Adduci, James, 378
Adelstein, Bernard, 349
Adonis, Joe. *See* Doto, Joe
Aeschylus, 1
AFL, 15, 67, 351, 356
AFL-CIO, 9, 13, 67, 88, 347, 355
Agca, Mehmet Ali, 293
Aggie, Billy, 342
Agnew, Spiro, 178
Agro, Salvatore, 371
Aguirre, Felix, 172
Ahern, Frank, 384
Aiuppa, Joseph, 362
Akros Dynamics, 160
Alaimo, Dominick, 302
Alamotel, 51
Albert, Carl, 390
Alberto, Mr., 32
Alcatraz federal penitentiary, 90
Alderisio, Felix, 94–95, 197, 269, 350, 365
Aleman, Jose, Jr., 44–46
Alessio, John, 172, 280, 283, 384, 402
Alex, Gus, 379, 387, 391–92
Alexander, William, 100, 150, 244, 255, 406
Ali, Muhammed, 227
Alinsky, Saul, 7, 281
Alkana, Irving, 78, 90
Allegra, Melchiorre, 318
Allegretti, James, 70, 72, 231
Allen, O. K., 41
Allen, Rosemary, 101
Allsop, Kenneth, 7, 281
Alo, Vincent (Jimmy Blue Eyes), 109
Aloi, Vincent, 323
Alongi, Dominick, 320
Ambassador Hotel, 273–74, 276–77, 280

American Academy of Forensic Sciences, 18
American Bar Association, 189, 373, 375
American Guild of Variety Artists, 126, 220,
    230–38, 256, 259, 404–5
AMLASH, 184
Ammirati, George, 370
Anastasia, Albert, 304, 320, 323, 356, 380
Anderson, Jack, 94, 160, 193, 225, 290
Angiulo, Jerry, 229, 290, 325, 342, 366, 377
Annenberg, Moe, 108
Annunzio, Frank, 198, 388
Anslinger, Harry, 16, 38
Anson, Robert Sam, 37, 39, 156, 164–65
Anzelmo, Salvatore, 348
Apalachin Mafia convention, 44, 77, 85, 88,
    158, 193, 229, 302–5, 309, 318–19, 327,
    344, 351, 387
Armstrong, Andrew, 128–29, 131, 235, 248,
    256
Armstrong, Louis, 222
Arnet, George, 248
Arthur, Chester A., 285–86, 295
Arthur's Farm, 337
Arvey, Jake, 379
Aschkenasy, Ernest, 25
Associated Booking Corp., 90, 222
Auction City, 350
Audubon Ballroom, 267–68
Aurelio, Thomas, 372
Aurelius, Marcus, 273
Ayo, Anthony, 202
Ayotte, Eugene, 319

Bachelor's III, 338
Badalamente, Salvatore, 197–98
Badger State Cheese Co., 399
Baer, Maish, 66, 70
Bailey, John, 100
Baioni, Larry, 332, 383
Baker, Robert B. (Barney), 85, 97, 109, 226,
    237, 382
Baker, Robert G. (Bobby), 153, 171, 193,
    195–97, 269, 273, 392, 398
Bakery and Confectionary Workers Union,
    381
Baletto, George, 370
Ball, Joe, 141

Bals, Frank, 380
Banca Privata Italiana, 293
Banco Ambrosiano, 293–94
Banister, Guy, 49–50, 53
Bankers Trust Co., 348
Baptist Foundation of America, 198
Barbara, Joseph, 229–30, 302–3, 319
Barboza, Joseph, 319–20, 324, 329, 332–33, 337–38, 364, 378
Barger, James, 24–25
Barnett, Ross, 286
Barrett, James, 337
Barrigan, James, 102
Barrow, Clyde, 169
Bartels, John, 371
Bas, Marvin, 97
Batchelor, Charles, 406
Batista, Fulgencio, 96, 160, 162–63, 202
Battaglia, Sam, 94–95, 365
Battle, W. Preston, 271
Baum, William, 398
Bauman, Roger, 55, 256
Bay of Pigs Invasion, 49–50, 156, 183
Beauboeuf, Alvin, 51–52
Becker, Edward, 42–43, 191–92, 198, 205, 212
Bella Napoli Cafe, 370
Belli, Melvin, 141, 282
Bello, Manuel, 374, 390
Bellotti, Francis, 383
Bellows, Charles, 375
Beneen, Senator, 329
Bennett, Harry, 10
Berkshire Downs Race Track, 382
Bertram, Lane, 256–58
Bianco, Nick, 323
Bickers, Benny, 92, 104, 205
Binaggio, Charles, 377–78
Binion, Lester "Benny", 92, 99
Bintliff, Russell, 165, 176
Bioff, Willie, 357
Bischoff, Willie, 92, 203
Bishop, Joey, 190
Bishop, Melvin, 12–13
Bissell, Richard, 163
Bivana, Joseph, 302
Blackstone, Milton, Advertising Agency, 221
Blackwell, Charles, 267
Blakey, G. Robert, 28, 94, 213, 251, 363
Blankenhorn, Heber, 13
Blankenship, D. L., 103–4
Blassingame, Walter, 221
Bliss, George, 354
Block, William, 96
Blodgett, Julian, 43
Bludhorn, Charles, 292
Blue Angel Club, 214
Blue Ribbon Dairy Co., 74
Blunt, Marvin, 298

Bob Wills Ranch House, 77
Boccia, Ferdinand, 324
Bogard, Albert, 35–36, 247
Boggs, Hale, 184, 390
Boiardo, Anthony, 28
Bolles, Don, 395
Bolt, Beranek and Newman, Inc., 24
Bommarito, Joe, 322
Bompensiero, Frank, 357
Bonanno, Joseph, Jr., 188, 373
Bonanno, Joseph, Sr., 188, 302, 373, 396
Bonds, Joe. *See* Locurto, Joseph
Bonventre, John, 302
Bookbinder, Walter, 374
Boos, George, 13
Bosch, Juan, 168
Bosco, Phil, 299
Boston Celtics, 338
Boston Patriots, 337–38
Bottus, Alex, 280–81, 401–3
Bowen, Ann, 188–89, 373
Bowers, Dr., 31
Bowers, Lee, 22–23, 32
Boyd, Jerry, 189, 373
Braden, Jim. *See* Brading, Eugene Hale
Brading, Eugene Hale, 54–56, 59, 61, 255–56, 259, 262, 271, 404
Bradley, Eugene, 59
Bradley, Marshall, 257
Branch, Johnny, 108, 115
Brant, Jeff, 278–79
Bravo, Nicholas, 9
Breen, James, 82
Brennan, William, 382
Brescia, Matty, 189–90, 221
Brewster, Benjamin Harris, 285
Brewster, Daniel, 170
Briggs Manufacturing Co., 12–13
Brill, Stephan, 47
Brocato, James, 87
Brocato, Robert, 87
Broccoli, Stephen, 289, 354
Brogna, Vincent, 374
Brooke, Edward, 265, 382
Browder, Edward, 201
Brown, Edmund, Jr. (Jerry), 191, 283
Brown, Edmund, Sr. (Pat), 283, 384
Brown, Morgan, 55, 256
Brown, Neil, 288, 315, 318, 370
Brown, Oran, 35–36
Brown, Tom, 123
Browne, George, 357
Bruner, Terry, 339
Brunker, Albert, 378
Bruno, Angelo, 345
Bruno, Angelo, Mafia Family, 344
Bruno, Emile, 53
Bryant, Ann, 254

Buccieri, Fiore, 322
Buchanan, Thomas, 2, 113
Buckley, Gerald, 322
Buckley, William, 18
Budge, Hamer, 390–91
Bufalino, Russell, 158, 302, 344, 389, 398
Bufalino, William, 344, 394
Buffa, Thomas, 323
Bugliosi, Vincent, 277
Bull-Pen Restaurant, 123
Bund, 66
Bunker, Jerry, 127
Burgess, Dale, 241
Busacca, Ciccio, 264
Buscetta, Tomaso, 179
Butler, George, 74–77, 96, 99, 239, 324–25
Butler, Norman, 267–68
Buttitta, Ignazio, 264
Byrd, Glen, 101
Byrne, Bobby, 337
Byron, David, 68

Cabana Hotel, 259
Cady, Dick, 395
Cahill, Thomas, 384
Cahn, William, 337
Cain, Richard, 379
Cairns, John, 69–70
Calamia, Leonard, 384
Calgrove, Mrs. Paul, 103
Califano, Marshall, 94
Cal Neva Lodge, 92
Calvi, Roberto, 294
Camarata, Pete, 69
Campagna, Louis, 6
Campisi, Joseph, 41, 72, 85–87, 89, 92, 99, 109,
    144, 190, 216, 223, 254, 258–59, 262,
    405, 407
Campisi, Sam, 85
Candy Barr. *See* Slusher, Juanita
Cangiano, Gus, 335
Cannone, Ignatius, 302
Cantalupo Realty Co., 321
Capezio, Tony, 66
Capone, Al, 6–7, 65–66, 72, 94, 101, 106, 108,
    222, 233, 237, 253, 266, 281, 309, 319,
    325, 329, 351, 369, 378, 381, 387, 396–97
Capone, John, 72
Capone, Matty, 66
Capone, Ralph, 66
Capri Hotel, 92, 95, 405
Capucci, Anthony, 343
Caracci, Frank, 86–88, 109, 212–16, 220, 222,
    225, 263, 392
Carillo, Anthony, 320
Carlin, Bruce, 111, 125–28, 130, 132, 249, 258
Carlin, Karen, 107, 111–12, 122–23, 125–32,
    134–35, 137, 144, 241, 258, 260, 262

Carlisi, Roy, 302–3
Carlson, E. E., 102–4, 406
Carnivali, Turiddu, 264
Carno, Nick, 216
Caro, Robert, 170, 195
Carona, Vic, 58
Carousel Club, 78, 83, 91–92, 95, 97, 100–105,
    107, 111, 113, 115, 117–18, 120–23,
    125–29, 131–32, 149, 200, 206, 213,
    219–20, 223, 226, 234–36, 240–43,
    246–49, 251–56, 258, 260, 306, 405–7
Carr, Mrs. Billy Chester, 256–57
Carr, Wagoner, 197
Carramusa, Carl, 322
Carroll, Roger, 55, 255
Carson, Robert, 389
Carter, Cliff, 170
Carter, Jimmy, 179–80, 288
Carter, John, 30
Cartier, Raymond, 1–2
Cascio, Paul, 214
Castellammarese War, 329
Castellano, Paul, 302–3
Castro, Fidel, 44, 49–50, 52–53, 57, 92, 94–95,
    156–57, 159–60, 162–64, 171, 184, 198,
    201–5, 207, 225
Castucci, Richard, 338
Catalanotte, Joe, 322
Cateno, Gerardo, 302
Cavagnaro, Joseph, 100
Cavallaro, Charles, 398
Cavallaro, Thomas, 398
Cecere, Daniel, 177
Cellar Door night club, 259–60, 262
Cellini, Dino, 92, 331
Central Intelligence Agency, 44, 57, 94, 156–57,
    159–60, 162–63, 165, 168, 180, 183–84,
    190, 204, 245
Cermak, Anton, 5–7, 16, 108, 281
Cerone, John, 322, 376
Cervantes, A. J., 377
Cervone, Bobbie, 353
Cesar, Thane Eugene, 278–81, 283, 401–2
Chambliss, Robert, 209
Chankalian, Armand, 371
Chapman, Bobby Joe, 404–5
Charach, Theodore, 278–80, 401–3
Chavez, Cesar, 275
Chavez, Frank, 88, 109, 274
Cheramie, Rose, 31, 143
Cherry, Dave, 205–6
Chicago Crime Commission, 345, 351, 387,
    396
Chicago Metropolitan Sanitary District, 354
Chisholm, Shirley, 312
Chivi, Charles, 302
Chotiner, Murray, 173, 176, 283
Christian, Jonn, 274

Christian Democratic Party, Italian, 328, 386
Chrysler Office Building (Detroit), 345
Chrysler Office Building (New York), 359
Churchill, Winston, 10
Churchill Farms Plantation, 42–44, 51, 60, 212
Cianflona, John, 399
Cimino, Dominic, 365
CIO, 12, 15
Cipango's, 92
Cirello, Joseph. *See* Civello, Joseph
Civella, Nick, 322
Civello, Joseph, 3, 41, 77, 82, 84, 88–89, 107, 109, 297–99, 302
Clark, Ramsey, 270
Clark, Robert, 188, 373
Clemente, Michelino, 40, 303
Clemons, Acquilla, 34
Coakley, Daniel, 383
Coffey, Melvin, 51
Coffman, Stella, 248
Cohen, Mickey, 90–91, 109, 141, 176, 253, 280, 282–83
Cohn, Roy, 193, 273
Cole, Jack, 236
Coleman, Delbert, 391
Colletti, James, 303
Colombo, Anthony, 394
Colombo, Joseph, 290, 319–21, 323, 374, 393–94
Colombo, Joseph, Mafia Family, 319–21, 323–24, 339, 370–71, 374, 384
Colonial Inn, 85, 201
Colson, Charles, 175
Columbia Records, 339
Columbia University, 168
Colvin, Hershey, 71
Common Laborers and Hod Carriers union, 303–4
Conduit Workers union, 359
Conforto, Janet, 102, 117, 213–15, 253–54
Congress on Racial Equality, 265, 268
Conley, Gene, 338
Connally, John, 17, 113, 128, 185–86, 220, 242
Connally, Nelly, 17, 19
Connell, Thomas, 96–97
Considine, Bob, 30
Constantino, Mark, 374
Continental Press, 96
Cook, Fred, 73, 172
Cooke, Leon, 67–68
Cooper, Grant, 281–82
Corallo, Tony, 359, 381
Cornman, Leon, 214
Corollo, Anthony, 320
Corona Breeding Farm, 275
Cosa Nostra. *See* Mafia
Costello, Frank, 87, 108, 169, 194, 197, 269, 312–13, 319, 359, 372, 380, 390, 396

Cotrini, Giuseppe, 92, 203
Cotter, William, 335
Covelli, Gerald, 375–76
Crafard, Larry, 107, 121–22, 129, 137, 144, 226, 246–48, 252, 306
Craig, Roger, 36, 143
Craig, Walter, 188–89, 198, 373
Craven, Robert, 100
Cressey, Donald, 229–30, 311, 314
Crimaldi, Charles, 326
Crosby, James, 171–72
Crowe, William. *See* DeMar, Bill
Cuban Revolutionary Council, 49, 53
Cucchiara, Frank, 303
Cudak, Robert, 319, 323, 343
Curry, Eileen, 82–83
Curry, Jesse, 22, 100, 123
Curtis, Carl, 41
Cushing, Richard Cardinal, 18
Cutrone, John, 323
Cy's Wee Wash It, 127

D'Agostino, Dominick, 303
D'Anna, Anthony, 10
D'Arco, John, 388
Dal-Tex Building, 54, 59, 262
Dale, Joy, 83
Daley, Richard, 379
Dalitz, Moe, 109, 388
Dalla Chiesa, Carlo, 294
Dallas Cowboys, 404
Dallas Criminal Courts Building, 54
Dallas Federal Parole Building, 55
Dallas Morning News Building, 113, 260–61
Dallas Police Building, 111, 114–15, 124, 132–36, 139, 260
Dallas Records Building, 54
Dallas Times Herald Building, 118, 121
Datacomp Corp., 197–98
Davis, George, 45
Davis, Sammy, 190
Dawson, William, 391–92
Dealey Plaza, 3, 19, 23–25, 32, 36, 54, 120, 210, 250, 262
Dean, John, 174–75, 178
Deauville Gambling Casino, 95
DeCarlo, Angelo (Ray), 177–78, 211, 339, 371–72
DeCavalcante, Sam, 290, 317, 353
DeCavalcante, Sam, Mafia Family, 398
DeCavalcante tapes, 177, 317, 322, 353
Decker, Bill, 22, 99–101, 136, 140–44
DeFeo, Mike, 391
DeGalindez, Jesus, 168
DeJohn, Nick, 76, 384
DeLamielleure, Albert, 13, 282
Del Charro Hotel, 193
Dellacroce, Aniello, 320, 347

Del Mar Race Track, 193, 275
Delmore, Nick, 352–53
DeLoach, Cartha, 192
DeLucia, Paul, 387–88
DeMar, Bill, 240–41, 245, 247
Demaris, Ovid, 68
DeMohrenschilt, George, 36
De Mooco, John, 303
Denet, Leo, 70
Department of Justice, 16, 38, 47, 94, 169, 176, 178–79, 190, 194, 196–97, 213, 222, 314, 356, 365, 379, 386
Department of Transportation, 314
DePaula, Frank, 338
DeSapio, Carmine, 381
Desaulnier, Edward, Jr., 374
Desimone, Frank, 303
DeStefano, Sam, 326, 372, 376
Detroit-Michigan Stove Works, 12
Deutsch, Sidney, 379
Dibrell, T. Kellis, 170
Dickey, O. C., 161
DiLeo, Lucas, 272
DiLorenzo, Matteo, 399
DiMase, Carmine, 371
Dioguardi, Johnny, 15, 323, 359
Dioguardi, Tommy, 359
DiPiazza, Sam, 272
DiPierro, Angelo, 277
Dirksen, Everett, 392
Ditta, Nick, 317
DiVarco, Joseph, 376
Dodd, Richard, 20–22
Dolan, James Henry, 232, 235–36, 404–5, 407
Donneroummas, Frank, 275–76
Donovan, William, 160–61
Doonesbury, 191, 283
Dorfman, Allen, 69, 94–95, 174–76
Dorfman, Paul, 67–69, 88, 94, 108
Dorman, Michael, 28, 75, 98, 289
Doto, Joe, 10, 201, 302, 380
Douglas, Helen Gahagan, 176
Douglas, William, 391
Dowe, Kenneth, 83, 123
Downtown Lincoln-Mercury dealership, 35
Doyle, Everett, 349
Dragna, Jack, 96, 206, 303
Dranow, Benjamin, 221
Dream Bar, 219, 232
Dream Lounge, 405
Drug Enforcement Administration, 85
Drury, William, 96–97
Dryer, Betty, 280
Duff, James, 385
Duffy, William, 315, 320, 364–65, 369
Dukakis, Michael, 182
Dulles, Allen, 163, 183–84
Dumont Corp., 197–98

Duncan, Glen, 115, 117
Dunn, Lt., 382
DuPont, Henry, 291, 333
Durso, Thomas, 369
Dyson, W. F., 255

Earle, George, 385
Eastland, James, 271
Ebb Tide Restaurant, 338
Eberhardt, August, 114
Eboli, Thomas, 320
Eden Roc Hotel, 93, 226
Edwards, George, 15–16, 312, 316, 322, 327, 330, 365
Edwards, Sheffield, 163
Egyptian Lounge, 85–86, 190, 258–59
Ehrlichman, John, 174–75
Eisenhower, Dwight, 156, 173
Elko, Stephen, 389
Ellington, Duke, 222
Ellis, Ben, 255
Ellis Park Race Track, 97
Elrod, Arthur, 379
Emerson, Wald, 280
Epstein, Ben, 69
Epstein, Edward, 57
Ervay Theater, 77
Ervin, Sam, 41, 189
Esposito, Frank, 322
Euzzino, Andrew, 352
Evola, Natale, 303

Faircloth, Earl, 251
Fair Play for Cuba Committee, 52
Falcone, Joseph, 303
Falcone, Pasquale, 339
Falcone, Salvatore, 303
Farmer, James, 268–69
Farrell, Lew. *See* Fratto, Luigi
Fascell, Dante, 360
Fast, Ernest, 231–32
Faye, Bobby, 233, 238
Federal Bureau of Investigation, *passim*
Federal Bureau of Narcotics, 91, 317, 332
Federici, Joseph, 253–55
Federici, Sandy, 253–55
Fensterwald, Bernard, Jr., 272–73, 282
Ferrie, David, 43, 49–53, 56–57, 61, 212, 271
Fillmon, Gloria, 254
Fine, John, 385
Fingerlakes Racetrack, 384
Fiorini, Frank. *See* Sturgis, Frank
Fithian, Floyd, 236
Fitzsimmons, Frank, 69, 174–76
Five Hundred Club, 212, 215–16
Flamingo Hotel, 391
Flood, Daniel, 158, 389
Flowers, Mr., 55

Floyd, "Pretty Boy", 169
Folies Bergere, 115
Fong, Hiram, 389
Food and Drug Administration, 310
Food Handlers union, 359
Ford, Gerald, 138–39, 143, 148, 179–80, 185, 288, 390
Ford, Henry, 10
Ford Motor Co., 10
Foreman, Leo, 372
Foreman, Percy, 270
Forsythe, Norman, 197
Fortas, Abe, 197
Four Seasons, 339
Fowler, Clayton, 244
Franklin National Bank, 172, 292–94
Franko, Frank, 398
Fratianno, James, 55, 232, 404
Fratto, Luigi, 382, 393
Frederici, Joseph. *See* Federici, Joseph
Friar's Club, 282
Fritz, Bill, 101, 114, 136
Frizzi, Guy, 324
Fry, John, 12
Fullerton Metals Co., 350
Furci, Frank, 165

Gage, Nicholas, 315
Gagliano, Frank, 320
Gaity Club, 70–71
Galba, Emperor, 181
Galente, Carmine, 179, 275, 332
Galiano, Dominic, 337
Gallagher, Cornelius, 228, 386
Gallina, Gino, 324, 387
Gallinaro, William, 321
Gallinghouse, G., 58
Gallo, Joseph, 320, 323, 358
Gallup Poll, 18
Gambino, Carlo, 179, 302–3, 317, 320, 343, 350, 359, 399
Gambino, Carlo, Mafia Family, 318, 320, 335–37, 345, 347, 350, 355, 376, 387, 399
Gandhi, Mahatma, 285
Garafalo, Bartholomew, 372
Garafola, Anthony, 335
Gardner, Mr., of Ambassador Hotel, 280
Gargano, Michael, 369
Gargotta, Charles, 377–78, 380
Garner, Darrell, 33–34
Garrison, Jim, 13, 31, 49, 56–61, 239, 273–74, 282
Genovese, Michael, 303
Genovese, Vito, 108, 144, 161, 169, 206, 229, 254, 303–4, 324, 380
Genovese, Vito, Mafia Family, 39, 88–89, 109, 177, 320, 334, 336, 343, 355, 380–81, 387, 398–400

Gentile, Nicola, 318, 328
Geoghegan, William, 38
Gershwin, George, 157
Gerth, Jeff, 171, 173, 347, 357
Gervais, Pershing, 57
Giancana, Sam, 46, 92–94, 96, 163, 197, 225, 227, 269, 379, 383, 387–88, 392
Giancana, Sam, Mafia Family, 379
Giardano, Tony, 352, 377
Gibbons, Harold, 47
Gibson, Kenneth, 378
Gilbain Building Co., 289, 354
Gill, G. Wray, 50–52, 56
Gill, James, 59
Glaser, Joseph, 90, 222–23, 233, 237–38, 263
Glickman, Bernie, 227
Glimco, Joseph, 352, 376
Glitta, Mike, 365
Golden, William, 399
Goldman, Peter, 267, 269
Goldstein, Frank, 66, 227, 238
Gordon, Waxey, 108
Gorman, Richard, 375–76
Gosper, John J., 285
Graffagnini, Nicholas, 88, 212, 214–15, 220
Grande Cheese Co., 399
Granello, Salvatore, 390
Grant, Eva, 29, 67, 78, 86, 90, 128, 131, 215, 219, 222, 226, 248, 259, 306, 405
Green, Milton, 358
Green, Shirley, 370–71
Greene, Bob, 395
Gregory, Dick, 271
Gremillion, Jack, 348
Gribler, Joe, 68–69
Griffin, Burt, 145, 183, 203, 207, 255
Gross, Murray, 333, 348
Groussard, Serge, 1–2
Gruber, Alexander, 91, 227, 237, 243, 252–53
Grutzner, Charles, 314
Guarnieri, Anthony, 303
Guccia, Bartolo, 303
Guglielmo, John, 92, 203
Gulf and Western Corp., 222, 292
Gurney, Edward, 321, 334
Guthman, Edwin, 274
Guthrie, Steve, 73–77, 83, 96, 99, 324–25
Guzik, Jake, 96–97
Gym Club, 66

H&H Restaurant, 66
Haber, Joyce, 221
Haggerty, Ed, 58
Haldeman, H. R., 174–76
Haley, Alex, 266
Halfen, Jack, 169, 393
Hall, Harry, 81–83, 105, 107, 116
Hall, Travis, 101

Hallmark, Garrett, 123
Hampco Meat Co., 197
Hand, Peter, 313
Hanes, Arthur, 271
Hannan, Eddie, 370
Hansen, T. M., 260
Hardee, Jack, 81–83, 105, 247
Hargis, Bobby, 26
Harper, Carl, 31
Harper, William, 276, 278–79
Harris, Louis, Poll, 56
Harvard University, 4, 295
Hatcher, Richard, 378
Hawkins, Ray, 100
Hayer, Talmadge, 267–69, 282
Hayes, Floyd, 369
Hazel Park Race Track, 345
Helen Bar, 14
Helmick, Wanda, 123
Hemming, Gerry, 205
Hennessey, David, 296, 315, 328
Henrici's Restaurant, 222
Hercules, Frank, 269
Hernando's Hideaway, 77
Herring, Charles, 169
Hersh, Seymour, 162
Hill, Gladwin, 90
Hill, Thomas, 118, 207
Hill's Liquor Store, 298, 300
Hoffa, Jimmy, 13, 37, 40, 45–48, 59–61, 67,
    84–85, 87–88, 90–91, 94–96, 118, 160,
    163, 170, 173, 175–76, 189, 193, 197, 209,
    218, 225–26, 230, 232, 253, 263, 269,
    273–75, 382, 385, 392–95
Holiday Inn Casino, 93
Holland, S. M., 19–24, 26
Holovachka, Metro, 358
Hoover, J. Edgar, 18, 148, 182–84, 192–96,
    198–99, 270, 273, 295, 384, 390, 407
Horner, Henry, 67
Horseshoe Club, 92
Hotel and Restaurant Employees union, 8,
    303
Houghton, Robert, 55, 275
House Assassinations Committee. *See* House
    Select Committee on Assassinations
House Judiciary Committee, 375
House Select Committee on Assassinations,
    4, 18–19, 21, 24–28, 31–33, 36, 40,
    42–45, 47–48, 50, 52–54, 62, 75–76,
    85–87, 93–96, 106, 114, 116, 122, 147,
    149, 163–64, 183, 187, 190, 192, 204,
    212–13, 215, 220, 225–26, 232, 237–38,
    247, 251, 253, 258, 271–72, 317, 388
House Select Committee on Crime, 52, 173,
    197–98, 347, 384
Howard, Tom, 29, 116, 122, 135–36

Howard Johnson's restaurant, Arlington,
    Texas, 220
Hoy, David, 240–41
Hubert, Leon, 145, 203, 207, 255
Huddleston, Walter, 351
Hudson, Charles, 376
Hudson, John, 204
Hughes, John, 265, 312
Humes, James, 185
Humphreys, Murray, 66, 387–88
Hundley, William, 194
Hunt, E. Howard, 156, 175
Hunt, H. L., 81, 145, 159, 168, 207, 255
Hunt, Lamar, 55, 207, 255–56
Hunt, Nelson Bunker, 55, 159, 207, 255–56
Hunt, Sam, 66
Hunt & Wesson Corp., 74
Hunter, Bill, 29, 122
Hunt Oil Co., 55, 207, 255–56
Husman, Governor, 91

Ice Pick Barney, 320
Ida, Joseph, 303
Igoe, Michael, 352, 376
Illinois Crime Commission, 70
Immigration and Naturalization Service, 87,
    203
Impelitteri, Vincent, 381
Inciso, Angelo, 15–16
Internal Revenue Service, 39, 58, 108, 172, 178,
    292, 326, 330, 382, 385, 391
International Alliance of Theatre Stage
    Employees, 94, 221, 357
International Brotherhood of Electrical
    Workers, 357
International Brotherhood of Teamsters, 8–9,
    13, 37–38, 45–47, 59, 67, 69, 84–85, 88,
    91–93, 95–97, 109, 143, 145, 160, 163,
    170, 173–76, 193, 195–98, 218, 220, 223,
    225–26, 230–32, 237–38, 253, 259, 263,
    269, 272–74, 282, 289, 291–92, 336, 347,
    349, 351, 353–54, 356–57, 359, 369, 382,
    385, 391, 393–95
International Longshoremen's Association, 8,
    289, 355–56, 387
International Union of Operating Engineers,
    8, 354
Investigative Reporters and Editors Group,
    395
Isaacs, Godfrey, 280
Italian-American Civil Rights League, 393–94
Ivey, J. T., 100

J&J Cartage Company, 397
Jace, Mike, 343
Jackson, George, 392

Jackson, Henry, 98, 178, 369
Jackson, William, 322
Jacobs, Clarence, 13–14
Jada. *See* Conforto, Janet
Jarnagin, Carroll, 241–43, 245, 247
Jaworski, Leon, 139
Jefferson, Thomas, 295
Jesus of Nazareth, 154, 264
Joesten, Joachim, 30, 159
John Birch Society, 118, 142, 146, 159, 207
John Paul I, Pope, 293
John Paul II, Pope, 293
Johnson, Blaney Mack, 200–201, 203
Johnson, Clemon, 20–21
Johnson, Lyndon, 18, 158–59, 167–71, 180, 184,
     193–98, 220, 262, 264, 288, 342, 363,
     386, 392, 398
Johnson, Thomas, 267–68
Johnston, Frank, 115
Jones, Clifford, 397
Jones, Janice, 102
Jones, Paul Roland, 67, 69, 74–77, 82, 84, 91, 96,
     99, 102, 109, 116, 138, 252, 324, 407
Jones, Penn, 30
Joseph, Ellis, 97
Joseph's Department Store, 350
Josephus, Flavius, 154

Kahoe, E. Michael, 316
Kaiser, Robert Blair, 275
Kaminsky, Eileen, 103, 139
Kantor, Seth, 91, 113–14, 220, 253
Kappler, Herbert, 177
Kattar, George, 382
Katzenbach, Nicholas, 18, 183, 195, 375
Kavner, Richard, 88
Kay, Kathy, 118–21, 137, 144
Kefauver, Estes, 10, 41
Kefauver Committee. *See* Senate Special
     Committee to Investigate Organized
     Crime in Interstate Commerce
Kehoe, John, 396
Kelly, Herbert, 101, 104
Kelly, Jack, 70, 116
Kenmore Hospital, 290
Kennedy, Caroline, 116, 139, 149
Kennedy, Jacqueline, 17, 19, 116, 149
Kennedy, John F., Airport, 289, 336
Kennedy, John F., *passim*
Kennedy, Regis, 51
Kennedy, Robert F., *passim*
Kenney, John, 293, 372
Kent State University, 24
Kenyatta, Charles, 269
Kerner, Otto, 266
Key Biscayne Bank, 171
Khrushchev, Nikita, 157, 164
Kilgallen, Dorothy, 30

Killam, Earl, 31
Killam, Hank, 30–31
Killam, Wanda, 30–31
Kilpatrick, John, 15–16
King, Martin Luther, Jr., 1, 18, 157, 194, 264,
     269–70, 272, 282, 311
King, Rufus, 98
Kirk, Travis, 136, 247
Kirkwood, Pat, 259–60, 262–63
Kistle, Oscar, 205
Kleindienst, Richard, 174
KLIF Radio Station, 117–20, 123, 145, 189, 222
Knapp Commission, 364
Knight, Russ. *See* Moore, Russ "Knight"
KNXT-TV, 54
Koethe, Jim, 29, 122
Kohlman, Herbert, 51
Kohn, Aaron, 40, 58–59, 79, 87, 93, 312–13, 315,
     338, 369
Korshak, Marshall, 379
Korshak, Sidney, 90, 190–92, 198, 205, 221–23,
     233, 238, 283, 292, 379, 390–93
Kreig, Margaret, 310
Ku Klux Klan, 271
Kutner, Louis, 76
Ky, Nguyen Cao, 165

L&P Milk Co., 74
Laborers' International Union of America, 8,
     68, 289, 351–52, 354, 359
Labriola, Paul, 74, 76–77
Labro, Phillippe, 114–15
Lacey, Frederick, 326, 360
La Charda, Salvadore, 272
La Costa Country Club, 174, 176, 388
La Duca, James, 303–4
La Fitte, Pierre, 397
Lagattuta, Samuel, 303
LaMonte, Frank, 89, 298–99
Landie, Sol, 322
Lane, Mark, 248–50
Lansky, Jake, 85, 92–93, 201, 203
Lansky, Meyer, 92–93, 108–9, 160, 171–72, 201,
     203, 290, 325, 331, 348, 384, 391, 405
Lanza, Joe, 304
LaPlaca, Peter, 318
La Proto, Salvatore, 304
Larasso, Louis, 303
Lardino, Danny, 74, 77
LaRocca, John, 303, 385
La Stella Restaurant, 44, 312, 320
LaTempa, Peter, 144, 161
Laundry Workers union, 8, 375
Law Enforcement Intelligence Unit, 364
Lawford, Peter, 190
Lawrence, Mary, 246–47, 259
Leavell, Joan, 102
Lee, H. L. *See* Oswald, Lee Harvey

Lee, Tony, 322
LeFore Insurance Company, 372
Lemoine, Peter, 320
Lepera, Patsy, 84, 227, 325, 334, 345
Lewis, Ben, 379
Lewis, Clint, 101
Lewisburg Federal Penitentiary, 275
Liberto, Frank, 272
Liberto, Liberto and Latch Produce Store, 272
Liberto, Salvatore, 272
Liberty Broadcasting Network, 189–90
Libonati, Roland, 273, 387–88
Licata, Nicola, 74
Licavoli, Peter, 322, 341, 373
Licavoli, Thomas, 385
Liddy, Gordon, 175
Liebler, Wesley, 186
Lindsay, John, 381
Lippmann, Walter, 18
Lipsky, Marcus, 74, 76
Lipton, Lewis, 172
Liston, Sonny, 226–27
Litchfield, Wilbur Waldon, 243–45, 247
LoCicero, Richard, 321
Locurto, Joseph, 78, 83, 102, 404, 406
Loeb, William, 394
Loesch, Frank, 7, 351
Lomax, Louis, 270
Lombardo, Peter, 14
Lombardozzi, Carmine, 303, 318, 359
Lombardozzi, John, 376
Long, Earl, 313–14
Long, Edward, 272–73, 282, 392
Long, Huey, 87, 312
Long, Russell, 59–60, 87, 170, 198, 392
Louisiana State Hospital, 31
Louisiana State University, 338
Loverde, Frank, 70–72
Lowell, Abbott Lawrence, 181
Lucas B&B Restaurant, 246–47, 259
Lucchese, Thomas, 336, 349, 371, 381
Lucchese, Thomas, Mafia Family, 359, 390
Luciano, Charles (Lucky), 161, 319
Luciano, Joseph, 385
Lufthansa Airlines, 336
Luparelli, Joseph, 318–19, 323–24, 342, 370–71
Lurie, Alfred, 221
Lyle, John, 6–7

McCarthy, Joseph, 193, 228, 295
McClellan, John, 38, 67, 193, 211, 231, 239, 288–89, 315, 321, 336, 341, 367, 395
McClellan Committee. *See* Senate Permanent Subcommittee on Investigations or Senate Select Committee on Improper Activities in the Labor or Management Field

McClory, Robert, 360
McCormack, Edward, 398
McCormack, John, 196, 389–91
McCowan, Michael, 282
McCoy, Alfred, 165
McCurdy, Danny, 117
McCurley, A. D., 22
McDade, Joseph, 168, 265, 311–12, 341
MacDonnell, Herbert, 277
Maceo, Sam, 92, 122
McFerren, John, 272
McGee, H. L., 135
McGovern's Bar, 69–71
McKeown, Robert, 202–3, 205
McKinney, Stewart, 106, 187
McKissick, Floyd, 265, 312
McLane, Alfred, 35
McLendon, Gordon, 118, 189–90, 221
McNamara, Robert, 157–58
McSwiggin, William, 329
McWillie, Lewis, 84, 90, 92–93, 96, 100, 107, 109, 190, 203–5, 207, 219–21, 223, 227, 238, 260, 405, 407
Mafia, *passim*
Mafia National Commission, 40, 44, 218, 314, 394
Magaddino, Anthony, 303–4
Magaddino, Stefano, 40, 179, 303–4, 317, 327
Magaddino, Stefano, Mafia Family, 327
Maggio, Peter, 344
Magliocco, Joseph, 303, 305
Maheu, Robert, 163
Majuri, Thomas, 304
Malatesta, Peter, 178
Malcolm X, 264–69, 282, 295, 311, 330, 341, 363
Malley, James, 106
Malone, Carlos, 97
Malone, William Scott, 200
Maloney, William, 354
Mancuso, Rosario, 304
Mancuso, Thomas, 338
Mannarino, Gabriel, 304
Manno, Pat, 74–75, 324
Manson, Charles, 277
Maranzano, Salvatore, 39, 329
Marcello, Carlos, 37, 40–44, 46–54, 56–61, 84, 86–87, 89, 94, 96, 108–9, 118, 145, 159, 169–70, 173, 176, 190–92, 209, 211–13, 215–18, 221, 225, 230, 232, 258, 263, 271–72, 274–75, 283, 312–13, 320
Marcello, Carlos, Mafia Family, 86–87, 144, 212, 216, 320, 355, 387, 407
Marcello, Joseph, Jr., 320
Marcello, Pete, 212, 214, 216, 219
Marchesi, Vincent, 223
Marcinkus, Paul, 294
Marcus, Greil, 283
Marcus, Jack, 83

Marcus, James, 381
Marcy, Pat, 373, 379, 388
Marie's Lounge, 271
Marino, Mario, 58
Markham, Helen, 33
Martens, Layton, 52
Martin, Dean, 190, 282
Martin, Jack, 50
Martin, Jim, 29, 122
Martin, John, 68
Martinez, Pauline Sierra, 163
Mason Tenders union, 353
Massachusetts Crime Commission, 98, 363
Mastriana, Louis, 331, 351
Matta, Giovanni, 386
Matthews, Elizabeth, 92, 223
Matthews, J. Neal, 169
Matthews, Russell, 91–92, 96, 99, 190, 205, 207, 223, 227, 404–5
Matula, Frank, 91, 253, 357
Maudlin, Shirley, 241–42
Maynard, Carl, 83
Mayor, Georgia, 261
Mazey, Emil, 13
Mazzei, Irwin, 72, 232–33, 238
Meagher, Sylvia, 150
Meany, George, 9, 15
Medica, Joe, 324
Medico, Phillip, 158, 344, 389
Medico, William, 157, 344, 389
Medico Industries, 157–58, 229, 304, 344, 389
Meli, Vincent, 397
Meltzer, Harold, 55
Menditto, Alexander, 372
Menolia, Guy, Jr., 379
Meredith, James, 286
Merindaceli, Duke of, 327
Methvin, Eugene, 311
Meyers, George, 68
Meyers, Larry, 259
Miami Heart Institute, 290
Michael's Dairies, Inc., 344
Michaels, Jimmy, 377
Mikado Club, 248
Miller, Austin L., 20
Miller, Dave L., 66, 405
Miller, Giles, 76
Miller, Isadore Max, 99, 405
Miller, Murray "Dusty", 93, 226, 238
Miller, William, 221, 237
Minutemen, 49, 57, 156–57, 274
Miranda, Michele, 304, 320
Mitchell, John, 170, 393
Modica, Joe, 382
Moldea, Dan, 88, 96, 175
Molinas, Jack, 339
Mollenhoff, Clark, 38, 173, 382, 391, 393
Monachino, Patsy, 304
Monachino, Sam, 304

Montana, John, 229, 303–4, 327
Montgomery, L. D., 111
Mooney, Nancy Jane, 33–34
Moore, Bobby Gene, 89–90, 298, 300
Moore, Edwin, 382
Moore, Elmer, 139–41, 256
Moore, Richard, 174
Moore, Russ "Knight", 115, 117–18
Moran, James, 380
Moran, Jim. *See* Brocato, James
Morelli, Frank (Butsey), and brothers, 182
Morgenthau, Robert, 326
Morici, Henry, 214
Morris, Edward, Jr., 70
Morris, Joseph F., 288, 329
Moschiano, Anthony, 369
Motel Drug Service, 127, 258
Motto, Daniel, 381
Moynihan, Daniel, 274
Muhammad, Elijah, 267
Mundt, Karl, 41, 231
Murchison, Clint, Jr., 168, 193, 197
Murder, Incorporated, 2, 323, 380
Murphy, Thomas, 20
Murray Packing Co., 350
Murret, Charles, 53, 212
Muskie, Edward, 171, 176
Mussolini, Benito, 161
Myers, Larry, 83
Mynier, Elaine, 204

Nadjari, Maurice, 368
Namath, Joe, 338
Nani, Sebastiano, 283, 384
Naples, Joey, 399
National Advisory Committee on Civil Disorders, 266
National Association for Air Freight, 336
National Association of Food Chains, 9
National Council on Crime and Delinquency, 341
Nautical Cafe, 325
Navasky, Victor, 38
Nazarian, Jackie, 323, 370
Nelson, Gary, 373
Newberry, Ted, 6
Newman, Morton William, 29, 76
Newman, Paul, 115
Newman, William, Jr., 21–22
New Orleans Metropolitan Crime Commission, 40, 58, 93–94, 213
New Orleans Saints, 338
New York Economic Club, 157
New York Hilton Hotel, 108, 213, 222
New York Jets, 338
New York State Joint Legislative Committee on Crime, 311, 372
Nichols, Roger, 197

Nichols Garage, 122–23, 128, 130–31, 137
Nicoletti, Chuck, 365
Nitti, Frank, 6, 66, 319
Nixon, Richard, 156, 162, 168, 171–80, 185, 283, 288, 295, 392
Noguchi, Thomas, 276–77
Notaro, Tony, 318
Nowlin, Duane, 55, 256
Noyes, Peter, 36, 49, 54–55

O'Brien, Carlton, 329–30
O'Brien, Gerald, 14
O'Brien, Judge, 298
O'Brien, Thomas, 387
O'Donnell, Kenneth, 158
O'Dwyer, William, 380
O'Halloran, Dorothy, 197
O'Sullivan, Frederick, 216
Occhipinti, Frank, 58
Ochs, Martin, 74
Odum, Bardwell, 245
Ogilvie, Richard, 354
Oglesby, Carl, 171
Old French Opera House, 212, 214, 216, 220, 222
Olivetto, Dominick, 304
Olsen, Harry, 118–21, 137, 262
Ormento, John, 302–4
Osticco, James, 304, 344
Oswald, Lee Harvey, 1–3, 6, 17–18, 26–27, 29–30, 33–36, 43, 50, 52–53, 56, 59, 61–62, 70, 76, 82–83, 86, 88, 95, 100, 106–7, 111–16, 118–25, 128, 132–39, 143–45, 149–50, 163–64, 182–87, 192, 194–95, 207, 209, 212, 225, 239–48, 259, 262–63, 271, 301
Oswald, Marguerite, 53–54, 244–47
Oswald, Marina, 53, 186, 245
Oswald, Russell, 390
Oxford, J. L., 22

Painters and Decorators union, 359
Palermo, Frank, 385
Palmer, Tom, 120, 126–27, 233, 235
Panitz, Meyer, 405
Panzarella, Edward, 371
Pappas, Ike, 117, 120
Paradise Island Casino, 172, 330
Paramount Pictures, 221
Parilli, Babe, 338
Parisi, Joe, 349, 380
Parker, Bonnie, 169
Parkland Hospital, 17, 21, 113–14, 139, 185, 262
Parr, George, 170
Parsons, Russell, 282–83
Partin, Edward, 46–47, 59, 118, 176, 274
Parvin, Albert, 390–91
Parvin, Albert, Foundation, 391

Parvin-Dohrmann Corp., 390–91
Pasley, Jerome, 396
Patman, Wright, 173, 348
Patriarca, Raymond, 229, 289, 317, 320, 324, 329–30, 333, 337, 342, 350, 354, 362, 366, 370, 377, 382–83, 390
Patriarca, Raymond, Mafia Family, 229, 319, 337
Patrick, Lenny, 68, 72, 90, 93, 96–97, 109, 138, 226–27, 379
Patrono, Johnny Ross, 405
Patrusky, Martin, 277
Patton, George, 161
Paul, Ralph, 78, 123–24, 131, 259
Paul VI, Pope, 293
Pecora, Nofio, 93–94, 109, 213, 215–16, 221, 226, 232, 404
Pellegrino, Rocco, 303
Pelligrino, Peter, 89
Pelou, Francois, 115
Pendergast, Tom, 377
Penn, Stanley, 360
Pentagon Papers, 167–68
People's Industrial Consultants, 174
Pepper, Claude, 173, 198, 291, 334, 347, 378, 384
Peppino, Don, 108
Pepsi-Cola Co., 165
Percy, Charles, 167, 291, 321, 342, 349, 374
Percy, Valerie, 342
Perrin, Robert, 206
Perrone, Gaspar, 12
Perrone, Santo, 12–14, 333
Persico, Carmine, 338, 370–71
Peterson, Henry, 356
Peterson, Virgil, 377, 396
Petrosino, Joseph, 328
Pettit, Tom, 136
Piccolo, Nicholas, 385
Piersante, Vince, 333, 366
Pike, Roy. *See* Ryan, Mickey
Pipefitters Local 562, 355
Pisciotta, Gaspare, 144
Pittman, Vail, 397
Pitts, Elnora, 134–35, 137
Plopi, Walter, 376
Poff, Richard, 341, 375
Polito, Joseph, 350
Polizzi, Al, 171
Polizzo, Angelo, 74
Polley, Stanley, 348, 367, 374, 389
Pollock, Seymour, 197
Polverino, Joseph, 177
Pope, Ralph, 16
Posner, Herman, 357
Powell, Adam Clayton, 367, 390
Powell, Nancy, 104, 126, 128–31, 251, 260
Powell, Paul, 383

Presser, Jackie, 176
Price, J. C., 23
Prio, Ross, 74, 399
Profaci, Joseph, 304
Progressive Drug Co., 347
Provenzano, Tony, 88, 175–76
Provincial Motel, 272
Proxmire, William, 180
Psychological Stress Evaluator, 147
Puzzangara, Joe, 323

Quaranta, Luigi, 385
Quinn, Paul, 365

Raft, George, 331
Ragen, James, 96, 138
Ramistella, Henry. *See* Donneroummas,
    Frank
Ramos Ducos, Leopoldo, 88, 143
Rankin, J. Lee, 147, 184, 249
Rao, Vincent, 304
Rare Earth, 339
Ratteni, Nick, 349
Ratterman, George, 361
Rava, Armand, 304
Ray, James Earl, 194, 270–72, 282
Ray, John, 270–71
Ray's Hardware Store, 93
Raymond, Michael, 28, 318–20, 333, 346,
    348–49, 360, 367, 374, 389
Reagan, Ronald, 176, 288
Rebozo, Bebe, 171
Rector, Milton, 341
Reddi-Wip Corp., 74
Redlich, Norman, 186
Reece, Gloria, 258
Reeves, Huey, 128, 130–31
Reid, Ed, 42–43, 60, 191–92, 212
Reles, Abe, 144, 380
Renda, Carl, 12, 14
Rennell, Lord, 162
Reprise Record Co., 220
Requena, Andres, 168
Resorts International, 171–72, 292
Reuther, Victor, 11–12, 14, 16
Reuther, Walter, 5, 9–16, 282
Revill, Jack, 134
Rex Carting Co., 349
Reynolds, Warren, 33–34, 240
Rheinstein, Fred, 115
Rhodes, James, 101–2, 385
Ricchiuti, William, 323, 335, 343
Riccobono, Joseph, 304
Rice Hotel, 256–57
Rich, Nancy Perrin, 32, 97, 101, 103–4, 143,
    205–6
Richey, Warren, 133–34
Riela, Anthony, 304
Riesel, Victor, 323, 355

Rimrock International Oil Co., 35
Rinaldi, Dominic, 371
Ritchie, Donald Joseph, 14–15
Riverside Hotel, 92, 221
Riviera Hotel, 90, 393
Rizzo, Vincent, 294, 334, 399
Roberts, Dennis, 340
Roberts, Donald, 133
Robertson, Vic, Jr., 114–15
Rockefeller, Nelson, 158
Rogers, Warren, 48, 58
Rogovin, Charles, 332
Romeo, Tony, 380
Roofers' Local 30, 8
Rooney, John, 390
Roosevelt, Franklin, 6
Roosevelt, James, 390
Roosevelt Raceway, 337
Roppolo, Carl, 42–43
Rosa, Joseph, 385
Rosata, Joseph, 304
Roschek, Urban, 71
Roselli, Johnny, 94, 96, 163, 204, 225, 263,
    281–82
Rosone, Roberto, 294
Ross, Barney, 65–66, 221–22, 233, 237, 253, 263
Ross Trucking Co., 349
Rothermal, Paul, 55, 256
Rothman, Norman, 92, 160, 203
Roulette Records, 339
Rourke, Alexander, 162
Rowley, James, 23
Rowntowner Inn, 58
Royal Coach Inn, 86
Royal Orleans Hotel, 51
Rozelle, Pete, 338
RSO Records, 340
Rubenstein, Fanny, 65
Rubenstein, Harry, 70–71, 214
Rubenstein, Hyman, 67, 69, 71, 82, 219, 226,
    405
Rubenstein, Jack. *See* Ruby, Jack
Rubenstein, Joseph, 65
Ruby, Jack, *passim*
Ruby, Sam, 253
Ruddy, Al, 393
Rushing, Ray, 134
Russell, Richard, 184
Russo, Anthony, 398
Russo, Joseph (Fatty), 228, 323, 370–71
Rutledge, John, 114
Ryan, Mickey, 72, 104, 256

S.G.S. Associates, 303, 359
Sacco, Nicola, 181–82
Sachs, Stephen, 170
Saia, Frank, 86–87
Saia, Sam, 53
Salas, Luis, 170

Salerno, Ralph, 5, 62, 64, 179, 192, 265–66, 312, 315, 341, 360, 386
Salvatore, Rocco, 365
Samish, Adrian, 383–84
Sands Hotel, 58
Sansone, Charlie, 298
Sansone, Tony, 377
Sans Soucie casino, 304
Santa Anita Race Track, 66, 94, 275
Santaniello, Leo, 383
Santos, Louis. *See* Trafficante, Santos, Jr.
Saperstein, Louis, 177
Saporito, Michael, 375–76
Saporito, Robert, 375–76
Sarkus, Raymond, 68
Sartor, William, 272
Saxbe, William, 399
Scalise, Joseph, 352
Scalish, John, 303–4
Scarborough Downs, 337
Scarne, John, 160
Scarpa, Gregory, 321
Schaeffer, James, 319, 335, 343
Schenck, Nicholas, 357
Schlesinger, Arthur, Jr., 18, 194
Schulberg, Budd, 392, 394–95
Schulman, Donald, 278–80
Schulman, Solly, 66
Schwartz, Louis, 371
Schweitzer, Mitchell, 374
Scialo, Dominick, 372
Sciandra, Angelo, 304
Sciortino, Patsy, 305
Scoggins, William, 34
Scolish, John. *See* Scalish, John
Scott, Peter Dale, 65
Scott Byron Motel, 44
Scotto, Tony, 355, 387
Scozzari, Simone, 305
Scranton, Paul, 45
Scrap Iron and Junk Handlers Union, 67–68
Secret Service, 17, 23, 50, 81, 125–26, 139, 141, 144, 186, 205, 207, 241, 256, 259–60, 262, 274
Securities and Exchange Commission, 292, 389–91
Securities Validation Corp., 291, 333
Security National Bank, 172
Seidband, Sidney, 80, 405
Seligman, Rabbi, 116
Senate Intelligence Committee. *See* Senate Select Committee to Study Government Operations with Respect to Intelligence Activities
Senate Permanent Subcommittee on Investigations, 3, 15, 35, 39, 162, 178, 193, 230, 282, 287, 314, 316, 333
Senate Rackets Committee. *See* Senate Permanent Subcommittee on Investigations

Senate Select Committee on Improper Activities in the Labor or Management Field (McClellan Committee), 39, 68, 74, 77, 211, 269, 325, 354, 357–58, 394–95
Senate Select Committee to Study Government Operations with Respect to Intelligence Activities (Senate Intelligence Committee), 18, 94, 163, 182–84, 192, 225
Senate Special Committee to Investigate Organized Crime in Interstate Commerce (Kefauver Committee), 10–12, 66, 73–74, 76, 87, 97, 99, 169–70, 314, 322, 325, 329, 344, 363, 378, 380
Senator, George, 29–30, 86, 121–22, 132, 134, 137, 144, 240, 306
Serpico, Frank, 367
Serritella, Vince, 365
Sharpe, Alton, 232–33, 238
Shaw, Clay, 56–58
Shaw, Donald, 362
Shaw, Robert, 186
Shenker, Morris, 377
Shepard, Charles, 370–71
Sheridan, Walter, 57, 173, 274
Sherman Hotel, 66, 222
Shippers, David, 376
Sho-Bar, 212, 214–16, 219–20
Shomberg, Lou, 348
Shore, Michael, 141, 220–23, 225–26, 238, 282
Shorman, Robert, 70, 101
Shoulders, Lou, 289, 351–52
Shusted, Thomas, 359
Sica, Joe, 55
Siciliano, Vincent, 353
Siefert, David, 95
Siegel, Bugsy, 85, 109
Silver Spur Club, 77, 107, 248, 407
Simmons, James, 20–22
.Simon's Garage, 119–20
Simpson, Johnny, 119–20
Sinatra, Frank, 92, 177–78, 190, 220–21, 282
Sindona, Michele, 292–94
Singleton, Penny, 232
Singleton, Ray, 102
Siragusa, Charles, 96
Sirhan, Sirhan, 27, 273, 275–79, 281–83
Sirica, John, 24, 28, 84, 319
Sixteenth Street Baptist Church, 209
Slater and Morill Shoe Co., 182
Slatin, Joe, 78
Slusher, Juanita, 90, 141, 299
Smaldone, Clyde, 55
Smaldone, Eugene, 55
Small Business Administration, 87, 94, 314
Smith, C. Arnholt, 172, 280–81, 402
Smith, Cecil, 372
Smith, D'Alton, 118, 173
Smith, Hugh, 102

Smith, Joe M., 21, 23
Smith, John, 133–34
Smith, L. C., 22
Smith, Mrs. Earl, 30
Smitherman, William, 396
Societa General Immobiliare, 292
Sol's Turf Bar, 81
Solomon, E. R., 81
Sorge, Santo, 35
Sorrentino, Pasqual, 373
Southland Hotel, 92, 121–22
Sovereign Club, 78, 101, 104
Spadolini, Giovanni, 294
Spinelli, Salvatore, 396
Sportsmen's Club, 331
Stalin, Joseph, 10
Standifer, Roy, 114
Stardust Hotel, 391
Stavola, Michael, 398
Stein, Charles, 271–72
Stella, Pasquale, 405
Stone, Walter, 330, 346, 354
Streisand, Barbra, 222
Strell, Bayard, 381
Sturgis, Frank, 160, 162
Sullivan, Jack, 170
Sullivan, William, 183, 192, 194
Surprise, Joey, 349
Surrey, Robert, 159
Swanton, John, 329
Sweig, Martin, 389–91
Szulc, Tad, 168

Tabet, Louis. See La Fitte, Pierre
Tacitus, 181, 198
Taglianetti, Louis, 317, 325
Taglianetti Airtels, 317, 325, 342, 382–83
Tameleo, Henry, 320, 324, 333, 337–38, 343, 350, 362, 382
Tanglewood Apartments, 253–54
Tannenbaum, Harold, 214–16
Tanner, Hans, 162
Tatum, Jack, 32–33
Taylor, Maxwell, 158
Teamsters union. See International Brother-
    hood of Teamsters
Telvi, Abraham, 323
Teresa, Vincent, 48, 109, 179, 182, 218, 290,
    318–20, 324, 330–31, 333, 335–36, 338,
    340, 343–44, 346, 350, 362, 366
Terminal Annex Building, 23
Termine, Sam, 53–54
Terranova, Cesare, 328
Testo, John, 358
Texas Adams Oil Co., 91
Texas School Book Depository Building, 17,
    19, 22–23, 25–26, 185, 261
Texas State Teachers College, 195
Thaller, Robert, 391

Thieu, Nguyen Van, 165
Thomas, Cary, 267
Thompson, Dolores, 201–2
Thompson, Josiah, 23–24
Thompson, Mary, 201–2
Three Dog Night, 339
Thunderbird Hotel, 92–93, 219, 221, 223, 405
Tice, Wilma, 114
Timphony, Frank, 57
Tippit, J. D., 17, 32–34, 186, 239–40, 247–50,
    262–63
Tisci, Anthony, 388
Tolson, Clyde, 194
Tonahill, Joe, 116, 139–41
Top of the Hill Club, 92
Torch Club, 70–71
Tornabe, Salvatore, 305
Torrio, Johnny, 108
Tortoriello, Frank, 253–54
Touhy, Roger, 6–7, 351
Tourine, Charlie, 331
Towler, Martin, 257
Town and Country Motel, 51, 272
Toy and Novelty Workers Union, 359
Trafficante, Santos, Jr., 37, 44–48, 61, 84, 92,
    94–96, 159, 163, 165, 203–5, 207, 209,
    218, 223, 225–26, 232, 238, 263, 274–75,
    304–5, 320, 404–5
Trafficante, Santos, Sr., 304, 318
Trammel, Connie, 255–56
Tramunti, Carmine, 179, 338
Tresca, Carlos, 161
Trescornia detention camp, 204
Tritle, T. A., 285
Tropical Tourist Court, 213, 215, 221, 226
Tropicana Hotel, Cuba, 35, 83, 92, 190, 203
Trujillo, Rafael, 168
Trupiano, Mike, 352
Turner, William, 274
Turnman, Reagan, 100
Turrigiano, Patsy, 305
Twentieth Century Industries, 347

U.S. Chamber of Commerce, 346
U.S. National Bank, 172, 280
U.S. President's Commission on Law Enforce-
    ment and Administration of Justice,
    285, 314
U.S. President's Commission on the Assassi-
    nation of President John F. Kennedy.
    See Warren Commission
Uecker, Karl, 276
Ullo, Joe, 339
Union Gastronomica, 88
United Auto Workers union, 9–16
United Farm Workers union, 9
United Mine Workers of America, 302
United Textile Workers union, 359

Valachi, Joseph, 3, 29, 39, 47, 107, 164, 189, 288, 317–18, 322, 327, 359, 380
Valente, Costenze, 305
Valente, Frank, 305
Vanzetti, Bartolomeo, 181–82
Vario, Leonard, 326
Vario, Paul, 326, 371
Vastola, Gaetano, 353, 398
Vatican, 293–94, 328
Vegas Club, 77–78, 90, 131, 149, 215, 234, 248, 299, 306, 404
Vertigo Key Club, 71
Veteran's Cabin, 253
Veterans Administration, 341
Vic Construction Co., 326
Viorst, Milton, 76
Visconti, Robert, 330
Vitale, John, 68–69
Vizzini, Cologero, 162
Vogue Credit Jewelers, 350
Voloshen, Nathan, 196, 348, 374, 389–91
Volpe, Angelo, 365

Wade, Henry, 103, 114–15
Waggenheim, Phil, 332
Wald, Jerry, 394
Waldo, Thayer, 115
Walker, Edwin, 142, 159, 273
Walker, Ira, 133–34
Wall, Breck, 100, 236
Wall, Charles, 318
Walthers, Buddy, 101
Ward, Charles, 59
Warehousemen's union, 353
Warner, Roger C., 125–26
Warren, Earl, 18, 118, 121, 139–43, 145–48, 184, 207, 249–50, 263, 283
Warren Commission, 3–4, 6, 18–21, 23, 26–27, 29–30, 32–34, 50, 56, 65–66, 68, 71–72, 75, 80, 82; 89–91, 100, 102–3, 106, 110, 113–14, 116, 118–19, 121–22, 124, 126, 129–30, 132, 134, 137–40, 142, 144–45, 147–48, 150, 153, 163, 179, 181–89, 192, 195, 198, 200, 203, 205, 207, 214, 236, 239–40, 244–45, 247–49, 252, 255, 259, 297, 406
Washington, George, 286, 294–95
Wasserman, Jack, 52
WBAP-TV, 133–34
Webb, Dell, 193
Weinberg, James, 74, 77
Weiner, Irwin, 94–96, 109, 141, 220, 225–26, 232, 236–38, 282, 404
Weinstein, Abe, 234
Weinstein, Barney, 234
Weisberg, Willie, 40
Weiss, George, 370
Weiss, Mark, 24–25
Weiss, Victor, 31

Weissman, Bernard, 248–50
Weitzman, Seymour, 22
Wertheimer, Mert, 85, 201
Westchester Carting Co., 349
Westgate-California conglomerate, 172
Whaley, William, 34–35
Whiskey Rebellion, 295
White, George. *See* Raymond, Michael
Wiener, Louie, 397
Williams, Bill, 257
Williams, Edward Bennett, 163, 194, 197, 269, 282, 292
Williams, Elmer, 7
Williams, Harold, 248
Williams, Paul, 323
Williams, Robert, 369
Willis, Phillip, 26–27
Wilner, Jack, 76
Wilson, John, Jr., 102–3
Wilson, O. W., 288, 324
Wilson, Will, 367
Winborn, Walter, 20
Winstead, Ralph, 13
Winter, Howie, 325
Winter-Berger, Robert, 196, 348, 374, 390–91
Wolfer, DeWayne, 276, 281
Wood, Leonard, 131
Woodard, James, 201–2
Woodward, Mary Elizabeth, 22
Wright, Edward, 375
Wuenche, Edward, 291, 334, 347

Yackovelli, Joseph, 319, 323–24, 370–71
Yale University, 295
Yanover, Jack, 220, 232, 405
Yaras, Dave, 90, 96–97, 138, 322
Yarborough, Ralph, 21
Young, Whitney, 265, 312
Youngblood, Rufus, 262
Younger, Evelle, 277, 283

Zagri, Sid, 170, 273
Zangara, Giuseppe, 6–7, 281
Zapas, Gus, 223
Zapruder, Abraham, 26
Zelmanowitz, Gerald, 177–79, 211, 292, 326, 339, 371–72, 374
Zerelli, Joseph, 87–88
Zerelli, Joseph, Mafia Family, 212
Zerilla, Anthony, 317
Zicarelli, Joe, 168, 228, 338, 386
Zicari, Emanuel, 305
Ziegler, Dennis, 354
Zito, Frank, 305
Zito, Joseph, 398
Zoppi, Tony, 190, 198, 221, 238, 260–61
Zuckerman, Nate, 70
Zuta, Jack, 101
Zwillman, Longy, 302